HUMAN RIGHTS IN THE
WORLD COMMUNITY

Pennsylvania Studies in Human Rights
Bert B. Lockwood, Jr., Series Editor
A complete list of books in the series is available from the publisher.

HUMAN RIGHTS in the WORLD COMMUNITY

Issues and Action

FOURTH EDITION

Edited by

Burns H. Weston

and

Anna Grear

PENN

UNIVERSITY OF PENNSYLVANIA PRESS

Philadelphia

Published by
University of Pennsylvania Press
Philadelphia, Pennsylvania 19104-4112
www.upenn.edu/pennpress

Printed in the United States of America on acid-free paper
10 9 8 7 6 5 4 3 2 1

Library of Congress Cataloging-in-Publication Data
ISBN 978-0-8122-4738-1

To the memory and in honor of

Richard Pierre Claude

Burns and I dedicated this book, rightly, to the memory of Richard Pierre Claude, coeditor of the first three editions. It is with great sadness that the publishers and I now mark the death of Burns Weston on October 29, 2015.

Burns worked on the publication you hold in your hand right up until the very last day of his life, and his unexpected death came as a tragic and shocking loss to people all over the world, as the hundreds of tributes in response to the news so richly reflected. Many of those expressing their grief simply found it impossible to accept that such a ferociously bright life-force had left the world. Burns was an outstanding scholar and human being, utterly passionate in his commitment to a profoundly human rights-centered ethic, untiring, fiercely independent of mind, courageous and generous of heart. It is my fervent hope that this book inspires those who wrestle with the seriousness of the questions it deliberately provokes, and that somehow—in some way—the energy of mind of Burns Weston will touch its readers and demand a response. The twenty-first-century world situation urgently needs those who are, like Burns, filled with fiery passion for justice, unafraid to be critical of the status quo, and courageous enough to work tirelessly for a better future history.

—Anna Grear

Contents

PART II: ACTION

A Warm Welcome from the Editors

Dear Reader,

We welcome you to what we hope will be for you a thought-provoking—and ultimately active—engagement with the fundamentally important, complex issues encompassing the world of human rights now and in the foreseeable future. Why? Because, on final analysis, human rights are about the alleviation of human suffering, responses to deprivations and degradations that signify fundamental disrespect toward, and injustice to, human beings; and in today's confused and conflicted world, the human rights task—more accurately, struggle—is ever more urgent and demanding.

We are filled with compassionate outrage at the very thought of imposed human suffering, not just at high-profile, egregious violations of human rights, but, as well, at the accretion of those almost banal, "normalized" day-to-day forms of disrespect that amount to human rights failures. We are particularly passionate about human rights as responses to injustice; and as international human rights lawyers we are, of course, much concerned with how international human rights law addresses these issues. As legal scholars, with two lifetimes of human rights thought and active engagement between us, we hope that, just maybe, we can make a difference—through our scholarship, our teaching, and our active engagement in and with the issues. Perhaps you also have been shocked by humanity's capacity for inhumanity toward other human beings and have yourself developed a similar human rights passion. If so, we hope this book will provide you with further sources of reflection and at least some guide to what surely must be a long list of many unanswered questions. But if not, we hope this book will help you cultivate and sustain an intelligent, informed, and critical engagement with the great human rights issues of our time, and a compassionate connection to human rights energies and efforts working to resolve them.

On our own personal journey, we have discovered that human rights are far from straightforward. Indeed, they exhibit a fiery mix of impulses, values, tensions, and paradoxes in which a whole gamut of questions arises. Many of the most important of these inhabit this text.

To help you engage with some of these questions, we have supplied Questions for Reflection and Discussion following each of the thirty-nine essays making up the bulk of our text—questions we believe will be helpful in analyzing the essays, in provoking new thinking, and in stimulating fresh research beyond the scope of the existing literature. The questions have been devised, too, with the general reader as well as classroom student in mind. It is our hope that the book will be of interest to the general reading public as well, for the issues canvassed in this book are relevant for every thoughtful individual.

We invite you to approach these questions with an open mind—truly thoughtfully, in a spirit of self-questioning as well as critique. If there is one thing that human rights teaching and scholarship has taught us, it is the vital importance of staying open to the conflicting energies flowing through this most fascinating and urgent of contemporary subjects. For it is in questioning that new insights are born, and nothing could be more important for our shared human futures than learning to live well with questions because they—and our own ability to remain unthreatened by differing viewpoints—are key to searching out new horizons of mutual acceptance in the midst of complex issues, and to the search for new and renewing choices of action.

To help you on your way, we have prepared "A General Introduction to Our Book" set forth immediately below, to introduce you to the twenty-first-century context in which our text is located and in which burning contemporary human rights questions arise. Thereafter, in "An Essential Guide to Use of Our Book," we detail a series of technical advisories that are important—indeed, critical—to your effective use and understanding of our text. These preliminary passages are "Must Reads." If you ignore them, you will seriously undermine your understanding of this book, its deliberate omissions, and its pedagogic purposes. You also will miss vital information intended for your benefit as you begin this particular human rights journey.

A GENERAL INTRODUCTION TO OUR BOOK

This is the fourth edition of *Human Rights in the World Community: Issues and Action*. Since its first publication in 1989, students of human rights on every continent have witnessed a large array of states undertaking reform, becoming "emerging" or "reemerging" democracies, and proclaiming support for the promotion and protection of international human rights. The second edition, published in 1992—soon after, and in recognition of, the dismantling of the Berlin Wall—reflected a post-Cold War aspiration, widely and optimistically shared, to displace the then sterile ideological posturing of superpower rivalry with a lively and constructive global human rights culture. This hope was manifest at the landmark World Conference on Human Rights held in Vienna in 1993. Among other things, the Conference called "on all States and institutions to include human rights, humanitarian law, democracy and rule of law as subjects in the curricula of all learning institutions in formal and non-formal settings."[1]

The third edition, substantially revised and published in 2006, was intended to facilitate human rights education and to do so in support of the international resolves that were voiced in the 2000 Millennium Declaration pursuant to which United Nations member states pledged that they would spare no effort to promote democracy and strengthen the rule of law, as well as respect for internationally recognized human rights and fundamental freedoms.[2] Since then, terrorist networks have made even the most powerful states feel vulnerable, tempting some observers to surmise that countering terrorism should displace human rights as a priority on the global agenda. Moreover, only five years after the Millennium Declaration, over forty countries (by UN accounts) were scarred by violent conflict—a continuing trend, alas, fraught with tragic human cost. Challenges to human rights world-

---

1. World Conference on Human Rights, Vienna Declaration and Programme of Action, endorsed by the 48th session of the General Assembly at its 85th plenary meeting by Resolution 48/121 of 20 December 1993, fully referenced in Documentary Appendix B, at www.uichr.org/WestonGrear.
2. Adopted by the UNGA 8 September 2000, fully referenced in Documentary Appendix B, at www.uichr.org/WestonGrear.

wide have featured wars, genocides, crimes against humanity, and reports of torture attributable to every country, including the United Kingdom and the United States, two countries that have long espoused the world rule of law. Such deadly assaults on the prospects for a humane world order have told the international community that it was (and remains) time to relearn the core message of the 1945 UN Charter and the 1948 Universal Declaration of Human Rights (UDHR)[3]—to wit, that the global struggle for justice undertaken through peaceful means centrally includes everyone working for the recognition and implementation of human rights as the cornerstone of world peace.

This fourth *wholly revised* edition of *Human Rights in the World Community: Issues and Action* is compiled in full awareness that the familiar threats to human rights remain deeply embedded and troubling. Additionally, it speaks to an era marked by the growing perils of climate change, the ominous shadows of nuclear proliferation, and the far-reaching impacts of an extensive and crippling global financial crisis that has deepened the gap between rich and poor the world over. As this edition reveals, in reading after reading, the need for human rights has never been more urgent nor, at the same time, their paradoxes more vexing or complex.

In this connection, we importantly note, numerous readings in this volume refer to "neoliberal economics and politics," "neoliberal globalization," the "neoliberal world order," and the like. Neoliberalism is a crucial theme in this fourth edition precisely because the context in which the edition has been compiled reflects deepening public concern with the seemingly unrelenting trends of an economic philosophy or ideology that currently defines and dominates a form of globalization that, especially since the end of the Cold War and according to increasingly many, has had and continues to have profoundly negative impacts upon the lives and human rights of individuals and groups everywhere, producing empirically verifiable and destabilizing levels of human vulnerability on multiple scales. It is important, therefore, briefly to define "neoliberalism" at this introductory stage.

One of the most useful and extensive explorations of the term is that offered by Dag Einar Thorsen and Amund Lie.[4] Drawing on their definition, neoliberalism emerges as a set of political commitments in which the primary (possibly even the sole) legitimate responsibility of the state is to protect individual market-based freedoms, at the national level and the international level where a global system of free trade guarantees commercial freedom and densely protected property rights. Thorsen and Lie emphasize that neoliberalism is not—despite its name—merely a revival of liberalism, but is

> best perceived . . . as a radical descendant of liberalism "proper," in which traditional liberal demands for "equality of liberty" have been bent out of shape into a demand for total liberty for the talented and their enterprises. In this, neoliberalism resembles the parallel phenomenon of "neoconservatism," which is not, either, a new form or recent revival of traditional conservatism, but rather a new and unique, and decidedly more uncompromising, set of political ideas.[5]

Accordingly, neoliberalism can be seen as an ideological commitment to total economic freedom, a demand for the state to stay out of the market and for an order of rights fundamentally committed to the prioritization of commercial freedom and interests and the sanctity of property rights above all else—especially for powerful corporations. The

3. Adopted by the UNGA 10 December 1948, reprinted and fully referenced in Documentary Appendix A, at www.uichr.org/WestonGrear.
4. Dag Einar Thorsen and Amund Lie, "What Is Neoliberalism?" University of Oslo Discussion Paper 2006, http://folk.uio.no/daget/neoliberalism.pdf (accessed 25 June 2015).
5. Ibid., 16.

phenomenon is accompanied by widespread enclosure (privatization) of formerly public spaces, functions, and utilities and by the general "rolling back of the state" such that the state's core contemporary role is as facilitator of market imperatives.

In addition to this neoliberal imprint on globalization, it is important to read this fourth edition also against two other centrally important backdrops: the climate crisis and the dangers presented by the proliferation of nuclear weapons. Along with the savage levels of poverty and spiraling forms of inequality now afflicting the human condition, these two existential threats present a very serious challenge to human beings—indeed to the future condition of Planet Earth itself. Humanity, at this point in the twenty-first century, stands at a highly strategic juncture—laden with threats. But the time is ripe also with opportunity for creating a different kind of world together, a more humane world that builds upon currently insurgent schools of thought in economics, digital technology, and human rights—indeed, in human governance itself—which, jointly and separately, are expanding our sense of the possible.

In 2005, in a report entitled "In Larger Freedom," UN Secretary-General Kofi Annan, taking both challenges and opportunities into account, sought to set a direction for our time:[6]

> We have it in our power to pass on to our children a brighter inheritance than that bequeathed to any previous generation. We can halve global poverty and halt the spread of major known diseases in the next 10 years. We can reduce the prevalence of violent conflict and terrorism. We can increase respect for human dignity in every land. And we can forge a set of updated international institutions to help humanity achieve these noble goals. If we act boldly—and if we act together—we can make people everywhere more secure, more prosperous and better able to enjoy their fundamental human rights.[7]

The years since these words have revealed the urgent need to take them very seriously; and one important—indeed paramount—way to do so is to encourage and facilitate human rights education on a widespread basis.[8] This human rights education necessarily involves facing human rights failures, hypocrisies, and contradictions. It involves recognizing the patterns and the measure of the immense challenges and pressures facing human rights realization in an age of deepening global crises. It also involves responding to signs of hope emerging across the globe—among the administrators and faculties of educational institutions, in the offices and corridors of commercial establishments and governmental secretariats, and in the streets, the market places, and the cyberspaces of Internet solidarities and new forms of social connection in the search for global justice.

Like its predecessors, this fourth edition brings a wide range of human rights materials together in one place for classroom use in many disciplines, including but not limited to international law and relations, economics, political science, sociology, history, philosophy, religion, and of course education itself (witness, for indicative example, the Abbreviations listed at the beginning of this book). Relying on a broad distinction between *issues* associated with international human rights problems and *action* that seeks to implement human rights norms and standards, nine chapters each contain essays by leading scholars and activists, preceded by an editors' introduction designed to orient the reader in the larger context in which the essays fit. To save on limited space, we have abridged most of the essays

---

6. See the epigraph to this volume.
7. Report of the Secretary-General for Decision by Heads of State and Government, "In Larger Freedom: Towards Development, Security and Human Rights for All," September 2005, para. 1, http://www.un.org/largerfreedom (accessed 23 May 2015).
8. See, e.g., The People's Movement for Human Rights Learning, "Global Appeal for Human Rights Learning," 10 December 2004, http://www.pdhre.org/global-appeal.html (accessed 15 May 2015).

substantially; and to facilitate ease of use as well as save space, we have largely dispensed with ellipses, bracketed editorializing, and most footnotes. In all instances, however, we have remained otherwise faithful to the original language and intent of each author.

At the website found at www.uichr.org/WestonGrear (our dedicated website, courtesy of The University of Iowa Center for Human Rights) is a bibliography of selected human rights books. We also include an annotated filmography updated through early 2015 at least. Additionally, because of the huge advances made in digital technology since the third edition of this book in 2006, and because we believe that human rights and wrongs are made tangible by eyewitness experience, we strongly recommend recourse to television and other visual arts (including theater and dance) as important teaching devices and tools in our exploding Information Age—likewise music and musical commentary. One way or another, and as many before us have proven, we all can and should become eyewitnesses to human rights triumphs and tragedies.

Human rights is not an abstract field of study. It is a field of work, a fundamental element of the search for a more humane global order, a way of life. It requires everyone's commitment, effort, and support. Thankfully no one has to begin from scratch. The United Nations took the first step with the UDHR in 1948, formulating internationally defined norms to which all states and peoples could commit, and its progeny have proliferated ever since, establishing and clarifying standards that form the basis on which the study and practice of human rights are rooted. Hence the two documentary appendices noted above.

Of course, whether the world is up to the task of building a world community respectful of human dignity remains to be seen. That it should try to do so, however, is imperative and beyond debate—particularly in an age of environmental/climatic, political/strategic, and economic/equity crises and pressures. A particularly credible case for this view is made by those who have seen its opposite: an Argentine judge, for example, who served on the court that convicted military rulers in his country for human rights violations between 1976 and 1983, has argued that it is time to view human rights from a global perspective. According to Justice Jorge Antonio Bacqué:

> It has become obvious that technological idiocy, unbridled fanaticism and Realpolitik have pushed humanity, for the first time in its history, to the brink of a precipice where the mode and conditions of life are at risk. This danger may be averted only by paying unconditional respect to human dignity.[9]

We agree. We must add, however, that human dignity cannot be understood without compassionate attention to the needs of the radically interdependent and interpenetrating global order in which we all now live, one that is, regrettably, filled with unparalleled climatic, strategic, and economic challenge. It is imperative and urgent that we attend to the material conditions, the socially and ecologically embedded actualities of the human situation in a world in unprecedented peril. The time is not for abstractions. The time now is for a new law and politics of compassion. It is, indeed, for this reason that we dedicate this fourth edition to our former coeditor, mentor, and friend, the late Richard Pierre Claude, whose compassionate attention to human dignity was and forever remains an inspiration to us all.

We welcome you!

Burns H. Weston
Anna Grear

---

9. Supreme Court of Argentina, Buenos Aires, Judgment of 22 June 1987 (*Causa No. 547 incoada en virtue del Decreto No. 280/84 del Poder Ejecutivo Nacional*). Constitutionality of the Law of "Due Obedience," Justice Jorge Antonio Bacqué, dissenting. The full opinion is published in English in "Supreme Court of Argentina, Buenos Aires," *HRLJ* 8 (1987): 430–71.

An Essential Guide to Use of Our Book

As we explained in our immediately preceding "Warm Welcome," we have worked hard to contextualize for you, our reader, many of the deepest human rights struggles currently animating global politics, law, economics, and of course human consciousness in an age of climate change, nuclear threat, and massive poverty and economic disparity. It is our hope that with this book we have succeeded in providing you with an apt, rich, timely, and thought-provoking resource from which you can benefit for years to come—or at least for the immediately foreseeable years to come. No doubt our fast-changing world will require a fifth edition within a few years.

Meanwhile, however, our potential success with this edition depends foremost upon your willingness to mine the depths of the book in its many details as fully as possible. To this end, we here enumerate a series of five essentials—and we do mean essentials—that can help you do precisely that. Please remember that our central pedagogical aim is to provoke discussion and to enable you, our reader, to question your own assumptions and perspectives—and those of others, too.

First, if you have not done so already, be sure to read our immediately preceding "Warm Welcome" in its entirety. Note especially our call to take very seriously the Questions for Reflection and Discussion that we have prepared and placed at the end of each reading. They are designed to invite critical engagement with the readings and their themes. Also note our summary clarification of the meaning of "neoliberalism" (xiii–xiv). As we explained, many of the authors represented in our text refer to "neoliberal economics and politics," "neoliberal globalization," the "neoliberal world order," and so on. It is important to be familiar with the meaning of this crucial and recurring terminology from the very outset.

Second, read each of the chapter introductions, nine in all, that provide you with (a) contextual information pertinent to the particular subject matter of each chapter, and (b) a brief summary of what we think each of the authors in each chapter is seeking to accomplish. A word to the wise: read them to get in on the ground floor of each chapter's readings.

Third, use continuously the two documentary appendices set out at www.uichr.org/WestonGrear (our previously noted website, courtesy of The University of Iowa Center for Human Rights) that register the many treaties, declarations, resolutions, and other human rights instruments commonly or uniquely cited throughout our book and forming or purportedly forming part of the ever-emerging international law of human rights.

Documentary Appendix A reprints and fully references (a) the provisions of the United Nations Charter that are directly and indirectly pertinent to human rights, and (b) all the provisions of the leading human rights instruments known as "the International Bill of Human Rights"—the 1948 Universal Declaration of Human Rights (UDHR), the 1966

International Covenant on Economic, Social and Cultural Rights (ICESCR), and the 1966 International Covenant on Civil and Political Rights (ICCPR)—but exclusive of some concluding technical/ritual provisions in each of the covenants and their optional protocols (all fully referenced, however, in Documentary Appendix B).

Documentary Appendix B identifies both the original and primary parallel references of the many human rights and related instruments that, in addition to the International Bill of Human Rights, detail the doctrines, principles, and rules upon which the world community struggles to build a social and legal order respectful of human dignity.

You would be well advised to master Documentary Appendix A and to familiarize yourself as much as possible with the instruments referenced in Documentary Appendix B, especially the 1948 Convention on the Prevention and Punishment of the Crime of Genocide and the following seven instruments which, together with the UDHR, ICESCR, and ICCPR reprinted in Documentary Appendix A, are designated by the Office of the UN High Commissioner for Human Rights (OHCHR) as "the core international human rights instruments"—all of them (the Genocide Convention, UDHR, ICESCR, and ICCPR included) available online via the OHCHR website at http://www.ohchr.org/EN/ProfessionalInterest/Pages/InternationalLaw.aspx (accessed 22 July 2015):

- International Convention on the Elimination of All Forms of Racial Discrimination (ICERD, 21 December 1965);
- Convention on the Elimination of All Forms of Discrimination against Women (CEDAW, 18 December 1979);
- Convention against Torture and Other Cruel, Inhuman or Degrading Treatment or Punishment (CAT, 10 December 1984);
- Convention on the Rights of the Child (CRC, 20 November 1989);
- International Convention on the Protection of the Rights of All Migrant Workers and Members of Their Families (ICMWF, 18 December 1990);
- International Convention for the Protection of All Persons from Enforced Disappearance (CPPED, 20 December 2006); and
- Convention on the Rights of Persons with Disabilities (CRPD, 13 December 2006).

Fourth, if at times you are confused by the alphabet soup of acronyms and initials present in much of our text, or have trouble remembering what they all mean, join the crowd. But not to worry. We have prepared a List of Abbreviations and their meanings for you (xxvii–xxxi). Though we cannot guarantee that we have caught all of them, we believe we have caught most of them, and certainly all the most important. Do consult the list whenever you have the need. We do. So why not you?

Finally, we are very aware that not all our readers will be familiar with all the legal dimensions of our book, and that many might be a bit hazy about even some of the field's basics. We have tried hard to keep this in mind as we put our book together. But if at times you find you need further assistance along these lines, we recommend that you refer to any one or more of the following five highly readable and informative summary texts—the first two focused on international law generally, the final three on international human rights law specifically:

- Sean D. Murphy, *Principles of International Law*, 2nd ed. (St. Paul, Minn.: Thomson/West, 2012);
- David Ott, *Public International Law in the Modern World* (London: Pittman, 1987);
- Thomas Buergenthal, Dinah Shelton, and David P. Stewart, *International Human Rights in a Nutshell*, 4th ed. (St. Paul, Minn.: West, 2009);

- Dinah L. Shelton, ed., *The Oxford Handbook of International Human Rights Law* (Oxford: OUP, 2013);
- Dinah L. Shelton, *Advanced Introduction to International Human Rights Law* (Northampton, Mass.: Edward Elger, 2014); and
- David Weissbrodt and Connie de la Vega, *International Human Rights Law: An Introduction* (Philadelphia: University of Pennsylvania Press, 2007).

All these texts are readily available in most university and law (especially academic) libraries, and they are available online as well.

And so: Onward! Needless to say, though we say so anyway, we hope and trust that our book will prove useful and energizing to you. If questions arise that you cannot answer for yourself—either with some research or with the help of a tutor—feel free to email either or both of us: Weston at burns-weston@uiowa.edu>; Grear at <GrearA1@cardiff.ac.uk>.

Once again, welcome!

About the Authors

Seyla Benhabib is Eugene Mayer Professor of Political Science and Philosophy at Yale University and former director of Yale's Program in Ethics, Politics, and Economics.

Fiona Beveridge is Professor of Law in the School of Law and Social Justice (within the Faculty of Humanities and Social Sciences) at the University of Liverpool.

Claudia Card is Emma Goldman Professor of Philosophy at the University of Wisconsin-Madison.

Richard Pierre Claude was Professor of Political Science Emeritus at the University of Maryland at the time of his writing. He also was Founding Editor of *Human Rights Quarterly.*

Wade M. Cole teaches sociology at the University of Utah, currently focused mainly on the impact of global human rights norms, treaties, and institutions on country-level practices.

Karen Engle is Minerva House Drysdale Regents Chair in Law and Co-Director and Founder of the Rapoport Center for Human Rights and Justice at the University of Texas.

Tony Evans is Professor of Global Politics in the Department of Politics at the University of Winchester. His research interests focus on the politics of human rights, historically and in the current era.

Richard Fairbrother, a former research associate of Robert McCorquodale (below), is currently Head of Research and Visit Support at the Australian Embassy in Beijing, having previously worked for the Australian Department of the Prime Minister and Cabinet.

Richard A. Falk is Albert G. Milbank Professor of International Law and Practice Emeritus at Princeton University and Visiting Professor of Global and International Studies at the University of California at Santa Barbara. From 2008 to 2014, he served as UN Special Rapporteur on "The situation of human rights in the Palestinian territories occupied since 1967."

Judy Fudge is Professor and Lansdowne Chair in Law at the University of Victoria in British Columbia.

Conor Gearty is Professor of Human Rights Law, former Director of the Centre for the Study of Human Rights, and currently head of the Institute of Public Affairs at the London School of Economics.

Anna Grear is Professor of Law and Theory at Cardiff University, Adjunct Associate Professor of Law at the University of Waikato, New Zealand, and Founder and Director of the Global Network for the Study of Human Rights and the Environment (GNHRE).

Cindy Holder is Associate Professor of Philosophy at the University of Victoria, British Columbia.

Paul Hunt, a native of New Zealand who served as UN Special Rapporteur on the right to health from 2002 to 2008, is a professor and member of the Human Rights Centre at the

University of Essex, UK, and Adjunct Professor at the University of Waikato, New Zealand.

Bonny Ibhawoh is Associate Professor of History at McMaster University in Hamilton, Ontario, where he teaches also in the Institute on Globalization and the Human Condition.

Michael Ignatieff, a Canadian writer, teacher, and former politician, is Edward R. Murrow Professor of Practice at the Kennedy School of Government at Harvard University, where from 2000 to 2005 he directed the school's Carr Center for Human Rights.

Ratna Kapur is Professor of Law at the Jindal Global Law School in Delhi, Titular Head of the Centre for Feminist Research in New Delhi, and a member of the visiting faculty of the Geneva School for International Relations and Diplomacy.

Harold Hongju Koh is Sterling Professor of International Law at Yale Law School, former twenty-second Legal Adviser of the U.S. Department of State (2009–2013), and former Dean of Yale Law School (2004–2009). He served as U.S. Assistant Secretary of State for Democracy, Human Rights and Labor from 1998 to 2001.

Scott Leckie is Director of the Melbourne, Australia, office of the Geneva-based Displacement Solutions, working to assist people who are displaced from their homes due to conflict or climate change.

Richard B. Lillich was Howard W. Smith Professor of Law at the University of Virginia and a member of the *American Journal of International Law* Board of Editors at the time of his writing.

Stephen P. Marks is François-Xavier Bagnoud Professor of Health and Human Rights at the Harvard School of Public Health, where he also directs the Program on Human Rights in Development.

Susan Marks is Professor of International Law at the London School of Economics.

Robert McCorquodale is Director of the British Institute of International and Comparative Law, Professor of International Law and Human Rights at the University of Nottingham, and a barrister at Brick Court Chambers in London.

Daniel Moeckli teaches International Law and State Law at the University of Zurich and is a Fellow of the University of Nottingham Human Rights Law Center.

Siobhan Mullally is Professor of Law at University College Cork, Ireland.

Martha C. Nussbaum is Ernst Freund Distinguished Service Professor of Law and Ethics at the University of Chicago.

Jordan J. Paust is Mike and Teresa Baker Law Center Professor of International Law at the University of Houston Law Center.

Christopher N. J. Roberts is Associate Professor of Law and an affiliated faculty member of the Department of Sociology at the University of Minnesota.

Douglas Roche, elected Chair of the UN Disarmament Committee at the 43rd General Assembly in 1988, served as a Member of the Canadian Parliament, Canadian Ambassador for Disarmament, and Visiting Professor at the University of Alberta during his career.

Dinah L. Shelton is Manatt/Ahn Professor of International Law at the George Washington University Law School. In 2009, she became the first woman nominated by the United States to membership on the Inter-American Commission on Human Rights, on which she served a four-year term and during which she served as President of the Commission.

Penelope Simons is Associate Professor of Law at the University of Ottawa—Common Law Section.

Margaret R. Somers is Professor of Sociology and History at the University of Michigan.

Jonathan Todres is Associate Professor of Law at Georgia State University College of Law in Atlanta.

Felisa L. Tibbitts is Founder and Senior Advisor of Human Rights Education Associates (HREA), which she directed from 1996 to 2011, and Lecturer in the Department of International and Transcultural Education of Teachers College of Columbia University.

Ineke van der Valk specializes in the study of racism and Islamophobia as a researcher in the Department of Political Science at the University of Amsterdam.

Jeremy Waldron is University Professor at New York University School of Law.

Burns H. Weston is Bessie Dutton Murray Distinguished Professor of Law and Founder and Senior Scholar of the Center for Human Rights at the University of Iowa.

Hannah Wittman is Associate Professor in the Faculty of Land and Food Systems at the University of British Columbia.

Acknowledgments

As with most books, especially books intended for classroom use in whole or in part, their authors and editors come away deeply indebted to many upon completion. We are no different. We cannot thank enough a great number of persons, who over four editions now, have given of themselves generously, often beyond what we had a right to expect.

Former contributors, colleagues, and friends who enhanced the first three editions with valuable contributions, comments, and other scholarly insights must be recognized again due to the intellectual sustainability of their ideas which continued to resonate in the making of this new fourth edition: George Andreopoulos, Upendra Baxi, Anne Bayefsky, Eva Brems, Hilary Charlesworth, Ellen Dorsey, Asbjørn Eide, Richard Falk, David Forsythe, Maryellen Fullerton, Lisa Hajjar, Laurie Handrehan, Stephen Hansen, Hurst Hannum, Hidetoshi Hashimoto, Rhoda Howard-Hassmann, Bernardo Issel, Edy Kaufman, Evan Kennedy, George Kent, Shulamith Koenig, Harold Koh, Maivân Lâm, Paul Lauren, Richard Lillich, Stephen Marks, Paul Martin, Mahmood Monshipouri, Rachel Neild, Diane Orentlicher, Jordan Paust, Michael Ratner, Douglas Roche, Luis Rodríguez-Rivera, Arjun Sengupta, Dinah Shelton, Jon Van Dyke, Justin van Fleet, Claude Welch, Adrien Wing, and of course Richard Pierre Claude.

We thank also all the contributors to this edition for granting us permission to publish new or revised excerpts of their works—but mostly, of course, for the intellectual energy of their ideas. Among them, however, we are particularly indebted to Richard Falk, Stephen Marks, Dinah Shelton, and Felisa Tibbitts for their above-and-beyond-the-call-of-duty willingness to volunteer entirely or virtually new essays to fill gaps that we knew they were uniquely qualified to do. They did so consummately in every sense, and for this they have our deep, enduring appreciation.

Never to be overlooked, of course, is the support given us by The University of Iowa College of Law Dean Gail Agrawal, Assistant Dean for Finance and Administration Gordon Tribbey, and Director of Financial Aid and Research Assistantships Susan Palmer who generously provided us with much-needed research assistant help. Grateful thanks are extended also to Cardiff University Law School for the generous provision of sabbatical time to Anna Grear, without which time this book could not have met its deadline.

Similarly deserving of grateful mention is Grace Tully, Burns Weston's secretarial assistant at The University of Iowa, for coming to our rescue on countless occasions—always expert, always prompt, always with a cheerful smile. Additionally, we thank Vicki Burgess, likewise at The University of Iowa, for vital help in unraveling the (unnecessary) mysteries of MS Word; and, for indispensable deliverance as well, the wonderful librarians of The University of Iowa College of Law, especially Donald Ford, and those of Cardiff University and the University of Waikato—always a blessing to scholars (though insufficiently recognized by many) who, like deer in the headlights, are not infrequently perplexed about how and where to go to find "that book with the black cover and gold embossing."

On final analysis, however, it is our former and present research assistants who merit our most passionate applause; and given that this book has been on track for over three years, they are quite a few: Damian Bakula, Brittany Bermudez, Lisa Castillo, Joshua Despain, Chelsea Moore, Ma Jin, Zachary Nichols, Carolyn Warner, and Alparslan Zora at The University of Iowa College of Law; and Keakaokawai Hemi at the University of Waikato Faculty of Law. Their energy, resourcefulness, and enthusiasm supplied us not only with a satisfying endorsement of our enterprise, but, as well, with friendships about which we care much. Damian Bakula is particularly to be singled out not simply for his acuity, creativity, and diligence over the last two years when our work was especially intense, but also for his generosity, sensitivity, and all-around kindness that is, we know from experience, decidedly uncommon.

We cannot close, however, without thanking The University of Iowa Center for Human Rights (www.uichr.org) for varieties of moral and logistical help—about some of which its staff may not even be aware so daily dedicated have they been to the success of this book. No small thanks can be tendered for providing us with vital website backup and extension, and for using and testing this and prior editions in the Center's human rights teaching. Reassuring institutional support rarely comes greater than this.

In sum, we have been exceedingly fortunate. To everyone mentioned, thank you. And to those human rights scholars upon whom we have leaned and from whom we have gleaned much, we salute you.

Abbreviations

ACHPR	African Charter on Human and Peoples' Rights
ACHR	American Convention on Human Rights
AICHR	Association of Southeast Asian Nations Intergovernmental Commission on Human Rights
AIR SC	All India Reporter, Supreme Court
AJICL	*African Journal of International and Comparative Law*
AJIL	*American Journal of International Law*
AJILS	*American Journal of International Law Supplement*
AOA	Agreement on Agriculture
APSR	*American Political Science Review*
ASEAN	Association of Southeast Asian Nations
ASIL	American Society of International Law
AU	African Union (formerly Organization of African Unity or OAU)
AYBIL	*Australian Yearbook of International Law*
Basdevant	Jules Basdevant, ed., *Traités et conventions en rigueur entre la France et les puissances étrangères 1814–1914*, 4 vols. (1918–22)
Bevans	Charles I. Bevans, ed., U.S. *Treaties and Other International Agreements of the U.S.*, 1 (1776–1917), 2 (1918–30), 3 (1931–45), 4 (1946–49)
BFSP	British and Foreign State Papers
BGBl	*Bundesgesetzblatt*
BIT	Bilateral Investment Treaty
Brownlie	Ian Brownlie, ed., *Basic Documents in International Law* (Oxford: Clarendon, 1967–)
BYBIL	*British Yearbook of International Law*
C, Cd, Cmd, Cmnd, Cm	UK Command Papers 1870–99, 1900–1918, 1919–56, 1956–86, 1986–present (respectively)
CAT, UNCAT	Convention against Torture and Other Cruel, Inhuman or Degrading Treatment or Punishment; *also* Committee against Torture
CED	Committee on Enforced Disappearances
CEDAW	Convention on the Elimination of All Forms of Discrimination against

	Women; *also* Committee on the Elimination of All Forms of Discrimination against Women
CERD	Committee on the Elimination of Racial Discrimination
CESCR	Committee on Economic, Social and Cultural Rights
CHR, UNCHR	UN Commission on Human Rights
CRC	Convention on the Rights of the Child; *also* Committee on the Rights of the Child
CRPD	Convention on the Rights of Persons with Disabilities
CSW	Commission on the Status of Women
CTS	Canadian Treaty Series
CUP	Cambridge University Press
DRD	Declaration on the Right to Development
EBRD	European Bank for Reconstruction and Development
ECA	*European Conventions and Agreements*, 1st ed. (Strasbourg: 1st ed. 1971; 2nd ed. 1993) (vol. 1, 1949–61; vol. 2, 1962–70)
ECHR	European Convention on Human Rights and Fundamental Freedoms
ECOSOC	UN Economic and Social Council
ECtHR	European Court of Human Rights
EHRR	European Human Rights Reports (of ECtHR judgments and decisions)
EJIL	*European Journal of International Law*
ESC	European Social Charter
ESCR	Committee on Economic, Social and Cultural Rights (established under International Covenant on Economic, Social and Cultural Rights)
ETS	European Treaty Series
EU	European Union
EYB	*European Yearbook*
FAO	UN Food and Agriculture Organization
Friedman	Leon Friedman, *The Law of War: A Documentary History* (New York: Random House, 1972)
GA, UNGA	UN General Assembly
GAOR, UN GAOR	UN General Assembly Official Records
GATS	General Agreement on Trade in Services
GATT	General Agreement on Tariffs and Trade
HGA	Host (State) Government Agreement
HHRJ	*Harvard Human Rights Journal*
HILJ	*Harvard International Law Journal*
HRC	Human Rights Committee; UN Human Rights Council (*see also* UNHRC)
HREA	Human Rights Education Associates
HRLJ	*Human Rights Law Journal*

HRQ	*Human Rights Quarterly*
HRR	*History Records Register*
Hudson	Manley O. Hudson, ed., *International Legislation*, 9 vols. (Washington, D.C.: Carnegie Endowment for International Peace, 1931–50)
HUP	Harvard University Press
IACHR	Inter-American Commission on Human Rights
IACtHR	Inter-American Court of Human Rights
ICC	International Criminal Court
ICCPR, CCPR	International Covenant on Civil and Political Rights
ICERD	International Convention on the Elimination of All Forms of Racial Discrimination
ICESCR, CESCR	International Covenant on Economic, Social and Cultural Rights
ICJ	International Court of Justice
ICLJ	*International and Comparative Law Journal*
ICLQ	*International and Comparative Law Quarterly*
ICMW, ICMWF	International Convention on the Protection of the Rights of All Migrant Workers and Members of Their Families
ICPED	International Congress on Population, Education and Development
ICPPED	International Convention for the Protection of All Persons from Enforced Disappearance
ICRC	International Committee of the Red Cross
ICRPD	International Convention on the Rights of Persons with Disabilities
ICTY	International Criminal Tribunal of Yugoslavia
ILC	International Law Commission
ILM	*International Legal Materials*
ILO	International Labour Organization
ILO CR	ILO Conventions and Recommendations 1919–66
IMF	International Monetary Fund
IOI 1A	*International Organization and Integration*, vol. 1A (The Hague: Nijhoff, 1981)
IPCC	Intergovernmental Panel on Climate Change
JDI	Journal du Droit International
JHRE	*Journal of Human Rights and the Environment*
JICL	*Journal of International and Comparative Law*
JORF	*Journal Officiel de la République Françaisefrançaise*
LNTS	League of Nations Treaty Series
Mezh	*Mezhdunarodnoe pravo v izbrannykh dokumentakh*
Misc	UK Command Papers, Miscellaneous Series
NYUP	New York University Press
NZTS	New Zealand Treaty Series

OAS	Organization of American States
OASTS	Organization of American States Treaty Series
OAU	Organization of African Unity (now African Union or AU)
OECD	Organization for Economic Cooperation and Development
OHCHR	Office of the UN High Commissioner for Human Rights
OJEC	*Official Journal of the European Communities*
OUP	Oxford University Press
Parry	Clive Parry, ed., *The Consolidated Treaty Series* (Dobbs Ferry, NY: Oceana Publications, 1969)
PAULTS	Pan-American Union (Organization of American States) Treaty Series
Peaslee	Amos J. Peaslee, *International Governmental Organizations: Constitutional Documents*, 3rd ed. (The Hague: Nijhoff, 1974–76)
PKOs	Peacekeeping Operations
PRSP	Poverty Reduction Strategy Papers
PUP	Princeton University Press
RCDIP	*Revue Critique de Droit International Privé*
RES, Res	Resolution
Roberts & Guelff	Adam Roberts and Richard Guelff, eds., *Documents on the Laws of War*, 2nd ed. (Oxford: Clarendon, 1989)*RTAF Recueil des Traités et Accords de la France*
Rüster & Simma	Bernd Rüster and Bruno Simma, eds., *International Protection of the Environment: Treaties and Related Documents* (Dobbs Ferry, N.Y. Oceana, 1975–82)
R2P	Responsibility to Protect
SAARC	South Asian Association for Regional Cooperation
SATS	South African Treaty Series
Schindler & Toman	Dietrich Schindler and Jiří Toman, eds., *The Laws of Armed Conflicts: A Collection of Conventions, Resolutions and Other Documents*, 3rd ed. (Leiden: Nijhoff, 1988)
SDIA	International Treaties and Conventions (Australia)
SLAPP	Strategic Law Suits Against Public Participation
SOCHUM	Social, Humanitarian and Cultural Committee (UNGA Third Committee)
SPT	Subcommittee on Prevention of Torture
SRSG	Special Representative of the Secretary-General
SSSR	*Sbornik deistvuyuschikh dogovorov, soglashenii I konventsii zaklyuchenny kh SSSR s inostrannymi gosudarstvami*
STAT, Stat	U.S. Statutes at Large
TLCP	*Transnational Law and Contemporary Problems*
TNC	Transnational Corporation
TRIPS	Trade-Related Aspects of Intellectual Property Rights
TS	Treaty Series (U.S. Department of State)
TWAIL	Third World Approaches to International Law

UDHR	Universal Declaration of Human Rights
UKTS	UK Treaty Series
UNCAT, CAT	UN Convention against Torture and Other Cruel, Inhuman or Degrading Treatment
UNCHR	UN Commission on Human Rights
UNDP	UN Development Programme
UNDRIP	UN Declaration on the Rights of Indigenous Peoples
UNEP	UN Environment Programme
UNESCO	UN Educational, Scientific and Cultural Organization (see also CESCR and UNESCR)
UNESCR	UN Committee on Economic, Social and Cultural Rights
UNFPA	UN Fund for Population Activities
UNHCHR	UN High Commissioner for Human Rights
UNHCR	UN High Commissioner for Refugees
UNHRC, HRC	UN Human Rights Council
UNICEF	UN Children's Fund (formerly International Children's Emergency Fund)
UNSC	UN Security Council
UNTS	UN Treaty Series
UPR	Universal Periodic Review
USC	U.S. Code
USDSB	United States *Department of State Bulletin*
VBD	*Verträge der Bundesrepublik Deutschland: Multilaterale Verträge* (ser. A, vol. 1)
VDPA	Vienna Declaration and Programme of Action
VJIL	*Virginia Journal of International Law*
WCED	World Commission on Environment and Development
Weston & Carlson	International Law & World Order: Weston's & Carlson's Basic Documents, http://referenceworks.brillonline.com/browse/international-law-and-world-order. *Note*: Most academic law libraries offer free access.
WFS	World Food Summit
WHO	World Health Organization
WPC	World's Poorest Countries
WTO	World Trade Organization
YBHR	*Yearbook of Human Rights*
YBUN	*Yearbook of the United Nations*
YJIL	Yale University Press

What we must offer

is a vision of human rights

that is foreign to no one

and native to all.

—KOFI ANNAN

Part I
ISSUES

Chapter One

International Human Rights: Issues and Overviews

A new ideal has triumphed on the world stage: human rights. It unites left and right, the pulpit and the state, the minister and the rebel, the developing world and the liberals of Hampstead and Manhattan. Human rights have become the principle of liberation from oppression and domination, the rallying cry of the homeless and the dispossessed, the political programme of revolutionaries and dissidents. But their appeal is not confined to the wretched of the earth. Alternative lifestyles, greedy consumers of goods and culture, the pleasure-seekers and the playboys of the Western world, the owner of Harrods, the former managing director of Guinness Plc as well as the former King of Greece, have all glossed their claims in the language of human rights.
  —Costas Douzinas, *The End of Human Rights* (2000)

THE ideal of human rights has captured the global imagination, yet the meaning of human rights—as the readings in this chapter imply—is never closed. The human rights ideal means radically different things to different people, and it is in part this very semantic openness that explains the extraordinary success of human rights as concept and language. However, as the quotation above also implies, this openness also renders human rights complex and paradoxical. Human rights, it seems, can be understood—simultaneously—as the language of both the oppressed and the oppressor. They represent our deepest hopes for respect, inclusion, and equality of significance, yet they have also a "dark side," as Ratna Kapur argues in this chapter.[1] Human rights harbor haunting ambiguities, some of which this book (and chapter) invite you, the reader, to explore. Human rights implicate issues (hotly debated) and forms of action (fraught with contestation) that engage very different value systems, political aspirations, and personal attachments that nonetheless manifest themselves while invoking the world's dominant ethical language.

There is no doubting the power and importance of human rights. On any given day, we are likely to be confronted by one or more news stories about their claimants, their successes, their betrayals, their defenders. In the contemporary world situation, would-be human rights defenders unite, increasingly through the Internet and social media, to call

---

1. See Reading 6 (Kapur) in this chapter.

for better conditions for countless human beings all over the planet. Human suffering and the blatant injustice of outright disrespect have a profound power and frequently evoke an outraged solidarity of protest in response. At their best, human rights reflect an emphatic and "creaturely" impulse to reach out and stand with the victim, to raise an outcry as creatures of blood and bone confronted by the suffering of others. Again in the words of Costas Douzinas:

> Human rights are the utopian element behind legal rights. . . . There is a poetry in human rights that defies the rationalism of law: when a burnt child runs from the scene of an atrocity in Vietnam, when a young man stands in front of a tank in Beijing, when an emaciated body and dulled eyes face the camera from behind the barbed wire of a concentration camp in Bosnia, a tragic sense erupts and places me, the onlooker, face to face with my responsibility, a responsibility that does not come from codes, conventions or rules but from a sense of personal guilt for the suffering in the world, of obligation to save humanity in the face of the victim.[2]

And so it is that defenders of human rights seek to call forth a fundamental and radical degree of human respect. They seek to protect the homeless, to call for adequate health provision for all, or for an end to torture enacted near and far. They call for free speech, fair elections, and the rule of truly democratic law. The denizens of the global human rights community reach across cultural and social differences to unite with Brazilian and other indigenous peoples fighting to safeguard their native homelands against colonization and dispossession; with Bulgarian women protesting efforts to lure them into international sex trafficking; with Ukrainians standing up to corrupt autocracy in favor of political democracy; with Indian women standing against a culture of rape with impunity; with children marching against abusive and exploitative child labor. The cast of characters is endless: Amazonian tribes, Burmese peasants, Congolese women, Russian gay men and lesbians, Tibetan monks, and multiple others—all speaking out against repressive state practices, unjust laws, and corrupt state partnerships with powerful transnational corporations.

In the twenty-first century, the ideal of human rights—as a basic, compassionate response to human disrespect and the suffering produced by multiple forms of oppression—shapes the aspirations and behaviors of all sorts of people in all kinds of situations. However, as is also brutally clear to twenty-first-century eyes, the full realization of human rights worldwide remains a distant dream. For all the human rights "progress" narratives shaping globally deployed discourse and policy, and for all the passionate, rising energies of global civil society, a truly just world order is barely on the horizon.

Yet the search for the core meaning of social justice from local to global and all points in between has never been more critical. The human rights project that began in response to the experience of Nazi atrocity and unfolded in a panoply of internationally defined human rights norms and procedures persists. As Adolfo Pérez Esquivel put it on receiving the Nobel Peace Prize as long ago as 1980, "The last few decades have seen a more extended and internationalized conscience in respect of human rights, such that we are confronted with and increasingly forced toward a deeper understanding of what the struggle for human rights means."[3]

And make no mistake: this *is* a struggle. It is a struggle of theory and worldview, between

---

2. Costas Douzinas, *The End of Human Rights: Critical Legal Thought at the Turn of the Century* (Oxford: Hart, 2000), 245.
3. Adolfo Pérez Esquivel, Afterword to Paul Williams, ed., *The International Bill of Rights* (Glen Ellen, Calif.: Entwhistle, 1981), 105–8, 105.

conflicting and contestable understandings; and a struggle, too, of situated action, a frequently confusing mixture of progressive and regressive impulses and dynamics. And yet, for all their ambiguities and contradictions (some would say hypocrisies), and precisely because, at their best, human rights capture the visceral energies of a shared human heart cry for justice and respect, the struggle must go on and in whatever form deemed appropriate for person, time, and place—as a challenge to state sovereignty; as an agenda for preferred world policy; as a standard for assessing national and international behavior; as a worldwide populist movement for fundamental change in human governance worldwide.

In a very real sense, the struggle has never been more important. There is genuine doubt that human rights can even survive.[4] Human rights face a crisis of authority: "Despite its legal and political success," writes Conor Gearty, "the idea of 'human rights' has been looking more and more like an awkward and ill-fitting relative at the philosophical house parties of recent years, standing in the corner and muttering about reality and 'a sense of moral obligation' while all about the young thinkers are jiving away grabbing what truth they can from the wordplay swirling about."[5] Human rights, it often is said, is a subject in a search for foundations adequate to meet the doubts of the age.

On the other hand, the struggle for human rights meanings also reflects the successful internalization of human rights into law, into legal structures both national and international, all over the world. Yet here, too, lurks crisis. Given that human rights are primarily a response to the marginalized, the oppressed—those suffering from a radical lack of respect and sometimes deprived even of basic human decencies, it is sobering to recall that law is by and large shaped predominantly by the interests of the powerful. Indeed, as human rights are successfully legalized, a gap opens up between their central impulse and what human rights become in practice, both in terms of who can access and operationalize human rights law, and in terms of—to say the least—visibly inconsistent enforcement patterns. The struggle for human rights further deepens when we take into account what Gearty calls "the crisis of national security."[6] Since 9/11, we have witnessed, across and beyond the Western world, the consolidation of a state of permanent "exception," a more or less constant state of emergency in the so-called "war on terror." This permanent crisis state, moreover, threatens to deepen as the social and environmental fallouts of climate change become more apparent. How will the state respond to food shortages, water shortages, and mass movements of refugees within and from beyond national boundaries? What will happen to human rights when, as a panel of U.S. military officials cautioned in 2007, climate change produces "mega-droughts, famine, widespread rioting and a threat to global security surpassing that of terrorism"?[7] The signs thus far are not encouraging.[8] The struggle for human rights meanings has never been more urgent.

4. Conor Gearty, *Can Human Rights Survive?* (Cambridge: CUP, 2006).
5. Ibid., 11.
6. Ibid., 12.
7. Peter Schwartz and Doug Randall, *An Abrupt Climate Change Scenario and Its Implications for United States National Security* (Arlington, Va.: U.S. Department of Defense, 2007), cited in David Nibert, "The Fire Next Time: The Coming Cost of Capitalism, Animal Oppression and Environmental Ruin," *JHRE* 3, 1 (2012): 141–58, 156.
8. It was reported that on 22 May 2014 the U.S. House of Representatives passed an amendment to the National Defense Authorization Bill that would bar the Department of Defense from using funds to assess climate change and its implications for national security. The sponsor of the amendment, Representative David McKinley (R-W.Va.), is quoted as saying in a memo to his House colleagues that "The climate is obviously changing; it has always been changing. With all the unrest around the [world], why should Congress divert funds from the mission of our military and national security to support a political ideology?" Kate Sheppard, "House Directs Pentagon to Ignore Climate Change," *Huffington Post*, 23 May 2014.

In this introductory first chapter, we seek to provide a deeper understanding of what the struggle for human rights means by looking at the topic from seven broad vantage points. Between them, these vantage points richly suggest the complexity and power of the idea of human rights, as well as its haunting ambiguities.

First, we review human rights in the context of changing historical concepts and international law. Burns Weston, in the opening essay, explores the concept and content of human rights as the idea of human rights has evolved over the ages and especially since World War II. His underlying supposition is that human rights, while having achieved widespread consensus about their meaning and application, are nonetheless not a corpus of fixed thought and action but, rather, a set of assumptions and choices that are open to constant rethinking because of ever evolving ideas, conditions, and needs.

Second, Anna Grear introduces the question of different perspectives—or framings—of human rights, pointing to the tensions between the oft-assumed dominant narrative in which human rights unfold as an arc of human progress and the narratives, positions, and subjectivities that the dominant framing of human rights excludes or marginalizes. Grear's essay points the reader toward the existence of multiple critiques of human rights and to the contestability and paradoxes of human rights.

Third, and illustrating one approach to the need for open-minded human rights "rethinking," is an essay by Martha Nussbaum that introduces us to the "capabilities approach" to human rights, laying out a framework for understanding the Universal Declaration of Human Rights in terms of the ways its provisions may be understood to enable people to achieve their individual promise and community-based potential. Her concern is to conceptualize and use human rights as a tool for human empowerment, especially in the context of those "capabilities" that help to define what it means to be human (itself a fraught and difficult question).

The question of the meaning of human rights is thoroughly at stake in the fourth reading; we look to the argument, prominent in the post-Cold War 1990s and early twenty-first century, between those who insist that local practices and traditions should determine the existence and scope of rights promised to individuals and groups versus those who contend that no amount of difference among diverse individuals and cultures should be allowed to obscure the essential universality of human rights. In a unique essay, "Universalism Versus Cultural Relativism: An Appeal for Respectful Decision-Making," Burns Weston asserts that proponents of the universality of human rights, a viewpoint to which he subscribes, cannot convincingly succeed without approaching cultural pluralism in a manner that is consistent with the core value of human rights: respect. To this end, he therefore outlines a "methodology of respect" for the resolution of competing relativist-universalist claims.

Fifth, Robert McCorquodale and Richard Fairbrother locate human rights in the pressurized materialities of contemporary globalization. They unflinchingly direct their sights at the conflicting implications of globalization for human rights, which are inevitably caught up in the complex political, economic, social, civil, and cultural dynamics of a globalizing world. The authors suggest the inability of international human rights law to deal adequately with the changes to state sovereignty accelerated by globalizing processes. For these authors, vast accumulations of economic power present a particular challenge to human rights realization.

Sixth, Ratna Kapur exposes the "dark side" of human rights in the twenty-first century by examining three normative claims on which the human rights project is based. Kapur is explicit in her challenge to the idea of human rights as progress. She questions the idea that human rights are "universal" and "inclusive" and points to the troubling way in which the liberal subject of rights constructs an "Other"—an other marginalized and excluded by the project of human rights, and reflective of its dark side. In this sense, Kapur picks up and develops certain themes in Grear's analysis.

Finally, Margaret Somers and Christopher Roberts introduce the role for a revived sociology of rights. They, too, locate human rights in contemporary materialities, pointing to the fact that deepening global poverty, floods of refugees, and the escalating awareness of human rights abuses deliver a powerful call for new approaches to human rights, in particular a sociological approach that commits itself—explicitly—to moving the focus toward questions of social relationship. Rights, in other words, must not be understood as something an individual possesses, but understood as relational constructs. In short, theirs is a move that allows for a vivid appreciation of differential social situations and disparities. Understood in this way, a sociology of rights delivers a much-needed critique of traditional human rights theory.

Each of these readings is intended to provoke engagement and questioning. Taken together they provide a glimpse into aspects of the ambiguities, promises, and contradictions of human rights as a powerful global ideal and meta-value. At the end of each reading, the reader is urged to reflect, discuss, and debate after studying the text critically and carefully, taking into account the questions posed—a method of interrogating and working toward a suitably nuanced understanding of human rights adopted throughout this volume.

1. BURNS H. WESTON *Human Rights: Concept and Content*

Human rights are rights that belong to an individual or group of individuals simply for being human, or as a consequence of inherent human vulnerability, or because they are requisite to the possibility of a just society. Whatever their theoretical justification, human rights refer to a wide continuum of values or capabilities thought to enhance human agency or protect human interests and declared to be universal in character, in some sense equally claimed for all human beings, present and future.

It is a common observation that human beings everywhere require the realization of diverse values or capabilities to ensure their individual and collective well-being. It also is a common observation that this requirement—whether conceived or expressed as a moral or a legal demand—is often painfully frustrated by social as well as natural forces, resulting in exploitation, oppression, persecution, and other forms of deprivation. Deeply rooted in these twin observations are the beginnings of what today are called "human rights" and the national and international legal processes associated with them.

Reprinted from Burns H. Weston, "Human Rights," in *Encyclopædia Britinnica Online* (2013). Copyright © 2013 Encyclopædia Britannica.

HISTORICAL DEVELOPMENT

The expression *human rights* is relatively new, having come into everyday parlance only since World War II, the founding of the United Nations in 1945, and the adoption by the UN General Assembly of the Universal Declaration of Human Rights in 1948 (UDHR). It replaced the phrase *natural rights,* which fell into disfavor in the nineteenth century in part because the concept of natural law (to which it was intimately linked) had become controversial with the rise of legal positivism. Legal positivism rejected the theory, long espoused by the Roman Catholic Church, that law must be moral to be law. The term *human rights* also replaced the later phrase the *rights of Man,* which was not universally understood to include the rights of women.

ORIGINS IN ANCIENT GREECE AND ROME

Most students of human rights trace the origins of the concept of human rights to ancient Greece and Rome, where it was closely tied to the doctrines of the Stoics, who held that human conduct should be judged according to, and brought into harmony with, the law of nature. A classic example of this view is given in Sophocles' play *Antigone*, in which the title character, on being reproached by King Creon for defying his command not to bury her slain brother, asserted that she acted in accordance with the immutable laws of the gods.

In part because Stoicism played a key role in its formation and spread, Roman law similarly allowed for the existence of a natural law and with it—pursuant to the *jus gentium* ("law of nations")—certain universal rights that extended beyond the rights of citizenship. According to the Roman jurist Ulpian, for example, natural law was that which nature, not the state, assures to all human beings, Roman citizens or not.

It was not until after the Middle Ages, however, that natural law became associated with natural rights. In Greco-Roman and medieval times, doctrines of natural law concerned mainly the duties, rather than the rights, of "Man." Moreover, as evidenced in the writings of Aristotle and St. Thomas Aquinas, these doctrines recognized the legitimacy of slavery and serfdom and, in so doing, excluded perhaps the most important ideas of human rights as they are understood today—freedom (or liberty) and equality.

The conception of human rights as natural rights (as opposed to a classical natural order of obligation) was made possible by certain basic societal changes, which took place gradually beginning with the decline of European feudalism from about the thirteenth century and continuing through the Renaissance to the Peace of Westphalia (1648). During this period, resistance to religious intolerance and political and economic bondage; the evident failure of rulers to meet their obligations under natural law; and the unprecedented commitment to individual expression and worldly experience that was characteristic of the Renaissance all combined to shift the conception of natural law from duties to rights. The teachings of Aquinas and Hugo Grotius on the European continent, the Magna Carta (1215) and its companion Charter of the Forests (1217), Petition of Right (1628), and English Bill of Rights (1689) in England were signs of this change. Each testified to the increasingly popular view that human beings are endowed with certain eternal and inalienable rights that never were renounced when humankind "contracted" to enter the social order from the natural order and never were diminished by the claim of the "divine right of kings."

NATURAL LAW TRANSFORMED INTO NATURAL RIGHTS

The modern conception of natural law as meaning or implying natural rights was elaborated primarily by thinkers of the seventeenth and eighteenth centuries. The intellectual, and especially the scientific, achievements of the seventeenth century (including the materialism of Hobbes, the rationalism of Descartes and Leibniz, the pantheism of Spinoza, and the empiricism of Bacon and Locke) encouraged a distinctly modern belief in natural law and universal order and, during the eighteenth century—the so-called Age of Enlightenment, inspired by a growing confidence in human reason and in the perfectibility of human affairs—led to the more comprehensive expression of this belief. Particularly important were the writings of Locke, arguably the most important natural-law theorist of modern times, and the works of the eighteenth-century thinkers known as the philosophes, who, centered mainly in Paris, included Montesquieu, Voltaire, and Jean-Jacques Rousseau. Locke argued in detail, mainly in writings associated with the English Glorious Revolution (1688–89), that certain rights self-evidently pertain to individuals as human beings (because these rights existed in the hypothetical "state of nature" before humankind entered civil society); that chief among them are the rights to life, liberty (freedom from arbitrary rule), and property; that, upon entering civil society, humankind surrendered to the state—pursuant to a "social contract"—only the right to enforce these natural rights and not the rights themselves; and that the state's failure to secure these rights gives rise to a right to responsible, popular revolution. The philosophes, building on Locke and others and embracing many and varied currents of thought with a common supreme faith in reason, vigorously attacked religious and scientific dogmatism, intolerance, censorship, and social and economic restraints. They sought to discover and act upon universally valid principles governing nature, humanity, and society, including the inalienable "rights of Man," which they treated as a fundamental ethical and social gospel.

Not surprisingly, this liberal intellectual ferment exerted a profound influence in the Western world of the late eighteenth and early nineteenth centuries. Together with the Glorious Revolution in England and the resulting Bill of

Rights, it provided the rationale for the wave of revolutionary agitation that swept the West, most notably in North America and France. Thomas Jefferson, who had studied Locke and Montesquieu, gave poetic eloquence to the plain prose of the seventeenth century in the Declaration of Independence proclaimed by the thirteen American colonies on 4 July 1776:

> We hold these truths to be self-evident, that all men are created equal, that they are endowed by their Creator with certain unalienable Rights, that among these are Life, Liberty and the Pursuit of Happiness.

Similarly, the marquis de Lafayette, who won the close friendship of George Washington and who shared the hardships of the American Revolution, imitated the pronouncements of the English and American revolutions in the Declaration of the Rights of Man and of the Citizen of 26 August 1789, proclaiming that "men are born and remain free and equal in rights" and that "the aim of every political association is the preservation of the natural and imprescriptible rights of man."

In sum, the idea of natural rights, forebear to the contemporary notion of human rights, played a key role in late eighteenth- and early nineteenth-century struggles against political absolutism. It was, indeed, the failure of rulers to respect the principles of freedom and equality that was responsible for this development.

"NONSENSE UPON STILTS": THE CRITICS OF NATURAL RIGHTS

The idea of natural rights was not without its detractors, however. In the first place, because it was frequently associated with religious orthodoxy, the doctrine of natural rights became less attractive to philosophical and political liberals. Additionally, because they were conceived in essentially absolutist terms, natural rights were increasingly considered to conflict with one another. Most importantly, the doctrine of natural rights came under powerful philosophical and political attack from both the right and the left.

In England, for example, conservative political thinkers such as Edmund Burke and David Hume united with liberals such as Jeremy Bentham to condemn the doctrine, the former out of fear that public affirmation of natural rights would lead to social upheaval, the latter out of concern lest declarations and proclamations of natural rights substitute for effective legislation. In his *Reflections on the Revolution in France* (1790), Burke—a believer in natural law who nonetheless denied that the "rights of Man" could be derived from it—criticized the drafters of the Declaration of the Rights of Man and of the Citizen for proclaiming the "monstrous fiction" of human equality, which, he argued, serves but to inspire "false ideas and vain expectations into men destined to travel in the obscure walk of laborious life." Bentham, one of the founders of utilitarianism, was no less scornful. "Rights," he wrote, "is the child of law; from real law come real rights; but from imaginary laws, from 'law of nature,' come imaginary rights. . . . Natural rights is simple nonsense; natural and imprescriptible rights (an American phrase) . . . [is] rhetorical nonsense, nonsense upon stilts." Agreeing with Bentham, Hume insisted that natural law and natural rights are unreal metaphysical phenomena.

This assault on natural law and natural rights intensified and broadened during the nineteenth and early twentieth centuries. John Stuart Mill, despite his vigorous defense of liberty, proclaimed that rights ultimately are founded on utility. The German jurist Friedrich Karl von Savigny, England's Sir Henry Maine, and other "historicalist" legal thinkers emphasized that rights are a function of cultural and environmental variables unique to particular communities. The English jurist John Austin argued that the only law is "the command of the sovereign" (a phrase of Hobbes). And the logical positivists of the early twentieth century insisted that the only truth is that which can be established by verifiable experience and that therefore ethical pronouncements are not cognitively significant. By World War I there were scarcely any theorists who would defend the "rights of Man" along the lines of natural law. Indeed, under the influence of nineteenth-century German idealism and parallel expressions of rising European nationalism, there were some—the Marxists, for example—who, though not rejecting individual rights altogether, maintained that rights, from whatever source derived, belong to communities or whole societies and nations preeminently.

THE PERSISTENCE OF THE NOTION

Although the heyday of natural rights proved short, the idea of rights nonetheless endured. The abolition of slavery, the implementation of factory legislation, the rise of popular education and trade unionism, the universal suffrage movement—these and other examples of nineteenth-century reformist impulses afford ample evidence that the idea was not to be extinguished, even if its a priori derivation had become a matter of general skepticism. But it was not until the rise and fall of Nazi Germany that the idea of human rights truly came into its own. Many of the gruesome atrocities committed by the Nazi regime had been officially authorized by Nazi laws and decrees, and this fact convinced many that law and morality cannot be grounded in any purely idealist or utilitarian or other consequentialist doctrine. Certain actions, according to this view, are absolutely wrong, no matter what the circumstances; human beings are entitled to simple respect, at least.

Today the vast majority of legal scholars and philosophers— particularly in the liberal West— agree that every human being has, at least in theory, some basic rights. Indeed, except for some essentially isolated late nineteenth- and early twentieth-century demonstrations of international humanitarian concern, the last half of the twentieth century may fairly be said to mark the birth of the international as well as the universal recognition of human rights. In the charter establishing the United Nations, for example, all member states pledged themselves to take joint and separate action for the achievement of "universal respect for, and observance of, human rights and fundamental freedoms for all without distinction as to race, sex, language, or religion." In the UDHR, representatives from many cultures endorsed the rights therein set forth "as a common standard of achievement for all peoples and all nations." And in 1976 the International Covenant on Economic, Social and Cultural Rights (ICESCR) and the International Covenant on Civil and Political Rights (ICCPR), each approved by the UN General Assembly in 1966, entered into force and effect. Together with the UDHR and their additional protocols, these documents came ultimately to be known as core elements of the "International Bill of Human Rights."

DEFINING HUMAN RIGHTS

To say that there is widespread acceptance of the principle of human rights is not to say that there is complete agreement about the nature and scope of such rights or, indeed, their definition. Among the basic questions that have yet to receive conclusive answers are the following: whether human rights are to be viewed as divine, moral, or legal entitlements; whether they are to be validated by intuition, culture, custom, social contract, principles of distributive justice, or as prerequisites for happiness or the achievement of human dignity; whether they are to be understood as irrevocable or partially revocable; and whether they are to be broad or limited in number and content. Even when the principle of human rights is accepted, there are controversies: whether human rights are a way of privileging narrowly conceived special interests over the common interest; whether they are the political tools of predominantly progressive elites; whether they are a stalking horse for Western economic imperialism; and so forth. It is thus sometimes claimed that there exists no universally agreed upon theory or even understanding of human rights.

THE NATURE OF HUMAN RIGHTS: COMMONLY ACCEPTED POSTULATES

Despite this lack of consensus, a number of widely accepted (and interrelated) postulates can assist in the task of defining human rights. Five in particular stand out, though not even these are without controversy.

First, regardless of their ultimate origin or justification, human rights are understood to represent both individual and group demands for political power, wealth, enlightenment, and other cherished values or capabilities, the most fundamental of which is respect and its constituent elements of reciprocal tolerance and mutual forbearance in the pursuit of all other such values or capabilities. Consequently, human rights imply both claims against persons and institutions impeding the realization of these values or capabilities and standards for judging the legitimacy of laws and traditions. At bottom, human rights qualify state sovereignty and power, sometimes expanding the latter even while circumscribing the former (as in the case of certain economic and social rights, for example). Increasingly, human rights are said also to qualify "private sovereignty" (as in the case, for example, of challenging the impunity of overbearing business enterprises, protecting family members from domestic violence, and holding nonstate terrorist actors to account).

Second, human rights are commonly assumed to refer, in some vague sense, to "fundamental," as distinct from "nonessential," claims or "goods." In fact, some theorists go so far as to limit human rights to a single core right or two—for example, the right to life or the right to equal opportunity. The tendency is to emphasize "basic needs" and to rule out "mere wants."

Third, reflecting varying environmental circumstances, differing worldviews, and inescapable interdependencies within and between different value or capability systems, human rights refer to a wide continuum of claims, ranging from the most justiciable (or enforceable) to the most aspirational. Human rights partake of both the legal and the moral orders, sometimes indistinguishably. They are expressive of both the "is" and the "ought" in human affairs.

Fourth, most assertions of human rights—though arguably not all (freedom from slavery, genocide, or torture are notable exceptions)—are qualified by the limitation that the rights of individuals or groups in particular instances are restricted as much as is necessary to secure the comparable rights of others and the aggregate common interest. Given this limitation, which connects rights to duties, human rights are sometimes designated "prima facie rights," so that ordinarily it makes little or no sense to think or talk of them in absolutist terms.

Finally, if a right is determined to be a human right, it is understood to be quintessentially general or universal in character, in some sense equally possessed by all human beings everywhere, including in certain instances even the unborn. In stark contrast to the divine right of kings and other such conceptions of privilege, human rights extend in theory to every person on Earth, without regard to merit or need, simply for being human or because they mitigate inherent human vulnerability or are requisite to social justice.

In several critical respects, however, all these postulates raise more questions than they answer. For instance, if, as is increasingly asserted, human rights qualify private power, precisely when and how do they do so? What does it mean to say that a right is fundamental, and according to what standards of importance or urgency is it so judged? What is the value of embracing moral as distinct from legal rights as part of the jurisprudence of human rights? Do nonjusticiable rights harbor more than rhetorical significance? If so, how? When and according to what criteria does the right of one person or group of people give way to the right of another? What happens when individual and group rights collide? How are universal human rights determined? Are they a function of culture or ideology, or are they determined according to some transnational consensus of merit or value? If the latter, is the consensus in question regional or global? How exactly would such a consensus be ascertained, and how would it be reconciled with the right of nations and peoples to self-determination? Is the existence of universal human rights incompatible with the notion of national sovereignty? Should supranational norms, institutions, and procedures have the power to nullify local, regional, and national laws on capital punishment, corporal punishment of children, "honor killing," veil wearing, female genital cutting, male circumcision, the claimed right to bear arms, and other practices? For some in the human rights debate, this raises a further controversy concerning how such situations comport with Western conceptions of democracy and representative government.

In other words, though accurate, the five foregoing postulates are fraught with questions about the content and legitimate scope of human rights and about the priorities, if any, that exist among them. Like the issue of the origin and justification of human rights, all five are controversial.

THE CONTENT OF HUMAN RIGHTS: THREE "GENERATIONS" OF RIGHTS

Like all normative traditions, the human rights tradition is a product of its time. Therefore, to understand better the debate over the content and legitimate scope of human rights and the priorities claimed among them, it is useful to note the dominant schools of thought and action that have informed the human rights tradition since the beginning of modern times.

Particularly helpful in this regard is the notion of three "generations" of human rights advanced by the French jurist Karel Vasak. Inspired by the three themes of the French Revolution, they are the first generation, composed of civil and political rights (*liberté*); the second generation of economic, social, and cultural rights (*égalité*); and the third generation of solidarity or group rights (*fraternité*). Vasak's model is, of course, a simplified expression of an extremely complex historical record, and it is not intended to suggest a linear process in which each generation gives birth to the next and then dies away. Nor is it to imply that one generation is more important than another, or that the generations (and their categories of rights) are ultimately separable. The three generations are understood to be cumulative, overlapping, and, it is important to emphasize, interdependent and interpenetrating.

LIBERTÉ: CIVIL AND POLITICAL RIGHTS

The first generation, civil and political rights, derives primarily from the seventeenth- and eighteenth-century reformist theories noted above (i.e., those associated with the English, American, and French revolutions). Infused with the political philosophy of liberal individualism and the related economic and social doctrine of laissez-faire, the first generation conceives of human rights more in negative terms ("freedoms from") than positive ones ("rights to"); it favors the abstention over the intervention of government in the quest for human dignity. Belonging to this first generation, thus, are rights such as those set forth in Articles 2–21 of the UDHR, including freedom from gender, racial, and equivalent forms of discrimination; the right to life, liberty, and security of the person; freedom from slavery or involuntary servitude; freedom from torture and from cruel, inhuman, or degrading treatment or punishment; freedom from arbitrary arrest, detention, or exile; the right to a fair and public trial; freedom from interference in privacy and correspondence; freedom of movement and residence; the right to asylum from persecution; freedom of thought, conscience, and religion; freedom of opinion and expression; freedom of peaceful assembly and association; and the right to participate in government, directly or through free elections. Also included are the right to own property and the right not to be deprived of it arbitrarily—rights that were fundamental to the

interests fought for in the American and French revolutions and to the rise of capitalism.

Yet it would be wrong to assert that these and other first-generation rights correspond completely to the idea of "negative" as opposed to "positive" rights. The right to security of the person, to a fair and public trial, to asylum from persecution, or to free elections, for example, manifestly cannot be assured without some affirmative government action. What is constant in this first-generation conception is the notion of liberty, a shield that safeguards the individual—alone and in association with others—against the abuse of political authority. This is the core value. Featured in the constitution of almost every country in the world and dominating the majority of international declarations and covenants adopted since World War II (in large measure due to the brutal denial of the fundamentals of civic belonging and democratic inclusion during the Nazi era), this essentially Western liberal conception of human rights is sometimes romanticized as a triumph of the individualism of Hobbes and Locke over Hegel's glorification of the state.

ÉGALITÉ: ECONOMIC, SOCIAL, AND CULTURAL RIGHTS

The second generation, composed of economic, social, and cultural rights, originated primarily in the socialist tradition, which was foreshadowed among adherents of the Saint-Simonian movement of early nineteenth-century France and variously promoted by revolutionary struggles and welfare movements that have taken place since. In large part, it is a response to the abuses of capitalist development and its underlying and essentially uncritical conception of individual liberty, which tolerated, and even legitimized, the exploitation of working classes and colonial peoples. Historically, economic, social, and cultural rights are a counterpoint to the first generation, civil and political rights, and are conceived more in positive terms ("rights to") than in negative ones ("freedoms from"); they also require more the intervention than the abstention of the state for the purpose of assuring the equitable production and distribution of the values or capabilities involved. Illustrative are some of the rights set forth in Articles 22–27 of the UDHR, such as the right to social security; the right to work and to protection against unemployment; the right to rest and leisure, including periodic holidays with pay; the right to a standard of living adequate for the health and well-being of self and family; the right to education; and the right to the protection of one's scientific, literary, and artistic production.

But in the same way that not all the rights embraced by the first generation (civil and political rights) can be designated as "negative rights," so not all the rights embraced by the second generation (economic, social, and cultural rights) can be labeled as "positive rights." For example, the right to free choice of employment, the right to form and to join trade unions, and the right to participate freely in the cultural life of the community (Articles 23 and 27) do not inherently require affirmative state action to ensure their enjoyment. Nevertheless, most of the second-generation rights do necessitate state intervention, because they subsume demands more for material than for intangible goods according to some criterion of distributive justice. Second-generation rights are, fundamentally, claims to social equality. However, in part because of the comparatively late arrival of socialist-communist and compatible "Third World" influence in international affairs, but more recently because of the ascendency of laissez-faire capitalism and the globalization of neoliberal, free-market economics since the end of the Cold War, the internationalization of these "equality rights" has been relatively slow in coming and is unlikely to truly come of age any time soon. On the other hand, as the social inequities created by unregulated national and transnational capitalism become more and more evident over time and are not directly accounted for by explanations based on gender or race, it is probable that the demand for second-generation rights will grow and mature, and in some instances even lead to violence. Indeed, this tendency was apparent already at the beginning of the 2010s, most notably in the widespread protests against austerity measures in Europe as the euro-zone debt crisis unfolded and in wider efforts (including social movements such as the "Occupy" movement) to regulate intergovernmental financial institutions and transnational corporations to protect the public interest.

FRATERNITÉ: SOLIDARITY OR GROUP RIGHTS

Finally, the third generation, composed of solidarity or group rights, while drawing upon and reconceptualizing the demands associated with the first two generations of rights, is best understood as a product of both the rise and the decline of the state since the mid-twentieth century. Foreshadowed in Article 28 of the UDHR, which proclaims that "everyone is entitled to a social and international order in which the rights set forth in this declaration can be fully realized," this generation appears so far to embrace six claimed rights (although events of the early twenty-first century arguably suggest that a seventh claimed right—a right to democracy—may be in the process of emerging). Three of the claimed rights reflect the emergence of nationalism in the developing world in the 1960s and '70s and the "revolution of rising expectations" (i.e., its demand for a global redistribution of power, wealth, and other important values or capabilities): the right to political, economic, social, and cultural self-determination; the right to economic and social development; and the right to participate in and benefit from "the common heritage of mankind" (shared Earth and space resources; scientific, technical, and other information and progress; and cultural traditions, sites, and monuments). The three remaining claimed solidarity or group rights—the right to peace, the right to a clean and healthy environment, and the right to humanitarian disaster relief—suggest the impotence or inefficiency of the state in certain critical respects.

All of these claimed rights tend to be posed as collective rights, requiring the concerted efforts of all social forces, to a substantial degree on a planetary scale. However, each of them also manifests an individual dimension. For example, while it may be said to be the collective right of all countries and peoples (especially developing countries and non-self-governing peoples) to secure a "new international economic order" that would eliminate obstacles to their economic and social development, so also may it be said to be the individual right of every person to benefit from a developmental policy that is based on the satisfaction of material and nonmaterial human needs. It is important to note, too, that the majority of these solidarity rights are more aspirational than justiciable in character and that their status as international human rights norms remains somewhat ambiguous.

Thus, at various stages of modern history, the content of human rights has been broadly defined, not with any expectation that the rights associated with one generation would or should become outdated upon the ascendancy of another, but expansively or supplementally. The history of the content of human rights reflects evolving and conflicting perceptions of which values or capabilities stand, at different times and through differing lenses, most in need of responsible attention and, simultaneously, humankind's recurring demands for continuity and stability. Such dynamics are reflected, for example, in a rising consensus that human rights extend to the private as well as to the public sector—i.e., that non-state as well as state actors must account for their violations of human rights. Similarly reflecting the continuing pressure for human rights evolution is a current suggestion that there exists a "fourth generation" of human rights consisting of women's and intergenerational rights (the rights of future generations, including existing children) among others.

LEGITIMACY AND PRIORITY: LIBERTÉ VERSUS ÉGALITÉ

The fact that the content of human rights has been broadly defined should not be taken to imply that the three generations of rights are equally accepted by everyone. Nor should broad acceptance of the idea of human rights suggest that their generations or separate elements have been greeted with equal urgency. The ongoing debate about the nature and content of human rights reflects, after all, a struggle for power and favored conceptions of the "good society."

First-generation proponents, for example, are inclined to exclude second- and third-generation rights from their definition of human rights altogether or, at best, to regard them as "derivative." In part this is because of the complexities involved in putting these rights into operation. The suggestion that first-generation rights are more feasible than other generations because they stress the absence over the presence of government is somehow transformed into a prerequisite of a comprehensive definition of human rights, such that aspirational claims to entitlement are deemed not to be rights at all. The most compelling explanation for such exclusions, however, has more to do with ideology or politics than with operational concerns. Persuaded that egalitarian claims against the rich, particularly where collectively

espoused, are unworkable without a severe decline in liberty, first-generation proponents, inspired by the natural law and laissez-faire traditions, are committed to the view that human rights are inherently independent of organized society and are necessarily individualistic.

Conversely, second- and third-generation defenders often look upon first-generation rights, at least as commonly practiced, as insufficiently attentive to material—especially "basic"—human needs and, indeed, as being instruments in service to unjust social orders, hence constituting a "bourgeois illusion." Accordingly, if they do not place first-generation rights outside their definition of human rights, these partisans tend to assign such rights a low status and to treat them as long-term goals that will come to pass only after the imperatives of economic and social development have been met, to be realized gradually and fully achieved only sometime vaguely in the future.

This liberty-equality and individualist-collectivist debate was especially evident during the period of the Cold War, reflecting the extreme tensions that then existed between liberal and Hegelian-Marxist conceptions of sovereign public order. Although Western social democrats during this period, particularly in Scandinavia, occupied a position midway between the two sides, pursuing both liberty and equality—in many respects successfully—it remains true that the different conceptions of rights contain the potential for challenging the legitimacy and supremacy not only of one another but, more importantly, of the sociopolitical systems with which they are most intimately associated.

THE RELEVANCE OF CUSTOM AND TRADITION: THE UNIVERSALIST-RELATIVIST DEBATE

With the end of the Cold War, however, the debate took on a more North-South character and was supplemented and intensified by a cultural-relativist critique that eschewed the universality of human rights doctrines, principles, and rules on the grounds that they are Western in origin and therefore of limited relevance in non-Western settings. The viewpoint underlying this assertion—that the scope of human rights in any given society should be determined fundamentally by local, national, or regional customs and traditions—may seem problematic, especially when one considers that the idea of human rights and many of its precepts are found in all the great philosophical and religious traditions. Nevertheless, the historical development of human rights demonstrates that the relativist critique cannot be wholly or axiomatically dismissed. Nor is it surprising that it should emerge soon after the end of the Cold War. First prominently expressed in the declaration that emerged from the Bangkok meeting held in preparation to the second UN World Conference on Human Rights convened in Vienna in June 1993 (which qualified a reaffirmation of the universality of human rights by stating that human rights "must be considered in the context of . . . national and regional particularities and various historical, cultural and religious backgrounds"), the relativist critique reflects the end of a bipolar system of alliances that had discouraged independent foreign policies and minimized cultural and political differences in favor of undivided Cold War loyalties.

Against the backdrop of increasing human rights interventionism on the part of the UN and by regional organizations and deputized coalitions of states (as in Bosnia and Herzegovina, Somalia, Liberia, Rwanda, Haiti, Serbia and Kosovo, Libya, and Mali, for example), the relativist viewpoint serves also as a functional equivalent of the doctrine of respect for national sovereignty and territorial integrity, which had been declining in influence not only in the human rights context but also in the contexts of national security, economics, and the environment. As a consequence, there remains sharp political and theoretical disagreement about the legitimate scope of human rights and about the priorities that are claimed among them.

INHERENT RISKS IN THE DEBATE

On final analysis, however, this legitimacy-priority debate can be dangerously misleading. Although useful for pointing out how notions of liberty and individualism have been used to rationalize the abuses of capitalism and Western expansionism and for exposing the ways in which notions of equality, collectivism, and culture have been alibis for authoritarian governance, in the end the debate risks obscuring at least three essential truths that must be taken

into account if the contemporary worldwide human rights movement is to be understood objectively.

First, one-sided characterizations of legitimacy and priority are very likely, at least over the long term, to undermine the political credibility of their proponents and the defensibility of the rights they regard as preeminently important. In an increasingly interdependent global community, any human rights orientation that does not support the widest possible shaping and sharing of values or capabilities among all human beings is likely to provoke widespread skepticism. The period since the mid-twentieth century is replete with examples, among them the official U.S. position that only civil and political rights—including the rights to own property and to invest in processes of production and exchange—can be deemed legally recognizable rights.

Second, such characterizations do not accurately reflect reality. In the real world, virtually all societies, whether individualistic or collectivist in essential character, at least consent to, and most even promote, a mixture of all basic values or capabilities. U.S. President Franklin Delano Roosevelt's Four Freedoms (freedom of speech and expression, freedom of worship, freedom from want, and freedom from fear) is an early case in point. A later demonstration is found in the Vienna Declaration and Programme of Action of the 1993 conference mentioned above, adopted by representatives of 171 states. It proclaims that, "While the significance of national and regional particularities and various historical, cultural and religious backgrounds must be borne in mind, it is the duty of States, regardless of their political, economic and cultural systems, to promote and protect all human rights and fundamental freedoms."

Finally, in the early twenty-first century, none of the international human rights instruments in force or proposed said anything about the legitimacy or priority of the rights they address, save possibly in the case of rights that by international covenant are stipulated to be "nonderogable" and therefore, arguably, more fundamental than others (e.g., freedom from arbitrary or unlawful deprivation of life, freedom from torture and from inhuman or degrading treatment and punishment, freedom from slavery, and freedom from imprisonment for debt). To be sure, some disagreements about legitimacy and priority can derive from differences of definition (e.g., what is "torture" or "inhuman treatment" to one may not be so to another, as in the case of punishment by caning or waterboarding or by death). Similarly, disagreements can arise also when treating the problem of implementation. For instance, some insist first on certain civil and political guarantees, whereas others defer initially to conditions of material well-being. Such disagreements, however, reflect differences in political agendas and have little if any concep-

tual utility. As confirmed by numerous resolutions of the UN General Assembly and reaffirmed in the Vienna Declaration and Programme of Action, there is a wide consensus that all human rights form an indivisible whole and that the protection of human rights is not and should not be a matter of purely national jurisdiction. The extent to which the international community actually protects the human rights it prescribes is, on the other hand, a different matter.

QUESTIONS FOR REFLECTION AND DISCUSSION

1. Where do human rights come from and for whom are they intended? It is commonly said that human rights are rights that one holds merely for being human. In *The End of Human Rights: Critical Legal Thought at the Turn of the Century* (Oxford: Hart, 2000), 372, Costas Douzinas comments that "it is not so much that humans have rights but that rights make human." This implies, Douzinas notes, that the granting and/or denial of rights results in a hierarchy of humanity, with those at the bottom accorded few rights and those at the top many or more. Do you agree? Disagree? What does Weston say?

2. Michael Freeman, in *Human Rights: An Interdisciplinary Approach* (Cambridge: Polity, 2002), 61, argues that it is not enough to say that human beings possess human rights simply for being human because "It is not clear why one has any rights simply because one is a human being." If you agree with Freeman, what theoretical rationale for human rights do you propose? Given that human rights are presumed to be, in Weston's words, "quintessentially universal in character," bear in mind the importance (necessity?) of a rationale to which all peoples and cultures can subscribe. Is such a rationale or theory possible? What does Weston say? In this regard, consider also Burns H. Weston, "The Theoretical Foundations of Intergenerational Ecological Justice: An Overview," *HRQ* 34 (2012): 251–66, esp. 260–65.

3. Members of indigenous cultures in Africa and elsewhere believe that individual rights do not exist independently of a group structure; witness the Xhosa saying, "umntu ngumntu ngabantu" ("a person is a person because of other people"). Other societies share a similarly collective concept of human identity and rights. Judeo-Christian and Islamic societies contend, on the other hand, that individual rights and duties are derived from divine sanction or from "nature." Given such radically different assumptions about the origins of rights, is it possible for the world's cultures to arrive at mutually comprehensible human rights accords? Can it fairly be argued that the individualistic ontology of the contemporary West has led not only to the development of individual human rights, but also to the abrogation of those rights by the West among peoples who do not share the same precepts? For possible answers to these questions, see Somers and Roberts in Reading 7.

4. Why is it important to inquire into the nature and scope of human rights? Do the following two statements by Weston provide any guidance?

"if a right is determined to be a human right it is quintessentially general or universal in character, in some sense equally possessed by human beings everywhere, including in certain instances even the unborn."

"the legitimacy of different human rights and the priorities claimed among them are necessarily a function of context. Because different people located in different parts of the world both assert and honor different human rights demands according to many different procedures and practices, these issues ultimately depend on time, place, institutional setting, level of crisis, and other circumstance."

Can these two statements be reconciled? Does the latter statement necessarily imply that the universalist project reflected in the former is illegitimate?

5. If, as Weston contends, human rights "qualify state power" and, in addition to being "quintessentially universal," are "fundamental" in character, addressing needs rather than "mere wants," why is it considered permissible to place limits on them? Consider, for guidance in answering this question, Article 29 of the UDHR and Article 4 of the ICCPR. By the same token, under what circumstances, if any, is it permissible to sit by while human rights are violated?

6. It has been argued that the idea of universally applicable human rights is essentially a modernist idea, and that cultural relativism and contextuality critiques have undermined its theoretical foundations. If as Andrei Sakharov once wrote, "The defense of human rights is a clear path toward the unification of people in our turbulent world," might one object that this "defense" is a form of new imperialism, albeit one imposed with the best of intentions? How might traditional modernist notions of universal human rights be reimagined to respond to such critique? See, in this connection, Jack Donnelly, *Universal Human Rights in Theory and Practice* (Ithaca, N.Y.: Cornell University Press, 1989).

7. Are economic, social, and cultural rights really "rights"? Is it better to think of these second-generation "rights" as social "goals"? Why? Why not? For assistance, see Reading 16 (Leckie) in Chapter 4.

8. If economic, social, and cultural rights are rights, is the right to property—important in the liberal West and proclaimed in Article 17 of the UDHR—among them? If so, why is it not recognized in the ICESCR? Is it because economic, social, and cultural rights really are not rights after all and that the right to property should be treated the same as life and liberty and thus be considered among first-generation civil and political rights? If so, why is the right to property also not recognized in the ICCPR? Is it because civil and political rights are not really "rights" either and that they, too, are better thought of as "social goals"? If so, is the right to property a right at all? Examine each of the aforementioned instruments. Also substantiate your response with an argument drawing on sources wherever possible.

9. Are so-called "communitarian" or "solidarity" ("third-generation") rights really "rights"? Or is it better to think of them as social "goals"? Why? Why not? Consider Philip Alston, "A Third Generation of Solidarity Rights: Progressive Development or Obfuscation of International Human Rights Law?" *Netherlands International Law Review* 29 (1992): 307–22, 322:

> In many respects the concept of third-generation rights smack rather too strongly of a tactical endeavor to bring together, under the rubric of human rights, many of the most pressing concerns on the international agenda and to construct an artificial international consensus in favour of human rights by appealing to the favorite concerns of each of the main geopolitical blocs. . . . In sum, the concept of third generation solidarity rights would seem to contribute more obfuscation than clarification in an area that can ill afford to be made less accessible to the masses than it already is.

Consider also the conundrum posed in Question 8 above, and reflect on how your answers to it compare with Professor Alston's observation.

10. It has been suggested that there is a "fourth generation" of human rights consisting of women's rights, the rights of future generations, rights of access to information, and the right to communicate. Does this make sense? Is a "fourth generation" of human rights a valid category of rights? If so, and if it contains women's rights, what does this imply about existing first-generation rights as they apply to women? What is signified by placing women's human rights alongside the rights of future generations? Consider the readings by Anna Grear and Ratna Kapur in this chapter, as well as Reading 14 (Beveridge and Mullally) in Chapter 3. What potential answer to the questions here do such perspectives imply?

11. Might new human rights emerge in the future? New generations of rights? Why, how, and with what effect? Why not?

12. John Locke (1632–1704) once suggested that everyone has "property in [their] own person" and that "nobody has a right but to himself [sic]." Does it make sense to expand the notion of property rights to rights in one's person? Why? Why not? Would such an expansion make property rights redundant with other rights? Why and which rights? Why not? How might your answer to this question affect your answer to the issue of a "fourth generation" of rights in Question 10 above? Is possible redundancy necessarily a liability?

13. In "The International Human Rights Movement: Part of the Problem?" *HHRJ* 15 (1999): 101–25, 108, David Kennedy has argued that the human rights movement has achieved a level of hegemony that has effectively crowded out other, possibly more effective modes of understanding, communicating, and acting. Kennedy notes that human needs not framed in the vocabulary of the human rights movement often go unattended. Do you agree? If so, which needs are unattended? Why? How might the human rights movement respond to Kennedy's critique? Consider Reading 3 (Nussbaum), in this chapter.

14. Is it possible and/or desirable to set a hierarchy or priority of rights or categories of rights? Why and according to what criteria? Relative importance? Utilitarian benefit? Why not? Should economic, social, and cultural rights be secured before civil and political rights? Before solidarity rights? The other way around? Some other sequence? Why? Why not?

15. Former Indian prime minister Indira Gandhi once said that "it is not individuals who have rights but states." What might Mohandas Gandhi (no relation) say about this? What arguments can you make for and against this assertion? Is the claim that the state is a substitute for the traditional communal group—ergo the embodiment of the people—sufficient to justify the statement? Why? Why not?

2. ANNA GREAR *"Framing the Project" of International Human Rights Law: Reflections on the Dysfunctional "Family" of the Universal Declaration*

Frames are principles of selection, emphasis and presentation composed of little tacit theories about what exists, what happens, and what matters.

> —Todd Gitlin, *The Whole World Is Watching: Mass Media in the Making and Unmaking of the New Left*

To frame is to select some aspects of a perceived reality and make them more salient in a communicating text.

> —Robert M. Entman, "Framing: Toward Clarification of a Fractured Paradigm"

The task of "framing the project" of international human rights law is daunting to say the least. First, there is the sheer enormity and complexity of the international human rights law "project"; adequately mapping the subject and its key related issues is impossible in a whole book, let alone a short reading. Second, it is daunting be-

Excerpted with changes by permission of Cambridge University Press from Anna Grear, " 'Framing the Project' of International Human Rights Law: Reflections on the Dysfunctional 'Family' of the Universal Declaration," in Conor Gearty and Costas Douzinas, eds., *The Cambridge Companion to Human Rights Law* (London: CUP, 2012), 17–35. Copyright © 2012 Cambridge University Press. Epigraphs: Todd Gitlin, *The Whole World Is Watching: Mass Media in the Making and Unmaking of the New Left* (Berkeley: University of California Press, 2003), 6; Robert M. Entman, "Framing: Toward Clarification of a Fractured Paradigm," *Journal of Communication* 43, 4 1993): 51–58.

cause every framing inevitably involves selection—if not pre-selection—through the conscious (and/or unconscious) placing of focus upon features or factors considered to be significant and/or valuable. As Gitlin puts it, framing is a way of choosing, underlining, and presenting "what exists, what happens and what matters." In this sense, the founding instrument of international human rights law (the Universal Declaration of Human Rights) functions as a particularly potent form of framing, for it selects aspects of perceived reality, making them not just salient but symbolically central to the entire philosophical, moral, juridical order designated by the term "international human rights law."

Framings, it should be noted, are inescapable—and draw attention to selected aspects of a perceived "something" at the expense of a host of other candidates for attention, producing, in the process, a set of muted or even invisible "others"—a whole range of unfocused-on factors, features, or (for the primary purpose of the discussion here) subjectivities. Framing choices in international human rights law are particularly influential. While there is a certain complex truth in the idea that the UDHR and its normative progeny deploy "human being" as a foundational category, it is also the case that the "human" of international human rights law is, in fact, a highly complex construction taking the form of a "universal" human subject that has been observed to (re)produce a range of "others" as marginalized subjects. Thus, much as a family photograph might reveal the unconscious favoritisms or over-sights of the parent holding the camera, the fram-ing of international human rights law's universal subject suggests a degree of dysfunction or frac-ture attending the "human family" evoked by the aspirational text of the UDHR.

This argument, however, will have to wait awhile. In "framing the project" of international human rights law we must surely first introduce at least a rudimentary outline of the project drawn from mainstream, traditional accounts and introduce the project's broad textual self-enunciation and institutional structure.

FRAMING THE PROJECT: TRADITIONAL ACCOUNTS

Traditional accounts of the international human rights law project converge to locate it in a rich amalgam of natural law, positive law, and an unprecedented international "consensus" "on substantive norms with high moral voltage"[1] at the end of the Second World War. It is generally agreed that the 1945 UN Charter effectively brought human rights into the sphere of interna-tional law—in the process achieving the simulta₁-neous internationalization of human rights and the birth of the "human individual" as a subject, rather than an object, of international law. This development is generally attributed with author-itatively establishing the idea, in normative terms at least, that ensuring respect for human rights would no longer be entrusted solely to the power of the nation-state. Ever since the relatively sparse first enunciation in the UN Charter of an interna-tional order of human rights, the UN has widely been seen as being instrumental in an apparently ceaseless and expanding process of international human rights standard-setting through an almost kaleidoscopic proliferation of instruments and treaties.

Of all these instruments and treaties, how-ever, one stands out as the iconic matrix from which all international human rights standards take their symbolic and juridical life: the UDHR. Since its formulation, the influence of the UDHR

has been impressive. It has been praised for giv-ing life to an entire generation of post-colonial states, for providing the rights-centered template for a host of new constitutional documents, and is credited with being the normative source of over two hundred international human rights instruments. The centrality of the UDHR as the frame within which the international human rights project unfolds, therefore, is indisputable, its practical influence undeniable: as Donnelly puts it, "For the purposes of international action, 'human rights' means roughly 'what is in the Universal Declaration of Human Rights.'"[2]

Traditional accounts of international human rights law also emphasize a series of phases or stages of standard-setting that reflect (and for the purposes of this discussion at least) pre-figure critiques of the UDHR. The initial vigor of the standard-setting activities reflected by the drafting of the UDHR cooled noticeably in the light of Cold War politics, producing a marked lull in the production of human rights docu-ments, unbroken except for the simultaneously adopted 1948 Genocide Convention until the 1965 adoption of the International Convention on the Elimination of All Forms of Racial Dis-crimination (ICERD), a development that quite naturally reflects the concerns of the newly de-colonized nations then swelling the ranks of UN membership and influencing the preoccupations of the international community.

In 1966, there was a fresh phase of general or universal standard-setting through which the rights of the UDHR found further enunciation in two international legal documents, in narrow chronological order, the International Covenant on Economic, Social and Cultural Rights (ICE-SCR) and the International Covenant on Civil and Political Rights (ICCPR). The dichotomous separation between these two "categories" of rights is often traditionally explained as reflecting a Cold War ideological rift, but for many, the sep-aration also reflects perceived differences between the categories of rights in terms of their relative justiciability, putative operation as primarily "neg-ative" or "positive" rights and relative enforceabil-ity. Together, the UDHR, ICESCR, and ICCPR are referred to as the "International Bill of Rights,"

---

1. Boaventura de Sousa Santos, *Toward a New Legal Common Sense: Law, Globalization and Emancipation* (London: Butterworths, 2000), 260.

2. Jack Donnelly, *Universal Human Rights in Theory and Practice* (Ithaca, N.Y.: Cornell University Press, 2003), 22.

and are supplemented, further expressed (or im-plicitly criticized—depending on one's chosen frame) by further standard-setting exercises re-sulting in a proliferation of international human rights treaties focusing upon either specific rights (such as the UN Convention against Torture and Other Cruel, Inhuman or Degrading Treatment or Punishment) or (perhaps more critically for pres-ent purposes) *specific rights-holders* (such as the Convention on the Elimination of All Forms of Discrimination against Women (CEDAW)).

This almost "carnivalistic"[3] expansion in the number of international UN human rights trea-ties has been accompanied, at different times and rates, by the incremental spread and matu-ration of a set of regional international human rights regimes: the European Convention on Human Rights and Fundamental Freedoms (ECHR) (adopted in 1950, which embraces only civil and political rights); the American Conven-tion on Human Rights (ACHR) (which excludes economic and social rights but later gave them normative space in the form of a separate proto-col); the African Charter on Human and Peoples' Rights (Banjul Charter) (adopted by the Organi-zation of African Unity in 1981—embracing all categories of rights in one culturally distinctive document). There is also a neonate and cultur-ally distinctive Arab and Muslim regional system (expressed in the Arab Charter on Human Rights, adopted by the Council of the League of Arab States in 1994 and which entered into force in 2008). No matter to what degree such human rights regimes operate at differing stages of jurid-ical and institutional maturity and reflect radi-cally differing regional and cultural commitments and histories, it is notable that they all, without exception, explicitly affirm their normative con-tinuity with the iconic UDHR.

FRAMING THE PROJECT: CRITICAL ACCOUNTS

The UDHR and the international human rights system, as has already been implied, is also subject to a range of critiques, some of which are now well embedded within mainstream human rights scholarship and debate. The most famous

of these reflects cultural relativist arguments de-constructing the "universalism" of human rights, arguments which emerge from a range of alter-native framing positions, including, most nota-bly, "Asian values," Islam, and postmodernism.[4] Within such accounts, there is a closely related and oft-repeated accusation that the UDHR is an instrument of "Western cultural imperialism," a mere Trojan horse for the imposition of "West-ern" commitments upon "non-Western" cul-tures. This critique is intimately related to the idea that the UDHR is Eurocentric in both origin and formulation.

Such critiques, in turn, are addressed by de-fenses of international human rights universal-ism resting on a variety of claims. It is argued, for example, that the UDHR Drafting Committee was more internationally diverse than is often assumed, and that the values in the UDHR reflect at least a thin convergence or "justificatory min-imalism"[5] centered on values viewed as being common to or at least conceptually derivable from many, if not most, great human philosoph-ical and religious traditions. Donnelly argues, for example, that "Christians, Muslims, Confucians, and Buddhists; Kantians, Utilitarians, Pragma-tists, and neo-Aristotelians; liberals, conserva-tives, traditionalists, and radicals, and many other groups as well, come to human rights from their own particular path."[6] Moreover, the de facto universality implied by the almost universal international recognition of the UDHR is also cited as evidence of its contemporary legitimacy as a common standard of achievement for all peoples. It is pointed out, furthermore, that the Vienna Declaration and Programme of Action af-firms universalism, construing it a value capable of respecting cultural variation and specificity while at the same time retaining an important primacy in order to defend against culturally de-rived violations of the minimum standards set forth by international human rights norms. In this sense, as Donnelly has argued, we can un-

---

3. Upendra Baxi, *The Future of Human Rights* (Oxford: OUP, 2006), 46.

4. For pertinent cultural relativism discussion, see Reading 4 (Weston) in this chapter.
5. Joshua Cohen, "Minimalism About Human Rights: The Most We Can Hope For?" *Journal of Political Philos-ophy* 12, 2 (2004): 190–213, 213.
6. Jack Donnelly, "Human Dignity and Human Rights," in *Protecting Dignity: An Agenda for Human Rights*, Swiss Initiative to Commemorate the 60th Anniversary of the Universal Declaration of Human Rights, www.udhr60 .ch/report/donnelly-Human Dignity_0609.pdf, 7.

derstand international human rights norms to be "relatively universal."[7]

There exist, of course, a range of other critiques—some of which are related to those already noted. The criticism, for example, that civil and political rights are incipiently favored over economic and social rights within the institutional mechanisms of international human rights law, a fact taken to reflect a fundamental ideological privileging of liberal constructs of rights descended from the commitments of the "West," remains painfully apt, particularly in the contemporary globalized context. It has been argued, relatedly, that the entire international human rights law project stands discursively colonized by the project of neoliberal capitalism and the hegemonic power of transnational corporations within the international legal order. Such arguments can be linked to earlier criticisms of rights discourse, particularly perhaps to the Marxist claim that human rights are individualistic tools of the capitalist project. Such critiques, taken together, strongly imply that the hierarchies and asymmetries observable in international human rights law (and further reflected, in substantive terms, by the differing strengths of enforcement mechanisms available for different categories of rights) reflect agendas far removed from the affirmation of the equal worth and dignity of all members of the "human family." This criticism, moreover, remains undeflected—even in the context of the so-called "third generation" (or "solidarity") rights, such as the human right to a clean environment.

Other telling discrepancies are also noted, centered upon excoriating denouncements of the selective deployment of international human rights standards by Western states, particularly in the late twentieth and early twenty-first centuries: for example, the use of human rights-based justifications for the "legitimation" of Western (and NATO) incursions into the sovereignty of certain states, especially those states whose aims and interests are considered inimical to those of the capitalist "West." There is a shocking disjunction, for example, between the "humanitarian" NATO intervention in Kosovo and abject failure

of the Western powers to intervene to prevent the highly publicized and appalling genocide in Rwanda. Such discrepant practices are sometimes cited as evidence of a self-serving realpolitik deploying the mantle of human rights.

There are many available critical framings of international human rights law. In fact, there are so many that the only safe conclusion that we can draw, as an intermediate matter, is that international human rights law, in both theory and practice, is riven with contradictions, disputations, rival framings, and oppositional accounts. The mainstream frame or account is vociferously disputed—and, just as it is challenging to provide a comprehensive map of the main documents and institutional mechanisms of international human rights law, it is even more difficult, arguably, to provide a complete account of all the critiques internal and external to international human rights law's vast and apparently illimitable discursive field.

AN INTERPOSITION—FRAMING THE "FRAMES"

What should be noted, at this stage of our reflection, is the contingency of all the available accounts and framings of international human rights law, mainstream and critical. All the accounts we have introduced (and those we have not) are "framings." They all come complete with their own epistemic limitations and closures. However, there is arguably one important general difference observable between "mainstream" and "critical" accounts—or, at least, those critical accounts embracing the inescapability of epistemic limitation—and it is this: such critical accounts are based on an explicit reflexivity that attempts to respond to the partiality and contingency of framings themselves. Generalizations are never safe, but it is possible to assert with some degree of plausibility nonetheless that many "mainstream" accounts of the international human rights law project imply a degree of "progressiveness" in the international human rights law trajectory. Genuinely critical accounts, by contrast, tend continuously to problematize it—as well as the narratives and framings on offer. This is not to suggest that critical accounts invariably end in a terminus of radical, paralyzing relativism. Human rights emerge from critical accounts as "ideas" (albeit powerful,

7. Jack Donnelly, "Cultural Relativism and Universal Human Rights," *HRQ* 6, 4 (1984): 400–419, 419. But see also the critique of this offered by Michael Goodhart, "Neither Relative Nor Universal: A Response to Donnelly," *HRQ* 30, 1 (2008): 183–93.

world-shaping ideas) which are revealed as being semantically elusive "placeholders in a global conversation that allows a constant deferral of the central defining moment in which rights themselves will be infused with substance."[8] Such accounts emphasize the sense in which the very meaning of human rights is always "up for grabs." They amply suggest the ambivalence of human rights: their Janus-faced capacity for producing and cloaking privilege and yet, simultaneously, their capacity for the unveiling of oppression. Critical accounts of human rights underline the sense in which human rights are always (to borrow the words of Douzinas) "floating signifiers":[9] their promise constantly draws the human imagination forwards, but is ever-deferred, always "not yet."

ONE CONTINGENT REFRAMING

We have already noted the centrality of the iconic UDHR to the entire edifice of human rights law and mentioned its production of a universal human rights bearer. A central paradox of international human rights law rests on the construction of this universal "human subject." Despite the fact that the UDHR clearly enshrines its rights as belonging to all members of the "human family," to "everyone," it is far from clear, as we shall see, that all human beings find themselves fully embraced or represented by the universal human rights subject. In fact, there is arguably a dysfunction or fracture at the heart of the "human family" of the UDHR—and it is this observation that forms the inspiration for this particular framing of the international human rights law project.

It is clear on various accounts, including its own, that the UDHR attempts to respond to the need to protect the human being understood qua human being. If we combine the emphasis of the UDHR preamble with the language of Article 2, this inclusive aspiration becomes clear: the invocation of terms such as "everyone" and "the human family" is supported by the *explicit*

delegitimation of forms of discrimination based upon any putative distinctions or subdivisions between human beings:

> *Everyone* is entitled to all the rights and freedoms set forth in this Declaration, *without distinction of any kind*, such as race, color, sex, language, religion, political or other opinion, national or social origin, property, birth *or other status*. Furthermore, no distinction shall be made on the basis of the political, jurisdictional or international status of the country or territory to which a person belongs, whether it be independent, trust, non-self-governing or under any other limitation of sovereignty.

It is clear from this that no putative basis for distinction, even those centered upon the nation-state itself, should form a legitimate basis for the denial of human rights. This emphasis is unsurprising in so far as certain scholarship has revealed the central concern driving the drafters of the UDHR to be an explicit reaction to the biocentric, racist, and species-segmenting abuse of state power by the Nazi state (which was itself conceived of as a species-specific entity: as an "Aryan" organic body of which Hitler was the head). This argument, emerging from Morsink's careful analysis of the records of the deliberations of the drafting committees,[10] is lent further plausibility by the preamble's immediate reference to the "barbarous acts which have outraged the conscience of mankind." Although, inevitably, this view is contested, it seems relatively clear that the affirmation of the fundamental commonality of the human race was a conscious aim of the drafters and that the UDHR explicitly emphasizes the unacceptability of selective segmentations and discriminatory practices and violations, whether those were primarily driven by awareness of Nazi laws and practices or were also responding to wider sociohistorical patterns and trajectories.

The UDHR aspiration for human familial inclusion and the explicit rejection of discrimination based on subdivisions in the human family is accompanied, it will be argued here, by an enduring paradox consisting in the directly contradictory (re)production, within international human rights law, of an entire range of outsider

8. Alicia Ely-Yamin, "Empowering Visions: Towards a Dialectical Pedagogy of Human Rights," *HRQ* 15, 4 (1993): 640–85, 663.

9. Costas Douzinas, *The End of Human Rights: Critical Legal Thought at the Turn of the Century* (Oxford: Hart, 2000), 253–61.

10. Johannes Morsink, "World War Two and the Declaration," *HRQ* 15 (1993): 357–405, 357.

or marginalized subjectivities. The puzzle of this contradictory state of affairs seems to hinge on a fundamental contradiction inherent in the figuration of the abstract form of human nature deployed as the "universal" subject of rights.

Linking the abstract human being of the UDHR with the abstract man of the earlier French Declaration, Douzinas argues that "Once the slightest empirical or historical material is introduced into abstract human nature, once we move from the declarations onto the concrete embodied person, with gender, race, class and age, human nature with its equality and dignity retreats rapidly."[11] We should pause to note, moreover, the *patterned nature of the specificities* in relation to which equality and dignity retreat. Such *patterned retreat* in the face of embodied empirical and historical particularity is especially troubling for the international human rights law project, for as Otto suggests, such critique *"goes to the heart* of the post-World War II discourse of universal human rights which, *as its most fundamental premise*, purports to apply *equally, without distinction*, to *'everyone'* (Article 2 UDHR). [Despite this, t]he allegedly universal subject of human rights law . . . reproduces hierarchies, including those of [gender], race, culture, nation, socio-economic status and sexuality."[12]

It seems that the universal human rights subject installed at the heart of the international human rights law project appears to (re)produce the very hierarchies and discriminatory patterns that the UDHR itself explicitly rejects. This presents, clearly, something of a conundrum, and despite the proliferation of a range of "identity"-inclusive documents, such as CEDAW, patterns of marginalization remain obdurately real and installed within international human rights law. The evidence for the reality and impact of these marginalized subjectivities emerges from various sources which we do not have space to examine more closely here, but it is worth nothing that even at the origins of the UDHR, marginalization was a historically real problem. For example, women, in particular, were marginalized in the drafting process: the Commis-

sion on the Status of Women (CSW) had to fight hard just to achieve a shift away from the language of the rights of "all men" toward the rights of "all human beings." This limited concession, moreover, entailed the explicit rejection of the explicitly sexuate and more inclusive formulation sought by the CSW—that of "all people, men and women."[13] It is of note that the masculine pronoun remains stubbornly dominant throughout the text of the UDHR, which is also completely silent on the issues of gendered violence and reproductive rights. Critics have noted, moreover, that women's equal rights are semantically tied to the context of the family (Article 16 UDHR) and that there is a problematic further muting of women's rights claims through the traditional liberal public/private divide —itself a profound barrier to genuine female rights enjoyment—and uncritically installed at the heart of the international human rights law project.

In a sense, the *very need* for CEDAW and other treaties directed at particular groups or "identities" of rights-claimants reflects the existence of marginalized and hierarchically constructed subjectivities within international human rights law. It is precisely the felt/lived sense of exclusion, hierarchical marginalization, or invisibility that has driven women and a range of marginalized others to seek the specific enumeration of their rights. This dynamic strongly suggests the (re)production of what we can with a high degree of accuracy label as *"nonuniversal* human subjectivities" (those deemed inherently *incapable* of representing all humanity).

The evidence suggests though, that the existing universal, far from being universal in reality, despite its claim to be inclusively representative, is a radically "nonuniversal universal," an abstract construct enacting familiar exclusions historically linked to certain much criticized conceptual and ideological features of Western thought. In short, the philosophical foundations of the universal human subject enact a certain kind of "tilt." This point is not without its irony. It has been noted by Morsink that the urgent ethical humanitarian sensibility driving the UHDR drafters was such that "they did not need a philosophical argument in addition to the ex-

11. Douzinas, *The End of Human Rights*, note 9, 96.
12. Diane Otto, "Disconcerting 'Masculinities': Reinventing the Gendered Subject(s) of International Human Rights Law," in Doris Buss and Ambreena Manji, eds., *International Law: Modern Feminist Approaches* (Oxford: Hart, 2005), 105–30, 105–6; emphasis added.

13. See Johannes Morsink, "Women's Rights in the Universal Declaration," *HRQ* 13 (1991): 299.

perience of the Holocaust"[14] to justify the UDHR. Yet, despite their ethical humanitarian energy, moral outrage, and high degree of empathy with victims of human violation, the drafters of the UDHR, in attempting to inaugurate a new age of international, ethical, and juridical concern predicated on the important concept of inclusive universality, turned (naturally enough perhaps) to the preexisting formula of abstract universalism enshrined in Western philosophy, and in particular, to the iconic French Declaration of the Rights of Man and of the Citizen (French Declaration).

The universal subject or "man" of the French Declaration has, of course, its own philosophical foundations and antecedents. Its formulation, for example, is radically continuous with the philosophical, political, and rights-based discursivity of John Locke, and with earlier philosophical assumptions concerning the primacy of "man's nature" as being quintessentially "rational." The rational man of the French Declaration, as Douzinas's argument above implies, is the direct progenitor of the universal "human being" of the UDHR. In fact, there are extensive continuities between the UHDR and the earlier French Declaration. Marks has argued that the proclamation of rights in the French Declaration had a "major impact on the form and content of the UDHR proclaimed 160 years later, and subsequently, on the current codex of internationally recognized human rights."[15] The assertion that all "men are born and remain free and equal in rights" (Article 1 of the French Declaration) becomes, in Article 1 of the UDHR, the statement that all "human beings are born free and equal in dignity and rights"—an almost identical formulation, as Hunt suggests, but for the exchange of "human beings" for "men."[16] The drafters of the UDHR reached out, then, for the preexisting symbols of rich human rights imaginary at the heart of which stood an abstract universal.

The abstract universal "man"/"human being" is conceived of as being essentially "neutral"— representative of all humanity. Closer inspection, however, reveals this "neuter" universal to be a cipher that is never neutral, never empty, because its essential rationality comes laden with philosophical and ideological provenance—most especially a long-standing coimbrication of rationality and maleness. Inevitably, then, this abstract universal is gendered. (We have already noted the related struggle of the CSW to change the language from "men" to "human beings" in the UDHR drafting process.) If we pause to reflect once more on the fact that, as Douzinas points out, "universal" dignity and equality rapidly retreat once the abstract human subject takes on materiality or concrete form, we can begin to grasp the essence and implications of the problem. The universal seems to be constructed as neutral, yet the retreat of dignity and equality is precisely along the well-worn conduits of discriminatory species-segmentation so familiar in our long human history of inequalities, diminutions, degradations, marginalizations, oppressions, and violence.

The marginalized subjectivities revealed by such realities suggest, just as a photographic negative might, the precise contours of the construct covertly privileged by the neuter-impossibility of the "universal *one*" of human rights. The marginalization of "women, humans of color, children, humans with disabilities, humans who are older or poor, and those with different sexual orientations"—those with long histories of exclusion— points ineluctably toward a hidden "insider"—the "one" who is most definitely "*not*" any of these. It is as if a great invisible figure inhabits the universal. The figure revealed by the patterned retreat of particularity in international human rights law emerges from the ebb, as "natural man" or "natural human being"—in "his" materialization, however, bearing a predictable set of particularities. "He" (for this is a construct not a living man) emerges as the male, the property-owning, the European, and the white. To claim this is simply to insist that international human rights law, in this particular regard, is no real exception to the history of rights struggles before it, although this paradox is all the more troubling in international human rights law, where the issue is both more complex (the UDHR explicitly

14. Ibid., 358.
15. Stephen P. Marks, "From the 'Single Confused Page' to the 'Decalogue for Six Billion Persons': The Roots of the Universal Declaration of Human Rights in the French Revolution," *HRQ* 20 (1998): 459–514, 460.
16. Lynn Hunt, *The French Revolution and Human Rights: A Brief Documentary History* (New York: Bedford/St. Martin's, 1996). The text of the American Declaration of Independence (1776) declares "all men" to be "created equal, . . . endowed by their Creator with certain unalienable Rights, . . . among these are Life, Liberty and the pursuit of Happiness."

denounces discrimination) and *more telling (for the same reason)*.

History is where ideology breaks cover. The paradoxes of the universal are reflected in a long history of rights settlements, history revealing a pattern (not just in the UDHR) of rights being born of visceral, critical reactions against a violently uneven status quo or an immense injustice—followed by their institutional crystallization, at which point their radical potential is muted or foreclosed (albeit not completely; thankfully their critical energy is never entirely exhausted in the process). Even in revolutionary France, where rights talk was at its most universalistic and liberationist, the initial institutional settlement strongly reflected the priorities of the powerful: the "rights of man" were granted, paradigmatically to the male, rational property-owning citizen—notwithstanding vigorous and open debate concerning the rights of slaves, Calvinists, Jews, and homosexuals and the attempts by some women to gain rights to active political citizenship.[17]

By the time of the UDHR, as the text itself reflects, there was a widely accepted awareness of just such past discriminatory patterns—yet, as we have seen, discriminatory patterns remained installed in the drafting process itself (at least concerning gender), and remain problematically installed within the cognitive and ideological architecture of the abstract "universal subject" of international human rights. A key challenge related to these patterns concerns a tendency in abstractionism toward (incomplete) disembodiment. The construct of the universal human being simply does not do justice to the full complexity, the sheer fleshy variability and multiple forms, colors, shapes, and sex/genders of the embodied human personality in all its vulnerability. The thin "nonuniversal universal" cannot do justice to the "thick" humanity of the entire human family. There is, quite simply, no protection in the UDHR for the human being qua human being, a fact representing a profound ethical failure lying at the heart of the most putatively humanitarian of rights regimes.

Lest readers think this statement too strong, let us pause to reflect with Hannah Arendt in *The Origins of Totalitarianism* on the fact that human rights "based on the assumed existence of a human being as such broke down at the very moment when those who professed to believe in [them] were for the first time confronted with people who had lost all other qualities and specific relationships—except that they were still human."[18] This breakdown concerns, paradigmatically, "the refugee"—the very figure who should most embody any *international* human rights subjectivity genuinely founded on the radical presence of the human being qua human being *as such*. Yet Article 14 of the UDHR, examined closely, fails to guarantee the refugee the right to enter another country, producing a lacuna signaling the radical failure of the promise of the universal in the stark light of the very moment when the promise of full inclusion in the "human family" of the UDHR is most necessary for juridically naked, dislocated human beings fleeing war, economic privation, environmental devastation, or tyranny. Article 14 arguably announces, or amplifies, the dysfunction lying at the heart of international human rights law concerning the discrepancy between the avowedly universalist aspirations of the UDHR and the fractured reality of its patterned (re)production of marginalized subjectivities.

In Arendt's terms, the fact that the UDHR fails to embrace the embodied vulnerable particularity of the human being qua human being, and the fact that the UDHR "family" remains haunted by international human rights law's multiple "others," signals a "void" at the heart of international human rights law. This "void" (and its historical and contemporary resonances) amply suggests, moreover, dark intimations of the radically differential distributions of life and death in the well-defended patterns and practices of injustice now characterizing our global age of corporate capital predation. Indeed, the specter of deepening climate injustice and its (as-yet) differential distribution of privation, immiseration, cultural destruction, and radical human dislocation points, if anything, to the continuing salience of Arendt's lament.

What use then, we might ask, are international human rights, if they fail precisely at the point where they are called upon in the very name of the juridically naked, embodied, vulnerable humanness so poignantly exposed? Was

---

17. Ibid.

18. Hannah Arendt, *The Origins of Totalitarianism* (New York: Harcourt, 1971), 299.

achieving this very nakedness not the precise aim of the Nazi programme of stripping away both citizenship and legal personhood—a process that assiduously preceded the procedurally regulated extermination of Jews and other victims in the camps of the Third Reich and which, through the imposition of "juridical death" opened the way for the practices of Holocaust so foundational, on one reading at least, to the inception of the UDHR as an outraged reaction to it?

How, then, are we to answer this call for human rights meaning? Arguably, human rights break their promise when they fail to be bearers of outrage and compassion. It is arguably at the very moment of experienced "nakedness," in the face of the "void" itself, in the "felt" gap between the "now" and the "not yet," in the savage contradiction between human rights promise and human rights betrayal, that the illimitable energy and paradox of human rights returns. For it is in the very experiential realities of the betrayal of the promise of the universal, in the viscerally felt failures of inclusion, in the embodied, lived senses of marginalization, exclusion, or excision

that human energies surge back into the space of human rights failure, articulating new words, breathing (literally) a pain that reawakens human rights as an endless contestation concerning the constitution of the "human family." Hope lies, perhaps, in the idea that international human rights law has not yet exhausted the critical energy of human rights as an endlessly recursive interaction concerning inclusions and exclusions in which every inclusion necessarily creates new, unforeseen exclusions, and in which every lived exclusion births new claims for inclusion. Perhaps in this sense, we can render legible the "void" of international human rights law, with Rancière, as being precisely that fragile but persistent space of hope in which international human rights are "the rights of those who have not the rights that they have and have the rights that they have not."[19]

19. Jacques Rancière, "Who Is the Subject of the Rights of Man?" *South Atlantic Quarterly* 103 (2004): 297–310, 302

QUESTIONS FOR REFLECTION AND DISCUSSION

1. What are "framing choices" and are they "inescapable"? Why? Why not?
2. Why are framing choices in international human rights law particularly influential?
3. What, according to Grear, are the central elements of the mainstream, traditional account of human rights? And which critical accounts does she refer to? What is the pivotal difference, for the purpose of her argument, between mainstream and critical accounts?
4. Grear cites Donnelly's quote "For the purposes of international action, 'human rights' means roughly 'what is in the Universal Declaration of Human Rights.'" Is this still the case?
5. Consider the criticism of the UDHR as Western cultural imperialism. Is "imperialism" the proper term for this criticism? How can the West best reconcile its contemporary view of universal human rights with its recent history of colonialism?
6. Grear writes: "We have already noted the centrality of the iconic UDHR to the entire edifice of human rights law and mentioned its production of a universal human rights bearer. A central paradox of international human rights law rests on the construction of this universal 'human subject.' Despite the fact that the UDHR clearly enshrines its rights as belonging to all members of the 'human family,' to 'everyone,' it is far from clear, as we shall see, that all human beings find themselves fully embraced or represented by the universal human rights subject. In fact, there is arguably a dysfunction or fracture at the heart of the 'human family' of the UDHR—and it is this observation that forms the inspiration for this particular framing of the international human rights law project." What is this fracture, and how does it reveal itself in practice? If you are unfamiliar with the issues, you could cross-refer to Reading 14 (Beveridge and Mullally) for assistance in answering this question.
7. Could the language offered by the Committee on the Status of Women (CSW) ("all human beings, men and women") have addressed the central concern identified by Grear's framing of the dysfunctional family of the UHDR? Or would this simply have installed a new abstract universal—this time of a binary nature? What arguments can you find to support the view that the CSW formulation would have helped? What arguments against?

8. Costas Douzinas writes: "Once the slightest empirical or historical material is introduced into abstract human nature, once we move from the declarations onto the concrete embodied person, with gender, race, class and age, human nature with its equality and dignity retreats rapidly."[20] What does he mean? Can you think of examples? Is his argument strengthened or weakened by the provision of multiple specific treaties addressing the rights of "minority" categories of human being?

9. Grear presents a compelling argument for the inherent inequality that accompanies singling out groups to be declared "equal" as human beings to the unnamed "insider" (presumably a European heterosexual male). What would be the best way to approach this phenomenon in the construction of amendments to treaties and other legal texts in the future?

10. What does Arendt's observation reveal about international human rights law? Do you see this particular limit of international human rights law as being problematic? Or not? Why? Why not?

11. What, in the light of this reading and the reading before it, *are* human rights? Are they any one thing? How would you define them—and why? What value choices inform your choice? How would you draw out different aspects of their nature and function and relate those to each other? Are human rights meanings inherently contestable? Why? Why not?

12. Is the trope of the "universal" human being useful or misleading? Substantiate your answer with argument, drawing on specific materials and sources.

20. Douzinas, *The End of Human Rights*, note 9, 96.

3. MARTHA C. NUSSBAUM *Capabilities, Human Rights, and the Universal Declaration*

The language of rights has a moral resonance that makes it hard to avoid in contemporary political discourse. But it is certainly not on account of its theoretical and conceptual clarity that it has been preferred. There are many different ways of thinking about what a right is, and many different definitions of "human rights." For example, rights are often spoken of as entitlements that belong to all human beings simply because they are human, or as especially urgent interests of human beings as human beings who deserve protection regardless where people are situated. The dominant tradition has typically grounded rights in the possession of rationality and language, thus implying that nonhuman animals do not have them, and that mentally impaired humans may not have them. Some philosophers have maintained that sentience, instead, should be the basis of rights; thus, all animals would be

rights-bearers. In contrast to this entire group of natural-rights theorists, there are also thinkers who treat all rights as artifacts of state actions. The latter position would seem to imply that there are no human rights where there is no state to recognize them. Such an approach appears to the holders of the former view to do away with the very point of rights language, which is to point to the fact that human beings are entitled to certain types of treatment whether or not the state in which they happen to live recognizes this fact.

There are many other complex unresolved theoretical questions about rights, including difficult theoretical questions about what rights are to be understood as "rights to." When we speak of human rights, do we mean, primarily, a right to be treated in certain ways? A right to a certain level of achieved well-being? A right to certain resources with which one may pursue one's life plan? A right to certain opportunities and capacities with which one may, in turn, make choices regarding one's life plan? Political philosophers who debate the nature of equality commonly tackle a related question head on, asking whether the equality most relevant to political distribution should be understood primarily as equality of well-being, or equality of resources, or equality of opportunity, or equality of capabilities. The language of rights to some extent cuts across this debate and obscures the issues that have been articulated, particularly in distinguishing between "positive" and "negative" rights.

Thus, one might conclude that the language of rights, including that of the Universal Declaration of Human Rights, is not especially informative, despite its uplifting character, unless its users link their references to rights to a theory that answers at least some of these questions. It is for this reason, among others, that a different language has begun to take hold in talk about people's basic entitlements. This is the language of capabilities and human functioning which was in some ways anticipated in the UDHR even though its authors came from diverse cultural backgrounds and did not use this language per se. As this essay seeks to demonstrate, rethinking the UDHR in terms of human capabilities and functioning enhances rather than questions the validity of most of the normative pronouncements of that text and suggests public policy directions for the UDHR's second fifty years.

The application of the capabilities approach to international human rights standards has accelerated in recent years. Since 1993, the Human Development Reports of the United Nations Development Programme have assessed the quality of life in the nations of the world using the concept of people's capabilities, or their abilities to do and to be certain things deemed valuable. Under the influence of economist/philosopher and Nobel laureate Amartya Sen, they have chosen that conceptual framework as basic to inter-country comparisons and to the articulation of goals for public policy. In 1997, this concern with human capabilities merged into a new policy of a rights-based approach to development, approved in November 1997, and set out in the UNDP publication *Integrating Human Rights with Sustainable Human Development.*[1]

Along with Sen, I have been among those who have pioneered what is now called the "capabilities approach," defending its importance in international debates about welfare and quality

of life. In a variety of contexts, we argue that the capabilities approach is a valuable theoretical framework for public policy, especially in the international development context. We commend it to both theoreticians and practitioners as offering certain advantages over approaches that focus on opulence—GNP per capita, or welfare—construed in terms of utility or desire-satisfaction, or even the distribution of basic resources. Similar efforts using different theoretical starting points have been articulated in the public policy approach of the so-called New Haven School of Jurisprudence[2] and research on the intersection of basic needs and human rights.[3]

[*Eds.*—The author next traces the recent application of the capabilities approach by various human rights theorists, then continues.]

But there still are some large questions to be answered. The relationship between the two concepts of capabilities and rights remains as yet underexplored. Does the capabilities view supplement a theory of rights, or is it intended to be a particular way of capturing what a theory of rights captures? Is there any tension between a focus on capabilities and a focus on rights? Does the capabilities view help us to answer any of the difficult questions which have preoccupied theorists of rights? Does the capabilities view incline us to opt for any particular set of answers to the various questions about rights, or any particular conception of rights? Finally, is there any reason, other than a merely rhetorical one, why we should continue to use the language of rights in addition to the language of capabilities?

[*Eds.*—The author next considers the "antecedents and argument" of the "capabilities approach," describing the approach and the motivation for its introduction, asking how it contrasts with other ways of thinking about entitlements, and briefly clarifying the connection

2. See, e.g., Myres S. McDougal, Harold D. Lasswell, and Lung-chu Chen, *Human Rights and World Public Order: The Basic Policies of an International Law of Human Dignity* (New Haven, Conn.: YUP, 1980).
3. See, e.g., Johan Galtung, *Human Rights in Another Key* (Oxford: Blackwell, 1994); Johan Galtung and Anders H. Wirak, "Human Needs, Human Rights and the Theories of Development," in *Indicators of Social and Economic Change and Their Applications*, Reports and Papers in Social Science 37 (Paris: UNESCO, 1976).

1. See UN Development Programme, *Integrating Human Rights with Sustainable Human Development: A UNDP Policy Document* (New York: UNDP, January 1998).

between it and liberal theories of justice. In particular, she stresses "the essential element of equality." She asks: "What does it mean when the UDHR affirms that 'Everyone is entitled to all the rights and freedoms set forth in this Declaration, without distinction of any kind, such as race, colour, sex, language, religion, political or other opinion, national or social origin, property, birth or other status?'" She concludes: "I believe that the most illuminating way of thinking about the capabilities approach is that it is an account of the space within which we make comparisons between individuals and across nations as to how well they are doing. This idea is closely linked with the idea of a theory of justice, since one crucial aim of a theory of justice typically is to promote some desired state of people."]

We argue that the most appropriate space for comparisons is the space of capabilities. Instead of asking "How satisfied is person A," or "How much in the way of resources does A command," we ask the question: "What is A actually able to do and to be?" In other words, about a variety of functions that would seem to be of central importance to a human life, we ask: "Is the person capable of this, or not?" This focus on capabilities, unlike the focus on GNP, or on aggregate utility, looks at people one by one, insisting on locating empowerment in this life and in that life, rather than in the nation as a whole. Unlike the utilitarian focus on satisfactions, it looks not at what people feel about what they do, but about what they are actually able to do. Finally, unlike the focus on resources, it is concerned with what is actually going on in the life in question: not how many resources are sitting around, but how they are actually going to work in enabling people to function in a fully human way.[4]

This relatively objective standard of empowerment for each individual to understand and achieve capabilities has practical implications for human rights action strategies. Recent approaches to human rights education stress the distinction between the static teaching of abstract human rights concepts and the transformative pedagogy that engages learners in analyzing the causes of their deprivation and in taking control of the

transformation of that reality until they attain a higher level of capability. This idea was captured in a definition agreed upon at a regional workshop on human rights education in the Asia-Pacific region in 1994: "Human rights education is a participative process of developing knowledge, values and skills that will enable people to develop their potentials and emancipate themselves from oppressive social realities."[5] Similarly, Richard Claude defined human rights education as "a process through which people and/or communities increase their control or mastery of their lives and the decisions that affect their lives."[6] Such transformative pedagogies have been developed and applied especially in community-based human rights education and for the secondary level as well. Their aim is the practical realization of the theoretical potential revealed by the capabilities approach to human rights insofar as they teach affected populations to reject as inadequate the utilitarian goal of the greatest good and even the liberal goal of Rawls's primary goods and advocate instead the empowerment of each individual to become capable of actually functioning in the fully human way defined in the international human rights texts. Enabling people to develop their potential captures the essence of the capabilities approach.

[*Eds.*—The author next addresses the "central human capabilities" and their correlation to human rights. In so doing, she introduces a list which she contends "can be convincingly argued to be of central importance in any human life, whatever else the person pursues or chooses."]

The central capabilities are not just instrumental to further pursuits; they are held to have value in themselves, in making a life fully human. But they are held to have a particularly central importance in everything else we plan and choose. In that sense, central capabilities play a role similar to that played by Rawls's primary goods; they support our powers of practical reason and choice, and have a special importance in making

---

4. In this sense, the approach takes its inspiration from Marx's discussion of fully human functioning in several early works in which he was, in turn, much influenced by Aristotle.

5. Quoted in Richard Pierre Claude, *Educating for Human Rights: The Philippines and Beyond* (Quezon City: University of the Philippines Press, 1996), 198.
6. Richard Pierre Claude, *The Bells of Freedom: With Resource Materials for Facilitators of Non-Formal Education and 24 Human Rights Echo Sessions* (Addis Ababa: Action Professionals Association for the People, 1996), 7.

any choice of a way of life possible. They thus have a special claim to be supported for political purposes in societies that otherwise contain a great diversity of views about the good. The basic point of the account is to put forward something that people from many different traditions, with many different fuller conceptions of the good, can agree on as the necessary basis for pursuing their good life.

The list is therefore an attempt to summarize the empirical findings of a broad and ongoing cross-cultural inquiry. As such, it is open-ended and humble; it can always be contested and remade.

Here is the current version of the list,[7] revised as a result of recent visits to development projects in India. Most of the central capabilities correspond to the essence of the rights proclaimed in the UDHR which, in turn, have been reaffirmed by the expanding membership of the international community and resoundingly reaffirmed in their entirety on the fiftieth anniversary of the UDHR. Their mention in the international texts contributes to the cross-cultural basis of the list, and in this sense the UDHR becomes a source, an evidentiary element, in defining the good. To illustrate this correlation, Table 1 records both the basic capabilities that I have identified and the corresponding article of the UDHR.

This list is, emphatically, a list of separate and indispensable components. We cannot satisfy the need for one of them by giving a larger amount of another. All are of central importance and all are distinct in quality and thus may be understood, in the official language of rights of the United Nations, as "universal, indivisible and interdependent and interrelated,"[8] which is often ritualized rhetoric in compromise resolutions on human rights but which, in the context of central human capabilities, acquires practical significance. Practical reason and affiliation are of special importance because they both organize and suffuse all the other capabilities, making

their pursuit truly human. The individual importance of each component limits the trade-offs that it will be reasonable to make, and thus limits the applicability of quantitative cost-benefit analysis. At the same time, the items on the list are related to one another in many complex ways. One of the most effective ways of promoting women's control over their environment, and their effective right of political participation, is to promote women's literacy. Women who can seek employment outside the home have more resources in protecting their bodily integrity from assaults within it.

In practice, human rights are viewed either as legal entitlements that are immediately justiciable before courts or as guiding aspirational principles that all branches of government should keep in mind as general propositions even if not as specific prescriptions to resolve specific cases. Commonly, the issue of these competing approaches to human rights is erroneously reduced to the distinction made at the time of the elaboration of the two 1966 covenants between, on the one hand, civil and political rights which supposedly are freedoms from state interference and immediately applicable and justiciable, and, on the other hand, economic, social, and cultural rights which are claims against the state for benefits to be provided progressively as resources allow. Rightist thinkers have attempted a philosophical justification of this approach. A more recent development assumes that all human rights—civil, cultural, economic, political, and social—are not only interdependent but of equal legal and moral validity, and thus focuses on the nature of obligations to realize rights. According to this view, the duty-holder (usually the state) has the triple obligation to "respect" (not to commit a violation), to "ensure respect" or to "protect" (not to allow others to violate), and to "fulfill" (provide the means to realize). Depending on the object of the right (freedom from torture or access to education, for example), one or the other of these obligations predominates. Without all three, human rights remain abstractions that the right-holder possesses in theory but does not enjoy in practice. The distinction between capability and functioning underlies this approach to obligation in the human rights field.

But how are capability and functioning related? If we were to take functioning itself as the goal of public policy, the liberal would rightly

7. The list is compatible with, but less abstract and more detailed than, the four "welfare values" (wealth, well-being, skills, enlightenment) and four "deference values" (power, respect, rectitude, affection) on which the commonly called New Haven School of Jurisprudence is premised. See McDougal et al., *Human Rights and World Public Order*.
8. Vienna Declaration and Programme of Action, 5.

TABLE 1

1. *Life*. Being able to live to the end of a normal length; not dying prematurely, or before one's life is so reduced as to be not worth living.	Article 3 on right to life.
2. Bodily Health. Being able to have good health, including reproductive health; to be adequately nourished; to have adequate shelter.	Article 25, further defined in Article 12 of the ICESCR as the "highest attainable level of physical and mental health."
3. Bodily Integrity. Being able to move freely from place to place; to be secure against violent assault, including sexual assault and domestic violence; having opportunities for sexual satisfaction and for choice in matters of reproduction.	Articles 3, 4, 5 and 13, although domestic violence, sexual satisfaction, reproductive choice were not sufficiently well established in 1948 for the overwhelmingly male drafters to include them.
4. Senses, Imagination, and Thought. Being able to use the senses; being able to imagine, to think, and to do these things in a "truly human" way, a way informed and cultivated by an adequate education, including, but by no means limited to, literacy and basic mathematical and scientific training. Being able to use imagination and thought in connection with experiencing and producing expressive works and events of one's own choice, religious, literary, musical, and so forth. Being able to use one's mind in ways protected by guarantees of freedom of expression with respect to both political and artistic speech and freedom of religious exercise. Being able to have pleasurable experiences and to avoid non-beneficial pain.	Article 18 on freedom of thought, conscience, and religion; Article 19 on freedom of opinion and expression; Article 26 on the right to education, which "shall be directed to the full development of the human personality"; Article 27 on participation in cultural life.
5. Emotions. Being able to have attachments to things and people outside ourselves; to love those who love and care; right to marry and found a family are for us, to grieve at their absence; in general, to love, to grieve, to experience longing, gratitude, and justified anger. Not having one's emotional development blighted by fear and anxiety. Supporting this capability means supporting forms of human association that can be shown to be crucial in their development.	Articles 12 and 16, although privacy, non-interference with family and the right to marry and found a family are manifestations of a much broader idea of capabilities regarding emotions.
6. Practical Reason. Being able to form a conception of the good and to engage in critical reflection about the planning of one's life. This entails protection for the liberty of conscience and religious observance.	Article 18 on freedom of thought, conscience, and religion.
7. Affiliation.	
A. Friendship. Being able to live for and to others, to recognize and show concern for other human beings, to engage in various forms of social interaction; to be able to imagine the situation of another and to have compassion for that situation; to have the capability for both justice and friendship. Protecting this capability means, once again, protecting institutions that constitute such forms of affiliation, and also protecting the freedom of assembly and political speech.	Article 1, mentioning "spirit of brotherhood" [sic]; Article 18 on thought and conscience; Article 19 on opinion and expression; Article 20 on peaceful assembly and association; Article 29 on duties to the community and respect for the rights of others and "just requirements of morality, public order and general welfare in a democratic society."

B. Respect. Having the social bases of self-respect and non-humiliation; being able to be treated as a dignified being whose worth is equal to that of others. This entails provisions of non-discrimination on the basis of race, sex, ethnicity, caste, religion, and national origin.	Article 1, on equality in dignity and rights; Article 2 on non-discrimination.
8. Other Species. Being able to live with concern for and in relation to animals, plants, and the world of nature.	This concern is found in international environmental instruments and in several draft texts on human rights and the environment, but not in the UDHR except by implication in Article 28.
9. Play. Being able to laugh, play, and enjoy recreational activities.	Article 24 relative to rest and leisure.
A. Political. Being able to participate effectively in political choices that govern.	Article 21 on political participation; Article 19 on speech; Article 20 on association of one's life; having the right of political participation, protections of free speech and association.
B. Material. Being able to hold property (both land and, movable goods); having the right to employment; having freedom from unwarranted search and seizure.	Article 17 on property; Article 23 on right to work and free choice of employment; Article 12 on non-interference in privacy, family, home or correspondence

judge that we were precluding many choices that citizens may make in accordance with their own conceptions of the good, and perhaps violating their human rights. A deeply religious person may prefer not to be well nourished, but instead prefer to engage in strenuous fasting. Whether for religious or for other reasons, a person may prefer a celibate life to one containing sexual expression. A person may prefer to work with an intense dedication that precludes recreation and play. Am I declaring, by my very use of the list, that these are not fully human or flourishing lives? And am I instructing government to nudge or push people into functioning of the requisite sort, no matter what they prefer?

It is important that the answer to these questions is no. Capability, not functioning, is the political goal. Capability must be the goal because of the great importance the capabilities approach attaches to practical reason. It is perfectly true that functionings, not simply capabilities, are what render a life fully human: if there were no functioning of any kind in a life, we could hardly applaud it, no matter what opportunities it contained. Nonetheless, for political purposes it is appropriate for us to strive for capabilities, and those alone. Citizens must be left free to determine their course after they have the capabilities. The person with plenty of food may always

choose to fast, but there is a great difference between fasting and starving, and it is this difference that we wish to capture.

I can make the issue clearer by pointing out that there are three different types of capabilities that figure in my analysis. First, there are what I call *basic capabilities*: the innate equipment of individuals that is the necessary basis for developing the more advanced capability. Most infants have from birth the basic capability for practical reason and imagination, though they cannot exercise such functions without a lot more development and education. Second, there are *internal capabilities*: that is, states of the person herself that are, so far as the person herself is concerned, sufficient conditions for the exercise of the requisite functions. A woman who has not suffered genital mutilation has the internal capability for sexual pleasure; most adult human beings everywhere have the internal capability to use speech and thought in accordance with their own conscience. Finally, there are *combined capabilities*, which I define as internal capabilities combined with suitable external conditions for the exercise of the function. A woman who is not mutilated but is secluded and forbidden to leave the house has internal but not combined capabilities for sexual expression—and work, and political participation. Citizens of repressive nondemocratic regimes have the internal but not the combined capability to exercise thought and speech in accordance with their conscience.

The aim of public policy is the production of combined capabilities. This idea means promoting the states of the person by providing the necessary education and care, as well as preparing the environment so that it is favorable for the exercise of practical reason and the other major functions. The UDHR expresses this idea clearly in Article 28: "Everyone is entitled to a social and international order in which the rights and freedoms set forth in this declaration can be fully realized." The most philosophically coherent interpretation of this article, and potentially the most powerful exhortation of the UDHR for the second half century of its life, is based on the capabilities approach. Specifically, the human rights of the UDHR and its progeny cannot be realized unless and until the social, economic, and political conditions prevailing domestically and internationally ensure each rights-holder the combined capability to exercise the rights he or she may desire. This means that their internal capabilities (called "human potential" in many human rights texts) are combined with the social order, including the legal regime and the economic and social conditions, so that they can express a controversial idea, attain sexual pleasure, secure free public education, or escape from poverty if they wish.

This explanation of the types of capability clarifies the link between capabilities and human rights. We can see, by this time, that there are two rather different relations that capabilities have to the human rights traditionally recognized by international human rights instruments. In what follows, I shall understand a human right in the same way as the UDHR, namely as involving an especially urgent and morally justified claim that a person has, simply by virtue of being a human, and independently of membership in a particular nation, or class, or sex, or ethnic or religious or sexual group.

First, there are some areas in which the best way of thinking about rights is to see them as combined capabilities to function in various ways. The right to political participation, the right to religious free exercise, the freedom of speech, the freedom to seek employment outside the home, and the freedom from unwarranted search and seizure are all best thought of as human capacities to function in ways that we

then go on to specify. The further specification will usually involve both an internal component and an external component: a citizen who is systematically deprived of information about religion does not really have religious liberty, even if the state imposes no barrier to religious choice. On the other hand, internal conditions are not enough: women who can think about work outside the home, but who are going to be systematically denied employment on account of sex, or beaten if they try to go outside, do not have the right to seek employment. In short, to secure a right to a citizen in these areas is to put them in a position of capability to go ahead with choosing that function if they should so desire.

Of course, there is another way in which we use the term "right" in which it could not be identified with a capability. We say that A has "a right to" seek employment outside the home, even when her circumstances obviously do not secure such a right to her. When we use the term "human right" this way, we are saying that just by virtue of being human, a person has a justified claim to have the capability secured to her: so a right in that sense would be prior to capability, and a ground for the securing of a capability. "Human rights" used in this sense lie very close to what I have called "basic capabilities," since typically human rights are thought to derive from some actual feature of human persons, some untrained power in them that demands or calls for support from the world.

On the other hand, when we say, as we frequently do, that citizens in country C "have the right of free religious exercise," what we typically mean is that this urgent and justified claim is being answered, that the state responds to the claim that they have just by virtue of being human. It is in this sense that capabilities and rights should be seen to be equivalent: as I have said, combined capabilities are the goals of public planning.

Why is it a good idea to express rights, so understood, in terms of capabilities? I think this approach is a good idea because we then understand that what is involved in securing a right to people is usually a lot more than simply putting it down on paper. We see this very clearly in India, for example, where the Constitution is full of guarantees of Fundamental Rights that are not backed up by effective state action. Thus, since ratification women have had rights of sex equality—but in real life they are unequal not only de facto, but also de jure. In short, thinking in terms of capability gives us a benchmark in thinking about what it is really to secure a right to someone.

There is another set of rights, largely those in the area of property and economic advantage, which seem to me analytically different in their relationship to capabilities. Take, for example, the right to a certain level of income, or the right to shelter and housing, expressed in Article 25(1) of the UDHR as the "right to a standard of living adequate for the health and well-being of himself and of his family, including food, clothing, housing and medical care." These are rights that can be analyzed in a number of distinct ways, in terms of resources, or utility, or capabilities. We could think of the right to a decent level of living as a right to a certain level of resources; or, less plausibly, as a right to a certain level of satisfaction; or as a right to attain a certain level of capability to function.

Once again, we must distinguish the use of the term "right" in the sentence "A has a right to X," from its use in the sentence "Country C gives citizens the right to X." All human beings may arguably have a right to something in the first sense, without being in countries that secure these rights. If a decent living standard is a human right, then American citizens have that right although their state does not give them, or secure to them, such a right. So far, then, we have the same distinctions on our hands that we did in the case of the political liberties. But the point I am making is that at the second level, the analysis of "Country C secures to its citizens the right to a decent living standard" may plausibly take a wider range of forms than it does for the political and religious liberties, where it seems evident that the best way to think of the secured right is as a capability. The material rights may, by contrast, plausibly be analyzed in terms of resources, or possibly in terms of utility.

An interesting controversy erupted during the Second United Nations Conference on Human Settlements (Habitat 11) in Istanbul, in June 1996. The United States delegation strongly resisted efforts to include in the final document any reference to the "right to housing" as such. It proposed instead that the text refer to "adequate shelter for all" and "enablement." While the concept of "enablement" may be seen as an element of the concept of capabilities and functionings, it does not address the responsibility of the state when the real estate industry, acting under the law of supply and demand, fails to make a significant dent in the problem of homelessness. It is here that the link between the human rights language and capabilities makes practical sense. The concept of "enabling environment" leaves open the possibility that an environment that holds out the potential for alleviating homelessness fails to do so in fact. The state is off the hook because the enabling environment—here the free operation of the real estate industry—exists. The concept of capabilities restores the obligation of result and makes it possible to talk of a right to housing.

Indeed this is the approach of the International Covenant on Economic, Social and Cultural Rights. The right in question is expressed in Article 11(1) in language similar to the UDHR: the "right of everyone to an adequate standard of living for himself and his family, including adequate food, clothing and housing, and to the continuous improvement of living conditions." However, the Covenant further stipulates in the same article that the "States Parties will take appropriate steps to ensure the realization of this right, recognizing to this effect the essential importance of international co-operation based on free consent." The first part of this provision suggests that states parties must place persons within their jurisdiction in the position of being capable of having shelter, while suggesting, in the second part, that voluntarily given foreign aid and technical cooperation through Specialized Agencies is most likely going to be necessary for poor countries to realize this right. Moreover, as provided in Article 2(1), the entire Covenant is conditioned by the general obligation of each state party

> to take steps, individually and through international assistance and cooperation, especially economic and technical, to the maximum of its available resources with a view to achieving progressively the full realization of the rights recognized in the present Covenant by all appropriate means, including particularly the adoption of legislative measures.

The reference to resources is crucial. The adoption of legislative measures, except with regard to legislation allocating resources for the national budget, is only marginally relevant to the issue of capabilities expressed in terms of allocation of resources.

Here again, however, I think it is valuable to

understand these rights, insofar as we decide we want to recognize them, in terms of capabilities. That is, if we think of a right to a decent level of living as a right to a certain quantity of resources, then we get into the very problems I have pointed to; that is, giving the resources to people does not always bring differently situated people up to the same level of functioning. If you have a group of people who are traditionally marginalized, you are probably going to have to expend more resources on them to get them up to the same living standard—in capability terms—than you would for a group of people who are in a favorable social situation.

Analyzing economic and material rights in terms of capabilities would thus enable us to understand, as we might not otherwise, a rationale we might have for spending unequal amounts of money on the disadvantaged, or creating special programs to assist their transition to full capability. This way of thinking has also practical implications for understanding what states parties must do to comply with their obligations under the International Covenant on Economic, Social and Cultural Rights. The acknowledgment on paper of the right is not sufficient; securing the right as a capability is closer to meeting the duties imposed on the state by the Covenant.

At the same time, the language of rights still plays four important roles in public discourse, despite its unsatisfactory features. First, rights language reminds us that people have justified and urgent claims to certain types of urgent treatment, no matter what the world around them has done about them. Second, the language of rights tells people right away that we are dealing with an especially urgent set of functions, backed up by a sense of the justified claim that all humans have to such things, by virtue of being human. This is the essence of the role of the UDHR; it reaffirms in a list of normative propositions the claims that people may consider fundamental to their humanness. Third, rights language has value because of the emphasis it places on people's choice and autonomy. It helps us to lay extra emphasis on this very important fact: that what one ought to think of as the benchmark are people's autonomous choices to avail themselves of certain opportunities, and not simply their actual functionings. Finally, the language of rights limits the areas that can be bargained away in a policy compromise. For example, a wide range of justifiable limitations may be placed on freedom of speech for reasons of public safety, order, morals, national security, and other reasons, but rights language precludes the policy option of replacing freedom of speech with a residual principle of censorship.

The capabilities approach discussed in this essay builds on an understanding of human rights only vaguely alluded to in the UDHR. Nevertheless, it fits well within the normative framework of the UDHR and offers a valuable tool for assessing compliance with the rights it reaffirms and that are set out in the numerous instruments that have built upon it.

QUESTIONS FOR REFLECTION AND DISCUSSION

1. In "The International Human Rights Movement: Part of the Problem?" *HHRJ* 15 (2002): 101–25, David Kennedy theorizes that the human rights movement may create more harm than good, stating that

> The human rights movement proposes itself as a vocabulary of the general good—as knowledge about the shape of emancipation and human possibility that can be "applied" and "enforced." As an emancipatory vocabulary, it offers answers rather than questions, answers that are not only outside political, ideological and cultural differences, but also beyond the human experience of specificity and against the human capacity to hope for more, in denial of the tawdry and uncertain quality of our available dreams about and experience with justice and injustice. Rather than enabling a discussion of what it means to be human, of who is human, of how humans might relate to one another, it crushes this discussion under the weight of moral condemnation, legal adjudication, textual certainty and political power. (111)

Do you agree with Kennedy? Would a capabilities approach avoid the issues he raises? That is, would it enhance the discussion of human rights (i.e., increase the number of questions asked) or would it hurt the discussion (i.e., provide too many answers)? If so, how?

2. Nussbaum observes that "there are difficult theoretical questions about what rights are to be understood as 'rights to.'" She continues: "When we speak of human rights, do we mean, primarily, a right to be treated in certain ways? A right to a certain level of achieved well-being? A right to certain resources with which one may pursue one's life plan? A right to certain opportunities and capacities with which one may, in turn, make choices regarding one's life plan?" How do you answer these questions?

3. Nussbaum acknowledges that the language of rights "cuts across [the] debate [about] the nature of equality," but argues that, in the process, it "obscures" important issues embedded in it—for critical example, "whether the equality most relevant to political distribution should be understood primarily as equality of well-being, or equality of resources, or equality of opportunity, or equality of capabilities." She concludes, therefore, that "the language of rights . . . is not especially informative, despite its uplifting character," and thus recommends (together with her long-time collaborator Amartya Sen) "a different language [to] talk about people's basic entitlements," to wit, "the language of capabilities and human functioning." What is the language of capabilities and human functioning? Does it really differ in kind from human rights discourse or is it implicit in it? Substantiate your response with argument.

4. Do you agree with Nussbaum that a different language or approach is needed, one that is based on capabilities as opposed to rights? If so, does this mean that talk about people's basic entitlements in terms of rights is fundamentally a waste of time? Note Nussbaum's assertion that "rethinking the UDHR in terms of human capabilities and functioning enhances rather than questions the validity of most of the normative pronouncements of that text and suggests public policy directions for the UDHR's second fifty years." Does this imply an acceptance of rights and rights talk not simply as a fact of life but perhaps even a necessity? If so, what, precisely, is the relationship between rights and capabilities? Do capabilities enhance rights? If so, how?

5. Nussbaum asks: "is there any reason, other than a merely rhetorical one, why we should continue to use the language of rights in addition to the language of capabilities?" Taking into account the questions for reflection and discussion posed so far, what is your answer? Why?

6. Fundamentally, Nussbaum's capabilities approach to human rights and functioning is about empowerment. "Citizens must be left free to determine their course after they have the capabilities," Nussbaum states. Is it fair to suggest that this injunction has a distinctly Western individualistic ring to it, perhaps inappropriate for communitarian (usually non-Western) cultures? And what about citizens who do not have the requisite empowerment capabilities? For example, does an Islamic woman living in, say, Saudi Arabia have a right to be free from physical abuse by her husband if she has no capability to exercise such a right? What are Nussbaum's answers to these questions? What are yours?

7. Are there capabilities that are not discussed in Nussbaum's table that you believe should be included? What are they, and how are they distinct from those she discusses?

8. Nussbaum notes the conflict between certain human rights and the human choice to live in a manner inconsistent with these rights in her examination of functionality versus capability. Can you think of specific national laws or policies regarding human rights that conflict with human capabilities? What about in countries with strong reputations for respect of human rights? Is it possible to avoid these conflicts?

9. Nussbaum argues that the language of human capabilities and functioning should be used to ensure that a person is *not* forced to exercise a right against her or his will. Is this to say that there is a human right not to partake of a human right? Do you think the term "right" implies that an option *must* be exercised?

10. Does the capabilities approach contain an inherent endorsement of—or requirement for—affirmative action programs? If so, does the failure to provide such programs constitute a violation of human rights? If so, whose?

11. Who, in the capabilities approach to human functioning, is the enabler of individual and group capabilities? The state? International institutions? Subnational entities? The private sector (corporations, trade unions, professional associations, nongovernmental organizations, academic institutions, faith-based groups)? The family? The individual? Some of the above? All of the above? Does it matter? Why and how?

4. BURNS H. WESTON *Universalism Versus Cultural Relativism: An Appeal for Respectful Decision-Making*

DELIMITATION OF THE PROBLEM

Values are preferred events, "goods" we cherish; and the value of respect, "conceived as the reciprocal honoring of freedom of choice about participation in value processes," is "the core value of human rights."[1] In a world of diverse cultural traditions that is simultaneously distinguished by the widespread universalist claim that "human rights extend in theory to every person on earth without discriminations irrelevant to merit,"[2] the question thus unavoidably arises: when, in international human rights decision-making, are cultural differences to be respected and when are they not?

There is a long history of occasions in which the universal validity of moral judgments has been called into question. Table 1, listing cultural practices well known for the cross-cultural controversies they can and do often generate, demonstrates how this is so.[3] And the more global modernization unfolds and culture con-

tact grows, the more are such occasions likely to arise and insist upon answers.

By way of illustration, consider the practices of child betrothal and fixed marriage widespread in the two-thirds world or Global South. Sooner or later one must ponder Article 16 of the Universal Declaration of Human Rights proclaiming that men and women of full age, without any limitation due to race, nationality or religion, have the right to marry and found a family and only with the free and full consent of the intending spouses. Similarly, in light of communitarian traditions prevalent in sub-Saharan Africa that define an individual's existence and status primarily with reference to birthright, sex, age, and group membership, or alternatively, the occasional Hindu and Muslim traditions of segregating women (harem, purdah), one must puzzle over the reach of the UDHR guarantees of equality and nondiscrimination irrespective of "race, colour, sex, language, religion, political or other opinion, national or social origin, property, birth or other status" (Article 2). Such illustrations of the possible nonuniversality of alleged universal human rights are of course many and in no way restricted to Global South settings. The long-standing resistance of the capitalist countries, particularly the United States, to economic and social rights, and of the communist countries, past and present, to civil and political rights, attest to this fact. So too do the abortion and nuclear weapons policies in the industrialized world, challenging the "right to life set forth in UDHR Article 3, just as do the practices of infanticide and female sacrifice (e.g., sati) in "premodern" societies. And when one adds to the mix that disagreements over claimed universal human rights exist not only in their substantive identification but, as well, in their interpretation and enforcement, the argument of cultural relativism—that there are no overarching moral truths and that local customs and traditions therefore fundamentally determine the existence and scope of rights in any given society—may be seen to loom large.

The issue remains with us today. Since 1989 especially, when cultural variabilities were freed from the silencing grip of Cold War loyalties, it has been forcefully argued in several—particularly Asian—quarters that, as Pascal observed some three centuries ago, what may be

Excerpted with changes by permission of Transnational Publishers from Burns H. Weston, "The Universality of Human Rights in a Multicultured World: Toward Respectful Decision-Making," in Burns H. Weston and Stephen P. Marks, eds., *The Future of International Human Rights* (Ardsley, N.Y.: Transnational, 1999), 65–99. Copyright © 1999 Transnational Publishers.

1. Ibid., 451. The authors impose an individualistic perspective on the meaning of this "core value." They write: "respect is defined as an interrelation *among individual human beings* in which they reciprocally recognize and honor each other's freedom of choice about participation in the value processes of the world community or any of its component parts" (emphasis added).
2. See Reading 1 (Weston) in this chapter. Reconsidering this phrase, I am today inclined to add "capability" to "merit" (and possibly also "basic need" insofar as it is not a function of "capability") as potentially a permissible basis for discrimination in otherwise equal arenas of claim and decision.
3. The practices—neither exhaustively nor altogether unambiguously stated—are listed in alphabetical order according to the physical and behavioral dimensions of human existence. The inner existential (spiritual) dimension of human existence does not seem apt for separate categorization inasmuch as all cultural practices for which relativist claims have been or might be made appear to affect the human psyche in some way, mental or psychological torture most directly of course.

TABLE 1

PHYSICAL PRACTICES	BEHAVIORAL PRACTICES

1. Abortion
 a. Mandatory
 b. Permitted, prohibited
2. Cannibalism
3. Corporal disfigurement
 a. Foot binding
 b. Genital cutting
  (1) Male (e.g., circumcision)
  (2) Female genital cutting (FGC, a/k/a FGM and FGS)[1]
 c. Scarring, tattooing
4. Corporal punishment
 a. Public (state imposed/sanctioned)
  (1) Amputation
  (2) Caning, flogging, lashing, spanking, whipping
  (3) Death/execution
   Electric chair
   Firing squad
   Hanging
   Lethal injection
   Stoning
 b. Private (e.g., familial)
  (1) Spanking, slapping, whipping
  (2) Honor killing
5. Euthanasia
6. Genocide, ethnic cleansing
7. Imprisonment
 a. Life
 b. Solitary
 c. Hard labor
8. Infanticide
9. Torture (physical, mental)
	1. Banishment, ethnic cleansing, ostracization
	2. Discrimination, segregation
	 a. Age
	 b. Caste/class
	 c. Ethnicity
	 d. Gender, sexual orientation
	 e. Health (e.g., HIV, lepers)
	 f. Merit/basic need
	 g. Nationality
	 h. Political opinion
	 i. Race
	 j. Religion
	3. Divorce, separation
	 a. Unilateral
	4. Dress codes
	 a. Body covering
	 b. Veil wearing
	5. Marriage
	 a. Arranged child marriage
	 b. Bride price, dower
	 c. Forced marriage
	 d. Homosexual
	 e. Polygamy/polygyny
	6. Slavery, forced labor
	7. State-sponsored deprivations
	 a. Civil/political deprivations
	  (1) Assembly, association
	  (2) Expression, opinion, speech
	  (3) Other
	 b. Economic/social deprivations
	  (1) Education
	  (2) Employment
	  (3) Other

1. Female genital cutting (FGC) is a value-neutral term I borrow from the *New York Times* and other media to avoid the pre-judgment bias of "female genital mutilation" or FGM. I choose the term in lieu of female genital surgery because this latter implies a greater degree of precision and refinement in the practice than I believe is empirically warranted overall.

truth on one side of the Pyrénées may be error on the other ("Vérité au-deçà des Pyrénées, erreur au-delà").[4] In the wake of such assertions, there has ensued not a little debate among governmental officials, scholars, and others about the extent to which cultural particularities should be allowed to determine the existence and scope of rights promised to individuals and groups by the UDHR and related universalist human rights instruments.

A survey of the literature reveals that the vast majority of commentators choose not an analytically neutral position but, rather, one that

champions one side of the debate or the other. It also reveals that the greatest number—most of them intellectually indebted or sympathetic to Western thought and tradition—come down, not surprisingly, on the side of universalism.[5] Hence, the widespread Western skepticism that greeted the 2012 ASEAN Human Rights Declaration, the first ever in the region, with its distinct tilt toward cultural relativism.[6] If not criticized for preventing transnational moral judgments altogether, cultural relativism is repeatedly denounced as "a new excuse for an old

4. Blaise Pascal, *Pensées* (1897; Paris: Garnier-Flammarion, 1976), 135.

5. See, e.g., Michael Freeman, *Human Rights: An Interdisciplinary Approach* (Cambridge: Polity, 2002), chap. 6 and the references cited therein.
6. See, e.g., Reading 27 (Weston) in Chapter 6.

strategy,"[7] used "to justify limitations on speech, subjugation of women, female genital mutilation, amputation of limbs and other cruel punishment, arbitrary use of power, and other violations of international human rights conventions."[8] Where once the old Adam of territorial sovereignty served generally to prevent foreign "humanitarian intervention" into "the domestic jurisdiction," now cultural relativism is seen increasingly to substitute in this role, invoked to prevent transnational judgments about genocide, ethnic cleansing, torture, rape, and other such acts of human rights violation wherever they occur.

Are these choices and conclusions unequivocally favoring universalism over relativism legitimate? In a critical sense, I think not, though not because they are the result of simplistic a priori reasoning or even that they are wrong. To the contrary, as Martha Nussbaum has pointed out, relativism, as a normative thesis about how we should make moral judgments, suffers from major conceptual problems of its own making:

> First, it has no bite in the modern world, where the ideas of every culture are available, internally, to every other, through the internet and the media. . . . Many forms of moral relativism . . . use an unrealistic notion of culture. They imagine homogeneity where there is really diversity. . . . Second, it is not obvious why we should think the normative thesis true. Why should we follow the local ideas, rather than the best ideas we can find? Finally, normative relativism is self-subverting; for, in asking us to defer to local norms, it asks us to defer to norms that in most cases are strongly non-relativistic. Most local traditions take themselves to be absolutely, not relatively true. So in asking us to follow the local, relativism asks us not to follow relativism.[9]

Furthermore, sympathetic (Westerner) that I am to the expansion and invigoration of univer-

sal human rights norms and practices, I am much taken by the idea that universalist international human rights law can and should serve as a basis for rendering cross-cultural normative judgments.

My concern is that, without an analytically neutral approach for deciding when cultural differences are to be respected and when not, the credibility and defensibility of pro-universalist choices and conclusions and their particularistic objectives are undermined and thus make the idea of universalist international human rights law as a basis for rendering moral judgments very difficult, perhaps even unworkable on occasion. One-sided assertions of legitimacy and priority, by definition discounting the centrality of the value of respect in human rights, invite countervailing charges of cultural imperialism (defending against real or imagined claims of cultural superiority—colonizing) and cultural ethnocentrism (defending against real or imagined claims of cultural bias—Westernizing), and thus defeat the core goals they seek to achieve. True, cultural relativists also express themselves in ways that subvert their own credo—as when, for example, non-Western and sometimes even Western proponents of cultural pluralism evince absolutist outrage at the supposed moral decay of the West. But this is only to prove my point. Any human rights orientation that is not genuinely in support of the widest possible embrace of the value of respect in the prescription and application of human rights norms in a multicultured world is likely to provoke widespread skepticism if not unreserved hostility.

It is of course tempting to argue that international human rights law itself settles the issue. In human rights convention after human rights convention, after all, states have committed themselves to the universality of human rights, and as required by the foundational international law principle *pacta sunt servanda* they are duty bound to uphold that universality. This argument, however, falls woefully short of the cross-cultural challenge.

First, not all states, certainly not all relativist states, have ratified even some of the core international human rights instruments, thus thwarting the *pacta sunt servanda* argument ab initio. Second, much of international human rights law, particularly as it relates to such first-generation rights as are reflected in the International Covenant on Civil and Political Rights, is

7. Anne E. Bayefsky, "Cultural Sovereignty, Relativism, and International Human Rights: New Excuses for Old Strategies," *Ratio Juris* 9 (1996): 42–59, 42.
8. Jerome J. Shestack, "The Philosophical Foundations of Human Rights," *HRQ* 20 (1998): 201–34, 231.
9. Martha C. Nussbaum, *Women and Human Development: The Capabilities Approach* (Cambridge: CUP, 2001), 49.

Western inspired, thus fueling the conflict rather than resolving it. Third, all human rights instruments are filled with ambiguity and indeterminacy, sometimes deliberately to ensure signature and ratification, and thus require interpretation to inform the *content* of universalism even when the *concept* of it has been accepted. Finally, when their plenipotentiaries are not signing human rights treaties and voting for human rights resolutions merely for public relations purposes, states, including states that profess the universality of human rights, typically hedge their bets via reservations, statements of understanding, and declarations so as to ensure that certain practices deemed central to their legal or other cultural traditions will not be rendered unlawful or otherwise anachronistic.

In sum, the invocation of international human rights law does not of itself settle the relativist-universalist debate; and there is, thus, no escaping that claims of cultural relativism demand and deserve thoughtful responses. Given the centrality of the value of respect in human rights, the onus is on the human rights advocate to provide a reasoned and intelligent—respectful—response to them.

But how is this to be done in a particular case? How do we reach the conclusion that a particular claim of universalism should trump a competing claim of cultural relativism or vice versa?

The remainder of this chapter explores this question, detailing a *methodology of respect* according to which competing relativist-universalist claims can be assessed objectively and thereby hopefully escape allegations of cultural imperialism and ethnocentrism—ever mindful, however, of my own vulnerability to cultural bias at least insofar as I rely on analytical concepts that derive from my own culture to describe and assess realities in others. I begin by delineating the observational standpoint that I believe is needed to render human rights judgments about particular cultural practices in transnational settings in an objectively respectful manner.

DELINEATING THE OBJECTIVE OBSERVATIONAL STANDPOINT

The observational standpoint required to resolve a relativist-universalist controversy in a genuinely respectful manner is, I believe, that of

rational persons of diverse identity (creed, gender, race, etc.) acting privately (i.e., not as state representatives) and in their personal self-interest relative to the policies or values they believe should define the world public order of which they are a part, but behind a veil of ignorance as to the particular circumstances of their own personal condition within that order. Persons familiar with legal philosophy will recognize the influence here of neo-Kantian John Rawls. The true principles of justice, Rawls argues, are those of fairness—to wit, those that free and rational persons concerned to further their own interests would accept in an *initial position* of equality as defining the fundamental terms of their association.[10] While a purely hypothetical starting point, this intellectual device does greatly minimize, even if it does not eliminate altogether, the influence of the biases and prejudices of the observer or decision-maker. The assumption is of thinking men and women who, each in their private capacity in some original social setting, but without knowledge of the details of their own physical and social identity, freely choose a public order that is fair to all in its distribution of benefits (rights) and burdens (duties) because, rationally contemplating their own self-interests, they choose a public order that will not cause anyone, including of course themselves, to be disadvantaged in the real world; they choose principles of governance that are good for all, not simply for some or a few. The result is a set of public order value preferences that transcend parochial interest and selfish motive, a blueprint of basic values or fundamental laws that can win the assent of persons everywhere, and thereby facilitate respectful decision when it comes to legal and moral judgments about particular cultural practices across national boundaries.

Is this proposed observational standpoint subject to criticism for being too Western inspired, too individualistically oriented? After all, Rawls comes from a long tradition of discourse dating back to the Enlightenment that, at an earlier time of flourishing, had no apparent conceptual difficulty in promoting rights and the rule of law

---

10. See John Rawls, *A Theory of Justice* (Cambridge, Mass.: Belknap Press of Harvard University Press, 1971), 11.

in the West while colonizing and subjugating much of the rest of the world.

But this argument, I submit, misses an important point. Merely because Rawls's "initial position" decision-makers may be acting individually and behind a "veil of ignorance" as to their actual positions does not mean that they are acting individually and behind a "veil of ignorance" as to their potential positions. Rational individuals denied self-knowledge can foresee the possibility that they may belong to social groups not necessarily Western in origin or outlook. The essential thrust of the observational standpoint is its dedication to a world public order that will most guarantee the fairest distribution of benefits and burdens among all social groups as well as all individuals and thereby ensure that groups as well as individuals benefit as much as possible and suffer the least possible disadvantage.

In short, an observational standpoint that identifies more with the human species as a whole than with the primacy of any of its individual or group parts constitutes, at least for anyone committed to global justice, an ideal to be pursued even if it is never to be fully realized. Hence the observational standpoint recommended here. Absent the core value of respect at the center of all inquiry into the relativist-universalist debate, there is no extending human rights values of any kind without rancor, possibly even violence.

THE POSTULATION OF BASIC WORLD ORDER VALUES

So what map of basic values, what fundamental principles of decision-making, should our "initial position" decision-makers choose to guide their transnational judgments about particular cultural practices? The core of it may be quickly and briefly stated. To be consistent with the observational standpoint recommended above, it cannot represent the exclusive interests of a particular segment of the world community only; the basic values or decision-making principles must reflect an inclusive approach to humankind's great diversity, and thus, as a guide for transnational judgments about particular cultural practices, it should embrace the following self-interested desiderata:

- the widest possible shaping and sharing of all the values of human dignity, including

but not limited to (political) liberty and (socioeconomic) equality,
- without discrimination of any kind save that of merit and basic need (e.g., physical/mental handicap, rank poverty) in many though not necessarily all instances, conditioned by the truism that, in a world of finite possibility, "most assertions of human rights . . . are qualified by the limitation that the rights of any particular individual or group in any particular instance are restricted as much as is necessary to secure the comparable rights of others and the aggregate common interest."[11]

It need here be added only that, in choosing this policy guide to respectful relativist-universalist decision, our "initial position" decision-makers might substitute Martha Nussbaum's (and Amartya Sen's) language of "capabilities"[12] to think upon the values of human dignity not in terms of abstract goals but, rather, in terms of the concrete and more readily measurable needs that all people must have satisfied to fulfill at least the minimal requirements of human dignity however defined.

THE INTELLECTUAL TASKS OF THE RELATIVIST-UNIVERSALIST DECISION

It is tempting to argue that local practices that are indisputably destructive of the values (or capabilities) of human dignity must be altogether rejected and that such rejection should not be confused with disrespect for cultural differences or the principles of sovereignty that afford them protection. I have in mind such policies and practices as genocide, ethnic cleansing, imposed starvation, torture, systematic rape, arbitrary execution, slavery, forced labor, and racial apartheid. If they are not entirely without cultural basis in the first place, these policies and practices are now so widely condemned that they no longer can be justified by any local custom or rationale.

However, to ensure fully respectful cross-cultural judgment generally, it is, I believe, essential first to embrace all the intellectual tasks that seem required to resolve, from an "initial position" policy-oriented perspective, a particu-

11. See Reading 1 (Weston) in this chapter.
12. See Reading 3 (Nussbaum) in this chapter.

lar relativist-universalist controversy: (1) the clarification of community policies relevant to the specific cultural practice at issue, (2) the description of past trends in decision relevant to that practice, (3) the analysis of factors affecting these trends, (4) the projection of future trends in decision relevant to the specific cultural practice in question, and (5) the invention and evaluation of policy alternatives to that practice.

An analytical flow chart of these relevant intellectual tasks looks as follows:

Clarification of Community Policies
↕
Description of Past Trends in Decision
↕
Analysis of Factors Affecting Decision
↕
Projection of Future Trends in Decision
↕
Invention and Evaluation of Policy Alternatives

Although they are presented in logically sequenced order here, they must be applied configuratively (as the two-way arrows suggest), each task informing and being informed by the others, to achieve as comprehensive a contextual analysis as possible. The goal is to test each dimension of policy-oriented inquiry for its ability to contribute to rational but respectful choice in decision, and to obtain guidance in the development of international community policy relative to the practices in question. But note: preliminarily one must address the threshold question of whether or not the practice in question is a *cultural* practice as distinct from one that might be, say, *idiosyncratic* to the particular governing elite involved. If the latter, then the relativist-universalist issue is by definition not implicated, and a decision about the practice may be taken according to potentially different policy criteria. In today's world, the policies and practices of genocide, ethnic cleansing, imposed starvation, torture, systematic rape, arbitrary execution, slavery, forced labor, and racial apartheid would not and should not qualify for such deferential intellectual treatment.

CLARIFICATION OF COMMUNITY POLICIES

Table 1 lists cultural practices well known for the cross-cultural controversies they generate or

might generate. The policy issue most fundamentally underlying each of the two categories concerns the intensity and scope of power exercised by one group of people (public or private) relative to another in the administration of the practice in question. This comes as no surprise, of course, because it is alleged abuses of power that characterize most if not all human rights controversies.

Spanning the two categories, however, though not coextensive with them, are at least two other dimensions of human experience that merit attention; they suggest yet more exact ways to identify at least the principal policies that are at stake when cross-cultural normative judgments are ventured: the societal functions of (1) punishment and (2) social differentiation. Regarding punitive practices, relativist-universalist disagreement centers essentially on the severity of the punishment in question or, alternatively, its proportionality vis-à-vis the alleged precipitating transgression, thus on community policies that regulate resort to coercion in the administration of cultural practices. Regarding socially differentiating practices, disagreement centers mainly on the justification given for the differentiation in question, thus on community policies that regulate the legal and moral rationales of cultural administration. Significantly, these policies tend to be gender-based and favor men over women (patriarchy) in many if not most instances. Women's issues lie both directly and indirectly at the heart of many relativist-universalist controversies, particularly at the intersection between masculine hegemony and women's sexual and reproductive identities. As feminist scholar Arati Rao has observed, "No social group has suffered greater violation of its human rights in the name of culture than women."[13]

From a policy-clarifying standpoint, some of these practices are less easily diagnosed than others. Exceedingly difficult, for example, is the matter of abortion, though less because of the emotional politics that surround the practice (in the United States at least) than because of fundamental disagreement on what it means to be human, thus disagreement on whether it is the

13. Arati Rao, "The Politics of Gender and Culture in International Human Rights Discourse," in Julie Peters and Andrea Wolper, eds., *Women's Rights, Human Rights* (New York: Routledge, 1995), 167–75, 169.

human rights of the fetus that are at stake (the right to life or pro-life position) or the human rights of the mother (the right to liberty or pro-choice position). Adding to the complexity is the matter of mandatory or forced abortion as a function of population control. It is likely that both pro-life and pro-choice proponents would agree that forcing a woman to have an abortion without her consent is a clear violation of human rights—but whose human rights espoused by whom?

Also complicating policy clarification are the competing philosophical traditions of individualism (liberty) and communitarianism (equality). Typically they are invoked to prioritize civil and political (first-generation or negative) rights, on the one hand, or economic and social (second-generation or positive) rights, on the other, even to the complete denial of one generation in favor of the other, thus to the disregard of the fundamental indivisibility that exists between each. But they have served also to rationalize most, perhaps even all, the physical and behavioral practices that have proven controversial in the cross-cultural setting. Exalting liberty and equality to the disregard of other principles or values, they have diverted responsible attention from the centrality of respect in human rights decision-making and thus thwarted clear-headed thinking about the relativist-universalist choice.

Consider, for example, a cultural practice that privileges one group over another. If equality is to serve as our policy guide, it follows that relativist defenses of the practice must be rejected. All of which will seem reasonable enough if the local differentiation is based on, for example, gender or race and we shun gender- or race-based discrimination or segregation as incompatible with equality. But what if it is based on, say, age, basic need, capability, or merit? What decision then? The point is, of course, that notions of equality do not of themselves provide a reliable exit from the relativist-universalist conundrum. Caught up in a swirl of normative tautology, we are not any closer to the objective understanding we seek. For this we must be guided by something else.

Similar confusion sometimes accompanies the cross-cultural assessment of physical practices (at least in theory). Consider, for example, the Islamic (*Qisas*) practice of hand amputation for thievery in formerly theocratic Afghanistan and imprisonment for thievery in the secular United States. Clearly each practice contradicts the individualist value of liberty. But given the widespread acceptance of deprivations of liberty for socially deviant behavior, surely it is not this infringement that inclines us to reject a relativist defense of the theocratic culture in the first instance, nor to accept a relativist defense (depending on other variables) vis-à-vis the secular culture in the second instance. The issue here is not whether liberty may be infringed, but to what extent, in what proportion. Thus, just as notions of equality do not of themselves provide reliable exit from the relativist-universalist conundrum, neither do notions of liberty. For this we again must be guided by something else.

This something else (or guide to respectful decision) is, of course, that map of basic values or fundamental principles of decision-making that our hypothetical initial position decision-makers would choose behind a veil of ignorance to ensure the greatest possible equal distribution of rights and duties within the public order of which they are a part—to wit, all the values (or capabilities) of human dignity postulated to be appropriate and necessary for national and transnational judgments about particular cultural practices. Only by relating these broad goals to specific instances of relativist-universalist controversy—e.g., hand amputation in Afghanistan or outright execution in the United States—will it be possible to ensure respectful decision about the competing values of cultural pluralism and universalist principle. True, the task of relating these goals to specific cultural practices is no easy one. Nor is it made easier by the fact that, behind the relativist-universalist debate and evident on *both* sides of it, there lurks a hidden or unstated agenda less to ensure cultural pluralism than to further the interests of the private and public governing elites who, in the post-Cold War phenomenon we inadequately call "globalization," are engaged in a grand struggle for local-to-global economic and political influence and control. To the dishonor of those who pursue it, this agenda commonly reflects a shameful disregard of the Other—the "huddled masses, yearning to breathe free"[14]—who typically are the victims of globalization's highly uneven, in-

14. Emma Lazarus, "The New Colossus," in *The Poems of Emma Lazarus* (Boston: Houghton Mifflin, 1889) (from the inscription on the Statue of Liberty in New York Harbor), 202–3.

deed unjust, distribution of economic benefits and burdens and whose pain always must be central to human rights discourse and action. The relativist-universalist debate is not merely a conflict between differing cultural and universal norms; it is, in many ways, a high-level confrontation between competing conservative and liberal versions of capitalism, none of which is a priori superior to the other, especially when expressed in cultural terms. Neither the relativist nor the universalist thus may dismiss the other's claims without a reasoned response. The policies that underwrite their claims must be understood for what they are and properly measured for their compatibility with the wider public order goals that our neutral initial position decision-makers would choose to ensure respectful decision when rendering cross-cultural moral judgments.

A DESCRIPTION OF PAST TRENDS IN CROSS-CULTURAL DECISION

A key task in cross-cultural decision-making is to describe past trends in decision relevant to the particular cross-cultural controversy. An understanding of past cross-cultural decision can reveal the extent to which the world community has actively denounced/supported, passively opposed/tolerated, or otherwise disapproved/condoned the particular practice across space and time, and thereby reveal the extent to which one should or should not take serious objection to it. In addition, assuming a desire to repeal or reform a local practice in keeping with some universalist perspective, past trends can instruct us on the cross-cultural difficulties that are likely to be encountered when subjecting provisional formulations of the desirable to the discipline of the possible; they encourage sensitivity to the potential for excessively burdensome demands for change, a particularly important concern where developing countries are involved.

THE ANALYSIS OF FACTORS AFFECTING CROSS-CULTURAL DECISION

Next it is important to analyze the factors that have influenced decisional trends in relativist-universalist controversy and thus also the case at hand. It is important because such analysis helps

us to understand not only how and why relevant precedents were reached but also what factors are likely to serve as useful indicators for present and future decisions, particularly as they may prove useful in guiding our evaluation and recommendation of policy alternatives. The following conditioning factor forays, organized around the principal elements of social process (*who does what to whom, why, when, and where, with what capabilities, how, and with what short- and long-term results*), should help to clarify what I have in mind—understanding that it is seldom the investigation of one conditioning factor alone but, rather, the in-depth exploration of all of them both severally and jointly that is going to provide the cumulative, comprehensive knowledge that is needed to reach the respectful decision that is our objective.

Participants

In all cultural practices, individual human beings are the ultimate actors, either because they are themselves the *masters* of the practice or its *servants*, or because they are affiliated with a group that is either way directly involved.[15] If only just to comprehend the practice, therefore, it is important to ask, as an anthropologist or historian might do, such descriptively oriented questions as: Who are the key participants in the practice? Who is responsible for the practice, who are its principal masters? Who is the object of it, who are its primary servants? What biological characteristics (race, sex, age, sexual orientation), culture (ethnicity, nationality), class (wealth, power), interest (group membership), or personality (authoritarian, submissive) may be attributed to each? And so forth. But partici-

15. There are no perfect words of common usage to identify the key participants in cultural practices. Therefore, for lack of more suitable alternatives and for purely descriptive purposes (that is, free of bias or preference), I adopt the term "master" to refer to those persons who define, execute, administer, and otherwise govern cultural practices, and the term "servant" to refer to those persons who follow or who are expected to follow such practices. It must be understood, however, that neither the masters nor servants of cultural practices are restricted to their most distinctive participatory characteristics. On many occasions, the same participant or participants perform both roles simultaneously.

patory questions such as these, helping us to understand the identity and roles of the different participants involved, can also greatly assist the issue of whether or not to honor a cultural practice, particularly where the resolution of that issue turns on the legal and moral rationales given for social differentiation. Indeed, together with other considerations, they may, in such instances, prove decisive in the given case.

Consider, for example, the practice of racial apartheid in pre-1990 South Africa. In addition to violating our general "initial position" postulate of nondiscrimination in the shaping and sharing of all values, the fact that it privileged minority whites of European origin over majority blacks of indigenous origin obviously had much to do with the world's having outlawed it. If, in other words, only privileged persons make the relevant decisions about a claimed cultural practice, then, in light of the postulated public order values noted above, a high level of scrutiny to the cultural practice should be expected; likewise if only one group benefits from the practice—particularly if the benefit is at the expense of another group or if only one group loses. If, on the other hand, the practice involves a broad cross-section of society participating in decision-making about it, including its servants as well as its masters, one might tentatively conclude that the practice has some at least prima facie legitimacy.

Perspectives

Individuals and groups who participate in cultural practices bring to them variable predispositional perspectives: objectives (value demands), identities (for whom values are demanded), and expectations (about the fulfillment or nonfulfillment of demanded values). Together with environmental factors, these perspectives affect cross-cultural judgment about the legitimacy of a given practice from the standpoint of our initial position decision-makers; be they of the masters or the servants of the cultural practice in question, they are thus important to identify and clarify. What are the objectives, identities, and expectations of the master(s) of the practice? The servant(s)? To what extent do the former affect the fulfillment or nonfulfillment of the latter and vice versa? Are the perspectives of the master(s) construc-

tive and expansionist, believed to increase aggregate values for all, or are they defensive, intended to protect the existing values of exclusive groups? Are the perspectives of the servant(s) opposed to the given practice, or are they in support of it? Does the master of a given practice seek power, wealth, or some other value at the expense of the servant? Does the servant willingly acquiesce to such demands? Unwillingly? Do the identities of the participants relate to the common interest of all members of the culture or only to the interests of a few? Do all or some of the participants, masters and servants alike, perceive an intrinsic value in fulfilling their role in the cultural practice? If so, which ones? Are they conditioned to personal/social security or insecurity as part of their daily routine? And so forth.

It is of course not only the express or stated perspectives of the participants that must be taken into account. In a world where processes of socialization commonly promote the internalization and toleration of patterns of inequality, it is of utmost importance to question the extent to which acquiescence to the given practice in issue is freely given. In such cases, if we are to be consistent with the postulated public order goals of our initial position decision-makers, a high level of scrutiny is warranted.

Situations

Spatial, temporal, institutional, and crisis-level features of social process also set the parameters within which cultural practices must be judged. Is the practice confined to a single country or subnational unit or does it extend across national frontiers to embrace whole regions or continents? Is it of long-standing or short duration, sporadic or continuous, thriving or dying out? Does it operate exclusively in the private sphere—say, as part of the institution of the nuclear family or clan—or is it initiated and/or sanctioned by governmental, religious, or other institutions of national scope and sway?[16] Is it a function of emergency situations or is it an ev-

16. Increasingly in today's world, the private-public dichotomy is, of course, by no means as clear cut as once it was. The family, for example, is a state-sanctioned form; the state governs marriage laws, blood laws, divorce, and much more.

eryday organic occurrence? Consider in these lights, for example, resort to the death penalty in the United States; female genital cutting recently outlawed in Egypt and reportedly on the decline in Kenya and Côte d'Ivoire; female "honor killings" in Jordan in violation of Jordanian public policy; and the curtailment of civil liberties in the presence of civil conflicts or terrorism or in the wake of national disasters. If the practice extends broadly geographically, or has been around for centuries or is growing in use, or is sponsored or actively supported by national governmental or religious institutions, or is a function of normal everyday life, might it not deserve at least prima facie deference? By the same token, if it is geographically confined, relatively new or dying out, carried out without church/state participation or approval, and/or implemented only or mainly during "manufactured crises," surely greater skepticism regarding claims of "cultural tradition" would be warranted. Guiding our assessment of these considerations, of course, are the public order goals postulated by our "initial position" decision-makers.

BASES OF POWER

Potentially, all values (the "welfare values" of wealth, well-being, skills, and enlightenment, on the one hand, and the "deference values" of power, respect, rectitude, and affection, on the other)[17] may be, alone or in combination, bases of power to ensure the continuity or discontinuity of given cultural practices. They are, indeed, the essential components of empowerment in any social process. Careful scrutiny of their availability to the masters and servants of a cultural practice in any given case would seem axiomatic. Notably requiring attention is the availability or nonavailability of particular values (or capabilities) in the absolute sense. Often this will explain both the intensity and the character of selected courses of action or inaction—the en-

17. For this typology, I am intellectually indebted to the germinal work of Harold D. Lasswell and Abraham Kaplan, *Power and Society: A Framework for Political Inquiry* (New Haven, Conn.: YUP, 1950): "By 'welfare values' we mean those whose possession to a certain degree is a necessary condition for the maintenance of the physical activity of the person. . . . Deference values are those that consist in being taken into consideration (in the acts of others and of the self)" (55–56).

forcement (execution or maintenance) of a cultural practice, on the one hand; its reception (acceptance or toleration), on the other—and thus the cross-cultural deference that should or should not be extended to it. Even more important, perhaps, are the relative value positions of the masters and servants of a cultural practice since significant disparities between them, relative to each other and to the wider community of which they are a part, might well tip the scales of cross-cultural judgment. It is well known, for example, that such masters of cultural practices as family clans, ethnic and religious groups, and governments commonly possess greater effective influence (power) and control more resources and personnel (wealth, enlightenment, skill) than the servants of such practices. In such circumstances, one's evaluative guard must be up. Bearing in mind the postulated public order goals of our "initial position" decision-makers, a cultural practice that continues because those with the most resources are able to force others to submit to it should be subject to intense scrutiny, as in the case, for example, of caste-based social arrangements in which only "upper" caste members may hold positions of power and influence while "lower" caste members are relegated to laborious jobs and poor living conditions. The examples are of course legion.

STRATEGIES

The strategies employed by both the masters and the servants of cultural practices commonly embrace the whole range of instruments of policy—diplomatic, ideological, economic, and military—that invariably are available to public and private officials. Typically the masters of cultural practices will resort to some or all of them to ensure the vitality and continuity of such practices, and the servants of them will do likewise either for the same reasons or, alternatively, to resist their continued exercise. Thus, because the type of strategy employed may sometimes shape cross-cultural judgment about a given practice and therefore its acceptability within the social framework within which it is exercised, it is useful to ask what strategies the participants employ to secure their objectives. For example, again recalling the public order goals postulated by our "initial position" decision-makers, one might legitimately look askance at cultural practices whose continued maintenance depends upon, say, bribery and other corrupt measures (economic instrument) or resort to the use of force (military instrument).

As implied, however, the type of strategy employed is less relevant than the differing degrees of coerciveness and persuasiveness with which it is employed. In the case of masters of cultural practices, responsible attention should address alleged abuses of power that manifest coercive or disproportionate means of enforcing cultural practices; and in the case of servants of cultural practices, it is well to consider the intensity of commitment or resistance to the practice, ergo to the degree of persuasiveness or coerciveness with which it is greeted by them. If a practice is carried out or served voluntarily, all other things being equal, it warrants at least prima facie deference or respect in cross-cultural decision-making. Likewise, if it is violently resisted, its legitimacy is in doubt.

OUTCOMES AND EFFECTS

Perhaps most important to cross-cultural judgment about given cultural practices are the short-term outcomes and long-term effects of the interactions between the masters and servants of the cultural practice in question. When all is said and done, it is the balance sheet of net value gains and losses, both short- and long-term, absolute and relative, that results from the practice that commonly determines whether that practice is to be honored or dishonored in cross-cultural judgment. Hovering over that balance sheet is the issue of necessity—the necessity of the value losses relative to the gains for cultural diversity or pluralism.

The following kinds of "outcome" questions are thus exceedingly pertinent. Does the continued exercise of the practice spell a "win-win" outcome for the participants involved? A "win-lose" outcome? If the latter, who "wins" and who "loses," and in what ways? In other words, if the continued exercise of the cultural practice can be seen essentially to reflect the shared aspirations of persons engaged in a cooperative community enterprise (a "win-win" outcome), then at least preliminary deference should be shown that practice. If on the other hand, its continued exercise may be concluded to benefit only a small group of "winners," say, at the expense of

a large group of "losers," then a high degree of scrutiny is warranted, particularly when the "losers" manifest distinctive "minority" identity. Even if the masters of a cultural practice do not intend a discriminatory result, the postulated public order goals of our "initial position" decision-makers compel us to account for the fact of discriminatory deprivation or nonfulfillment as such.

As for the long-term effects of the cultural practice in dispute, which potentially can impact beyond the immediate participants involved, again cross-cultural decision-making must take heed. Suppose, for example, that the continued exercise of a given cultural practice were to result in racially discriminatory outcomes that would spark instability and violent uprisings in large parts of the country involved, even perhaps beyond. What then? If we are faithful to the postulated public order goals of our "initial position" decision-makers, then, logically, cross-cultural decision-making should look upon the practice with skepticism. Suppose, however, that the opposite were true, i.e., that the continued exercise of the cultural practice—say, discriminations based on merit or basic need—were to have a net positive effect for the society in question as a whole. Then, just as logically and based on the same criteria, cross-cultural decision-making should display at least initial great deference.

The point is, of course, that cultural practices can have both beneficial and detrimental outcomes and effects relative to the postulated public order goals of our "initial position" decision-makers. Precise characterization of them and therefore cross-cultural judgment about them will hinge at least in part on whether and how one appraises their short- and long-term consequences.

GENERAL CONDITIONS

If cross-cultural decision-making is to respond adequately to the vicissitudes of our times, it must account not only for the primary characteristics of the particular relativist-universalist case, but also for those influential general conditions of the larger global context within which those characteristics live. Of course, the wider context is ever-changing. Moreover, what may be relevant in that context for one relativist-universalist controversy may not be germane for another. Nevertheless, certain features of the world scene, many of them contradictory, may prove especially significant and therefore worthy of at least passing consideration when attempting cross-cultural judgment—at the present time, for example, the accelerating socioeconomic "globalization" of the world, commonly on unequal terms as between "modern" and "traditional" peoples and cultures; or widespread disillusionment with democratic processes born of intercivilizational/intercultural tensions and unrewarded experiment; or transnational messianic terrorism and responses to it that pit fundamentalist Islamic values against Western Judeo-Christian values and vice versa. Comprehensive assessment of such "secondary" contextual conditions would seek richer indication of their specific relevance to diverse cultural practices and to the fundamental policies that are deemed pertinent in relation to them.

THE PROJECTION OF FUTURE TRENDS IN CROSS-CULTURAL DECISION

The projection of probable future developments relative to given cultural practices—in the sense of the broad trend, not the particular instance—is an important variable in cross-cultural decision-making for at least two reasons. First, it can help us see whether continuation of the practice will reveal movement toward or away from the postulated public order goals of our initial position decision-makers. If so, the practice merits at least prima facie deference; if not, then the opposite. Second, to minimize the diminution of cultural pluralism where continuation of a given practice reveals movement away from the postulated goals of our initial position decision-makers, it can help creativity in the invention and evaluation of alternatives to the manner in which the given cultural practice is exercised so as to make it comport with our postulated public order goals while simultaneously preserving its essence. This is no easy decisional task. No simpleminded extrapolation of the past, it requires a disciplined analysis of all the relevant features of the practice under scrutiny and of the primary and secondary contextual factors that condition it.

THE INVENTION AND EVALUATION OF ALTERNATIVES

The final intellectual task of respectful decision-making in relativist-universalist controversies relates to the deliberate search for, and assessment of, alternatives either to the given cultural practice itself or to the manner in which it is exercised in cases where it may be found that the practice or, more precisely, its manner of exercise is at odds with the postulated public order goals of our initial position decision-makers. It is the last task toward which all the preceding intellectual tasks accumulate and therefore the one to be pursued after all of its predecessors have been credibly exhausted. The point is that the ultimate goal of respectful decision-making in the relativist-universalist context is not to declare a winner, but, rather, to enhance the possibility of ensuring the world's rich diversity (cultural pluralism) while at the same time serving the values of human dignity as defined by the postulated public order goals of our initial position decision-makers. Thus, where on final analysis a particular cultural practice is found to conflict with those goals in the manner of its exercise but not necessarily in its innate purpose or social function, one would look to encourage or reward initiatives that can make the practice consistent with the values of human dignity embedded in the goals. A case in point is found in the rites of female passage and sexual purification in sub-Saharan Africa, where, for generations, these rites have been administered via female genital cutting. Recently in Kenya and the Côte d'Ivoire, for example, the focus of responsible attention has shifted to emphasize the innate purpose of the ritual rather than the modality of its implementation and thus to preserve the ritual and simultaneously lessen or eliminate its severity. To the extent feasible, respectful decision-making in cross-cultural context should seek integrative solutions characterized by maximum gains and minimum losses for all sides of the relativist-universalist debate; it should seek diversity in unity.

APPRAISALS AND RECOMMENDATION

In the preceding pages, I have sought to outline in at least impressionistic fashion the key intellectual tasks and inquiries required to serve respectful decision in relativist-universalist contests. To say that they are the *key* intellectual tasks and inquiries, however, is not to say that they constitute *all* the study that is needed. Additionally critical is an honest assessment of the very decision process pursuant to which that judgment is being rendered. As any sophisticated law student knows, who decides what, why, when, where, and how often has as much and sometimes more to do with the resolution of legal controversies as the facts and pertinent doctrines, principles, and rules themselves. Indeed, for precisely this reason, a thorough approach to respectful decision in the relativist-universalist context would identify and analyze that process just as it would identify and analyze the process of decision in any controversy—that is, not simply as just one more factor generally conditioning the controversy, but, rather, as a separate yet intimately interrelated central part of the total social process surrounding the controversy that merits discrete analysis in its own right. The core value of respect demands at a minimum that the process of cross-cultural decision-making itself prove its own legitimacy when it comes to challenging, possibly eliminating altogether, a demonstration of cultural pluralism.

In any event, one thing is certain: if one is to take seriously the proposition that respect is the core value of all human rights, cross-cultural decision-making about relativist-universalist controversies must reflect the complexity of life itself, implicating a whole series of interrelated activities and events that are indispensable to effective inquiry and, thus, rational and respectful choice in decision. Accordingly, I join other human rights theorists and activists in advocating dialogue across cultures and societies. But not only ethical or moral dialogue. Also needed is that kind of cross-cultural dialogue that can yield substantial consensus on the many factual and policy-oriented questions that absolutely must be asked—hopefully in keeping with the *methodology of respect* that I have urged here—so as to guarantee that the core value of respect will be present in all relativist-universalist decision-making.

QUESTIONS FOR REFLECTION AND DISCUSSION

1. Human rights are the rights to which everyone is entitled, it is said, simply for being human; they are universal by definition. How, then, is it possible to talk about cultural relativism in relation to them? Can the notions of universal human rights and cultural relativism logically coexist? Why? Why not?

2. Does the cultural relativist critique signal the exclusionary implications of the "abstract human universal" that Grear identified in Reading 2? What explains the perceived disjuncture between the prima facie universalist aspirations of the UDHR and the practical and political outworkings of a universalism experienced by certain groups as exclusionary? How would you seek to resolve this dilemma?

3. In "Cultural Relativism and Universal Human Rights," *HRQ* 6, 4 (1984): 400–419, Jack Donnelly identifies cultural relativism as a doctrine that holds that (at least some) variations (in the observance of human rights) are exempt from legitimate criticism by outsiders, a doctrine that is strongly supported by notions of communal autonomy and self-determination (400). In "International Human Rights and Cultural Relativism," *VJIL* 25 (1985): 869–98, Fernando R. Tesón argues that the right of self-determination should not be allowed to deny human rights, that the relativist version of self-determination is a rationalization for oppression. Who do you think is right? Is either right, in terms? Is there a way of reconciling their views? Why? Why not?

4. By asserting the uniqueness of their cultures, non-Western countries or groups may be reclaiming their dignity and national self-esteem from their past experiences of colonial domination by the West and its attendant cultural denigration of the colonized. Does Weston address this possibility? How? How adequately? How not? Substantiate your answer with arguments drawn from the text and from any other specific sources of which you are aware.

5. Weston observes that the value of respect is the core value of all human rights. What does this mean? What are its implications for the theory and practice of human rights? What is its relevance to the relativist-universalist debate? To cross-cultural decision-making?

6. According to one observer, the expectation of equal cultural recognition is inherent

in all modern democratic societies because it is grounded in the Enlightenment value of equal dignity. Charles Taylor, "The Politics of Recognition," in Amy Gutmann, ed., *Multiculturalism and the Politics of Recognition* (Princeton, N.J.: PUP, 1992), 25–73, 27. The legitimate challenge of recognition, according to Taylor, is all too often co-opted by the politics of difference, which demands the same respect for all cultures based merely on the fact that they are different. Do you agree with Taylor? How might we know when the politics of difference is co-opting the challenge of recognition—if it is?

7. Is it possible to ensure cultural pluralism and at the same time insist on cultural universalism? Does Weston's methodology of respect provide an answer? If so, how? And to what degree? If not, why not?

8. In "Human Rights in the Twenty-First Century: Take a Walk on the Dark Side" (Reading 6 in this chapter), Ratna Kapur writes that "The human rights promise of progress, emancipation, and universalism has been exposed as myopic, exclusive, and informed by a series of global panics, especially a panic over national security, sexual morality, and cultural survival in the contemporary period. . . . How has a project that held out the promise of a grand spicy fete mutated into an insipid appetizer?" More specifically, she argues that Western liberalism has belied its own intellectual heritage by practicing what she calls "discriminatory universality." Is Weston's foregoing essay an example of the myopia and exclusivity that Kapur decries? Is his proposed "methodology of respect" a Trojan horse for just another liberal attempt at "discriminatory universality"? How? How not?

9. Weston's methodology of respect is an attempt to formulate an analytically neutral approach for deciding when cultural differences are to be respected and when they are not. Is neutrality important? Did he succeed? Is it possible?

10. To apply Weston's methodology premised on respect for the cultures of other peoples, it is helpful, arguably even necessary, to know these cultures well. However, as Michael Freeman remarks in *Human Rights: An Interdisciplinary Approach* (Cambridge: Polity, 2002), it is difficult for outsiders to have this knowledge because governments and intellectual elites often act as gatemasters, offering an official version of the people's culture to the outside world (110). Does Weston's methodology overcome this difficulty? How? How not?

11. Consider the wearing of the burka by women practiced in some Islamic traditions. Proceed through Weston's five-step model for evaluation. At what decision do you arrive? Why?

12. Would it profit Westerners to apply Weston's methodology of respect to cultural practices of their own countries that arguably are in violation of universal human rights principles? If so, what might some of these practices be? Having identified a relevant practice, apply Weston's methodology to it. Does the analysis assist in determining the status of the practice? How? How not?

13. Weston ends his analysis with the statement that the ultimate goal of respectful decision making in the relativist-universalist context is not to declare a winner, but to enhance diversity and serve the values of human dignity. Cannot declaring a winner actually further universal human rights? Or does it merely excuse cultural practices that deserve to be overruled or modified as a result of the five-step model for evaluation? Why? Why not? Explain.

5. ROBERT MCCORQUODALE AND RICHARD FAIRBROTHER *Globalization and Human Rights*

The focus of this chapter is the effect of globalization on protection of human rights, particularly protection of human rights through international human rights law. Examples from Africa are primarily used because the impact can be seen most clearly there. In this analysis, the consequences of globalization, including both the opportunities and dangers it creates, are considered not only with regard to the protection of human rights, but also in terms of globalization's effect on the international legal order, of which international human rights law forms a part.

GLOBALIZATION

Globalization is a contested term and there is no one accepted definition of it. Clearly, it is a political, social, and cultural process, but "It is foremost an economic process."[1] Cerny defines the economic process of globalization in the following way:

It . . . create[s] permissive conditions for a range of distinct but intertwined structural trends—that is, it expands the playing field within which different market actors . . . interact. It transforms the international economy from one made up of holistic national economies interacting on the basis of *national* "comparative advantage" into one in which a variety of "*competitive* advantages" are created in ways which are not dependent on the nation-state as social, economic, and/or political unit.[2]

As Cerny's definition suggests, economic globalization is seen in terms of "markets" where the

actors in the market have changed, as have the goods and services on offer.

The establishment of globalized economic institutions has been both a symptom of and a stimulus for globalization. The development of the World Bank, the International Monetary Fund, regional development banks such as the European Bank for Reconstruction and Development (EBRD), and, more recently, multilateral trade institutions such as the World Trade Organization (WTO) indicates the trend away from the dominance of the state as the exclusive unit of analysis in international affairs. Acknowledging this trend, the World Bank has stated that:

The state still defines the policies and rules for those within its jurisdiction, but global events and international agreements are increasingly affecting its choices. People are now more mobile, more educated, and better informed about conditions elsewhere. And involvement in the global economy tightens constraints on arbitrary state action, reduces the state's ability to tax capital, and brings much closer financial market scrutiny of monetary and fiscal policies.[3]

Globalization has thus been transformative in terms of a reconceptualizing of state sovereignty within both international relations and international law.

Of course, states have never had exclusive control over their economic, legal, political, and security affairs. However, the current trend of globalization differs from past transnational influences on state sovereignty in the scale and speed of its operation. As Luke notes:

a "transnational" flow of goods, capital, people and ideas has existed for centuries; it antedates even the rise of modern nation-states. However, this historical flow . . . tended to move more slowly, move less and more narrowly than the rush of products, ideas, persons and money that develops with jet transportation,

Excerpted with changes by permission of Johns Hopkins University Press from Robert McCorquodale with Richard Fairbrother, "Globalization and Human Rights," *Human Rights Quarterly* 21 (1999): 735–66. Copyright © 1999 Johns Hopkins University Press.

1. Alex Y. Seita, "Globalization and the Convergence of Values," *Cornell International Law Journal* 30 (1997): 429–91.
2. Phillip G. Cerny, "Globalization and Other Stories: The Search for a New Paradigm for International Relations," *International Journal* 51 (1996): 617–37, 626 (note omitted).

3. World Bank, *World Development Report 1997* (1997), 12.

electronic telecommunication, massive decolonization and extensive computerization.[4]

Yet, while the current globalization is different, it is not analytically detached from its historical origins. Despite some claims to the contrary,
the philosophical oppositions that characterized
the Cold War remain integral to many debates
concerning globalization today.

Nonetheless, the end of the Cold War represents a new analytical phase in world history.
In today's globalization, the actors involved are
not only states but also transnational corporations and intergovernmental institutions. Indeed, of the world's 100 biggest economies [as of
2009], only 56 were states; the remaining [44]
economies are corporations. Thus heads of states
may have much less impact on both individuals
and world events than those in charge of transnational corporations. As Luke explains:

> who sets the pace in automobile output, who
> controls the Earth's computer software pro-
> duction, . . . who leads international money
> markets or who directs world telecommuni-
> cation systems is materially far more impor-
> tant to most individuals, households and
> firms than who holds the state leadership in
> Guatemala, Germany, Ghana or Greece.[5]

Current globalization operates in diverse ways.
Falk offers a bifurcated view of globalization: "glo-
balization-from-above reflect[s] the collaboration
between leading states and the main agents of
capital formation . . . [of] the New World Order"[6]
and concerns the activities of transnational corporations, international economic organizations,
and other similar developments. In contrast, "glo-
balization-from-below" includes popular participation at local levels, the building of civil societies,
and the enhancement of nongovernmental organizations as part of "the strengthening over time
of the institutional forms and activities associated
with global civil society."[7] Falk appropriately locates human rights in this latter branch.

INTERNATIONAL HUMAN RIGHTS LAW

At one time, governments dealt with those
within their jurisdiction as they wished and resisted all criticisms of their actions by claiming
that human rights were matters of "domestic jurisdiction." Now human rights are an established
part of international law.

International human rights are [themselves]
globalized. They operate beyond all borders and
all state mechanisms. They have become part of
the discourse in almost all societies, speaking to
both the elites and the oppressed, to institutions,
and to communities.

However, this globalized characterization of
human rights is subject to criticism by those who
argue that international human rights law does
not reflect universal values, but rather Western,
European ones. While a critique of human rights
as globalized or universal goes beyond the scope
of this article, it is important to realize the context
within which human rights have developed and
are developing. Human rights (though that term
was not originally used) developed in the context
of certain historical, social, political, and philosophical situations in Europe. They "are one of
the monumental legacies left by the Enlightenment. They are one of those grand narratives . . .
that spoke the Truth about the world in order to
change it, and that promised a final reconciliation
at the end of modernity."[8] Theorists from many
perspectives have shown the problems with this
assumption of what is "the Truth" in human
rights, because "in its current form, human rights
law naturalizes and legitimizes the subjugating
and disciplinary effects of European, masculinist,

4. Timothy W. Luke, "New World Order or Neo-World
Orders: Power, Politics and Ideology in Information-
izing Glocalities," in Mike Featherstone et al., eds.,
Global Modernities (London: Sage, 1995), 91–107,
99–100.
5. Ibid., 103. Also, "the secretary general of Amnesty
International and the chief executive officer of Royal
Dutch Shell cast far longer shadows on the international stage than do the leaders of Moldova, Namibia,
or Nauru. The state may not be quite ready to wither
away, but it's not what it used to be." Peter J. Spiro,
"New Global Communities: Nongovernmental Organizations in International Decision-Making Institutions,"
Washington Quarterly 18 (1995): 45–56, 46 (note
omitted).
6. Richard A. Falk, "The Making of Global Citizenship,"
in Jeremy Brecher et al., eds., *Global Visions: Beyond the
New World Order* (Boston: South End Press, 1993), 39–
50, 93.

7. Ibid.
8. Rolando Gaete, "Postmodernism and Human Rights:
Some Insidious Questions," *Law and Critique* 2 (1991):
149–70, 149.

heterosexual and capitalist regimes of power."[9] Thus, besides the general problem of the lack of enforcement of international human rights law, there is also a debate about whether an international system for protecting human rights is inappropriate and invasive if human rights are dependent on their cultural context. In addition, international human rights law, despite its concern with the protection of the rights of humans, remains largely contained within a state-based framework where the responsibility for violations of human rights is by states alone. These criticisms have made some impact on the understanding of human rights. Thus, while the international legal framework for the protection of human rights is based on a universal approach, some account is now taken of the diversity of cultures; both the international instruments and the international human rights tribunals make allowance for each state's "margin of appreciation." Nevertheless, the globalized aspect of human rights can be seen most clearly in the universal power of the rhetoric of "human rights." According to Williams:

> For the historically disempowered, the conferring of rights is symbolic of all the denied aspects of their humanity: rights imply a respect that places one in referential range of self and others, that elevates one's status from human body to social being. . . . "Rights" . . . , deliciously empowering to say . . . , is the magic wand of . . . inclusion and exclusion, of power and no power. The concept of rights, both positive and negative, is the marker of citizenship, our relation to others.[10]

Because this rhetoric is heard worldwide, it is necessary to understand it in terms of the types of rights affected by economic globalization.

ECONOMIC RIGHTS AND ECONOMIC GROWTH

Economic rights include the individual right to an adequate standard of living and the individual and group right to development. The right to an adequate standard of living concerns access to the basic essentials for sustaining life, including food, shelter, clothing, and health care. Accordingly, it can be argued that economic growth will increase protection of economic rights because economic growth brings increased access to health care, food, and shelter, either directly through employment and increased income or indirectly through the improvement and extension of these facilities to more people. For most developing states, particularly those in Africa, economic growth is often fostered through large-scale external investment. This investment comes from globalized economic institutions, such as intergovernmental institutions, including the World Bank and the IMF, or transnational corporations. This argument, therefore, concludes that economic growth through globalization leads to the protection of economic rights such as the right to an adequate standard of living and the right to development.

However, the reality is somewhat different in most instances. There are at least three reasons for this: the type of investment, the basis for investment decisions, and the type of economic growth.

First, a great deal of the investment arising from globalized economic sources for the purposes of "development" is allocated only to certain types of projects, such as the building of dams, roads, and runways, and the creation of large-scale commercial farms. There is little or no investment in primary health care, safe drinking water, and basic education. Furthermore, these globalized investment-based projects "create some risks of (legally cognizable) harm to some categories of project-affected people, and some projects generate many risks of very serious harms to many people."[11] The World Bank itself has [long] recognized the risks involved. [For example, with regard to large-scale irrigation projects, it has admitted] that

> Social disruption is inevitable in large-scale irrigation projects. . . . Local people often find

9. Diane Otto, "Rethinking Universals: Opening Transformative Possibilities in International Human Rights Law," *AYBIL* 18 (1997): 1–36, 35. Similar arguments can be made with respect to neoclassical economics generally because it emerged from the same philosophical foundations as human rights. See Stephen Toulmin, *Cosmopolis: The Hidden Agenda of Modernity* (New York: Free Press, 1990).
10. Patricia J. Williams, *The Alchemy of Race and Rights* (Cambridge, Mass.: HUP, 1991), 164.

11. James C. N. Paul, "The Human Right to Development: Its Meaning and Importance," *John Marshall Law Review* 25 (1992): 235–65, 238.

that they have less access to water, land and vegetation resources as a result of the project. Conflicting demands on water resources and inequalities in distribution can easily occur both in the project area and downstream . . . altering the distribution of wealth.[12]

An example of this occurred when representatives of the Penan people of Malaysia told [former] senator [and later] U.S. vice president Al Gore: "We are not being killed by weapons, but when our lands are taken, it is the same as killing us."[13] The type of investment generated by globalized economic institutions tends to infringe on economic rights rather than protect them.

Second, decisions about investment by these globalized organizations are based almost exclusively on financial concerns, including generating profits for banks and other transnational corporations. Such concerns external to the state in which the investment is made fail to focus on social welfare within the state. A classic example of this decision-making process is seen in an infamous internal World Bank memo:

> shouldn't the World Bank be encouraging more migration of the dirty industries to the [less developed countries]? . . . The measurement of the costs of health impairing pollution depends on the foregone earnings from increased morbidity and mortality. From this point of view, a given amount of health-impairing pollution should be done in the country with the lowest wages. I think the economic logic behind dumping a load of toxic waste in the lowestwage country is impeccable and we should face up to that. . . . I've always thought that under-populated countries in Africa are vastly under-polluted; their air quality is probably vastly inefficiently [high] compared to Los Angeles or Mexico City.[14]

This memo, written by then World Bank chief economist [and later U.S. deputy treasury secretary and treasury secretary] Lawrence Summers, makes excellent neoclassical economic logic. But this logic [has] disastrous consequences for environmental and human rights protection. For example, U.S.-based chemical companies exporting pesticides banned in the United States to developing states by altering production techniques and changing production sites to avoid strict U.S. labeling laws means that unlabeled containers of hazardous pesticides then become available for purchase over the counter in, for example, parts of Africa. Often, due to lack of proper information [for] consumers, the pesticides are improperly used and the containers are reused to carry drinking water.

In a globalized economy, the patience of investors to obtain returns on their investment is considerably reduced. In Africa, where long-term investment in infrastructure is needed, investors from developed states can be harsh in their economic decisions. For example, a French diplomat apparently said that "Economically speaking, if the entire black Africa, with the exception of South Africa, were to disappear in a flood, the global cataclysm will be approximately nonexistent."[15]

In broader human rights terms, globalized economic institutions often implement plans that hurt those whose economic rights are most vulnerable. For example, Howard notes that "In Africa today, schools are closing down as governments retrench in the face of structural adjustment programmes imposed by the International Monetary Fund."[16] Because the government is the largest employer in most African states, "Not only do thousands of people lose their jobs . . . , but often all services are drastically cut, especially those of the already underfunded health sector."[17] Those who are the worst affected when

12. World Bank, "Technical Paper 140," in *Environmental Assessment Sourcebook*, vol. 2 (Washington, D.C.: World Bank, 1991), 96.

13. As quoted in Brian B. A. McAllister, "The United Nations Conference on Environment and Development: An Opportunity to Forge a New Unity in the Work of the World Bank Among Human Rights, the Environment, and Sustainable Development," *Hastings International and Comparative Law Review* 16 (1993): 689–744, 691.

14. See "Let Them Eat Pollution," *Economist*, 8 February 1992, 66 (quoting a World Bank memo by Lawrence Summers). See also "Pollution and the Poor," *Economist*, 15 February 1992, 18.

15. Victor Chesnault, "Que faire de l'Afrique noire?" *Le Monde*, 28 February 1990, 2, quoted in Michael Chege, "Remembering Africa," *Foreign Affairs* 71, 1 (1992): 146–63, 148.

16. Rhoda E. Howard, "Civil Conflict in Sub-Saharan Africa: Internally Generated Causes," *International Journal* 51 (1996): 27–33, 32.

17. Mahmood Monshipouri, *Democratization, Liberalization & Human Rights in the Third World* (Boulder, Colo.: L. Rienner, 1995), 54 (quoting Fran Hoskin). See also Anne Orford, "Locating the International: Military and Monetary Interventions After the Cold War," *HILJ* 38 (1997): 443–85, 464–75.

governments are forced to change their priorities are usually the poor, women, and agricultural workers. For example, Zimbabwe used to provide free education for all until adherence to an IMF structural adjustment program caused this to end. As a result, many Zimbabwean girls are no longer being educated because parents make gender-based financial choices. This occurs despite the clear evidence that the education of girls is an investment that "yield[s] the highest rate of return in a developing country."[18]

Indeed, structural adjustment programs have significant gender impact, and often fail to withstand criticism in the same economic terms that they purport to uphold. The UN Special Rapporteur on the Realization of Economic, Social and Cultural Rights reported [as early as 1992] that "Structural adjustment programs continue to have a significant impact upon the overall realization of economic, social and cultural rights, both in terms of the ability of people to exercise them, and of the capability of governments to fulfil and implement them. . . . Human rights concerns continue to be conspicuously underestimated in the adjustment process."[19]

The fact that the economic decision-making process is being taken away from governments and put in the hands of financial "experts" in globalized economic institutions also means that the people and the governments of developing states are not effectively involved in decisions affecting their lives. This has an impact on both state sovereignty and human rights. People are not able to exercise their right to development because they are not afforded the opportunity to participate in decisions concerning their development. In addition, governments, as well as minorities within a state, are marginalized as power is transferred to bureaucrats and special interest groups. This impact is compounded with increasing privatization of public functions and public goods. As a result, the ability of governments to protect human rights, even if guaranteed by a constitution and enforced by an independent judiciary, becomes more restricted.

The third and final reason that globalization does not necessarily promote economic rights is because there are different types of economic growth. The UN Human Development Report 1995 dealt with the impact of damaging forms of economic growth. It found that damaging economic growth includes "that which does not translate into jobs, that which is not matched by the spread of democracy, that which snuffs out separate cultural identities, that which despoils the environment, and growth where most of the benefits are seized by the rich."[20] An example of damaging economic [growth] is where crops are planted for export to gain foreign exchange revenue while the people are deprived of their staple diet. This has happened in both Zimbabwe and Brazil, [and is directly] contrary to the right of self-determination which provides that "In no case may a people be deprived of its own means of subsistence."[21]

Another kind of damaging economic growth in which the benefits of economic growth are seized by the rich was exemplified in South Africa during the apartheid regime. There, economic growth was for many years achieved through the exploitation of a large unskilled, insecure, dispossessed, and dependent work force consisting of oppressed blacks. Thus globalization can have the effect of increasing economic inequality when the economic interests that are protected are those of the rich and economically powerful, who are usually the elite urban males.

In sum, economic globalization can lead to improved conditions for those in developing states, but it can also encourage economic exploitation and oppression. Globalization may lead to apparent improvements in economic growth, but at a cost to the economic rights of

---

18. Josette L. Murphy, *Gender Issues in World Bank Lending* (Washington, D.C.: World Bank, 1995), 22 (note omitted).
19. The Realization of Economic, Social and Cultural Rights, Final Report Submitted by Mr. Danilo Türk, Special Rapporteur, UN Doc. E/CN.4/Sub.2/1992/16 (1992).

20. Larry Elliott, "Bridging the North-South Divide," *Guardian Weekly* (Manchester), 11 August 1996, 14 (describing the conclusions of the UNDP Report). One form of damaging growth can be where governments attempt to attract foreign investment by "improving" the physical appearances of cities, such as the extermination of street children in Latin America and the perfunctory cleaning up of slum housing by eviction of low-income tenants in Atlanta prior to the 1996 Summer Olympics.
21. International Covenant on Economic, Social and Cultural Rights (ICESCR), Art. 1(2), and International Covenant on Civil and Political Rights (ICCPR), Art. 1(2).

many within a state. The influence of the economic philosophies of the globalized economic institutions is such that even the concepts of human rights can be affected. For example, the right to development is now partly defined on the notion that "development" means industrialization, westernization, and economic growth. Only a very few of the globalized economic institutions take human rights issues directly into account in their investment decisions, though this may be changing. If human rights issues are not taken into account in these investment decisions, it is likely that human rights will become more endangered as a consequence of those decisions.

POLITICAL RIGHTS AND INTERNATIONAL INVESTMENT

There has been debate concerning the relationship between economic globalization and the protection of political rights, the strengthening of civil society and institution building, and the development of democracy. The main arguments supporting both a positive and a negative relationship will be canvassed here in turn.

It was argued by a former UN Secretary-General that there is a positive relationship between democracy and development:

> Democracy and development are linked in fundamental ways. They are linked because democracy provides the only long-term basis for managing competing ethnic, religious, and cultural interests in a way that minimizes the risk of violent internal conflict. They are linked because democracy is inherently attached to the question of governance, which has an impact on all aspects of development efforts. They are linked because democracy is a fundamental human right, the advancement of which is itself an important measure of development. They are linked because people's participation in the decisionmaking processes which affect their lives is a basic tenet of development.[22]

There is some research to support this argument.[23]

Another argument supporting a positive relationship between economic globalization and democracy suggests that globalized economic institutions, including transnational corporations, tend to demand that certain conditions exist in a state before they are willing to invest and that these conditions lead to the protection of political rights. These investment conditions, sometimes called "democratic governance" requirements, can include the acceptance of the rule of law, clear and transparent practices by government and local institutions, and international dispute resolution. Thus, it is argued, these investment conditions ensure that there is a democratic system, including judicial guarantees of human rights and political institutions. The apparent links between setting these conditions and democracy are found in instruments such as the Charter of Paris, where "democracy has as its foundation respect for the human person and the rule of law."[24] Similarly, in the opinion of the Inter-American Court of Human Rights, judicial protection and political institutions are essential to the preservation of democracy and the rule of law.[25] The rule of law is crucial because "in a society governed by law, the legal system can be a means for people to protect themselves from bureaucratic abuse, commercial exploitation, and official lawlessness which are generally the lot of the poor and powerless."[26]

In contrast, there are arguments that find a negative relationship between economic globalization and political rights. The record of the globalized economic institutions in using their investment to foster democracy has been poor. This may be due in part to the pervasive distrust of outsiders by ruling elites, as well as relatively weak "civil societies" and the fragility of many

22. Development and International Economic Cooperation: An Agenda for Development, Report of the Secretary-General, U.N. GAOR, 48th Sess., Agenda Item 91, 120, UN Doc. A/48/935 (1994).

23. See, e.g., Robert Barrow, *Determinants of Economic Growth: A Cross-Country Empirical Study* (Cambridge, Mass.: MIT, 1997), 52, 59–61.
24. Charter of Paris for a New Europe, adopted by the Conference on Security and Co-operation in Europe at Paris, 21 November 1991.
25. *Eds.*—See Judicial Guarantees in States of Emergency (Arts. 27(2), 25, 8 of American Convention on Human Rights), Advisory Opinion OC-9/87, 6 October 1987, Inter-Am. Ct. H.R. (Ser. A) No. 9 (1987).
26. Geoffrey Budlender, "Lawyers and Poverty: Beyond Access to Justice," in *Second Carnegie Inquiry into Poverty and Development in Southern Africa*, Carnegie Conference Paper 91, 1984, 7.

developing states. Indeed, globalization, through the creation of international or regional trade and economic institutions, can lead directly to a feeling of loss of political power by groups within states. [It] also leads to the fostering of "tribalism and other revived or invented identities and traditions which abound in the wake of the uneven erosion of national identities, national economies, and national state policy capacity."[27]

In addition, many of the funding conditions imposed by the globalized economic institutions, such as economic structural adjustment programs, require strong government action for smooth implementation. Authoritarian and military governments are favored by external investors as the best suited to implement these policies successfully, thereby putting new democracies at risk. Indeed, the World Bank's characterization of a credible legal system [capable of holding governments accountable] is solely market focused. There is no recognition of other reasons for law, including protection of human rights and maintenance of ordered, settled communities.

Furthermore, the investment conditions imposed by the globalized economic institutions can lead to distortion of the energies and resources of governments. Even the instances of apparent links between investment and democracy have been said to emerge from financial concern over repayment of loans and not from a broader interest in the establishment of democracy. Similarly, a case study of the former Yugoslavia traced some of the causes of the conflict there to actions by the globalized economic institutions which stripped that state of many of its functions and led people to seek other sources of community.[28]

Despite these facts, it is still recognized that "In the new global order unleashed by the collapse of communism, Africans [and other developing States] have little choice but to pull their own weight by meeting the most exacting standards in domestic governance and economic competitiveness."[29]

The implications from this quotation, as well as the Yugoslavian case study, are twofold. On the one hand, there is an encouraging move away from the use of developing states as places for political ideological conflict and military

bases to an acknowledgment that economic decision making requires consideration of human rights. On the other hand, the economic philosophies expounded in developed states rarely consider the cultural and social ramifications for developing states. In addition, under the pressure of the globalized economic institutions, governments in developing states often lack any effective sovereign power to make decisions to protect minorities or to preserve important cultural and social elements within communities.

It is only in recent years that globalized economic institutions have begun to take into account noneconomic factors such as human rights, environmental degradation, and cultural fragmentation in their investment decisions. This may be due partly to broader human rights concerns and partly to economic considerations.

While transnational corporations can have a powerful influence in reforming political conditions, this is only likely to occur where such reform is in the corporations' own interests. Transnational corporations are primarily subject to control by their major shareholders. Arguably, however, they are subject [also] to the power of the market in terms of the interests of consumers and can therefore be forced, for example, to consider human rights or environmental issues due to strong consumer boycotts. However, this approach is not uniformly applicable [and, in any case, tends to favor consumers in developed nations—a] selective reaction that is inconsistent with human rights because human rights are applicable worldwide and are [also] not limited to matters that only affect consumer groups.

Further, while transnational corporations can greatly assist the effectiveness of international sanctions such as those previously in force against South Africa, which can lead to improved protection of human rights, [transnational corporations] may also choose to ignore [such] international actions. Thus, while opportunities for enhanced human rights protection can emerge from pressure on globalized economic institutions to take more account of human rights issues, so far this pressure (and the resultant impact) has been piecemeal and inconsistent.

Finally, many of the arguments claiming a positive relationship between economic globalization and political rights confuse democracy with human rights. The terms are not synonymous [and] there is no generally accepted human "right to democracy." . . . [Moreover], human rights are

27. Cerny, "Globalization and Other Stories," 619 (alteration in original).
28. See Orford, "Locating the International," 457.
29. Chege, "Remembering Africa," 149.

much more and diverse than simply being about democracy or civil and political rights.

Accordingly, it is possible to argue that there is a positive relationship between economic globalization and the protection of political rights [But this argument, taken at face value, is misleading.]. [While] the globalized economic institutions have been seeking to make the relationship a positive one by placing democratic governance conditions on investment and taking some account of noneconomic factors in their decision making, the arguments that the relationship is a negative one are strong. These arguments raise questions about the legitimacy of the democratic governance conditions and the seriousness with which human rights issues, and the nebulous concept of "democracy," are taken into account by both global economic institutions and transnational corporations. It would appear that instead of creating order, rule of law, and protection of human rights, globalization can create conditions for disorder, authoritarian rule, and disintegration of the state entity with consequent violations of human rights.

CULTURAL RIGHTS AND GLOBAL COMMUNICATION

One of the sectors that has been an integral part of economic globalization is the communications industry. Not only has it become a global industry in and of itself, but also it has been a major factor in the globalization of other industries. The worldwide high-speed communications systems developed in recent years have propelled globalization. Information transmitted almost instantly by satellites and computer networks gives economic and political decision makers a worldwide and real-time view. The Internet particularly operates beyond any real state control and transcends territorial boundaries.

As a result, information about human rights abuses is disseminated around the world much more quickly and easily, thereby reducing the effectiveness of state internal security regimes. Indeed, as early as 1976, the European Court of Human Rights recognized that "Freedom of expression [is] one of the essential foundations of" a democratic institution,[30] and that the commu-

nications industry, by providing information, is a vital part of the protection of human rights.[31] This globalized communications system can provide human rights groups with information, assistance, and support in their resistance to oppression. Human rights nongovernmental organizations, such as Amnesty International, flourish in an information-rich environment. When people know about human rights and are aware of human rights abuses, they are more likely to seek to protect them. In addition, the globalized communications system reduces the ability of governments to hide their activities, including acts which violate human rights, from public scrutiny. This exposure can lead to changes in policy by the state concerned.[32] In addition, information provided by the globalized communications industry can lead to international pressure on, or even action against, that state by other states.

However, a difficulty that arises with the impact of the globalized communications industry on the protection of human rights is that the information that it provides is full of both noises and silences. So much information is available so quickly that it is inconceivable that something could happen without someone being aware of it. But there are also dangers. Events [can] get lost in what Der Derian calls the "signal/noise ratio: information overload."[33]

An additional concern arises from the consequences of the information provided by the globalized communications industry. This is seen in the "CNN effect," where the globalized communications industry [predominantly] shapes what is seen and, in doing so, shapes the bases for decision-making. This has the potential for skewed decision-making because decisions based on CNN coverage, as many are, may be made on insufficient, or insufficiently objective, information. In addition, certain information may be given greater priority than others for the personal business purposes of media owners. This is of increasing concern in an era when control of

30. *Handyside Case*, 24 Eur. Ct. H.R. (ser. A) 23 (1976).

31. See *Autronic AG v. Switzerland*, 12 Eur. H.R. Rep. 485 (1990).
32. *Eds.*—It also can galvanize civil movements seeking directly to confront oppressive regimes, as revealed by the "Arab Spring"—suggesting the particular power of social networking sites and mechanisms.
33. James Der Derian, *Antidiplomacy: Spies, Terror, Speed, and War* (Cambridge, Mass.: Blackwell, 1992), 141–69.

the globalized communications industry is held by a few groups, who are largely based in the developed states. As Alleyne has commented:

> Because politics is about power, we say that the global flow of news is political: it reflects and determines the international configuration of power. . . . In the case of global news flows, therefore, those with power are those who can determine the very definition of news. Power also rests with those whose voices and perspectives are heard the most.[34]

Alleyne's comment applies to all those who control communications, both the globalized communications industry and governments. Governments can and do regulate and control communications, as seen during apartheid South Africa [and in many more recent situations[35]]. However, the extent to which governments can continue to regulate communications, and hence maintain sovereignty within their states may depend on who gets access to information technology. The speed of developments in communications technology and the expense involved [suggest the danger of a digital divide whereby economically disempowered people] in developed states and in developing states stand in very real danger of missing most of the advantages of global communications technology. Meanwhile, the impact on the human rights of those in developing states by the globalized communications industry controlled from developed states may already have been felt. It has been argued that

> Under conditions of very scarce resources [as in many developing States], the emulation of the socio-cultural systems and especially the consumption patterns of [developed States] means first of all that the provision of basic foodstuffs, health services, clothing, housing, drinking water, education, reliable transportation and the like is neglected. It furthermore means that production processes tend to be utilised which

actually may increase unemployment and underemployment; and that, in fact, resources are wasted in products subject to planned obsolescence. Moreover, to the extent that the satisfaction of foreignoriented consumption wants requires inputs from abroad, continuing dependence on [developed] countries and their constitutions (especially transnational enterprises) that can provide these inputs remains almost unavoidable.[36]

This view indicates not only the possible consequences on the protection of human rights of a globalized communications industry, but also the way in which industry tends to offer a particular economic and political philosophy, where the primacy of the markets and of certain civil and political rights (such as the rights of freedom of speech, fair trial, and political participation) are constantly propounded to the detriment of economic rights.

One particular impact of the globalized communication industry is on the protection of cultural rights, especially of minorities. Some cultures are brought to life by this industry by being recorded and transmitted on the international communications network, albeit usually from the perspective of the developed state. A successful transnational corporation must take some account of the local culture, and many cultures may be more tenacious and adaptable over time than had been thought. Furthermore, global communications can enable cross-fertilization of ideas which can nurture and support group[s] working in apparent isolation in their own state.

However, there is the risk that the diverse voices of women, indigenous groups, refugees, and ethnic minorities may be silenced. A type of homogenized, universal, Americanized culture aided by the globalized communication industry may develop. The extent to which this has already occurred is tabulated in the respected magazine, the *Economist*, which, for more than [two] decade[s], has produced a "Big Mac Index" in which the price of a Big Mac produced by McDonald's is used, with an increasing degree of seriousness, as an international currency benchmark. The index uses data

34. Mark D. Alleyne, *International Power and International Communication* (New York: St. Martin's, 1995), 67–69.
35. *Eds.*—For example, the suppression of news from Turkey concerning the 2013 Istanbul protests by state-friendly media. It was largely through international coverage, social network sites, tweets, and blogs that the news made its way into the consciousness of the wider international community.

36. Karl P. Sauvant, "From Economic to Socio-Cultural Emancipation: The Historical Context of the New International Economic Order and the New International Socio-Cultural Order," *Third World Quarterly* 3 (1981): 48–61, 58–59.

from the vast array of states in which McDonald's foods are sold and is based on the notion of "purchasing power parity" by which an American dollar should buy the same amount of goods in all states. The existence of this index shows the depth of the impact of globalization throughout the world, including the extent to which cultures are subject to external pressures to change.

The globalized communications industry enables globalization and propounds certain market-based philosophies shared by the globalized economic institutions and transnational corporations. It offers opportunities for the protection of human rights through its ability to provide information. However, globalization of the communications industry also presents [important] dangers.

CONCLUSIONS

Economic globalization simultaneously creates opportunities and presents challenges for the international legal protection of human rights. While there are understandable concerns about both economic globalization and the international legal protection of human rights in terms of their philosophical bases, both are part of the process of globalization in which political, economic, social, civil, and cultural relationships are not restricted to territorial boundaries and are not solely within the control of any one state. As a result, globalization and the international legal order are opportunities to end the absolute sovereignty of the state, and, hence, to further the realization that how a state deals with those within its territory is no longer a matter exclusively within the domestic jurisdiction of a state. It is now a matter of legitimate international concern.

Nevertheless, international human rights law, caught within its framework of state responsibility for human rights violations, is unable to deal fully with the changes to state sovereignty accelerated by the process of globalization. Where the violator of human rights law is not a state or its agent but is, for example, a globalized economic institution or a transnational corporation, international human rights law finds it difficult to provide any redress to the victim. In such cases, international human rights law focuses on the responsibility of a state to adopt constitutional,

legislative, judicial, administrative, and other measures to ensure that human rights within its territory are protected, no matter who the perpetrator may be. However, this approach tends to be ineffective where a state is unwilling or unable to take these measures due to the possible effect on investment by globalized economic institutions. Therefore, international human rights law needs to take the opportunities presented by globalization to develop a more flexible framework within which responsibility for human rights violations is not [merely] state-based; states must provide appropriate mechanisms for all individuals, groups, and others to have standing to bring claims for any violation of human rights.

The other major opportunity offered by economic globalization for the protection of human rights emerges from the decision-making processes of the globalized economic institutions. As has been indicated, human rights issues are now occasionally taken into account by these institutions. This is occurring for a variety of reasons, including perceptions of increased likelihood of returns on investment, fear of consumer boycotts, pressure from nongovernmental organizations, and, possibly, concern for the rights of human beings. Furthermore, a relationship between human rights and economic growth, development, and political institutions is recognized, so that these issues are no longer seen as separate or discrete from one another.

However, pressure still needs to be exerted to ensure that the globalized economic institutions do take international human rights law explicitly into account in all stages of their decision making. Because economic globalization is generated by a philosophy in which markets must be allowed to flourish while states are relegated to the role of assisting this flourishing, any benefits for human rights protection tend to be incidental and fragmentary. Accordingly, the dangers of economic globalization for human rights can outweigh these incidental benefits. This was made clear in a report by the UN Secretary-General [more than two decades ago]:

> Development strategies which have been oriented merely towards economic growth and financial considerations have failed to a large extent to achieve social justice; human rights have been infringed, directly and through the

depersonalization of social relations, the breakdown of families and communities, and of social and economic life.[37]

Furthermore, there is the possibility of the fragmentation of states. This fragmentation is fostered by shifting the decision-making processes away from governments and people to globalized economic institutions and transnational corporations which have a limited interest in the social and cultural welfare or the human rights of people in developing states.

Another danger of economic globalization is its impact on the concepts and application of human rights. [One] example [is] seen in the right to development where only certain types of development, such as the construction of transportation infrastructures, have been included within the concept of this right; another is seen in the dominance of globalization's focus on certain rights (civil and political) to the virtual exclusion of other rights. But the greater danger is that the values of the international community, embodied in the international legal order and created to protect human rights, are themselves being challenged by the values of the global economic free market. As Alston observes:

> In the world of globalization, a strong reaction against gender and other forms of discrimination, the suppression of trade unions, or the denial of primary education or health care, can often require not only showing that the relevant practices run counter to human rights standards but also a demonstration that they are offensive to the imperatives of economic efficiency and the functioning of the free market. . . . In some respects the burden of proof has shifted—in order to be validated, a purported human right must justify its contribution to broader market-based "vision" of a good society.[38]

It is these challenges to the values established by international human rights law that must be countered if the human rights of all are to be protected. These values need to be constantly asserted and given meaning because, as Eleanor Roosevelt said:

> Where after all, do universal human rights begin? In small places, close to home—so close and so small that they cannot be seen on any map of the world. Yet they are the world of the individual person: the neighbourhood he lives in; the school or college he attends; the factory, farms or office where he works. Such are the places where every man, woman, or child seeks equal justice, equal opportunity, equal dignity without discrimination. Unless these rights have meaning there, they have little meaning anywhere.[39]

There are a number of opportunities for human rights to be asserted within the current international community. This includes advocating for the inclusion of human rights in international treaties, demanding that human rights be considered in the making of foreign policy, and insisting that the activities of transnational corporations are consistent with international human rights law. It is vital that those who seek to protect human rights, particularly through the international legal system, are aware of the opportunities and dangers of globalization for the protection of human rights. Only then can they seek to ensure that the dangers are diminished and the opportunities are taken.

---

37. Question of the Realization of the Right to Development: Global Consultation on the Right to Development as a Human Right, Report Prepared by the Secretary-General Pursuant to Commission on Human Rights Resolution 1989/45, U.N. ESCOR, Comm'n on Hum. Rts., 46th Sess., Agenda Item 8, I 153, UN Doc. E/CN.4/1990/9/Rev.1 (1990).
38. See Philip Alston, "The Myopia of Handmaidens: International Lawyers and Globalization," *EJIL* 8 (1997): 435–48, 442.
39. Celina Romany, "State Responsibility Goes Private: A Feminist Critique of the Public/Private Distinction in International Human Rights Law," in Rebecca Cook, ed., *Human Rights of Women: National and International Perspectives* (Philadelphia: University of Pennsylvania Press, 1994), 90 (quoting Eleanor Roosevelt). [*Eds.*— One may correctly assume Mrs. Roosevelt did not intend to marginalize or otherwise demean women in her use of male-gendered pronouns in this statement.]

QUESTIONS FOR REFLECTION AND DISCUSSION

1. What is globalization? What key characteristics of it do you think have the greatest implications for human rights (positive or negative), and why? Substantiate your arguments by drawing on the text and if possible, alternative sources you are aware of.

2. How, according to McCorquodale and Fairbrother, has globalization "been transformative in terms of a reconceptualizing of state sovereignty within both international relations and international law"?

3. McCorquodale and Fairbrother, citing Otto, argue that "in its current form, human rights law naturalizes and legitimizes the subjugating and disciplinary effects of European, masculinist, heterosexual, and capitalist regimes of power." Can you think of examples that support this argument? That undermine it? On what research or information are your examples based?

4. Evaluate the claim that "economic growth through globalization leads to the protection of economic rights such as the right to an adequate standard of living and the right to development." What evidence do McCorquodale and Fairbrother provide that might help you in this task?

5. There is "debate concerning the relationship between economic globalization and the protection of political rights, the strengthening of civil society and institution building, and the development of democracy." Do you believe globalization extends or undermines democracy? Do you think economic globalization strengthens political rights and civil society or weakens them? Where? On what research, evidence, and reasoning is your position based?

6. *H*as economic globalization strengthened or weakened substantive respect for social and economic human rights? *How? How* not? Upon what research, evidence, and reasoning is your position based? Substantiate your answer with specific sources wherever possible.

7. What implications do you think the pervasive influence of corporations upon the WTO, the IMF, and other international institutions has for the future of human rights? Upon what do you base your view?

8. McCorquodale and Fairbrother state that transnational corporations can have some influence in promoting economic growth and human rights. *A*ccording to them, however, their positive influence is limited by the fact that shareholders of corporations prioritize profits over anything else. Outcries from consumers of human rights concerns can to some degree influence corporations to alleviate those concerns, because good consumer relations tend to benefit profits. Consider the public outcry surrounding *A*pple, Inc. and its major manufacturer of the iPhone and iPad in China, Foxconn. In 2010, more than a dozen workers committed suicide. Since then, *A*pple, Inc. and Foxconn have responded to outcry from mostly Western consumers by putting in place a plan to alleviate health concerns, reduce overtime hours, and improve compensation. Given this example, do you agree with McCorquodale and Fairbrother or not? Do transnational corporations like *A*pple, Inc. have more or less influence in promoting economic growth and human rights than McCorquodale argues? *A*re outcries from consumers a strong or weak mechanism for improving human rights?

9. McCorquodale and Fairbrother refer to the "CNN effect." What is it? Is it a good or bad thing from a human rights standpoint? Upon what do you base your view?

10. Do you agree that the Internet means the state is made more accountable for human rights abuses, or can you see situations in which the state has managed successfully to turn the Internet into a source of control or to control the Internet so as to mute its effectiveness as a mode of accountability? Give examples and suggest why they support your position.

11. Does the increase in social networking undermine or deepen the Internet as a source of human rights information and communication? Does it facilitate or divert attention from human rights and other critical issues (e.g., the climate crisis and nuclear proliferation)? Upon what do you base your views?

12. On balance, do you think globalization is a positive or negative force for the promotion of human rights? In respect of which rights, in which respects, and on the basis of what examples or evidence?

13. It is possible that the McCorquodale and Fairbrother essay will leave some wondering how, exactly, the international system and particularly the international legal system can solve or mitigate the many problems mentioned. Have you any suggestions?

6. RATNA KAPUR *Human Rights in the Twenty-First Century: Take a Walk on the Dark Side*

We have witnessed an extraordinary prolifer-ation of human rights law in the course of the twentieth century and the beginning of this mil-lennium. Contrary to popular belief, business is booming at the United Nations, with its entou-rage of resolutions, declarations, and conventions that now deal with a broad range of abuses across the globe—including racial discrimination, wom-en's rights to equality, the rights of children, and the rights of indigenous groups—all aided and abetted by nongovernmental organizations, in-cluding faith-based groups, women's groups, and other social justice initiatives. There is a sense that the international community is dealing with these "problems" seriously and handling them with great speed and efficacy.

Yet, the outward sense of progress, of some-thing being done, of a social justice project being pursued in the name of human rights, is emerg-ing as a somewhat disingenuous and illusory en-deavor. The record of human rights since their proclamation in the eighteenth century has been less than stellar. Indeed, the legal interventions that have been pursued in the name of human rights are perhaps the most explicit examples we have to date of how the assumptions that more law equals more equality and freedom, and that human rights is an optimistic and hopeful pur-suit, are quite mistaken. In fact, the proliferation of laws in the name of human rights serves at times to remind us how our good intentions, passions, and progressive "swords may have turned into boomerangs."[1] The human rights promise of progress, emancipation, and univer-salism has been exposed as myopic, exclusive, and informed by a series of global panics, espe-cially a panic over national security, sexual mo-rality, and cultural survival in the contemporary period. What happened to the dissidence and

rebellious spirit of human rights? How has a project that held out the promise of a grand spicy fete mutated into an insipid appetizer?

In this essay, I unpack three normative claims on which the human rights project is based and expose its dark side.[2] In the first section, I set out the larger context within which human rights has taken shape, especially the claim that human rights is part of modernity's narrative of progress—that is, human rights represents a step forward in the progress of human development and civiliza-tional maturity. In the second part, I interrogate the assumption that human rights are universal, challenging its dehistoricized, neutral, and inclu-sive claims. In the third part, I examine the at-omized, insular liberal subject on which the human rights project is based and its correlating assumptions about the "Other," who needs to be cabined or contained lest she destabilizes or un-dermines this subject. In the final part of the ar-ticle, I make some tentative proposals as to how we can engage with human rights once its dark side is exposed.

NARRATIVE OF PROGRESS

The establishment of human rights in the mid-twentieth century as part of a modern proj-

1. Janet Halley and Wendy Brown, eds., *Left Legalism/ Left Critique* (Durham, N.C.: Duke University Press, 2002), 4.

2. My focus on three normative claims is not exhaus-tive. There are a number of other concerns about the field that are not addressed in this article; see, for ex-ample, David Kennedy, *The Dark Side of Virtue: Reassess-ing International Humanitarianism* (Princeton, N.J.: PUP, 2004). Kennedy lists a host of other pragmatic worries regarding the field. Some of these include a critique of the way human rights has come to occupy the space of emancipatory possibilities, and also effectively margin-alize any other emancipatory projects; the narrow focus of human rights on the state, leaving the severe harms produced by nonstate actors unaddressed; the generalizing vocabulary of human rights that papers over political, ideological, and cultural differences; pro-motion of a "one size fits all" politics; centering the relationship between the state and individual, equat-ing the structure of the state, which enforces, grants, recognizes, implements, and remedies violations, with freedom; and the false sense of satisfaction that emerges when building a human rights movement comes to be equated with the human rights project. He states that signing up to the cause does not bring an end to the practice.

ect of international institutions was a critical moment. It brought into being the possibility that states could no longer shelter behind the fig leaf of sovereignty for violations committed against individuals. State sovereignty could be cast aside and a state's acts subjected to human rights scrutiny. It was a new form of interventionism that emboldened the liberal internationalist and his or her belief in the virtue of law and principle of universality. Human rights marked a point of arrival—a step in the progress of human development.

This belief in the transformative and progressive potential of human rights is contingent on an assumption that we have, as a civilized world, moved forward, and that the coming together of nation-states in the recognition of universal human rights is a critical part of the liberal project that seeks to advance individual rights and human desires. It is a narrative that is driven by a persistent belief that history has a purpose and direction coupled with an assumption that the world has emerged from a backward, more uncivilized era. Indeed, it reflects the metamorphosis of civilization from the primitive, into a modern and evolved form, and this progress has emanated from the heart of Europe. It has mostly been achieved except in some of the outposts of the empire. This new emboldened project has received a major impetus in the post-Cold War era in the form of liberal internationalism, which no longer faces any ideological resistance. A veneration of these ideals and hubris born of the profound belief in this justice-seeking project has come to characterize the practice in the field. There is a real earnestness on the part of well-intentioned activists, practitioners, judges, and even politicians that they are pursuing a progressive, even righteous, goal.

Those who do not necessarily regard human rights as such a neat and tidy project—as a project that is progressive let alone transformative—have challenged this narrative of progress. The view that the international recognition of human rights marks an end to an ignorant past and enables the realization of freedom and equality is challenged as empirically and theoretically flawed: in purely factual terms more human rights violations have been committed in the twentieth century, which was ostensibly the most human rights focused century, than at any

other point in human history.[3] As the late Jacques Derrida stated, "No degree of progress allows one to ignore that never before in absolute figures, have so many men, women and children been subjugated, starved or exterminated on earth."[4] And it continues.

There is a dark side to human rights work, which has been exposed by, among others, postcolonial scholars, feminists, and new scholars in international law. These scholars have examined the costs of this work, revealing some of the resulting, often unanticipated damage done. What has emerged is how it is possible to read the virtuous script of human rights against the grain, to read another narrative into the story line that was, perhaps, never intended by those who inspired the project, or to accord a meaning to it that counters or subverts any progressive reading it might have had. Original intent is invariably not knowable. But even if it was, and however well intentioned, it does not necessarily continue to inform the constitutive basis of the human rights project—as progressive, emancipatory, and liberating. As put by Kennedy, "virtue does not always move in the direction of the virtuous."[5]

Perhaps partly because of these limitations, as well as the powerful hold [of national] sovereignty, there is another more reactionary critique of human rights that has emerged. In its crude form, this critique views human rights as a corrosive tool that has eroded the legitimacy conferred or exercised through sovereignty, and threatened national and social cohesion. According to this view, we have entered the age of uncertainty and instability. Today the global flows of human beings across borders, immorality of sex, "bogus" refugees, single-parent families, absence of faith, homosexuality, and welfare mothers have in part brought about the demise of history and an end to progress. In contrast, a more sophisticated, nuanced position is emerging, which seeks to engage with human rights

3. Costas Douzinas, *The End of Human Rights: Critical Legal Thought at the Turn of the Century* (Oxford: Hart, 2000), 2.
4. Jacques Derrida, *Spectres of Marx: The State of the Debt, the Work of Mourning, and the New International*, trans. Peggy Kamuf (New York: Routledge, 1994), 85, quoted in Douzinas, *The End of Human Rights*.
5. Kennedy, *The Dark Side of Virtue*, note 2, xix–xx.

discourse to pursue a very reactionary and conservative agenda.

These responses exemplify how human rights are a contested terrain and not one that can simply be read in linear terms. I want to expand on this idea that human rights is an arena where different visions of the world are fought out and how this struggle is obscured in linear accounts of human rights. In the contemporary period, there is an explicit example of this complex narrative in the context of the bombing of Afghanistan in October 2001. The attacks took place amid a cacophony of claims by Western leaders that this was a "crusade" against the "evildoers," that "Western civilization was superior to Islam" and part of the war on terror, which according to one United States general was a "Christian battle against Satan." These claims were wrapped in a strong, bold argument in favor of self-defense, including the right to preemptive strikes. Subsequently, as Vasuki Nesiah argues, there has been a subtle mutation of the discourse on the part of those countries which participated in the Afghanistan offensive, from self-defense to human rights, providing the tool for legitimizing the operation that had initially seemed so suspect.[6] The muscle flexing and macho talk, the language of evil, darkness, and crusades that permeated the initial representation of the military conquest, came to be superseded by the gentler tones of women's rights, peace, religious freedom, and democracy that ultimately provided legitimacy for the intervention.[7]

Thereafter, it was but one small step toward Iraq. Once again the initial narrative of conquest and occupation is gradually being overwritten by claims of "freedom on the march," where human rights are being equated with democratization and freedom projects, and the pursuit of "infinite justice." Images of shock and awe were replaced by congregations of Iraqi men and women, struggling in the constituent assembly to bring some form of governance to Iraq and draft a constitution. The language of human rights and democracy was somewhat muted, if not actually countered, by the daily civilian atrocities committed by the occupying forces and the insurgency, the failure of the newly formed government of national unity to restore law and order, the continuous questioning over the legality of the war, as well as the prison humiliations and abuses at Abu Ghraib and the massacre of Iraqi civilians by U.S. marines in Haditha.[8] Perhaps the jury is still out on this one—it is too early to say whether Iraq can be successfully rescripted as a noble endeavor by the altruistic West, in particular the United States, to bring democracy and freedom to the Middle East. Yet for some in the United States, this claim appears self-evident.

These critiques, as well as the reactionary possibilities of human rights, constitute some of the theoretical and practical tensions that characterize human rights law and disrupt the idea that human rights is one long and steady march toward progress.

DISCRIMINATORY UNIVERSALITY

In this section, I unpack the normative assumptions that inform the notion of universality to which human rights claims are tethered. The human rights project is based on the assumption that all humans are entitled to enjoy human rights without regard to distinction. It is a claim that regards human rights as being based on notions of objectivity, neutrality, and inclusion.

Yet when we examine the Enlightenment project, the precursor to the human rights movement, it exposes a history of how claims to universality and inclusion have coexisted with exclusion and subordination. Recall the moment when Europe was in the midst of a struggle for liberty, equality, and freedom, but Europe's "Others" continued to be subjugated under the weight of colonialism and slavery. Even within Europe, gender and racial apartheid established a hierarchy of what and who constituted the liberal subject—the white, Christian, propertied male. While there is an assumption that certain political practices are in-

6. See Vasuki Nesiah, "From Berlin to Bonn to Baghdad: A Space for Infinite Justice," *HHRJ* 17 (2004): 75–98, 75. Nesiah demonstrates how humanitarian intervention has not only constrained violence and militarism, but also buttressed and complemented it.
7. Ibid., 95.

8. Ellen Knickmeyer, "In Haditha: Memories of a Massacre," *Washington Post*, 27 May 2006, A1; Daniel Henninger, "The Indictment of U.S. Troops Was Inevitable," *Wall Street Journal*, 2 June 2006, A18.

deed universal, such as liberty, equality, and freedom, these ideals seem to stumble and falter at the moment of their encounter with the unfamiliar, the "Other" or difference. These values meet with some of the same difficulties today in their encounters with difference and unfamiliarity. Universality is always accompanied by what Denise da Silva evocatively describes as "the other side of universality."[9]

While there is some concern over the universalist claims of human rights in light of the harms and exclusions that have characterized its liberal antecedents, there remains a deep commitment to the project and faith in its universal application. The exclusions of the past are regarded as moments of profound inconsistency in what liberalism stands for and how it has operated, for example, in relation to women and other socially disadvantaged groups. As some feminist scholars have argued, it is, in fact, a failure of liberal thinkers to follow their own thought through to its progressive end.[10] For example, subordination by sex was deemed to be natural and the subject of sex ignored by liberal political philosophers and their theories of justice. It is only through feminism's role in unmasking inequalities in familial arrangements that the promise of liberalism for women is being brought about, and the liberal internationalist endeavor to promote women's human rights globally strengthened.[11] It is the result of manipulation that can be corrected through the gradual process of inclusion of these previously excluded groups. Independence from colonial rule fought and won through the invocation of civil and political rights is used as another example to substantiate this position.

Yet this search to restore liberalism to its pristine elegance and original features is an elusive one, for its history belies the possibility of any such origins. International law coupled with its humanitarian zeal was structured by the colonial encounter and its distinction between the civi-

lized and uncivilized.[12] The search for a standard to both explain and justify the exclusion of non-European subjects from international law in the nineteenth century was based on the prevailing and uninterrogated assumption that European states were civilized. In order to gain entry into the community of international law and family of civilized nations, outside communities had to strive to resemble the European.

Revisiting the colonial encounter is critical in order to understand the limitations and possibilities of human rights in the contemporary period. It is essential for human rights advocates to embrace this history. Assertions about the universality of human rights simply deny the reality of those whom it claims to represent and speak for, disclaiming their histories and imposing another's. Thus, the liberal tradition from which human rights have emerged not only incorporates arguments about freedom and equal worth but—and this is the core of my argument—it also incorporates arguments about civilization, cultural backwardness, and racial and religious superiority. Further, human rights remain structured by this history. This dark side is intrinsic to human rights, rather than something that is merely broken and can be glued back together.

TROUBLING SUBJECTS

The liberal subject lies at the heart of the human rights endeavour. This subject is free, unencumbered, self-sufficient, and rational, existing prior to history and social context. However, given the arguments already presented about the situatedness of human rights and its liberal underpinnings, it is evident that the sovereign, autonomous subject is unable to survive without the existence of an "Other." A host of subjects continue to be denied inclusion into the project, or entitled access only to the extent that they resemble the familiar subject of human rights discourse.

There are at least three different ways in

9. Denise da Silva, "Toward a Critique of the Socio-Logos of Justice: The Analytics of Raciality and the Production of Universality," *Social Identities* 7 (2007): 421–54, 421.

10. Martha C. Nussbaum, *Sex and Social Justice* (New York: OUP, 1999). See also Martha C. Nussbaum, *Hiding from Humanity: Disgust, Shame, and the Law* (Princeton, N.J.: PUP, 2005).

11. Nussbaum, *Sex and Social Justice*, 65.

12. Martti Koskenniemi, *The Gentle Civilizer of Nations: The Rise and Fall of International Law, 1870–1960* (Cambridge: CUP, 2002), chap. 2; Antony Anghie, "Finding the Peripheries: Sovereignty and Colonialism in Nineteenth Century International Law," *HILJ* 40 (1990): 1–81, 1; Antony Anghie, *Imperialism, Sovereignty and the Making of International Law* (Cambridge: CUP, 2005).

which the "Other" has been addressed in relation to rights discourse. The first is through the
assumption that the difference can be erased and
the "Other" tamed and assimilated through
some form of cultural or racial strip. The second
is to treat the difference as natural and inevitable. And finally, there is the response that justifies incarceration, internment, or even
annihilation of the "Other" because of the threat
it poses. These are not rigid and absolute categorizations, but frequently overlap and leak into
one another. And all these responses are present
in the contemporary moment.[13]

Assimilation is integral to the liberal tradition.
It is accompanied by cultural erasure and plays
out on a host of sites. In the context of the colonial encounter in India, assimilation took the
form of learning how to imitate the colonial
power. The "universal" principles of liberty,
equality, and freedom were contingent on the
native's ability to conform or be trained into civilization. The native was entitled to certain rights
and benefits to the extent that he could reinvent
himself as an Englishman. Yet that standard remained an elusive one, often unattainable, for no
matter how hard, the native struggled to mimic
the "master" at the cost of her own subjectivity.

In the contemporary period, this response is
found in the proliferation of new citizenship and
nationality laws being enacted throughout Europe and elsewhere. These laws reflect a simultaneous fear of the "Other," while also providing
an opportunity to enable these "Others" to be
part of the universal project of rights and acquire
legitimacy through the process of assimilation

and their permanent translation into a familiar
medium.

The second response of naturalizing or essen-
tializing the difference has a rich genealogy. In
the context of the colonial encounter the "Other"
was treated as lacking the capacity to reason, incapable of decision-making, culturally and morally inferior. The difference justified not only the
denial of a host of legal rights and benefits to the
native, but also of sovereignty. It was this "rule
of colonial difference" that essentialized the difference between the colonizer and the colonized,
and served to justify the imperial presence even
when espousing a commitment to universal
ideas and institutions.[14]

Finally, there is the response of incarceration,
internment, or elimination, where the "Other" is
cast as completely outside of Western liberal democracy, defined as a threat to the nation-state—
as backward, uncivilized, and dangerous. These
subjects are legitimately denied human rights
protections, as they are cast in opposition to such
values and protections. In the civilizing mission of
Empire, the lack of conformity to the project
could result in death and even annihilation. In
the contemporary period there are countless examples of difference being cast as a threat, con-
taminant, or evil to be contained and purged
should it prove too threatening. This somewhat
bloated subject includes the Islamic, regarded as a
threat to the mythical Caucasian, Christian West;
the homosexual, who is destroying civilization,
family, and faith as we know it; the sex worker,
with her contaminating agenda; and the migrant
subject, intent on disrupting the social cohesion of
distinctive Western states. *All* these responses to
the "Other" are not confined to tyrannical dictatorships or oppressive fundamentalisms. They are
located in the heartland of the "homeland"—in
the epicenter of the liberal democratic state. A
spectacular array of legal tools are being crafted in
the form of antiterrorism and antimigration laws
to deal with these new "Others." These initiatives
are intended to reestablish the moral, cultural,
and national certainties of the past as well as the
security of the sovereign nation-state and sovereign subject. The threat per se justifies the creation of new categories—such as "unlawful
noncitizens" and the explicit policy of incarcera-

13. This analysis parallels some of the arguments presented in a large body of recent scholarship on citizenship and nationality. One stream of this literature
argues in favor of a global or world citizenship, given
that there is evidence that citizenship is no longer (and
should no longer be) bounded by the nation-state as
well as the emergence of a universal human rights regime. Some scholars argue that the conferment of
rights and benefits on human beings, regardless of
their citizenship status, constitutes part of our moral
obligation. Yet it is not at all self-evident that appeals
to international human rights law bound to conceptions of a "global" or "world" citizen would inevitably
rescue an unlawful noncitizen and accord him/her a
recognition that transcends the monopoly power of
nation-states to determine who counts and who does
not. And as argued in this article, universalist claims of
human rights have been unmasked as operating along
the same axis of inclusion and exclusion that characterized their liberal antecedents.

14. Partha Chatterjee, *The Nation and Its Fragments: Colonial and Postcolonial Histories* (Princeton, N.J.: PUP, 1993).

tion of asylum seekers in Australia; or the detention of the newly created "enemy combatants" by the United States in Guantanamo Bay. Through these gestures, the "Other" is being transformed into a manipulative, dangerous, and contaminating force that can justify a "shoot-to-kill" policy to protect the state and its citizens, even if it involves collateral damage.

In all these instances we are declaring new nonhumans, or lesser humans, as well as superhumans. These hierarchies and rankings are produced in and through the discourse of rights, which produces the human and social subject.

The commitment to human rights is not necessarily a commitment to a social justice project that is unequivocally liberatory or emancipatory. The "dark side" also constitutes this project. Sometimes, the dark side is obscured, as Western, liberal democratic states project themselves as well ordered, law abiding, and demonstrably tolerant, and human rights are cast as something that is needed out there—in the less developed, nondemocratic, illiberal world. When George Bush walks into a mosque immediately after the September 11 attacks to ensure that there is no backlash in the form of violence inflicted on Muslims in the homeland, or when Tony Blair boldly asserts that the Muslim community will be embraced and diversity defended after the recent London bombings, the self-controlled, democratic, liberal values are presented as stable, coherent, and intact, as examples of how "civilized" free states behave. Yet this particular narrative obscures how these very same states are able to export the dark side of the liberal project. Countries such as the United States, with its muscular military arsenal and monetary strength, are able to export the dark side, push it out of the ranch, sending it in the contemporary moment to places like Guantanamo, Iraq, or Abu Ghraib.

The ability of some powerful democratic nations to export the "dark side" deflects attention from the ways in which the possibilities for disorder and instability are produced in and through the discourse of rights, which sets out the terms for inclusion and exclusion.

TAKE A WALK ON THE "DARK SIDE":
TENTATIVE PROPOSALS

This article is not arguing in favor of an outright rejection of human rights nor serving as an apology for a realist position on human rights. Human rights are radical tools for those who have never had them [and seem] a preferable, though a flawed ideal, to no rights at all. It is a very useful vocabulary. Yet, it is also important to confront the "dark side" of this project. There is a need to address the complicity of human rights in making the world less stable, less peaceful, more divisive, more polluted, and more violent. Who is accountable when human rights interventions actually harm more than they help? The dark side enables everyone to use the vocabulary of human rights, while at the same time advance agendas that may not be emancipatory ones at the end of the day. To use the words of Costas Douzinas, "human rights are being reduced to a body without a soul, without a political vision or moral purpose."[15]

Despite all that is known about the inadequacies of human rights, there continues to be an appeal to them as so much political hope has been invested in the project. It is an approach that has been characterized as a "Yes I know. But . . ." politics. The critique is suspended out of concern that it will create anxiety, fear, and even nihilism. Yet after the most atrocious century and nothing encouraging to inspire us at the beginning of this one, it is also difficult to formulate a persuasive argument for returning to the ideals of classical liberalism—progress, universality, and free will. The equation of critique with pessimism, and progress with optimism, is quite mistaken. To question human rights is not to side with the inhuman, the antihuman, and evil. What is required at this moment is neither an arrogant triumphalism nor hopeless despair, but rather, thoughtful reflection. What happens when the faith in human rights is eroded? Where does that leave us? It is much better to confront these difficult questions than to cling to old tattered frameworks or a project that now exists in its broken form.

I propose some tentative, though by no means comprehensive thoughts about how we might move in a more creative and constructive direction.

First, we need to move beyond debates between the universal character of human rights and their historical particularity. More important as a starting point is to recognize that human

15. Douzinas, *The End of Human Rights*, note 3, 4.

rights are a site of power and that resort to the vocabulary of human rights is indeed very powerful. It is this power in the hands of those who use it that must be understood—not its ability nor lack of ability to transform people's lives, nor its potential to bring about change. Because it is powerful, it matters who brandishes this sword. Human rights advocates need to realize that they also wield power once they participate in the terrain, and can be implicated in perpetuating its dark side.

Second, there needs to be a reorientation in human rights scholarship and education. It is not only useful, but critical, for human rights scholars and advocates to consciously draw on the experience of the postcolonial world. This is obligatory in order to revise both our thinking and understanding of human rights that has been so dominated by Western pontification about the project, tied down to liberal utopian visions, or claims that human rights are something needed only "over there," in the developing, less civilized world. To draw on the experiences requires understanding and learning from the postcolonial engagement with rights that are informed by the legacies of the colonial encounter. It is, after all, in the postcolonial world where the dark side has been most obviously played out. It is an experience that provides insights into how the marshy zones of exclusion were and continue to be produced. They were not simply imposed through brute force, but in and through rights discourse.

Finally, a major shift in the location of the project, who is telling the story and how the story is told, can provide a different and critical trajectory from which to view human rights. I [appeal to] the urgency of re-reading human rights from alternative locations, the excluded zones or from the perspective of excluded subjects through the example of three contemporary issues.

The first concerns the current moment of economic globalization and neoliberal governmentality. While the G8 talks of increased aid to Africa it completely ignores the emergence of new market actors in that continent and the relevance of economic globalization and trade. While entrenching the "native" in a victim subject position through a focus on poverty alleviation can be regarded as laudable, it is also nonthreatening and sustains the imperial messianic myth. The language of rights and humani-

tarianism once again obscures a counternarrative, based on sustaining unequal trade and market relations, and the fear of competition from cheaper labor markets. It reproduces a colonial anxiety. In the mid-eighteenth century this was played out explicitly when the East India Company subordinated a flourishing international trade in handicrafts and textiles by Indian merchants by cutting off the thumbs of 200 highly skilled, local textile weavers. It ruined the indigenous industry and served the interests of the British mercantile community. Concerns about the neoliberal project aside, the demand for free trade from poorer nations and the assertion of their identity as market actors is producing a similar consternation, which cannot be met with responses of charity. What challenges are posed to human rights—to its dark side as well as its relevance—when we read the narrative from the perspective of these new market actors? To what extent are new emancipatory spaces being provided by globalization rather than human rights? To what extent are human rights being aligned with neoliberalism and inclusion into the market?

A second, related issue concerns the arrival of the non-West onto the shores of the "West." While this presence takes many forms—on the catwalk, through celluloid and spicy cuisine—it is the specter of cross-border movements that are causing jitters. Today, these movements are being addressed implicitly through more stringent immigration, anti-trafficking, and anti-terror laws. They are also being addressed through ludicrous schemes such as the one devised by European countries to organize joint charter flights, dubbed "Migrant Air," to pick up and deport illegal migrants back to their home countries at less cost and greater speed. Such initiatives will not curtail cross-border movements. The transnational migrant will continue to move clandestinely if legal routes are not available, as demand and the free flow of labor are necessary corollaries to the free flow of capital. These cross-border movements are in fact producing a paradox where the security of the transnational migrant is perhaps less threatened by people smugglers and traffickers, than by the current international system of human rights protection offered to people who move as migrants, refugees, or asylum-seekers. How can the story of human rights be told from the perspective of transnational migrants? What then are the obligations states have toward the economic migrant in the context of economic globalization?

Finally, religion is another example of a contemporary issue that needs to be addressed from a different perch. God is out of the closet and on the loose everywhere. The assumed opposition between religion and human rights that is presented as hallowed truth is neither helpful nor indeed accurate. It seems impossible for human rights to retain its secular credentials in a world where religion has seeped into the public domain, into conversations about security, HIV/AIDs, the family, homosexuality, gender equality, and the "war on terror." The liberal democratic states of the West are increasingly revealing themselves to be deeply faith-based. The French state has invoked the rights to secularism, liberty, and equality to justify a ban against the wearing of headscarves by Muslim girls studying in French state-run schools. Yet such interventions are exposed as exclusive and majoritarian, where acceptance is based on the performance of a cultural disrobing, forcing a choice on the part of the liberal (Christian) democratic state between the right to education and the right to expression and freedom of religion, while the girls themselves want both.

Can human rights be articulated in ways that do not perpetuate these polarizations and false dichotomies? The answer to this question lies in learning from contexts that have engaged with these tensions. Freedom of religion and gender equality has operated with commitments to secularism in postcolonial, democratic countries such as India. It is a country where vast multitudes of deities coexist with vast multitudes of people. You bump into them (gods and people) on the street, trip over them on the sidewalk, they sit with you in taxis and attend street parades where they are the constant cause of traffic jams. No matter where you go, there they are! Women in religious minority communities are constantly renegotiating the boundaries and contesting the meaning of equality, understandings of secularism, and the right to religious freedom, attempting to delink their meanings from their majoritarian moorings or capture by Hindu nationalists. These engagements attest to the importance of challenging the unhelpful dichotomies between religion and rights, the complex and contradictory nature of the human rights terrain, and why the meanings of rights need to be constantly monitored, revisited, and interrogated.

My critique of human rights is intended to be productive and to articulate a different cosmology in which to understand the place of human rights in our contemporary world. The battle to recapture the progressive and transformative terrain of human rights cannot be simply "won," but the centering of excluded subjects, excluded zones, and excluded histories can bring the project back to a space of greater optimism and lesser despair. Ultimately, it is an effort to put some life back into a project in desperate need of resuscitation and to give this body a soul.

QUESTIONS FOR REFLECTION AND DISCUSSION

1. What, precisely, does Kapur mean by the "dark side" of the human rights project?
2. Kapur argues that "in purely factual terms more human rights violations [were] committed in the twentieth century, which was ostensibly the most human rights focused century, than at any other point in human history." Can you think of examples of human rights violations that support this argument? Of twentieth-century human rights progress that might outweigh Kapur's claim? Upon what research or information are your examples based?
3. Is it acceptable for any country to use human rights-based pretexts for waging war? Does such a basis for war render the human rights project hypocritical? How? How not?
4. Consider Kapur's narration of the U.S. wars in Afghanistan and Iraq. Kapur argues that the United States initially justified its actions by relying on national security, but later justified its actions by relying on human rights and emancipation of the local population. Is this a "dark side" of human rights or is it "merely" the hijacking of human rights to justify an unrelated action? Did international law and human rights scholars contribute to the ease with which states can use human rights to further their own goals? Last, would it be in the strategic interest of human rights to promote the use of force, especially on the scale of wars like Iraq or Afghanistan, or does the current UN stricture on the use of force provide the better alternative to war? How or how not?

5. How, according to Kapur (and a wide range of other scholars) is "universality discriminatory"? Looking at world society today, can you see evidence that human rights progress means greater equality between human beings and between human societies? Support your answer with examples.

6. What does Kapur mean by the "Others"? Are you among them? Can there ever not be "Others"? Why? Why not?

7. Kapur identifies three existing responses to the "Others" of human rights. What are they? Can you see examples of these strategies operating in contemporary society? What are they? What evidence can you supply to support your answer?

8. Kapur writes:

after the most atrocious century and nothing encouraging to inspire us at the beginning of this one, it is difficult to formulate a persuasive argument for returning to the ideals of classical liberalism—progress, universality, and free will. The equation of critique with pessimism, and progress with optimism, is quite mistaken. To question human rights is not to side with the inhuman, the antihuman, and evil. What is required at this moment is neither an arrogant triumphalism nor hopeless despair, but rather, thoughtful reflection. What happens when the faith in human rights is eroded?

First, what trajectories in politics and economics, both global and national, can you see that may support Kapur's argument that there is nothing at the beginning of the twenty-first century to inspire us that it is likely to be any better than the "atrocious" twentieth century? *Second*, can you find any evidence to the contrary? If so, what? *Third*, what happens when faith in human rights is eroded? Does such erosion matter? Why? Why not?

9. Kapur argues that we can learn how to address certain human rights dilemmas by studying those societies (postcolonial in the main) where people already negotiate the tensions. She also suggests that centering "excluded" subjects, zones, and histories is a way of recovering some kind of human rights optimism. How would you bring the "soul" back to the "body" of human rights? What strategies would you employ, and why?

10. In Reading 4, Weston states that "In a world of diverse cultural traditions that is simultaneously distinguished by the widespread universalist claim that 'human rights extend in theory to every person on earth without discriminations irrelevant to merit,' the question thus unavoidably arises: when, in international human rights decision making, are cultural differences to be respected and when are they not?" What do you think Kapur's response to this question would be, and why?

11. Climate change and nuclear proliferation may be viewed as the two greatest threats facing humankind today. Might one or both signal severe implications for, in particular, Kapur's "Others"? If so, how so? If not, how not? Are Kapur's "Others" the most likely of affected persons and communities to have the least resilience to withstand or survive climate and nuclear catastrophe? Why? Why not? What evidence and sources can you deploy in support of your answer?

12. Does economic globalization hold out hope of spaces of emancipation? If so, in what ways? Or does it reenact the colonial dynamic central to Kapur's analysis of the "dark side" of human rights? Support your answers with examples.

13. How does Kapur's analysis resonate with that of Grear concerning the universality of human rights (Reading 2 in this chapter)? How does it differ? And how might Nussbaum's capability thesis address Kapur's concerns, if at all? Support both your answers with evidence drawn from the relevant readings in this chapter.

14. In the light of Kapur's viewpoint, consider McCorquodale and Fairbrother's analysis of the relationship of economic and democratic growth to human rights (Reading 5 in this chapter). Are there "dark sides" of globalization, transnational corporations, structural adjustment programs, development projects, etc.? What do McCorquodale and Fairbrother say?

72 *Issues*

7. MARGARET R. SOMERS AND CHRISTOPHER N. J. ROBERTS *Toward a New Sociology of Rights: A Genealogy of "Buried Bodies" of Citizenship and Human Rights*

In the years since the Universal Declaration of Human Rights, human rights have swung a broad arc, ducking and dodging the theoretical challenges, political struggles, and historical obstacles—above all, entrenched institutionalized American racism, exceptionalism, and the Cold War—that continuously dogged and impeded their legitimization, especially in the United States. And while the human rights trope was never completely abandoned—it emerged from time to time in struggles over race and the death penalty, living wages, welfare eligibility, and similar issues—in the United States the language of rights has been safely confined to civil and political rights and that of human rights completely silent on domestic rights abuses.

THE REDISCOVERY OF DEMOCRACY AND THE TRIUMPH OF NEOLIBERALISM: 1989 AND THE POST-9/11 WORLD

AMERICAN EXCEPTIONALISM TODAY

Although human rights discourse has proliferated at an astonishing pace over the past two decades, the U.S government's dogged rejection of human rights in the domestic context persists today. It carries out a strict practice of compartmentalization, which reserves human rights concerns for other places. A well-known example of this simultaneous foreign embrace and domestic disregard is the State Department's annual reports on human rights. Respected sources of information about human rights practices around the world, they contain one notable absence: the United States.

The U.S. failure to ratify important international human rights treaties is also well known. Of the nine international human rights treaties deemed core by the Office of the UN High Commissioner for Human Rights (OHCHR), the United

States has ratified only three.[1] Moreover, just because it ratified a treaty does not mean that the United States has accepted it in full; states may ratify with reservations, essentially amending or nullifying entire parts of the text. The United States ratified the International Convention on the Elimination of All Forms of Racial Discrimination (ICERD), for example, with the stipulation that it does not apply to the United States.

NEOLIBERALISM AND AMERICAN EXCEPTIONALISM

The triumph of capitalism in 1989 bestowed neoliberal policies with a new triumphalism that valorized property rights on the one hand and denigrated socioeconomic rights on the other. International Monetary Fund (IMF) and World Bank loan practices and foreign aid reflected this higher level of commitment to free market ideology and market fundamentalism, and in return for support the developing world was literally compelled toward austerity, structural readjustment, and the end of social safety nets. A historic rise in global poverty and social inequality has followed. Moreover, with neoliberalism's increasing global hegemony, the International Covenant on Economic, Social and Cultural Rights (ICESCR) has had to fight continuously for recognition, while the International Covenant on Civil and Political Rights (ICCPR) is especially celebrated in capitalist democracies for its support of individual and property rights. Market fundamentalism's harmful effects on human well-being have spurred a strong response from researchers and advocacy groups championing the cause of international human rights. But while the push for global equality has been presented at the highest levels in human rights terms (e.g., the United Nations), the U.S govern-

1. The United States has ratified the ICCPR, ICERD, and CAT [*Eds.*—but has not ratified the ICESCR, CEDAW, CRC, ICPRMWF, ICPED (ICPPED), or CRPD as of this writing.]. See http://www2.ohchr.org/english/law (accessed 15 June 2015) for the text of these treaties and https://treaties.un.org/Pages/Treaties.aspx?id=4&subid=A&lang=en (accessed 15 June 2015) for links to the country by country signatory and ratification status for each treaty. See also III Weston and Carlson.

0Excerpted with changes by permission of the *Annual Review of Law and Social Science* from Margaret R. Somers and Christopher N. J. Roberts, "Toward a New Sociology of Rights: A Genealogy of 'Buried Bodies,' of Citizenship and Human Rights," *Annual Review of Law and Social Science* 4 (2008): 385–425, 400–406. Copyright © 2008 Annual Review of Law & Social Science.

ment has yet to recognize or adopt such a frame for its own social inequality.

AMERICAN EXCEPTIONALISM AND HUMAN RIGHTS REVIVED

If U.S. crime rates and incarceration statistics were not enough, Hurricane Katrina provided evidence of the confluence of the most enduring forms of American exceptionalism: racial exclusion and rejection of socioeconomic rights. Perhaps because the government's nonresponse to the Katrina tragedy so clearly inflicted widespread human rights violations on full American citizens, it seems also to have stimulated African American intellectuals and social justice advocates to revive long-repressed struggles over internationally recognized human rights and to adopt a new language of human rights to address this ongoing post-Hurricane Katrina narrative of abandonment, poverty, and social exclusion. Clearly, a profound change is in the works when Ron Daniels, president of the Institute of the Black World Twenty-First Century, declares that the guiding principle for the Martin Luther King–Malcolm X Community Revitalization Initiative is the "conviction that every person in this country is entitled to enjoy certain basic human rights, *as articulated in the Universal Declaration of Human Rights.*"[2] Daniels mobilized this international human rights vision in a call for Black America to revive the concept of a Domestic Marshall Plan to "reverse the deterioration of the nation's dark ghettos—most immediately, to restore New Orleans' exiled population." Daniels is not abandoning the struggle against "racism, poverty and inequality as dramatically exposed by Katrina." Rather, he is renarrating these familiar social problems under the unfamiliar (to Americans) rubric of international human rights, especially with reference to the UDHR, which has until now served almost exclusively as the rallying cry for "elsewhere." The crush of neoliberal social policies appears to have prompted the once-dedicated civil rights community to adopt a new American human rights agenda to push back against poverty and socioeconomic inequality.

2. See Dr. Ron Daniels, "A Domestic Marshall Plan to Transform America's 'Dark Ghettos,'" *Black Scholar* 37, 1 (2007).

[*Eds.*—Against the foregoing backdrop, the authors next turn their attention to what they call *the rediscovery of citizenship and the new citizenship studies.* Largely responsible for this rediscovery, they observe, is the widespread use of the citizenship concept as an "institutional proxy" for the normative study of human rights, at least among skeptical and relativist sociologists and others uncomfortable with the ontology, morality, and evaluation of natural and human rights as classically conceived—citing Bryan Turner's germinal "Outline of a Theory of Human Rights," *Sociology* 176 (1993). They point also to "The resurgence of republicanism" which "led to a rediscovery of political identities and practices based not on the isolated self but in the context of political membership and citizenship," citing especially Michael Walzer, *Obligations: Essays on Disobedience, War, and Citizenship* (New York: Clarion, 1970) and Sheldon S. Wolin, *Politics and Vision: Continuity and Innovation in Western Political Thought* (Boston: Little, Brown, 1960). But the authors notably credit "neoliberalism's success in the 1980s and 1990s in waging a 'personal responsibility crusade' that led not just the left but also some mainstream thinkers to revalorize social citizenship rights too long taken for granted"; also the "radical transformation of the federal judiciary over the past quarter century and its role in denying rights that many had thought were firmly established or implied by rights already recognized." The authors proceed: "In light of the privileged status of the rights of property and a commercially oriented interpretation of freedom of speech, the liberal left began to see the Supreme Court as responsible for a demoralizing assault against many of the civil and political rights that [were assumed to have been] foundational to democratic citizenship rights." The authors write: "the expansion of conservative legal doctrine reliably drowns out or limits the assertion of rights that ordinary citizens were thought to have possessed," citing Cass R. Sunstein, "The Right-Wing Assault: What's at Stake, What's Already Happened, and What Could Yet Occur," *American Prospect* (Suppl.) 14 (2003): A2–4. The authors then continue.]

CITIZENSHIP AND CIVIL SOCIETY

Arguably, it was the Eastern European democratic movements of the 1980s (Solidarity in Poland, Charter 77 in Czechoslovakia, the revolutions of 1989–1991, the fall of the Berlin Wall, and the collapse of the Soviet state) that catalyzed the (re) turn to citizenship studies. The rediscovered civil society concept served as both normative ideal and practical site for democratic rights claims. As a third sphere, not reducible to the ruthless individualism of unregulated capitalism or the tyranny of the communist state, it was a novel political and social terrain, a springboard for rights-claiming popular mobilizations. The civil society concept was also an attempt to define and make available for future rights claimers an empirical explanation for the success of the revolutions that overturned communism and valorized democratic rights throughout the world. In seeking to understand the demise of communism and the requisites of state-building, civil society theorists pointed to the significance of social organization and associational life—both formal (e.g., civic clubs) and informal (underground communities of shared resistance). Civil society, in short, was the heart of a reinvigorated citizenship rights ideal.

MULTICULTURAL REALITIES AND QUESTIONS OF EXCLUSION

Porous national boundaries and global labor movements of immigrants from poor to rich countries, and from postcolonial societies to metropolises, have made most advanced Western societies multicultural; they are thus subject to citizenship pressures. Long overdue recognition has come to indigenous peoples, national minorities, and the socially excluded who, despite the formal status of citizenship, have long been excluded from most of its rights and privileges. Their frequent claims to unfulfilled rights and constitutional obligations are immediately recognizable as the inclusionary claims of citizenship. More contested are the implications of social exclusion. Claims to redistribution have refocused attention on arguments regarding the foundational nature of social and economic citizenship rights, now theorized as interdependent and in constant tension with civil and political rights.

CITIZENSHIP AND RECOGNITION/IDENTITY POLITICS

Living in a multicultural world challenges traditional understandings of the rights and ob-

ligations of citizenship. Whereas social inclusion has traditionally been a rights claim made under the principle of redistribution, the right to recognition—the right to be acknowledged by others as moral equals—mobilized many excluded groups in the 1980s–1990s. Recognition movements pierced the illusory veil of universality to reveal the deep fissures of race, gender, sexuality, and ethnicity that form the fault lines of contemporary advanced political cultures. Identity politics thus push the limits of political/ juridical citizenship by advocating group rights, diversity rights, environmental rights, and rights of disability, race, gender, and sexual difference. Intense attention to recent Supreme Court decisions concerning sexuality and racial diversity demonstrates the challenge these rights claims pose for existing definitions of citizenship.

POSTNATIONAL CITIZENSHIP

Citizenship studies have been roiled by theories of postnationalism. Globalization has also raised postnational citizenship questions, as many believe it has shifted power away from nation-states toward the decentered global market place, where business and finance capital operate in a zone outside the reach of any global polity or international political/legal entity. New literature has thus theorized about "cosmopolitan citizenship,"[3] a "postnational constellation,"[4] and "denationalized citizenship."[5] In this cornucopia of recent studies, citizenship's relationship with human rights has rarely made an appearance.

ANTHROPOLOGY REEMERGES

Half a century after the American Anthropological Association (AAA) declined to endorse the

3. See Seyla Benhabib, *Another Cosmopolitanism* (New York: OUP, 2006); Benhabib, "Twilight of Sovereignty or the Emergence of Cosmopolitan Norms? Rethinking Citizenship in Volatile Times," *Citizenship Studies* 11 (2007): 19–36; Martha C. Nussbaum (with respondents), in Joshua Cohen, ed., *For Love of Country: Debating the Limits of Patriotism* (Boston: Beacon, 1996).
4. Jürgen Habermas, "Remarks on Legitimation Through Human Rights," *Philosophy and Social Criticism* 24 (1998): 157–71.
5. Linda Bosniak, *The Citizen and the Alien: Dilemmas of Contemporary Membership* (Princeton, N.J.: PUP, 2006).

original draft of the UDHR, their anxieties have proved to be both prescient and shortsighted. Their prescience applies primarily to the U.S. government, which has admonished their political antagonists to respect human rights while in practice committing or colluding with some of the worst atrocities of the last half century (Guatemala, Pinochet's Chile, Iraq, etc.), including its current dismissal of the Geneva Convention rules against torture and the attempt to repeal habeas corpus for many foreigners and some U.S. citizens. That all this has been concurrent with unqualified support for the Egyptian, Saudi Arabian, and Pakistani regimes (and their appalling human rights records) reveals a level of hypocrisy that has turned many against the very principles of human rights and so-called humanitarian interventions. Whether the United States has behaved thus in the name of democratization or of stopping genocide, for many critics U.S. actions are often perceived as nothing short of neocolonial, neoliberal forms of global exploitation. At the same time, AAA comparisons of the UDHR with nineteenth- and twentieth-century European colonialism seem shortsighted when one considers the West's woeful record of enforcement of the UDHR and its abject deference to national sovereignty.

All the more striking, then, is the degree to which anthropologists have taken a radical turn and reemerged as major interlocutors and scholarly advocates for global human rights scholarship. Although recent anthropological work acknowledges some of the global/local dilemmas that prompted early anthropologists to dismiss human rights, pioneering scholars suggest that a more nuanced, dynamic, and complex conception of culture may sidestep the long-standing relativist debates that have pitted culture against human rights. While approaches to human rights that emphasize autonomy, individualism, and bodily integrity are sometimes perceived as incompatible with local cultures, it does not necessarily follow that indigenous peoples will reject a more robust and relational conception of human rights when tailored to the local context. Merry describes a process of "vernacularization"[6] through which cultural translators appropriate global norms and apply them within an appro-

priate cultural form at the local level. In some contexts, then, human rights have emerged as local knowledge, and prime among these rights is the right to preserve indigenous cultures in which local rights reside. Local knowledge has also been put to use in the interest of civic repair through truth and reconciliation commissions with the hope of vindicating human rights without the social disruptions that would accompany serious sanctions for violations.

TOWARD A NEW SOCIOLOGY OF RIGHTS

Just as the Eastern European revolutions brought new attention to the issues of citizenship and political rights, so too do increasing levels of global poverty, stateless refugees, genocidal civil wars, and human rights abuses justified by the war on terror appear to be reuniting the arc of the human rights story with the plodding linearity of the social sciences. As if waking up from a long sleep, a far-flung assortment of social science scholars are beginning to train their focus on a new human rights agenda. With few exceptions, however, these disparate sociological endeavors operate in isolation.

What must a sociology of rights entail if it is to bring added value to the field? We believe that at minimum it must deliver a self-conscious commitment to challenge, negotiate, and transcend the obstacles, dichotomies, ambiguities, and intractabilities that have so long impeded a sociology of rights project. A sociology of rights must navigate between normative, philosophical foundationalism and empirical, explanatory positivism; between universal, purportedly natural/human rights and the particularistic institutionalism of citizenship, culture, and exclusivity of membership; between the privileging of civil/legal/political rights and the devalued, often demonized, socioeconomic rights. Rights—whether human or citizenship rights or other kinds—are the label we use to characterize certain kinds of social arrangements. To move the focus of rights away from what the individual possesses to the individual's position in a fluid network of social relations is to begin to construct the social foundations of rights. A sociology of rights thus foregrounds the relationality of rights. Rights as relationships brings a distinct added value to current thinking and underscores the sociological critique of traditional rights theory:

6. Sally Engle Merry, *Human Rights and Gender Violence: Translating International Law into Local Justice* (Chicago: University of Chicago Press, 2006), 44.

Individualist interpretations of rights are bound to go wrong precisely because they must ignore the relational nature of life. For example, race and gender are social constructs, depending for their coherence on the existence of oppositions between blacks and whites, men and women. If these concepts are coherent only because each is accompanied by its opposition, an individualist understanding of rights cannot get very far.

CONCLUDING THOUGHTS

Attention to rights poses both a challenge and an opportunity for the social sciences. Perhaps more than any other area, fully understanding the character, prevalence, institutionalization, and impact of rights requires attention to both the positive and the normative, to the global and the local. Conceptual underbrush still must be cleared, and the mechanisms by which rights are constituted and have their effects must be further elucidated. The coercive power of states must be reconceptualized in light of the power of ideology and philosophy, and the situations in which the latter can most matter must be understood.

Thus, law appears to be a rough draft not only of existing social theory, but also of theory that has yet to be written. Subaltern social and political struggles are only partially recorded in law, if they ever make it to the legal system in the first instance. After 1948, the brief exuberance for human rights quickly sputtered in the United States with the realization that the discourse of civil rights was the only viable means for political struggles to become written into law. Sixty years later, events such as Hurricane Katrina provide dramatic evidence to the contrary; here, the language of citizenship rights proves to be sorrowfully inadequate. Ron Daniels seized an opportunity (and a longing) by deploying the language and institutions of human rights to confront the overwhelming rightlessness of Katrina victims. In the United States—a stronghold of legal resistance toward recognizing human rights as a domestic concern—the effect of this strategy remains to be seen. Perhaps social reality has outpaced existing law's capacity and/or will to recognize new rights claims to recognition and inclusion. What is clear is that social scientists can no longer avoid the challenges of theorizing human rights, now the dominant mode of expression of human suffering and social injustice throughout the world. The moment is ripe to seize; there are so many more buried bodies that await the telling of their stories.

QUESTIONS FOR REFLECTION AND DISCUSSION

1. The authors accuse the United States of exceptionalism when it comes to the recognition and enforcement of human rights nationally and internationally. They are especially critical of the U.S. domestic track record: "the U.S. government's dogged rejection of human rights in the domestic context persists today. It carries out a strict practice of compartmentalization, which reserves human rights concerns for other places." Do you agree? Disagree? What evidence informs your view? Would Michael Ignatieff (Reading 37) agree? Disagree?

2. What do you think explains American "exceptionalism" relative to human rights, and is it justifiable? How would you justify it? For potential help, consult Reading 37 (Ignatieff) cited in the preceding question.

3. Is the United States bound to recognize certain human rights based upon customary international law absent ratification of corresponding human rights treaties? What, if any, human rights rise to the level of *jus cogens* (Latin for "cogent law," i.e., compelling or peremptory norm(s) deemed to be fundamental, overriding principles of law and policy from which no derogation is lawfully permitted, e.g., prohibitions on aggression, slavery, torture, genocide)?

4. Consider why it is that nearly a century of "Jim Crow" laws imposing racial segregation on black U.S. citizens have never been popularly, let alone officially, characterized as "apartheid laws" as in South Africa. Is it possible in the United States today, where the majority of African Americans are consigned to underdeveloped neighborhoods, poor schools, and low-income wages, to speak of present-day economic apartheid vis-à-vis black Americans? Would this be legitimate discourse? How would Somers and Roberts answer this question? Do you agree with them? Why or why not?

5. The authors cite Hurricane Katrina (2005) as "dramatic evidence" that the handling of the crisis by governmental authorities paid little attention to the civil and political rights of Katrina's victims. Do you agree? Disagree? Would they have written less emphatically had they been writing after Hurricane Sandy (2008), which was handled in quite opposite fashion? More emphatically? In any case, what explains the difference between the two? Did race have anything to do with it? The different socioeconomic status of the respective victims? If so, what does this reveal, if anything, about the status of civil and political rights in the United States? Socioeconomic rights?

6. Do you believe that economic, social, and cultural rights differ from civil and political rights with respect to any potential justification for their differential treatment? Does the claimed indivisibility of all categories of international human rights mean that differences in treatment are no longer justifiable? Support your answer with an argument drawing, where possible, upon sources and evidence.

7. How might citizenship claims based on identity politics be nurtured by human rights law and discourse? Would this be a valuable contribution to discussions of citizenship, or not? Give reasons for your answer.

8. How do human rights extend any protection for human beings beyond the parameters of citizenship? Do they? Or do they fail in this regard? Does it matter, either way? Support your answer with reasons.

9. In what ways, if any, do civil society movements give content to (a) civil and political rights, (b) socioeconomic rights, (c) human rights generally, and (d) the meaning of citizenship?

10. To what extent is globalization a challenge and to what extent an opportunity for a reinvigoration or reinvention of citizenship? For a reinvigoration or reinvention of human rights? Support your answer as fully as possible with an argument drawing upon sources and evidence.

11. Somers and Roberts write: "Thus, law appears to be a rough draft not only of existing social theory, but also of theory that has yet to be written. Subaltern social and political struggles are only partially recorded in law, if they ever make it to the legal system in the first instance." Can you think of any contemporary examples of subaltern social and political struggles that are either (a) partially recorded in law or (b) excluded from the legal system entirely? If so, does your answer imply that law is an adequate tool for social justice aspirations—or a limit on them? Support your answers as fully as you can, drawing upon any sources and/or evidence available to you.

Chapter Two

Basic Decencies

IN this chapter, we consider some grave problems raised by recent world history: genocide, human trafficking, and torture. There are multiple forms of radical disrespect and violence in the contemporary world, but each of the subjects in this chapter represents a particularly iconic example of a failure to respect basic human decencies, calling into question fundamental assumptions about "core" values allegedly "shared" within the contemporary international legal order. In short, the readings in this chapter concern violations of the root value of simple human respect or, more precisely, present-day deprivations of human respect that show utter contempt for the most rudimentary of human values: survival, security, and equality in the pursuit of life—and notwithstanding a wide measure of "moral consensus" concerning the evil of these atrocities.

Suffering characterizes much of human history, but during the twentieth century and the first two decades of the twenty-first, humanity has managed to propagate misery of the most grotesque forms on a global scale. For the purposes of the present chapter, the particular acts and forms of human-against-human violation on which we have chosen to focus further highlight the contradictions and paradoxes surrounding human rights as signaled in the Introduction and readings in Chapter 1. It is shocking to realize that the "age of human rights" is characterized by an unprecedented degree of human rights violations, some of which inaugurated human rights energies in international law, but many of which betrayed the international human rights promise at the very deepest level.

The record of these centuries speaks volumes about the precarious fragility of human empathy and concern. The twentieth century witnessed two devastating world wars, which, complete with indiscriminate fire bombings and atomic blasts, claimed sixty million lives and inaugurated the era of international human rights as a direct reaction to the "barbarous acts" that shocked the conscience of humankind. But notwithstanding the high-minded ideals and aspirations of international human rights law, policy, and discourse that emerged from the ashes of these wars and their associated barbarities, the trajectory of imposed human suffering continues to unfold. The twentieth and twenty-first centuries are littered with genocides, mass purges, arbitrary killings, and barbarous acts of torture. What Adolph Hitler and Josef Stalin enacted during the Second World War found hideously familiar echoes in the later barbarity of Idi Amin (Uganda), Pol Pot (Cambodia), Slobodan Milošević (Serbia), Saddam Hussein (Iraq), Augustin Bizimungu (Rwanda), Janjaweed militia leader Musa Hilal (Sudan), and Bashar al-Assad (Syria)—and to which may now be added the private sector barbarisms of the terrorist Islamic State of Iraq and the Levant (ISIL in Syria and Iraq) and Boko Haram (Nigeria). Forced transportation of people under slavery, and the extensive, industrialized, and coercive transport of human beings into labor and concentration camps under the Nazi regime find a disturbing resonance in the commercialized human trafficking of the contemporary era. The core patterns of indecency at the heart of genocide, trafficking, and torture continue in the twenty-first century—even, in the case of torture, in the name of human rights. Multiple forms of invidious marginalization continue to be expressed through the practices of Western state-sanctioned torture, extensive and spiraling levels of human trafficking, and a raft of other forms of violence, exploitation, oppression, and control, whether driven by state imperatives, rogue elements, or corporation-sponsored territorial expansionism in resource-rich developing countries. The picture is certainly a shameful one.

Against this appalling background, however, there is some good news. Though unparalleled in its treachery, our era is also the first in which people all over the world are trying to do something about human rights violations on a global and regional scale. For example, in the name of human rights, insistence on basic decency and equality has established a minimum global standard that is now an integral part of contemporary international law doctrine, even if not always of national and international policy. And that doctrine is deployed by a wide range of advocates and communities calling for redress in the name of human rights. There are, in short, normative standards to which the oppressed and their defenders can turn for argumentative and moral support. Thus does the Preamble to the UN Charter, responding to death camps, torture chambers, abused minorities, and helpless peoples fleeing misery and oppression, reaffirm faith in fundamental human rights, in the dignity and worth of the human person, in the equal rights of men and women and of nations large and small. This, along with the Universal Declaration of Human Rights (UDHR) and the normative reach of its many human rights treaty offspring, now operationalized through hundreds of provisions and procedures the world over, provide more than human rights rhetoric. There now exist, for example, a permanent (though yet uncertain) International Criminal Court, several increasingly robust regional human rights systems, a wide variety of intergovernmental human rights institutions and mechanisms, and countless nonprofit human rights organizations dedicated to bringing political and ethical pressure to bear upon abuses of power.[1]

The emergence of human rights into international law was a decisive moment. As is well known, the first big step from human rights rhetoric to consequential action was taken at Nuremberg in 1945, when Nazi leaders captured as criminals of war were convicted not only for violations of the laws and customs of war, a time-honored standard imposed by military victors, but also for crimes against humanity. The Nazi leaders captured by the victorious Allied powers were convicted for political, racial, and religious persecutions committed against *any* civilian population (i.e., German citizens as well as other nationals), and their convictions were ruled justified whether or not in violation of the domestic law of the country where perpetrated.[2]

In other words, in contrast to pre-World War II times when international law allowed each equal sovereign an equal right to be monstrous to his [or her] subjects,[3] the Nazi laws of Germany, however authoritative, provided no legal defense. Accordingly, international legal accountability achieved (albeit in an incomplete and imbalanced way) a breach in

1. For details, see Chapters 6–8.
2. Article 6(c) of the Agreement for the Prosecution and Punishment of the Major War Criminals of the European Axis Powers and Charter of the International Military Tribunal (8 August 1945).
3. Tom J. Farer, "Introduction," in Paul Williams, ed., *The International Bill of Human Rights* (Glen Ellen, Calif.: Entwhistle, 1981), xiii.

national sovereignty that opened the way toward international accountability for human rights violations in the future. As Leo Gross once put it, these (Nuremberg) trials were in a profound sense a demonstration against the totalitarian subjection of the individual to nationalized truth; they were a protest against the erasure of the individual as a subject, mediate or immediate, of international law, and as a responsible member of the international community.[4] The human rights of individuals, in this moment, were made visible matters of international concern: human rights were internationalized and international law was humanized.

THE CRIMES OF GENOCIDE

Drawing on the principles of Nuremberg, the United Nations developed the 1948 Convention on the Prevention and Punishment of the Crime of Genocide.[5] The Convention defines genocide as acts committed with intent to destroy in whole or in part, a national, ethnical, racial, or religious group as such,[6] and the Contracting Parties to it confirm that, even if perpetrated by a government against its own inhabitants, it is a crime under international law that they undertake to prevent and punish.[7] Genocide is a violation of human rights on hideous scale.

Philosopher Claudia Card's essay in this chapter explores the fundamental evil of genocide. Drawing a careful distinction between genocide and "other mass murders," Card develops the hypothesis that *social death*—that is to say, the calculated removal of the identity, relationships, and meaning that make up social vitality—is "utterly central to the evil of genocide, not just when a genocide is primarily cultural but even when it is homicidal on a massive scale."

Card argues that what distinguishes genocidal murder from mass murder in the general sense (hideous as it is) is the centrality of *social death* to genocide, which aims precisely at the obliteration of a group's *social vitality*—at the obliteration of identity, relationships, and meaning, a strategy amounting to the violent interruption of human social existence and at disabling a group's capacity for intergenerational continuity. The inexorable logic of this position implies, Card argues, that social death can *aggravate* physical death, even mass murder. By removing the interconnected webs of social import and significance that give death meaning in a given society, social death means that death itself is rendered "indecent."

The logic of Card's analysis points toward continuities discernible between genocidal intent and other forms of hatred manifesting in the social exclusion, marginalization, and even the cultural "death" of groups through the obliteration of their significant relationships and cultural understandings and languages. Genocide can be seen as the extreme and evil end of a spectrum moving between mass killings animated by the goal of social obliteration and, at the other end of the spectrum, multiple forms of "othering"—even mundane but oppressive forms—enacted upon the groups and individuals. That we can recognize, all too easily, the tendencies of our own Western liberal cultures in relation to marginalized

4. Leo Gross, "The Punishment of War Criminals: The Nuremberg Trial," *Netherlands International Law Review* 2, 4 (1955): 356–74.
5. Concluded 9 December 1948, one day before the adoption of the UDHR.
6. Convention on the Prevention and Punishment of the Crime of Genocide, Art. 2.
7. Ibid., art. 1.

groups, populations, or subjectivities should give us, as readers of Card's argument, more than a moment's thoughtful pause. The fundamentally rejecting impulses that reach their nadir as the evil, homicidal energies of genocide are at stake also in multiple other forms of social hatred, including infinitely more duplicitous, polite ones. Such "othering" impulses form a central element also in the phenomenon of human trafficking.

HUMAN TRAFFICKING: FROM THE INDECENCY OF SLAVERY TO THE OUTRAGE OF A GLOBAL TRADE IN HUMAN BEINGS

Jonathan Todres takes "othering" as his central analytical motif in his exploration of the phenomenon of contemporary human trafficking. Linking trafficking unambiguously with slavery, Todres argues that despite the universal condemnation of slavery as a gross violation of human rights, human trafficking is a global growth industry, worth billions and billions of U.S. dollars worldwide.

Todres identifies "otherness" ("the quality of being not alike, being distinct or different from that otherwise experienced or known") as a root cause of not only trafficking itself, but as seriously, a cause of international "inaction and [of] the selective nature of responses to the abusive practice of human trafficking." Othering, in other words, presents a dynamic that lies at the heart of legal failure to address the outcomes of othering processes. This is perhaps unsurprising, in so far as othering devalues the "other" and amounts to the facilitating not only of active abuse and exploitation but also a passive failure to appreciate, respond to, and address the violations of the "other." A devalued other cannot be properly seen as a meaningfully injured party: devaluation reduces the significance of both the other and her/his wounds.

CONFRONTING TORTURE AND DISAPPEARANCES

Torture, like genocide and slavery, is a profound affront to the fundamental value of respect that lies at the heart of human rights law, policy, and discourse. Article 3 of the Universal Declaration of Human Rights (UDHR) states that "Everyone has the right to life, liberty and security of person"; and Article 6 of the International Covenant on Civil and Political Rights (ICCPR) specifies that "no one shall be arbitrarily deprived of his [sic] life." In his book, *The Right to Life in International Law*, former deputy high commissioner for human rights B. G. Ramcharan shows that the word *arbitrarily* was carefully chosen with the intention of providing the highest possible level of protection to the right to life and to confine permissible deprivations therefrom to the narrowest of limits.[8] In remarks to the Committee Against Torture in April 2001, in which he ably reviewed some relevant historical literature and recounted an important 12-point torture prevention program adopted as a model guide by Amnesty International, Dr. Ramcharan concluded unequivocally, quoting Article 2(2) of the 1984 Convention against Torture and Other Cruel, Inhuman or Degrading Treatment or Punishment (CAT): no exceptional circumstances whatsoever,

---

8. Bertrand G. Ramcharan, *The Right to Life in International Law* (The Hague: Nijhoff, 1985).

whether a state of war or a threat of war, internal political instability or any other public emergency, may be invoked as a justification of torture.

Jeremy Waldron's argument in this chapter addresses the travesty that governmental reliance on torture is far from being a thing of the past. His starting point is a direct focus upon the appalling revelations of the extensive violations enacted in the Abu Ghraib prison in Iraq while it was under U.S. control. However, more dishonoring for Waldron than the explicit images of sexual humiliation, dogs, hoods, wires, and beatings was the fact that the situation at Abu Ghraib resulted from broader U.S. policy commitments and determinations: the Abu Ghraib violations were not isolated incidents, but part of an extensive pattern of practice. Yet for Waldron there is an even more troubling and revealing fact: that these brutal acts took place "not just in the fog of war, but against a legal and political background set by discussions among lawyers and other officials in the White House, the Justice Department, and the Department of Defense about how to narrow the meaning and application of domestic and international legal prohibitions relating to torture." In other words, U.S. lawyers and state officials sought deliberately to use positive law and legal argument to narrow the meaning of torture in a way that would *facilitate* it. Waldron is explicit: "I want to place particular emphasis on the fact that these efforts to modify the prohibition on torture have been undertaken by lawyers."

In confronting this fact, Waldron conducts an extensive analysis of the status of the prohibition on torture and the arguments raised in defense of narrowing the scope of the meaning and application of the relevant law. Waldron argues that "were we to put up for acceptance as an integral part of the main body of human rights law the proposition that people may be tortured in times of emergency, I think people would sense that the whole game was being given away, and that human rights law itself was entering a crisis."

Torture, like genocide and trafficking, is a particularly clear and direct example of the violent and fundamental denial of basic human decency. This chapter does not assert that fundamental denials do not exist elsewhere. They most assuredly do, and many will be revealed in the chapters that follow. But genocide, human trafficking, and torture, taken together or apart, do provide a powerful illumination of that against which human rights law, policy, and discourse must stand firmly opposed.

8. CLAUDIA CARD *Genocide*

This essay develops the hypothesis that social death—the loss of social vitality (identity, relationships, meaning)—is utterly central to the evil of genocide, not just when a genocide is primarily cultural but even when it is homicidal on a massive scale. It is social death that enables us to distinguish the peculiar evil of genocide from the evils of other mass murders. If my hypothesis is correct, the term "cultural genocide" is probably both redundant and misleading—redundant if the social death present in all genocide implies cultural death as well, and misleading if "cultural genocide" suggests that some genocides do not include cultural death.

GENOCIDE, WAR, AND JUSTICE

Genocide need not be part of a larger war, although it commonly is. But it can be regarded as itself a kind of one-sided war, a profoundly unjust kind of war, perniciously unjust, an injustice that is also an evil. Of course, not all injustices are evils. Some injustices are relatively tolerable—unjust salary discriminations, for ex-

Excerpted with changes by permission of Indiana University Press from Claudia Card, "Genocide and Social Death," in "Feminist Philosophy and the Problem of Evil," special issue, *Hypatia* 18, 1 (Winter 2003): 63–79. Copyright © 2003 Indiana University Press.

ample, when the salaries in question are all high. An injustice becomes an evil when it inflicts harms that make victims' lives unbearable, indecent, or impossible, or that make victims' deaths indecent. Injustices of war are apt to fall into this category. Certainly genocide does.

THE CONCEPT OF GENOCIDE

"Genocide" combines the Greek *genos* for race or tribe with the Latin *cide* for killing. The term was coined by Raphael Lemkin, an attorney and refugee scholar from Poland who served in the United States War Department.[1] He campaigned as early as the 1930s for an international convention to outlaw genocide, and his persistence resulted in the United Nations Genocide Convention of 1948. Although this convention is widely cited, the first state to bring a case to the World Court under the convention was Bosnia-Herzegovina in 1993.[2] It was not until 1998 that the first verdict interpreting that convention was rendered, when the Rwanda tribunal found Jean-Paul Akayesu guilty on nine counts for his participation in the genocide in Rwanda in 1994.[3]

The *term* "genocide" is thus relatively new, and the Holocaust is widely agreed to be its paradigmatic instance. Yet Lemkin and many others find the *practice* of genocide ancient. Instances of apparent genocide range from the Athenians' annihilation [and enslavement] of the people of Melos in the fifth century B.C.E. (recorded by Thucydides) and the ravaging of Carthage by Romans in 146 B.C.E. (also listed by Lemkin as the first of his historical examples of wars of extermination) through mass killings in Bangladesh, Cambodia, and East Timor in the second half of the twentieth century. Controversies are ongoing over whether to count as genocidal the

1. See Raphael Lemkin, *Axis Rule in Occupied Europe: Laws of Occupation, Analysis of Government, Proposals for Redress* (Washington, D.C.: Carnegie Endowment for International Peace, Division of International Law, 1944).
2. See Application of the Convention on the Prevention and Punishment of the Crime of Genocide (*Bosnia and Herzegovina v. Serbia and Montenegro*), 1993 ICJ General List No. 91.
3. See Diane F. Orentlicher, "Genocide," in Roy Gutman and David Rieff, eds., *Crimes of War: What the Public Should Know* (New York: Norton, 1999), 153–57.

annihilation of indigenous peoples in the Americas and Australia (who succumbed in vast numbers to diseases brought by Europeans), Stalin's induced mass starvation of the 1930s (ostensibly an economically motivated measure), and the war conducted by the United States in Vietnam.

Controversies over the meaning of "genocide" lead naturally to the closely related question of whether genocide is ethically different from nongenocidal mass murder. The practical issue here is whether, and if so, why it is important to add the category of genocide to existing crimes against humanity and war crimes. Crimes against humanity were important additions to war crimes in that, unlike war crimes, they need not be perpetrated during wartime or in connection with a war, and they can be inflicted by a country against its own citizens. But given that murder of civilians by soldiers is already a war crime and a human rights violation, one may wonder whether the crime of genocide captures anything that they omit.

Arguably, genocide does capture something more. What distinguishes genocide is not that it has a different kind of victim, namely, groups. Rather, the kind of harm suffered by individual victims of genocide, in virtue of their group membership, is not captured by other crimes.

The definition of "genocide" is currently in such flux that the Association of Genocide Scholars asks members on its information page to specify which definition they use in their work. A widely cited definition is that of the 1948 UN Convention on the Prevention and Punishment of the Crime of Genocide:

> Genocide means any of the following acts committed with the intent to destroy, in whole or in part, a national, ethnical, racial or religious group, as such: (a) killing members of the group; (b) causing serious bodily or mental harm to members of the group; (c) deliberately inflicting on the group conditions of life calculated to bring about its physical destruction in whole or in part; (d) imposing measures intended to prevent births within the group; (e) forcibly transferring children of the group to another group.

Every clause of this definition is controversial.

Israel Charny and others criticize the UN definition for not recognizing political groups, such as the Communist Party, as possible targets of genocide.[4] Political groups had been, in fact, recognized in an earlier draft of the genocide convention, and Chalk and Jonassohn do recognize political groups as targets of genocide in their historical survey.[5] Some scholars, however, prefer the term "politicide" for these cases and reserve the term "genocide" for the annihilation of groups into which one is (ordinarily) born—racial, ethnic, national, or religious groups. Yet, one is not necessarily, of course, born into one's current national or religious group, and either one's current or one's former membership can prove fatal. Further, some people's political identity may be as important to their lives as religious identity is to the lives of others. And so, the distinction between "genocide" and "politicide" has seemed arbitrary to many critics. A difficulty is, of course, where to draw the line if political groups are recognized as possible victims. But line drawing is not a difficulty that is peculiar to political groups.

The last three clauses of the UN definition—conditions of life intended to destroy the group "in whole or in part," preventing births, and transferring children—count as genocidal many acts that are aimed at cultural destruction, even though they are not homicidal. "Preventing births" is not restricted to sterilization but has been interpreted to include segregation of the sexes and bans on marriage. Social vitality is destroyed when the social relations—organizations, practices, institutions—of the members of a group are irreparably damaged or demolished. Such destruction is a commonly intended consequence of war rape, which has aimed at family breakdown. Although Lemkin regarded such deeds as both ethnocidal and genocidal, some scholars prefer simply to call them ethnocides (or "cultural genocides") and reserve the term "genocide" (unqualified) for events that include mass death. The idea is, apparently, that physical death is more extreme and therefore, presumably, worse than social death. That physical death is worse, or even more extreme, is not obvious, however, but deserves scrutiny, and I will return to it.

Even the clauses of the UN definition that specify killing group members or causing them serious bodily or mental harm are vague and can cover a wide range of possible harms. How many people must be killed for a deed to be genocidal? What sort of bodily harm counts? (Must there be lasting disablement?) What counts as "mental harm"? (Is post-traumatic stress sufficient?).

Although most scholars agree on including intention in the definition of genocide, there is no consensus regarding the content of the required intention. Must the relevant intention include destruction of all members of a group as an aim or purpose? Would it be enough that the group was knowingly destroyed, as a foreseeable consequence of the pursuit of some other aim? Must the full extent of the destruction even be foreseeable, if the policy of which it is a consequence is already clearly immoral? Bedau makes much of the content of the relevant intention in his argument that whatever war crimes the United States committed in Vietnam, they were not genocidal because the intent was not to destroy the people of Vietnam as such, even if that destruction was both likely and foreseeable.[6]

Charny, however, objects to an analogous claim made by some critics who, he reports, held that because Stalin's intent was to obtain enough grain to trade for industrial materials for the Soviet Union, rather than to kill the millions who died from this policy, Stalin's famine was not a genocide. Charny argues that because Stalin foresaw the fatal consequences of his grain policies, those policies should count as genocidal.[7] Charny appears to reject as ethically insignificant a distinction between intending and "merely foreseeing," at least in this kind of case. His position appears to imply that the foreseeability of the peasants' mass death is enough to constitute genocidal intent, even if it was not intended instrumentally toward Stalin's aims.

Some controversies focus on whether the intent was "to destroy a group as such." One might argue with Bedau that the intent is "to destroy a group as such" when it is not just accidental that

4. See Israel Charny, "Toward a Generic Definition of Genocide," in George Andreopoulos, ed., *Genocide: Conceptual and Historical Dimensions* (Philadelphia: University of Pennsylvania Press, 1994), 64–94.
5. See Frank Chalk and Kurt Jonassohn, eds., *The History and Sociology of Genocide: Analyses and Case Studies* (New Haven, Conn.: YUP, 1990).

6. Hugo Adam Bedau, "Genocide in Vietnam?" in Virginia Held, Sidney Morgenbesser, and Thomas Nagel, eds., *Philosophy, Morality, and International Affairs* (New York: OUP, 1974).
7. Charny, "Toward a Generic Definition of Genocide," note 4.

the group is destroyed in the process of pursuing a further end. Thus, if it was not just accidental that the peasant class was destroyed in the process of Stalin's pursuit of grain to trade for industrial materials, he could be said to have destroyed the peasants "as such," even if peasant starvation played no more causal role in making grain available than killing the fetus plays in removing a cancerous uterus. Alternatively, some argue that the words "as such" do not belong in the definition because, ethically, it does not matter whether a group is deliberately destroyed "as such" or simply deliberately destroyed.

Further, one might pursue the question of whether it is really necessary even to be able to foresee the full extent of the consequences in order to be accurately described as having a genocidal intent. Historian Steven Katz argues that the mass deaths of Native Americans and Native Australians were not genocides because they resulted from epidemics, not from murder.[8] The suggestion is that the consequences here were not reasonably foreseeable. However, David Stannard, American Studies scholar at the University of Hawaii, finds the case less simple, for it can be argued that the epidemics were not just accidental.[9] Part of the controversy regards the facts: to what extent were victims deliberately infected, as when the British, and later Americans, distributed blankets infected with smallpox virus? And to what extent did victims succumb to unintended infection stemming from ordinary exposure to Europeans with the virus? But, also, part of the controversy is philosophical. If mass deaths from disease result from wrongdoing, and if perpetrators could know that the intolerably destructive consequences had an uncontrollable (and therefore somewhat unpredictable) extent, then, does it matter, ethically, whether the wrongdoers could foresee the full extent of the consequences? One might argue that it does not, on the ground that they already knew enough to appreciate that what they were doing was evil.

What is the importance of success in achieving a genocidal aim? Must genocide succeed in eliminating an entire group? An assault, to be homicide, must succeed in killing. Otherwise, it is a mere attempt, and an unlawful attempted homicide generally carries a less severe penalty than a successful one. While "genocide" does not appear to be analogous to "homicide" in that way, there may still be room for some distinction between genocide and attempted genocide if we distinguish between partially formed and fully formed intentions, or if we distinguish among stages in carrying out a complex intention. But in paradigmatic instances of genocide, such as the Holocaust, there are always some survivors, even when there is clear evidence that the intention was to eliminate everyone in the group. There is general agreement that at least some mass killing with that wrongful intention is genocidal. The existence of survivors is not sufficient to negate fully formed genocidal intent. Bedau observes, however, that there is a certain analogy between "genocide" and "murder" that enables us to contrast both with homicide. Both genocide and murder include wrongfulness in the very concept, whereas a homicide can be justifiable. Homicide is not necessarily unlawful or even immoral. In contrast, genocide and murder are, in principle, incapable of justification.

On my understanding of what constitutes an evil, there are two basic elements: (1) culpable wrongdoing by one or more perpetrators and (2) reasonably foreseeable intolerable harm to victims. Most often the second element, intolerable harm, is what distinguishes evils from ordinary wrongs. Intentions may be necessary to defining genocide. But they are not always necessary for culpable wrongdoing, as omissions—negligence, recklessness, or carelessness—can be sufficient. When culpable wrongdoing *is* intentional, however, its aim need not be to cause intolerable harm. A seriously culpable deed is evil when the doer is willing to inflict intolerable harm on others even in the course of aiming at some other goal. If what is at stake in controversies regarding the meaning of "genocide" is whether a mass killing is sufficiently evil to merit the opprobrium attaching to the term "genocide," a good case can be made for including assaults on many kinds of groups inflicted through many kinds of culpable wrongdoing. Yet that leaves the question of whether the genocidal nature of a killing has special ethical import, and if so, what that import is and how, if at all, it may restrict the scope of "genocide." I turn to these and related questions next.

8. See Steven Katz, *The Holocaust in Historical Context* (New York: OUP, 1994).
9. See David E. Stannard, *American Holocaust: The Conquest of the New World* (New York: OUP, 1992) and "Uniqueness As Denial: The Politics of Genocide Scholarship," in Alan S. Rosenbaum, ed., *Is the Holocaust Unique?* (Boulder, Colo.: Westview, 1996).

THE SPECIFIC EVILS OF GENOCIDE

Genocide is not simply unjust; it is also evil. It characteristically includes the one-sided killing of defenseless civilians—babies, children, the elderly, the sick, the disabled, and the injured of both genders along with their usually female caretakers—simply on the basis of their national, religious, ethnic, or other political identity. It targets people on the basis of who they are rather than on the basis of what they have done, what they might do, even what they are capable of doing. (One commentator says genocide kills people on the basis of *what* they are, not even *who* they are.)

Genocide is a paradigm of what Israeli philosopher Avishai Margalit calls "indecent" in that it not only destroys victims but first humiliates them by deliberately inflicting an "utter loss of freedom and control over one's vital interests."[10] Vital interests can be transgenerational and thus survive one's death. Before death, genocide victims are ordinarily deprived of control over vital transgenerational interests and more immediate vital interests. They may be literally stripped naked, robbed of their last possessions, lied to about the most vital matters, made witnesses to the murder of family, friends, and neighbors, made to participate in their own murder, and if female, they are likely to be also violated sexually.[11] Victims of genocide are commonly killed with no regard for lingering suffering or exposure. They, and their corpses, are routinely treated with utter disrespect. These historical facts, not simply mass murder, account for much of the moral opprobrium attaching to the concept of genocide.

Yet such atrocities, it may be argued, are already war crimes, if conducted during wartime, and they can otherwise or also be prosecuted as crimes against humanity. Why, then, add the specific crime of genocide? What, if anything, is not already captured by laws that prohibit such things as the rape, enslavement, torture, forced deportation, and the degradation of individuals? Is any ethically distinct harm done to members of the targeted group that would not have been done had they been targeted simply as individuals rather than because of their group membership? This is the question that I find central in arguing that genocide is not simply reducible to mass death, to any of the other war crimes, or to the crimes against humanity just enumerated. I believe the answer is affirmative: the harm is ethically distinct, although on the question of whether it is worse, I wish only to question the assumption that it is not.

Specific to genocide is the harm inflicted on its victims' social vitality. It is not just that one's group membership is the occasion for harms that are definable independently of one's identity as a member of the group. When a group with its own cultural identity is destroyed, its survivors lose their cultural heritage and may even lose their intergenerational connections. To use Orlando Patterson's terminology, in that event, they may become "socially dead" and their descendants "natally alienated," no longer able to pass along and build upon the traditions, cultural developments (including languages), and projects of earlier generations.[12] Social death can even aggravate physical death by making it indecent, removing all respectful and caring ritual, social connections, and social contexts that are capable of making dying bearable and even of making one's death meaningful. In my view, the special evil of genocide lies in its infliction of not just physical death (when it does that) but social death, producing a consequent meaninglessness of one's life and even of its termination. This view, however, is controversial.

[*Eds.*—The author next takes issue with African American and Jewish philosopher Lawrence Mordekhai Thomas, who argues that American slavery natally alienated slaves—born severed from most normal social and cultural ties that connect one with both earlier and later generations—but that the Holocaust did not natally alienate Jews because many Jews survived the Holocaust and "the central tenets of Judaism . . . endured in spite of Hitler's every intention to the contrary."[13] For Card, however, analyzing

---

10. Avishai Margalit, *The Decent Society*, trans. Naomi Goldblum (Cambridge, Mass.: HUP, 1996), 115.
11. Men are sometimes also violated sexually (usually by other men), although the overwhelming majority of sex crimes in war, including genocide, are perpetrated by men against female victims of all ages and conditions.

12. Orlando Patterson, *Slavery and Social Death* (Cambridge, Mass.: HUP, 1982), 5–9.
13. See Lawrence Mordekhai Thomas, *Vessels of Evil: American Slavery and the Holocaust* (Philadelphia: Temple University Press, 1993), 150–57.

Thomas's position through the lens of social death, the critical question is not "simply whether the traditions survived but whether individual Jewish victims were able to sustain their connections to those traditions." While agreeing "that slaves who are treated as nonpersons have (practically) no socially supported ties not only to a cultural heritage but even to immediate kin (parents, children, siblings) and peers" and that "Hereditary slavery yields a paradigm of natal alienation," Card points out that many Holocaust survivors were unable to sustain their specific social/cultural connections because "many lost entire families, their entire villages, and the way of life embodied in the *shtetl* (eastern European village), "Some could not produce more children because of medical experiments performed on them in the camps," and "Many . . . lost access to social memories embodied in such cultural institutions as libraries and synagogues." She adds: "More clearly, those who were made stateless before being murdered were certainly treated, socially, as nonpersons. National Socialist decrees robbed them of social support for ties to family, peers, and community, stripped their rights to earn a living, own property, attend public schools, even ride public transportation, and on arrival at the camps they were torn from family members. Although they were not born to social death, they were nevertheless intentionally deprived of all social vitality before their physical murder." Card thus concludes that the concept of "genocide" qua "social death" applies to both slavery and the Holocaust. She then continues:]

Most immediate victims of genocide are not born socially dead. But genocides that intentionally strip victims of the ability to participate in social activity, prior to their murders, do aim at their social death, not just their physical death. In some cases it may appear that social death is not an end in itself but simply a consequence of means taken to make mass murder easier (concentrating victims in ghettos and camps, for example). When assailants are moved by hatred, however, social death may become an end in itself. Humiliation before death appears often to have been an end in itself, not just a means. The very idea of selecting victims by social group identity suggests that it is not just the physical life of victims that is targeted but the social vitality behind that identity.

If the aim, or intention, of social death is not accidental to genocide, the survival of Jewish culture does not show that social death was not central to the evil of the Holocaust, any more than the fact of survivors shows that a mass murder was not genocidal. A genocide as successful as the Holocaust achieves the aim of social death both for victims who do not survive, and to a degree and for a time, for many survivors as well. Thomas's point may still hold that descendants of survivors of the African diaspora produced by the slave trade are in general more alienated from their African cultures of origin than Holocaust survivors are from Judaism today. Yet it is true in both cases that survivors make substantial connection with other cultures. If African Americans are totally alienated from their African cultures of origin, it is also true that many Holocaust survivors and their descendants have found it impossible to embrace Judaism or even a Jewish culture after Auschwitz. The survival of a culture does not by itself tell us about the degree of alienation that is experienced by individual survivors. Knowledge of a heritage is not by itself sufficient to produce vital connections to it.

The harm of social death is not, so far as I can see, adequately captured by war crimes and other crimes against humanity. Many of those crimes are defined by what can be done to individuals considered independently of their social connections: rape (when defined simply as a form of physical assault), torture, starvation. Some crimes, such as deportation and enslavement, do begin to get at issues of disrupting social existence. But they lack the comprehensiveness of social death, at least when the enslavement in question is not hereditary and is not necessarily for the rest of a person's life.

Still, it is true that not all victims of the Holocaust underwent social death to the same extent as prisoners in the camps and ghettos. Entire villages on the Eastern front were slaughtered by the Einsatzgruppen (mobile killing units) without warning or prior captivity. Yet these villagers were given indecent deaths. They were robbed of control of their vital interests and of opportunities to mourn. Although most did not experience those deprivations for very long, inflicted en masse these murders do appear to have produced sudden social death prior to physical extermination. The murders were also part of a larger plan that included the death of Judaism, not just the deaths of Jews. Implementing that plan included gradually stripping vast numbers of Jews of social vitality, in some places over a period of years, and it entailed that survivors, if there were any, should not survive as Jews. The fact that the plan only partly succeeded does not negate the central role of social death within it or the importance of that concept to genocide.

If social death is central to the harm of genocide, then it really is right not to count as a genocide the annihilation of just any political group, however heinous. Not every political group contributes significantly to its members' cultural identity. Many are fairly specific and short-lived, formed to support particular issues. But then,

equally, the annihilation of not just any cultural group should count, either. Cultural groups can also be temporary and specialized, lacking in the continuity and comprehensiveness that are presupposed by the possibility of social death. Some mass murders—perhaps the bombings of 11 September 2001—do not appear to have had as part of their aim, intention, or effect the prior soul murder or social death of those targeted for physical extermination. If so, they are mass murders that are not also genocides. But mass murders and other measures that have as part of their reasonably foreseeable consequence, or as part of their aim, the annihilation of a group that contributes significantly to the social identity of its members are genocidal.

QUESTIONS FOR REFLECTION AND DISCUSSION

1. Card's core thesis is that social death is central to the evil of genocide and that it is social death that distinguishes the peculiar evil of genocide from the evils of other mass murders. What is "social death"? And where, if at all, is it evident in the world today?

2. What are the linkages, if any, between discrimination, the destruction of group social vitality, genocide (see Lemkin's definition), and human rights? Support your answer with an argument carefully built upon an accurate discussion of the text, and draw, where possible, upon other sources you are aware of or have been able to find.

3. As noted by Card, Article 2 of the 1948 Convention on the Prevention and Punishment of the Crime of Genocide defines "genocide" to mean:

any of the following acts committed with intent to destroy, in whole or in part, a national, ethnical, racial or religious group, as such:
(a) Killing members of the group.
(b) Causing serious bodily or mental harm to members of the group.
(c) Deliberately inflicting on the group conditions of life calculated to bring about its physical destruction in whole or in part.
(d) Imposing measures intended to prevent birth within the group.
(e) Forcible transferring children of the group to another group.

On the basis of this official legal definition, did seventeenth- through mid-twentieth-century colonialism/imperialism (largely European, later including the United States) constitute or generate genocide? What of the bringing of Christianity to indigenous peoples? What of the "carpet" or "saturation" bombings of German cities by Allied forces during the Second World War—or the U.S. atomic bombings of Hiroshima and Nagaski? What of the dumping of toxic waste in developing countries by developed nations? What of the employment by transnational corporations of security forces to drive local populations off their ancestral lands and thereby win control over valuable natural resources? What of economic and political policies adopted by national and international financial institutions that inflict foreseeably severe harms upon economically vulnerable social classes—including, in some cases, severe privation and death? In each case, substantiate your response by making an argument. What differences would you wish to make between any of the examples given in this set of questions? Would you, in each case, reach different conclusions if the basis of your analysis were rooted in Lemkin's definition of "genocide" rather than in Card's—and vice versa? Does Card's argument that the distinguishing evil of "genocide" is "social death" make a difference to the outcome of your analysis?

4. If, with respect to the case of Hiroshima and Nagasaki, you were to conclude that the U.S. atomic bombings there did not constitute acts of genocide, might you conclude

differently were it incontrovertibly proven, as Gar Alperovitz, Lionel R. Bauman Professor of Political Economy at the University of Maryland, has argued in *Atomic Diplomacy: Hiroshima and Potsdam: The Use of the Atomic Bomb and the American Confrontation with Soviet Power* (New York: Simon and Schuster, 1965), that the first use of these terrible weapons was unnecessary, that this was understood by decision-makers at the time, and that there was very substantial though not absolutely definitive evidence that by late summer 1945 the decision was primarily influenced by strategic considerations related to Soviet expansionism in Eastern Asia? Why? Why not?

5. Why, in Card's view, do war crimes and crimes against humanity fail to capture the specific and particular evil of genocide? Do you agree with her? Disagree?

6. Like Card, Diane Orentlicher in "Genocide" (note 3) observes that political groups are not protected under the 1948 Genocide Convention, and bemoans this fact, pointing out that political groups can be as identifiable and vulnerable as national, ethnical, racial, or religious groups recognized under the Convention. Card, however, argues that "If social death is central to the harm of genocide, then it really is right not to count as a genocide the annihilation of just any political group, however heinous." Do you agree with Card? Why? Why not? If you disagree, does this mean that you believe that Card's equation of "genocide" with "social death" is inadequate or insufficient for definitional purposes? How so?

7. Is persecution of people on the basis of sexual orientation capable of being classified as genocide? What about crimes against humanity?

8. The United States did not ratify the 1948 Genocide Convention until 1988, and then with reservations that are somewhat disabling. By the time the United States ratified the convention, 97 other UN members had already done so. "Such resistance is interesting," observes Card, "in view of questions raised during the interim regarding the morality of U.S. conduct in Vietnam." What does Card mean by this?

9. Why did it take so long for the United States to ratify the Genocide Convention? Could U.S. Senate rules and a "Solid Democratic South" dominated by conservative politicians have had something to do with it, much as the "Solid Republican South" dominated by conservative politicians operates in U.S. politics today? If so, what does this imply for (a) U.S. constitutionalism and (b) U.S. leadership in the advancement of international human rights? Might some form of racism be lurking in the background? A form of isolationism or exceptionalism—such as described in Reading 7 (Somers and Roberts) in Chapter 1? Or is it all a matter simply of changing the Senate rules?

10. On numerous occasions, the former UN Commission on Human Rights (replaced by the UN Human Rights Council in 2006 as the principal UN mechanism and the forum charged to promote and protect human rights) failed to condemn acts of genocide due in part to some of its own members being states known or alleged to have committed genocide. In your view, did this failure of the UNCHR have the effect of condoning genocidal activity? Or was it merely a result of a coincidence of UNCHR membership without normative consequence? In any event, do you agree that membership on the UN Human Rights Council should be restricted to states without a genocidal history? Why? Why not? Can you identify any state without a history that, from some perspective, could be characterized as "genocidal"? If so, which state, and on what basis?

11. Even in recent times, as is well known, the 1948 Genocide Convention has been breached with disturbing frequency, including by states parties to the Convention. Given these facts, what legal or other significance does the Convention have? Is it law today, or merely the illusion of law?

12. What is the significance of classifying crimes aimed at destroying a group "genocide"? What difference does the classification make?

9. JONATHAN TODRES *Law, Otherness, and Human Trafficking*

A gross violation of human rights, slavery has been condemned globally and is viewed by most as a terrible relic of the past. Yet the incidence of human trafficking—a modern form of the slave trade[1]—persists and, in fact, continues to grow. Today, human trafficking is a multibillion dollar industry.[2] While the international community has turned its focus to human trafficking in recent years, progress on the issue has been slow and selective. A central reason for this limited success is the prevailing conception of the problem, which, in turn, forms the basis of the law developed to combat human trafficking.

I submit that "otherness"—the quality of being not alike, being distinct or different from that otherwise experienced or known[3]—is a root cause of both inaction and the selective nature of responses to the abusive practice of human trafficking. It facilitates the abuse and exploitation of particular individuals and operates across multiple dimensions to reinforce a conception of a virtuous "Self" and a lesser "Other." To successfully combat human trafficking, it is essential to recognize and acknowledge all facets of the Self, including its responsibility in fostering or tolerating the conditions under which the Other can be exploited.

This article attempts to unpack the impact of otherness on the prevailing understanding of human trafficking and legal responses to it, with a view to developing a more effective approach to combating this modern form of slavery.

[*Eds.*—The author next examines the definition and complexities of "otherness" and the process of "othering." Drawing on feminist legal scholarship, postcolonial feminism, critical race theory, and other critical legal studies, he discusses how otherness operates to render certain individuals, groups, and populations in all countries vulnerable to the exploitation of human trafficking. Othering, he observes, "operates across multiple dimensions, including race, gender, ethnicity, class, caste, culture, and geography" and results in "a devaluation of certain individuals, communities, and even nations, and a privileging of those who are members of the dominant group, class, or country."[4] Exposing otherness and its impact, he argues, "is therefore the first step toward developing more effective measures to combat this trade in persons." In this regard and in particular, the author focuses on the othering that takes place in the Global North. While acknowledging that othering occurs virtually everywhere in the world, the othering that is fostered and sustained by the Global North, he observes, has by virtue of that region's dominance in the international arena "particularly far-reaching implications, including the shaping of international agendas and treaties." The author then turns his attention to the legal responses to human trafficking in the present world order, both international and national.]

LEGAL RESPONSES TO HUMAN TRAFFICKING

Today, the "rule of law" is advanced as a necessary component for just societies. Inherent in that push is an assumption that law is objective

Excerpted with changes by permission of the *Santa Clara Law Review* from Jonathan Todres, "Law, Otherness, and Human Trafficking," *Santa Clara Law Review* 49 (2009): 605–72. Copyright © 2009 Santa Clara Law Review.

1. I refer to human trafficking as a modern form of slavery because, while parallels between the two exist, trafficking does not map precisely onto the nineteenth-century slave trade (states openly sanctioned slavery, whereas today law prohibits human trafficking). For so many victims of human trafficking, however, the experience equates to enslavement.
2. The profits realized by trade in human beings trails only the arms trade and drug trade. The potential for profit from human trafficking is immense in part because, unlike with arms and drugs, which an individual can sell only once, a human being can be sold repeatedly. Traffickers earn an estimated five to ten billion dollars each year.
3. Princeton WordNet, Otherness, http://wordnet web.princeton.edu/perl/webwn?s=OTHERNESS [*Eds.*—accessed 17 June 2015].

4. *Eds.*—The author adds: "Some populations experience 'intersectional othering' because they possess multiple characteristics that are devalued in the current global power structure. For example, poor women of color in developing countries confront othering across potentially all of the above mentioned dimensions, giving them little or no voice in shaping the dominant understanding of human trafficking or appropriate remedies to the problem."

and just. We know that this is often not the case. After all, law governed Nazi Germany, entrenched apartheid in South Africa, and protected the institution of slavery in the United States and elsewhere. Whether it was anti-Semitic laws of 1930s Germany, racist laws of South Africa's apartheid era, or Jim Crow laws in the United States, the law has been utilized throughout history to institutionalize the views of those in power that certain individuals count as whole persons, while others are something less than human.

In more recent history, scholars from various disciplines have demonstrated that law is shaped by, and reflects, human biases. Legal systems were built on bifurcated conceptions of the dominant group and the subaltern. Ratna Kapur explains, "the liberal project could reconcile promises of universality with exclusions in practice through a clear and persuasive logic. Rights and benefits were linked to the capacity to reason, and the capacity to reason was tied to notions of biological determinism, racial and religious superiority, and civilizational maturity."[5] Thus, systematic exclusion through law was accepted as applied to some. Even when the intent to exclude was not explicit, the dominant discourse or regime operated to establish legal structures that further entrenched the privileging of some and exclusion of others.

In other words, throughout history, societies have developed legal systems that simultaneously promote equality for some and permit, or even promote, enslavement or exploitation of others. But shortcomings in the development of law do not mean that law serves solely as an obstacle. Attempting to foster progress, the international community, dating to the early twentieth century, has proffered legal measures aimed at combating human trafficking. The efficacy of these legal developments, however, is compromised by the failure to account for the impact of otherness.

INTERNATIONAL LEGAL RESPONSES TO HUMAN TRAFFICKING

In the past decade, the international community has launched major initiatives aimed at combating human trafficking. It has promul-

5. Ratna Kapur, "The Citizen and the Migrant: Postcolonial Anxieties, Law, and the Politics of Exclusion/Inclusion," *Theoretical Inquiries Law* (2007): 537–70, 541.

gated two significant international treaties on the issue—the Protocol to Prevent, Suppress and Punish Trafficking in Persons, Especially Women and Children, Supplementing the United Nations Convention against Transnational Organized Crime, and the Optional Protocol to the Convention on the Rights of the Child on the Sale of Children, Child Prostitution and Child Pornography. This effort has been coupled with other international treaties—e.g., the Rome Statute of the International Criminal Court, and ILO Convention No. 182 Concerning the Prohibition and Immediate Action for the Elimination of the Worst Forms of Child Labor—that, while not focusing only on trafficking, recognize the grave nature of the offense of human trafficking.

These legal measures have been supplemented by major international and regional policies and programs that reinforce the international legal requirements set forth in the new multilateral treaties. Together, these steps evidence a commitment by the international community to address this modern form of slavery.

The important issue is the degree to which these measures have been effective. These new developments, [reflecting] something of a renewed focus, build upon—intentionally or not—the historical approach to trafficking. I highlight the most salient elements of the historical development, features that evidence the presence of othering and exclusion to the detriment of particular populations. Following that, I return to the most recent legal developments to examine the same questions.

HISTORICAL VIEW

In examining the historical development of international legal measures to combat human trafficking, two key concepts emerge. First is that from the outset the aim was not to guard against the trafficking of all persons, but rather only white women (and girls). While that has long since been remedied formalistically in international law, its legacy has not. Second, the historical development of the law evolved to understand trafficking as fundamentally linked with prostitution. Though numerous individuals are trafficked for prostitution, the linkage between the two has led, in many instances, to overlooking the extent to which persons are trafficked for other forms of exploitation.

To begin, the early international treaties on human trafficking focused on "white slave traffic" and preventing "procuring of women or girls for immoral purposes abroad."[6] The International Agreement for the Suppression of White Slave Traffic of 1904 and the International Convention for the Suppression of the White Slave Traffic of 1910 evidence by name that international concern was only for white women and girls.

When used in these early conventions, the term "white slave" was not new. It was first used in the earlier part of the nineteenth century to refer to English factory workers, but fell into disuse until it was resurrected in 1870 by Victor Hugo.[7] In a letter to the British social reformer Josephine Butler, Hugo wrote, "the slavery of black women is abolished in America; but the slavery of white women continues in Europe."[8] Accordingly, the 1902 Paris Conference, which led to the 1904 treaty, focused on "traite des blanches" (or "trade in whites") in discussing the importance of abolition of the international trafficking in women. Women of color, as well as men and boys, were not on the liberal agenda.

In 1910, delegates to the Madrid Conference finally questioned the label, noting it failed to cover women of color. However, the conference decided to keep the white slave term "because it had become a household word."[9] While public awareness campaigns and social movements depend on easily recognizable slogans to carry their message and enhance the likelihood of their success, this decision demonstrated that increasing the chance of success of a campaign to protect white women was of greater value to the international community than calling attention to the fact that women of color (as well as men and boys) were being exploited. In all likelihood, that exclusion does not happen with such ease unless those being excluded are considered less important—a devalued Other. Subsequent treaties, such as the 1921 International Convention for the Suppression of the Traffic in Women and Children, made incremental progress by abandoning the term "white slave traffic" and by including children of both genders. However, this history of overlooking devalued populations continues to play out today.

The second historical lesson is that the linking of trafficking and prostitution led to overlooking the extent to which persons are trafficked for other forms of exploitation. Following the early international treaties, the next landmark step occurred in 1949, with the adoption of the Convention for the Suppression of the Traffic in Persons and of the Exploitation of the Prostitution of Others.[10] While the 1949 Convention represented a step forward by being the first gender-neutral convention on trafficking and by dropping the requirement that trafficking have an international nexus to be a crime, it also focused solely on trafficking for purposes of prostitution and failed to cover labor trafficking. Conventions developed to combat forced labor were seen as distinct and not employed in the trafficking context. Thus, reinforced by an otherness-driven notion of the iconic victim-subject, the law on human trafficking came to neglect those trafficked for work in sweatshops or on farms, as domestic servants, for forced marriages, or for use in armed conflict.

The legacy of these two historical developments—exclusion of certain populations of color from protection in the early years, and linking trafficking only to prostitution—is reflected in the new law emerging today.

CURRENT LAW

Today, the international legal framework on human trafficking—set forth in greatest detail in the Trafficking Protocol and the CRC Protocol—requires states to combat human trafficking through: (1) criminalization and prosecution of acts of trafficking, (2) development of trafficking

6. See, e.g., International Agreement for the Suppression of White Slave Traffic (18 May 1904); International Convention for the Suppression of the White Slave Traffic (4 May 1910); International Convention for the Suppression of the Traffic in Women and Children (30 September 1921); Convention for the Suppression of the Traffic in Persons and of the Exploitation of the Prostitution of Others (21 March 1950).
7. Nora V. Demleitner, "Forced Prostitution: Naming an International Offense," *Fordham International Law Journal* 18 (1994): 163–97, 165 (quoting Victor Hugo letter).
8. Ibid. Apparently Hugo and others believed the mere act of adopting the Reconstruction Amendments meant slavery of black women ended and only white women now suffered harm.
9. Ibid.
10. Hereinafter 1949 Convention.

prevention programs, and (3) provision of assistance to victims of trafficking. A review of current law reveals important manifestations of otherness, further entrenching an approach that ultimately hampers efforts to combat human trafficking.

First, the strongest obligations under international law are tied to the first requirement, that of criminalization of acts of trafficking. Article 5 of the Trafficking Protocol includes the following mandatory language: "each State Party shall adopt such legislative and other measures as may be necessary to establish as criminal offences the conduct set forth in the Protocol's definition of 'trafficking in persons.'" In contrast, while Article 9 of the Trafficking Protocol requires that states parties "shall establish comprehensive policies, programmes and other measures" to prevent human trafficking, it immediately weakens that obligation by setting forth in Article 9(1)–(2) that "States Parties shall endeavour to undertake measures such as research, information and mass media campaigns and social and economic initiatives to prevent and combat trafficking in persons."

Similarly, with respect to assisting victims of trafficking, Trafficking Protocol Article 6(3) requires only that "each State Party shall consider implementing measures to provide for the physical, psychological and social recovery of victims of trafficking in persons." Juxtaposed against flat obligations to criminalize acts of trafficking, the weaker language on prevention and assistance expresses a lesser commitment. This lesser expectation or obligation under international law to assist those who have been harmed or are at risk of harm has two important results. First, as states seek to implement or comply with international law, they have focused their resources on complying with obligations to criminalize trafficking and have done less to assist vulnerable populations as less is required. In other words, to the extent a state intends to comply with international law, it knows it can fulfill its obligations even with minimal efforts with regard to assisting victims or developing prevention measures. Second, as mentioned above, law has an expressive function—reflecting a societal expression of what is valued—and thus international law that expresses a lower priority on assisting marginalized persons reaffirms the otherness-shaped perspectives and values held by citizens.

Some critics might maintain that there are

"practical" reasons for the different levels of obligation in these two protocols that form the core international law on human trafficking—e.g., it is easier to pass legislation to criminalize an act than to ensure victims receive assistance. However, when the international community decides on a lesser obligation for a particular step, it articulates the view that it is acceptable for states to exert less effort implementing those provisions. Second, the assertion that it is easier to criminalize trafficking than assist victims relies on a comparison of unequal outcomes. Both areas require states to adopt laws or regulations—in the case of the former, criminal law; in the case of the latter, laws or regulations that establish and support assistance programs. Laws to assist victims can be adopted with the same ease as new criminal law provisions. Ensuring full implementation of each law—that is, ensuring that all who violate anti-trafficking laws are punished and all who are victims are provided assistance—is a separate issue, and it is unclear that achieving the former is any easier than achieving the latter. Certainly there are generalized questions about the enforcement mechanisms of international law, but that does not fully explain why the international community agrees on the one hand that the elimination of human trafficking requires action on three fronts (protection, prevention, and prosecution) but creates law that permits states to do less vis-à-vis the two steps that would assist marginalized communities.

Other proponents of maintaining differential obligations might suggest that criminalization ties to negative rights, whereas prevention and assistance to victims likely involve positive rights that require resources, and thus the language was intended to provide flexibility for resource-constrained states. In fact, civil and political rights require resources just as economic, social, and cultural rights do. Moreover, had the treaty required that states shall implement measures to assist victims, such language would not have dictated a level of resources, but would have made it impossible for a state to "consider" but ultimately reject measures to assist victims of trafficking. Mandatory language also would have had the expressive function of stating that assistance to victims and prevention measures carry the same import as criminal statutes.

When mapped on the otherness-shaped understanding of human trafficking, the differential obligations make more sense. Flat obligations to criminalize fit with the dominant understanding that the problem primarily is a relatively small number of deviant actors who need to be punished (and the dominant group can be the savior by punishing those deviants). Lack of prioritization of assistance to victims and prevention also fits with an understanding of human trafficking that is based on a world view that does not fully value the trafficked Other.

This lesser valuation of the Other in current international law on the issue is reminiscent of the tiered priorities of the early treaties aimed at ending the white slave trade. In 2005, the Council of Europe adopted a treaty to combat human trafficking.[11] Its focus is on trafficking of persons in Europe, where a larger percentage of the victims are white. In the Council of Europe treaty, Member States agreed to stronger language on prevention and assistance to victims. Thus states that had participated in the drafting of Trafficking Protocol and CRC Protocol just a few years earlier now were willing to make a stronger commitment to the victims of trafficking. It is possible they had learned more was needed. It is also possible that those states related more to the European victims and were motivated to do more to help them.

Further, under the current international legal regime on human trafficking, what is "generally accepted" as the international definition of trafficking is enshrined first in a protocol to a treaty on organized crime.[12] That organized crime is involved in, and benefits from, human trafficking is not to be denied, but this placement reflects a narrow conception of the issue as caused by a limited number of deviants who bear no connection to the Self. By focusing on prosecuting bad actors, the dominant group reinforces its self-perception as savior, even while providing little real assistance to most trafficking victims or those who might be at risk of being trafficked.

The placement of anti-trafficking provisions within the framework of a treaty on organized crime also suggests that trafficking occurs solely because of organized crime, which diverts our attention from the role played by each of us in society in tolerating the societal conditions that facilitate this trade in persons. The reality is that the problem of human trafficking goes well beyond the actions of underground organized criminal networks. Yet the Trafficking Protocol relies upon definitions in the underlying Convention on Transnational Organized Crime, and thus it addresses only those acts of trafficking that are transnational in nature and involve an organized criminal group. These definitions serve to limit the scope of the Trafficking Protocol, leaving intracountry trafficking beyond the treaty's reach, even though it harms a greater number of victims.

Finally, the historical focus on sex trafficking at the expense of victims of labor trafficking is evidenced here as well. Not only has international law given less attention to labor trafficking, discussions of trafficking and prostitution have often led to a conflation of the two. As a result, questions and discussion of consent are imported into dialogue on trafficking. Proposals and critiques of the definition of human trafficking have led, in some instances, to a conflating of the terms trafficking, smuggling, migration, and even prostitution. The definitional questions are further complicated as a result of the narrow perception of the iconic victim-subject.

The above discussion is not intended to suggest that current international legal measures are all counterproductive. However, the actual progress would seem to be less significant than the dominant narrative suggests. This is due in part to the fact that mainstream conclusions are built upon an understanding of the issue that overlooks the impact of otherness. So, weaknesses in the law (e.g., lesser obligations on assistance and prevention; omitting labor trafficking in some instances; and failure to cover intracountry trafficking victims and others who do not fit the prototypical victim profile) go unchallenged. Understanding how otherness has infused our international legal responses to human trafficking can help bring to the forefront the gaps in the international legal regime. Similar benefits emerge from an analysis of the impact of otherness at the national level.

11. See Council of Europe Convention on Action against Trafficking in Human Beings.
12. See Protocol to Prevent, Suppress and Punish Trafficking in Persons, Especially Women and Children, Supplementing the United Nations Convention against Transnational Organized Crime (15 November 2000).

NATIONAL LAW ON HUMAN TRAFFICKING: THE U.S. EXAMPLE

[*Eds.*—The author here focuses on the United States as a case study to illustrate how otherness affects national law on human trafficking. The historical U.S. approach, he writes, "resembles the early international efforts discussed above and similarly incorporates a racialized and gendered othering into the law." In recent years, he observes "there has been a renewed commitment by the U.S. government to make progress in combating human trafficking" such that "the U.S. federal government has adopted several significant pieces of legislation in the past decade, and at least thirty states now have their own law on human trafficking."[13] However, the "modern" U.S. approach, formally launched with the 1998 anti-trafficking directive from President Clinton, the author perceives to "[reflect] an otherness-shaped understanding of human trafficking." The United States, he observes, citing the Trafficking Victims Protection Act of 2000 (TVPA) and its subsequent reauthorizations,[14] follows "a law enforcement model," targeting sex trafficking much more than labor trafficking, and focuses primarily on the international aspects of the problem, emphasizing prosecutions and border controls that have "done little to reduce the incidence of trafficking, in part because a very small percentage of traffickers have been prosecuted and because tougher criminal sanctions do not address root causes of vulnerability of particular populations." He notes in particular the federal legislation that has been strengthened to facilitate prosecutions of sex tourists on their return home,[15] finding it wanting despite its "laudable" intent (and limited success) because it reinforces "the perception that the problem is caused by a select number of aberrant men who travel overseas to engage in such illegal acts." The U.S. law enforcement approach, he maintains, "overlooks more effective ways of addressing the issues, instead relying on a narrative that has the virtuous Self rescuing victims from deviant others." As evidence, he points to the TVPA mandatory annual U.S. review of other countries' progress in combating human trafficking, premised on the viewpoint that the problem lies with other countries and thus perpetuating "the narrative of the virtuous Self and the lesser Other." To the same end, he points out that while foreign victims of trafficking are able to receive assistance (pursuant to an oft-praised element of the TVPA, the T-visa), "similarly situated domestic victims" typically are not—thus building on concepts of otherness that "serve to reinforce the idea that the problem is . . . with the Other, and the Self, if at all involved, is so only as 'rescuer.'"]

ENFORCEMENT OF THE LAW

The impact of otherness is not limited to legislation on human trafficking. Building on the otherness-rooted law, those seeking to enforce the law—from police, to prosecutors, to judges—further add their own, often subconscious, perceptions of the Other into the mix, frequently exacerbating the problem. Many law enforcement officials exhibit "a particular type of myopia in which they only see a person as a victim if they, themselves, have rescued her."[16] In fact, most victims are not rescued but rather find their own way out of a brothel, sweatshop, farm, or other exploitative setting, after suffering physical, emotional, psychological, or sexual abuse, and eventually present at a shelter, health clinic, or other service provider.

In short, many cases reinforce the need to better account for the impact of otherness on legal responses to human trafficking. To the extent that individuals or peoples are devalued or

---

13. One might fairly question why the United States took a particular interest in human trafficking in the 1990s. There is at least some evidence that U.S. action was tied to the increase in human trafficking in Europe, following the fall of the Soviet Union. See *Briefing on the Trafficking of Women and Children in the United States and Europe, Commission on Security and Cooperation in Europe*, 106th Cong. (1999) (testimony of Rep. Chris Smith) (noting about 4,000 of the 50,000 women and children trafficked into the United States annually come from the former Soviet Union and Eastern Europe); 145 Cong. Rec. S7835–6, S7843 (1999) (statement of Sen. Wellstone) (discussing in detail women trafficked from the former Soviet Union, while mentioning more briefly young girls being sold by their families in Thailand).

14. See Trafficking Victims Protection Act of 2000, Pub. L. No. 106-386, 114 Stat. 1464 (2000).

15. See 18 U.S.C.A. §§2421–2424 (West 2008). The United States is one of a number of countries that has adopted legislation criminalizing sex tourists' actions; others include Australia, Belgium, Canada, Denmark, Finland, France, Germany, Iceland, New Zealand, Norway, Sweden, and the UK.

16. Dina F. Haynes, "(Not) Found Chained to a Bed in a Brothel: Conceptual, Legal, and Procedural Failures to Fulfill the Promise of the Trafficking Victims Protection Act," *Geographical Immigration Law Journal* 21 (2007): 337–81, 349.

dehumanized, the legal process is compromised. Moreover, devaluation of victims' circumstances, experiences, and options in these cases reinforces and furthers the ongoing othering of certain peoples. When this othering is encapsulated in judicial opinions, the law reinforces a collective consciousness built on the Self/Other dichotomy. Making significant, meaningful progress on these issues will take much more than just a continuation of current policies. The next section sets out considerations that, I submit, will foster a more effective approach to combating human trafficking.

ACCOUNTING FOR OTHERNESS TO ADDRESS HUMAN TRAFFICKING

In recent years, new "mainstreaming" efforts have been underway to foster gender equality and to fully account for the needs of children. The Beijing Platform of Action launched a mandate for all governments and nongovernmental actors to mainstream a gender perspective into all policies and programs.[17] As the ILO describes:

Mainstreaming a gender perspective is the process of assessing the implications for women and men of any planned action, including legislation, policies or programmes, in any area and at all levels. It is a strategy for making the concerns and experiences of women as well as of men an integral part of the design, implementation, monitoring and evaluation of policies and programmes in all political, economic and societal spheres, so that women and men benefit equally, and inequality is not perpetuated.[18]

Similar efforts have been advanced in the children's right arena, including, for example, a children's rights sensitive approach to urban development. The process involves contemplating the impact on children of any decision at any stage in urban planning and also involving children's perspectives in the process.

Drawing upon the principles of these and other efforts, I suggest that we need to develop a similar approach of mainstreaming the Other and the experience and voice of the Other. To be clear, mainstreaming does not suggest assimilation of views, but rather a full accounting and incorporation of the full range of perspectives.

I propose that the following seven questions be a part of any process for developing, implementing, monitoring, and evaluating anti-trafficking law, policies, programs, or initiatives. Designed to develop better responses to the incidence of human trafficking, ultimately they have utility in addressing other forms of exploitation.

1. WHAT IMPACT WILL THE LAW/POLICY/PROGRAM HAVE ON SUBALTERN COMMUNITIES?

Developers of anti-trafficking laws, policies, and programs need to ask how subaltern communities and individuals will be affected. The impact of new anti-trafficking initiatives on historically disadvantaged individuals and communities, including persons of color, women, children, refugee and internally displaced persons, and others, must be considered on an ongoing basis at every stage in the process. Related to this, an assessment of the impact on the subaltern communities necessarily means asking the question of how bias shapes the initiative in question. Doing so requires asking not if but how bias against these communities is either addressed or further entrenched by a new initiative.

2. HOW WILL THE INITIATIVE ADDRESS THE SELF'S ROLE IN SUSTAINING TRAFFICKING?

Advocates working to combat human trafficking have called attention to the need to address the demand side of the equation. Addressing demand-side issues in a way that accounts for otherness means reexamining several commonly held beliefs.

First, we need to rethink who is creating the demand and recognize that it is not only the pedophile or other sexually deviant outsider who creates demand, but rather the "everyman" (and on occasion female customers) when the issue is

17. See Fourth World Conference on Women, 15 September 1995, Beijing Declaration and Platform for Action, Fourth World Conference on Women, UN Docs. A/CONF.177/20, A/CONF.177/20/Add.1.
18. ILO, Definition of Gender Mainstreaming, http://www.ilo.org/public/english/bureau/gender/newsite2002/about/defin.htm [*Eds.*—accessed 6 June 2015]. See also World Health Organization, "What Is 'Gender Mainstreaming'?" http://www. who.int/gender /mainstreaming/en [*Eds.*—accessed 6 June 2015].

sex trafficking. Addressing demand for sex trafficking means examining broader societal views that promote the acceptability of sexual exploitation and objectification of certain individuals.

Second, addressing demand means recognizing that trafficking is not restricted to trafficking for sexual purposes. Individuals are trafficked for a range of reasons, including forced labor. Who benefits from the forced labor? Essentially all of us who purchase goods made by companies that rely on or benefit from cheap, exploited labor.

Finally, the role of the Self (or dominant group) on the supply side must be examined. When the root causes of vulnerability are examined, it must be asked what role the dominant group plays in entrenching inequality and heightening vulnerability of particular populations.

3. What Impact Do Subaltern Communities Believe the Initiative Will Have? What Role Will They Have in Developing the Initiative?

The current discourse on human trafficking tends to conflate poverty with lack of agency. The resulting picture is that of a voiceless, helpless victim. That perception must change. Subaltern communities at risk must be involved in the development of initiatives. They offer insights that those who are part of the dominant power structure do not see or struggle to appreciate. If those in the dominant power structure do not consult subaltern communities and allow them to shape solutions, anti-trafficking efforts will fail to realize their potential. Moreover, the first question above of how subaltern communities will be affected by a new law or policy cannot be answered solely by those in the dominant group in society. To do so runs the risk of preserving or reinforcing inequalities and marginalization while celebrating supposed progress.

4. Does the Initiative Account for Both Short- and Long-Term Factors?

A number of scholars have highlighted the need for antitrafficking initiatives to address both short-term and long-term factors. Efforts to combat human trafficking must account for both "structural" and "proximate" factors. Structural factors include economic factors (e.g., globaliza-

tion, poverty, market economies, migration), social factors (e.g., inequality, discrimination and marginalization, prostitution), ideological factors (e.g., racism, xenophobia, gender and cultural stereotyping), and geopolitical factors (e.g., war, civil strife, conflict). Proximate factors include: legal and policy aspects (e.g., inadequate national and international legal regimes, poor law enforcement, immigration laws, labor laws), rule of law (e.g., corruption, state complicity in supporting trafficking), and inadequate partnership between civil society and state (e.g., weak education campaigns, low public awareness, lack of state accountability).

To date, insufficient attention has been centered on understanding why particular communities are more vulnerable to exploitation. Once the focus is shifted to underlying causes, we can begin to see, for example, that in conflict-affected countries, human trafficking "is also precipitated by the collapsed economic conditions . . . where women face extreme poverty, economic discrimination, and lack of sustainable incomes. With limited or no resources, women [and children] become easy prey for recruiters." Ethnic minorities are often particularly at risk, as discrimination marginalizes and heightens vulnerability.

Addressing structural factors also means looking at economic, social, and cultural rights, as they are crucial to strengthening communities. Lack of health rights, education rights, labor rights and other economic, social, and cultural rights push members of communities deeper into poverty and more risky situations. Fully valuing all rights requires overcoming the Western conception of a hierarchy of rights and the view that civil and political rights are more important than economic, social, and cultural rights. Structural issues—poverty, discrimination, lack of fulfillment of economic and social rights, and so on—present not just in day-to-day practices and relationships but also in the law. Accounting for short-term and long-term factors means reviewing current law to assess whether it fully accounts for both and building such a review into the development of future legal measures.

5. Does the Initiative Help the Dominant Groups Come to Better Understand/Know the Other?

Too frequently, law and policy are developed from a reliance on anecdotal evidence of a few compelling cases (which resonates with lawmakers because such examples play on otherness-shaped ideas of the victims). Women in developing countries are often represented as "thoroughly disempowered, brutalized, and victimized: a representation that is far from liberating for women."[19] This stereotype "recreates the imperialist move that views the native subject as different and civilizationally backward. The image that is produced is that of a truncated Third World woman who is sexually constrained, tradition-bound, incarcerated in the home, illiterate, and poor."[20] While it is true that many victims of trafficking have been disempowered in important respects, it is also true that other victims present very differently. Anti-trafficking strategies that assume all victims are "similarly oppressed" can have the unintended result of "perpetuating the exclusion of the very constituency they claim to represent, through cultural, religious, or sexual 'Othering.' "

A more sophisticated understanding of subaltern communities and their experience is crucial to combating human trafficking. As Gayatri Spivak writes, "there is a distinction between the superficial desire to 'learn about' the Other and the desire to 'know' the non-West through conscious and assiduous study and participation."[21] The dominant group must come to know the Other. This means hearing the diversity of voices and experiences of the Other, and hearing the experience of those trafficked so that the dominant group may come to better understand the impact of its actions on the marginalized. Thus, at every stage of developing responses to human trafficking, a fundamental question must be whether the process is bringing us closer to knowing the Other.

6. Does the Initiative Reflect an Appreciation of the Common Experience?

Nearly 150 years ago, Giuseppe Mazzini wrote that "your first duties, first, not as to time, but as to importance—because unless you understand these, you can only imperfectly fulfill the rest—your first duties are towards Humanity."[22] This call for a sense of the common experience has been obstructed by otherness, which serves to create a distance between the Self and the Other and to frustrate any development of a sense of a shared humanity. To mitigate otherness's harmful effects, we need to bridge that gap and restore an understanding of the common experience. Martha Fineman has suggested this in writing about the "vulnerable subject" and arguing for reclaiming the term "vulnerab[ility]" to represent "a universal, inevitable, enduring aspect of the human condition that must be at the heart of our concept of social and state responsibility."[23] The question must be asked of any new anti-trafficking initiative whether it reflects a sense of shared humanity, whether it addresses the experience of the vulnerable as we would want it addressed were we the vulnerable, as ultimately we all are.

19. Ratna Kapur, "The Tragedy of Victimization Rhetoric: Resurrecting the 'Native' Subject in International/Post-Colonial Feminist Legal Politics," *HHRJ* 15 (2002): 1–37, 6.
20. Ibid. For discussion of the "victim subject" in the context of violence against women, see 18–22.
21. Ratna Kapur, *Erotic Justice: Law and the New Politics of Postcolonialism* (London: Glass House Press, 2005), 5 (quoting Gayatri Spivak).
22. Giuseppe Mazzini, *The Duties of Man* (1862; New York: Funk and Wagnalls, 1892), 44. [*Eds.*—A politician, journalist, and activist for the unification of Italy, Mazzini was also an early advocate of a United States of Europe. Professor Todres comments further:] While Mazzini's language and thought reflected, in many respects, the nineteenth-century European intellectual mindset, he also moved beyond that in recognizing the exclusion of at least one Other, by closing his famous book with a reminder to his fellow countrymen: "In bidding you farewell, I will remind you of another duty, not less solemn than that which binds you to achieve and preserve the freedom and unity of your Country. Your complete emancipation can only be founded and secured upon the triumph of a Principle—the principle of the Unity of the Human Family. At present day one half of the Human Family is, by a singular contradiction, declared civilly, politically and socially unequal, and excluded from the great Unity. To you who are seeking your own enfranchisement and emancipation in the name of a Religious Truth, to you it belongs to protest on every occasion and by every means against this negation of Unity. The Emancipation of Women, then must be regarded by you as necessarily linked with the emancipation of the workingman. This will give to your endeavors the consecration of a Universal Truth" (146).
23. Martha A. Fineman, "The Vulnerable Subject: Anchoring Equality in the Human Condition," *Yale Journal of Law and Feminism* 20 (2008): 1–23, 8.

7. The "Then What?" Question

The final step aims to provide a safety net in cases where the above questions do not result in a full accounting for otherness. For example, when a victim of trafficking is "rescued," given temporary shelter, and then repatriated to her home country, then what? If she returns to a community where there remain no opportunities for a life much beyond subsistence, then what? She is likely to look for other opportunities, as most of us would, and may be as vulnerable to exploitation as before. The same question must be asked when domestic victims of trafficking are removed from harmful settings and returned to their home communities. The "then what" question serves to ensure that, as we develop responses to human trafficking, we think through the implications of new laws and policies and their impact on communities and that we include a significant component that addresses structural issues.

CONCLUSION

To develop effective responses to the problem of human trafficking, we need to transform our approach to this issue and related ones. As Kapur writes, "transformative politics can only emerge if we are willing to think from different locations and more creatively."[24] Part of that requires truly getting to know the Other, hearing the voice of the Other, and allowing the Other to share in control of the process.

24. Kapur, *Erotic Justice*, 11.

QUESTIONS FOR REFLECTION AND DISCUSSION

1. Todres argues that "with its attendant devaluation of the Other, [otherness] facilitates the abuse and exploitation of particular individuals [and] operates across multiple dimensions to reinforce a conception of a virtuous 'Self' and a lesser 'Other.' Drawing on Kapur's argument in Chapter 1, Reading 6, can you expand upon the likely nature of that "Other"? And that "Self" of which Todres writes? What themes would you expect to attend the social assumption of "otherness"? Of "selfness"? And why?

2. According to Todres, how does "othering" affect the international legal order? What additional evidence can you find either for or against his viewpoint in this regard?

3. Many victims of human trafficking never cross international borders. What steps could/should be taken to enhance enforcement of domestic human trafficking?

4. Todres argues that it is today believed that "the 'rule of law' is . . . a necessary component for just societies." What about unjust societies, such as un-benign authoritarian or totalitarian societies? Is not the "rule of law" necessary for them as well? What does Todres say? What do we mean by "rule of law"? Is it consistently followed in democratic societies? At home? Abroad?

5. How might "othering" function in contemporary legal practices reflecting anxieties around national security?

6. Todres argues that the "modern" U.S. approach to curb human trafficking "has been marked by several characteristics, each of which reflects an otherness-shaped understanding of human trafficking." What are those characteristics?

7. What criticisms does Todres level at current laws addressing human trafficking? Do you think there are other potential reasons for the way the law is set up? If so, what are they?

8. Prostitution is illegal in most jurisdictions. Therefore, sex trafficking victims are also perpetrators of the crime of prostitution. What challenges might this pose for combatting sex trafficking?

9. How, according to Todres, might it be possible to develop more effective responses to human trafficking?

10. Analyze each of Todres's seven questions to be addressed when dealing with trafficking. In your view, how helpful is each one and why? On what basis are you making an assessment? What evidence supports your response in each case?

11. Kapur argues that "transformative politics can only emerge if we are willing to think from different locations and more creatively." How might this be achieved? Are you able

to think from the perspective of those you see as different to you? If you cannot, what do you think prevents you from being able to do so? What are the challenges that such a strategy faces (a) at the individual level, (b) at the collective social level, and (c) in law? For each answer you provide to these questions, provide reasons in support of the position you take.

12. What mechanisms and processes do you think would best ensure that all voices and perspectives are heard in relation to trafficking? Draw on Todres, further reading, and evidence to support your response.

10. JEREMY WALDRON *Torture and Positive Law*

My starting point is the dishonor that descended upon the United States early in 2004 as a result of revelations about what happened under American control in Abu Ghraib prison in Iraq. That dishonor involved more than the Abu Ghraib nightmare itself—the photographs of sexual humiliation, the dogs, the hoods, the wires, the beatings. What took place there was not just a result of the depravity of a few poorly trained reservists, but the upshot of a policy determined by intelligence officials to have military police at the prison "set favorable conditions" (that was the euphemism) for the interrogation of detainees.

The dishonor intensified when it was revealed that abuses were not isolated in this one prison, but that brutal interrogations were also being conducted by American officials elsewhere. We know now that a number of captured officers in Iraq and Afghanistan were severely beaten during interrogation by their American captors, and in one case killed by suffocation. We know too that terrorist suspects, enemy combatants, and others associated with the Taliban and Al Qaeda held in the camps at Guantanamo Bay were interrogated using physical and psychological techniques that had been outlawed by the European Court of Human Rights after their use by British forces against terrorist suspects in Northern Ireland in the early 1970s,[1] and outlawed by the Israeli Supreme Court after their

use by security forces in Israel against terrorist suspects in the 1990s.[2]

Above all, my starting point is the realization that these abuses took place not just in the fog of war, but against a legal and political background set by discussions among lawyers and other officials in the White House, the Justice Department, and the Department of Defense about how to narrow the meaning and application of domestic and international legal prohibitions relating to torture.

It is dispiriting as well as shameful to have to turn our attention to this issue. In 1911, the author of the article on "Torture" in the *Encyclopedia Britannica* wrote that "The whole subject is now one of only historical interest as far as Europe is concerned." But it has come to life again. With the growth of the ethnic-loyalty state and the security state in the twentieth century, the emergence of anticolonial insurgencies and other intractable forms of internal armed conflict, and the rise of terrorism, torture has returned. It is not just a rogue-state, third-world, banana-republic phenomenon: the use of torture has in recent decades disfigured the security policies of France (in Algeria), Britain (in Northern Ireland), Israel (in the Occupied Territories), and now the United States (in Iraq, Afghanistan, and Cuba).

Perhaps what is remarkable is not that torture is used, but that it (or something very close to it) is being defended, and by well-known American jurists and law professors. [*Eds.*—The author then describes the writings of professors John Yoo at the University of California at Berkeley School of Law, Alan Dershowitz at Harvard Law

Excerpted with changes by permission of *Columbia Law Review* from Jeremy Waldron, "Torture and Positive Law: Jurisprudence for the White House," *Columbia Law Review* 105 (2005): 1681–750. Copyright © 2005 Columbia Law Review.

1. See *Ireland v. United Kingdom*, 25 Eur. Ct. H.R. (ser. A) at 41, 94 (1978).

2. See *Pub. Comm. against Torture in Israel v. Israel*, (1999) IsrSC 53(4).

School, and Judge Jay Bybee of the Ninth Circuit Federal Court of Appeals, formerly a law professor at Louisiana State University and the University of Nevada, each of whom as well as others, the author observes, have sought "to narrow or modify" the prohibitions on torture in the context of "the war on terror" and "an active doctrine of preemptive self-defense."][3]

I want to place particular emphasis on the fact that these efforts to modify the prohibition on torture have been undertaken by lawyers.

Sure, our primary objection to torture ought to be out of consideration for the potential victims of the treatment that Yoo, Dershowitz, and Bybee appear to condone. But the defense of torture is also shocking as a jurisprudential matter. At the very least, it indicates the necessity of our thinking more deeply about the nature of the rule against torture, its place in our legal system, and the responsibilities that lawyers (particularly lawyers working in government) have to uphold the integrity of our law in this regard.

[*Eds.*—The author next lays out a four-part discourse. The remainder of this extract focuses principally on Parts I and II.]

I. LEGAL DEFINITIONS

THE TEXTS AND THE PROHIBITIONS

The law relating to torture comprises a variety of national, regional, and international norms. The basic provision of human rights law is found in the 1966 International Covenant on Civil and Political Rights (ICCPR) ("the Covenant"):

3. See Memorandum from John Yoo, Deputy Assistant Att'y Gen. and Robert Delahunty, Special Counsel, to William J. Haynes II, Gen. Counsel, Dep't of Def. I, 9 January 2002 (on file with *Columbia Law Review*); Alan Dershowitz, *Shouting Fire: Civil Liberties in a Turbulent Age* (Boston: Little, Brown, 2002), 470–77; Alan Dershowitz, *Why Terrorism Works: Understanding the Threat, Responding to the Challenge* (New Haven, Conn.: YUP, 2002), 132–63; Alan Dershowitz, "Tortured Reasoning," in Sanford Levinson, ed., *Torture: A Collection* (Oxford: OUP, 2004), 257–80, 257; Memorandum from Office of the Assistant Att'y Gen. to Alberto R. Gonzales, Counsel to the President (1 August 2002) (on file with *Columbia Law Review*) (hereinafter Bybee Memorandum).

Article 7 provides that "No one shall be subjected to torture or to cruel, inhuman or degrading treatment or punishment."

Article 4 provides that "In time of public emergency which threatens the life of the nation and the existence of which is officially proclaimed," the States Parties "may take measures derogating from their obligations under the Covenant," but also insists that "No derogation from [Article 7] may be made under [such circumstances]."

The United States ratified the Covenant in 1994, though with the following reservation:

the United States considers itself bound by Article 7 to the extent that "cruel, inhuman or degrading treatment or punishment" means the cruel and unusual treatment or punishment prohibited by the Fifth, Eighth, and or Fourteenth Amendments to the Constitution of the United States.

This is part of a pattern of reservations from human rights conventions in which the United States asserts its right to rely on its own constitutional law in any case of overlap with international human rights law where the international standards might prove more demanding.

Besides the Covenant, we have also to consider a more specific document—the international 1984 Convention against Torture (CAT) ("the Convention"). This instrument requires states to "take effective legislative, administrative, judicial or other measures to prevent acts of torture in any territory under its jurisdiction," and to "ensure that all acts of torture are offences under its criminal law."

Again there is a nonderogation provision (implying in effect that states must establish an absolute rather than a conditional or derogable ban on torture), and again there is a similar reservation relating to cruel, inhuman, and degrading treatment in the U.S. ratification of the Convention. In addition, the Convention goes beyond the Covenant (not to mention regional human rights instruments such as the 1950 European Convention on Human Rights (ECHR), in that it attempts in Article I (1) to give a definition of torture:

For the purposes of this Convention, the term "torture" means any act by which severe pain or suffering, whether physical or mental, is intentionally inflicted on a person for such purposes as obtaining from him or a third person information or a confession, punishing him for an act he or a third person has committed or is suspected of having committed, or intimidating or coercing him or a third person, or for any reason based on discrimination of any kind, when such pain or suffering is inflicted by or at the instigation of or with the consent or acquiescence of a public official or other person acting in an official capacity. It does not include pain or suffering arising only from, inherent in or incidental to lawful sanctions.

This definition, particularly in its reference to the intentional infliction of severe pain, was the starting point of the discussion by Jay Bybee and others.

In pursuance of its obligations under the Convention, the United States has enacted legislation forbidding torture outside the United States by persons subject to U.S. jurisdiction.[4] The anti-torture statute makes it an offense punishable by up to twenty years imprisonment to commit, or conspire or attempt to commit torture. The offense is also punishable by death or life imprisonment if the victim of torture dies as a result. Moreover, §2340(1) of the statute defines torture as follows:

"torture" means an act committed by a person acting under the color of law specifically intended to inflict severe physical or mental pain or suffering (other than pain or suffering incidental to lawful sanctions) upon another person within his custody or physical control.

There is in §2340(2) an additional definition of "severe mental pain and suffering" in terms of "prolonged mental harm" caused by or resulting from the threat of death, physical torture, or the administration of mind-altering substances to oneself or others.

Finally, there are the four 1949 Geneva Conventions, which deal with the treatment of various categories of vulnerable individuals in circumstances of armed conflict. The best-known provision is Article 17 of the third Geneva Convention, which provides that "No physical or mental torture, nor any other form of coercion, may be inflicted on prisoners of war to secure from them information of any kind whatever." In addition, the four Geneva Conventions share a common Article 3, which provides as follows:

Persons taking no active part in the hostilities, including members of armed forces who have laid down their arms . . . shall in all circumstances be treated humanely . . . .

. . . the following acts are and shall remain prohibited at any time and in any place whatsoever with respect to the abovementioned persons:
(a) violence to life and person, in particular murder of all kinds, mutilation, cruel treatment and torture; . . .
(c) outrages upon personal dignity, in particular humiliating and degrading treatment. . . .

Common Article 3 applies to all the persons the Geneva Conventions protect, which include not just prisoners of war, but wounded soldiers, shipwrecked sailors, detained members of irregular forces, and so on.

These provisions, together with the protections that law routinely provides against serious assault and abuse, add up to an interlocking set of prohibitions on torture. They are what I have in mind when I refer to "the prohibition on torture" (or "the rule against torture"), though sometimes one element in this interlocking set, sometimes another, will be most prominent in the arguments that follow.

RULES AND BACKGROUNDS

What is the effect of these provisions? How should we approach them as lawyers? Should we use the same strategies of interpretation as we use elsewhere in the law? Or is there something special about the prohibitions on torture that requires us to treat them more carefully or considerately?[5]

John Yoo has suggested that the Geneva Conventions, read literally, apply to some captives or

---

4. See 18 U.S.C. § 2340 (2000). It is assumed that ordinary provisions of criminal and constitutional law sufficiently prohibit torture within the United States.

5. *Eds.*—These questions occupy the remainder of this essay and the article from which it is derived.

detainees but not others, and that they do not apply to Al Qaeda and Taliban detainees in the war on terror. What sort of reading, what sort of interpretive approach is necessary to reach a conclusion like that? To answer this question, it is helpful to invoke the old distinction between *malum prohibitum* and *malum in se*—two ways in which a legal prohibition may be regarded.

On the *malum prohibitum* approach, we may think about a given legal provision as introducing a prohibition into what was previously a realm of liberty. Overparking is a *malum prohibitum* offense: it consists of violating the letter of the regulations. If the regulations had not been enacted, there would be no offense. And the corollary of this is that anything that is not explicitly prohibited by the regulations remains as free as before.

The other approach is a *malum in se* approach. Some things are just wrong, and would be wrong whether positive law prohibited them or not. So, for example, a statute prohibiting murder characteristically does not make unlawful what was previously permissible; it simply expresses more clearly the unlawfulness of something that was impermissible all along. It follows that consulting the statutory provision in a rigidly textualist spirit might be inappropriate; it certainly would be inappropriate if one were assuming that anything not prohibited by the exact terms of the text must be regarded as something that one was entirely free to do.

All we need to make sense of *malum in se* and distinguish it from *malum prohibitum* is to discern some preexisting normative background to the prohibition that is legally recognizable. That normative background may be a shared moral sense or it may be some higher or background law: natural law, perhaps, or international law. We should note, however, that the distinction between *malum in se* and *malum prohibitum* is not clear cut. Even in our parking example, there will have been some background reasons governing the way it was appropriate to park even before the regulations were introduced: do not park unsafely or inconsiderately, do not block access, and so on. These reasons do not evaporate when the explicit regulations are introduced.

Now let us apply these distinctions to the rule against torture. I think it is obvious that the U.S. anti-torture statute cannot plausibly be construed according to the *malum prohibitum* model. It does not represent the first introduction of a prohibition into an area that was previously un-

regulated. On the contrary, the statute fulfilled a treaty obligation that the United States already had under the Convention, and it also applied and extended the spirit of existing criminal law. It gave definition to an existing and legally recognized sense of the inherent wrongness of torture. Something similar is true of the Convention itself and also of the Covenant, neither of them to be conceived as new pieces of positive international law encroaching into what was previously an unregulated area of freedom. Like all human rights instruments, they have what Gerald Neuman has called a suprapositive aspect, "conceived as reflections of nonlegal principles that have normative force independent of their embodiment in law, or even superior to the positive legal system."[6] Though they are formal treaties based on the actual consent of the states that are party to them, they also represent a consensual acknowledgment of deeper background norms that are binding on nations anyway, treaty or no treaty.

It might be thought that the Geneva Conventions are a special case because they are designed to limit armed conflict. That is, one might think that armed forces are normally at liberty to do anything they like to enemy soldiers in time of war—bombard, shoot, kill, wound, maim, and terrify them—and that the function of the Geneva Conventions is precisely to introduce a degree of unprecedented regulation into what would otherwise be a horrifying realm of freedom. Under this reasoning, the *malum prohibitum* approach is appropriate, and therefore we have no choice but to consult the strict letter of the texts of the Conventions to see exactly what is prohibited and what has been left as a matter of military freedom.

John Yoo's memorandum approaches the Geneva Conventions in that spirit. He implies that absent the Conventions we would be entitled to do anything we like to enemy detainees; grudgingly, however, we must accept some limits (which we ourselves have negotiated and signed up for). But we have signed up for no more than the actual texts stipulate. When we run out of text, we revert to the default position, which is that we can do anything we like.

6. See Gerald L. Neuman, "Human Rights and Constitutional Rights: Harmony and Dissonance," *Stanford Law Review* 55 (2003): 1863–1900, 1868.

Yoo's approach is wrong in three ways. First, its narrow textualism embodies a bewildering refusal to infer anything along *ejusdem generis* lines from the existing array of categories and standards. Professor Yoo proceeds as though the methods of analogy, inference, and reasoned elaboration—the ordinary tools of the lawyerly trade—are utterly inappropriate in this case. In any case, the Geneva Conventions, like the Convention against Torture and the International Covenant, respond to a strongly felt and well-established sense that certain abuses remain beyond the pale even in emergency situations or situations of armed conflict. There are certain things that are not to be done to human beings and these international instruments represent our acknowledgment by treaty of that fact.

Second, Professor Yoo asserts that the United States cannot regard itself as bound by norms of customary international law or even *jus cogens* norms of international law;[7] he thinks that we must regard ourselves as having a free hand to deal with detainees except to the extent that the exact letter of our treaty obligations indicates otherwise. But such argument as he provides for this assertion relies on the *malum prohibitum* approach, which, as we have already seen, is inappropriate in this area.

Third, Yoo's analysis lacks a sense of the historic context in which the conventions governing captives and detainees were negotiated and reformulated in 1949. In part a response to a preexisting patchwork of rules with piecemeal coverage, the 1949 conventions were negotiated precisely to prevent this sort of exploitation of loopholes, and it is quite discouraging now to see American lawyers arguing for the inapplicability of the Conventions on grounds that are strikingly similar—new forms of warfare, new types of nonstate entity, etc.—to those invoked by Germany in that period.

THE INTEREST IN CLEAR DEFINITIONS

Let me turn now to the word "torture" itself in these various provisions of municipal and international law. Some of the provisions—the Covenant, for example—offer no elucidation of the term. The Covenant just prohibits torture; it does not tell us what torture is. It seems to proceed on the theory that "we know it when we see it,"[8] or that we can recognize this evil using a sort of visceral "puke" test.[9]

Well, the trouble is that we seem to puke or chill at different things. The response to the Abu Ghraib scandal indicated the lack of any settled consensus in this matter. Muslim prisoners were humiliated by being made to simulate sexual activity with one another; they were beaten and their fingers and toes were stomped on; they were put in stress postures, hooded and wired, in fear of death if they so much as moved; they were set upon or put in fear of attack by dogs. Was this torture? Many commentators thought it was, but others resisted the characterization, preferring the word "abuse" or "hazing."

Unlike the Covenant, the Convention and the U.S. anti-torture statute offer more than just a term and an appeal to our intuitions. Their definitional provisions analyze torture as a certain sort of action, performed in a certain capacity, causing a certain sort of effect, done with a certain intent, for a certain purpose, and so on. Now, I have some harsh things to say about the quest for definitional precision. But for now I want to consider a kind of complaint about definitional looseness (and an attempt to narrow the definition of "torture") that goes well beyond [the] business of analyzing the elements of the offense.

Both the Convention and the anti-torture statute refer to the intentional infliction of "severe" pain or suffering. Since pain can be more or less severe, evidently the word "severe" is a site for contestation between those who think of torture in very broad terms and those who think of it in very narrow terms. The word looks as though it is supposed to restrict the application of the word "torture." But as with a requirement to take "reasonable care" or a constitutional prohibition on "excessive" bail, we are not told where exactly severity is on the spectrum of pain, and thus where the prohibition on torture is supposed to kick in.

---

7. *Eds.*—Latin for "cogent law," i.e., compelling or peremptory norm(s) deemed to be fundamental, overriding principles of law and policy from which no derogation is lawfully permitted (e.g., prohibitions on aggression, slavery, torture, and genocide).

8. This is what Justice Potter Stewart said, notoriously, about obscenity in *Jacobellis v. Ohio*, 378 U.S. 184, 197 (1964).

9. Oliver Wendell Holmes once said that a law was constitutional unless it made him want to "puke."

We might ask: what is the point of this restriction? Why narrow the definition of torture so that it covers only severe pain? . . . What do those who are dissatisfied with the vagueness of the phrase "severe pain or suffering" have in mind? What would be a more determinate definition? Presumably, it would be some measure of severity, something to turn the existing vague standard into an operationalized rule.

But first I want to discuss the very idea of such precision. I think the argument in favor of precision goes like this: if the terms of a legal prohibition are indeterminate, the person to whom the prohibition is addressed may not know exactly what is required of him, and he may be left unsure as to how the enforcement powers of the state will be used against him. The effect will be to chill that person's exercise of liberty as he tries to avoid being taken by surprise by enforcement decisions.

Is this a compelling argument? We should begin by recalling that the prohibitions on torture contained in the Geneva Conventions and in the Convention against Torture apply in the first instance to the state and state policy. Is the state in the same position as the ordinary individual in having a liberty interest in bright lines and an interest in not having its freedom of action chilled? I don't think so. We set up the state to preserve and enlarge our liberty; the state itself is not conceived as a beneficiary of our libertarian concern. Even the basic logic of liberty seems inapplicable. In the case of individuals, we say that everything that is not expressly forbidden is permitted. But it is far from clear that this principle should apply to the state. Indeed, constitutional doctrine often works the other way around; in the United States, everything not explicitly entrusted to the federal government is forbidden to it; it does not have plenary power.

However, although the prohibition on torture is intended mainly as a constraint on state policy, soldiers and other officials do also have an interest as individuals in anticipating war crimes or other prosecutions. The anti-torture statute purports to fulfill the obligations of the United States under the Convention by defining torture as an individual criminal offense. Many would say that inasmuch as that statute threatens serious punishment, there is an obligation to provide a tight definition. If that obligation is not fulfilled, they will say, then lenity requires that the defendant be given the benefit of whatever ambiguity we find in the statute. The doctrine of lenity, then, is the basis of the demand for precision.

Against this, however, we need to remember that the charge of torture is unlikely to be surprising or unanticipated by someone already engaged in the deliberate infliction of pain on prisoners. The potential defendant is one who already knows that he is inflicting considerable pain; that is his intention. The question he faces is whether the pain is severe enough to constitute torture. It seems to me that the working definition in the anti-torture statute already gives him all the warning he needs that he is taking a huge risk in relying upon casuistry about "severity" as a defense against allegations of torture.

It is important to understand that torture is a crime of specific intent: it involves the use of pain deliberately and specifically to *break the will* of the subject. We therefore should be suspicious about the attempt that the Bush administration made to pin down a definition of torture and to try to stipulate precisely the point of severity at which the prohibition on torture is supposed to kick in. Far from being the epitome of good lawyering, we might suspect an attempt to weaken or undermine the prohibition, by portraying it as something like a speed limit which we are entitled to push up against as closely as we can. These suspicions are confirmed, I think, by the character of the actual attempts that have been made to give the prohibition on torture this sort of spurious precision.

[*Eds.*—The author then discusses the Bybee Memorandum. After careful, analysis—including Judge Bybee's failure to consider that, in *Ireland v. United Kingdom*,[10] the European Commission on Human Rights had concluded that five techniques of interrogation virtually identical to those used by the Bush administration constituted, in combination, torture and not just inhuman or degrading treatment, and that both these categories of conduct are absolutely prohibited under the European Convention on Human Rights—the author concludes that Bybee's legal work is a "disgrace" when one considers the service to which his analysis was put. "Bybee's mistakes," he observes "distort the character of the legal prohibition on torture and create an im-

---

10. *Eds.*—See note 1.

pression that there is more room for the lawful infliction of pain in interrogation than a casual acquaintance with the anti-torture statute might suggest." The author adds: "Fortunately, someone in the Administration felt that he had gone too far: This part of Bybee's memorandum was not incorporated into the Haynes memorandum (although most of the rest of it was), and much of the Bybee approach to the definition of torture appears to have been rejected by the Administration in its later deliverances on the subject."]

II. ILLEGAL ABSOLUTES

LEGAL CONTINGENCY: IS NOTHING SACRED?

I now want to step back from all this and ask: what is it about these definitional shenanigans that seems so disturbing? After all, we know there is an element of contingency and manipulation in the definition of any legal rule. As circumstances change, amendments in the law or changes of interpretation seem appropriate. Why should the law relating to torture be any different?

Well for one thing, we seem to be dealing in this case with not just fine tuning, but a wholesale attempt to gut our commitment to a certain basic norm. Even so, we still have to acknowledge that the life of the law is sometimes to change or reinterpret whole paradigms (particularly in constitutional law). Why is it so shocking in this instance?

The question can be generalized. Law in all its features and all the detail of its terms and application is contingent on politics and circumstances. Nothing is beyond revision or repudiation. Why then do we have this sense that something sacred is being violated in the Bybee Memorandum, in John Yoo's arguments, or in the proposal Alan Dershowitz invites us to consider? Can we make sense—without resorting to religious ideas—of the idea of a noncontingent prohibition, a prohibition so deeply embedded that it cannot be modified or truncated in this way?

There are some fairly well-known ways of conceiving the indispensability of certain legal norms. We have already considered the distinction between *mala in se* and *mala prohibita*. There is legal philosopher H. L. A. Hart's idea of "the minimum content of natural law"—certain kinds of rules that a legal system could not possibly do without, given humans as they are and the world as it is.[11] Less philosophically, we understand that there are things that in theory lawmakers might do but are in fact very unlikely to do. As author and literary critic Leslie Stephen put it, "If a legislature decided that all blue-eyed babies should be murdered, the preservation of blue-eyed babies would be illegal; but legislators must go mad before they could pass such a law, and subjects be idiotic before they could submit to it."[12] Besides, there are various legal ways to diminish the vulnerability of a norm to revision, redefinition, or repeal.[13]

Yet, for a culture supposedly committed to human rights, we have amazing difficulty in even conceiving—without some sort of squirm—the idea of genuine moral absolutes. Academics in particular are so frightened of being branded "unrealistic" that we will fall over ourselves at the slightest provocation to opine that of course moral restraints must be abandoned when the stakes are high enough. Extreme circumstances can make moral absolutes look ridiculous, and those in our position cannot afford to be made to look ridiculous.

THE DERSHOWITZ STRATEGY

This tendency is exacerbated by the way we pose the question of torture to ourselves. Professor Dershowitz asks: what if on September 11 law enforcement officials had arrested terrorists boarding one of the planes and learned that other planes, then airborne, were heading toward unknown occupied buildings? Would they not have been justified in torturing the terrorists in their custody—just enough to get the information that would allow the target buildings to be evacuated? How could anyone object to the use of torture if it were dedicated specifically to saving thousands of lives in a case like this? That

11. H. L. A. Hart, *The Concept of Law*, 2nd ed. (Oxford: Clarendon, 1994), 193–200.
12. Leslie Stephen, *The Science of Ethics*, 2nd ed. (New York: Putnam, 1907), 137.
13. *Eds.*—The author points to three: a constitutional prohibition; an authoritative denomination of *jus cogens* status (see note 7); and a nonderogation clause revoking *explicitly* times of emergency extenuations.

is the question that Dershowitz and others regard as a useful starting point in our thinking about torture. The answer it is supposed to elicit is that torture can never be entirely out of the question, if the facts are clear and the stakes are high enough.

Should it worry us that once one goes down this road, the justification of torture—indeed, the justification of anything—is a matter of simple arithmetic coupled with the professor's ingenuity in concocting the appropriate fact situation? Dershowitz concedes the point, acknowledging that there is something disingenuous about his own suggestion that judicial torture warrants would be issued to authorize nothing but nonlethal torture. If the number of lives that can be saved is twice the number necessary to justify nonlethal torture, why not justify lethal torture or torture with unsterilized needles? Indeed, why just torture? Why not judicial rape warrants? Why not terrorism itself? The same kind of hypotheticals will take care of these inhibitions as well.

Still, this concern alone does not dispose of Dershowitz's question. Might we be willing to allow the authorization of torture at least in a "ticking bomb" case where we are sure that the detainee we are proposing to torture has information that will save thousands of lives and will give it up only if subjected to excruciating pain?

For what it is worth, my own answer to this question is a simple "No." I draw the line at torture. I suspect that almost all of my readers will draw the line somewhere, to prohibit some actions even under the most extreme circumstances—if it is not torture of the terrorist, they will draw the line at torturing the terrorist's relatives, or raping the terrorist, or raping the terrorist's relatives, all of which can be posited (with a logic similar to Dershowitz's) to be the necessary means of eliciting the information. Then the boot is simply on the other foot: why is it so easy to abandon one absolute (against torturing terrorists) while remaining committed to other absolutes (against, for instance, raping terrorists' relatives)? We can all be persuaded to draw the line somewhere, and I say we should draw it where the law requires it, and where the human rights tradition has insisted it should be drawn.

But in any case, one's answer is less important than one's estimation of the question. An affirmative answer is meant to make us feel patriotic and tough minded. But the question that

is supposed to elicit this response is at best silly and at worst deeply corrupt. It is silly because torture is seldom used in the real world to elicit startling facts about particular ticking bombs; it is used by American interrogators and others to accumulate lots of small pieces of relatively insignificant information which may become important only when accumulated with other pieces of similar information elicited by this or other means. And it is corrupt because it attempts to use a farfetched scenario, more at home in a television thriller than in the real world, deliberately to undermine the integrity of certain moral positions.

Some replies to Dershowitz's question—and to my mind, they are quite convincing—say that even if the basic fact situation he posits is no longer so fantastic given the bizarre horrors of September 11, nevertheless the framing of the hypothetical is still farfetched, inasmuch as it asks us to assume that torture warrants will work exactly as Professor Dershowitz says they should work. The hypothetical asks us to assume that the power to authorize torture will not be abused, that intelligence officials will not lie about what is at stake or about the availability of the information, that the readiness to issue torture warrants in one case (where they may be justified by the sort of circumstances Dershowitz stipulates) will not lead to their extension to other cases (where the circumstances are somewhat less compelling), that a professional corps of torturers will not emerge who stand around looking for work, that the existence of a law allowing torture in some cases will not change the office politics of police and security agencies to undermine and disempower those who argue against torture in other cases, and so on. Yet, what we know about Abu Ghraib and other recent cases is that against the background of any given regulatory regime in these matters, there will be some who are prepared to "push the envelope," trespassing into territory that goes beyond what is legally permitted. In addition, there will always be some depraved individuals who act in a way that is simply abusive *relative to whatever authorization is given*. There is, as Henry Shue notes, "considerable evidence of all torture's metastatic tendency."[14] In the last hundred

14. Henry Shue, "Torture," *Philosophy and Public Affairs* 7 (1978): 124–43, 143.

years or so it has shown itself not to be the sort of thing that can be kept under rational control. Indeed, it is already expanding.

The important point is that the use of torture is not an area in which human motives are trustworthy. Sadism, sexual sadism, the pleasure of indulging brutality, the love of power, and the enjoyment of the humiliation of others—these all-too-human characteristics need to be kept very tightly under control, especially in the context of war and terror, where many of the usual restraints on human action are already loosened. Remember too that we are not asking whether these motives can be judicially regulated in the abstract. We are asking whether they can be regulated in the kind of circumstances of fear, anger, stress, danger, panic, and terror in which, realistically, the hypothetical case must be posed.

Considerations like these might furnish a pragmatic case for upholding the rule against torture as a legal absolute, even if we cannot make a case in purely philosophical terms for a moral absolute. However, we should not stop there. Though I think the pragmatic case for a legal absolute is exactly right, we should explore the idea that certain things might just be repugnant to the spirit of our law, and that torture may be one of them. Specifically, I am prepared to make and explore the claim that the rule against torture plays an important emblematic role so far as the spirit of our law is concerned.

[*Eds.*—Next, in Part III of the article from which this essay is derived, the author probes the idea that the rule against torture may have extraordinary legal force, and defends "the proposition that torture is utterly repugnant to the spirit of our law"; that "narrowing or otherwise undermining the definition of torture might deal a body blow to the *corpus juris* that would go beyond the immediate effects on the mentality of torturers and the terror and suffering of their victims"; and that, therefore, the rule against torture should operate in our law as an "archetype," *as a rule that has significance not just in and of itself, but also as the embodiment of a pervasive principle.* Finally, in Part IV, he extends his analysis to consider the relation between prohibitions on torture and the idea of the rule of law—to which we now turn.]

IV. THE STATE

"ENGINE OF STATE" AND THE RULE OF LAW

Let us first consider the relationship between law and state. I have been arguing that the prohibition on torture is a legal archetype emblematic of our determination to break the connection between law and brutality and to reinforce its commitment to human dignity, even when law is at its most forceful and its subjects are at their most vulnerable. But in its modern revival, torture does not present itself as an aspect of legal practice. It presents instead as an aspect of state practice, by which I mean it involves agents of the state seeking to acquire information needed for security or military or counterinsurgency purposes, rather than (say) police, prosecutors, or agents of a court seeking to obtain information which can then be put to some forensic use.

The suggestion that Professor Dershowitz raises, with its specific provision for judicial torture warrants, involves introducing torture into the fabric of the law. But even Dershowitz is primarily concerned with judicial authorization of state torture for state purposes, not judicial authorization of state torture as a mode of input into the criminal process. So what is the relevance of my legal archetype argument to a practice which no one proposes to connect specifically with law? Why be so preoccupied with the trauma to law of what is essentially a matter of power?

One point is that "engines of state" and "engines of law" are not so widely separated. Even if one were to take the view that what is done by American officials in holding cells in Iraq, Afghanistan, or Guantanamo Bay is done in relation to the waging of war in a state of emergency rather than as part of a legally constituted practice, the thought that torture (or something very like torture) is permitted would be a legally disturbing thought. The warning has been sounded often enough: do not imagine that you can maintain a firewall between what is done by your soldiers and spies abroad to those they demonize as terrorists or insurgents, and what will be done at home to those who can be designated as enemies of society.

You may say that there is a distinction between what we do when we are at war and what we do in peacetime, and we should not be too paranoid that the first will infect the second. But is it really a basis for confidence in regard to the sort of war in which we are said to be currently involved—a war against terror as such, a war without end and with no boundaries, a war fought in the American homeland as well as in the cities, plains, and mountains of Afghanistan and Iraq?

A second point is that although we are dealing with torture as "an engine of state," still the issue of legality has been made central. Maybe there are hard men in our intelligence agencies who are prepared to say, "just torture them, get the information, and we will sort out the legal niceties later." But even if this is happening, a remarkable feature of the modern debate is that an effort is being made to see whether the law can be stretched or deformed to actually authorize this sort of thing. The effect on law, in other words, is unavoidable.

A third point addresses the issue of the rule of law—the enterprise of subjecting "the engines of state" to legal regulation and restraint. We hold ourselves committed to a general and quite aggressive principle of legality that law does not just have a little sphere of its own in which to operate, but expands to govern and regulate every aspect of official practice. I believe the prohibition on torture operates as an archetype not only of various parts of American constitutional law and law enforcement culture generally but of the ideal we call the rule of law. That agents of the state are not permitted to torture those who fall into their hands seems an elementary incident of the rule of law as it is understood in the modern world. If this protection is not assured, then the prospects for the rule of law generally look bleak indeed.

AN ARCHETYPE OF INTERNATIONAL LAW

I think a case can be made that the prohibition on torture also operates as an archetype in [international law, particularly in international humanitarian law and the law of human rights]. Consider, for example, the treatment of prisoners in wartime. We implicitly understand that while prisoner-of-war camps are uncomfortable, there is something inherently unlawful about the torture of prisoners. This is not just because of the stringency of the provision itself. Torture of prisoners threatens to undermine the integrity of the surrender/incarceration regime.

If we can torture prisoners, then we can do anything to them, and if we can do anything to them, then the willingness of defeated soldiers to surrender will be quite limited. The whole enterprise of attempting to mitigate the horrors of war by making a provision for an *hors de combat* status for individual soldiers in the face of certain defeat depends on their confidence, underwritten by law, that surrender and incarceration is better than death in combat. But torture (or interrogation practices that come close to torture) threatens that confidence and thus the whole basis of the regime.

What about human rights law? Certainly torture is widely understood as the paradigmatic human rights abuse. It is the sort of evil that arouses human rights passions and drives human rights campaigns. Now it is true that even human rights advocates accept the idea that rights are subject to interpretation, as well as the limitation to meet "the just requirements of morality, public order and the general welfare in a democratic society."[15] And few are so immoderate in their human rights advocacy that they do not accept that "In time of public emergency which threatens the life of the nation" the human rights obligations of the state may be limited. People are willing to accept that the human rights regime does not unravel altogether when detention without trial is permitted, when habeas corpus is suspended, or when free speech or freedom of assembly is limited in times of grave emergency. But were we to put up for acceptance as an integral part of the main body of human rights law the proposition that people may be tortured in times of emergency, I think people would sense that the whole game was being given away, and that human rights law itself was entering a crisis.

But what if we are only proposing to violate not the rule against torture but only the international norm relating to cruel, inhuman, or degrading treatment? Can that be abandoned without wider damage to the human rights regime? I have serious doubts about this. For one thing, the Bush administration enjoyed toying with the redescription of a considerable amount of what was previously regarded as torture to recategorize as merely—merely!—"cruel, inhuman, and degrading treatment." The human rights

15. UDHR, art. 29(2).

community is not easily fooled, and it would be an archetypal blow to its endeavor if the rule which in fact prohibits torture were to unravel under this sort of definitional pressure. For another thing, we must not become so jaded that the phrase "cruel, inhuman, and degrading treatment" simply trips off the tongue as something much less taboo than torture. The word "inhuman" means much more than merely "inhumane." "Inhuman treatment" means what it says, and its antonymic connection with the phrase "human rights" is not just happenstance. To treat a person inhumanly is to treat that person in a way that no human should ever be treated. On this basis it would not be hard to argue that the prohibitions on inhuman treatment in the Universal Declaration of Human Rights, the Covenant, and the ECHR are as much a paradigm of the international human rights movement as the absolute prohibition on torture.

We also need to consider the effect on the international human rights regime of the collapse of the archetype in relation to the United States in particular. That is, we need to consider the demoralizing impact of defection from the antitorture consensus by not just another rogue state but the world's one remaining superpower. The expressed willingness of one very powerful state to subject itself to legal restraint where its interests are most gravely at stake sends a message that international law is to be taken seriously. But the abandonment of the archetype by such a state sends a message too—that international law may be of no account if even the most powerful regime, the one that can most afford to sustain damage, is willing to dispense with legal restraint for the sake of a tactical advantage.

CONCLUSION

One final caveat. There are all sorts of reasons to be concerned about torture, and I am under no illusion that I have focused on the most important. The most important issue about torture remains the moral issue of the deliberate infliction of pain, the suffering that results, the insult to dignity, and the demoralization and depravity that is almost always associated with this enterprise whether it is legalized or not. By thinking about the prohibition as an archetype, I reach a clearer and more substantive sense of what we aspire to in our jurisprudence: a body of law and a rule of law that renounces savagery and a state that pursues its purposes (even its most urgent purposes) and secures its citizens (even its most endangered citizens) honorably and without recourse to brutality and terror.

QUESTIONS FOR REFLECTION AND DISCUSSION

1. Waldron's "starting point" in this essay concerns the realization that forms of illegal abuse of prisoners by the United States has taken place at the hands of lawyers, in particular governmental lawyers. Do you think it is acceptable for lawyers—or anyone in government, indeed—to narrow (a) the meaning and (b) the applicability of international legal prohibitions relating to torture? Why? Why not? Substantiate your answer as fully as possible with an argument drawing on relevant facts and sources.

2. Waldron asks of ICCPR Articles 4 and 7: "What is the effect of these provisions? How should we approach them as lawyers? Should we use the same strategies of interpretation as we use elsewhere in the law? Or is there something special about the prohibitions on torture that requires us to treat them more carefully or considerately?" How does Waldron answer them, and why? How do you answer these questions, and why?

3. Waldron notes that the current torture preventions were negotiated in the historic context of the wake of World War II, which was fought almost exclusively between well-organized national militaries. Today's conflicts are typically quite the opposite. What are the implications of this change? Should rules of war (including the treatment of prisoners) be adapted because of it? How and why? Does the context of the "war against terror" make a difference to the acceptability of the state use of torture? If so, how and with what effects? If not, why not and with what effects?

4. How does Waldron counter the arguments of law professors Yoo and Dershowitz? Do you find his counter-arguments convincing? Which side of the argument offers the more compelling case, and why?

5. As we have learned, ICCPR Articles 4 and 7 combine to make the prohibition on torture and cruel, inhuman, or degrading treatment or punishment absolute (a rarity in international human rights). In 1994, as Waldron points out, the United States ratified the ICCPR but subject to the following reservation:

> the United States considers itself bound by Article 7 to the extent that "cruel, inhuman or degrading treatment or punishment" means the cruel and unusual treatment or punishment prohibited by the Fifth, Eighth, and or Fourteenth Amendments to the Constitution of the United States.

Was the United States legally justified in, in effect, derogating from Article 7 by insisting on a constitutional standard less "demanding" (Waldron's word) than that provided by the ICCPR? If so, why, and was it wise? If not, why not?

6. Waldron asserts that the "prohibition on torture [is] archetypal of our particular legal heritage, as well as a certain sort of commitment to the rule of law [and to] international law, particularly in international humanitarian law and the law of human rights." Does your understanding of American history cause you to agree with Waldron? Disagree? What implications flow from Waldron's characterization? Does it influence state practice? Does it even matter?

7. David Cole and James X. Dempsey, in *Terrorism and the Constitution: Sacrificing Civil Liberties in the Name of National Security* (New York: New Press, 2002, 2006), observe at 175–76 that "this is not the first time our nation has responded to fear by asserting unchecked power, trampling rights, targeting immigrants and treating individuals as suspect because of their group identities rather than their personal conduct." Itemizing the World War I and II imprisonment of dissidents and immigrants—and U.S. citizens of Japanese descent, as well as citing the excesses of anti-communist paranoia under McCarthyism, they note that "All of these measures are now seen as mistakes. Yet the post-9/11 response . . . features many of the same mistakes of principle." Against this background, do you think that weakening the absolute prohibition on torture is an acceptable legal development? Support your answers with reasons and evidence insofar as you can.

Cole and Dempsey further note that "as we face new threats to our security, we also confront new threats to our liberties. Information technology is an important tool in fighting terrorism, but the combination of the vast aggregations of personal data generated by daily life in the digital age and the government's largely unchecked access to that information threatens privacy as never before"; and they argue that in the light of this heightened sense of vulnerability felt by us "all," the U.S. government efforts since 9/11 fail "to strike a proper balance between liberty and security." Against this background, do you trust that the United States—or any government committed to fighting terrorism—will abstain from resort to torture or cruel, inhuman, or degrading treatment or punishment? Again, support your answers with reasons and evidence insofar as you can.

8. After the end of World War II, writes Wayne Morrison in *Jurisprudence: From the Greeks to Post-Modernism* (Oxford: Cavendish, 1977), 312–13, there was an immense sense of "jurisprudential shock." "Positive law," he argues, "was exposed as only too easily the instrument of a legislative reason which attained ideological power. It was difficult to hide from the fact that from a legal perspective the decrees promulgated by the Nazis were valid law." He asks the question: "Had the jurisprudential imagination of legal positivism helped to make the evil of the Nazi regime a slowly acceptable banality?" Can positive law become the instrument of a legislative reason in the service of a gradually deepening banality of cruelty? In the light of this question, is Waldron's argument a vital corrective to the gradual erosion of a standard to which positive law must remain accountable? If so, what standard and where is it drawn from? If not, how are basic standards of respect to be maintained in the face of the weakening of what Waldron argues is an archetypal commitment of the rule of law, international law, and international human rights law? Where, on the spectrum between a constitutional landscape of profound respect for human life and the nadir of Nazi law, do you think U.S. policy sits relative to the potential legalization of torture? What distinctions can you draw? What might Waldron argue?

9. How should individuals accused of torture be treated? Waldron refers to the Abu Ghraib situation on a number of occasions. Were you to research the procedures followed and the punishments assessed in the Abu Ghraib and related cases (which you are

encouraged to do), would you expect that the U.S. service members involved were punished appropriately, got off lightly, or were not punished at all?

10. On final analysis, is the debate about torture a legal one or a moral one? Either way, might it not be morally repugnant even to debate the acceptability of torture? Does such debate legitimate torture as a practice? Is this a problem, or not? Substantiate your answers with reasoning, drawing upon any relevant, reliable sources of evidence.

Chapter Three

Participatory Rights

IN this chapter, we focus on the centrality of the complex and contested arena of so-called "first-generation" or "negative" rights that facilitate inclusion in the political community. We begin with a brief reflection on the role of respect at the core—and genesis—of human rights claims because this is pivotal for understanding the power of participation in the political community howsoever conceived.

Fundamental to human rights, in the raw moments when they first emerge as new claims, is a sense of outrage, suffering, or discomfort in response to a status quo that commonly belittles, marginalizes, excludes, or otherwise violates the sensibilities of human beings. Human rights claims are authored, in the deepest sense, by human beings in struggle, as a response to diverse forms of injustice and failures of human decency—indeed, to profound disrespect, whether enacted on rights-claimants themselves or on groups or communities whose suffering or oppression is witnessed by others who then become advocates on their behalf.

When rights discourse first emerged with full political force in the eighteenth century, it was precisely this kind of outraged, empathic response that, as historian Lynn Hunt's careful historical expositions reveal,[1] ignited the power of rights-based argument. Rights arguments arose from a new public sensibility provoked by the excesses of state torture (particularly the notorious Calas affair in 1762 France, an expression of Catholic religious intolerance[2]), a sensibility that was, in turn, fed by emergent forms of social awareness stimulated by the birth of the epistolary novel and the development of ordinary portraiture—developments that brought the human subjectivity of others into a fresh, intimate proximity for the first time. In sum, human rights consciousness in the eighteenth century was a response to a growing sense of shared humanity and outrage against disrespect, symbolized most prominently by public spectacles of brutal state torture and execution.

Thus human rights, notwithstanding the complexity and tensions in their history, may clearly be seen as arising first as claims against varying forms and degrees of fundamental disrespect, and that central to these forms of disrespect is the role of state power in relation to personhood. Indeed, it is to the relationship between state power and "citizen" in particular that civil and political rights first directed themselves as the modern state itself came into being, born with the mythic bond of the social contract fathered by the germinal philosophers of liberalism: Locke, Hobbes, and Rousseau.

---

1. Lynn Hunt, *Inventing Human Rights: A History* (New York: Norton, 2008).
2. Ibid., 70–112, especially 70–76 for details.

Civil and political rights are accordingly fundamental to the institutional order of the state. They represent important aspirations and guarantees (albeit imperfect, limited, and frequently betrayed) of civil and political respect. While such rights are flawed by the under-inclusivity of the universal "man" (now "human" or "person"), they assume at their respectful core the fundamental value of individual and group inclusion and participation in the civic order—and *in a way that counts*. This chapter addresses core issues attending civil and political human rights and the degree to which they can be said to be truly inclusive or participatory.

Opening the chapter is a reading drawn from an iconic essay by the prematurely late Richard B. Lillich, who, noting their predominance in the Universal Declaration of Human Rights, introduces us to the international standards designed to safeguard life, liberty, and security of the person as well as equality under and appertaining to the rule of law—i.e., civil rights. Lillich explains how these and other rights (the right to a remedy, to a fair trial, to presumption of innocence, to freedom of movement, to nationality, to marry and found a family) are protected under international law so as to ensure everyone's claims for respect and equal participation in society. Civil rights, which with political rights make up what are called "first-generation" rights, are "commonly considered to be," Lillich asserts, "the most basic and fundamental of all human rights." However controversial this assertion, Lillich nonetheless provides important interpretative insights and an informative backdrop for the readings that follow in this chapter and beyond.

Daniel Moeckli next engages with the idea of equality and non-discrimination—a sense of fairness so fundamental that even children and animals can be seen to possess the potent impulse underlying the notion, which Moeckli rightly identifies as deeply "intuitive." At the same time, however, he rightly acknowledges that the notion of equality is in reality, extremely "abstract" and "complex," pointing out that it can, in fact, be formulated in a variety of different ways. Yet, abstract and complex though it may be, the notion of equality is, Moeckli observes, foundational to international human rights law and therefore presents a central challenge to human rights policy in every instance at every level of social organization where it is valued: how best to give "equality" substance in practical, juridically applicable ways. Of course, this problem is not unique to international human rights law, Moeckli acknowledges. Accordingly, he addresses precisely how the challenge of formulating and applying the concept has been handled in international human rights law. Finding that multiple standards have emerged, he finds troubling gaps and inconsistencies, perhaps the most vital of which concern spiraling global—especially economic—inequalities. For Moeckli, in other words, "equal rights" remains "an unfulfilled promise for large sections of the [world's] population"—a key response to which, he argues, must be "to ensure that all people can participate on an equal basis in all areas of economic, social, and political life, including in the very decisions on how equality should be realized."

The challenge of ensuring that all voices are included in a discussion of what equality should mean and look like in practice is, however, a very difficult one to address. Ineke van der Valk addresses one central challenge: racism, arguing that racism is a key ideological driver of inequality, injustice, violence, and structural disadvantage. It is also, she contends, a "threat to global peace," noting that the social construction of "race" as a political category emerged not during but after the rights revolutions in France and America when, in the late nineteenth and early twentieth centuries, the concept of "race" had acquired so much political significance that it was deployed, not just to explain racial differences, but "to *justify* inequalities at the political level" (emphasis added)—a development fully reflected in, for two egregious examples, the programmatic massacres in Europe in the Armenian Genocide and Jewish Holocaust operationalized by the political racism of the Ottoman Empire and

Nazi state respectively. Racism, however, is more generally a "typical expression of group dominance" and, as Van der Valk points out, not confined to "overt and violent forms of social domination and exclusion but [also operationalized in] more indirect and subtle forms expressed in daily practices." Racism emerges from Van der Valk's analysis as a dynamic, evolving social practice with pernicious implications for global solidarity and peace, reflected by, among other things, the fact that "The same means of communication that have played such an important role in the development of globalization contribute to the ongoing reproduction of the phenomenon of racism on a world scale [facilitated by] means of communication [that] penetrates the remote corners of the world, favoring tendencies toward ethnic conflict."

Racism, of course, does not stand alone as an offense against human rights values. While it is true that the evils of apartheid in South Africa epitomized for many for a long time what a human rights violation "looks like," history both before and after the UN system came into being makes clear that multiple other forms of radical disrespect enacted on the basis of contestable differences between human beings pose serious challenges to "simple human respect" on a global basis, among them "sex difference," which has long been a central basis for forms of structural disrespect based on the construction and interpretation of difference.

Fiona Beveridge and Siobhan Mullally in this chapter directly address the "body politics" implicated in the struggle for "women's human rights." Noting the continued and widespread feminist criticism of appeals to rights and to rights-based concepts "as a tool for addressing the oppression of women," they point out that international human rights law has considerable difficulties "accommodating women's 'differences.'" They draw upon the well-known fact that women's human rights are marginalized within international human rights law and discourse, and that "abuse of women's human rights [is] perceived [to be] a cultural, private, or individual issue, not a political matter requiring State action." Recognizing the pervasive nature of female marginalization as both conceptual and institutional, they observe that

> the main international organs have dealt with violations of women's human rights only in a marginal way, while women's bodies have been rendered almost invisible within mainstream human rights law. This exclusion of women's bodies is apparent both in the failure of international human rights law to respond to violence against women and in the lack of any clear understanding or consensus on a woman's right to bodily integrity.

The authors clearly support the development of a right to bodily integrity, but at the same time evince an important strategic awareness of the double-edged nature of rights themselves. Women, it seems, occupy a problematic and ambivalent space in international human rights law and policy discourse, a fact reflected in a long history of exclusion, marginalization, and oppression of women in both the public and private spheres—a distinction that itself is central to the operationalization of sexual oppression, as Beveridge and Mullally make clear.

The birth of the public sphere is intimately related to the simultaneous rise of rights and the modern state—noted above—which emerged in the early modern political settlements between sovereigns and populations in Europe as Europe moved toward modernity. The formation of the modern polity is a theme important for Seyla Benhabib's contribution to this chapter. She notes not only the authorship of rights in struggle (as we do above) but also the fact that "since the seventeenth century, democracy and the consolidation of the modern nation-state have marched together, at times contradicting and at times supplementing each other." Addressing the struggles for inclusion that characterize the history of the modern state, Benhabib implies the driving force of participation for political rights discourse when she references the "democratic struggles of propertyless males, artisans, farmers, and workers to win suffrage [which] gave way in the early twentieth century to the struggle of women, and non-Christian and non-White colonial peoples to be included within the boundaries of the demos."

Benhabib points out that the traditional synthesis between freedoms and institutional relationships is breaking down—and the crisis this represents, she argues, is not the crisis of democracy, but "the crisis of the territorially circumscribed nation-state formation." This is a crisis starkly revealed by transnational migration and displacement—phenomena likely to become more pervasive, moreover, as the climate crisis unfolds. The flood of contemporary refugees and immigrants is rapidly becoming, we suggest, a core motif—and one of the most destabilizing problems—of the globalized order: immigration debates currently rage in Global North countries, and respect for the human rights of immigrants is set to become an even more contested issue as pressures mount.

Benhabib writes that "The old political structures may have waned but the new political forms of globalization are not yet in sight." She continues: "We are like travelers navigating an unknown terrain with the help of old maps, drawn at a different time and in response to different needs. While the terrain we are traveling on, the world-society of states, has changed, our normative map has not." Accordingly, she highlights the "growing normative incongruities between international human rights norms, particularly as they pertain to the 'rights of others'—immigrants, refugees, and asylum-seekers—and continuing assertions of territorial sovereignty." Benhabib's contribution thus confronts her readers with the now-famous failure of inclusion and respect at the heart of international human rights law identified by Hannah Arendt.[3] Writing of refugees, Arendt laments the fact that "the conception of human rights based upon the assumed existence of a human being as such, broke down the very moment when those who professed to believe in it were for the first time confronted with people who had indeed lost all other qualities and specific relationships—except that they were still human." Arendt's critique drives at the idea that beyond the national rights of citizenship, human rights betray their most fundamental promise: "The world found nothing sacred in the abstract nakedness of being human."

If, as Benhabib's analysis suggests, refugees, immigrants, and asylum-seekers threaten to expose the limits and inadequacies of an aging world order—then, in the light of Arendt's critique, it is possible to see such dislocated human beings as the return of the repressed unconscious of international human rights law itself, exposing the dark lacuna at the heart of the state-centric system. And while Benhabib's response is to turn to a form of cosmopolitan world citizenship, questions remain concerning whether even global citizenship—and human rights as components of such extended citizenship—can become genuinely inclusive or whether such attempted solutions will simply replicate familiar patterns of exclusion, reenacting Arendt's lacuna, perhaps in more complex, refracted ways. Thus the central question persists: how can the order of rights guarantee simple, inclusive respect and genuine political participation for all human beings within and beyond the boundaries of the nation-state in a complex global age? The answers seem by no means clear.

3. Hannah Arendt, *The Origins of Totalitarianism* (New York: Harvest, 1968), 299.

11. RICHARD B. LILLICH *Civil Rights*

This essay is basically a description *cum* commentary of those international norms which purport to guarantee and protect one bundle of rights: the civil rights of individuals. These rights, commonly considered the most basic and fundamental of all human rights, will be familiar to readers versed in United States constitutional law, for, as Professor Henkin once recalled, "most of the Universal Declaration of Human Rights (UDHR), and later the International Covenant on Civil and Political Rights (ICCPR), are in their essence American constitutional rights projected around the world."[1]

Since these rights find their expression in Articles 3–18 of the 1948 UDHR[2]—restated, supplemented, and occasionally modified by companion articles in the 1966 ICCPR, the 1950 European Convention for the Protection of Human Rights and Fundamental Freedoms, the 1969 American Convention on Human Rights, and the 1981 African Charter on Human and Peoples' Rights—for the sake of convenience they are considered here in the order they appear in the UDHR.

Before beginning this survey, however, the human rights to be reviewed must be placed in proper juridical perspective. Specifically, what is their status under contemporary international law, and what restrictions may states impose upon their enjoyment? Unless these questions can be answered satisfactorily, human rights, no matter how nicely phrased, can have little real meaning in or effect upon the lives of individuals.

As to the first question, it now may be argued persuasively that substantial parts of the UDHR, a UN General Assembly resolution adopted in 1948 without dissent and originally thought not to give rise to international legal obligations, have become, over the past third of a century, part of customary international law binding upon all states. This view, first advanced solely by legal scholars but subsequently supported by the statements of international conferences, by state practice, and even by court decisions,[3] now appears to have achieved widespread acceptance. Indeed the suggestion has even been made that the UDHR has "the attributes of *jus cogens*,"[4] a statement that, in the opinion of this writer, goes too far if intended to imply that all rights enumerated in it have this character.[5] There is little doubt, however, that many of the human rights to be discussed—the prohibition of slavery being just one example—not only reflect customary international law but also partake of the character of *jus cogens*. This conclusion is particularly valid when the right in question appears in both the UDHR and the ICCPR. The latter, of course, is binding conventional law only between states parties to it, but many of its provisions now can be said to have helped create norms of customary international law, including ones having *jus cogens* status—binding even states which have yet to ratify it.

Excerpted with changes by permission of Oxford University Press from Richard B. Lillich, "Civil Rights," in Theodore Meron, ed., *Human Rights in International Law: Legal and Policy Issues* (New York: Oxford University Press, 1984), 115–69. Copyright © 1984 Oxford University Press.

1. Louis Henkin, "Rights: American and Human," *Columbia Law Review* 79 (1979): 405–25, 415. *Eds.*—These constitutional rights date back at least to the Magna Carta of 1215, later to be cultivated and refined by the English and French revolutions as well as the American Revolution.

2. *Eds.*—Note: the author does not here address UDHR Articles 19 (freedom of opinion and expression), 20 (freedom of assembly), and 21 (right to governmental participation), each of which, along with Articles 3–18, are commonly understood components of "first-generation" civil *and* political rights. It may be assumed, however, that many—though not all—of the author's *general* findings and opinions about Articles 3–18 apply also to these three articles.

3. See, e.g., *Filártiga v. Peña-Irala*, 630 F.2d 876, 882 (2nd Cit. 1980), where the Court of Appeals for the Second Circuit held that "the right to be free from torture . . . has become part of customary international law, *as evidenced and defined by the Universal Declaration of Human Rights*" (emphasis added). For discussion of this important decision and its aftermath, see Chapter 7, Reading 33 (Grear and Weston).

4. *Eds.*—Latin for "cogent law," i.e., compelling or peremptory norm(s) deemed to be fundamental, overriding principles of law and policy from which no derogation is permitted (e.g., prohibitions on aggression, slavery, torture, genocide).

5. Rosalyn Higgins (formerly judge and president of the International Court of Justice), writing about human rights treaties but reasoning along lines applicable to the UDHR as well, makes a similar point. See Rosalyn Higgins, "Derogations Under Human Rights Treaties," *BYBIL* 48 (1976–77): 281–320, 282.

With respect to the second question, the restrictions a state may impose upon an individual's internationally protected human rights come in two tiers, both of which must be kept in mind in determining the protection afforded by particular guarantees. On the first tier of restrictions, both the UDHR and the ICCPR contain provisions limiting the rights guaranteed therein. The former contains a general limitations clause, Article 29(2), which provides that in the exercise of their rights and freedoms, everyone shall be subject only to such limitations as are determined by law solely for the purpose of securing due recognition and respect for the rights and freedoms of others and of meeting the just requirements of morality, public order, and the general welfare in a democratic society.

In the ICCPR, as [former World Court Judge] Rosalyn Higgins has pointed out, the references to the need for rights to be exercised in conformity with morality, public order, general welfare, etc., appear not as a general clause but as qualifications to specific freedoms. The specific limitations (or, as she aptly terms them, clawback clauses)[6] in the ICCPR relating to civil rights are contained in Articles 12(3), 14(1), and 18(3). One can only endorse the warning that such limitations can be highly dangerous (from the point of view of human rights).

On the second tier of restrictions, which is relevant to the ICCPR alone, Article 4(1) thereof permits states parties to derogate from (i.e., suspend or breach) certain obligations "In time of public emergency which threatens the life of the nation and the existence of which is officially proclaimed." No derogation may be made, however, from the human rights contained in Articles 6, 7, 8(1), 8(2), 11, 15, 16, and 18, evidence that at least some of these rights may have attributes of *jus cogens*.[7] Nevertheless, as in the case of the limitation clauses discussed in the preceding paragraph, the fact that a wide variety of important rights—for example, the right to liberty and

security of person guaranteed by Article 9(1)—may be rendered temporarily "inoperative" by means of derogation must be kept in mind when assessing the degree of protection actually afforded individuals by the language of Articles 3–18 of the UDHR.[8]

[*Eds.*—The author next analyzes the civil and political rights of individuals set forth in the UDHR: rights to life, liberty, and security of person (art. 3); prohibition of slavery and servitude (art. 4); prohibition of torture and cruel, inhuman, or degrading treatment or punishment (art. 5); right to legal recognition (art. 6); rights to equality before the law and to nondiscrimination in its application (art. 7); right to a remedy (art. 8); prohibition of arbitrary arrest, detention, or exile (art. 9); right to a fair trial (art. 10); presumption of innocence and prohibition of ex post facto laws (art. 11); right to privacy (art. 12); right to freedom of movement (art. 13); right to asylum (art. 14); right to a nationality (art. 15); right to marry and found a family (art. 16); right to own property (art. 17); and freedom of thought, conscience, and religion (art. 18). While the author strongly supports these asserted rights, his analysis is noteworthy for being meticulous and measured. In almost every instance, he correctly points out, these rights, as propounded in the UDHR, the ICCPR, and their regional offspring, are fraught with complexity, high levels of abstraction, and ambiguity, and thus pose major interpretative challenges to judicial and political decision-making. He also emphasizes, however, the international community's unequivocal decision in the ICCPR to limit to a relative few those rights that may be deemed nonderogable (and therefore, in his judgment, top ranked)—that is, rights that may not be suspended by a state even in time of public emergency: right to life; freedom from torture and cruel, inhuman, or degrading treatment or punishment; freedom from slavery and involuntary servitude; freedom from debtor

---

6. By a clawback clause is meant one that permits, in normal circumstances, breach of an obligation for a specified number of public reasons. It thus differs from a derogation clause such as Article 4(1) of the ICCPR, which allows suspension or breach of certain obligations in circumstances of war or public emergency.
7. Reservations to the ICCPR, to the extent that they are directed to the rights guaranteed in these seven articles, presumably have no force or effect if these rights actually have acquired *jus cogens* status.

8. An issue is raised by the use of the words arbitrary or arbitrarily throughout the UDHR and the ICCPR. These words, it now seems clear, should be construed to prohibit not only illegal but also unjust acts. Thus, despite the fears of some observers, a state cannot impinge upon an individual's internationally protected human rights simply by enacting legislation making its acts legal on the domestic plane.

prison; freedom from ex post facto laws; and freedom of thought, conscience, and religion. Additionally, he asserts that only the following rights may be deemed part of customary international law: the right to life; freedom from slavery and involuntary servitude; freedom from torture and cruel, inhuman, or degrading treatment or punishment; rights to equality before the law and to non-discrimination in its application; freedom from arbitrary arrest and detention; presumption of innocence; and freedom of thought, conscience, and religion. He accepts, too, that freedom from arbitrary arrest and detention and presumption of innocence may now be considered norms of customary international law (and therefore potentially nonderogable). However, the author is hesitant to extend this status to such other procedural due process rights as the right to a remedy, the right to a fair trial, and freedom from ex post facto laws. Indeed, taking into account "uncertainties about [its] contours and content," he qualifies even the right to be free from arbitrary arrest and detention as customary international law only and then to the extent of its "basic core prohibition."[9] The author then continues, focusing mostly on "civil" as distinct from "political" rights.]

RIGHTS TO EQUALITY BEFORE THE LAW AND TO NON-DISCRIMINATION IN ITS APPLICATION (ARTICLE 7)

UDHR Article 7 reads: "All are equal before the law and are entitled without any discrimination to equal protection of the law. All are entitled to equal protection against any discrimination in violation of this Declaration and against any incitement to such discrimination." Language almost identical with the first sentence of Article 7 is found in the first sentence of Article 26 of the ICCPR; the second sentence of Article 26, however, contains the following variation: "In this respect, the law shall prohibit any discrimination and guarantee to all persons equal and effective protection on any ground." Language paralleling the first sentence of Article 7 is found in Article 24 of the American Convention, while the European Convention contains no directly corresponding provision.

Almost from the beginning, the words equal protection of the law caused confusion. According to one member of the Third Committee[10] during debates on the draft Universal Declaration, "it was not clear whether they meant that there should be laws which should be applied equally or that all were equally entitled to the protection of whatever laws existed." This lack of clarity, in the view of some observers, persists under the ICCPR. Professor Robertson analyzes and evaluates the alternative interpretations as follows:

> Broadly speaking, two quite different meanings seem possible: that the substantive provisions of the law should be the same for everyone; or that the application of the law should be equal for all without discrimination. The former interpretation would seem unreasonable; for example, in most countries women are not required to perform military service, while it is unnecessary that the law should prescribe maternity benefits for men. It would seem, therefore, that the meaning rather is to secure equality, without discrimination, in the application of the law, and this interpretation is borne out by the *travaux préparatoires*.[11]

This interpretation is consistent with the approach taken in UDHR Article 2 and Article 2(1) of the ICCPR, both of which mandate non-discriminatory treatment, but only insofar as the rights set out in the respective human rights instrument are concerned. Articles 7 and 26, therefore, while specifically guaranteeing one important civil right to all persons on a non-discriminatory basis, surely cannot be read to constitute a general norm of non-discrimination invocable in other contexts. Properly limited, however, the right considered in this subsection

9. *Eds.*—It must be noted, however, that Professor Lillich's original essay was penned in 1984 and that it is likely that he would have had a less skeptical, more positive assessment today.

10. *Eds.*—The Third Committee, shorthand for the Social, Humanitarian, and Cultural Committee (SOCHUM) of the UN General Assembly, is charged with matters relating to a wide range of social, humanitarian affairs, and human rights issues that have worldwide impact or significance.

11. Arthur H. Robertson and J. G. Merrills, *Human Rights in the World: An Introduction to the Study of the International Protection of Human Rights*, 4th ed. (Manchester: Manchester University Press, 1972), 39.

probably now has become customary international law.

RIGHT TO A REMEDY (ARTICLE 8)

This unique article, added at the last minute by the Third Committee to fill a supposed lacuna in the draft Universal Declaration, guarantees all persons "the right to an effective remedy by the competent national tribunals for acts violating the fundamental rights granted him *by the constitution or by law.*" Since "human rights without effective implementation are shadows without substance,"[12] there is no doubt that the right to a remedy is an extremely important one. For this reason, despite assertions that such a right was superfluous or would prove of little value, it has been included not only in the UDHR and the ICCPR, but in the European Convention and American Convention as well. Its importance, however, depends greatly upon the scope of the substantive rights it is designed to protect. Here there is considerable variation in the language of the relevant articles.

The UDHR, quoted above, guarantees an effective domestic remedy for acts which violate rights granted by the constitutions or laws of the various states. Thus, in contrast with Article 7, whose reach extends only to acts in violation of the UDHR, Article 8's scope is potentially much broader. Since the ambit of the rights granted by domestic constitutions and domestic law generally is larger (at least on paper) than that of the rights enunciated in the UDHR, the right to a remedy contemplated by Article 8 may be regarded as a broad one indeed.

Unfortunately, both the ICCPR and the European Convention are more restrictive in this regard. Effective remedies are guaranteed by Article 2(3)(a) of the ICCPR only to vindicate the "rights or freedoms as herein recognized," i.e., recognized by the ICCPR. Similarly, Article 13 of the European Convention guarantees an effective remedy only for "rights and freedoms as set forth in this Convention." The American Convention, on the other hand, provides the person seeking relief the best of all possible worlds: Article 25(1) combines the approaches of the UDHR, ICCPR, and European Convention, requiring states to accord prompt and effective relief "against acts that violate . . . fundamental rights recognized by the constitution or laws of the state concerned or by the Convention."

[*Eds.*—Quoting Sir James Fawcett, former President of the now erstwhile European Commission of Human Rights, the author next observes that Article 13 of the European Convention (quoted above) has been interpreted to reveal "a basic confusion of thought as to the real purpose and function of the article."[13] The author then adds that, given the general confusion surrounding the scope of the right to a remedy in the European Convention and the continuing doubts concerning its meaning more broadly, "it can be said with reasonable assurance that it is not part of customary international law."[14]]

PROHIBITION OF ARBITRARY ARREST, DETENTION, OR EXILE (ARTICLE 9)

UDHR Article 3, it will be recalled, establishes not only the right to life, but also the right to liberty and security of person. The ICCPR handles these rights in two articles, 6(1) and 9(1), the latter of which, in addition to guaranteeing "the right to liberty and security of person," provides, inter alia, that "No one shall be subjected to arbitrary arrest or detention." "Protection against arbitrary arrest and detention"— "is clearly the central feature of any system of guarantees of the liberty of the individual."[15] Indeed, the drafters of the UDHR considered the prohibition of arbitrary arrest and detention so important that rather than treating it as just one liberty interest, they devoted a separate article to it, demonstrating their intention to establish it as

12. John Humphrey, "Report of the Rapporteur of the International Committee on Human Rights," in *Report of the Fifty-Third Conference [of the International Law Association] Held at Buenos Aires, Argentina, August 25 to August 31, 1968* (London: International Law Association, 1969), 457. Humphrey's remarks echo the more poetic words of Justice Holmes: "Legal obligations that exist but cannot be enforced are ghosts that are seen in the law but are elusive to the grasp." *The Western Maid*, 257 U.S. 419, at 433 (1922).

13. James E. S. Fawcett, *The Application of the European Convention on Human Rights* (Oxford: Clarendon, 1969), 232.
14. But see note 8.
15. Francis G. Jacobs, *The European Convention on Human Rights* (Oxford: OUP, 1975), 75.

an independent human right. Thus, Article 9 of the UDHR provides that "No one shall be subjected to arbitrary arrest, detention or exile."

The *travaux préparatoires*, revealing an understandable reluctance to define "arbitrary" and an enthusiastic endorsement of an amendment adding "exile" to the draft Declaration's proscription against "arbitrary arrest or detention," indicate that most members of the Third Committee were pleased with the article's "eloquent brevity" and content to leave it to the ICCPR to spell out its general terms. The ICCPR, in Article 9, fulfills their expectations by elaborating in considerable detail the rights to be accorded a person who has been arrested or detained. Most of these rights also are protected by Article 5 of the European Convention and Article 7 of the American Convention in "substantially similar terms."

After the language quoted above, Article 9(1) of the ICCPR concludes with the following sentence: "No one shall be deprived of his liberty except on such grounds and in accordance with such procedure as are established by law." The purpose of this provision is to require states to spell out in legislation the grounds on which an individual may be deprived of his liberty and the procedures to be used. With the freedom of action of the executive branch of government thus restricted, Yoram Dinstein observes, "Not every policeman (or other state functionary) is entitled to decide at his discretion, and on his own responsibility, who can be arrested, why and how."[16] Nor is any detention allowed by law permissible, as a literal interpretation of the provision might suggest. Just as an arrest may not be arbitrary—defined as "unjust" and not merely "illegal"—so too must a detention not be arbitrary. The deprivation of liberty therefore must be not only in accordance with law, but also in conformity to the principles of justice.

The balance of ICCPR Article 9 defines certain guarantees applicable in case of any arrest or detention, plus certain special guarantees applicable when a person is arrested or detained on a criminal charge. Space dictates that these guarantees be listed here rather than fully evaluated. In the first, general category are the following:

16. Yoram Dinstein, "The Right to Life, Physical Integrity and Liberty," in Louis Henkin, ed., *The International Bill of Rights: The Covenant on Civil and Political Rights* (New York: Columbia University Press, 1981), 414–37, 430.

Article 9(2): "Anyone who is arrested shall be informed, at the time of arrest, of the reasons for his arrest and shall be promptly informed of any charges against him."

Article 9(4): "Anyone who is deprived of his liberty by arrest or detention shall be entitled to take proceedings before a court, in order that court may decide without delay on the lawfulness of his detention and order his release if the detention is not lawful."

Article 9(5): "Anyone who has been the victim of unlawful arrest or detention shall have an enforceable right to compensation."

In the second category—special guarantees applicable to persons arrested or detained on criminal charges—Article 9(3) provides that such persons "be brought promptly before a judge" and thereafter "be entitled to trial within a reasonable time or to release." Additionally, it establishes a presumption that persons awaiting trial shall not be detained in custody; their release, however, may be made subject to guarantees of appearance, the most common of which presumably would be bail.

Interpretative guidance as to the meaning of most of the above provisions can be obtained from the nascent practice of the UN Human Rights Committee established under the ICCPR as well as the more developed practice of the European Court of Human Rights under Article 5 of the European Convention. Given the differences in wording, however, the latter must be used with care. In any event, taking into account uncertainties about the contours and content of the prohibition of arbitrary arrest and detention, plus the fact that states may derogate therefrom under Article 4(2) of the ICCPR, it seems unlikely that little more than the basic core prohibition can be said to constitute part of customary international law at present.

RIGHT TO A FAIR TRIAL (ARTICLE 10)

This article, which along with its companion, UDHR Article 11, guarantees individuals "the basic right to a fair trial in both civil and criminal matters," enunciates a very important right, for the implementation of all other rights depends upon the proper administration of justice. In its entirety Article 10 reads as follows: "Everyone is entitled in full equality to a fair and public hearing by an independent and impartial tribunal, in the determination of his rights and obligations and of any criminal charge against him." Two preliminary points should be made with respect to this language. First, it lumps together both criminal and civil proceedings, despite cogent arguments for their being treated separately, the potential for abuse of state power obviously being greater where the rights of an accused—as opposed to a mere party in civil lawsuit—are concerned. Second, it is so terse that it offers little help when applied to the facts of particular cases. Hence, here more than elsewhere, guidance as to the meaning of the right must be obtained from parallel provisions in subsequent international human rights instruments and the decisions of competent bodies interpreting them.

The requirements of a fair trial in criminal proceedings, the sole concern of this subsection, can be divided somewhat arbitrarily into four general categories: the character of the tribunal, the public nature of the hearing, the rights of the accused in the conduct of his defense, and, lastly, a miscellaneous collection of other prescriptions.

The first category, the character of the tribunal, obviously is of prime importance. Article 10 requires tribunals to be "independent and impartial," as do Article 14(1) of the ICCPR and Articles 6(1) and 8(1) of the European Convention and American Conventions, respectively. As Professor Harris has put it,

> These are obvious and overlapping requirements. The primary meaning of "independent" is independence of other organs of government in the sense of the doctrine of the separation of powers: in particular, a judge must not be subject to the control or influence of the executive or the legislature. . . . The requirement that the court must be "impartial" needs little implication. It is reflected in the universally accepted doctrine that no man may be a judge in his own cause and is an obvious characteristic for a court to possess.[17]

Whether such independence and impartiality can be assured when a state resorts to ad hoc or special tribunals, as frequently occurs after revolutions or in national emergencies, is a doubtful proposition: for this reason, it is disappointing that Article 10 does not speak directly to this point. In contrast, Article 14(1) of the ICCPR and Article 8(1) of the American Convention add the requirement that the tribunal be "competent," a word which, according to the *travaux préparatoires* of the former, "was intended to ensure that all persons should be tried in courts whose jurisdiction had been previously established by law, and arbitrary action so avoided." Article 8(1) of the American Convention goes one step further, specifically stating that a trial must be conducted by a tribunal "previously established by law." Arguably, this requirement can be read into the "independent and impartial" language of the UDHR.

The second category, the public nature of the hearing, also is of importance in protecting individuals from arbitrary proceedings. The drafters of Article 10 of the UDHR inserted the words "and public" between the words "fair" and "hearing" to insure the openness of trials, a procedure conducive to their fairness. Moreover, despite language in the *travaux préparatoires* that "There were circumstances in which a secret trial might be acceptable," Article 10 itself acknowledges no such exception. Article 14(1) of the ICCPR, however, closely tracked by Article 6(1) of the European Convention, contains a wide range of exceptions. Article 14(1) reads, inter alia, as follows: "The Press and the public may be excluded from all or part of a trial for reasons of morals, public order (*ordre public*), or national security in a democratic society, or when the interest of the private lives of the parties so requires, or to the extent strictly necessary in the opinion of the court in special circumstances where publicity would prejudice the interests of justice." Such language, as Professor Fawcett remarks with respect to Article 6(1) of the European Convention, is so broad that "it is doubtful whether the requirement of public hearing under the Convention is likely in practice to yield much protection."[18]

The rights of the accused in the conduct of his defense, the third category, presents the converse of the above. Rather than the ICCPR undercutting a broad and unqualified right found

---

17. David J. Harris, "The Right to a Fair Trial in Criminal Proceedings as a Human Right," *ICLQ* 16 (1967): 352–78, 354–56.

18. Fawcett, *The Application of the European Convention*, 150.

in the UDHR, here the ICCPR spells out at length in Article 14(3) just what rights an accused has in a criminal proceeding. In brief, they are the right to be informed promptly of the charge against him; the right to have adequate time and facilities to prepare a defense and to communicate with counsel; the right to be tried without undue delay; the right to be tried in his presence and to defend himself in person or through counsel; the right to cross-examine witnesses against him and to summon witnesses on his own behalf; the right to an interpreter; and the right not to be compelled to testify against himself. Roughly similar guarantees are found in Article 6(3) of the European Convention and Article 8(2) of the American Convention. As is apparent, they generally reflect the procedural due process rights developed by the U.S. Supreme Court from the Fifth and Fourteenth Amendments to the U.S. Constitution.

The fourth and here final category comprises a number of miscellaneous rights, none of which are set out in the UDHR, which generally are thought to contribute to a fair trial in criminal proceedings. In the order in which they appear in Article 14 of the ICCPR, they are: the right of juveniles to be tried under special procedures; the right to appeal one's conviction and sentence; the right to compensation when one is convicted through a miscarriage of justice; and the right not to be subjected to double jeopardy. The fact that none of these rights is mentioned in the European Convention (and only three are guaranteed by the American Convention) suggests that they are part of conventional rather than customary international law, a status they are likely to retain until the ICCPR becomes so widely accepted as to be generally norm-creating. Moreover, without the interpretative assistance of the ICCPR, the right to a fair trial provided for in Article 10 of the UDHR seems too generally phrased to constitute a customary international law rule capable of application in concrete cases.

PRESUMPTION OF INNOCENCE AND PROHIBITION OF EX POST FACTO LAWS (ARTICLE 11)

This article, closely related to Article 10 of the UDHR, also is concerned with the rights of the accused in criminal proceedings. It establishes the presumption of innocence and proscribes ex post facto offences. These important and distinct guarantees are discussed separately.

Article 11(1) provides that "Everyone charged with a penal offence has the right to be presumed innocent until proved guilty according to law in a public trial at which he has had all the guarantees necessary for his defense." Since the latter part of this sentence is redundant, in view of the rights accorded accused by Article 10, it was omitted when the language of Article 11(1) was adopted, almost *in haec verba*, as Article 14(2) of the ICCPR. Language almost identical to Article 11(1) is contained in Articles 6(2) and 8(2) of the European Convention and American Convention respectively. Thus, there is unanimous consensus supporting the presumption of innocence in criminal proceedings; surely therefore it has become part of customary international law.

Little difficulty has been encountered so far in applying the principle under the European Convention, although, as Professor Jacobs cautions, it has a slightly different meaning in the civil law than it has at common law:

The principle of the presumption of innocence is reflected in English law in the rule placing the burden of proof on the prosecution. But it cannot be equated with that rule, to which there are in any event numerous exceptions. Under the inquisitorial system of criminal procedure found in many of the Contracting Parties to the European Convention, it is for the court to elicit the truth in all cases. What the principle of the presumption of innocence requires here is first that the court should not be predisposed to find the accused guilty, and second that it should at all times give the accused the benefit of the doubt, on the rule *in dubio pro reo*.[19]

While the principle thus concerns primarily the behavior of judges, the admissibility in evidence of prior convictions and the effect of pretrial publicity have been alleged, so far unsuccessfully, to violate the right to be presumed innocent. Other such allegations can be anticipated as this right is tested under the ICCPR and the American Convention.

19. Jacobs, *The European Convention on Human Rights*, 113.

Article 11(2), which proscribes ex post facto offenses, requires quoting in full. It states:

No one shall be held guilty of any penal offence on account of any act or omission which did not constitute a penal offence, under national or international law, at the time when it was committed. Nor shall a heavier penalty be imposed than the one that was applicable at the time the penal offence was committed.

Two points here are worth noting: first, the reference to international law, inserted "to exclude doubts as to the Nuremberg and Tokyo trials" and "to ensure that no one shall escape punishment for a criminal offence under international law by pleading that his act was legal under his own national law"; and, second, the extension, in the second sentence, of the nonretroactivity principle to increased penalties.

Article 15(1) of the ICCPR, from which there may be no derogation according to Article 4(2), closely follows Article 11(2); thus it may be argued convincingly that customary international law now prohibits both ex post facto offenses and penalties. Moreover, Article 15(1) adds a sentence designed to guarantee an accused the benefits of ex post facto legal reforms: "If, subsequent to the commission of the offence, provision is made by law for the imposition of a lighter penalty, the offender shall benefit thereby." Article 15(2) of the ICCPR also adds an entirely new and arguably superfluous provision justifying past and authorizing future international war crimes trials: "Nothing in this article shall prejudice the trial and punishment of any person for any act or omission which, at the time when it was committed, was criminal according to the general principles of law recognized by the community of nations." Articles 7 and 9 of the European Convention and American Convention respectively are based upon Article 11(2) of the UDHR and Article 15 of the ICCPR, albeit both contain one or more variations.

While the primary purpose of such ex post facto provisions is to prohibit retrospective penal legislation, a secondary purpose is to preclude "the courts from extending the scope of the criminal law by interpretation." Thus the former European Commission, construing Article 7 of the European Convention, noted that it "does not merely prohibit—except as provided in paragraph (2)—retroactive application of the criminal law to the detriment of the accused," but it "also confirms, in a more general way, the principle of the statutory nature of offences and punishment . . . and prohibits, in particular, extension of the application of the criminal law *in malam partem* by analogy."[20] It further added that,

although it is not normally for the Commission to ascertain the proper interpretation of municipal law by national courts . . . , the case is otherwise in matters where the Convention expressly refers to municipal law, as it does in Article 7. . . . [U]nder Article 7 the application of a provision of municipal penal law to an act not covered by the provision in question directly results in a conflict with the Convention, so that the Commission can and must take cognisance of allegations and of such false interpretation of municipal law.

The above remarks, according to Castberg, "clearly keep the door open for preventing under Article 7 not only the application of criminal law by analogy, but also extensive interpretations."[21] The various proscriptions against ex post facto offenses certainly offer an opportunity to develop a similar body of restraints against retroactive judicial as well as legislative action.

---

20. *X v. Austria, 1965 Yearbook of the European Convention on Human Rights* (Eur. Ct. Hum. Rts.), 190, 198.
21. Fredde Castberg, *The European Convention on Human Rights* (Dobbs Ferry, N.Y.: Oceana, 1974), 130.

QUESTIONS FOR REFLECTION AND DISCUSSION

1. Lillich states that the civil and political rights of individuals are "commonly considered to be the most basic and fundamental of all human rights." Do you agree? What evidence can you adduce to support your response? Irrespective of your answer to the first question, should civil and political rights be considered to be the most fundamental of all human rights? Why or why not? Would persons in developing countries agree? Would Kapur (Reading 6 in Chapter 1) agree?

2. In "Distinguishing Criteria of Human Rights," in Karel Vasak, ed., *The International Dimensions of Human Rights* (Westport, Conn.: Greenwood Press for UNESCO, 1982), 43–59, 50, Theo C. van Boven recounts the discussion of the drafters of the two international covenants on human rights:

> those who favoured the drafting of two separate instruments argued that civil and political rights were enforceable, or justiciable, and immediately applicable, while economic, social and cultural rights were to be progressively implemented . . . they drew the attention to the fact that civil and political rights, being "legal" rights, required different means and methods of implementation (namely through complaints procedures) than economic, social and cultural rights, which were program rights and could best be implemented through a system of periodic reports.

Are first-generation rights more "legal" than second-generation rights? If so, in what sense? Does the fact that socioeconomic and cultural rights may require "different means and methods of implementation" make them any less legal? Why? Why not? Support your answer with arguments/reasons drawn from relevant materials and sources.

3. Should means or relative efficiency of implementation of rights be the basis for deciding what are "most basic and fundamental" among human rights? Why? Why not? Support your response with reasons/arguments drawn from relevant materials and sources.

4. Lillich is at pains to identify which treaty-prescribed civil and political rights have become part of customary international law. Why?

5. Lillich notes the prohibition of slavery as an example of a right having *jus cogens* status. Consider the other rights discussed in the essay. Which of these also have *jus cogens* status, and which do not? Why do those lacking *jus cogens* status fall short?

6. How would you define and distinguish "equal protection of the law" and "equality under the law"?

7. Lillich notes the presence of "derogation" and "limitation" (or "clawback") clauses in the ICCPR and analogous regional instruments, allowing states to excuse themselves from their obligations under these agreements. What is the difference between these two types of clauses? Why do they exist? What is their utility? Are they desirable? Necessary? From the standpoint of wanting to enhance human rights, which type is better? Why? What are your criteria?

8. Considering all the ways in which civil and political guarantees can be lawfully circumvented, what is their status under contemporary international law?

9. It is necessary, surely, that states be able to function effectively during public emergencies. But is it necessary that they be allowed to suspend or curtail human rights guarantees in the process? A customary international law "doctrine of margin of appreciation" extends to states a certain degree of latitude in determining the existence of a public emergency. Is such a doctrine desirable? If it is, in respect of which rights is it desirable? Undesirable? And based on which specific considerations? Are there any rights or prohibitions that should be immune from suspension? What are they? In each case, support your answer with reasons and with any further evidence drawn from materials or sources you have been able to find to supplement your reading of Lillich.

10. Rights cast at high levels of abstraction, such as "the right to life," present interpretive problems. Does "right to life" guarantee protection against, say, capital punishment, voluntary euthanasia, or abortion? Conscriptive military service? Should it? All? Some? If only some, according to what differentiating criteria? Why do you think drafters include rights as abstract as "right to life"?

11. Are civil rights inherently captured by any particular concept of democracy?

12. Do you see any clear diversions from the international legal rights described in the article and the rights provided in your own domestic legal system (or other national legal systems with which you are familiar)? If so, what are they and what makes them inconsistent?

12. DANIEL MOECKLI *Equality and Non-Discrimination*

The notion that all human beings are equal and therefore deserve to be treated equally has a powerful intuitive appeal. It is one of the central ideals of the Enlightenment and at the heart of liberal theories of the state. It is included in the key human rights instruments; and the Vienna Declaration and Programme of Action, adopted by the World Conference on Human Rights in 1993, describes it as "a fundamental rule of international human rights law."[1]

What this fundamental rule entails in practice, however, is difficult to establish. Equality can be formulated in different ways, and deciding which concept of equality to use is not a question of logic but a political choice. In this sense, equality is an "empty idea"—it does not answer the questions of who are equals and what constitutes equal treatment. The challenge, therefore, is to give substance to the abstract notion of equality by translating it into concrete legal formulations that make clear which forms of unequal treatment are legitimate because they are based on morally acceptable criteria and which ones are wrongful. This essay explains how this challenge has been addressed in international human rights law.

THE MEANING OF EQUALITY AND NON-DISCRIMINATION

The terms "equality" and "non-discrimination" have often been used interchangeably and described as the positive and negative statement of the same principle: whereas the maxim of equality requires that equals be treated equally, the prohibition of discrimination precludes differential treatment on unreasonable grounds. In recent years, however, there has been an increased emphasis on the positive formulation. This shift in terminology highlights that equality implies not only a negative obligation not to discriminate, but also a duty to recognize differences between people and to take positive action to achieve real equality. Thus, whereas "non-discrimination" corresponds to the more limited concept of formal equality, usage of the term "equality" stresses the need for a more positive approach aimed at substantive equality.

FORMAL EQUALITY

Formal equality refers to Aristotle's classical maxim according to which likes must be treated alike.[2] This notion of equality as consistency focuses on the process rather than the outcome: equality is achieved if individuals in a comparable situation are treated equally, regardless of the result. However, this idea of equality raises the question of when two cases can be said to be alike. It is inevitable that laws and government action classify persons into groups that are treated differently. Under a progressive taxation system, for example, people are treated differently according to their income. In states with a juvenile justice system, people are treated differently according to their age. These distinctions are generally seen as perfectly legitimate. But which differences in treatment are legitimate and which ones are not? The principle that likes should be treated alike does not, by itself, answer this question.

There are other problems with the concept of equality as consistency. First, since it is not concerned with the outcome, it does not matter whether two parties are treated equally well or equally badly.[3] Second, inconsistent treatment can only be demonstrated if the complainant can find a comparably situated person who has been treated more favorably. Third, treating people apparently consistently regardless of their differing backgrounds may have a disparate impact on particular groups. A law which, in the famous words of Anatole France, "forbids the rich as well as the poor to sleep under bridges, to beg in the streets, and to steal bread" will in fact entrench inequality.[4]

1. UN Doc. A/CONF.157/23 (25 June 1993), para. 15.

2. Aristotle, *The Nicomachean Ethics of Aristotle* (1911) Book V3, paras.1131a–b.
3. See, e.g., *Palmer v. Thompson*, 403 U.S. 217 (1971).
4. Anatole France, *Le Lys rouge* (Paris: Calmann-Lévy, 1894), ch. 7.

Substantive Equality

Proponents of a substantive conception of equality recognize that a merely formal notion of equality as procedural fairness can perpetuate existing patterns of disadvantage. Drawing on values such as human dignity, distributive justice, and equal participation, they argue that equality must go beyond consistent treatment of likes. There are two main variants of substantive equality: equality of opportunity and equality of results.

According to the notion of equality of opportunity, true equality can only be achieved if people are not only treated equally but are also given the same opportunities. Like competitors in a race, everyone should be able to begin from the same starting point. Equality of opportunity requires the removal of barriers to the advancement of disadvantaged groups, such as upper age limits for employment that may disadvantage women with childcare responsibilities. According to a broader, substantive understanding of the concept, it may also require positive measures such as training. But equality of opportunity does not aim to achieve equality of outcome. Once the race has started, everyone is treated the same.

Equality of results goes further than this and aims to achieve an equal distribution of social goods such as education, employment, healthcare, and political representation. It recognizes that removing barriers does not guarantee that disadvantaged groups will in fact be able to take advantage of available opportunities. Abolishing upper age limits, for example, does not, by itself, ensure that more women with childcare responsibilities will be able to apply for jobs.

These differing conceptions of equality find their reflection in different forms of legal regulation. No legal system relies exclusively on simply one approach to equality.

EQUALITY AND NON-DISCRIMINATION IN INTERNATIONAL LAW

The right to equality and non-discrimination gives concrete expression to the basic idea on which the whole international human rights system is founded: that all human beings, regardless of their status or membership of a particular group, are entitled to a set of rights. Since it underlies all other human rights, equality is often described not only as a "right" but also as a "prin-ciple." The foundational significance of equality is reflected in the fact that it is proclaimed in the very first article of the Universal Declaration of Human Rights (UDHR): "All human beings are born free and equal in dignity and rights."

Sources

Article 1(3) of the UN Charter makes it clear that one of the basic purposes of the UN is the promotion of the equal guarantee of human rights for all without any distinction. Numerous instruments aimed at the realization of this notion have been adopted under the auspices of the UN. The general human rights instruments guarantee the right to equality and non-discrimination in several of their provisions.[5] As far as the specialized human rights treaties are concerned, at least three are specifically devoted to addressing certain forms of discrimination,[6] and two at least partly pursue the same objective and contain explicit provisions on equality and non-discrimination.[7] The only global human rights treaties without explicit non-discrimination clauses are the Convention against Torture and Other Cruel, Inhuman or Degrading Treatment or Punishment (CAT) and the International Convention for the Protection of All Persons from Enforced Disappearance.

The right to equality and non-discrimination is also guaranteed by all major regional human rights instruments.[8] In addition, a range of specialized regional treaties, provide protection against particular forms of discrimination.[9]

Finally, it is now widely acknowledged that, at the very least, the right to non-discrimination on the grounds of race, sex, and religion binds all states, irrespective of their ratification of human

---

5. See UDHR arts. 1, 2(1), and 7; ICCPR arts. 2, 3, and 26; ICESCR arts. 2(2) and 3.
6. See ICERD, CEDAW, and the CRPD.
7. See CRC arts. 2 and 28; ICRMW arts. 1(1), 7, 18, 25, 27, 28, 30, 43, 45, 54, 55, and 70.
8. See ACHPR arts. 2, 3, 18(3)–(4), and 28; ACHR arts. 1 and 24, the American Declaration of the Rights and Duties of Man, art. II; the Arab Charter on Human Rights, arts. 2, 9, and 35; ECHR art. 14 and Protocol No. 12; and the Charter of Fundamental Rights of the European Union, arts. 20, 21(1), and 23.
9. E.g., the Protocol to the African Charter on Human and Peoples' Rights on the Rights of Women in Africa and the Inter-American Convention on the Elimination of All Forms of Discrimination against Persons with Disabilities.

rights treaties, because it has become part of customary international law. The Inter-American Court of Human Rights has gone further than this and held that also the guarantee against discrimination on other grounds, including language, political or other opinion, national, ethnic or social origin, nationality, age, economic situation, property, civil status, birth, or any other status, forms part of general international law and, indeed, is a norm of *jus cogens*[10] that cannot be set aside by treaty or acquiescence.[11]

Scope: Subordinate and Autonomous Norms

Non-discrimination provisions can be subdivided into subordinate and autonomous (or freestanding) norms. *Subordinate norms* prohibit discrimination only in the enjoyment of the rights and freedoms otherwise set forth in the respective instrument. An example of a subordinate norm is ICCPR Article 2(1), which states:

> Each State Party to the present Covenant undertakes to respect and to ensure to all individuals within its territory and subject to its jurisdiction the rights recognized in the present Covenant, without distinction of any kind, such as race, colour, sex, language, religion, political or other opinion, national or social origin, property, birth or other status.

Other subordinate norms include UDHR Article 2(1), ICESCR Article 2(2), CRC Article 2 (1), ICRMW Article 7, ACHR Article 1, ACHPR Article 2, and ECHR Article 14.[12]

UDHR Article 7, ICCPR Article 26, ICERD Articles 2 and 5, ACHR Article 24, and ACHPR Article 3, on the other hand, are *autonomous norms*: they guarantee non-discrimination not only in the context of other rights but in general. For example, ICCPR Article 26 provides:

> All persons are equal before the law and are entitled without any discrimination to the equal protection of the law. In this respect, the law shall prohibit any discrimination and guarantee to all persons equal and effective protection against discrimination on any ground such as race, colour, sex, language, religion, political or other opinion, national or social origin, property, birth or other status.

The UN Human Rights Committee (HRC)[13] elaborated on the scope of this provision in *Bröeks v. The Netherlands*[14] when it emphasized that "Article 26 does not merely duplicate the guarantees already provided for in Article 2," but instead "prohibits discrimination in law or in practice in any field regulated and protected by public authorities."[15] The Committee confirmed this finding in its General Comment 18.[16] Thus, states parties to the ICCPR have a general obligation neither to enact legislation with a discriminatory content nor to apply laws in a discriminatory way.

Prohibited Grounds of Distinction

Which grounds of distinction are unacceptable and should therefore be prohibited? There

10. *Eds.*—Latin for "cogent law"; compelling or peremptory norms deemed to be fundamental, overriding principles of law and public policy, from which no derogation is ever permitted (e.g., prohibitions on aggression, slavery, torture, genocide).

11. OC/18, *Juridical Condition and Rights of the Undocumented Migrants*, IACtHR Series A No. 18 (2003) paras. 100–101 and 173.4.

12. As the ECHR does not contain an autonomous norm in addition to its subordinate provision in Article 14, the jurisprudence of the European Court of Human Rights interpreting it is of particular importance. According to the European Court, in order to invoke Article 14 ("The enjoyment of the rights and freedoms set forth in this Convention shall be secured without discrimination on any ground such as sex, race, colour, language, religion, political or other opinion, national or social origin, association with a national minority,

property, birth or other status"), an applicant must show that the facts of the case fall "within the ambit" of another substantive Convention right. *Rasmussen v. Denmark* (1984) 7 EHRR 371, para. 29. [*Eds.*—Noteworthy, however, as the author further comments, is that "Protocol 12, which entered into force in 2005 but has not been widely ratified so far, contains a non-discrimination guarantee that is not limited to the enjoyment of Convention rights." On the other hand, he adds, "this guarantee is still narrower than the general right to equality before the law and equal protection of the law under ICCPR Article 26 in that it only applies to the enjoyment of rights set forth by (national) law."]

13. Established pursuant to ICCPR art. 2(1) to oversee the implementation of the ICCPR.

14. UN Doc. CCPR/C/29/D/172/1984 (9 April 1987).

15. Ibid., at para. 12.3.

16. HRC, General Comment 18, UN Doc. HRI/GEN/1/Rev.9 (Vol. I) 195, para. 12.

is no straightforward answer to this question as, depending on one's moral and political views, any criterion may be regarded as either relevant or irrelevant. There is certainly broad consensus today that normally a person's inherent characteristics such as race, color, or sex are not acceptable criteria for differential treatment. In addition, grounds such as membership of a particular group, holding certain beliefs, and national or social origin are outlawed by most human rights treaties. But as is evident from a comparison between the ICCPR, adopted in 1966, and the ICRMW, adopted in 1990, what is seen as unacceptable can change over time: the ICRMW has considerably expanded the list of prohibited grounds by adding the criteria of conviction, ethnic origin, nationality, age, economic position, and marital status. Today, further criteria, including disability and sexual orientation and gender identity would have to be added.

Equality and non-discrimination norms vary widely in their approaches to defining the prohibited grounds of distinction. A first type of norm provides for *a general guarantee of equality*, without specifying any particular prohibited grounds. ACHR Article 24, for instance, simply states: "All persons are equal before the law. Consequently, they are entitled, without discrimination, to equal protection of the law."

A second category of norms uses a diametrically opposed approach: these norms contain an *exhaustive list* of prohibited grounds. The CEDAW, for instance, prohibits only distinctions based on "sex" (Article 1), the ICERD those based on "race, colour, descent, or national or ethnic origin" (Article 1(1)), and the CRPD those based on "disability" (Articles 1 and 5). Article 2(2) ICESCR, Article 2(1) CRC, and Article 1 ACHR contain lists that are much longer but still fixed.

Steering a middle course, there is a third category of norms that contain a list of prohibited grounds but one that is *open ended*. For instance, ECHR Article 14 and its Protocol 12 prohibit "discrimination on *any* ground *such as* sex, race, colour, language, religion, political or other opinion, national or social origin, association with a national minority, property, birth or other status." Similarly, UDHR Article 2(1), ICRMW Articles 1(1) and 7, and ACHPR Article 2 provide for non-discrimination "without distinction of *any* kind." As a consequence, even distinctions made on grounds that are not explicitly listed

may engage these provisions. The European Court of Human Rights sometimes does not even find it necessary to state the particular ground of distinction involved when considering a case under ECHR Article 14.

The text of ICCPR Article 26 ("discrimination on *any* ground *such as* race, colour, sex, language, religion, political or other opinion, national or social origin, property, birth or other status") suggests that this provision is also open ended. Nevertheless, the HRC has often been at pains to fit a particular distinction within one of the listed grounds, be it the specific ones or the broad rubric of "other status." Thus, it has found that the reference to "sex" also includes "sexual orientation"[17] and that "other status" covers grounds such as nationality, age, and marital status.[18] But it has never clarified how it decides whether a difference in treatment comes within the reference to "other status." Its efforts to apply one of the listed grounds suggest that the Committee regards the list of Article 26 as exhaustive and it has accordingly stated that an applicant is required to show that the difference in treatment was based on one of the enumerated grounds.[19]

DIRECT AND INDIRECT DISCRIMINATION

At the heart of all non-discrimination norms is the formal equality requirement that likes should be treated alike. It is therefore clear that international human rights law prohibits direct discrimination. But human rights bodies and courts have acknowledged that the requirement of consistent treatment is not sufficient to achieve true equality: not only discriminatory treatment but also a discriminatory outcome (indirect discrimination) is prohibited. It is important to note that international human rights law prohibits both intended and unintended discrimination. Whether there has been a difference in treatment or result is the first question that a

---

17. *Toonen v. Australia*, UN Doc. CCPR/C/50/D/488/1992 (31 March 1994) para. 8.7.
18. See *Gueye v. France*, UN Doc. CCPR/C/35/D/196/1985 (3 April 1989) para. 9.4; *Schmitz-de-Jong v. The Netherlands*, UN Doc. CCPR/C/72/D/855/1999 (16 July 2001); *Danning v. The Netherlands*, UN Doc. CCPR/C/OP/2 (9 April 1987).
19. *BdB v. The Netherlands*, UN Doc. CCPR/C/35/D/273/1988 (2 May 1989) para. 6.7.

court needs to assess when considering a discrimination claim under international human rights law. Once a prima facie case of direct or indirect discrimination has been made out, the court must decide whether there is a justification for the difference in treatment or outcome. This second element of the test is discussed below ("Justified and Unjustified Distinctions").

DIRECT DISCRIMINATION

Direct discrimination occurs when a person, *on account of one or more of the prohibited grounds*, is treated less favorably than someone else in comparable circumstances. Thus, the complainant must show, first, that others have been treated better because they do not share the relevant characteristic or status and, second, that these others are in a comparable, or, in the terminology of the European Court of Human Rights, "analogous"[20] or "relevantly similar"[21] situation. In practice, international human rights bodies often tend to merge the comparability test with the test as to whether there is an objective justification for the difference in treatment, explained below.

A classic example of direct discrimination is when members of a certain ethnic group are denied access to a public facility, such as a swimming pool, which is open to everyone else. But most cases of direct discrimination are not as straightforward as this. More often, direct discrimination occurs covertly: the "discriminator" will not admit that the difference in treatment was based on a prohibited ground, making it difficult for the complainant to provide sufficient evidence. Furthermore, it may not always be easy to identify a person who is in a comparable situation. How can a woman establish pay discrimination when there are no men doing the same job?

INDIRECT DISCRIMINATION

Indirect discrimination occurs when a practice, rule, or requirement that is outwardly "neutral," that is, not based on one of the prohibited grounds of distinction, has a dispropor-

tionate impact on particular groups defined by reference to one of these grounds. The concept has its origins in U.S. and European Community (EC) law but has now also found its way into the jurisprudence of international and regional human rights bodies.

The HRC recognized the possibility of indirect discrimination, albeit without explicitly referring to the concept, for the first time in 1989 in *Singh Bhinder v. Canada*.[22] Only much later in 2003 in *Althammer v. Austria*, a case concerning the abolition of household benefits that affected retired persons to a greater extent than active employees, did the HRC expressly refer to the concept of "indirect discrimination."[23]

Similarly, it was only in 2007 that the European Court of Human Rights, in its groundbreaking ruling in *DH and others v. Czech Republic*, came up with an explicit definition of "indirect discrimination." Several Roma children had complained that the manner in which statutory rules governing assignment to schools were applied in practice resulted in the placement of a disproportionate number of Roma pupils in "special schools" for children with "mental deficiencies." Referring to the definition of "indirect discrimination" in EC law, the Grand Chamber of the European Court stated:

> The Court has already accepted in previous cases that a difference in treatment may take the form of disproportionately prejudicial effects of a general policy or measure which, though couched in neutral terms, discriminates against a group. . . . such a situation may amount to "indirect discrimination," which does not necessarily require a discriminatory intent.[24]

20. *Lithgow v. UK* (1986) 8 EHRR 329, para. 177.
21. *Fredin v. Sweden* (1991) 13 EHRR 784, para. 60.

22. UN Doc. CCPR/C/37/D/208/1986 (9 November 1989). The case concerned a Sikh who was dismissed from his employment because he refused to comply with a legal requirement that safety headgear be worn at work, as his religion required him to wear only a turban. While the Committee found that the legislation could amount to de facto discrimination because, though neutral in that it applied to all persons without discrimination, it disproportionately affected persons of the Sikh religion, it nevertheless found no violation of ICCPR Article 26 as the safety headgear requirement was based on reasonable and objective grounds.
23. UN Doc. CCPR/C/78/D/998/2001 (8 August 2003) para. 10.2.
24. 24. App. No. 57325/00, Judgment of 13 November 2007, para. 184.

The African Commission on Human and Peoples' Rights seems also to have recognized the concept of indirect discrimination.[25]

DISCRIMINATORY INTENTION

In some legal systems, such as the United States, complainants need to show a discriminatory intention or purpose to establish discrimination. There is no such requirement under international human rights law. That both intended and unintended discrimination—not to be confused with direct and indirect discrimination[26]—are prohibited under international law is apparent from the explicit definitions of discrimination contained in some of the human rights treaties. The ICERD defines discrimination as any distinction based on one of the listed grounds "which has the purpose *or effect* of nullifying or impairing the recognition, enjoyment or exercise, on an equal footing, of human rights and fundamental freedoms."[27] The CEDAW definition is almost identical.[28] The HRC, in its General Comment on non-discrimination, has adopted the same definition for the purposes of the ICCPR and has made it clear in its jurisprudence that discriminatory intention is not a necessary element of discrimination.[29] Equally, the European Court of Human Rights has indicated that discrimination under Article 14 ECHR may also relate to the *effects* of state measures.[30]

JUSTIFIED AND UNJUSTIFIED DISTINCTIONS

Once it is established that there has been a difference in treatment or outcome, the next question that needs to be answered is whether there is a justification for it. As explained above, it is to some extent inevitable that states classify people into different groups. The crucial question is whether there are objective and reasonable criteria for these distinctions.

THE JUSTIFICATION TEST

The HRC, in its General Comment on non-discrimination, has stressed that, for the purposes of the ICCPR, "not every differentiation of treatment will constitute discrimination, if the criteria for such differentiation are reasonable and objective and if the aim is to achieve a purpose which is legitimate under the Covenant."[31] But it is in the jurisprudence of the European Court of Human Rights that the criteria for distinguishing between justified and unjustified distinction have been most clearly articulated. The Court interpreted ECHR Article 14 for the first time in the *Belgian Linguistics Case* and has since repeatedly confirmed those conclusions:

> the Court, following the principles which may be extracted from the legal practice of a large number of democratic states, holds that the principle of equality of treatment is violated if the distinction has no objective and reasonable justification. The existence of such a justification must be assessed in relation to the aim and effects of the measure under consideration, regard being had to the principles which normally prevail in democratic societies. A difference of treatment in the exercise of a right laid down in the Convention must not only pursue a legitimate aim: Article 14 is likewise violated when it is clearly established that there is no reasonable relationship of proportionality between the means employed and the aim sought to be realised.[32]

This two-limb test, requiring that any difference in treatment must (1) pursue a legitimate

25. *Purohit and Moore v. The Gambia*, Communication No. 241/2001, 16th Activity Report (2002) paras. 53–55.

26. It is true that these concepts will often correlate, but this is not always the case—e.g., the direct exclusion of pregnant women and mothers from certain types of work where the intention is to protect the respective groups rather than to discriminate against them. On the other hand, a "neutral" criterion such as a literacy test for job applicants may well be used as a pretext for excluding certain ethnic groups, amounting to intended indirect discrimination.

27. Art. 1(1) (emphasis added).

28. Art. 1.

29. See, e.g., *Simunek et al. v. The Czech Republic*, UN Doc. CCPR/C/54/D/516/1992 (19 July 1995) para. 11.7; *Adam v. The Czech Republic*, UN Doc. CCPR/C/57/D/586/1994 (23 July 1996) para. 12.7.

30. *Case Relating to Certain Aspects of the Laws on the Use of Languages in Education in Belgium (Belgian Linguistics Case) (No. 2)* (1968) 1 EHRR 252, para. 10.

31. HRC, General Comment 18, UN Doc. HRI/GEN/1/Rev. 9 (Vol. I) 195, para. 13.

32. Ibid., para. 10.

aim and (2) be proportionate, is very similar to the test used in the context of other rights to assess the permissibility of limitations. The test formulated by the European Court has been adopted, explicitly or implicitly, by most other human rights bodies.

In terms of what exactly this test involves, its first limb will not usually be very difficult for states to meet: most distinctions can be argued to pursue some aim that qualifies as legitimate, for example the protection of public order or tailoring the education system to children's differing learning capabilities. More difficult to satisfy is the second element of the test, the proportionality requirement. This requirement reflects the basic notion that a fair balance ought to be struck between the interests of the community and respect for individual rights. A wide range of factors may need to be considered to assess proportionality, including the suitability of a distinction to achieve the aim pursued, the availability of alternative means, and the question of whether the disadvantage suffered by the affected individuals or groups is excessive in relation to the aim. While this assessment inevitably turns on the specific facts of a given case, international human rights bodies have been consistent in their characterization of certain reasons as not sufficient to justify differential treatment; these include, among others, mere administrative inconvenience, existence of a long-standing tradition, prevailing views in society, or convictions of the local population.[33]

STANDARD OF REVIEW

The stringency with which human rights courts or bodies review the existence of a justification will vary according to a number of factors.

Most important, certain grounds of distinction are generally regarded as inherently suspect and therefore require particularly strict scrutiny. The grounds attracting the greatest degree of attention and most likely to be declared unjustified are race, ethnicity, sex, and religion.

[*Eds.*—The author then documents the verity of his strict scrutiny finding: first in respect of race (citing the widespread ratification of the ICERD, the general acceptance of racial non-discrimination as forming part of customary international law, and the endorsement of the strict scrutiny standard by the European Commission and Court[34] and by the Inter-American Commission on Human Rights[35]); next in terms of ethnicity (citing the European Court's 2005 judgment in *Timishev v. Russia*[36]); third relative to sex (citing "a wealth of international treaties addressing the problem of sexual discrimination, including the CEDAW," and decisions of the Inter-American Commission[37] and European Court[38]); finally, the suspect nature of distinctions based on *religion* (citing the unanimous adoption by the UN General Assembly of the Declaration on the Elimination of All Forms of Intolerance and Discrimination Based on Religion or Belief and the European Court's finding that "Notwithstanding any possible arguments to the contrary, a distinction based essentially on a difference in religion alone is not acceptable").[39]]

As far as other grounds of distinction are concerned, it is difficult to discern a consistent approach in international case law. Lists of suspect classifications are, in any event, not fixed but can change as international law on these matters develops. Given the recent emergence of new international norms against discrimination on grounds such as disability, sexual orientation, and age, it seems likely that these classifications will soon be regarded as suspect, if they are not already regarded as such.

Apart from the ground of distinction, the intensity of review may also depend on a number of other factors. For example, most courts and human rights bodies tend to apply a lenient stan-

33. See *Gueye v. France,* note 18, para. 9.5; *Müller and Engelhard v. Namibia,* UN Doc. CCPR/C/74/D/919/2000 (26 March 2002) para. 6.8; *Bröeks v. The Netherlands,* note 17; *Inze v. Austria* (1988) 10 EHRR 394, para. 44.

34. *East African Asians v. UK* (1973) 3 EHRR 76, paras. 207–8; *Cyprus v. Turkey,* App. No. 25781/94, Judgment of 10 May 2001, para 306.

35. Case 11.625, *María Eugenia Morales de Sierra v. Guatemala,* IACommHR Report No. 4/01 (19 January 2001) para. 36.

36. *Timishev v. Russia,* App. nos. 55762/00 and 55974/00, Judgment of 13 December 2005, para. 58.

37. *María Eugenia Morales de Sierra v. Guatemala,* note 35, para. 36.

38. *Abdulaziz, Cabales and Balkandali v. UK* (1985) 7 EHRR 471, para. 78.

39. *Hoffmann v. Austria* (1993) 17 EHRR 293, para. 36.

dard as far as matters of social or economic policy are concerned, whereas classifications affecting fundamental individual interests entail particularly strict scrutiny. Furthermore, it will generally be more difficult for states to justify direct rather than indirect discrimination. The Declaration of Principles on Equality, an important but nonbinding document signed by numerous human rights and equality experts, states that "direct discrimination may be permitted only very exceptionally."[40]

EVIDENCE AND PROOF

According to established human rights jurisprudence, it is up to the individual complaining of discrimination to establish a difference in treatment or outcome, the ground of distinction, and the existence of comparably situated groups. Having done so, the burden of proof shifts to the state to show that there is a justification for the distinction.

In cases of alleged indirect discrimination, however, complainants may find it very difficult to prove that a neutral measure has a disproportionate impact on particular groups. Therefore, the European Court of Human Rights has held that less strict evidential rules should apply in these cases.[41] Yet *often* the data required to establish a presumption that a measure has a discriminatory effect can only be collected by state authorities. The UN treaty bodies therefore regularly stress in their concluding observations that states have a duty to collect and analyze relevant statistical data, disaggregated by grounds of distinction. Such a duty to gather information has also been included in the Declaration of Principles on Equality.[42]

POSITIVE ACTION

As with any other human right, the right to equality and non-discrimination entails state obligations of different types. The *obligation to re-*

spect requires states to refrain from any discriminatory action and to ensure that all their laws and practices comply with the right to non-discrimination. The *obligation to protect* imposes a duty on states to prevent discrimination by non-state actors. According to the consistent jurisprudence of the UN treaty bodies, this means that states must introduce comprehensive legislation prohibiting discrimination in fields such as employment, education, healthcare, housing, and the provision of goods and services.

However, an exclusively prohibitory approach is severely limited in that it focuses on discrimination understood as individual, isolated events that can be remedied through penalizing the perpetrators and compensating the victims. In fact discrimination is often the consequence of deeply embedded patterns of disadvantage and exclusion that can only be addressed through changes to social and institutional structures. Accordingly, it is now well established in international human rights law that it is not sufficient for states to have anti-discrimination legislation in place. Instead, they also have an *obligation to promote, guarantee, and secure* equality by taking proactive steps to eliminate structural patterns of disadvantage and to further social inclusion. This obligation, often referred to as the duty to take "positive action," may cover a huge variety of legislative, administrative, and policy measures, ranging from the restructuring of institutions to the provision of "reasonable accommodation"[43] for individuals in particular circumstances, from educational campaigns to the use of public procurement to promote equality, and from the "mainstreaming"[44] of equality issues in public policy to encouraging participation of affected groups in relevant decision-making processes.

One important aspect of "positive action" is "affirmative action programmes" or, as they are generally called in international law, *special measures of protection.* These are "measures aimed specifically at correcting the position of members of a target group in one or more aspects of their

40. See Equal Rights Trust, Declaration of Principles on Equality, http://www.equalrightstrust.org/ endorse/index.htm [*Eds.*—accessed 16 June 2015], Principle 5.
41. *DH v. Czech Republic*, note 24, para. 188.
42. Declaration of Principles on Equality, note 40, Principle 24.

43. For a definition of "reasonable accommodation," see CRPD, art. 2.
44. For "gender mainstreaming," that is, the integration of a gender perspective in all legislation and public policies, see Report of the Fourth World Conference on Women, A/Conf.177/20 (1995), strategic objective H.2.

social life, in order to obtain effective equality."[45]
In their strongest form, such special measures
involve the preferential treatment of members of
a previously disadvantaged group over others in
the allocation of jobs, university places, and
other benefits (often referred to as "positive" or
"reverse discrimination").

Although such preferential treatment is
clearly incompatible with a formal notion of
equality, international human rights law permits
it, thus recognizing that it may be legitimate to
prioritize the achievement of substantive equality over the requirement of consistent treatment.
ICERD Article 1(4), for example, provides:

> Special measures taken for the sole purpose
> of securing adequate advancement of certain
> racial or ethnic groups or individuals requir-
> ing such protection as may be necessary in
> order to ensure such groups or individuals
> equal enjoyment or exercise of human rights
> and fundamental freedoms shall not be
> deemed racial discrimination, provided, how-
> ever, that such measures do not, as a conse-
> quence, lead to the maintenance of separate
> rights for different racial groups and that they
> shall not be continued after the objectives for
> which they were taken have been achieved.

The CEDAW contains a similar provision in
Article 4(1). For purposes of the ICCPR, the HRC
has made it clear that special measures are permissible as long as they meet the general justification test described above, that is, as long as
they pursue a legitimate aim in a proportionate
manner.[46] Proportionality in this context means,
among other things, that the preferential treatment must be introduced for the benefit of genuinely disadvantaged groups, be temporary, and
cease once the objectives have been achieved,
and not result in the maintenance of separate
rights for different groups.

Not only does international human rights law
permit, but to some extent it even *requires*, states
to adopt special measures of protection. As the

HRC's General Comment on non-discrimination
states: "the principle of equality sometimes requires States parties to take affirmative action in
order to diminish or eliminate conditions which
cause or help to perpetuate discrimination prohibited by the Covenant."[47]

That states may need to adopt special measures has also been highlighted by the Committee on Economic, Social and Cultural Rights. As
far as racial groups and women are concerned,
the duty follows from Article 2(2) ICERD and
Article 3 CEDAW, respectively. At the regional
level, the Inter-American Court of Human Rights
has observed that "States are obliged to take affirmative action to reverse or change discriminatory situations that exist in their societies to the
detriment of a specific group of persons,"[48] while
the European Court has stressed that "a failure
to attempt to correct inequality through different
treatment" may amount to a violation of the
right to non-discrimination.[49]

CONCLUSION

The concept of equality and non-discrimination
in international human rights law has evolved
significantly since the adoption of the UDHR.
Detailed legal standards have been drawn up
and human rights bodies and courts have developed a rich jurisprudence, giving concrete substance to the notion of equality. Nevertheless,
considerable gaps, inconsistencies, and uncertainties remain.

The most important challenge, however, is to
ensure that every human being is in fact able to
enjoy her or his right to equality. In a world in
which the average income of the richest 20 percent is about fifty times that of the bottom 20
percent and the 500 richest people earn more
than the poorest 416 million,[50] equal rights remain an unfulfilled promise for large sections of
the population. Recent developments in international human rights law are evidence of a growing recognition that, while prohibitions of

45. Progress report on the concept and practice of affirmative action by the Special Rapporteur of the Sub-
Commission on the Promotion and Protection of
Human Rights, UN Doc. E/CN.4/Sub.2/2001/15 (26
June 2001) para. 7.
46. E.g., *Stalla Costa v. Uruguay*, UN Doc. CCPR/
C/30/D/198/1985 (9 July 1987) para. 10; *Jacobs v. Belgium*, UN Doc. CCPR/ C/81/D/943/2000 (7 July 2004)
para. 9.5.

47. Note 31, para. 10.
48. *Juridical Condition and Rights of the Undocumented Migrants*, note 11, para. 104.
49. *Stec and Others v. UK*, App. nos. 65731/01 and
65900/01, Judgment of 12 April 2006, para. 51.
50. UN Development Programme, *Human Development
Report 2005*, 36–37.

discrimination play a crucial role in achieving equality, states also have an obligation to proactively tackle structural patterns of disadvantage—in other words, that formal and substantive approaches to equality need to be combined.

One key component of such a proactive strategy must be to ensure that all people can participate on an equal basis in all areas of economic, social, and political life, including in the very decisions on how equality should be realized.

QUESTIONS FOR REFLECTION AND DISCUSSION

1. In what sense is "equality an empty idea"?

2. Do you agree that "equality" and "non-discrimination" are simply different ways of expressing the same idea, or can you see nuances of emphasis that the terms bring into play that drive at different aspects of the basic idea of fairness? What difference does it make—if any—to focus upon non-discrimination as opposed to "equality"? Do the terms imply the need to look at anything in particular? Substantiate your answers as fully as you can.

3. What is the difference between formal and substantive equality? Does it matter? Why? Why not?

4. Which is preferable: equality of opportunity or equality of results? Support your answer with reasons and examples.

5. What are the international legal sources of the principle of equality? In the light of an analysis of the language of the relevant legal sources, what conceptions of equality do they indicate? Can you discern different conceptions of equality contained within different norms and rules? If so, which conceptions inhabit which rules/norms? You are encouraged to look up the relevant treaties to answer this question.

6. Which grounds of distinction are unacceptable as a basis for discrimination and should therefore be prohibited? On what basis and in accordance with which values? Are there any grounds of distinction that you consider an acceptable basis on which to discriminate? What, and why?

7. Why is the concept of indirect discrimination necessary? How does it relate, if at all, to unintentional discrimination?

8. In what way is the European doctrine of proportionality helpful, and how does it operate?

9. Moeckli states that "discrimination is often the consequence of deeply embedded patterns of disadvantage and exclusion that can only be addressed through changes to social and institutional structures. Accordingly, it is now well established in international human rights law that it is not sufficient for states to have anti-discrimination legislation in place. Instead, they also have an obligation to promote, guarantee, and secure equality by taking proactive steps to eliminate structural patterns of disadvantage and to further social inclusion."

How might Moeckli's observation resonate with the arguments of Todres (Reading 9) concerning "othering"? What might explain "deeply embedded patterns of disadvantage and exclusion"? Can you identify any such patterns within the structures of the global order? If so, what are they? If you can identify any, is international human rights law relevant to them? Why? Why not?

10. What group or groups in need are left unprotected by the anti-discrimination framework described in this essay, if any? What barriers prevent their full participation in society?

11. Affirmative action policies are often highly controversial and criticized for being, as Moeckli describes, "incompatible with a formal notion of equality." Reconsider what the ideal affirmative action policy for your community would look like, requiring that it accord entirely with Article 1(4) of the ICERD. Is this policy better than the status quo? Why? Why not?

12. Moeckli divides state obligations related to human rights into three categories: obligation to respect, obligation to protect, and the obligation to promote, guarantee, and secure. Are these obligations fulfilled by the legal practices of your country, state/province, or city? If so, how so? If not, why not, and what do you propose should be done about it?

13. INEKE VAN DER VALK *Racism: A Threat to Global Peace*

Doubtless surprising to many but nonetheless true, a definition of racism that can be accepted unanimously does not exist. Noteworthy in this regard is the inescapable fact that neither the International Bill of Human Rights,[1] nor the three leading regional human rights conventions in Europe, the Americas, and Africa as amended,[2] nor even the 1965 International Convention on the Elimination of All Forms of Racial Discrimination (ICERD) invoke the term, referring instead to "race" or to "racial discrimination." Thus, for example, does Article 1(1) of the ICERD provide that, "In this Convention, the term 'racial discrimination' shall mean any distinction, exclusion, restriction or preference based on race, colour, descent, or national or ethnic origin which has the purpose or effect of nullifying or impairing the recognition, enjoyment or exercise, on an equal footing, of human rights and fundamental freedoms in the political, economic, social, cultural or any other field of public life."[3] In part, this preference for the term "racial discrimination" in lieu of "racism" may be attributed to a desire to avoid semantic confrontation with a once popular belief that "racism" should be confined more or less to the World War II Nazi concept of race and racial superiority.[4] In any event, all of these instruments have as their ultimate goal the elimination of racism in

social discourse and behavior in manifold settings. All the more reason, therefore, that the concept "racism"—controversial in definition ergo controversial in application—be well and widely understood.

The concepts of race and racism are of relatively recent origin. Although ideas about human differences on the basis of color and phenotypic characteristics already occurred in earlier societies, the present meaning of the concept of "race" became current only toward the end of the eighteenth century subsequent to the French and American revolutions. The notion of "race" thus originated in modern times and has changed with the evolution of modern society.

After the Reformation, explanations of the origin of peoples in terms of religion or reason were increasingly displaced by a racial discourse in which anatomy, bloodlines, climate, geographical location, and language were central. The development of the natural sciences and of the related principles of categorization contributed to this development.

According to Bulmer and Solomos,[5] "race" had three central meanings:

- humanity is composed of different groups, each with its own common physical characteristics;
- these groups have different origins;
- racial boundaries have cultural and social significance.

Distinctions between and negative evaluations of phenotypic differences in skin color, in hair color, in the color and shape of eyes, in the shape of the skull, and so on have for a long time been a central element of the ideology of racism. These kinds of differences were used as explanations for differences in culture and in mental properties. By the late nineteenth and early twentieth centuries this mode of thinking was common in the Western world. It was developed in academia and spread throughout society. It was used to justify practices such as slavery and colonialism. "Race" was construed as a social fact and thus as an object of scientific inquiry.

By the late nineteenth and early twentieth

1. I.e., the 1948 Universal Declaration of Human Rights (UDHR), 1966 International Covenant on Economic, Social and Cultural Rights (ICESCR), and 1966 International Covenant on Civil and Political Rights (ICCPR).
2. I.e., the 1950 European Convention for the Protection of Human Rights and Fundamental Freedoms, the 1969 American Convention on Human Rights, and the 1981 African Charter on Human and Peoples' Rights.
3. *Eds.*—For extended discussion of the prohibition of racial and other forms of discrimination, see Reading 12 (Moeckli) in this chapter.
4. See Matthijs Hisschemöller, Troetje Loewenthal, and Marja Vuijsje, "Het slopen van het bolwerk" (The Demolition of the Rampart), in Matthijs Hisschemöller, ed., *Een bleek bolwerk* (A Pale Rampart) (Amsterdam: Pegasus, 1988), 137–50.

5. Martin Bulmer and John Solomos, eds., *Racism* (Oxford: OUP, 1999), 7.

centuries the concept of "race" acquired major political significance, too. "Race" as a dominant and widely accepted ideological concept in Western thought was no longer only used to explain differences but, in particular, also to justify inequalities at the political level. The shift to a political implementation of racist doctrines at the national level was made in the thirties by the National Socialists under the leadership of Adolph Hitler. This development culminated in genocide during the Second World War, when the Nazis killed six million Jews and at least two hundred thousand Gypsies in gas chambers.

After the Second World War, at the request of the United Nations Educational, Scientific and Cultural Organization (UNESCO), authorities in the social sciences examined the concept of race. In their declaration of 1950, they argued that "race" is less a biological phenomenon than a social myth:

> for all practical social purposes "race" is not so much a biological phenomenon as a social myth. The myth of "race" has created an enormous amount of human and social damage. In recent years it has taken a heavy toll in human lives and caused untold suffering. It still prevents the normal development of millions of human beings and deprives civilization of the effective co-operation of productive minds. The biological differences between ethnic groups should be disregarded from the standpoint of social acceptance and social action. The unity of mankind from both the biological and social viewpoints is the main thing.[6]

"Race" is a social construction invented by people. It is first and foremost a discursive category, "the organizing category of those way[s] of speaking, systems of representation, and social practices (discourses) which utilize a loose, often unspecified set of differences in physical characteristics—skin color, hair texture, physical and bodily features, and so forth—as *symbolic markers* to differentiate one group socially from another."[7] The UNESCO statement advocated drop-

ping the term "race" and replacing it by the more neutral term "ethnic group." "Race" no longer existed; that is to say, science abandoned the concept. Racism, however, did continue to exist.

The concept "racism" is much younger than the concept "race." The first scientific use of the concept of racism is often attributed to the German Jewish scientist Magnus Hirschfeld. He used it in the title of a book that was published in 1938 in which he criticized racial thinking. In Western Europe the term first appears in the dictionaries in the thirties. Since then, racism has remained a contested notion.

It is often argued that even now a generally accepted definition of "racism" is lacking. Historical research has shown that this concept has taken different forms in different national contexts. Historically, racism has also varied in signification. It should be noted, however, that many other complex social phenomena equally lack an accepted definition, as with sexism, for example. Different disciplines, such as economics, sociology, and social psychology, have developed different theories about the phenomenon on the basis of their specific perspectives. Thus, a definition of racism that can be accepted unanimously does not exist. We may, however, offer a global outline with some contours, including the properties of the phenomenon that are the object of frequent discussions in the academic world.

RACISM AS EXPRESSION OF GROUP DOMINANCE

The most important and most far-reaching forms of social inequality today are related to group relations based on gender, class, and ethnic background. (Inequality on the basis of age, sexual orientation, and physical or mental handicap also plays a role.) Historically, specific mechanisms of group dominance have produced and reproduced these forms of social inequality. Racism is a typical expression of group dominance. Racism as a system of social inequality implies that social groups do not have equal access to and control over material and immaterial social resources. At the material level, these resources include employment, income, and housing. Immaterial resources, however, are of equal concern, including education, knowledge, information, and access to the social networks and means of communication instrumental in

6. Ashley Montagu, "UNESCO Statement on Race by Social Scientists," in Montagu, *Race, Science and Humanity* (New York: Van Nostrand Reinhold, 1963), 172.
7. Stuart Hall, "The Question of Cultural Identity," in Stuart Hall, David Held, and Tony McGrew, eds., *Modernity and Its Futures* (Cambridge: Polity, 1993), 273–326.

public debates (such as the media, politics, the judicial system, the educational system, and the welfare sector). Crucial for understanding the phenomenon of racism is the observation that racism not only refers to overt and violent forms of social domination and exclusion but also to more indirect and subtle forms expressed in daily practices, including through the discursive practices of journalists, opinion makers, writers, politicians, and teachers who, few from ethnic minorities, legitimate social inequality and the daily organization of dominance and exclusion. It should, however, be stressed that racism is not considered a mental property of individual persons, but rather a dynamically changing dimension of social practices.

The different historical manifestations of racism have always been intimately linked to the different economic functions that the labor of the targeted groups fulfilled in the socioeconomic system. Wilson identifies the following characteristics of capitalism feeding racism: the exploitation of subordinated groups, the existence of extreme inequality, the monopolistic and private ownership of productive property, the struggle between capital and labor, the development of hierarchical labor structures, and the presence of reserve armies of labor. Though not everywhere the same in substance, structure, process, and effect, racism develops and increases where human exploitation, extreme inequality, and oppression exist—in particular where structures of inequality overlap with differences of color or origin. Disdain and denigration have historically functioned to justify and legitimize oppression and inequality.

HISTORICALLY SPECIFIC IDEOLOGICAL CONSTRUCTION

Since the Second World War, racism has been conceptualized as an irrational prejudice according to which other groups are considered inferior on the basis of biological-racial characteristics. Racism, however, is not a personality disorder or irrational prejudice. Although prejudice is an important underlying attitude, racism is a historically specific ideological construction. It changes with time and with the economic-political and sociocultural conditions in which it functions. Consequently, it has to be studied in its specific historical and social context.

Thus, racism is not a uniform, static, transhistorical phenomenon, but a complex, contradictory, multifaceted, and dynamic phenomenon that adapts itself to the conditions in which it functions. It is more than an ideology. It also involves discriminatory practices and discriminatory effects in the functioning of elements of the social structure, such as institutions. Racism, in its broad sense, also includes anti-Semitism and modern forms of ethnocentrism and xenophobia such as Islamophobia. Racism has many dimensions such as the cultural, sociopsychological, sociopolitical, and economic and should be studied on each level. Cutting through these different dimensions, discourse is central.

CENTRAL DIMENSIONS OF MEANING

Power and Group Polarization

As we have seen before, power is a central (sociological) characteristic of racism. By power we mean social, economic, political, and/or cultural power vis-à-vis domination/submission between social groups.

The reference to biological differences has been dropped since the Second World War, but it continues to function as an (unexpressed) criterion for dividing people into groups. It is not explicitly referred to in argumentation, however. Today, cultural issues are more central to the arguments that racist discourse uses to characterize "us" as superior and "them" as inferior. An important similarity between prewar racism and contemporary racism, however, is the representation of differences as "natural"—unchangeable, not socially constructed. This is equally the case with biological differences and cultural differences. This "naturalness" is another central dimension that can be discerned.

Naturalness

The theory of naturalism, especially as elaborated by those who in the nineteenth century advocated scientific racism, argues that the distinction between social groups (differentiated according to sex, class, and social background) is naturally given, not socially constructed. It is assumed that humanity may naturally be divided into different (unequal) social groups. This thinking in terms of the natural properties of groups implies that there is no consideration of the nature of social relations, such as current relations of power, while the main focus is on the intrinsic characteristics of different groups. In a racist perspective, the "natural" replaces the "social" or "political."

The process of racist signification has predominantly the effect of transforming the other into the "Other" (as when the Nazis required of Jewish people the wearing of a visible yellow star), and always the difference is mystified, presented as inherent to the empirical reality of the observable or of the supposed deviance from the dominant culture. The content of this process varies and has become less simplistic over time (e.g., "they are lazy"—of colonial labor origin—giving way to "they are not able to raise their children"—referencing growing criminality among inner-city street gangs and immigrant youth). But one constant has remained: the indicia of the Other continue to be predominantly phenotypical (i.e., color of the skin or eyes, hair texture, etc.), although in recent times secondary cultural markers play the differentiating role (e.g., *djellebah* or headscarf for Muslims).

BIOLOGICAL AND/OR CULTURAL DIFFERENCES

Since the nineteenth century, biological characteristics (such as skin color, and later also hair and eye color, and even measurements of skulls and noses) were studied to explain cultural differences. It is not accidental that in the period between the two world wars cultural anthropologists played an important role in the scientific underpinning of racism as well as in its refutation. The debate on "race" among scientists engaged in the development of scientific racism was hardly ever about physical characteristics alone. It was almost always interwoven with cultural interpretations and psychological speculations about human nature and its potential. Race, culture, and language were considered to be different expressions of an inherited identity.

In the 1920s, the American cultural anthropologist Franz Boas and his followers were the first to plead for the separation of "race" and "culture." From that point onward the debate on "nature" versus "nurture" and the theory of cultural relativism developed, with the relationship between what people are given at birth and what

they acquire by education and socialization occupying a central position in this nature/nurture debate. Barkan shows that the work of these cultural anthropologists has been of utmost importance in refuting (scientific) racism. Racism did not disappear, but "racial differences are viewed in cultural terms, not biological; xenophobia has become more egalitarian and the strife is no longer waged in the name of superiority."[8]

It is important to appreciate that racism manifests different emphases according to time and place. The central position of biology should be considered as characteristic of the racism of a specific historical period. Today, a range of cultural and religious differences function as pillars sustaining the stereotypes and prejudices that play a dominant role in contemporary racism. This many-sidedness of racism gives rise to a recent tendency in science not to speak about "racism" in the singular but about "racisms" in the plural. Racisms vary according to the central position occupied by biological or cultural characteristics and in the patterns of articulations linking racism to ideologies of nation, gender, and class. These variations depend on historically determined, contextual differences between the social formations in which racism functions and on the "target group." The historical relation between physical characteristics and cultural properties in racist discourse is not simple, but complex. Different gradations exist, both historically and today.

DENIAL

Denial may be considered a central element of contemporary forms of racism. This may be explained by the fact that racism has become an unacceptable ideology in accordance with more general norms that developed after the Second World War.

In many Western European countries, racism has been declared taboo. Those who openly admit to racist ideologies are excluded. Admittedly this stance has positive effects, but it has also a darker side. The exclusive conceptualization of racism as open and blunt has marginal-

8. Elazar Barkan, *The Retreat of Scientific Racism: Changing Concepts of Race in Britain and the United States Between the World Wars* (Cambridge: CUP, 1992), xii.

ized those forms of anti-racism that address its structural dimensions and less spectacular everyday expressions, giving the impression that there was no longer any racism in society because it was not allowed to be there. Those who argued that this was not the case were considered oversensitive or on the extreme left, which was subsequently identified with the extreme right.

Today, as noted at the outset, the term "discrimination" is preferred to the term "racism," a preference that resulted in part from a desire to avoid a conceptualization of race that identified with the Nazi's inhumane theories of superiority before and during World War II.[9] From this perspective, race and racism were directly linked like two sides of the same coin, with racism being viewed as merely a function of fascism. Following World War II and prompted in part by the end of the colonial era that unraveled after it, the concept of racism came to be viewed at best as a characteristic of extremist groups on the margins of society. From this perspective arose the unfortunate paradox that contemporary forms of racism, particularly when denied, are not always recognized as such.

NEW RACISM

Contemporary forms of racism are often characterized as modern racism or new racism. Martin Barker, in his study of the new racism in the UK, points to two changes in the postwar ideological legitimization of racist practices. First, the superiority of one's own culture and nation is no longer emphasized either openly or straightforwardly; racist practices are now legitimized on the basis of so-called "principal otherness." Second, presumed biological-genetical differences are also replaced by differences between cultures or nations, represented as homogenous entities.[10] "Race" is coded as culture or ethnicity. Barker characterizes the new racism as pseudo-biological culturalism. In this vision, the building blocks of the nation are not the economy or politics, but human nature: "It is part of our biology

and our instincts to defend our way of life, traditions and customs against outsiders—not because these outsiders are inferior, but because they belong to other cultures."[11] As we have seen above, a shift in the racist discourse from phenotypical characteristics to sociocultural properties has been developing since the 1920s. Influenced by the Second World War this tendency has deepened and generalized. This is why a relativization of contemporary cultural racism as "new racism" is imperative.

Contemporary racism is also characterized as "racism without race." Practices or ideas are characterized as racist if they are "oriented in intention or effect towards the production, reproduction or affirmation of unequal relations."[12] Such racism is more about exclusion than overt dominance.

STIGMATIZATION

A common characteristic for different groups that are socially excluded is the sociopsychological process of stigmatization to which they are subjected. The recognition of difference and the consequent devaluation of others in terms of their deviance and the assumed threat they pose along with the anxiety, aversion, depersonalization, and dehumanization that results, are all central to processes of stigmatization that transform others into "stereotypic caricatures."[13]

PREJUDICE AND THE ROLE OF EMOTIONS

A key attitude in racism is the social cognitive phenomenon of prejudice. Early definitions of prejudice emphasize its "bad" character in different ways; it is a "rigid or inflexible attitude," an "overgeneralized attitude," an "unjust attitude," an "irrational attitude," and so on. In the 1980s more neutral, nonpejorative definitions began to be used, but always the negative character of the attitude was foregrounded.

Duckitt distinguishes four levels of causation

9. See note 4.
10. Martin Barker, *The New Racism* (London: Junction, 1981); "Het Nieuwe Racism" ("The New Racism"), in Anet Bleich and Peter Schumacher, eds., *Nederlands Racisme* ("Dutch Racism") (Amsterdam: Van Gennep, 1984), 62–85.

11. Ibid., 78.
12. David T. Wellman, "Toward a Sociology of White Racism," in Bulmer and Solomos, eds., *Racism*, note 5, 190.
13. Todd F. Heatherton et al., eds., *The Social Psychology of Stigma* (New York: Guilford, 2000).

in relation to prejudice, presenting prejudice as both a social and simultaneously an individual phenomenon. First, he argues, certain psychological processes ensure that every human has the potential to be prejudiced. Second, the activation of this potential is determined by social and intergroup dynamics of contact and interaction in specific social situations and societies. Third, prejudiced attitudes are socially transmitted. Fourth, individual differences influence people's susceptibility to prejudice, thereby creating different, varying outcomes to the mechanisms of social influence involved in the transmission of prejudices.[14] Just like cognitions, emotions may also be communicated to others through *emotional contagion*, a process in which people in interaction catch each other's emotions. Emotional contagion may in particular be witnessed and is most frequently studied in parent-child interactions, therapeutic sessions, educational interaction, and interaction between lovers. Emotional contagion, however, also occurs on a mass scale, where in many historical events "fear, hysterical grief and anger have swept through communities."[15] They refer for example to mass reactions to the Black Death in the Middle Ages and to the Holocaust in modern times.

Today, the mass media can potentially spread emotions on a scale previously unthinkable. Since politics crucially involves power, and emotional contagion is not restricted to small-scale interpersonal communication, we may assume that processes of emotional contagion play a role in political practices as well, particularly since the mass media are involved. Given the dialectical relationship between emotions and cognitions, I assume that these processes of emotional contagion consequently may inform, and so reinforce, the beliefs and opinions of the public in the same way as the congruent social cognitions that are transmitted. There is, moreover, ample evidence of emotional factors such as anxiety, aggressiveness, frustration, and feelings of hostility and dissatisfaction influencing individual's susceptibility to prejudice.[16] Emotions thus not

only exert their influence by dialectically informing the cognitions of an actor, but also have a more direct effect on the cognitions of the public through the process of emotional contagion. It is in terms of this dual function that the role of emotions has to be integrated into a theoretical framework used to explain the production, reproduction, and mechanism of ideologies such as racism and its underlying attitude of prejudice.

DOMAINS

A distinction may be made between four important domains in and through which racism is produced and reproduced: elite racism, everyday racism, institutional racism, and politically organized racism, all of which are antithetical to the core value of respect that underlies all human rights.

- Social elites working in the most important social sectors, such as politics, policy sectors, the media, educational institutions, and welfare institutions, preformulate (so to speak) racist ideologies, often in hidden terms.
- The concept of everyday racism was developed to explain the integration of racism in everyday situations and practices. Problematization, marginalization, and exclusion are important effects of everyday racism.
- The concept of institutional racism pertains to the discriminating effects of institutional rules and procedures that marginalize and exclude people from non-Western groups; practices that are institutionalized while the ideology is no longer explicitly articulated; and when racist discourse has lost its explicit racist content but the original meaning is reflected in other words.
- Politically organized racism is the racism of xenophobic, anti-immigrant parties that have come up and developed since the beginning of the 1980s in a number of European countries and elsewhere. Generally speaking, these right-extremist parties, while not questioning the democratic system as such, reject the established sociocultural and sociopolitical system. They are populist in that frequently, in their support of traditional values, they appeal to the common sense of ordinary people. At the

14. John Duckitt, *The Social Psychology of Prejudice* (New York: Praeger, 1992).
15. Elaine Hatfield, John T. Cacioppo, and Richard L. Rapson, *Emotional Contagion* (Cambridge: CUP, 1994), 122.
16. Duckitt, *The Social Psychology of Prejudice*, note 14, 161–217.

same time, however, they are authoritarian, anti-egalitarian, and opposed to the integration of immigrant communities, commonly mobilizing xenophobic and racist sentiments.

ARTICULATION

The scientific literature about inequality according to class, gender, and ethnic background discusses the ways in which different discourses relating to the production and reproduction of systems of social inequality are intermingled and have common characteristics. This is not only the case for contemporary discourse, but also for historical discourse. This intermingling, and the related reciprocal influences of different discourse, is referred to with the concept "articulation."

As I have sought to show above, the entanglement of different discourses about groups that are subject to social exclusion is historically complex. The concept of "articulation" was developed in order to better explain the mechanisms that play a role in the interweaving of these ideologies and practices. Robert Miles argues that articulation occurs where an ideology shares certain characteristics with other ideologies, for example in the case of racism and sexism. The shared characteristic in this case is the representation of a naturalized division of humankind in terms that make it inherent and universal.[17]

Historically, racism and classism have had a complementary origin and impact. Where the assumed superiority of the white race legitimated the repression and exclusion of other "races," it also has led to the repression and exclusion of elements within one's own "race" considered a threat to its quality. Groups of particular concern are criminals, the mentally ill, nomadic groups, and people viewed as antisocial. With regard to this point, Hitler's fascism showed great excesses but has never been exclusive. In the United States, sterilization campaigns directed at so-called "antisocials" occurred until the beginning of the 1970s. In the Netherlands, antisocial families were reeducated in special camps or neighborhoods. In both cases, the influence of eugenic thinking may be

identified. The refutation of racism after the Second World War has never been total and undivided. The notion of "racial supremacy" and the elevation of race as the highest criterion were evidently refuted. Yet the existence of "races," the inequality of different "races" and attempts to improve the "race" continued to be defended.

Both phenomena, racism and classism, are historically rooted in the process of nation formation. In this process, different groups (differentiated according to class, gender, or ethnic-cultural background) were represented as naturally distinct and different from the dominant group, thus legitimizing their exclusion. Both ideologies share, with sexism, a historical function, namely legitimizing exclusion by white, dominant male elites. Articulation characterizes the relationship between these ideologies; similarities and parallels do exist, but so do differences and contradictions. To equate them would testify to reductionism. It would remind one of the traditional, orthodox, Marxist framework of thought, in which race was subsumed by class, as a result of which it was assumed that the solution to the race question would be a logical, self-evident consequence of the expected class revolution. Theoretically, this viewpoint has long been out of date, and unmasked as Eurocentric.

CONCLUDING THOUGHTS

Racism is a highly complex social phenomenon that can be studied only on an interdisciplinary basis, if only to do justice to the complex, multidisciplinary nature of human rights. In this essay I have discussed briefly its function as well as some of its key dimensions and mechanisms while at the same time attending to its history and related mechanisms of social exclusion. Broadly based on racisms in the West, it is, I believe, nonetheless a discussion highly relevant to peoples and cultures everywhere, ergo to human dignity everywhere. While there are differences, of course, expressions of racism in various parts of the world may be seen as increasingly characterized by similarity. Particularly under the influence of modern-day globalization, social, economic, and cultural systems tend more and more to converge. The twenty-first-century revolution in communications technology also plays an important role in this

17. Robert Miles, *Racism* (London: Routledge, 1989), 87–90.

regard. And all this has, in turn, consequences not only for racism, trending toward homogeneity, hence facilitating the spread of ethnic conflict, but also for the norms, institutions, and procedures of human rights law and policy that—East, West, North, and South, and from local to global—have developed to combat it. Knowledge and understanding of this ugly phenomenon and its impact upon human rights struggles against it thus remain imperative.

QUESTIONS FOR REFLECTION AND DISCUSSION

1. How does Van der Valk substantiate the claim that "The concepts of race and racism are of relatively recent origin"? Do you agree with her? Why? Why not?

2. Is "race" a social fact, or a social myth? Justify your answer by providing a reasoned argument drawing on relevant sources and materials.

3. Is the argument that "race" is a social "myth" just a form of imperialistic, flattening logic that ignores important biological and cultural distinctions? Why? Why not? What follows from your answer in terms of social organization, levels of respect between different groups, and for the implementation of human rights?

4. What is "racism"? What does Van der Valk say? Do you agree? Disagree? Why?

5. Van der Valk argues that "a distinction may be made between four important domains in and through which racism is produced and reproduced: elite racism, everyday racism, institutional racism, and politically organized racism." Can you think of examples? If not, does that mean that Van der Valk is mistaken? Or might there be other explanations for an inability to find examples? What might Van der Valk argue, faced with someone who cannot "see" the issue, or the forms, of racism that her analysis identifies?

6. Costas Douzinas and Adam Gearey argue in *Critical Jurisprudence* (Oxford: Hart, 2005), 198, that when law recognizes racial difference (as in racial segregation laws): "difference is emphasized, it becomes central to the recognition and treatment that the law accords and is construed normatively as a distance from normality, a lack of completeness. A surface characteristic, colour, is turned into the outward expression of a deeper inferiority and as the essence of personality. One aspect of appearance is picked up and becomes the defining property of character, ability and belonging. Colour overwhelms individual traits, qualities and attributes—all those elements that constitute concrete identities are set aside as insignificant. People are not just of colour, colour is the only quality that counts in their dealings with the law."

However, argue Douzinas and Gearey, such laws offend formal equality. Thus, when the legal system adopts "more or less extensive provisions against racial discrimination" such open discrimination on the basis of color becomes illegal. However, there is a double bind in this very move: "The social processes for the selection and conferral of benefits become 'colour blind,' racially neutral. In contrast to the earli[er] stage, colour, in theory at least, disappears. The law sees all in the same colour, white or gray, but certainly not black." Does color-blind law amount to a form of misrecognition? If so, why? If not, why not?

7. If the law "both recognizes and negates the difference of race" (Douzinas and Gearey, 200), can it really confront the "effects of persistent, tolerated and accumulated racism, which places minorities in a position of structural disadvantage"? Or does the non-acknowledgement of difference (through "color-blind law") undermine the social recognition of persons of color? What color does such a system assume as its norm? In your answers to these questions, offer reasoned arguments drawing on sources, materials, and evidence where possible.

8. How, if at all, are racism and classism related? How are they different? Is one any worse than the other?

9. What is the root cause of racial discrimination? Do you think race-based discrimination is natural or taught or maybe a bit of both? Consult Todres (Reading 9) as you think about this question.

10. What future is there for international human rights concerning race in a world of growing nationalisms? What resistance, if any, does international human rights law offer, either in theory (bearing in mind the arguments of Douzinas and Gearey) or in practice? Support your answers with evidence if you can.

14. FIONA BEVERIDGE AND SIOBHAN MULLALLY *International Human Rights and Body Politics*

Despite continued and widespread criticism of appeals to rights and rights-based concepts of international human rights law as a tool for addressing the oppression of women, the difficulties experienced in accommodating women's "differences" within that discourse and in articulating or responding to harms experienced uniquely by women serve to reveal its underlying gendered nature. Women's human rights have been marginalized, both institutionally and conceptually, from national and international human rights movements; abuse of women's human rights has been perceived as a cultural, private, or individual issue, not a political matter requiring state action.[1] The main international organs have dealt with violations of women's human rights only in a marginal way, while women's bodies have been rendered almost invisible within mainstream human rights law. This exclusion of women's bodies is apparent both in the failure of international human rights law to respond to violence against women and in the lack of any clear understanding or consensus on a woman's right to bodily integrity.

The objective of this essay is to examine existing feminist critiques of "rights" and to consider their relevance in relation to questions of body politics in international human rights law.

RIGHTS AND BODY POLITICS

If feminism can be defined as a tradition of questioning, then body politics questions have been the subject matter of much of this questioning. The relationship between "body politics" questions and law has been problematic on a number of levels—criticisms have ranged from general critiques of law (for its maleness, sexism,

irrelevance) to specific critiques regarding the appropriateness of law as a medium for the regulation of body politics. Much of the discussion has centered around the usefulness of rights law as a strategy for improving the position of women.

One area of criticism relates to the *form* of rights discourse epitomized by the perpetual opposition of "rights" to corresponding duties, freedoms, powers, and privileges. Essentially rights are portrayed as the property of individuals (or occasionally groups). Critics have argued that the assumption upon which this rights discourse is predicated of a society of free-willed individuals, motivated by self-interest, perpetually seeking prioritization of their own claims (rather than accommodation, negotiation, or some other form of compromise) is false, either because it misrepresents the way in which individuals operate generally, or because it misrepresents the way women in particular operate (i.e., that it is inherently sexist).

In reality, rights discourses, it is argued, oversimplify complex power relations. Rights are generally formulated in individual terms; although the invocation of rights to sexual equality may therefore solve an occasional case of inequality for individual women, the position of women generally remains unchanged. As Charlesworth et al. have put it, "Rights discourse is taxed with reducing intricate power relations in a simplistic way. The formal acquisition of a right, such as the right to equal treatment, is often assumed to have solved an imbalance of power. In practice, however, the promise of rights is thwarted by the inequalities of power."[2] The discourse of rights, it is argued, takes no account of the various factors implicated in women's oppression, assuming instead that the acceptance of rights claims is sufficient to make the "competition" fair.

This concept of the self as essentially separate from and antagonistic toward others conflicts with competing cultural conceptions of the self as "essentially connected" to others and ignores the fact that the self is "embedded" or "situated"

1. Charlotte Bunch, "Women's Rights as Human Rights: Toward a Re-Vision of Human Rights," *HRQ* 12 (1990): 486–98, 489.

2. Hilary Charlesworth et al., "Feminist Approaches to International Law," *AJIL* 85 (1991): 613–45, 635.

in existing social practices and that we cannot always stand back and opt out of those roles and relationships. The individualistic concept of the self on which rights discourse is based has led to problems for feminists particularly in relation to body politics. The self is abstracted not only from its social, economic, and cultural context but also from the physical body of the subject herself.

Further criticism of rights-based dialogue has centered on the claim that rights themselves, or the legal systems within which they operate, are inherently sexist. Catherine MacKinnon argues that sexuality is defined, at present, in terms of dominance and submission, specifically male dominance and female submission.[3] Female sexuality is distorted and manipulated to meet the interests of a sex that does not share female interests. The alienation of female sexuality has particular significance, because, as MacKinnon argues, one becomes a woman through the experience of sexuality. In a male-dominated society, sexuality is defined by men, the dominant class, in their interests, which include the organized expropriation of female sexuality for male use and its material consequences for women: rape, pornography, sexual harassment. Legal reforms through rights strategies are inadequate to challenge what MacKinnon sees as being an all-pervasive system of male domination. She goes on to make the even stronger claim that rights strategies are inherently limited because the law itself is fundamentally gendered. She argues that the law is "male," not merely substantively, but also formally. Substantively, it sees and treats women the way men see and treat women. Formally, its claims to objectivity and neutrality reflect a masculine mode of thinking. MacKinnon states: "when the state is most ruthlessly neutral, it will be most male; when it is most sex blind it will be most blind to the sex of the standard being applied. . . . The law is objective, therefore male."[4]

Rights discourse has also been criticized by feminists because of what is perceived as the in-herent indeterminacy of rights claims. Resorting to rights strategies, it is argued, raises the specter of provoking competing and often conflicting rights claims which potentially limit a woman's autonomy and control over her body to an even greater extent. Rights may produce counter-claims to other rights including, inter alia, fetal rights, children's rights, and men's rights to decide whether or not a biological offspring is born.

Another limitation on rights discourse, less seldom addressed, concerns its bluntness as an instrument. Some conflicts, either because of the nature of the relationships involved, or because of the nature of the subject matter, cannot be reduced satisfactorily to the paradigmatic paired oppositions of free-willed self-interested individuals of rights discourse.

Conflicts over the body involve issues of immense social, political, economic, sexual, and psychological complexity. The body is a complex social construct, whose meaning and significance changes from place to place and time to time (and sometimes very rapidly). Cultural diversity in the treatment of the body is immense. Women's bodies in particular have been a site of struggle, definition, and control and are extensively regulated and confined by societal mores and norms. Law has played an important contributing part in this process.

THE PUBLIC/PRIVATE DIVIDE

The exclusion of women's accounts of their experiences from legal discourse has been facilitated by the public/private dichotomy of liberal theory and practice. Contemporary liberalism expresses its commitment to liberty by sharply separating the public power of the state from the private relationships of civil society, and by setting strict limits on the state's ability to intervene in private life. However, as Carole Pateman notes, this division between private and public spheres is constructed as a division within the world of men.[5] Civil society is conceptualized by liberal theory in abstraction from domestic life, and so the latter remains "forgotten" in theoretical discussion. The domestic sphere is thus ren-

3. Catherine A. MacKinnon, "Feminism, Marxism, Method and the State: An Agenda for Theory," *Signs: Journal of Women in Culture and Society* 7, 3 (Spring 1982): 515–44.

4. Catherine A. MacKinnon, "Feminism, Marxism, Method and the State: Toward Feminist Jurisprudence," *Signs: Journal of Women in Culture and Society* 8, 4 (Summer 1983): 635–58, 658.

5. Carole Pateman, "Feminist Critiques of the Public/Private Dichotomy," in Anne Phillips, ed., *Feminism and Equality* (New York: NYUP, 1987), 103.

dered invisible within liberal theory and practice. The idea of the domestic sphere as constituting a separate sphere to which the concept of justice is not appropriate means that rights discourse has generally failed to transcend this notion of "separate spheres of justice" and has instead concerned itself with problems arising within the "public" rather than the domestic sphere.

Difficulties in articulating harms suffered by women within this conceptual framework have been exacerbated by the legal recognition of a right to privacy, a derivation of the classical liberal values of freedom and autonomy that serves to remove a sphere of action from the regulation or control of the state. Privacy was first utilized by feminists in the United States in the case of *Griswold v. Connecticut*[6] to gain a ruling that laws that denied access to contraception to married women violated the constitutional right of privacy. Initially this ruling was welcomed by feminists as a victory. However, it has since become clear that the right to privacy is a double-edged sword that has frequently been used to depoliticize many of the harms suffered by women. Commonly defined by the structure of the traditional family unit, complete with its power imbalances, it means, for example, that violence and rape within the family have traditionally been subjected to different tests of justice than similar acts committed outside that context. The public/private divide has been identified as central to this state of affairs; hence much feminist debate has focused on how to challenge this concept.

Ruth Gavison[7] distinguishes between "internal" and "external" critiques of the public/private divide. Internal critiques purport that a given version of the public/private distinction is wrong or mistaken (which creates negative effects) and should be reconstructed (to avoid these negative effects). . . . External critiques challenge the distinction itself, claiming "that there is no useful, helpful or valid way to draw the distinction."[8] MacKinnon states:

> For women the measure of the intimacy has been the measure of the oppression. This is why feminism has had to explode the private.

This is why feminism has seen the personal as political. The private is public for those for whom the personal is political. In this sense, for women there is no private, either normatively or empirically.[9]

She argues:

> the very place, the body; the very relations, heterosexual; the very activities, intercourse and reproduction; and the very feelings, intimate—form the core of what is covered by privacy doctrine. From this perspective, the legal concept of privacy can and has shielded the place of battery, marital rape, and women's exploited labour; has preserved the central institutions whereby women are *deprived* of identity, autonomy, control and self-definition.[10]

Rights serve to draw a distinction between public and private fields. Rights can render certain matters private, either through silence (the failure of law to specifically recognize particular claims), or through the invocation of a "privatizing" right (privacy, autonomy, freedom). Thus some claims are protected at the expense of others, by rendering some of the claims involved invisible to law. To leave the body in a "private" or "intimate" sphere, beyond legal control, is therefore to replicate the "invisibility" of women and women's bodies in dominant discourses of rights. Gender neutral rights discourses fail to take account of the deeply gendered nature of society: they are predicated on a public/private divide that is not gender neutral.

The dichotomies between public and private and between the state and civil society are reproduced *in international law* through traditional doctrines of state responsibility and a focus within international human rights law on direct state violations of individual rights.[11] Harms suffered by women at the hands of private individuals or within the family have been placed outside of the conceptual framework of international human rights and thus render invisible particular problems suffered by women: "women and men do not enjoy rights on an equal basis, which is the promise held out to women by the

6. 381 U.S. 49 (1965).
7. Ruth Gavison, "Feminism and the Public/Private Distinction," *Stanford Law Review* 45 (1992): 1–45.
8. Ibid.

9. Catherine A. MacKinnon, *Toward a Feminist Theory of the State* (Cambridge, Mass.: HUP, 1989), 191.
10. Catherine A. MacKinnon, *Feminism Unmodified* (Cambridge, Mass.: HUP, 1987), 101.
11. *Eds.*—Emphasis added.

major human rights instruments."[12] Where the particular problems faced by women have been addressed, the instruments (and related enforcement mechanisms) have generally been located on the periphery of the international human rights process.

The complexity of the debate is multiplied, however, in the international context as the argument finds an echo in the debate over cultural relativism.

[*Eds.*—The authors next address the cultural relativist claim that universal standards on women's rights threaten traditional practices and traditions which, cultural relativists assert, are a superior source of morality than so-called liberal norms devised largely in the West according to Western traditions and values—a perspective from which, the authors note, "it is easy to view the entire international human rights enterprise as imposed morality, and in the current international situation as neocolonialist." In any event, as the core value of all human rights is respect for others (including their cultures), the question inevitably arises (as the authors do in fact ask) whether there is, relative to the enforcement of human rights, sufficient consensus on the universal standard to compel its application in the specific instance. Yet even if so, the authors quickly remind, the public/private divide in contemporary human rights theory and practice still leaves women at severe disadvantage. Typically left out of human rights charters and seldom addressed in the fora that administer these instruments, they write, "questions of . . . private violence, rape, body alterations, reproduction . . . are [in fact] questions in respect of which the 'defense' of culture has been pleaded" and, indeed, issues that have caused "the cry of cultural relativism" to be raised "when women have sought to query this [state of affairs] to seek enlargement of the area of consensus."

Finally, the authors observe, "Feminists are deeply divided on the matter of cultural relativism. While some have argued that, "The cry against 'interference in culture' is used as a defense of men's rights, not of women's, . . . others have pointed to the cultural specificity of rights

discourse. The concept of human rights, it is argued, is a peculiarly western construct."[13] For still others, "the consequence of recognizing cultural differences between women means no more than that feminists should be 'cautious and contingent'[14] in advocating universalistic solutions . . . , shaping discourse in such a way that space remains for diversity between cultural groups. The immediate retort of radical feminists is that this space, a new form of private space, will be colonized by powerful (male) interest groups." One possible way out of this dilemma, the authors conclude, "is to recognize that the form of rights discourse, the language of rights, is not universal and need not be so. What may be asserted in the form of a rights claim in one society may be asserted in a more familiar form in another society. Concepts such as Raimundo Pannikar's 'homeomorphic equivalent'[15] come to mind here. This would enable feminism to allow space for diversity between cultural groups without abandoning the international agenda of the feminist project."[16]]

INTERNATIONAL HUMAN RIGHTS LAW

The rules making up the body of law referred to as international human rights law are couched in gender neutral terms. The International Bill of Rights[17] as well as the numerous other Conventions and Declarations making up mainstream human rights law provide that everyone is entitled to the rights provided for without any distinction on grounds, inter alia, of sex. No distinction is made between the nature of human rights violations suffered by women and men. This assumes of course that distinction is the problem and lack of distinction the solution.

12. Andrew Byrnes, "Women, Feminism and International Human Rights Law—Methodological Myopia, Fundamental Flaws or Meaningful Marginalisation," *AYBIL* 12 (1992): 205–40, 217.

13. Adamantia Pollis and Peter Schwab, "Human Rights: A Western Construct with Limited Applicability," in Pollis and Schwab, eds., Human Rights: Cultural and Ideological Perspectives (New York: Praeger, 1979) 1.
14. Annie Bunting, "Theorizing Women's Cultural Diversity in Feminist International Human Rights Strategies," *Journal of Law and Society* 20 (1993): 6–22, 18.
15. Raimundo Pannikar, "Is the Notion of Human Rights a Western Concept?" *Diogenes* 120 (1982): 75–102.
16. *Eds.*—For an alternative approach, see Reading 4 (Weston) in Chapter 1.
17. *Eds.*—i.e., the UDHR, ICESCR, and ICCPR.

The guarantees set out in the Bill of Human Rights may be interpreted so as to include protection against those injuries or assaults experienced mainly by women. Until recently, however, this has not occurred. In addition, where physical assault such as rape has been explicitly prohibited, it has not been punished as such. What have been perceived as "women's human rights" have been marginalized both institutionally and conceptually, from national and international human rights law.

Within the UN system, a separate institutional structure has been established to deal with violations of women's human rights. The culmination of this process was the adoption of the 1979 UN Convention on the Elimination of All Forms of Discrimination against Women (CEDAW), which represented the first significant challenge to a vision of human rights that traditionally excluded much of women's experience. Its adoption also underlined the exclusion of women from mainstream human rights law and the gendered nature of what claims to be an impartial and neutral body of rules.

However, the Convention falls far short of what many feminists would have hoped for. While provision has been made for individual complaints or interstate complaints, the number and scope of reservations entered by states parties has rendered the Convention largely ineffective. Many of these reservations invoke the primacy of traditional customs and practices and/or religious law, in particular the Shari'a, and no procedure is established for determining whether such reservations are compatible with the "object and purpose" of the Convention. They have, therefore, largely remained unchallenged.

Furthermore, CEDAW continues the "equal treatment" approach found in mainstream human rights law, that is, the belief that equality is best achieved by extending to women the same rights as are available to men.[18] Again the belief that distinction is the problem and lack of

distinction the solution is reiterated. This serves only to reinforce existing norms and values without in any way subverting the inherently gendered nature of the existing rules. Temporary "special measures" may be adopted under the Convention to eliminate any distinctions that have resulted from preexisting discriminatory practices and to "accommodate" women's childbearing capacities within the structures of the workplace. However, such measures are open to the criticism advanced by MacKinnon and others that this "special treatment" approach attempts to "compensate" women for their lack of correspondence with men, thereby reinforcing the belief that the male standard is the norm against which we are all to be measured.

A significant omission from the Convention is the failure to explicitly address the issue of violence against women. In fact, apart from some references to reproduction and the needs of pregnant women within the workplace, women's bodies are largely absent from the text of the Convention. Nor is any attempt made to articulate a right to bodily integrity. An attempt was made to correct this omission by the Committee on the Elimination of All Forms of Discrimination against Women which, in 1989, adopted a general recommendation on violence against women stating, inter alia, that the Convention requires states parties to protect women against violence of any kind occurring within the family, at the work place, or in any other area of social life.[19] In 1992 the Committee adopted a comprehensive recommendation on violence against women.[20] In its general comments, the Committee stated that the definition of discrimination contained in the Convention included gender-based violence and defined such violence as "violence that is directed against a woman because she is a woman or that affects women disproportionately." The particular rights and freedoms identified as being violated by the existence of gender-based violence included (a) the right to life; (b) the right not to be subject to torture or to cruel, inhuman, or degrading treatment or punishment; (c) the right to equal protection according to humanitarian norms in time of international or internal armed conflict; (d) the right

18. *Eds.*—As the authors note, "discrimination" is defined in CEDAW, Article 1 as "any distinction, exclusion or restriction made on the basis of sex which has the effect or purpose of impairing or nullifying the recognition, enjoyment or exercise by women, irrespective of their marital status, on a basis of equality of men and women, of human rights and fundamental freedoms in the political, economic, social, cultural, civil or any other field."

19. General Recommendation No.12, GAOR, 44th Session, Supp. No.37 (UN Doc. A/44/38), 1989.
20. General Recommendation No.19, GAOR, 47th Session, Supp. No.38 (UN Doc. A/47/38), 1992.

to liberty and security of person; (e) the right to equal protection under the law; (f) the right to equality in the family; (g) the right to the highest standard attainable of physical and mental health; and (h) the right to just and favorable conditions of work.

Further, it was stated that traditional attitudes by which women are regarded as subordinate to men perpetuate widespread practices involving violence, such as female circumcision; the effect of such practices on women's mental and physical integrity, the Committee stated, was to deprive them of the equal enjoyment, exercise, and knowledge of human rights and fundamental freedoms. This was a significant move beyond the stance adopted in its 1990 recommendation on female circumcision [which had framed the issue as being harmful to women's health rather than as a rights violation]. Finally, it was recommended that all states parties should ensure that laws against family violence and abuse, rape, sexual assault, and other gender-based violence give adequate protection to all women, and respect their integrity and dignity. Implicit within this recommendation is clearly an acceptance of a right to bodily integrity.

The identification of gender-based violence as a violation of a woman's human rights was reiterated in the Vienna Declaration and the Declaration on the Elimination of Violence against Women. Paragraph 30 of the Vienna Declaration identified discrimination against women as a gross and systematic violation of human rights. Paragraph 38 stresses the particular importance of working toward the elimination of violence against women in public and private life. Of particular interest is the reference to the need to eradicate any conflicts which may arise between the rights of women and the harmful effects of certain traditional or customary practices. The World Conference called on the General Assembly to adopt the UN draft Declaration on the Elimination of Violence against Women; this was duly adopted by the General Assembly without a vote on 20 December 1993. Violence against women is defined as "any act of gender-based violence that results in, or is likely to result in, physical, sexual or psychological harm or suffering to women, including threats of such acts, coercion or arbitrary deprivation of liberty, whether occurring in public or in private life" (Art. 1).

As Christine Chinkin points out, the refer-

ence to violence as "gender-based" emphasizes the "specificity" of the problem: "In other words, the right is not an adaptation of a right built on male experience."[21] Rape (including marital rape), female genital mutilation, and any form of violence within the family are all specifically identified as being prohibited by the Declaration. Another step taken by the Declaration is its clarification in Article 4 that custom, tradition, or religion cannot be used as a justification to avoid eliminating violence against women. The reference to "female genital mutilation" and "other traditional practices harmful to women" was included over the protest of some Islamic nations, particularly the Sudan. A clear attempt is also made to transcend the public/private dichotomy of international law. Violence occurring within the general community and in the family as well as any form of violence "perpetrated or condoned" by the state is within its scope. Article 4(c) exhorts states to "Exercise due diligence to prevent, investigate and, in accordance with national legislation, punish acts of violence against women, whether those acts are perpetrated by the State or by private persons."

The Declaration thus clearly departs from the traditional doctrine of state responsibility with its almost exclusive emphasis on the public sphere. Chinkin, however, points out that the main text of the Convention avoids making any clearly stated nexus between violence and human rights. Violence against women is defined in Articles 2 and 3 without any reference to human rights while Article 3 refers to human rights but not to violence against women. This, she argues, reflects the strong opposition to describing violence against women as a violation of human rights, which was expressed, in particular, by the United States and Sweden during the 1992 Intersessional Meeting of the Commission on the Status of Women. It was argued that human rights provide protection from actions in which there is direct state involvement and to extend rights discourse to cover "private" behavior would reduce the status of the whole human rights canon. Nonetheless, the Declaration is clearly an improvement on previous legal instruments. A further step toward the integration of "women's

21. Christine Chinkin, "Women's Rights as Human Rights Under International Law," paper presented at the W. G. Hart Legal Workshop, 1994.

rights" into the mainstream human rights agenda was the approval of the appointment of a special rapporteur on violence against women.

While the symbolic importance of these developments should be recognized, it must also be remembered that the instruments within which these advances have been made do not in themselves give rise to any binding legal obligations. At most they could be said to form part of the growing body of *lex ferenda* (future law) in the international sphere.

WOMEN'S RIGHTS AND HUMAN RIGHTS

The potential of human rights discourse as a venue for addressing the harms suffered by women is a matter of debate concerning both the substance and the form of that discourse. Some feminists have argued that the adversarial nature of rights discourse fails to address many of the concerns that arise especially with regard to issues surrounding the female body. The assertion of a rights claim frequently provokes competing and often conflicting rights claims leading to apparently indeterminate debates which, many feminists argue, detract attention from the underlying inequalities in power between the disputing parties. Furthermore, as Carol Smart points out, "the acquisition of a right in a given area may create the impression that a power difference has been resolved."[22] In addition it may be seen to legitimate existing inequalities. Such inequalities as do persist are then attributed to "natural" sex differences or different "free" choices.

As to the form of human rights theory and practice, the feminist critique of its public/private dichotomy is well documented.

Despite these difficulties, however, many feminist writers are reluctant to abandon the discourse of rights. The reasons include the motivational power of rights discourse and the symbolic importance of an assertion of a rights claim. The power of rights discourse to render visible issues and concerns previously silenced is in itself a strong attraction for feminists. Although the recognition of a woman's right to autonomy and self-determination may be a double-edged

22. Carol Smart, *Feminism and the Power of Law* (New York: Routledge, 1989), 144.

sword, it has served in some instances to protect women from interference by the state. The prevalence of rights discourse, particularly within international law, also means that feminists cannot avoid articulating their claims in the language of rights if those claims are to be acknowledged in international legal fora. There are, therefore, many reasons why feminists might seek to utilize international human rights law.

A RIGHT TO BODILY INTEGRITY

It is immensely difficult to cast such a right so that it can be of use to women seeking to assert control and choice over their bodies in the wide variety of cultural settings in which such struggles can be imagined. The right must be specific enough to make its meaning and its subject evident to those who will be charged with implementing or overseeing the application of the instrument in question, since experience has shown that gender neutral language and general formulations of rights are liable to be interpreted so as to exclude that which is the concern primarily of women. Yet it must be general enough to accommodate the wide range of body politics struggles which feminists would seek to assist. Law, for this purpose at least, should be regarded as process rather than as a static set of normative statements. And it is to assist in the shaping of that process in a variety of settings that the "right to bodily integrity" must be proposed.

From the analysis above it can be concluded that "privatizing" rights should be avoided where possible in favor of a positive statement of the right to bodily integrity against specified harms. Moreover a specific effort should be made to ensure that international law's own version of the public/private divide is overcome. This would entail placing states under a firm positive obligation to promote and maintain the conditions under which bodily integrity can be realized and to provide effective means of redress where bodily integrity is infringed. Most importantly, the state must be obliged to protect bodily integrity from interference by private individuals. A model for this can be seen in the General Assembly Resolution on Violence against Women. There is no reason why this obligation—to protect against violations by "private" individuals—should not be incorporated into the definition of the right to bodily integrity.

On a more general note, consideration should be given as to whether the specific content of the "right to bodily integrity" should be gender neutral or not. There are dangers in any course which involves recognizing explicitly that women are especially vulnerable to particular forms of harm. This would be regarded by many feminists as sending out undesirable signals about women's vulnerability, perpetuating images of women as victims. However, there are other ways to ensure that a "right to bodily integrity" reflects the experiences of women: the right might incorporate specific references to areas of body politics with which women have been concerned: reproduction, domestic violence, rape, female circumcision, to mention a few.

An alternative approach, perhaps less attractive, might be to focus on procedural rather than substantive aspects of the right to bodily integrity. Under this approach, aspects such as access to advice and information, education, and questions such as consent and choice might be addressed. Many feminist critics of rights strategies would dismiss this as inadequate to empower women in any real sense.

It is not possible to foresee to any degree the fate that might befall such a right once it became embedded in mainstream human rights documents. Constant vigilance would be required on the part of feminists to ensure that maximum capital was made of any opportunities thus presented. Constant vigilance would also be required to ensure that the bodies charged with the supervision and implementation of the human rights instruments in question, in their dialogue with states parties on the "right to bodily integrity," addressed the harms suffered by women.

QUESTIONS FOR REFLECTION AND DISCUSSION

1. Why are so many feminist commentators suspicious of rights discourse? What key areas of concern do Beveridge and Mullally identify with respect to this suspicion? Do you agree that there are grounds for suspicion of rights? Why? Why not? Do your grounds differ from those of feminist commentators? If so, in what respects? What values and assumptions is your argument calling on?

2. Are there layers of resistance that exist between international human rights law and women's rights? Yes? No? Be specific.

3. Beveridge and Mullally assert that "the domestic sphere is rendered invisible within liberal theory and practice." What does this mean? What is the authors' concern here?

4. According to Beveridge and Mullally, Christine Chinkin argues that there is "strong opposition to describing violence against women as a violation of human rights, which was expressed, in particular, by the United States and Sweden during the 1992 inter-sessional meeting of the Commission on the Status of Women." What, if anything, does such opposition reveal about the nature of human rights themselves?

5. What is the central feminist critique called the public/private divide? Do you agree with it? Why? Why not? Regardless, which critique of the public/private divide is more convincing: the "internal" or the "external" critique? Why?

6. Andrew Byrnes argues that "Women and men do not enjoy [human] rights on an equal basis, which is the promise held out to women by the major human rights instruments," Andrew Byrned, "Women, Feminism, and International Human Rights Law: Methodological Myopia, Fundamental Flaws, or Meaningful Marginalisation," *Australian Yearbook of International Law* 205 (1992): 217. How does the existence—and content—of CEDAW support this view or undermine it? Analyze the CEDAW provisions in the light of Beveridge and Mullally's argument to provide a cogent, well-supported and logical defense of your answers. Available at http://www.un.org/womenwatch/daw/cedaw/cedaw.htm or III Weston and Carlson III.C.12.

7. Why is it that women's rights are perhaps the most problematic category of concern for arguments about the rights of cultural minorities, whether in modern pluralistic democracies or in international human rights law? What, if anything, do the complexities of the relationship between women's rights and cultural relativism reveal about the fundamental assumptions of international human rights law, its central "subject of rights," and its relationship with collective values?

8. Beveridge and Mullally note that "What may be asserted in the form of a rights claim in one society may be asserted in a more familiar form in another society." Concepts such as Raimundo Pannikar's "homeomorphic equivalent" come to mind here. What examples, if any, can you find of rights that find expression in a different form in a non-Western society? Does it help to revisit Burns Weston's arguments concerning human rights and cultural relativism (Reading 4)? Why? Why not? Be specific.

9. Beveridge and Mullally argue that "What have been perceived as 'women's human rights' have been marginalized both institutionally and conceptually, from national and international human rights law." How do they seek to establish this claim? What examples do they give?

10. Beveridge and Mullally argue that CEDAW has been rendered "largely ineffective" in protecting women. What reasons do they give? Do you agree with them? Why? Why not?

11. Referring to CEDAW's "equal treatment" approach to women's rights, Beveridge and Mullally argue that it "serves only to reinforce existing norms and values without in any way subverting the inherently gendered nature of the existing rules." What do they mean by this? Do you agree with them? Why? Why not?

12. Religion, cultural tradition, and male-dominated politics are cited as barriers to the universal recognition of women's rights. Which of these do you think are the most difficult to overcome? Do you see any ways around these barriers?

13. On final analysis, are women's rights human rights? Who is the "human" of the UDHR? Draw on the readings you have encountered in this book to substantiate your answers.

15. SEYLA BENHABIB *Borders, Boundaries, and Citizenship*

DEMOCRATIC CITIZENSHIP AND THE CRISIS OF TERRITORIALITY

Modern liberal democracies owe their stability and relative success to the coming together of two ideals which originate in distinct historical periods: the ideals of *self-governance* and *territorially circumscribed nation-state*. Self-governance defines freedom as the rule of law among a community of equals who are citizens of the polis and who have the right to rule and to be ruled. This ideal emerges in fifth-century Athens and is revived throughout history in episodes such as the experience of self-governing city-states in the Renaissance, the Paris Commune of 1871, the anarchist and socialist communes of the Russian Revolution, and the Spanish Civil War.

The ideal of the territorially circumscribed nation-state, by contrast, conceives of the citizen first and foremost as the subject of *state-administration*, or more positively, as *the subject of rights and entitlements*. Originating with the tran-

sition from feudalism to the absolutist state, this experiment with good governance in a self-regulating civil society has been the defining conception of the social contract in the works of Thomas Hobbes and John Locke.

Since the seventeenth century, democracy and the consolidation of the modern nation-state have marched together, at times contradicting and at times supplementing each other. The democratic struggles of propertyless males, artisans, farmers, and workers to win suffrage gave way in the early twentieth century to the struggle of women, and non-Christian and non-White colonial peoples to be included within the boundaries of the demos. Along with the formal expansion of citizenship rights came the enrichment of the scope of rights from civil to political to social.[1] In this process, the ideal of self-governance was increasingly interpreted as the formal equality of citizens who now sought to realize the *equal value of their liberty* in terms of an equivalent schedule of rights and entitlements. The civic-republican ideal of self-governance,

Excerpted with changes by permission of Cambridge University Press from Seyla Benhabib, "Borders, Boundaries, and Citizenship," *Political Science and Politics* 38, 4 (2005): 673–77. Copyright © 2005 Cambridge University Press.

1. See T. H. Marshall, *Citizenship and Social Class and Other Essays* (London: CUP, 1950).

the exercise of freedom among equals in a public space, is connected—and I would argue necessarily—to the liberal ideal of citizenship as the practice and enjoyment of rights and benefits. Modern democracies seek to integrate these republican and liberal ideals into the practices of "private" and "public" autonomy. The private autonomy of citizens presupposes the exercise and enjoyment of liberty through a rights-framework which underwrites the equal value of their liberty; public autonomy is realized through the institutions of democratic self-governance in increasingly complex societies.

This relatively successful synthesis of republican and liberal-democratic ideals, or of public and private autonomy, is today in crisis. The crisis is not the crisis of democracy in the first place but rather the crisis of the territorially circumscribed nation-state formation.

It has now become commonplace in normative political thought as well as in the social sciences to foretell "the end of the nation-state" and "the demise of Westphalian conceptions of sovereignty." Yet contemporary developments are much more complicated than these phrases suggest, for even in the face of the collapse of traditional conceptions of state-sovereignty, monopoly over territory is exercised through immigration and citizenship policies. All pleas to develop "post-Westphalian" conceptions of sovereignty are empty, therefore, if they do not also address the normative regulation of peoples' movement across territorial boundaries.

From a normative point of view, transnational migrations bring to the fore the constitutive dilemma at the heart of liberal democracies: between sovereign self-determination claims on the one hand and adherence to universal human rights principles on the other. I argue that practices of political membership may best be illuminated through an internal reconstruction and critique of these dual commitments.[2]

The UN estimates that in 1910 roughly 33 million individuals lived in countries other than their own as migrants; by the year 2000 that number had reached 175 million. During this same period (1910–2000), the population of the world has grown threefold, from 1.6 to 5.3 bil-

lion. Migrations, by contrast, increased almost sixfold over the course of these ninety years. Strikingly, more than half the increase of migrants from 1910 to 2000 occurred in the last three decades of the twentieth century, between 1965 and 2000. In this period, 75 million people undertook cross-border movements to settle in countries other than that of their origin.[3]

While migratory movements in the latter half of the twentieth century have accelerated, the plight of refugees has also grown. There are almost 20 million refugees, asylum seekers, and "internally displaced persons" in the world. The resource-rich countries of Europe and the northern hemisphere face a growing number of migrants, but it is mostly nations such as Chad, Pakistan, and Ingushetia that are home to hundreds of thousands of refugees fleeing from wars in the neighboring countries of Central African Republic, Afghanistan, and Chechnya, respectively.

To ascertain such trends one need not commit to exaggerated claims about the end of the state system. The irony of current political developments is that while state sovereignty in economic, military, and technological domains has been greatly eroded, it is nonetheless vigorously asserted; national borders, while more porous, still keep out aliens and intruders. The old political structures may have waned but new political forms of globalization are not yet in sight. We are like travelers navigating an unknown terrain with the help of old maps, drawn at a different time and in response to different needs. While the terrain we are traveling on, the world-society of states, has changed, our normative map has not. The growing normative incongruities between international human rights norms, particularly as they pertain to the "rights of others"—immigrants, refugees, and asylum-seekers—and continuing assertions of territorial sovereignty are the novel features of this new landscape.

Since the 1948 Universal Declaration of Human Rights, an international human rights regime has emerged. I understand an "international human rights regime" to mean the development of interrelated and overlapping global

2. See Seyla Benhabib, *The Rights of Others: Aliens, Residents and Citizens*, John Robert Seeley Lectures 5 (New York: CUP, 2004).

3. UN Department of Economic and Social Affairs, Population Division, International Migration Report 2002, UN Doc. ST/ESA/SER.A/220, http://www.un.org/esa/population/publications/ittmig2002/ 2002ITTMIGTEXT22 -11.pdf (accessed 9 June 2014).

and regional regimes that encompass human rights treaties as well as customary and international soft law. Yet states' sovereignty to disregard treaties, to abide by or not implement them, goes unchecked. The UDHR recognizes a limited right to freedom of movement across boundaries: it recognizes the right to emigrate (that is, the right to leave a country), but not a right to immigrate (the right to enter a country) (Article 13). Article 14 anchors the right to enjoy asylum under certain circumstances, while Article 15 proclaims that everyone has "the right to a *nationality*." The second half of Article 15 stipulates that "No one shall be arbitrarily deprived of his nationality nor denied the right to change his nationality."[4]

The UDHR is silent on states' *obligations* to grant entry to immigrants, to uphold the right of asylum, and to permit citizenship to alien residents and denizens.[5] These rights have no specific addressees and they do not appear to anchor *specific* obligations of compliance on the part of second and third parties. Despite the cross-border character of these rights, the Declaration upholds the sovereignty of individual states. Thus a series of internal contradictions between universal human rights and territorial sovereignty are built right into the logic of the most comprehensive international law document in the world.[6]

The Geneva Convention of 1951 Relating to the Status of Refugees, and its Protocol, added in 1967, are the second most important international legal documents governing cross-border movements. Nevertheless, neither the existence of these instruments nor the creation of the United Nations High Commissioner on Refugees has altered the fact that this Convention and its

Protocol are binding on signatory states alone and can be brazenly disregarded by non-signatories and, occasionally, even by signatory states themselves.

In contemporary political philosophy two lines of thinking have emerged in response to these questions: the "law of peoples" model defended by John Rawls[7] and the model of cosmopolitan citizenship centered around a new law of nations,[8] as suggested by Jürgen Habermas.[9] The Rawlsian law of peoples makes tolerance for regimes with different understandings of the moral and religious good its cornerstone and compromises universal human rights claims for the sake of achieving international stability, whereas Habermas envisages the expansion of such universalistic claims in ever-widening networks of solidarity. Rawls takes the nation-state framework for granted;[10] Habermas seeks to transcend it along the model of the constitutionalization of international law. Both, however, have said relatively little about the dilemmas of democratic

4. *Eds.*—Article 12 of the International Covenant on Civil and Political Rights (ICCPR) is yet more limited than UDHR. It guarantees freedom of movement, including the right of persons to choose their residence and to leave a country, but these rights can be restricted where necessary to safeguard "national security, public order or health, and the rights and freedoms of others." It also recognizes a right of people to enter their own country, but guarantees no freedom to seek asylum and no right of nationality, although ICCPR Article 14(3) does provide that "Every child has the right to acquire a nationality."

5. *Eds.*—The same may be said of the ICCPR. See note 4.

6. *Eds.*—The ICCPR is further confirmation of this assessment—the more so for being a treaty while the UDHR is not.

7. John Rawls, *The Law of Peoples* (Cambridge, Mass.: HUP, 1999).

8. *Eds.*—Cosmopolitanism is a way of thinking which holds that all human beings, irrespective of personal circumstance, belong to a single community based on a shared morality of opposition to ethnic nationalism and religious fundamentalism. Traceable to Diogenes (c. 412 B.C.E.) and in more modern times to Immanuel Kant, its prominent contemporary exponents include Jürgen Habermas, the late Emmanuel Levinas, Jacques Derrida, and (in alphabetical order) Daniele Archibugi, Richard Falk, and David Held.

9. See Jürgen Habermas, "The European Nation-State: On the Past and Future of Sovereignty and Citizenship," in Ciaran Cronin and Pablo De Greiff, eds., *The Inclusion of the Other: Studies in Political Theory* (Cambridge, Mass.: MIT Press, 1998); Habermas, *Der Gespaltene Westen: Kleine Politische Schriften* (Frankfurt: Suhrkamp, 2004).

10. See Rawls's astonishing comment: "a democratic society, like any political society, is to be viewed as a *complete and closed social system*. It is complete in that it is self-sufficient and has a place for all the main purposes of life. It is also closed . . . in that entry into it is only by birth and exit from it is only by death." Thus, we are not seen as joining society at the age of reason, as we might join an association, but as being born into a society where we will lead a complete life." John Rawls, *Political Liberalism* (New York: Columbia University Press, 1993), 41 (emphasis added). Even if Rawls uses the model of a "complete and closed social system" as a *counterfactual* step in a thought experiment, designed to justify the principles of political liberalism, this initial step of abstraction has significant consequences for the rest of his argumentation.

citizenship in a post-Westphalian world. Yet one of the most pressing contemporary questions is access to citizenship rights, or the attainment of political membership rights by nonmembers.

The crises of the nation-state, along with globalization and the rise of multicultural movements, have shifted the lines between citizens and residents, nationals and foreigners. Citizenship rights today must be resituated in a transnational context. How can private and public autonomy be reconfigured? How can we do justice both to the republican ideal of self-governance and the liberal ideal of the equal value of liberty?

There is not only a tension, but often an outright contradiction between human rights declarations and states' sovereign claims to control their borders and to monitor the quality and quantity of admittees. There are no easy solutions to the dilemmas posed by these dual commitments. I will not call for the end of the state system nor for world-citizenship. Rather, following the Kantian tradition of cosmopolitan federalism, I will underscore the significance of membership within bounded communities and defend the need for "democratic attachments" that need not be directed toward existing nation-state structures alone. Quite to the contrary: as the institution of citizenship is disaggregated and state sovereignty comes under increasing stress, subnational as well as supranational spaces for democratic attachments and agency are emerging in the contemporary world, and they need to be advanced with, rather than in lieu of, existing polities. It is important to respect the claims of diverse democratic communities, including their distinctive cultural, legal, and constitutional self-understandings, while strengthening their commitments to emerging norms of cosmopolitical justice.

DISAGGREGATION OF CITIZENSHIP WITH THE EUROPEAN UNION

The concept of citizenship in the modern state can be analytically divided into three components: the collective identity of citizens along the lines of shared language, religion, ethnicity, common history, and memories; the privileges of political membership in the sense of access to the rights of public autonomy; and the entitlement to social rights and privileges. We are witnessing today an "unbundling" of these components. One can have political membership rights without sharing the common identity of the majority; one can have access to social rights and benefits without sharing in self-governance and without being a national.

Within the European Union, in which this disaggregation effect has proceeded most intensively, the privileges of political membership now accrue to all citizens of member countries of the Union who may be residing in territories other than those of their nationality. It is no longer nationality of origin but EU citizenship which entitles one to these rights. Citizens of the EU can vote and stand for office in local elections in their host countries; they can also participate in elections to the European Parliament. If they are long-term residents in their respective foreign countries, on the whole they are also entitled to an equivalent package of social rights and benefits.

The condition of EU's third-country nationals, whose countries of origin do not belong to the EU, is of course different. While European Union citizenship makes it possible for all EU citizens to vote, run for, and hold office in local as well as Union-wide elections, this is not the case for third-country nationals. Their entitlement to political rights remains attached to their national and cultural origins. Yet in this respect as well changes are visible throughout the EU: in Denmark, Sweden, Finland, and the Netherlands, third-country nationals can participate in local and regional elections; in Ireland these rights are granted at the local but not the regional level. In the UK, Commonwealth citizens can vote in national elections as well. In Spain and Portugal, reciprocity rights to vote in local elections are granted to certain third-country nationals (mainly those from South America).

The most important conclusion to be drawn from these developments is that the entitlement to rights is no longer dependent on the status of citizenship; legal resident aliens have been incorporated into civil and social rights regimes, as well as being protected by supra- and subnational legislations. The condition of undocumented aliens, as well as of refugees and asylum-seekers, however, remains in that murky domain between legality and illegality. In some cases, children of refugees and asylees can attend school; on the whole, asylees and refugees are entitled to certain forms of medical care. Undocumented migrants, by contrast, are cut off from rights and benefits and mostly live and work in clandestine ways. The conflict between *sovereignty* and *hospitality* has weakened in intensity but has by no means been eliminated. The EU is caught among contradictory currents which move it toward norms of cosmopolitan justice in the treatment of those who are *within* its boundaries, while leading it to act in accordance with outmoded Westphalian conceptions of unbridled sovereignty toward those who are on the *outside*. The negotiation between insider and outsider status has become tense and almost warlike.

The decline of the unitary model of citizenship should suggest neither that its hold on our political imagination nor that its normative force in guiding our institutions has grown obsolete. It does mean that we must be ready to imagine forms of political agency and subjectivity which anticipate new modalities of political citizenship. In the era of cosmopolitan norms, new forms of political agency have emerged that challenge the distinctions between citizens and long-term residents, insiders and outsiders.

RECONFIGURATIONS OF CITIZENSHIP AND SOVEREIGNTY

Democratic sovereignty is based on three regulative ideals: public autonomy, that is, that the people are the author as well as the subject of the laws; the ideal of a unified demos; and a self-enclosed and autonomous territory over which the demos governs. While territorial and economic self-sufficiency have been undermined by general developments in the world society of states, the ideal of the unified demos has become fractured through the increasing multiculturalism of the demos and growing transnationalism of national societies. The unity of the demos ought to be understood not as if it were a harmonious given, but rather as a process of self-constitution through more or less conscious struggles of inclusion and exclusion.

The core of democratic self-governance is the ideal of *public autonomy*. How can democratic voice and public autonomy be reconfigured? Can democratic representation be organized along lines going beyond the nation-state configuration? The new reconfigurations of national democracies are giving rise to subnational as well as transnational modes of citizenship.

Within the European Union in particular, there is a return to *citizenship in the city* as well as the *transnational institutions* of the EU. "Flexible citizenship," particularly in the case of Central American and South Asian countries, is another such attempt to multiply the voice and the sites for exercise of democratic citizenship.[11]

As a result of these developments, "alien suffrage" is increasingly practiced at the municipal and regional levels. In the Netherlands, for example, all foreign residents who are third-country nationals, that is, citizens of countries which are not EU members, obtain the right to vote and to organize political parties after five years of residency. What all these models have in common though is that they retain the principle of territorial membership for undergirding representation. Whether it is residency in cities such as Amsterdam, London, or Frankfurt, or dual citizenship between Mexico, El Salvador, the Dominican Republic, and the United States, the model of democratic representation is dependent upon access to, residency upon, and eventual membership within a circumscribed territory.

Representation can run along many lines besides territorial residency. Yet there is a crucial link between democratic selfgovernance and territorial representation. Precisely because democracies enact laws that are supposed to bind those who legitimately authorize them, the scope of democratic legitimacy cannot extend beyond the demos which has circumscribed itself as a people upon a given territory. Democratic laws require closure precisely because democratic representation must be accountable to a specific people. Imperial legislation, by contrast, was issued from a center and was binding as far as the power of that center to control its periphery extended. Empires have frontiers; democracies have boundaries.

There are also current developments, however, which point precisely toward the uncoupling of democratic voice and territorial representation. Ironically, along with the spread of cosmopolitan norms, we are witnessing a shrinking of the effectiveness of popular sovereignty and the emergence of sovereignty beyond the boundaries set by the rule of law. Vis-à-vis peoples' cross-border movements, the state re-

11. See Aihwa Ong, *Flexible Citizenship: The Cultural Logic of Transnationality* (Durham, N.C.: Duke University Press, 1999).

mains sovereign, albeit in much reduced fashion. Vis-à-vis the movement of capital and commodities, information, and technology across borders, by contrast, the state today is more hostage than sovereign.

In her analysis of economic globalization processes in Southeast Asia, Aihwa Ong recounts the creation of "multinational zones of sovereignty" in the form of growth triangles (GTs). The three GTs formed by linking neighboring countries are Indonesia-Malaysia-Singapore (Sijori), Indonesia-Malaysia-Thailand, and Brunei-Indonesia-Malaysia-Philippines. Transnational corporations such as Nike, Reebok, and Gap employ millions of women who work twelve hours a day and make less than two dollars a day. Ong observes that these

> growth triangles are zones of special sovereignty that are arranged through a multinational network of smart partnerships and that exploit the cheap labor that exists within the orbit of a global hub such as Singapore. It appears that GT workers are less subject to the rules of their home country and more to the rules of companies and to the competitive conditions set by other growth triangles in the region.[12]

Whether it is the growth triangles of Southeast Asia or the maquiladoras of Central America, this form of economic globalization results in the disaggregation of states' sovereignty with their own complicity. There is an uncoupling of *jurisdiction and territory* in that the state transfers its own powers of jurisdiction, whether in full knowledge or by unintended consequence, to nonstatal private and corporate bodies. The losers in this process are the citizens from whom state protection is withdrawn, or, more likely, who never had strong state protection in the first place, and who thus become dependent upon the power and mercy of transnational corporations and other forms of venture capitalists.[13]

Despite the great variation across countries with respect to the interactions of the global economy and states, one generalization can be safely made: economic globalization is leading to a fundamental transformation of legal institutions and of the paradigm of the rule of law. Increasingly, globalization is engendering a body of law which is self-generating and self-regulating but which does not originate through the legislative or deliberative activity of national legislators. Global law is transterritorial law, whose limits are set by " 'invisible colleges,' 'invisible markets and branches,' 'invisible professional communities,' 'invisible social networks.' "[14]

Law without a state? Or race to the bottom by states which have to cut back on welfare benefits and relax labor and environmental regulations to attract global capital? Surely, these are not the only alternatives with which globalization processes confront us. It is important to emphasize that sovereign states are players with considerable power in this process: they themselves often nurture and guide the very transformations which appear to curtail or limit their own powers.

Whether it be through the changing patterns of transnational migrations; through the emergence of growth triangles and new global forms of law without a state in the fluid global marketplace; or through the pressure to adapt state bureaucracies to the new capitalism, an epochal change is underway in which aspects of state sovereignty are being dismantled chip by chip. State jurisdiction and territoriality are uncoupled as new agents of jurisdiction in the form of multinational corporations emerge. In some cases, the state disburses its own jurisdiction to private agencies in order to escape the control of popular legislators—a process we became painfully familiar with through the George W. Bush administration's policy of "rendition," that is, of transporting to undisclosed foreign countries illegal enemy aliens and maybe even of prisoners of war.

Thus, we are caught in cross-currents that on the one hand extend the domain of citizenship by weakening the divisions between long-term residents and national citizens; on the other hand, popular democratic control, whether it be by citizens or residents, over nonstatal institutions that increasingly assume state-like functions, is decreasing. The disaggregation of citizenship and the disaggregation of sovereignty are part and parcel of the same landscape but

---

12. Ibid., 222.
13. *Eds.*—For further pertinent discussion along these lines, see Reading 38 (Grear) in Chapter 9.

14. Gunther Teubner, " '*Global Bukowina*': Legal Pluralism in the World Society," in Gunther Teubner, ed., *Global Law Without a State* (Brookfield, Vt.: Dartmouth, 1997), 3–28, 8.

have distinctive normative logics. Whereas dis-aggregated sovereignty means the escape of public power from the purview of the public autonomy of citizens, the disaggregation of citizenship means the extension of public autonomy to those who did not formerly possess it.

To assert popular sovereignty in an era of the twilight of state sovereignty means multiplying sites of citizenship at the subnational, national, and transnational levels. This will take various forms. Extending the vote to long-term residents at city and state levels has become necessary because the traditional coupling of voting rights with nationality is no longer convincing. Democratic legitimacy requires that all those whose interests are affected by collective decisions in which they have a stake—as workers, parents, residents—also have a say in these decisions. Long-term residency in a city, region, or state government makes one a stakeholder. Modern states regulated the circle of stakeholders through the category of nationality, but in view of the developments recounted, this is no longer plausible and functions more as a mechanism of exclusion than inclusion.

Multiplying sites of citizenship at the substate levels, though, is hardly an adequate measure to cope with many of the world's problems, ranging from security and arms control to combating poverty and disease, economic cooperation, ecological concerns, regulating the flow of electronic commerce and communication, etc. Advocates of multinational and transnational sites of citizenship distinguish between transnational governance and transnational government.[15] This distinction is intended to highlight the need for structures of cooperation and collective action coordination which go beyond the more familiar ones of interstatal organizations based on treaty obligations such as NATO, GATT, etc., and toward more closely integrated and more permanent institutions for addressing the world's problems. They require the partial delegation of certain forms of state sovereignty. Yet structures of transnational governance must remain ac-

countable to peoples who have their own governments. Democratic government must remain accountable to the citizens and residents they represent. A world state is rejected but a possible reconfiguration of state boundaries in the form of ever larger configurations of cooperation and popular sovereignty is possible.

Along with structures of transnational governance, which will remain accountable to democratically organized peoples, sites of citizenship can also be multiplied by instituting a world peoples' assembly in the United Nations to accompany the states which are represented. As fanciful as this may seem, it is not impossible to imagine a worldwide election of peoples' representatives to the UN, in addition to state-run delegations.

Finally, it is important to note that the world already has organizations of transnational cooperation that are marked by lack of transparency or of cosmopolitan values. The IMF, the World Bank, and the summit meetings of G7 and G8 are incipient structures of transnational governance without democratic accountability. If one applies the principle of democratic legitimacy to their functioning, it is clear that these organizations serve more the interest of donor countries than those whose livelihood and stakes in many parts of the world they affect. Here too there is a democratic deficit which must be bridged.

This sketchy vision of cosmopolitan federalism is not based on hostility toward the nation-state; quite to the contrary. Only within a framework of sub- and transnational modes of cooperation, representation, and collaboration is it possible to protect the fundamental values of liberal and republican liberty, that is, of private and public autonomy. The nation-state is the home of the modern citizen. The reconfiguration of citizenship beyond nation-state boundaries is necessitated by developments which themselves undermine the nation-state, even if they are blindly promoted by it as well. The innocuous term for these developments is globalization; the more ominous epithet is that of "empire." Cosmopolitan federalism is a project which attempts to rein in the forces of globalization while resisting the spread of empire and strengthening the democratic citizen.

15. See David Held, *Global Covenant: The Social Democratic Alternative to the Washington Consensus* (London: Polity, 2004).

QUESTIONS FOR REFLECTION AND DISCUSSION

1. Benhabib begins by asserting that "Modern liberal democracies owe their stability and relative success to the coming together of two ideals." What ideals? And do you agree with her assertion? Be precise in your response.

2. Benhabib states that "From a normative point of view, transnational migrations bring to the fore the constitutive dilemma at the heart of liberal democracies: between sovereign self-determination claims on the one hand and adherence to universal human rights principles on the other." What does she mean by this? Why is the question so salient for the twenty-first century? What does Benhabib say? If you need some help, consider reviewing Grear's argument (Reading 2) where she draws on Hannah Arendt's challenge to the limits of international human rights law.

3. Illustrative of the "constitutive dilemma" that Benhabib is at pains to describe, are transnational migrations and the plight of immigrants (aspiring or forced) which bring to the fore, Benhabib argues, the "crisis of territoriality" currently challenging state governance worldwide. What do you understand this to mean? What is, according to her, the "crisis of territoriality" and how does it affect migrants? Be specific.

4. What, according to Benhabib, explains the "crisis of territoriality"? Do you agree with her? Does she make a persuasive case? If so, how? If not, does this mean you do not believe there is the crisis she says there is? Again, be specific in your response. Substantiate your points carefully.

5. Whether or not you are persuaded that there exists a "crisis of territoriality" in today's world, there can be no denying that, given the brute statistics, there is a crisis—a large-scale human tragedy—when it comes to cross-border migrations. Who or what is responsible for this? Modern-day globalization? Individual states? Other forces? What does Benhabib say?

6. Benhabib says that international law, including international human rights law, is more or less feckless when it comes to migrant laborers, asylum seekers, and other challenges to the governance of cross-border movements. Do you agree? Disagree? Why? Note that, historically, refugees have had no legal right to sanctuary, only the right to *request* sanctuary. See, e.g., UDHR Article 14(1).

7. In any case, is modern-day globalization helpful to the millions of individuals who in recent years have left their homelands to settle in other countries? Unhelpful? Why? Whatever your viewpoint, frame your reasons clearly and precisely.

8. What is "globalization"? Is there a case, as Benhabib implies, for calling it a form of "empire"? Why? Why not? It might help to review McCorquodale and Fairbrother (Reading 5) and to leapfrog ahead to Evans (Reading 39).

9. Benhabib claims that "the state today is more hostage than sovereign." How does Benhabib support her claim? Do you agree or disagree? In any case, if true, does it help or hinder immigrants? Identify and explain factors that favor sovereignty and factors that challenge sovereignty in your answer.

10. Does globalization influence democratic decision-making? Does it strengthen or weaken democratic control over domestic policy decisions? What does Benhabib say? What do you say? Defend your answer with cogent arguments.

11. Benhabib contends that "economic globalization results in the disaggregation of states' sovereignty with their own complicity." Do you agree? Disagree? Either way, do you think it is or would be a good thing or bad thing? And what strategies exist, according to Benhabib, for responding to such a situation and to the dilemmas it may present? Do you find the possible strategies convincing? Why? Why not?

12. Benhabib also contends that "the crises of the nation-state, along with globalization and the rise of multicultural movements, have shifted the lines between citizens and residents, nationals and foreigners. Citizenship rights," she argues, "today must be resituated in a transnational context." In response to this description of the challenge, she then asks: "How can private and public autonomy be reconfigured? How can we do justice both to the republican ideal of self-governance and the liberal ideal of the equal value of liberty?" What is her answer? Your answer? Be precise in the formulation of your response.

13. What rights are universal and what rights are unique to citizens? It might help to think about "positive" versus "negative" rights—as explained in, for example, Reading 1 (Weston). Generally speaking, "positive" rights oblige action and "negative" rights oblige

inaction. Under what classification are noncitizens owed rights that ordinary citizens are not owed within a state? Are all states required to offer these additional rights to noncitizens falling within this classification? Why? Why not? Be specific.

14. Is the entitlement to human rights dependent upon citizenship in a given country? Should it be? Defend both of your answers by providing reasons/argument in support.

15. What new forms of political agency have emerged to challenge the distinctions between citizens and long-term residents, insiders and outsiders? What examples does Benhabib supply?

16. What implications do you think Benhabib's analysis has for the future of human rights? For all human rights? For some human rights? What are they and why? Whose human rights are most likely to be affected? How? Why?

Chapter Four

Basic Human Needs as Security Rights

IN this chapter, we turn to a set of values—basic human needs as security rights—that concern the right of individuals and groups to expect that governments will do something positive to support their fundamental needs, interpreted, as we shall see, in a range of ways. In the preceding chapter, we were concerned primarily with so-called "first-generation" human rights, conceived traditionally in terms of what the state may be prohibited from doing in relation to, mostly, civil and political entitlements—thus sometimes called "freedom from" or "negative" rights, and archetypally symbolized by, for example, the absolute prohibition on torture. Here, however, we are concerned principally with so-called "second-generation" human rights conceived mainly in terms of what the state shall affirmatively provide in relation to, mostly, economic, social, and cultural entitlements—thus sometimes called "rights to" or "positive rights" and archetypally symbolized by, for example, obligatory governmental provision of education or social security. Despite this shift of focus, readers will nonetheless notice here certain fundamental continuities: the centrality of the value of respect in human rights law, policy, and discourse is apparent—as is evidence of the pressures emerging from neoliberal globalization and the ascendancy of market values. Thus, the reader will find that "second-generation rights" are equally—if not more—affected by the deepening inequalities worldwide and by the uneven exposure of human beings to peril and privation visible in relation to "first-generation" human rights. The reader will further find that this unevenness traces patterns of discrimination and traditional modes of disempowerment, some of which have been identified in the first three chapters of this book.

This fourth chapter embraces two intimately connected themes foundational to meaningful human physical and social existence and to justice-based concerns. *Basic human needs* encompass those "social goods" that are essential to human subsistence—for example, food, clothing, shelter, medical care, and schooling. Public policies concerning these values are, as the chapter makes clear, critically important. Basic human needs speak to the duty of governments to respond to, and at least attempt to satisfy, the welfare requirements involved, albeit mindful of the constraints of limited resources. *Security rights*, meanwhile, refer to the rights of individuals and groups to enjoy reasonably reliable prospects of well-being and survival—for example, by relying on their rights as workers, and rights to food, health, education, and culture, the topics selected for special attention in this chapter not least because they often are discounted as "rights" in modern-day capitalist polities that tend generally to favor the achievement of social justice through the "the free market."

Because these "second-generation" rights are interconnected with other rights in holistic and interdependent ways, it is important to acknowledge them in the full array of human rights articulated by the Universal Declaration of Human Rights (UDHR). Indeed, it may even be more urgent than ever to do so, for, as becomes clear in many of the readings in this chapter, the process of contemporary globalization is producing deepening forms of structural inequality and global, unevenness, commonly the precursor of violent social unrest and revolution.

THE ARCHITECTURE OF HUMAN RIGHTS

The framers of the UDHR recognized that it should be taught to people worldwide for its thirty articles to take hold in human attitudes and practices. Addressing this necessity, French Nobel Laureate René Cassin, one of the drafters of the UDHR, argued that, for learning purposes, the structure of human rights can be visualized as a temple (or Asian pagoda, or African meeting hut) founded on four pillars.[1] Shown in Figure 1, first are *civil and personal rights*—the right of equality, rights to life, and liberty (arts. 1–11); then the *social rights* that belong to individuals in their relationships with the groups in which they participate—the rights to privacy; to family life and to marry; to freedom of movement within or outside the national state; to have a nationality; to asylum in case of persecution; to property; to freedom of religion (arts. 12–17); next the third pillar of *political rights*, exercised to contribute to the formation of government institutions or to take part in decision-making processes—freedom of conscience, thought, and expression; freedom of association and assembly; the right to vote and to stand for election; of access to government (arts. 18–21). And finally, the fourth category or pillar: *rights exercised in the economic and cultural area*—the rights to social security; to work and its employment rights; to rest and leisure; to an "adequate" standard of living; to health care; to education; and to participate freely in the cultural life of the community (arts. 22–27).

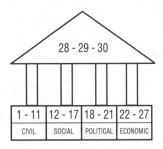

Figure 1.

Erected on these four pillars and found in the remaining three UDHR articles, there is a fifth section—what Cassin called the "pediment of the temple"—that encompasses harmonizing provisions designed to hold the entire structure together and calling on governments

1. René Cassin, "Historique de la Déclaration Universelle de 1948," in Cassin, *La Pensée et l'action* (Paris: CNRS, 1981), 109–21, 114.

to make arrangements in support of human rights. Article 28 proclaims the "entitlement" of "Everyone . . . to a social and international order in which the rights and freedoms set forth in this Declaration can be fully realized"—the premise being that governments have duties to foster a favorable social structure within which human rights can take root, and that international duties also call on prosperous states to assist the economic development of poorer states. Articles 29 and 30 set out, further, principles to harmonize rights—e.g., that they be exercised in ways that do not transgress the rights of others and do not conflict with other UN objectives (e.g., free speech should not be misused to disseminate war propaganda).

Seeing economic, social, and cultural rights in relation to other rights is essential, for harm is too often done by approaching a right's content with reference to a single category of rights exclusively. Such an approach is simplistic and fraught with danger, as well as analytically unjustifiable in the light of the overall UDHR framework. Indeed, for those aiming to work as human rights activists, policy-makers, or as scholars dealing with economic, social, and cultural rights issues, problem-solving is enhanced by understanding the holistic nature of the collection of human rights and by being "prepared to engage in category crossing and category combining."[2] Two perspectives can assist in this regard.

First, simply by imagining the partial or total collapse of just one of the rights pillars in our four-pillared human rights temple, we can see quickly the fundamental interdependence of the various pillars of rights that jointly hold up the temple. Consider, for example, the consequences to the right to health (Pillar 4) if all or part of pillars 1–4 were to collapse. Consider, for further example, the impact on: *equality* to safeguard access to medical care for all without regard to race, sex, or other status factors (Pillar 1, art. 3); *privacy*, essential for the security of one's health records (Pillar 1, art. 12); *freedom of movement*, necessary for health professionals to attend international conferences to improve their skills (Pillar 2, art. 13); *freedom of thought*, essential for scientific creativity in support of medical science advances (Pillar 3, art. 18); the *right to information and freedom of expression*, central to everyone's right to inquiry as pharmaceutical consumers and to criticize public health policy (Pillar 3, art. 19); everyone's *right to enjoy the advancements of science* (Pillar 4, art. 27). And what, indeed, might be the consequences if the temple's pediment itself were damaged or destroyed? What might happen to, for example, Article 28's promise of an *international order promotive of international cooperation*, including technology transfer?

Second, in addition to imagining how the loss of one right could lead to the loss of others, one must also understand that these various categories of rights ("generations," "pillars," or otherwise), while distinguishable, display significant overlaps. For example, freedom of speech, perhaps the ultimate symbol of individualism (freedom from governmental intervention), necessarily takes place in a group or social setting and, in any event, requires courts and other decision-making institutions (commonly at great public expense) to be safeguarded. The collective right to social and economic development is meaningless if it does not embody education rights for individuals. A people's cultural identity is preserved only if individuals are protected in their customary practices. And so on. In other words, the commonplace suggestion that traditional civil and political rights are individual rights (ostensibly "negative rights") and that socioeconomic and cultural rights are collective rights (ostensibly "positive rights") breaks down in the light of an analysis of the content of human rights. Classifying rights as individual or collective, negative or positive, etc.,

2. See, e.g., Craig Scott, "Toward the Institutional Integration of the Core Human Rights Treaties," in Isfahan Merali and Valerie Oosterveld, eds., *Giving Meaning to Economic, Social, and Cultural Rights* (Philadelphia: University of Pennsylvania Press, 2001), 7–38, 7.

is a useful first step in understanding their scope, content, and character. Such classifications, however, reflect ideological perspectives, and understanding this fact is important because such differences are real and significant both historically and contemporaneously. But it is precarious theoretically and therefore hazardous operationally to proceed as if rights categories are rigid, sealed, or straightforward, especially when it comes to the "nuts and bolts" hard work of implementing human rights "on the ground." As Burns Weston emphasizes in Reading 1 of Chapter 1, in an increasingly interdependent and interpenetrating global community, any human rights orientation that fails to recognize the essential interrelatedness of all human rights "is likely to provoke widespread skepticism." Ultimately, such an approach would undermine the potential of human rights as operational elements in the production of a humane global order, a potential which is in any case vulnerable to subversion, for as we have emphasized in our previous chapter introductions, human rights are—and remain—the subject of heated contestation, rich with ambiguity, and open to deployment as tools of exclusion as well as inclusion. Human rights can be used to bolster the power of the status quo or to serve emancipatory energies of protest and justice. What is more, human rights gain new meaning with each fresh iteration. Thus, while human rights express a vital aspiration for a just world order, they also retain a deep openness to multiple interpretations relative to their status and nature. In a very real sense, human rights are the *beginning* of a global justice conversation rather than its end.

BASIC NEEDS AS HUMAN RIGHTS

The interrelatedness of individual and collective rights and of political liberty and economic equality is particularly valuable in understanding second-generation rights—and particularly important in an age of market globalization. The issue is perhaps nowhere so evident as in the debate over appropriate goals for modernization in developing countries, conveniently depicted by Johan Galtung and Anders Wirak in a basic needs/human rights approach to balanced human development,[3] partially extrapolated in Table 1. Projected onto the national plane, the Galtung-Wirak approach points to the duty of governments to respect fundamental civil and political rights *and* provide needed goods and services to all on the basis of equality.

The classic debate as to whether capitalism or socialism or some combination of the two affords the most promising route to the fulfillment of this dutiful function of national governance is sometimes broadly characterized as a contest between freedom and bread. But even with the collapse of the Soviet Union, the demise of most authoritarian socialist regimes, and the ascendancy of neoliberal market ideology, the successor free and mixed market democracies must still attend to how the freedom-bread choice must be made. Writing in 2002, Michael Freeman noted that "there is now a widespread belief that free markets will do a better job" in meeting basic human needs—to which he tersely replied: "It is clear [that] unregulated markets will almost certainly not."[4] This is a conclusion increasingly reached in the years since Freeman expressed his view. Jack Donnelly, for one,

3. See Johan Galtung and Anders Helge Wirak, "Human Needs, Human Rights and the Theories of Development," in *Indicators of Social and Economic Change and Their Applications*, Reports and Papers in Social Science 37 (Paris: UNESCO, 1976), 7–34. See also Galtung and Wirak, "Human Needs and Human Rights: A Theoretical Approach," *Bulletin of Peace Proposals* 8 (1977): 251–58.
4. Michael Freeman, *Human Rights* (Malden, Mass.: Blackwell, 2002), 166.

TABLE 1: THE GALTUNG-WIRAK MODEL OF BASIC NEEDS AND HUMAN RIGHTS AND THE CORRESPONDING GOVERNMENT DUTIES TO PROVIDE GOODS AND SERVICES

VALUES	NEEDS/RIGHTS	GOODS/SERVICES
Security	Individual: against attack	Personal security
	Collective: against war and group destruction	Peace
		Self-determination
Welfare		
Physiological	Individual and collective	Food, water
Ecological	Climatic	Clothing, housing
	Somatic	Medical treatment
	Collective	Clean environment
Sociocultural	Self-expression, dialogue, preservation of group values	Schooling
		Cultural preservation
Freedom		
Mobility	Right to travel	Transportation
	Right to exchange information	Communication
Politics	Right to participate, choose, mobilize	Elections, parties, assemblies, meetings
	Rights of due process	Courts
Legal work	Right to work	Jobs
Identity		
Relation to self	Need for self-expression, creativity	Leisure
(individual needs)	Need for self-actualization to realize personal potential	Vacation
Relation to others	Need for sense of purpose	Religion, ideology, culture
(collective needs)	Need for affection, love, sex	Primary groups
	Need for association and support from others	Secondary groups

has staked out a strong position on this theme, arguing that human rights are required to modulate and "tame" the market as well as majoritarian democracy, restricting their operation to "a limited rights-defined domain."[5] That is, just as majoritarian democracy must be made to respect minority rights, so must market economies be tempered to ensure everyone's basic needs.[6] Donnelly concludes: "Only when the pursuit of prosperity is tamed by economic and social rights . . . does a political economy merit our respect."[7]

Despite the indivisibility of rights and the power of arguments such as that made by Donnelly, it is clear that socioeconomic rights lag behind civil and political rights in the degree to which they are in fact realized. Beginning this chapter, Scott Leckie observes that failures to protect free speech or violations of the absolute prohibition on torture invoke an almost instinctive awareness of the state's responsibility. But when people die of hunger or thirst or for want of physical shelter, the assumption is that some "nameless economic or 'developmental' force" is responsible, or that the victim of poverty or other deprivation is somehow to blame. Leckie argues that "societies increasingly blame victims of such violations for creating their own dismal fates, and in some countries, they are even characterized

5. Jack Donnelly, "Human Rights, Democracy, and Development," *HRQ* 21 (1999): 608–32, 630.
6. See, e.g., Amy Chua, *World on Fire: How Exporting Free Market Democracy Breeds Ethnic Hatred and Global Instability* (New York: Anchor, 2004). Cf. Andrew J. Nathan, "The Dynamics and Counterdynamics of Globalization," in Mahmood Monshipouri et al., eds., *Constructing Human Rights in the Age of Globalization* (Armonk, N.Y.: Sharpe, 2003), 111–236.
7. Donnelly, "Human Rights, Democracy, and Development," 630.

as criminals on this basis alone." In other words, despite the theoretical indivisibility and interrelatedness of all categories of human rights, when it comes to socioeconomic rights there is a marked tendency toward a reductive ideological response that simply sidelines the full significance of such rights. There is thus genuine reason to doubt that many of the political economies of the twenty-first century, in Donnelly's words, "merit our respect." After providing a careful review of the nature of violations and the categories of violators of socioeconomic rights, Leckie observes that the possibility of being deprived of social, economic, and cultural rights affects all of us. This fact alone, he hopes, might become the impetus for a change in how states and corporations view and act in the world.

Next, Judy Fudge points unequivocally to the globalized market economy as the context in which labor rights—and the welfare state generally—must now be understood. "Wealth is being created," she writes, "but too many countries and people are not sharing in its benefits . . . [and] have little or no voice in shaping the process." Fudge continues: "Seen through the eyes of the vast majority of women and men, globalization has not met their simple and legitimate aspirations for decent jobs and a better future for their children." In this situation, where labor rights have been superseded by neoliberalism's ideological faith in the market as the "best mechanism of distribution and service provision," international human rights law, policy, and discourse concerning labor rights has shifted by placing, she observes, a "renewed emphasis on social rights"—toward the status of "fundamental social rights." This dynamic, Fudge contends, is "part of the movement to recognize the social dimension of globalization and to re-embed the labor market in society." Thus, the language and logic of human and social rights reaches increasingly into the realm of labor law, placing a strong emphasis upon ameliorating the social costs of neoliberal logic. The question at stake for Fudge is whether or not the new rights discourse can adequately match the rapidly consolidating world of market regulation and deepening global inequality.

Like the labor and social rights, the right to health is a centrally important mode of protecting basic human well-being, and necessarily interdependent with other human rights. Paul Hunt, in Reading 18 in this chapter, provides an insider's view of how to assess the right to health from an international perspective. A former UN Special Rapporteur on the Right to Health, he clarifies key objectives of the right as well as related themes and interventions. In so doing, he addresses the by now familiar core dilemma of inequality of access to, and distribution of, critical resources, in this instance with reference to health and flourishing and with particular scrutiny upon disfavored immigrants and minorities. Human rights analysis, drawing on internationally defined standards, discloses how rights violations contribute to ill health and even undermine the right to life. Hunt's analysis reveals that over a half century after the adoption of the UDHR, violations of the right to health, the right to medical care, and the right to share in the benefits of scientific advances have proliferated far beyond that imagined in 1948. The UDHR drafters could not have foreseen such present-day issues as the maldistribution of medical services for life-saving drugs based on ethnic, racial, and national differences; DNA testing without regard to privacy; gene patenting that does not benefit gene contributors; pharmaceutical fraud and toxic dumping in less developed countries; and discrimination in access to education in the health professions and medicine. For these and myriad other such contemporary problems, we look to the UDHR to begin—but hardly to conclude—inquiry into applicable normative standards and enforcement mechanisms. Hunt concludes that the right to health—particularly at the international level—can, by adopting the ethic of shared responsibility, contribute directly to the goal of realizing global equity.

Health is fundamental to a human life worth living and thus intimately related to a wide range of normative and structural questions concerning the overall functioning of national and global society. Nutritional justice, for example, is fundamental to good health, and also a key node at which discrepancies between market power and deepening socioeconomic inequality collide. Centrally at stake, therefore, is the right to food—a claim fundamental to continuing human existence itself and increasingly of immense personal and political significance, urgent in the context of climate change which threatens global food security and demands swift reengagement with the question of food production. In her contribution to this chapter, Hannah Wittman examines the emergent framework of "food sovereignty" (arising from people's movements primarily) that is responding to the need to defend, on the one hand, "the right of peoples to healthy and culturally appropriate food produced through ecologically sound and sustainable methods," and, on the other, "their right to define their own food and agriculture systems." Food sovereignty also directly addresses the depersonalized market forces of corporate agribusiness by placing the needs and aspirations of human beings at the heart of food systems and policies, which tend to prioritize local and national economies and markets and food sustainability—understood, moreover, in "environmental, social and economic" terms. Importantly, food sovereignty also addresses the need for new social equalities—among different peoples generally, but manifestly between men and women, racial and religious groups, socioeconomic classes, generations, and so forth. Ultimately, Wittman leads the reader to a rich understanding of the present and future potential of community- and rights-based growing projects and movements. She suggests that the community-driven nature of food sovereignty has forged the conceptual and practical space for a new food imaginary—a "transformation of knowledge and ways of knowing" reflecting a research (and action) agenda "sure to expand exponentially in the face of urgent demands for alternative agricultural and food policy models that can address the imminent effects of global climate change."

In light of the complexities of globalization and the urgent social pressures of climate change, it is more vital than ever that the right to education, and to a human rights education in particular, be adequately valued. In "The Right to Education and to Human Rights Education," Richard Pierre Claude and Felisa L. Tibbitts examine the importance of education in the UDHR cluster of internationally defined human rights. Their account confirms that the right to education is multifaceted—as a social right in the community context—and that, when focused on human rights in particular, it promotes the full development of the human personality. As a socioeconomic right, it facilitates self-sufficiency and self-realization. And as a cultural right, especially now that the international community has directed education toward the building of a universal culture of human rights, it serves as a lodestar for empathy and respect at all levels of social organization.

Finally, in an essay on a closely related theme, Cindy Holder addresses the relationship between a human right to culture and the right of a group to flourish—or even to continue to exist. Holder argues that, in traditional terms, culture has been treated as an "object" by international legal instruments, but that an alternative conception of culture—one responsive to the empirical realities of the abuse of minorities' cultural rights—treats culture not as a "good" but as an "activity." This "activity" conception of the right emerges from international legal instruments addressing the rights of indigenous peoples, and protects the ability of individuals and communities to "engage in" culture—an engagement taken to be "as basic a component of human dignity as are freedom of movement, freedom of speech, and freedom from torture." Holder contends that this conception of the right has wide value for international human rights law and policy generally. In short, it frames "the role of cultural communities in the realization of human dignity as an important physical and political issue, not just a psychological one." In so doing, it reveals the coherence between the protection of the individual and the protection of a community—a revelation defusing the traditional tensions assumed to dominate the relationship (or "competition") between the human rights of individuals and the human rights of peoples. Holder's argument brings out the deep wrong of cultural violations, linking them deeply to a fundamental assault on the individual person—an assault as fundamental as any other denial of respect lying at the heart of human rights.

In sum, in their own ways, each of the readings in this chapter traces the dynamics of human rights as an impulse to protect what is required for meaningful human existence— to resist, in short, the unjust and disrespectful denial of basic needs and fundamental forms of human security. The urgency of such concerns could not be more contemporary or salient for human futures and for the future of human rights themselves.

16. SCOTT LECKIE *Another Step Toward Indivisibility: Key Features of Violations of Economic, Social, and Cultural Rights*

Moralists used to complain that international law was impotent in curbing injustices of nation-states, but it has shown even less capacity to rein in markets that, after all, do not even have an address to which subpoenas can be sent. As the product of a host of individual choices or singular corporate acts, markets offer no collective responsibility. Yet responsibility is the first obligation of both citizens and civic institutions.[1]

INTRODUCTION

Of all the domains where state and intergovernmental action on human rights have failed to achieve anything more than modest success, the development of effective measures for the prevention and remedying of violations of economic, social, and cultural rights must surely classify as one of the most glaring. Although the international community has consistently reiterated the proposition that all human rights are intertwined within a coherent system of law, responses to violations of economic, social, and cultural rights—both procedural and substantive—

have paled in comparison to the seriousness accorded infringements of civil and political rights.

This situation prevails even though perhaps no other human rights treaty is violated in as obdurate or frequent a way as the International Covenant on Economic, Social and Cultural Rights,[2] despite much conceptual and interpretive progress in this area of law over the past decade. This state of affairs has little, however, to do with the nature of the obligations and rights established in the ICESCR. Problems of perception and resolve, rather than any inevitable limitation of law or jurisprudence, have kept economic, social, and cultural rights wallowing in the relative purgatory of global efforts to secure human rights.

For instance, when someone is tortured or a person's right to speak freely is restricted, observers almost unconsciously hold the state responsible. However, when people die of hunger or thirst, or thousands of urban poor and rural

1. Benjamin R. Barber, *Jihad vs. McWorld: How the Planet Is Both Falling Apart and Coming Together and What This Means for Democracy* (New York: Times Books, 1995), 16.

2. The author notes: "Longtime member of the UN Committee on Economic, Social and Cultural Rights [and former member of the International Court of Justice] Bruno Simma was unfortunately far from erroneous when he declared that 'there hardly exists another human rights treaty which has been more frequently misinterpreted, downplayed or intentionally abused than the International Covenant on Economic, Social and Cultural Rights.'" Simma, "The Implementation of the International Covenant on Economic, Social and Cultural Rights," in Franz Matscher, ed., *The Implementation of Economic and Social Rights: International and Comparative Aspects* (Kehl am Rhein: Engel, 1991), 75–94, 79.

dwellers are evicted from their homes, the world still tends to blame nameless economic or "developmental" forces, or the simple inevitability of human deprivation, before placing liability at the doorstep of the state. Worse yet, societies increasingly blame victims of such violations for creating their own dismal fates, and in some countries, they are even characterized as criminals on this basis alone.

These truncated visions of human rights have been a major force in careening clear and irrefutable violations of economic, social, and cultural rights off the international and national human rights agendas. For reasons well known, most would recoil in horror at the deprivation of freedom of life when active violence is involved, but display considerably more tolerance when human suffering or death stem from preventable denials of the basic necessities of life such as food, health care, or a secure place to live. Ambivalence toward violations of economic, social, and cultural rights—whether by those entrusted with their implementation or those mandated to monitor compliance with them—remains commonplace.

There has been, despite such attitudes, some progress. The work of the Committee on Economic, Social and Cultural Rights (CESCR) has been instrumental in promoting greater action and attention to the ICESCR. New human rights instruments including these rights have been promulgated, as have certain institutional mechanisms within the UN and elsewhere. In 1995, European states promulgated a complaint procedure specifically designed to remedy violations of these rights within the framework of the Revised European Social Charter. In nearly all countries, constitutions and national legislation (while under threat of repeal in some) continue to recognize, either explicitly or implicitly, elements of, if not a broad range of, clearly elaborated economic, social, and cultural rights.

While a great deal has been accomplished, particularly if the world is viewed through the lens of international human rights law, there is certainly no room for complacency. Current political, social, and especially economic trends are not at all conducive to the prevention of violations of economic, social, and cultural rights, or even the preservation of rights already in place. The shock often required to activate the human rights community still rarely accompanies situations of severe social and economic injustice. Even when human rights bodies take action or

other criticism of violators is forthcoming, this action is frequently no match for what are increasingly perceived as larger state interests, in particular those linked to trade, market share, and misplaced notions of national security.

Nevertheless, when the practice of human rights institutions and the actual status of international law as currently written are examined (as distinct from what states actually do), the possibility of legal claims based on violations of economic, social, and cultural rights is nowhere near as limited as skewed perceptions of these rights may indicate. The legal, conceptual, economic, and political obstacles commonly associated with the procedural aspects of enforcing economic, social, and cultural rights are often overstated and tend to be couched in terms far more reflective of ideology or self-interest than the prevailing status of law. Translating the provisions and positive dictums of human rights law into concrete actions, however, remains one of the greatest challenges facing the human rights movement and the community of nations.

PRELIMINARY CONSIDERATIONS IN DETERMINING THE NATURE OF VIOLATIONS OF ECONOMIC, SOCIAL, AND CULTURAL RIGHTS

It is often argued that in the absence of a precise elaboration of the normative content of each economic, social, or cultural right, the determination of a violation of such norms will be difficult to conclude, except in extraordinary circumstances involving explicit abuses of power. Clearly identifying both the core and supplemental contents of economic, social, and cultural rights norms, as well as carrying out the equally important exercise of clarifying the obligations attached to each entitlement found under this group of rights have been primary concerns of the human rights community. Without first carefully distinguishing such prerequisites it is indeed difficult, if not foolhardy, to even attempt to delineate which deeds and inactions could constitute actual violations of these rights. To conclude that violations had occurred, it would seem reasonably obvious that an analyst would require at least some clarity regarding the entitlements and obligations involved.

The immense strides of recent years with respect to the delineation of the contents (both obligations and entitlements) of these rights have assisted in refining the identification and elaboration of violations of these norms, despite what many call the essentially "programmatic" nature of these guarantees. As national courts and institutions expand their attention to alleged violations of economic, social, and cultural rights and as similar advancement occurs within regional human rights systems, further clarity will emerge, both with respect to what is prohibited and what behavior is considered conducive or mandatory to ensure the full realization of these rights.

Although the arguments put forth by opponents of economic, social, and cultural rights have been more than adequately rebuffed, there remains some confusion as to whether widespread violations of economic, social, and cultural rights can be automatically declared when, for instance, a portion of society is ill fed, ill clothed, or ill housed. Additionally, questions remain as to whether a state's reduction in social expenditure automatically constitutes a violation of such rights. Many also question whether individual detriment, in addition to gross and systematic acts or omissions, constitutes a violation.

Preliminary answers can be found in the Limburg Principles on the Implementation of the International Covenant on Economic, Social and Cultural Rights,[3] which delineate the general contours of possible violations of these rights. The Limburg Principles have proven very useful to human rights advocates and have been particularly instrumental as an interpretive adjutant of the norms of the ICESCR in domestic legal spheres. Although the Principles that address violations clearly retain their pertinence today, expanding international attention toward understanding, clarifying, preventing, and remedying violations of these rights is a task of the utmost urgency.

STATE OBLIGATIONS

What are sometimes superficially understood as the uniquely noncommittal and vague state

obligation provisions of Article 2(1) of the ICESCR have been subjected to extensive interpretive and jurisprudential analysis yielding more than adequate clarity.[4] This coverage has made major inroads in generating the lucidity required to determine whether a state party to the ICESCR has complied with its obligations or not. The delineation of state obligations under the ICESCR to *respect, protect, and fulfill* these rights has received widespread support and is frequently applied to analyses of economic, social, and cultural rights.[5] Work on the right to housing, the right to health, the right to food, the right to education, and other rights has disaggregated the constituent elements of these rights based upon this now widely accepted interpretive tool.

Indeed, this methodology of outlining state duties has proven a durable means of establishing accountability on economic, social, and cultural rights, and has assisted greatly in work toward more clearly identifying, deconstructing, and redressing violations of these rights. Because human rights law must be viewed as constituting an indivisible and organic whole, all human rights contain corresponding obligations to respect, protect, and fulfill the right in question (including civil and political rights). Therefore each type of obligation is subject to violation.

What the UN International Law Commission (ILC) has called "obligations of conduct" and "obligations of result" must also be viewed as forming an inseparable and mutually inclusive way of understanding the nature of state obligations under the ICESCR in addition to providing a tool for discerning violations. Although it has been argued that the ICESCR exclusively creates obligations of result, a deeper analysis of these two notions reveals that they overlap with, rather than exclude, the other. With regard to the right to adequate housing, for example, duties of conduct could entail the development of a national housing strategy, whereas result-related duties would involve the achievement by states of specific targets (e.g., the elimination of homelessness within two years) within the framework of the housing strategy. Effectively, therefore, obligations to respect, protect, and ful-

3. The Limburg Principles on the Implementation of the International Covenant on Economic, Social and Cultural Rights, U.N. ESCOR, Comm'n on Hum. Rts., 43rd Sess., Agenda Item 8, UN Doc. E/CN.4/1987/17/ Annex (1987), reprinted in "The Limburg Principles on the Implementation of the International Covenant on Economic, Social and Cultural Rights," *HRQ* 9 (1987): 122–36.

4. See Philip Alston and Gerard Quinn, "The Nature and Scope of States Parties' Obligations Under the International Covenant on Economic, Social and Cultural Rights," *HRQ* 9 (1987): 156–229, 171.
5. *Eds.*—Emphasis added.

fill consist simultaneously of dimensions of obligations of conduct and obligations of result, all of which are subject to violation under human rights law.

PROGRESSIVE REALIZATION

In spite of the clarity thus derived regarding state obligations, governments and judiciaries in many countries still tend to view the entire ICESCR with clouded judgment, only giving priority to norms dealing with misguided notions of progressivity. Fundamentally, however, the determination of violations of economic, social, and cultural rights should not be hindered by the progressive realization provisions. It would be difficult to dispute that the full realization of *all* human rights will invariably be a progressive undertaking—for example, some of the rights enumerated in the International Covenant on Civil and Political Rights.[6] Although it is only under the ICESCR that the term "progressive" is utilized in the obligations regime, this does not affect the legal nature of the assumed duties, nor does it imply that no immediate obligations exist with regard to the ICESCR.[7] This principle places a burden upon states to show discernable progress toward the enjoyment by everyone of the rights established by the ICESCR.

The obligation of states to "take steps" indicates, inter alia, that states assume some immediate legal duties upon ratification of the ICESCR. General Comment No. 3 asserts that while the full realization of the relevant rights may be achieved progressively, steps toward that goal must be taken within a reasonably short time after the ICESCR's entry into force for the states parties.[8] If, therefore, a state fails to take steps, a violation will have occurred. The obligation to protect economic, social, and cultural rights also requires states to develop targeted, legally consistent, and sufficiently progressive policies toward securing those rights. The use of indicators as a means of monitoring and evaluating specific aspects of economic, social, and cultural rights appears to be increasingly accepted.

States cannot utilize the progressive norms as a pretext for failing to comply with the ICESCR, nor can they justify limitations or derogations of economic, social, and cultural rights on such grounds. Human rights advocates and monitors, however, will need to be increasingly vigilant in precluding states' suspicious reliance on this qualifier. For no matter how refined the notion of progress norms may become, it will always be at least a small (though increasingly surmountable) obstacle in the process of determining violations of the ICESCR. This is because the progressive realization clause will be increasingly embraced as an escape hatch by recalcitrant states as the substantive provisions of the ICESCR gain greater clarity and resonance within civil society.

New interpretations of this principle may need to be developed to widen the legal vision of public officials and courts to reflect the view that states must move as expeditiously as possible toward the realization of the rights found in the ICESCR. States must view, use, and act upon this standard as a positive basis for preventing or reversing any regressive policies, laws, or practices negatively affecting the full enjoyment of economic, social, and cultural rights. It implies, by necessity, an obligation of states to improve the overall enjoyment of particular rights, and it presumes a constantly expanding web of legal protection for all right holders.

The UN Committee on Economic, Social and Cultural Rights (CESCR) has followed such logic in several of its concluding observations. With re-

6. According to McGoldrick, the Human Rights Committee has interpreted Article 6 of the ICCPR as encompassing wide-ranging positive obligations, some of which are clearly of a progressive nature. For example, matters such as infant mortality, malnutrition, and public health schemes have been raised. This approach was echoed in the collective opinion of the HRC as expressed in its first General Comment on Article 6. Views under the Optional Protocol have also suggested that there is a preventive or positive aspect to Article 6. Dominic McGoldrick, *The Human Rights Committee: Its Role in the Development of the International Covenant on Civil and Political Rights* (Oxford: Clarendon, 1994), 346 (notes omitted).

7. Limburg Principle 21 provides that the obligation "to achieve progressively the full realization of the rights" requires states parties to move as expeditiously as possible toward the realization of the rights. Under no circumstances shall this be interpreted as implying for states the right to defer indefinitely efforts to ensure full realization. On the contrary, all states parties have the obligation to begin immediately to take steps to fulfil their obligations under the Covenant.

8. The Nature of States Parties Obligations, General Comment 3, adopted 13–14 December 1990, U.N. ESCOR, Comm. on Econ., Soc. & Cult. Rts., 5th Sess., 49th & 50th mtg., UN Doc. E/C.12/1990/8 (1990).

spect to compliance with the housing rights provisions of the ICESCR by the Dominican Republic, for example, the Committee has stressed that

> In order to achieve progressively the right to housing, the Government is requested to undertake, to the maximum of available resources, the provision of basic services (water, electricity, drainage, sanitation, refuse disposal, etc.) to dwellings and ensure that public housing is provided to those groups of society with the greatest need. It should also seek to ensure that such measures are undertaken with full respect for the law. In order to overcome existing problems recognized by the Government in its dialogue with the Committee, the Government is urged to give consideration to initiatives designed to promote the participation of those affected in the design and implementation of housing policies. Such initiatives could include: (a) a formal commitment to facilitating popular participation in the urban development process; (b) legal recognition of community-based organizations; (c) the establishment of a system of community housing finance designed to open more lines of credit for poorer social sectors; (d) enhancing the role of municipal authorities in the housing sector; (e) improving coordination between the various governmental institutions responsible for housing and considering the creation of a single governmental housing agency.[9]

With the degree of precision now afforded state obligations under the ICESCR, these duties can be analyzed within the well-established international legal framework obliging states "to take reasonable steps to prevent human rights violations and to use all the means at [their] disposal to carry out a serious investigation of alleged violations committed within [their] jurisdiction, to identify those responsible, to impose appropriate punishment and to ensure the victim adequate compensation."[10]

[*Eds.*—The author next discusses at great length the "specific features of violations of economic, social, and cultural rights," both theoretical and operational:

- *Terminology and Issues of Scale*, including "whether the term 'violations' constitutes an appropriate means of describing situations not in conformity with internationally recognized economic, social, and cultural rights";
- *Acts of Commission and Omission*, including (a) "Deliberately Retrogressive Measures"; (b) "The Decency Threshold" utilized by, e.g., the European Committee of Independent Experts in supervising the interpretation of imprecise language in the European Social Charter such that, for example, "any wage less than 68 percent of the average national wage, combined with compensatory measures, would not meet the 'decency threshold'"; (c) "Minimum Core Entitlements" (e.g., essential foodstuffs, essential primary health care, basic shelter and housing, basic education); (d) "Forced Evictions"; and (e) "Permeability [of all Human Rights], Equality Rights, and Non-Discrimination";
- *Legislative and Policy Spheres*; and
- *Public Expenditure and Resource Allocation*

The author then continues.]

VIOLATORS

The list of potential violators of economic, social, and cultural rights expands beyond actors linked directly to the state; it must be seen to include all entities capable of causing harm to the enjoyment of these rights.[11] Although third parties may possess fewer obligations than the states to which they are ultimately accountable, these entities cannot be considered immune

9. Report on the Tenth and Eleventh Sessions of the Committee on Economic, Social and Cultural Rights, U.N. ESCOR, Comm. on Econ., Soc. & Cult. Rts., 10th &11th Sess., Supp. No. 3, 91, 332–33, UN Doc. E/C.12/1994/20 (1994).
10. *Velásquez Rodríguez Case*, T 174, Case 7920, Ser. C, No. 4, Inter-Am. Ct. H.R. 35, O.A.S. Doc. OEA/Ser.L/V/III.19, doc. 13 (1988).

11. See The Realization of Economic, Social and Cultural Rights, Second Progress Report Prepared by Mr. Danilo Türk, Special Rapporteur, UN Doc. E/CN.4/Sub.2/1991/17, 52(e), at 18–19 (1991) ("legal obligations towards the realization of economic, social and cultural rights are multidimensional. At the macro-level they affect: (1) national and local governments and agencies, as well as third parties capable of breaching these norms; (2) the international community of states; and (3) intergovernmental organizations and agencies").

from duties to respect and protect the rights afforded individuals under human rights law. Nor can the state escape liability for failing to regulate social relations at this level. Potential violators can be categorized in five distinct groups: (1) the state and public actors; (2) private actors; (3) international financial and other institutions; (4) transnational corporations (TNCs); and (5) the international community.

THE STATE AND PUBLIC ACTORS

International law obliges states to refrain from acts, omissions, or other measures that result in violations of human rights within territory under their jurisdiction and in countries other than their own. This is the obvious essence of human rights law and obligations deriving therefrom. Analyses of economic, social, and cultural rights generally neglect linking the obligations connected to these rights with international legal principles of state responsibility, despite the obvious and fundamental relationship that exists in this regard. State responsibility applies to human rights issues when a state is in breach of the obligation to respect internationally recognized human rights norms that arise from treaties, custom, or *jus cogens*. States must not only respect such rights, but must ensure them as well; this implies an obligation to ensure compliance with international obligations by private persons and an obligation to prevent violations by them.[12]

This latter point was clearly reaffirmed in the often-cited *Velásquez Rodríguez* case, where the Inter-American Court of Human Rights emphasized that states compromise their responsibility when rights and freedoms are infringed on their territory; any impairment of such rights that can be attributed under the rules of international law to the action or omission of any public authority constitutes an act imputable to that state.[13] *Velásquez Rodríguez* dictated that not only is the state obligated to prevent, investigate, and punish any human rights violation carried out by an act of the public authority or by persons who abuse their position of authority, but also those result-

ing from an act not directly imputable to the state. For example, an act of a private person or by an unknown assailant is not directly imputable to the state, but as a consequence of the state's lack of due diligence in preventing the violation or in responding to it as required by the ICESCR, the acts are inferentially imputed to the state.

At the most basic level, state responsibility implies that when a state has violated a legal obligation, it is required to terminate the violation and to make reparation, including in appropriate circumstances restitution or compensation for loss or injury. States are also required to prevent impunity for such violations, whether such violations are attributable to intentional abuse of an obligation or *force majeure*. As the normative framework of state responsibility expands as it relates to human rights, it will be fundamental to ensure that adequate attention is given to all such principles with respect to preventing and redressing violations of economic, social, and cultural rights.

States will need to be held increasingly accountable for failures to adequately apply principles of due diligence in responding to or in structurally preventing human rights violations linked to economic, social, and cultural rights, for ignoring (as they often do with respect to the ICESCR) basic principles of *pacta sunt servanda*,[14] and for disregarding the contents of Articles 27, 31, and 46 of the Vienna Convention on the Law of Treaties. Extending the norms recognized as *jus cogens*[15] to include a more systematic and inclusive approach toward socioeconomic rights concerns—in line with enlarging state responsibility—should feature centrally in future efforts supporting the augmentation of these rights.

NONSTATE ACTORS

Traditional views of human rights law distinguish between public and private actors. This once widely accepted dichotomy, however, has become blurred such that private actors (often in conjunction with the state) may now be deemed liable for violations of economic, social, and cul-

---

12. See Ian Brownlie, *Principles of Public International Law*, 4th ed. (Oxford: Clarendon, 1990), 435.
13. *Velásquez Rodríguez Case*.

14. *Eds.*—Latin for "agreements must be kept."
15. *Eds.*—"Cogent law," compelling or peremptory norms deemed fundamental, overriding principles of law and policy from which no derogation is permitted (e.g., prohibitions on aggression, slavery, torture, genocide).

tural rights.[16] Human rights law has irrevocably entered the private domain. The horizontal effectiveness of rights ("Drittwirkung der Grundrechte") implies the existence of correlative state duties to ensure the protection of an individual's rights from violation by third parties not generally linked to the state.

The potential impact of actions by third parties to the overall satisfaction of economic, social, and cultural rights is substantial—perhaps even more so than with regard to civil and political rights. Employers, corporations, landlords, teachers, doctors, and any other citizen capable of violating an individual's rights because of neglect or encouragement by the state are increasingly being held accountable as notions of state responsibility expand beyond traditional confines.

INTERNATIONAL FINANCIAL AND OTHER INSTITUTIONS

For many years, the Bretton Woods institutions have faced serious and generally justifiable criticism for their active involvement in projects where human rights violations occurred and for the effective imposition of economic adjustment, fiscal, and other policies with equally detrimental effects. The World Bank and International Monetary Fund (IMF) exert considerable influence over the policy-making (and sometimes law-making) process in borrower countries, yet pay lip service at best to human rights obligations held either by states or these institutions themselves (pursuant to Articles 55 and 56 of the UN Charter). These institutions, as UN entities and subjects of international law, are bound by the UN normative framework. Despite this, however, the policies of the international finan-

cial institutions (IFIs) have resulted in substantial violations of economic, social, and cultural rights within a range of developing nations, particularly the poorest countries with the least economic or political leverage. Indirect violations of civil and political rights also may occur in the context of structural adjustment programs or large-scale project financing.

The creation of a World Bank Inspection Panel is a small step in the right direction, as was the recognition by the World Bank that it was itself bound by sanctions that the UN Security Council took against Serbia (in contrast to its previous decisions to skirt sanctions against the South African apartheid regime).[17] While these developments indicate that human rights concerns may have begun to enter the Bank's awareness, they are no guarantee that violations of economic, social, and cultural rights perpetrated directly or indirectly by the Bank or the IMF will cease. Convincing grounds exist for addressing the liability of these institutions with respect to such violations. The international human rights community will also need to bring attention to the potentially negative human rights consequences of decisions, practices, and policies pursued by the increasingly powerful World Trade Organization (WTO).

In addition to these financial and trade institutions playing potentially violative roles, a 1996 report alleges that the UN Security Council has been responsible for large-scale violations of economic, social, and cultural rights through, inter alia, the imposition of multilateral economic sanctions that indiscriminately and disproportionately harmed the civilian population of Iraq.[18] The report asks why it is that sanctions can be employed against a UN member state by the Council, which is obliged by the UN Charter to "promote and encourage respect for human rights" when such sanctions clearly violate the rights of civilians with a form of collective punishment. How is it possible that humanitarian law requires states to distinguish between military and civilian targets, yet sanctions can be applied without regard to

16. The UN Special Rapporteur on Impunity for Human Rights Violations stressed in 1996 that "Violations of economic, social, and cultural rights can also be perpetrated by private individuals. In the vast majority of States, such violations are punishable offenses or are, at any rate, subject to a procedure of civil compensation. It is for the State to devise an adequate legal framework." The Realization of Economic, Social and Cultural Rights, Second Interim Report on the Question of the Impunity of Perpetrators of Human Rights Violations, prepared by Mr. El Hadji Guissé, Special Rapporteur, U.N. ESCOR, Comm'n on Hum. Rts., Sub-Comm'n on Prevention of Discrimination and Protection of Minorities, 48th Sess., Agenda Item 8, at 33, UN Doc. E/CN.4/Sub.2/1996/15 (1996).

17. See Bruce Rich, *Mortgaging the Earth: The World Bank, Environmental Impoverishment and the Crisis of Development* (Boston: Beacon, 1994), 71.
18. Center for Economic and Social Rights, *Unsanctioned Suffering: An Assessment of United Nations Sanctions on Iraq* (New York: Center for Economic and Social Rights, 1996).

legal obligations or the human rights implications of decisions by the Security Council? This example indicates that the applicability of human rights norms to sanctions applied by the Security Council under Chapter VII of the UN Charter should be examined in light of possible violations of economic, social, and cultural rights.

TRANSNATIONAL CORPORATIONS (TNCS)

The world now finds itself in the midst of one of the greatest shifts in recorded history toward a concentration of economic power, such that of the 100 largest economies in the world [as of 1998], 51 are not nation-states but transnational corporations. As corporate power concentrates seemingly without end, political ideology becomes cloudy, and markets strive to merge into one, the world has become less, rather than more, equal. Income distribution both in and between states has rarely been more skewed. This growing inequality has occurred in conjunction with a proliferation of ethnic (and sometimes genocidal) conflicts; the slashing of public expenditure in order to balance budgets, achieve criteria for monetary union, or accede to the demands of global lenders; and the not uncommon repeal of legislation and policies supportive of economic, social, and cultural rights. All these occurrences gravely threaten continued economic and political stability.

Although the financial wealth and corresponding power of TNCs eclipse that of many states, they are under no obligation to finance the realization of rights, and are, in many respects, effectively nonaccountable to persons and groups potentially threatened by their activities. States and the international community should combine efforts to contain such activities through the establishment of legal standards capable of ensuring, at least in legal terms, that TNCs refrain from violating economic, social, and cultural rights.

THE INTERNATIONAL COMMUNITY

On the basis of Articles 55 and 56 of the Charter, unalterable legal obligations are held by states to promote and safeguard human rights throughout the international community. Combined with provisions from Articles 2, 11, 22, and 23 of the ICESCR (which stress the "essential importance" of international assistance and cooperation toward securing the rights recognized in this treaty), the Charter-based principles can be interpreted to imply that an obligation to provide international aid generally may be said to exist when another state is no longer capable of independently realizing the absolute minimum norms of economic, social, and cultural rights.

Human rights law has increasingly been interpreted as implying a right to humanitarian assistance for victims of armed conflict. Consequently, it has been argued that the international community is acquiring an emergent obligation to intervene in circumstances resulting in the massive denial and violation of economic, social, and cultural rights when the state generally responsible for preventing such violations is no longer capable or willing to provide such protection.

Should such assertions gain greater support in the years to come, these measures undoubtedly will play a large role in addressing past and pending violations of economic, social, and cultural rights. Short of accepting forfeiture of sovereignty, it would appear advantageous, at a minimum, were states to perceive themselves as obligated to submit petitions of complaint (in whatever form deemed appropriate and effective) in the event of alleged violations of economic, social, and cultural rights within their boundaries or carried out by other states.

CONCLUSIONS

> Our level of tolerance in response to breaches of economic, social, and cultural rights remains far too high. As a result, we accept with resignation or muted expressions of regret, violations of these rights. . . . We must cease treating massive denials of economic, social, and cultural rights as if they were in some way "natural" or inevitable.[19]

Despite the relatively clear status of human rights law, the international legal community has yet to come to terms with the fact that homelessness, hunger, social and economic exclusion, discrimination on the basis of poverty,

19. Philip Alston, "Excerpts from a speech to the plenary of the World Conference on Human Rights," reprinted in *Terraviva*, 22 June 1993.

displacement, illiteracy, unemployment, and many other social ills can and usually do constitute human rights violations. These violations are as serious, as worrying, and as threatening to the social and economic fabric of the world as any violation of human rights.

The contemporary nature of most efforts to secure economic, social, and cultural rights provides a great deal of space for innovative initiatives geared toward filling the gaps in international, regional, and national legal structures. If states are to continue to presume legitimacy within the rapidly globalizing world and are serious about the legal commitments they possess, there is no shortage of ways to augment the legal order such that violations of economic, social, and cultural rights occur less and less frequently. Possibilities of claiming economic, social, and cultural rights internationally or regionally and thus, in theory, redressing violations of these rights, must not be viewed as an act of ultimate futility. Reliance on human rights law has stopped planned violations from occurring and has, in some cases, provided relief to victims. The effectiveness of the remedial procedures that do exist, the frequency of their use, the seriousness accorded them by states, the range of coverage, and the degree to which any decisions stemming from them actually alter local circumstances, however, remain limited.

The difficulties associated with such tasks are well known and substantial, particularly if placed into the framework of current economic and social trends throughout the planet. A dereliction by states to secure and advance economic, social, and cultural rights both within and beyond their borders, may at first glance appear to be advantageous to national self-interest. However, if governments decide not to develop better assurances to prevent and repair violations of these rights against their citizens, such a decision would be at their eventual peril and in disregard for the legal obligations they already possess. Real self-interest will come not from rejecting new measures on economic, social, and cultural rights, but from continuing to build on and consolidate recent advances, finally completing the construction of mutually reinforcing structures of law that ultimately treat all people, all rights, and all violations equally.

All human rights violations, notwithstanding the perpetrator, victim, or extent of the violation, must be seriously considered as acts in disregard of human dignity and the rule of law. Everyone everywhere is a potential victim of violations of economic, social, and cultural rights. This fact, built as it is upon real or potential self-interest, may at the end of the day have the most marked impact upon the powers that be—whether states or corporations—to change ways of acting in and viewing the world. Such an impact would definitively alter behavior such that human rights, particularly economic and social ones, would be seen to be a source of stability, a springboard for peace, and finally, not just good for business, but imperative for a healthy world economy.

QUESTIONS FOR REFLECTION AND DISCUSSION

1. Leckie claims that "Although the international community has consistently reiterated the proposition that all human rights are intertwined within a coherent system of law, responses to violations of economic, social, and cultural rights—both procedural and substantive—have paled in comparison to the seriousness accorded infringements of civil and political rights." What evidence from prior readings in this book either supports or undermines Leckie's claim? Do you accept the claim? Why? Why not?

2. Leckie suggests that the lack of responses to violations of economic, social, and cultural rights may be due to lack of a government's resolve in addressing these issues. Do you think governments consciously hesitate to address such violations or that there is a fundamental misunderstanding of how these violations constitute human rights violations? What hesitations might there be? Is the argument of misunderstanding these violations legitimate?

3. Leckie argues that "The shock often required to activate the human rights community still rarely accompanies situations of severe social and economic injustice." Why might this be the case?

4. Do you think that it is correct to describe a state's failure to satisfy basic human needs as a human rights violation? Why? Why not? Draw on any relevant sources and materials you have been able to find.

5. Leckie argues that "in the absence of a precise elaboration of the normative content of each economic, social, or cultural right, the determination of a violation of such norms will be difficult to conclude." How would you standardize social, economic, and cultural rights? For example, what would you constitute as "adequate" housing? Would this definition be rigid, or take into account the culture of a given people (e.g., nomadic lifestyles) or economy of a state?

6. What, precisely, do you understand social, economic, and cultural rights to consist of, and how do you define the state's corresponding obligations? Be as precise as you can and draw upon the text of the ICESCR. How might the Limburg Principles be of assistance?

7. Is the text of the ICESCR a completely adequate guide to the meaning and content of state obligations vis-à-vis this category of human rights? Why? Why not?

8. Even if there is an adequate guide to the meaning and content of state obligations with respect to social, economic, and cultural rights, what can or should be done when a state fails to meet its obligations? Should other states impose sanctions? If so, how can the punishing state ensure that the sanctions do not untowardly affect the civilian population?

9. Leckie divides potential violators of socioeconomic rights into five distinct groups. What are they? Why does each category matter? Can you think of examples of the ways in which each relevant category of potential violators either has, or could, violate socioeconomic rights? Be specific.

10. How might Leckie's argument that "the policies of the international financial institutions (IFIs) have resulted in substantial violations of economic, social, and cultural rights within a range of developing nations, particularly the poorest countries with the least economic or political leverage" relate to earlier readings in this book? Be specific. Draw out any links you can think of and explain the relevance of any connections you discern.

11. How might neoliberal globalization bear upon the context of Leckie's argument? Readings 5 (McCorquodale-Fairbrother), 6 (Kapur), 35 (Simons), 38 (Grear), and 39 (Evans) might be of assistance in exploring this topic further and informing your response.

12. On final analysis, is the prioritization of "first-generation" civil and political rights over "second-generation" economic, social, and cultural rights as Leckie describes a legal choice or a moral one? The former? Why? The latter? Why? Also, is it a choice you support or not, and if so why? Explain precisely.

17. JUDY FUDGE *The New Discourse of Labor Rights: From Social to Fundamental Rights?*

Social rights are like paper tigers, fierce in appearance but missing in tooth and claw.
—Bob Hepple, "Enforcement: The Law and Politics of Cooperation and Compliance"

In *The Great Transformation*, political economist Karl Polanyi showed how during the Industrial Revolution British "society protected itself against the perils inherent in a self-regulating market system."[1] Polanyi's "double movement" captured the dynamic relationship between market expansion and social institutions and provided a way of understanding the relationship between Keynesian economic expansion and the emergence of the welfare state. Today, it can be used to explain the increased interest in social rights, "one of the side effects of globalization."[2]

Supranational trade agreements combined with and supported by neoliberal values and political arrangements have resulted in the transformation of the welfare state and an emphasis

Excerpted with changes by permission of *Comparative Labor Law and Policy Journal* from Judy Fudge, "The New Discourse of Labor Rights: From Social to Fundamental Rights?" *Comparative Labor Law and Policy Journal* 29 (Fall 2007): 29–66. Copyright © Comparative Labor Law and Policy Journal. Epigraph: Bob Hepple, "Enforcement: The Law and Politics of Cooperation and Compliance," in Hepple, ed., *Social and Labour Rights in a Global Context* (Cambridge: CUP, 2002), 19–54.

1. Karl Polanyi, *The Great Transformation* (Boston: Beacon, 1957), 67.
2. Simon Deakin, "Social Rights in a Globalized Economy," in Philip Alston, ed., *Labour Rights as Human Rights* (Oxford: OUP, 2005), 25.

on the market as the best mechanism of distribution and of service provision. The shift from a Fordist to a digital economy has restructured global and local labor markets and has led to increasing inequality.[3] According to the World Commission on the Social Dimension of Globalization,[4] a problem with the current process of globalization is that it is generating unbalanced outcomes, both between and within countries. Wealth is being created, but too many countries and people are not sharing in its benefits. They also have little or no voice in shaping the process. Seen through the eyes of the vast majority of women and men, globalization has not met their simple and legitimate aspirations for decent jobs and a better future for their children.[5]

The renewed emphasis on social rights in the mid-1990s was part of the movement to recognize the social dimension of globalization and to re-embed the labor market in society. It is another example of Polanyi's double movement.

The language and logic of human and social rights is increasingly used in the field of labor law. The International Labour Organization (ILO) 1998 Declaration of Fundamental Principles and Rights at Work[6] and the EU 2000 Charter of Fundamental Rights are two of the most prominent examples of characterization of labor rights as fundamental rights at the international and supranational level. The central challenge to the expansion of markets via globalization and neoliberalism has been "the struggle for social rights, not least labor standards, in pursuit of freedom."[7] As Simon Deakin has observed, "legal and constitutional mechanisms are increasingly

being used to assert social claims."[8] Law's prominence is a distinctive feature of contemporary discourse of social rights.

A core concern of the new discourse of labor and social rights in the world of work, therefore, is whether the "new rhetoric of social rights as embodied in institutions such as the ILO Declaration of Fundamental Principles and Rights and the EU Charter of Fundamental Rights match the reality of the new world of market regulation and growing global inequality."[9]

THE GENEALOGY OF LABOR AND SOCIAL RIGHTS

During the period after World War II, social rights were instituted as part of a wider effort to regulate the labor market and to reforge the links between family life and the economy. Social rights were part of a broader discourse about citizenship and the market, which is best captured in T. H. Marshall's influential account of the evolution of modern citizenship, published in 1950. The welfare state of the mid- to late twentieth century gave rise to a specific conception of social rights, one based on a model of social citizenship built on the platform of employment.

Marshall identified three distinctive elements of citizenship entitlements: civil, political, and social, which corresponded to distinctive sets of rights. According to him,

> The civil element is composed of the rights necessary for individual freedom—liberty of the person, freedom of speech, thought and faith, the right to own property and to conclude valid contracts, and the right to justice. . . . By the political element, I mean the right to participate in the exercise of political power, as a member of a body invested with political authority or as an elector of the members of such a body. . . . By the social element, I mean the whole range, from the right to a modicum of economic welfare and security to the right to share to the full in the

3. *Eds.*—A Fordist economy, named after Henry Ford, is an economic and social system based on industrialized forms of mass production.

4. *Eds.*—An independent and representative group established in 2002 by the ILO to find common ground on the question of the social dimension of globalization.

5. World Commission on the Social Dimension of Globalization, ILO, *A Fair Globalization: Creating Opportunities for All* (Geneva: ILO, 2004), http://www.ilo.org/public/libdoc/ilo/2004/.104B09_19_engl.pdf   [*Eds.*—accessed 14 January 2015].

6. *Eds.*—Adopted 18 June 1998, together with the Declaration's "follow-up" annex, known as the ILO Social Declaration.

7. Lord Wedderburn, "Common Law, Labour Law, Global Law," in Hepple, ed., *Social and Labour Rights in a Global Context*, 19–54, 54.

8. Deakin, "Social Rights in a Globalized Economy," note 2, 52.

9. Hepple, "Enforcement: The Law and Politics of Cooperation and Compliance," in Hepple, ed., *Social and Labour Rights in a Global Context*, 2

social heritage and to live the life of a civilized being according to the standards prevailing in society.[10]

The three categories of rights with different institutions corresponded to different stages in the development of the modern state. Civil rights, an eighteenth-century achievement, enabled workers to free their labor from the ties of the land, and provided a basis for the exchange of property and ideas. These rights were profoundly individual in character, and their fundamental value was liberty. The extension of the franchise in late nineteenth-century Britain marked the era of political citizenship and rights and added democracy to liberalism's core values. Social rights, meanwhile, are the distinctive contribution of the Keynesian welfare state, fusing citizenship rights "onto the welfare state form and an everwidening net of social policies that provided each citizen with a modicum of economic security and opportunities for social mobility."[11] A central feature of social rights is the decommodification of labor through the existence of a social safety net and labor standards that ameliorate the harshness of the market. Public services, typically delivered by a government bureaucracy, and trade unions were the institutional platforms for social rights and equality was the core value.

A distinctive feature of social rights is that they address "the inherent contradiction in liberal democracies between the promise of citizenship equality and the harsh inequalities generated by capitalist markets."[12] Marshall regarded social rights as an invasion of status into contract and the penetration of social justice into the market. This dimension of social rights leads to possible conflicts with civil rights, and it is the exercise of political rights that gives social rights their authority and legitimacy. The conflict between different generations of rights combined with social rights' dependence on the exercise of political rights helps to account for the problem-

atic legal status of social rights, a conflict that is most pronounced in common law liberal democracies.

Social rights have a much more ambiguous legal status than civil or political rights. Unlike civil rights, social rights are rarely justiciable, and if they are, courts have tended to be suspicious of them. Social rights were based on the "superstructure of legitimate expectations" in a society, and they depended on a system of public provision and required some form of collective financing. They were based more on public policy and union negotiation than on legal entitlement.

Social rights were the foundation of welfare states, and they were both inspired by and inspired international labor law. Labor rights were first recognized at the international level when the ILO was founded in 1919, during a period of profound labor unrest in many countries. They were seen as workers' rights and their role was to promote social justice and to provide minimum standards to workers as protection against the increased competition that was likely to occur with the expansion of international trade. However, in 1944 the constitutional objectives of the ILO were reviewed in light of the atrocity of "Concentration camps, in which not only genocide but also forced labour was rife. . . . In this context, workers' rights came to be viewed as human rights; they stemmed from a recognition of human dignity."[13] After World War II, the principle that labor is not a commodity became part of the ILO constitution and freedom of association and collective bargaining were recognized as fundamental rights. In 1946, the ILO became the first specialized agency of the UN and in 1948 the Universal Declaration of Human Rights recognized the freedom of association and the right to join trade unions as fundamental. Labor rights were explicitly recognized within the International Covenant on Economic, Social and Cultural Rights.

The political and economic basis for social rights began to be undermined in the 1970s, and by the 1980s the Keynesian welfare state was in a deep and irrevocable crisis. Neoclassical economics, which came into ascendancy in the 1970s, called into question the utility of Keynes-

10. T. H. Marshall, *Class, Citizenship and Social Development: Essays* (Garden City, N.Y.: Anchor, 1965), 78, reprinted in Christopher Pierson and Francis G. Castells, eds., *The Welfare State: A Reader* (Cambridge: Polity, 2000).
11. Janine Brodie, "Citizenship and Solidarity: Reflections on the Canadian Way," *Citizenship Studies* 6 (2002): 377–94, 378.
12. Ibid., 380.

13. Tonia Novitz, *International and European Protection of the Right to Strike: A Comparative Study of Standards Set by the International Labour Organization, the Council of Europe and the European Union* (Oxford: OUP, 2003), 99.

ian policies, and Milton Friedman, Robert Nozick, and Frederick von Hayek questioned the normative foundations of the welfare state, emphasizing individual civil rights as the route to human freedom. The ideological challenge to the welfare state was reinforced by the economic transformation that destabilized the Fordist production regime. Globalization, which was spurred by digital technologies, combined with neoliberalism to undermine both the sovereignty of the nation-state, which traditionally has been the main author of social welfare and labor legislation, and the traditional goals of labor protection and enhancing workers' agency through democratic participation.

Deeper economic integration across national boundaries placed constraints upon the ability of elected governments to develop and to implement policies that are at odds with the central tenets of neoliberalism. Promoted by such international financial institutions as the International Monetary Fund (IMF) and the World Bank, neoliberalism emphasized international free trade, deregulation (especially of labor markets), and privatization. Along with the Organization for Economic Cooperation and Development (OECD), these institutions blamed labor market rigidities for poor economic performance and especially for unemployment. They advocated a largely decentralized structure of bargaining and workplace norm setting within a market governed greatly by the property and contract rights of employers. They also urged countries to switch from passive labor market policies, such as unemployment insurance, to more active policies that involve workfare. Social rights were subordinated to civil rights and their scope contracted as their traditional institutional supports, trade unions and the welfare state, were weakened. Moreover, because they were not seen as engaging fundamental civil or political rights, social and labor rights were especially vulnerable to legislative retrenchment.

Globalization and neoliberalism have set in motion their own double movement. The gulf between social justice and international economic agreements has increasingly become a cause for concern, as it is perceived to be a source of social and political instability. However, proposals to link social clauses to trade agreements were rejected as they raised concerns from developing countries that such clauses were a form of disguised protectionism. In this context, the

ILO has become "a social mediator in the process of globalization."[14] At the UN World Summit for Social Development in Copenhagen in 1995 and the World Trade Organization Conference in Singapore in December 1996, world leaders reaffirmed the important role of the ILO with regard to basic workers' rights. In 1998, the International Labour Conference issued the Declaration on Fundamental Principles and Rights at Work and its follow-up, which is known as the Social Declaration.[15] Like the 1944 ILO Declaration of Philadelphia,[16] the Social Declaration and its follow-up impose a constitutional obligation that does not depend on voluntary acceptance and it recognizes that social justice and economic progress are inextricably linked.

The Social Declaration identifies four categories of fundamental rights at work: freedom of association and the effective recognition of the right to effective collective bargaining; elimination of forced and compulsory labor; effective prohibition of child labor; and elimination of discrimination in employment and occupation. At the same time, as the ILO has limited what it counts as core labor rights, it has also elevated them to the status of human or fundamental rights. This characterization emphasizes the universal nature of the standards selected as core rights and is intended to liberate them from analysis solely in economic terms. These rights are grounded in respect for human dignity and can no longer be trumped by economic efficiency; they "go to the essence of human dignity at work, touching upon bedrock values of freedom and equality."[17] According to the official story, the rights listed in the Declaration are regarded as core because they are essential for workers to engage freely in the market, and they are procedural rather than substantive in that they restrict the nature of contracting but they do not impose outcomes. The justification of core fundamental rights "which treats economic and social policies as mutually reinforcing, marks a significant shift from the priority given in earlier ILO conventions

---

14. Ibid., 104.
15. *Eds.*—See note 6.
16. *Eds.*—http://www.ilocarib.org.tt/cariblex/pdfs/ILO_dec_philadelphia.pdf [*Eds.*—accessed 24 January 2014].
17. Anne Trebilcock, "The ILO Declaration on Fundamental Principles and Rights at Work: A New Tool," in Roger Blanpain and Chris Engels, eds., *The ILO and the Social Challenges of the 21st Century: The Geneva Lectures* (The Hague: Kluwer Law, 2001), 105–16, 107.

to matters which were believed to have a direct effect on economic competitiveness, such as hours of work, night work, unemployment and minimum wage."[18] Moreover, the follow-up provides a promotional mechanism for achieving the fundamental rights, rather than supervisory procedures for ensuring compliance.

As the traditional vehicles for labor and social rights—trade unions and the welfare state—have lost their luster, labor and social rights have been cast in the language of international human rights. There has been a shift in the normative and conceptual grammar from that of international labor standards to that of international rights. Casting labor rights as international human rights transforms "the legal matter at hand into a moral one—the moral and unjust denial of human dignity" and places them on a new symbolic plane.[19]

In short, a conception of labor rights as "international rights" is gaining ground.[20] In this light, the task of international labor and social rights is to mitigate the distributional and social consequences of this phase of market expansion.

The most significant recent step in the constitutional recognition of social rights was the proclamation of the Charter of Fundamental Rights of the European Union in Nice in 2000. According to Jeff Kenner,

> the Charter's proclamation of indivisible values and its express reference to solidarity alongside dignity, equality and freedom, sends a clear message that the EU institutions, when carrying out their obligations, will be bound to take note of the more elevated position that economic and social rights now occupy.[21]

The solidarity rights the Charter contains go beyond the core rights in the ILO Social Declaration to include substantive rights or standards. They not only include central labor rights such as the right to consultation, collective bargaining, strike, protection against unfair dismissal, and fair and just working conditions, they also encompass "social security and assistance, health care, and access to services of general economic interest."[22]

The chief obstacle, however, of these new international labor and European rights is their lack of direct legal effect—they are not enforceable by the traditional method of individual complaints that are adjudicated. The ILO has adopted a promotional mechanism to monitor member state recognition of the Social Declaration, instead of utilizing the existing supervisory machinery. The method of enforcing social rights in the EU—the Open Method of Coordination (OMC)—is in many respects similar to that provided in the ILO follow-up, since it is based on benchmarking and peer pressure. The Charter is a proclamation by the European Parliament, Council, and Commission, and does not establish any new power or task for the Commission or member states of the Union, or modify the powers or tasks defined by the EU treaties.

These new labor and social rights are very different from those that emerged with the welfare state. Bob Hepple identifies four features of "the new dawn of social and labour rights."[23] First, these new labor and social rights depart from Marshall's traditional conception of social rights in that they are no longer opposed to the market, but rather are seen as integral to efficient and competitive markets. Social rights are conceptualized as institutionalized capabilities that enable people to participate effectively in the market. Second, social rights no longer impose positive obligations on the state to intervene and provide services or benefits but rather function as interpretive norms and principles of institutional design. Third, the law's role in achieving social rights is being redefined. There is a movement away from establishing standards, which are enforced by sanctions, to providing proce-

---

18. Bob Hepple, *Labour Laws and Global Trade* (Oxford: Hart, 2004), 59.
19. Boaventura de Sousa Santos, *Toward a New Common Sense: Law, Science and Politics in the Paradigmatic Transition*, 2nd ed. (Cambridge: CUP/Butterworths, 2002), 483.
20. Patrick Macklem, "The Right to Bargain Collectively in International Law: Workers' Rights, Human Rights, International Rights?" in Philip Alston, ed., *Labour Rights as Human Rights* (Oxford: OUP, 2005), 61–84, 63.
21. Jeff Kenner, "Economic and Social Rights in the EU Legal Order: The Mirage of Indivisibility," in Tamara Harvey and Jeff Kenner, eds., *Economic and Social Rights Under the EU Charter of Fundamental Rights* (Oxford: Hart, 2003), 1–25, 15.

22. Sandra Fredman, "Transformation or Dilution: Fundamental Rights in the EU Social Space," *European Law Journal* 12 (2006): 41–60, 56.
23. Bob Hepple, "Introduction," in Hepple, ed., *Social and Labour Rights in a Global Context*, 15.

dural rights to groups and individuals to participate in substantive standard setting and to monitor compliance. Fourth, the emerging structure of rights does not presuppose a contract of employment. The ILO conception of decent work is far wider than the domain covered by the standard employment relationship and Fordist labor law. A group of experts appointed by the European Commission have recommended moving "beyond employment" in formulating policy responses that will guarantee decent work for all workers.[24]

TROUBLING THE CONVENTIONAL TYPOLOGY: THE PLACE OF LABOR RIGHTS

In the new discourse of labor and social rights, these rights are seen as having an equivalent juridical status to civil and political rights. However, the idea that labor and social rights should have equivalent juridical status to civil and political rights is far from problem free.

THE CONVENTIONAL TYPOLOGY

The conventional typology tends to emphasize the difference between civil and political rights, on the one hand, and labor and social rights, on the other. As Dowell-Jones explains, "this classification creates an impression of there being a certain hierarchy at the heart of the international human rights system—that socio-economic rights are a later graft onto the 'pure' liberal theory of rights, which exudes shades of incompatibility between the two groups of rights."[25]

Civil rights are regarded as fundamental, universal, individual, absolute, and negative (in the sense that they are directed against the state and do not require the state to provide resources). They apply equally to everyone, and they are justiciable or enforceable in the courts. By contrast, social rights are seen as imposing different types of obligations, either positive obligations on the state to provide services or negative and

positive obligations on private actors. They can be individual or collective and they may require that people be treated differently. They impose conditional and indeterminate obligations that are programmatic in nature.

Yet, despite the weakness of reasons purporting to justify a *sharp* separation between civil, political, labor, and social rights and convincing attempts to highlight the artificiality of the distinction between different types of rights, either social rights are not included in state constitutions or, if they are, they are more weakly enforced.

CLASSIFYING LABOR RIGHTS

Labor rights trouble the traditional typology of rights, which breaks them into three categories or generations—civil, political, and social. In part, this is because there are different kinds of labor rights that correspond to different categories of general rights. However, even once their general character is determined, labor rights have distinctive elements (their collective nature and their application to the market) that require the traditional typology of rights to be revised and a new approach to classifying rights be developed.

Colin Crouch's definition of industrial citizenship captures a broad range of different types of labor rights. Industrial citizenship is

> the acquisition by employees of rights within the employment relationship, rights which go beyond, and are secured by forces external to, the position which employees are able to win purely through labour market forces.... These rights cover such matters as: individual rights to a safe and healthy working environment; to protection from arbitrary management action; to certain entitlements to free time; guarantees of some protection of standard of living in the case of inability to work as a result of loss of employment, poor health or old age; collective rights to representation by autonomous organizations in relations between employees and employers.[26]

24. See Alain Supiot, *Beyond Employment: Changes in Work and the Future of Labour Law in Europe* (Oxford: OUP, 2001).
25. Mary Dowell-Jones, *Contextualising the International Covenant on Economic, Social and Cultural Rights: Assessing the Economic Deficit* (Leiden: Nijhoff, 2004), 14.
26. Colin Crouch, "The Globalized Economy: An End to the Age of Industrial Citizenship?" in Ton Wilthagen, ed., *Advancing Theory in Labour Law and Industrial Relations in a Global Context* (Amsterdam: Royal Netherlands Academy, 1998), 152.

A complete list of labor rights would include also equal status rights such as the rights not to be subject to discrimination on the basis of race or sex. Thus, labor rights include *collective* civil and political rights as well as social rights available to individual employees.

Most labor rights fit within the general category of social rights. The bulk of them are recognized in the ICESCR. However, there is some overlap with traditional civil rights such as freedom of association and freedom from discrimination found in the International Covenant on Civil and Political Rights (ICCPR). Collective labor rights have proven to be the most difficult to categorize because industrial citizenship entails the collective use of civil rights in order to assert claims for social justice, yet individual civil rights are crucial for the emergence of trade unions. Collective labor (traditionally known as industrial) rights are inherently individualistic; "trade unions can only function properly if the rights of their individual members are subordinate to the rights of the collectivity."[27]

Collective labor rights have been recognized by the ILO and by the UN in the ICESCR, which suggest that they are regarded as a type of social right. However, some aspects of collective rights are also protected as basic civil rights. The ICCPR provides that everyone has the right to freedom of association, including the right to form and join unions. While the Human Rights Committee, which hears complaints under the ICCPR, initially was reluctant to interpret the provision to include collective bargaining and the right to strike, it has begun to move in the direction of recognizing collective labor rights. However, despite tentative steps to recognize collective labor rights as fundamental freedoms that are justiciable, typically they are regarded as social rights and, as such, not to be enforced by courts.

CAPABILITIES—THE NEW NORMATIVE GROUND FOR LABOR AND SOCIAL RIGHTS

Social rights have conventionally been understood as claims to resources in the form of income, services, or employment. Their role was redistributive, and they conflicted with the logic of the market, and, to a certain extent, with civil rights. Recently, several scholars have suggested that the work of economist and philosopher Amartya Sen can provide a better normative basis for labor and social rights for the ILO and for the EU. His conception of equality of capabilities is offered as a replacement for equality of resources and redistribution as the normative goal and metric of labor and social rights. One of the virtues of the concept of capabilities is that it makes social rights compatible with the market and with civil rights. This is a very important feature. According to Deakin, as "social rights in this juridical sense of the term have grown in importance, the issue of their reconciliation with civil and political rights, and with market-oriented guarantees of economic participation, has become more pressing."[28]

Brian Langille has explicitly invoked Sen's idea of freedom and his concept of capability as the normative basis of fundamental labor rights[29] [which he characterizes as "primarily procedural" and argues that] there is no trade-off between social justice and labor rights on the one hand and economic progress and the market on the other. Instead of seeing procedural rights as part of the ascendancy of neoliberalism, Langille asserts that it is important to understand the relationship between these rights and other substantive rights and freedoms. He refers to Sen's admonishment to distinguish between ends and goals and to remember that the goal is human freedom, by which he "means the real capacity for human beings to lead lives which we have reason to value."[30] He also emphasizes Sen's insight that different types of human freedoms, such as social, economic, and political, interact in complex mutually supportive ways. Labor rights and the market are valuable precisely because both institutions contribute to human freedom. Langille concludes that

on a view of human freedom as the end and the key means the core rights sound in what labour law theory has long known—that while

28. Deakin, "Social Rights in a Globalized Economy," note 2, 60.
29. Brian Langille, *What Is International Labour Law For?* (Geneva: International Institute for Labour Studies, 2005), 118, http://www.crimt.org/Publications/IILS_Report_2005.pdf [*Eds.*—accessed 14 January 2015].
30. Ibid., 432.

27. J. M. Barbalet, *Citizenship Rights, Struggle, and Class Inequality* (Minneapolis: University of Minnesota Press, 1988), 6.

there is much room for and need of other laws and institutions to make for a just workplace, the most valuable legal technique (instrumentally and as an end in itself) has always been, and is, to unleash the power of individuals themselves to pursue their own freedom.[31]

Langille's attempt to provide a new grounding for labor rights in Sen's conception of freedom and capabilities does not however address some crucial issues, [including the fact that "a purely procedural understanding of core labor rights runs the risk of abuse of power in unequal bargaining situations."].

A further concern is the individualistic emphasis of Langille's conception of fundamental labor rights. Although he stresses the normative significance of freedom of association and collective bargaining, he discusses them in terms of individual rights and their compatibility with the freedom of contract. Deakin, by contrast, specifically identifies the difficulty or danger that Sen's approach to capabilities (which focuses exclusively on the individual and the real or effective choices that are available to each person) poses to both the right to collective action and the principal institutions of the welfare state: collective bargaining, social insurance, and progressive taxation.[32]

However, the problem is not so much with Sen's concept of capability, but rather in assuming that the concept of capability provides a complete theory of social justice. Sen is very clear to acknowledge that

> although the idea of capability has considerable merit in the assessment of the opportunity aspect of freedom, it cannot possibly deal adequately with the process aspect of freedom, since capabilities are characteristics of individual advantages, and they fall short of telling us about fairness or equity in the processes involved, or about the freedom of citizens to invoke and utilize procedures that are equitable.[33]

In other words Sen's account does not tell us much about either the distribution of power in a society or the type of deliberative mechanisms needed to determine the set of human functionings a society values.

Despite the limitations to the capabilities approach, its strength is that it provides a bridge between the market (and the civil law rights of contract and property) and social rights. Jude Browne, Simon Deakin, and Frank Wilkinson "explore the potential for linking the economic notion of capabilities to the juridical conception of social rights."[34] They emphasize the market-creating role of social rights. They explain that on Sen's account it is not only the commodities over which an individual has control that are important for determining that individual's welfare, but also "the capability of that individual to achieve a range of functionings with the commodity also has to be considered."[35] A capability is a type of freedom to achieve a number of different things a person may value being or doing. Central to this conception of capability are the multiple and diverse characteristics of an individual's person, society, and environment.

The idea that Browne, Deakin, and Wilkinson pursue "is that social rights be understood as part of the process of 'institutionalizing capabilities,' that is to say, as providing mechanisms for extending the range of choice of alternative functions on the part of individuals."[36] They also suggest that the "'procedural' orientation of social law . . . forms a bridge to the idea of a social choice procedure of the kind which Sen sees as providing the most appropriate basis for the achievement of equality of capability."[37] Thus, they identify two categories of social rights: "(1) social rights as immediate claims to *resources* (financial benefits such as welfare payments) and (2) social rights as particular forms of *procedural* or institutionalized interaction (such as rules governing workplace relations, collective bargaining, and corporate governance)."[38] The first category of social rights can be seen as claims to commodities that can be converted by individuals into functionings. These are such traditional

---

31. Ibid., 120–21.
32. Deakin, "Social Rights in a Globalized Economy," 59–60.
33. Amartya Sen, "Work and Rights," *International Labour Review* 139 (2000): 119–28.
34. Jude Browne, Simon Deakin, and Frank Wilkinson, "Capabilities, Social Rights and European Market Integration," in Robert Salais and Robert Villeneuve, eds., *Europe and the Politics of Capabilities* (Cambridge: CUP, 2004), 205–21, 205.
35. Ibid., 207.
36. Ibid., 210.
37. Ibid.
38. Ibid.

social rights as sick and maternity pay. The second category of social rights is social conversion factors, such as collective bargaining and trade unions. These procedural rights, which support collective provision and collective mechanisms, are the means by which institutional environments can be shaped to ensure that all individuals can convert their endowments into a range of possible functionings. According to Simon Deakin,

> the primary *function* of social rights is to provide the conditions for substantive market access on the part of individuals, thereby promoting individual freedom but also enhancing the benefits to society of the mobilization, through the market, of economic resource. In terms of *form*, social rights are constructed around a particular combination of substantive and procedural norms.[39]

The idea of capabilities Deakin and his colleagues elaborate provides for a much more robust set of social rights, which include substantive labor rights such as the right to a minimum wage and maternity pay, than Langille's core fundamental labor rights. The significance of Browne, Deakin, and Wilkinson's conception of social rights is that they show that social rights, even those that are directly redistributive, function in the same way as civil and political rights.

Sen's concept of capabilities provides a framework for debating which labor and social rights ought to be considered fundamental[40] but needs to be supplemented by a theory of social choice, deliberative mechanisms, and a social theory about power in order to provide a full account of social justice and human rights. However, the appeal of the capabilities approach is that it links the normative ground of social rights (human freedom) directly to the welfare goal (market efficiency) by providing both a metric and a substantive value. The key concern is overcoming a conception of rights shared by Hayek and Marshall—that social rights conflict with the market. But the danger with this approach . . . is that it cedes a great deal of the moral terrain to

the market. As Hugh Collins points out, conceiving of social rights as market enabling may create a greater risk that social rights will be traded off against other welfare values. He cautions that

> at the very least, we need to be better convinced that the strategy that has so successfully augmented the moral force of civil and political rights by appeals to notions of human dignity, citizenship, social inclusion and solidarity should not also be applied to advocacy of social and economic rights.[41]

Thus, it is also important to consider the other values, such as democracy and solidarity, which along with distributive justice, provide the normative foundation of decent work.

CONCLUSION

Are fundamental labor and social rights a bulwark that protects the few remaining remnants of the welfare state from neoliberalism or are they an individualizing force that undermines more solidaristic forms of social cohesion? The answer to this question is not a foregone conclusion. Institutional economists and lawyers tend to treat norms as a solution to coordination problems rather than acknowledge that they reflect collective forms of power. From the latter perspective, which recognizes that "globalization is about the redistribution of power towards the interests of finance and industrial capital,"[42] the role of social rights is a political question. As this article has shown, there is nothing intrinsic in the legal form or normative content of labor and social rights that makes them incompatible with a market economy or the institutions of a liberal democracy. Thus, the crucial question is what social forces are capable of restoring a minimum balance between the economic rights of global capital and the labor and social rights of working people on an international level.

---

39. Deakin, "Social Rights in a Globalized Economy," note 2, 60.

40. *Eds.*—Sen's theory of capabilities was developed in part with Martha Nussbaum who, in Chapter 1, Reading 3, provides a glimpse of the theory as it relates to human rights generally.

41. Hugh Collins, "Book Review," *Industrial Law Journal* 35 (2006): 105–9, reviewing Simon Deakin and Frank Wilkinson, *The Law of the Labour Market: Industrialization, Employment and Legal Evolution* (Oxford: OUP, 2005).

42. Guy Standing, "Global Governance: The Democratic Mirage?" *Development and Change* 35 (2004): 1065–72, 1072.

QUESTIONS FOR REFLECTION AND DISCUSSION

1. Fudge suggests that "an increased interest in social rights" has been "one of the side effects of globalization." How do you explain this? How does Fudge explain it? Are there clues in other readings in this book that help explain it? If so, what? And how?

2. Fudge states that globalization in conjunction with "The shift from a Fordist to a digital economy has . . . led to increasing inequality." Do you agree? If so, how? If not, what are your counterarguments?

3. How, if at all, does T. H. Marshall's account of the three categories of human rights help to theorize the role of social rights in relation to the global market?

4. Fudge asserts that "Social rights have a much more ambiguous legal status than either civil or political rights." Do you agree? Why? Why not?

5. Does Fudge's claim that social rights have a more ambiguous status than civil and political rights survive Leckie's (Reading 16) analysis and argument? If so, how? If not, why not? Which of the two positions is more analytically satisfying, and why?

6. According to Fudge, "the problematic legal status of social rights" is "most pronounced" in common law democracies. Does Fudge give reasons for this assertion? What other reasons might there be for her assertion?

7. Fudge argues that globalization has "combined with neoliberalism to undermine both the sovereignty of the nation-state, which traditionally has been the main author of social welfare and labor legislation, and the traditional goals of labor protection and enhancing workers' agency through democratic participation." Does Benhabib's sketch of cosmopolitan federalism (Chapter 3, Reading 15) add anything to Fudge's critical account? Can it offer a potential solution to the challenges that Fudge identifies? Why? Why not?

8. The ILO Social Declaration identifies four categories of fundamental rights at work. What are they? How might they afford workers more protection? Do you find them satisfactory? If so, why? If not, why not, and what changes would you make?

9. How (and why) have labor rights been construed as fundamental rights? What core values might the status of fundamental rights protect, which labor rights cannot protect if they are seen as purely economic rights? Do you, in any case, accept a binary opposition between economic and fundamental rights? Why? Why not? What values inform your position? What suppositions does your argument rest on? Do these suppositions withstand further critical scrutiny? Why? Why not?

10. What are the four features of "the new dawn of social and labor rights" to which Fudge refers?

11. Does "industrial citizenship" contribute anything to the protection of labor rights as human rights? If so, what—and why? If not, why not?

12. What does a "capabilities approach" add to the discourse of labor rights? Do you prefer Sen's and Nussbaum's theoretical approach (see Chapter 1, Reading 3)—and why? Be as specific, precise, and detailed as you can be in your response.

13. Fudge asks whether "fundamental labor and social rights [are] a bulwark that protects the few remaining remnants of the welfare state from neoliberalism or an individualizing force that undermines more solidaristic forms of social cohesion." How do you respond to this question? Based on what evidence and for which reasons?

18. PAUL HUNT *The Right to Health: Key Objectives, Themes, and Interventions*

In September 2002, I was appointed Special Rapporteur on the Right to Health by the Chairperson of the UN Commission on Human Rights (precursor to today's UN Human Rights Council).[1] A few months after my appointment, I presented my preliminary report to the Commission. Because space does not permit an in-depth examination of the content of that report, I have chosen to focus here on some of the key objectives, themes, and interventions arising from the contemporary realization of the right to health. The full report, which includes an examination of the sources, contours, and content of the right to health, can be read in its entirety on the UN Commission on Human Rights website.[2] I emphasize briefly four crucial jurisprudential elements of the right to health that inform this discussion.

First, the right to health includes, but goes beyond, the right to health care. The right to health is an inclusive right, extending not only to timely and appropriate health care, but also to the underlying determinants of health, such as access to safe and potable water and adequate sanitation, healthy occupational and environmental conditions, and access to health-related education and information, including information on sexual and reproductive health.

Second, the right to health contains both freedoms and entitlements: freedoms include the right to control one's health, including the right to be free from nonconsensual medical treatment and experimentation. Entitlements include the right to a system of health protection (i.e., health care and the underlying determinants of health) that provides equality of opportunity for people to enjoy the highest attainable standard of health.

Third, the right to health imposes some immediate obligations: although subject to progressive realization and resource constraints, the right to health imposes various obligations of immediate effect. These immediate obligations include the guarantees of non-discrimination and equal treatment, as well as the obligation to take deliberate, concrete, and targeted steps toward the full realization of the right to health, such as the preparation of a national public health strategy and plan of action. Progressive realization means that states have a specific and continuing obligation to move as expeditiously and effectively as possible toward the full realization of the right to health.[3]

Fourth, the right to health gives rise to responsibilities in relation to international assistance and cooperation: states have an obligation to take steps, individually and through international assistance and cooperation, toward the full realization of the right to health. For example, states are obliged to respect the enjoyment of the right to health in other jurisdictions, to ensure that no international agreement or policy has an adverse impact on the right to health, and to make certain that their representatives in in-

1. *Eds.*—Because of the author's unique position with the former UN Commission and the responsibilities it assigned to him, we have left his verbal references to it untouched. Regarding his Commission responsibilities, the author writes (2–3): I am requested to do the following: • Gather, request, receive, and exchange right to health information from all relevant sources. • Dialogue and discuss possible areas of cooperation with all relevant actors, including governments; UN bodies; specialized agencies and programs, in particular the World Health Organization (WHO) and the joint UN Program on HIV/AIDS, as well as nongovernmental organizations (NGOs); and international financial institutions. • Report on the status of the realization of the right to health throughout the world, including laws, policies, good practices, and obstacles. • Make recommendations on appropriate measures to promote and protect the right to health. The Special Rapporteur is also mandated to apply a gender perspective, to pay special attention to the needs of children in the realization of the right to health, to take into account the relevant provisions of the Durban Declaration and Program of Action, and to bear in mind, in particular, General Comment No. 14 of the Committee on Economic, Social, and Cultural Rights (CESCR) and General Recommendation No. 24 of the Committee on the Elimination of Discrimination against Women (CEDAW).

2. See http://www.ohchr.org/english/issues/health/right (accessed 10 June 2015).

3. CESCR, General Comment 14 (see note 5) also uses the term "core obligations." On core obligations, see Audrey Chapman and Sage Russell, eds., *Core Obligations: Building a Framework for Economic, Social and Cultural Rights* (Brussels: Intersentia, 2002).

ternational organizations take due account of the right to health, as well as the obligation of international assistance and cooperation, in all policy-making matters.[4]

BROAD OBJECTIVES

Given the state of the right to health today, three broad interrelated objectives deserve particular attention:

1. *To promote—and to encourage others to promote—the right to health as a fundamental human right, as set out in numerous legally binding international human rights treaties, resolutions of the Commission on Human Rights, and the Constitution of the World Health Organization (WHO).* Although the right to health is a fundamental human right that has the same international legal status as freedom of religion or the right to a fair trial, it is not as widely recognized as these and other civil and political rights. Many different actors, such as governments, international organizations, and civil society groups, can help raise the profile of the right to health as a fundamental human right. While it may take some years before the right to health enjoys the same currency as other, more established human rights, a crucial goal should be to ensure that the right to health receives widespread recognition as a fundamental human right.

2. *To clarify the contours and content of the right to health in jurisprudential terms. What does the right to health mean? What obligations does it give rise to?* Although national and international jurisprudence on the right to health is growing, the legal content of the right is not yet well established. This is not surprising, given the historic neglect of the right to health, as well as other economic, social, and cultural rights. Thus, a second key objective is to clarify and explore the contours and content of the right to health by drawing first on the evolving national and international jurisprudence and second on the basic principles that animate international human rights law, such as equality, non-discrimination, and dignity of the individual.

3. *To identify good practices for operationalizing the right to health at the community, national, and international levels.* Once human rights are recognized and their legal content understood, their legal provisions must be operationalized. In other words, national and international norms must be translated into effective policies, programs, and projects. How to go about such a transition for the right to health is not readily evident, any more than it is for a number of other human rights. Fortunately, different jurisdictions can provide examples of good laws, policies, programs, and projects that reflect the right to health. While what works in one context might not necessarily work in another, lessons can be learned. Thus, collecting, analyzing, and promoting good practices on the right to health are important steps. These good practices may be found at the community, national, and international levels and may be related to various actors including governments, courts, national human rights institutions, health professionals, civil society organizations, and international organizations.

MAIN THEMES

The right to health extends across a wide, diverse, and at times highly complex range of issues. To make promoting the right to health more manageable, I suggest focusing on two interrelated themes (a) poverty and the right to health and (b) discrimination, stigma, and the right to health.

As affirmed in the 2000 UN Millennium Declaration, poverty eradication has become one of the key, overarching policy objectives of the UN, as well as of other international organizations and many states. Discrimination and stigma both continue to seriously constrain and undermine progress in the field of health. The themes of poverty, discrimination, and stigma especially affect issues of gender, children, and racial discrimination. These themes also lend themselves to an examination of other important issues, such as those relating to mental health and HIV/AIDS.

---

4. Note Judge Weeramantry's dissenting opinion in the Advisory Opinion of the International Court of Justice (ICJ) on the Legality of the Threat or Use of Nuclear Weapons in which, referring to Article 12 of the International Covenant on Economic, Social and Cultural Rights (ICESCR), he stated: "it will be noted here that the recognition by States of the right to health is in the general terms that they recognize the right of everyone and not merely of their own subjects. Consequently, each State is obligated to respect the right to health of all members of the international community." ICJ Reports (1996), 1: 144. [*Eds.*—For an overall assessment of the Court's Advisory Opinion, see Burns H. Weston, "Nuclear Weapons and the World Court: Ambiguity's Consensus," *TLCP* 7 (1997): 371–400].

POVERTY, HUMAN RIGHTS, AND THE RIGHT TO HEALTH

A growing body of literature and practice has emerged that focuses on the impact of human rights on poverty reduction. In brief, human rights empower the poor; help tackle discrimination and inequality; require the participation of the poor; underscore the importance of all rights in the struggle against poverty; render some policy choices (e.g., those with a disproportionately harmful impact on the poor) impermissible; emphasize the crucial role of international assistance and cooperation; and introduce the notion of obligation and thus the requirement of effective, transparent, and accessible mechanisms of accountability.

Less literature and practice exist on the contribution that the right to health specifically has made to poverty reduction and it is this issue that demands particular attention. A poverty reduction strategy based on the right to health would, for example, focus on improving poor populations' access to health services by, perhaps, identifying diseases that are particularly prevalent among the poor and creating immunization and other programs that are specifically designed to reach the poor; improving the effectiveness of public health interventions by, for instance, implementing basic environmental controls, especially for waste disposal in areas populated by the poor; reducing the financial burden of health protection on the poor, e.g., by reducing or eliminating user fees for the poor; and promoting policies in other sectors that bear positively on the underlying determinants of health, e.g., supporting agricultural policies that have positive health outcomes for the poor.

Ultimately, exploring the specific contribution the right to health makes to reducing poverty is important. This contribution has to be understood in the overall context of the contributions human rights, including non-discrimination, participation, international cooperation, and accountability, make to reducing poverty.

DISCRIMINATION AND STIGMA AND THE RIGHT TO HEALTH

Discrimination and stigma is a second key theme relevant to the right to health. Discrimination on the grounds of gender, race, ethnicity, and other factors is a social determinant of health. Social inequalities, fueled by discrimination and marginalization of particular groups, shape both the distribution of diseases and the course of health outcomes among those afflicted. As a result, the burden of ill health is borne by vulnerable and marginalized groups in society. At the same time, discrimination and stigma associated with particular health conditions, such as mental disorders, and diseases, such as HIV/AIDS, tend to reinforce existing social divisions and inequalities. Non-discrimination is among the most fundamental principles of international human rights law. The International Covenant on Economic, Social and Cultural Rights (ICESCR) proscribes

> any discrimination in access to health care and underlying determinants of health, as well as to means and entitlements for their procurement, on the grounds of race, colour, sex, language, religion, political or other opinion, national or social origin, property, birth, physical or mental disability, health status (including HIV/AIDS), sexual orientation and civil, political, social or other status, which has the intention or effect of nullifying or impairing the equal enjoyment or exercise of the right to health.[5]

As well as prohibiting discrimination on a range of specified grounds, such as race, color, sex, and religion, international human rights instruments also prohibit discrimination on the grounds of "other status." The Commission on Human Rights has interpreted this term to include health status. Thus, the Commission and the Committee on Economic, Social and Cultural Rights (CESCR) agree that states have an obligation to take measures against discrimination based on health status, as well as in relation to other prohibited grounds. With respect to the right to health, states have an obligation to ensure that health facilities, goods and services including the underlying determinants of healthcare are accessible to all, especially the most vulnerable or marginalized sectors of the population, without discrimination.

The links between stigma, discrimination, and denial of the right to enjoy the highest at-

5. CESCR, General Comment 14, The Right to the Highest Attainable Standard of Health, 11 August 2000, UN Doc. E/C.12/2000/4, at 18.

tainable standard of health are complex and multifaceted. Together, discrimination and stigma amount to a failure to respect human dignity and equality by devaluing those affected, often adding to the inequalities already experienced by vulnerable and marginalized groups. This increases people's vulnerability to ill health and hampers effective health interventions. The impact is compounded when an individual suffers double or multiple forms of discrimination based, for example, on gender, race, poverty, and health status.

Effectively promoting the right to health requires identifying and analyzing the complex ways in which discrimination and stigma have an impact on the enjoyment of the right to health of those affected, particularly women, children, and marginalized groups, such as racial and ethnic minorities, indigenous peoples, persons with disabilities, people living with HIV/AIDS, refugees, the internally displaced, and migrants. Promoting the right to health also requires gathering and analyzing data to better understand how various forms of discrimination are determinants of health, recognizing the compounding effects of multiple forms of discrimination, and documenting how discrimination and intolerance affect health and access to health care services. It will also require carefully balancing the need to address discrimination and stigma in relation to health by encouraging the desegregation of data and the development of policies and strategies to combat discrimination, while also ensuring that publication of such data does not perpetuate stigma. The impact of stigma and discrimination on the enjoyment of the right to health is best understood in relation to particular populations, such as women, racial and ethnic minorities, people with disabilities, and people living with HIV/AIDS.

SPECIFIC PROJECTS, ISSUES, AND INTERVENTIONS

Given the three previously identified broad objectives, as well as the themes of poverty and discrimination/stigma, what are examples of specific right-to-health projects, issues, and interventions that might be usefully pursued? Below, six possible interventions are briefly discussed that, in my opinion, deserve increased attention. Of course, many other compelling

right-to-health interventions could and should be undertaken by various actors. The following illustrations are designed to signal how the general objectives and themes already identified can be taken forward and made more specific.

POVERTY-REDUCTION STRATEGIES

Poverty is a global phenomenon experienced in varying degrees in all nations. An increasing variety of nations—higher-income, lower-income, and those in transition—are formulating strategies to reduce poverty. Thus, one intervention is to examine a selection of poverty reduction strategies through the prism of the right to health with a view to suggesting ways in which the health component might more effectively benefit the poor and reduce poverty.

Poverty Reduction Strategy Papers (PRSPs), derived from the Heavily Indebted Poor Countries (HIPC) initiative, are one category of antipoverty strategy. In 2001–2, WHO carried out a desk review of ten full PRSPs and three interim PRSPs. This preliminary study found little evidence of attempts to adapt national health strategies to meet the needs of the poorest populations. Very few PRSPs have built in any health indicators that would monitor their impact on poor people or regions. No PRSPs contain plans to include poor people in a participatory monitoring process. All of these shortcomings would have been, at least, attenuated if the right to health had been taken into account during the formulation of the relevant PRSP. Not surprisingly, the study also found that no PRSP mentions health as a human right.

An examination of antipoverty strategies should not only include WPCs (world's poorest countries) and lower-income states, but should also extend to some antipoverty strategies. Moreover, the poverty reduction strategy of a higher-income state should address two different constituencies: their own jurisdiction and developing states. In light of its obligation of international assistance, a higher-income state should consider what contribution it is making to reduce poverty in the countries of the Global South. Accordingly, one project or intervention is to examine, through the prism of the right to health, higher-income states' strategies for the reduction of poverty in both their jurisdictions and in countries of the South.

NEGLECTED DISEASES

Broadly speaking, diseases fall into three categories. Type I diseases, such as hepatitis B, occur in rich and poor countries alike, with large numbers of populations vulnerable to these diseases found in each. Type II, or "neglected," diseases include HIV/AIDS and tuberculosis and are found in both rich and poor countries but are disproportionately present in poor countries.

Type III, or "very neglected," diseases, such as river blindness and sleeping sickness, overwhelmingly or exclusively plague lower-income countries. According to a 2002 WHO report, *Global Defence Against the Infectious Disease Threat*, the "health impact of these . . . diseases is measured by severe and permanent disabilities and deformities in almost 1 billion people. . . . Their low mortality despite high morbidity places them near the bottom of mortality tables and, in the past, they have received low priority."[6] The report continues:

[These] diseases form a group because they affect almost exclusively poor and powerless people living in rural parts of low-income countries. While they cause immense suffering and often life-long disabilities, these diseases rarely kill and therefore do not receive the attention and funding of high mortality diseases, like AIDS, tuberculosis, and malaria. They are neglected in a second sense as well. Confined as they are to poor populations, all have traditionally suffered from a lack of incentives to develop drugs and vaccines for markets that cannot pay. Where inexpensive and effective drugs exist, demand fails because of an inability to pay. Neglected diseases impose an enormous economic burden in terms of lost productivity and the high costs of long-term care. . . . [These] diseases can help to guarantee that the next generation remains anchored in poverty. . . . The disabilities caused by most of these diseases are associated with great stigma.[7]

The lines separating these three disease categories are not rigid: some diseases straddle two categories. Malaria, for instance, falls between types II and III.

In the case of type I diseases, incentives for research and development exist in rich countries, e.g., the market mechanism, public funding of basic research, and patent protection for product development. Products get developed, and the main policy issue for poor countries is gaining access to those technologies, which tend to be high priced and patent protected. Although many vaccines for type I diseases have been developed during the past twenty years, there is little incentive to introduce them widely into poor countries because of anticipated low returns on such an investment.

Incentives for research and development of type II diseases do exist in rich-country markets, but funding globally is not commensurate with the disease burden. A particularly acute example of this involves vaccines for HIV/AIDS. Substantial research and development for these vaccines is underway because of rich-country market demand, but not in proportion to global need or addressed to the specific disease conditions of poor countries.

Type III diseases receive extremely little research and development, with essentially no commercial funding taking place in rich countries. Because of poverty, the market mechanism fails. Moreover, governments of poor countries lack the means to subsidize the needed research and development. Thus, research and development for diseases specific to poor countries tend to be grossly underfinanced. As the report from the WHO Commission on Macroeconomics and Health puts it: "The poor countries benefit from R&D (research and development) mainly when the rich also suffer from the same diseases."[8]

The imbalance between research on diseases of the poor (type II and especially type III) and on diseases of the rich has been documented for more than a decade. In 1990, the Commission on Health Research and Development noted what has become known as the "10/90 disequilibrium": only 10 percent of research and development spending goes into health problems that affect 90 percent of the world's population. Initiatives have been launched to address this imbalance, and some progress has been made but the initiatives remain profoundly underfunded. Recently, neglected diseases—a problem arising

6. WHO, *Global Defence Against the Infectious Disease Threat* (Geneva: WHO, 2002), iv.
7. Ibid., 96.

8. WHO, *Macroeconomics and Health: Investing in Health for Economic Development* (Geneva: WHO, 2001), 77.

from market and public-policy failures—have been given fresh impetus by a number of welcome developments, including adoption of the Declaration on the Trade-Related Aspects of Intellectual Property Rights (TRIPS) Agreement and Public Health and the work of the Global Fund to Fight AIDS, Tuberculosis, and Malaria.

In the final analysis, particular attention must be paid to the numerous right to health implications of neglected including very neglected diseases and the 10/90 disequilibrium, including non-discrimination, equality, the availability and accessibility of health facilities, goods and services (including drugs), international assistance and cooperation, and so on. Neglected diseases, very neglected diseases, and the 10/90 disequilibrium are human rights issues.

IMPACT ASSESSMENTS

Before a state introduces a new law or policy, it has to ensure that the new initiative is consistent with its existing national and international legal obligations, including those relating to human rights.[9] If a state has adopted poverty reduction as a major policy objective, it must ensure that any new law or policy is consistent with that policy goal. Rigorous policy-making demands that the distributional impact of reforms on the well-being of different groups in society, especially the poor and vulnerable, is analyzed. Such an analysis has to consider Intergovernmental Panel on Climate Change (IPCC)—before, during, and after implementation of any relevant policy—the intended and unintended consequences of an initiative, with a view to identifying appropriate mitigating or other measures. This socially responsible impact analysis is required of states and other actors in the context of national and international policies.

Of course, there are obstacles to preparing such rigorous analyses. According to authors of a 2002 International Monetary Fund publication, these obstacles include "Data limitations,

weak national capacity, and a lack of donor coordination."[10] They recommend that poverty and social impact analyses should be strengthened and suggest the international community should do more to develop institutional capacity at the national level for "development of alternative policy scenarios" and "preparation of poverty and social impact analysis."[11]

Despite these and other difficulties, different forms of impact analysis are increasingly common at the national and international levels. In the context of the European Union, there is a requirement to check that some policy proposals do not have an adverse impact on health and this has contributed to a growing literature on health impact assessments. In addition, the World Bank has prepared a lengthy guide, entitled *User's Guide to Poverty and Social Impact Analysis*.[12] Some civil society organizations have advocated the introduction of "poverty impact assessments" within the framework of the PRSP process. Human rights impact assessments have been suggested for many years, most prominently in the Vienna Declaration and Programme of Action, and a few actors have sought to put them into practice.

Appropriate impact analyses are one way of ensuring that the right to health, especially of marginalized groups, including the poor, is given due weight in all national and international policy-making processes. Accordingly, in the context of the right to health, continuing attention should be given to the different types of impact analyses with a view to identifying good practice for states and other actors.

THE WORLD TRADE ORGANIZATION AND THE RIGHT TO HEALTH

It is not possible in a commentary of this nature and length to adequately scrutinize the TRIPS Agreement and the General Agreement on Trade in Services (GATS) through the prism of the right to health, an exercise begun by the former High Commissioner for Human Rights in

9. According to the Vienna Declaration and Programme of Action: "Protection and promotion of human rights and fundamental freedoms is the first responsibility of Governments." Vienna Declaration and Programme of Action, 25 June 1993, UN Doc. A/CONF.157/24, pt. 1, at 1.

10. Sanjeev Gupta et al., *Is the PRGF Living Up to Expectations? An Assessment of Program Design*, Occasional Paper 216 (Washington, D.C.: IMF, 2002), 32.
11. Ibid., 35.
12. World Bank, *A User's Guide to Poverty and Social Impact Analysis* (Washington, D.C.: World Bank, 2003).

her reports of June 2001 and 2002. What is clear, however, is that both agreements have crucial bearings on the right to health. TRIPS, for example, affects issues of access to essential drugs and also international cooperation. As the Commission on Human Rights has observed: "Access to medication in the context of pandemics such as HIV/AIDS is one fundamental element for achieving progressively the full realization of the right of everyone to the enjoyment of the highest attainable standard of physical and mental health."[13]

The Declaration on the TRIPS Agreement and Public Health, adopted at the WTO Fourth Ministerial Conference in Doha during November 2001, was a significant development.[14] The Doha Declaration recognizes "the gravity of the public health problems afflicting many developing and least-developed countries, especially those resulting from HIV/AIDS, tuberculosis, malaria and other epidemics."[15] The Declaration stresses that TRIPS "can and should be interpreted and implemented in a manner supportive of WTO members' right to protect public health and, in particular, to promote access to medicines for all."[16] In this way, the Declaration reflects human rights perspectives, especially the right to health and the right to enjoy the benefits of scientific progress.

In a 2002 resolution, the UN Commission on Human Rights called on all states

> to ensure that their actions as members of international organizations take due account of the right of everyone to the enjoyment of the highest attainable standard of physical and mental health and that the application of international agreements is supportive of public health policies which promote broad access to safe, effective and affordable preventive, curative and palliative pharmaceuticals and medical technologies.[17]

In these circumstances, it is important to monitor and examine trade rules and policies in the context of the right to health, including implementation of the Doha Declaration.

The Right to Mental Health

In 2001, WHO estimated that 450 million people suffered from mental or behavioral disorders and that these disorders accounted for 12 percent of the global burden of disease.[18] Mental disorders, including schizophrenia, bipolar disorder, depression, mental retardation, and Alzheimer's disease and other dementias, are common in all countries. Poor and other marginalized groups tend to be disproportionately affected by these disorders in both higher-income and lower-income countries.

For a majority of the world's population, mental health care is geographically and economically inaccessible. Where it is accessible, there are significant disparities in the standards of care between and within countries. In many countries, mental health care often consists primarily of large psychiatric institutions that have limited provisions for community-based treatment and care.

A wide range of human rights violations reportedly occur in some institutions designated for the care and treatment of persons with mental disorders. These violations include torture and other cruel, inhuman, or degrading treatment, such as sexual exploitation. Stigma and discrimination surround those with mental disorders, including the real or perceived incapacity of persons with mental disorders to make decisions about the treatment of their illness. It is the combination of these interrelated issues that makes persons with mental disabilities particularly vulnerable to violations of their human rights.

Thus, more attention should be devoted to this neglected element of the right to health: the right to mental health.

Health Professionals

As providers of health services, health professionals play an indispensable role in the promo-

13. UNCHR, Res. 2002/32, at 1.
14. WTO, "Declaration on the TRIPS Agreement and Public Health," adopted by the Fourth Ministerial Conference, Doha, 14 November 2001, WT/MIN(01)/DEC/2.
15. Ibid., 1.
16. Ibid., 4.
17. UNCHR, Res. 2002/32, note 14, ¶ 6(b).

18. WHO, *World Health Report 2001: Mental Health. New Understanding, New Hope* (Geneva: WHO, 2001), 3.

tion and protection of the right to health. This role, as well as the difficulties impeding their practice, must not be overlooked.

In many countries, health professionals are poorly paid, work long hours, and must make do with shortages of equipment and obsolete facilities. Poor terms and conditions of employment are a major cause of "brain drain": the migration of medical practitioners mainly from the South to the North, but also from rural areas to urban settings within countries. While the exporting countries may accrue some benefits (e.g., financial remittances from expatriates), the potential adverse outcomes, including shortages of health professionals, absence of compensation, and a decline in quality of health care, are likely to outweigh the benefits. Poor terms and conditions also create incentives for better-trained medical practitioners to seek more favorable situations, often in the private sector, thereby depleting public health systems.

In some countries, professional activities have made health workers victims of discrimination, arbitrary detention, killings, and torture. These workers have also had their freedoms of opinion, speech, and movement curtailed. At particular risk are health professionals who work with victims of torture. Some health professionals have participated, often under duress, in human rights abuses, including torture and the preparation of false medical documentation to cover up human rights abuses.

Corruption is a problem in the provision of health services in some jurisdictions. While in some cases this problem derives from unsatisfactory employment terms and conditions, corruption in health services is not confined to health workers. Nor is it confined to one region of the world. Corruption is clearly disadvantageous to the poor and corrodes the right to health. "In many countries poor people report that they are asked to pay for medicine that should be available to them at no charge."[19] Interestingly, a 2002 IMF study of corruption in healthcare services concludes: "Participation of the poor in the decisions that influence the allocation of public resources would mitigate corruption possibili-

ties."[20] Although there are no quick solutions, corruption should be understood as an issue of both poverty and the right to health.

CONCLUSION

International human rights law, including the right to health, should be consistently and coherently applied across all relevant national and international policy-making processes. In the context of international policy-making, this fundamental principle is reflected in the Vienna Declaration and Programme of Action, as well as in the Secretary-General's reports: *Renewing the United Nations: A Programme for Reform* (1997), *Strengthening of the United Nations: An Agenda for Further Change* (2002), and *Road Map Towards the Implementation of the United Nations Millennium Declaration* (2001).[21] Moreover, the principle is also reflected in positions taken by the UN Commission on Human Rights, such as its resolution calling on states parties to the ICESCR to "ensure that the Covenant is taken into account in all of their relevant national and international policy-making processes."[22]

At the national level, the right to health can enhance health policies and also strengthen the position of health ministries. At the international level, the right to health can contribute to the realization of the Millennium Declaration's vision of global equity and shared responsibility. Thus, the consistent and coherent application of the right to health across all national and international policy-making processes is one of the most important challenges confronting those committed to the promotion and protection of this fundamental human right.

19. Deepa Narayan-Parker with Raj Patel et al., *Voices of the Poor: Can Anyone Hear Us?* (New York: OUP, 2000), 111.

20. Sanjeev Gupta, Hamid Davoodi, and Erwin Tiongson, "Corruption and the Provision of Health Care and Education Services," in George T. Ahed and Sanjeev Gupta, eds., *Governance, Corruption, and Economic Performance* (Washington, D.C.: IMF, 2002), 272.
21. Renewing the United Nations: A Programme for Reform, Report of the Secretary-General, 14 July 1997, UN Doc. A/51/950, 78-79; UN General Assembly, Strengthening of the UN: An Agenda for Further Change, Report of the Secretary-General, 9 September 2002, UN Doc. A/57/387, 48; Road Map Towards the Implementation of the United Nations Millennium Declaration, Report of the Secretary-General, 6 September 2001, UN Doc. A/56/326, 202, 204.
22. UNCHR, Res. 2002/24, para. 7.

QUESTIONS FOR REFLECTION AND DISCUSSION

1. According to the World Health Organization, health is *a state of complete physical, mental and social well-being and not merely the absence of disease or infirmity*. According to General Comment 14 on ICESCR Article 12 of March 2000, the right to health is the right of all people *to the highest attainable standard of health as a prerequisite for the full enjoyment of all other human rights*. Are these definitions too broad? Too narrow? Just right? Why? Why not?

2. Hunt begins his essay by emphasizing briefly "four crucial jurisprudential elements of the right to health." What are these elements?

3. Hunt asserts that "the right to health includes, but goes beyond, the right to health care." He also asserts that the "right to health contains both freedoms and entitlements . . . [including] the right to control one's health." What else does it include? What else should it include? How broad or how narrow would you interpret this right to be? For example, should it include the freedom of parents to refuse vaccinations for their children? The freedom to get an abortion? What does Hunt say? What does ICESCR Article 12 say? Are Hunt and Article 12 in agreement? Is one more expansive or inclusive than the other? If so, which one and how?

4. Is it reasonable to think of the right to health as involving, in addition to health care, the improvement of all the cultural, economic, environmental, and sociopolitical conditions that determine health status, e.g., inequality and poverty; race, gender, and minority relations; discrimination, and marginalization (especially in relation to HIV/AIDS); global environmental threats; labor; militarism; and consumerism and meaninglessness/disease-inducing lifestyles? Why? Why not? What evidence in support of your answer?

6. Hunt contends that the "right to health gives rise to responsibilities in relation to international assistance and cooperation." What responsibilities does this entail? How can these obligations be enforced?

7. As noted in Ichiro Kawachi and Bruce Kennedy, *The Health of Nations: Why Inequality Is Harmful to Your Health* (New York: New Press, 2002), 45, economic historians and epidemiologists who have been examining the correlation between health and wealth/poverty have suggested that:

> the requirements for maintaining good health are finite and do not keep rising with the level of economic development. . . . Up to a level of national income of about $5,000 per head (in 1990 US dollars), there is a steep linear relationship between money and higher life expectancy. Beyond that point, however, further growth does not produce more health, and the relationship between income and life expectancy flattens out.

Rather than wealth per se, researchers find, it is the absence of extreme income distribution disparities that make for better overall health across the societal spectrum (49–50). These findings suggest that poverty reduction alone may not be the best strategy for improving health in developing countries and that the most health-threatening consequence of WTO, IMF, and World Bank economic prescriptions for these countries is an increase in wealth disparities. In fact, the "health gap" between the world's rich and the world's poor is widening. See, e.g., David Legge, "Health Inequalities in the New World Order," in Richard Eckersley, Jane Dixon, and Bob Douglas, eds., *The Social Origins of Health and Well-Being* (Cambridge: CUP, 2001). How are these difficulties to be overcome? How do they relate to the "dark side" of rights in the twenty-first century as recounted by, for example, Kapur in Reading 6 of Chapter 1?

8. Hunt notes that research and development for "neglected" and "very neglected" diseases are inadequate or nonexistent. Can you think of ways that rich countries can be incentivized to research and develop treatments for these diseases? How can funding be increased?

9. In 1999, WHO's World Health Assembly instructed WHO's Director General to monitor the public health impact of international trade agreements (the WHO having been represented in the 1999 Seattle WTO Conference for the purpose of linking public health concerns to trade). While affirming its support for drug patent protection under the TRIPS Agreement (1869 UNTS 401, *reprinted in ILM* 33 (1994): 1197, and 4 Weston & Carlson IV.C.2d), WHO voiced its concern with the "obvious market failures that lead hundreds of

millions of people being left without access to essential drugs," as quoted in Yves Beigbeder, *International Public Health: Patients' Rights vs. the Protection of Patents* (Aldershot: Ashgate, 2004), 64. WHO pushed for delays in the implementation of TRIPS in favor of developing and least-developed countries and, with the help of key NGOs, fought to permit poor countries to import desperately needed patented drugs at reduced prices ("parallel imports") and to manufacture generic drugs without the agreement of the patent holder ("compulsory licensing"). In the following years, however, the implementation of these concessions was obstructed by developed countries and the pharmaceutical industry. The 2001 Doha WTO Ministerial Conference reaffirmed the inviolability of patent rights even in cases of extreme public health emergencies and created serious doubts as to whether parallel imports and compulsory licensing were permissible. In 2002, the U.S. representative to the WHO Executive Board was particularly critical of the WHO's emphasis on access to essential medicines and refused to support differential drug pricing for poorer countries on the grounds that it would stifle American research and innovation. Should trade laws be above international public health? Why? Why not? Substantiate your answers.

10. What implications does the global environmental crisis have for the human right to health? For example, the impact of environmental toxins on mental health? Can you think of other examples? And upon whom the duties of protection should fall?

11. According to the Intergovernmental Panel on Climate Change (IPCC), "the impacts of climate change will fall disproportionately upon developing countries and poor persons within all countries, and thereby exacerbate inequities in health status and access to adequate food, clean water, and other resources." Intergovernmental Panel on Climate Change, *Climate Change 2001: Synthesis Report: Contribution of Working Groups I, II, and III to the Third Assessment Report of the Intergovernmental Panel on Climate Change* (Cambridge: CUP, 2001), 3.33. What arguments might you make, drawing on the human right to health, concerning the need for a response to the disparities of climate change? Does the human right to health hold out any hope for climate-blighted communities? Why and how so? Why not?

12. Unlike many if not all of its economic peers, the United States does not officially recognize the human right to health. Why? Should it? Why? Why not?

19. HANNAH WITTMAN *Food Sovereignty: A New Rights Framework for Food and Nature*

In 1996, an international coalition of peasant, farmer, rural women's, and indigenous people's movements met in Tlaxcala, Mexico, to discuss their common concerns around the effects of an increasingly globalized and concentrated agri-food system on their livelihoods, communities, and ecologies. This coalition was consolidated in 1993 as La Via Campesina, or "peasant way" and now is one of the largest and most vibrant social movements in the world, encompassing more than 148 organizations in sixty-nine countries. At the Tlaxcala meeting, members of La Via Campesina proposed an alternative paradigm called "food sovereignty" as a concept and framework that both challenges the foundations of the cur-

rent agri-food order and proposes a set of concrete alternatives for both theory and practice.[1] Since the Tlaxcala conference, the concept of food sovereignty has garnered increasing attention, first from grassroots social movements and the nongovernmental sector, then in policy arenas, notably the 2002 World Food Summit and counter-summit, the NGO/CSO Forum on Food Sovereignty, in Rome. In 2007, an international forum on food sovereignty held in Nyéléni, Mali, attended by 500 representatives from eighty countries defined food sovereignty as

The right of peoples to healthy and culturally appropriate food produced through ecologi-

Excerpted with changes by permission of Berghahn Books from Hannah Wittman, "Food Sovereignty: A New Rights Framework for Food and Nature?" *Environment and Society: Advances in Research* 2 (2011): 87–105. Copyright © Berghahn Books 2011.

1. See María Elena Martínez-Torres and Peter M. Rosset, "La Vía Campesina: The Birth and Evolution of a Transnational Social Movement," *Journal of Peasant Studies* 37, 1 (2010): 149–75.

cally sound and sustainable methods, and their right to define their own food and agriculture systems. It puts the aspirations and needs of those who produce, distribute and consume food at the heart of food systems and policies rather than the demands of markets and corporations. It defends the interests and inclusion of the next generation. It offers a strategy to resist and dismantle the current corporate trade and food regime, and directions for food, farming, pastoral and fisheries systems determined by local producers and users. Food sovereignty prioritizes local and national economies and markets and empowers peasant and family farmer-driven agriculture, artisanal fishing, pastoralist-led grazing, and food production, distribution and consumption based on environmental, social and economic sustainability. Food sovereignty promotes transparent trade that guarantees just incomes to all peoples as well as the rights of consumers to control their food and nutrition. It ensures that the rights to use and manage lands, territories, waters, seeds, livestock and biodiversity are in the hands of those of us who produce food. Food sovereignty implies new social relations free of oppression and inequality between men and women, peoples, racial groups, social and economic classes and generations.[2]

In what follows, I examine the emergent framework of food sovereignty from a food regimes perspective, comparing its ontological and epistemological underpinnings with a "food security" agenda. This is followed by an exploration of rights-based approaches to food and food sovereignty, including the practice of rights and agrarian citizenship within an agrarian moral economy based on food sovereignty. I then review the demands and strategies of the food sovereignty movement: a new trade regime, agrarian reform, a shift to agroecological production practices, attention to gender relations and equity, and the protection of intellectual and indigenous property rights.

A FOOD REGIMES APPROACH

In the late 1980s, the concept of a "food regime" was introduced as a constellation or cluster of class and interstate power relations, norms, and institutional rules, and socioecological/ geographical specializations that link the global relations of food production and consumption to periods of capital accumulation. The first food regime, in force between 1870 and the 1930s, was characterized by the transfer of basic grains and livestock from settler colonies to Europe and Great Britain where they were used as "wage foods."[3] This system of exchange included the consolidation of national agricultural sectors in settler states including the United States, Canada, and Australia. The second food regime—from 1950s to 1970s—sent subsidized, surplus food from the United States via food aid to postcolonial "development states" to extend industrialization and attenuate the threat of communism, while an international division of specialized agricultural supply chains and commodity complexes was developed by agribusiness.

Transition from one food regime to another stems from a series of contradictory relations resulting in crisis, then in transformation to a successor regime. As norms and rules over the distribution of power and property are challenged, in many cases by social movements, stable relationships are disrupted and space opens for the emergence of alternative constellations of production and consumption practices, and mechanisms of control over food systems. For example, Bill Pritchard notes the importance of multilateral negotiations around agricultural trade within the World Trade Organization (WTO) in facilitating the breakdown of the second food regime. When national governments joined the WTO in 1995, they "relinquished their powers to unilaterally set their own food and agricultural policies." WTO requirements caused a major restructuring of food security and rural livelihood programs in developing countries, but "the main effect of bringing agriculture into the WTO was not to reform global agriculture in line with market rationalities, but to aggravate already existing uneven opportunities in

2. Nyéléni Forum for Food Sovereignty, 2007, Declaration of the Forum for Food Sovereignty,
Sélingué, Mali, 23–27 February. See www.foodsovereignty.org.

3. See Philip McMichael, "A Food Regime Genealogy," *Journal of Peasant Studies* 36, 1 (2009): 139–69.

the world food system"[4] as the effects of subsidy restructuring were felt to a much lesser extent in countries that were part of the Organization for Economic Cooperation and Development (OECD).

By the turn of the twenty-first century, this current but theoretically unconsolidated food regime has been alternately described as "neoliberal," "corporate," and "corporate-environmental," as a product of the divergent tensions within, and resistance to, the ongoing financialization and corporatization of global food networks. Resistance to a corporate food regime, characterized by what French activist-farmer José Bové has called "food from nowhere,"[5] has most visibly been manifested in the food sovereignty movement, with its emphasis on rights, autonomy, and "food from somewhere." In this regard, although certainly not yet a consolidated food regime, food sovereignty can be regarded as a new, alternative paradigm and driver of change challenging the current food regime, in its efforts to re-embed economic, environmental, and equity-related concerns around agricultural production, consumption, and trade.

FOOD SECURITY, THE RIGHT TO FOOD, AND AGRARIAN CITIZENSHIP

As argued by Philip McMichael, the food sovereignty approach can be distinguished as an "epistemic shift" in which value relations, approaches to rights, and a shift from an economic to an ecological calculus concurrently challenge the rules and relations of a corporate or neoliberal food regime. One of the most salient shifts has been in the value relations, justification regimes, and frames around the concept of food security as it has been challenged by new conceptualizations of food sovereignty. Food security— framed as a universal ideal to prevent world hunger—emerged as a post-World War II development principle enshrined in the 1948 Universal Declaration of Human Rights (UDHR) and the 1966 International Covenant on Economic, So-

cial and Cultural Rights (ICESCR).[6] As defined by the Food and Agriculture Organization (FAO), food security exists when "all people, at all times, have physical, social and economic access to sufficient, safe and nutritious food that meets their dietary needs and food preferences for an active and healthy life."[7] This definition of food security treats food as a problem of insufficient trade rather than hunger by privileging *access* to food rather than *control over* systems of production and consumption. In this conception, food is a tradable commodity rather than a right, and hunger simply a problem of distribution.

The way that food security is framed has significant implications for how agricultural and food policy is developed and challenged. For example, Patrick Mooney and Scott Hunt suggest several distinct collective action frames around food security that are in concurrent use.[8] A *hunger frame* corresponds to a corporate/neoliberal food regime, focusing on food aid and technological development to increase global food production. A *community frame* is associated with food sovereignty, addressing hunger by advocating more localized control over food and agricultural policy. Food sovereignty also pushes an *ethical frame* based on control over and access to food as an element of the confluence of economic, social, cultural, political, and environmental rights. This frame connects food as a

4. Bill Pritchard, "The Long Hangover from the Second Food Regime: A World-Historical Interpretation of the Collapse of the WTO Doha Round," *Agriculture and Human Values* 26, 4 (2009): 297–307, 300.
5. José Bové and François Dufour, *The World Is Not for Sale: Farmers Against Junk Food* (London: Verso, 2000).

6. Both the UDHR and ICESCR are reprinted and fully referenced in Documentary Appendix A. [*Eds.*—UDHR Article 25(1) provides that "Everyone has the right to a standard of living adequate for the health and well-being of himself and of his family, including food, clothing, housing and medical care and necessary social services, and the right to security in the event of unemployment, sickness, disability, widowhood, old age or other lack of livelihood in circumstances beyond his control." ICESCR Article 11 provides that "The States Parties to the present Covenant recognize the right of everyone to an adequate standard of living for himself and his family, including adequate food, clothing and housing, and to the continuous improvement of living conditions."]
7. This definition has been in use by FAO since 2001, as the latest of several modifications of the definition developed in 1974 at the World Food Summit: "availability at all times of adequate world food supplies of basic foodstuffs to sustain a steady expansion of food consumption and to offset fluctuations in production and prices."
8. Patrick H. Mooney and Scott A. Hunt, "Food Security: The Elaboration of Contested Claims to a Consensus Frame," *Rural Sociology* 74, 4 (2009): 469–97.

human right (a focus of consumer and aid policy) to the right to choose how and by whom that food is produced (a focus of agricultural/ national food policies and of early proponents of the food sovereignty framework like La Via Campesina). Referring to a 2008 report by the UN Human Rights Council (UNHRC) on creating a human rights framework for world food and nutrition security, which does not explicitly mention the concept of food sovereignty, Marcia Ishii-Eitemann argues that "ultimately, the HRCR concludes that the right to food can only be realized where the conditions enabling food sovereignty are guaranteed."[9] She further argues that the rights-based approach embedded in food sovereignty is "an explicitly moral enterprise that stands in contrast to the economic processes of market-driven globalization," noting that "this implies a radical shift from the existing hierarchical and increasingly corporate-controlled research system to an approach that devolves more responsibility and decision-making power to farmers, indigenous peoples, food workers, consumers and citizens for the production of social and ecological knowledge."[10]

The UN-based right-to-food approach has been critiqued for focusing on the individual human right to food, rather than the structural problems of agricultural development, food production, and consumption within the world economic system. For example, Farhad Mazhar et al. suggest that

> The affirmation of individual rights to food, while a useful demand in the political environments of the North, has not been incorporated wholeheartedly into the food sovereignty discourse because it does not directly address the right of communities to produce food and to retain command and control over local food systems. From a food sovereignty perspective, a focus on egocentric rights diverts attention from concrete economic and political relations such as corporate control over agricultural inputs and knowledge and economic policies that structure the global food system. It also runs the risk of reducing the issue of hunger

and malnutrition to a humanitarian problem for the rich countries to solve, a prospect unacceptable to societies with long and rich agrarian histories.[11]

Although the "elaborate legal architecture" of international rights-based approaches to food may not yet be enforceable or effective in addressing problems of world hunger, the food sovereignty framework offers an alternative policy arena in which to discuss the rights and obligations around food production and consumption. Above all, food sovereignty proponents demand to participate in decisions and have a voice in establishing food system structures and particular, place-based conceptions of rights.

The concept of agrarian citizenship creates explicit links between struggles for political and ecological rights and practices, bringing the rights of nature into the food sovereignty equation. The agrarian citizenship approach acknowledges a socioecological metabolism as a crucial law of motion in agroecological transformation, in which the advent of capitalism and relationships of unequal ecological exchange commodified nature, separated urban consumers from rural producers, disrupted traditional patterns of nutrient cycling, and contributed to both hunger and environmental degradation. Agrarian citizenship acknowledges the diverse voices of human actors within the food system, but also considers how these voices and practices interact with nature voice (such as changing weather patterns as a result of climate change). Political and ecological voices are actively reshaping food policy and practice, especially in light of the implications of climate change for agricultural systems. By focusing on ecologically sustainable food production and reconnecting producers and consumers via the localization of "food from somewhere," food sovereignty as part of an "agrarian regeneration movement" is increasingly presented as having theoretical potential to rework, repair, or heal the metabolic rift.[12]

9. Marcia Ishii-Eiteman, "Food Sovereignty and the International Assessment of Agricultural Knowledge, Science and Technology for Development," *Journal of Peasant Studies* 36, 3 (2009): 689–700, 698.
10. Ibid., 691 (original citation omitted).

11. Farhad Mazhar, Daniel Buckles, P. V. Satheesh, and Farida Akhter, *Food Sovereignty and Uncultivated Biodiversity in South Asia: Essays on the Poverty of Food Policy and the Wealth of the Social Landscape* (Ottawa: International Development Research Centre, 2007), 65.
12. Hannah Wittman, "Reworking the Metabolic Rift: La Vía Campesina, Agrarian Citizenship, and Food Sovereignty," *Journal of Peasant Studies* 36, 4 (2009): 819–40.

MOVING TOWARD FOOD SOVEREIGNTY: STEPS AND SUBSTANTIVE CONCERNS

TRADE LIBERALIZATION AND ALTERNATIVE TRADE REGIMES

The food sovereignty movement was born out of concerns about the effects of structural adjustment, trade liberalization, and a shift to an agricultural export orientation on local food economies, communities, and ecologies. There is a large literature on the role of structural adjustment on weakening agricultural investment and support measures in developing countries, leading to supply constraints and an increase in hunger to over one billion people in 2009. WTO protocols, including the Agreement on Agriculture,[13] prohibit price supports in the Global South while allowing developed countries to maintain key agricultural subsidies, leaving small farmers worldwide unable to "compete in markets where the prices for farm products fell substantially through the decade following implementation of WTO rules."[14] This period, along with its push to implement export-oriented agricultural systems in developing countries, was accompanied by a "race to the bottom" in terms of environmental and social policies. As demonstrated by Marta Rivera-Ferre[15] in a review of the implementation of industrial, export-oriented shrimp farming in Asia, Latin America, and Africa, large companies benefitted from external financing and bilateral aid, while mangrove forest degradation and land conflicts reduced local food security and generated social exclusion. Similar reviews evaluating the social and environmental effects of expanded soybean production for biofuels in Brazil highlight structural contradictions in the current food regime that set the stage for the emergence of a food sovereignty orientation aimed at localization and diversification of agricultural production and trade. Following the collapse of the Doha Round of the WTO,[16] food sovereignty advocates argue that a subsequent proliferation of bilateral free trade agreements "will only serve to promote unfair trading practices, lock [countries] into even greater trade liberalization than would be expected under the WTO, and negatively impact the majority of their fellow citizens and the local environment."[17]

While often perceived as "antitrade," the food sovereignty movement is actually engaged in deep, ongoing conversations about what kinds of trade relations will best serve the social, economic, political, and environmental principles of an alternative food paradigm. Themes and issues within this conversation include affirmative action, intellectual property rights, dumping, social, environmental, and labor laws and regulations, labeling, denomination of origin, slow food, fair trade, regional networks, farmer's markets, and community-supported agriculture, many of which do not explicitly link to a food sovereignty framework but express many of the same social and environmental goals. The vast alternative-food networks and local and regional food-supply chains literature emerging from Europe and North America covers these issues in great detail, but only rarely invokes food sovereignty. Conversely, little discussion of these issues is currently present in the extensive literature on trade and food sovereignty, most of which focuses on identifying trade as an obstacle to food sovereignty. A research challenge remains to connect these themes and provide case-based examinations of alternatives to the dominant trade-liberalization system.

13. *Eds.*—See WTO website at http://www.wto.org/english/docs_e/legal_e/14-ag_01_e.htm, accessed 6 February 2015.
14. Philip McMichael, "A Food Regime Analysis of the 'World Food Crisis,'" *Agriculture and Human Values* 26, 4 (2009): 281–95, 295.
15. Marta Rivera-Ferre, "Can Export-Oriented Aquaculture in Developing Countries Be Sustainable and Promote Sustainable Development? The Shrimp Case," *Journal of Agricultural and Environmental Ethics* 22, 4 (2009): 301–21.

16. *Eds.*—As explained by the WTO, "The Doha Round [officially launched in November 2001] is the latest round of trade negotiations among the WTO membership. Its aim is to achieve major reform of the international trading system through the introduction of lower trade barriers and revised trade rules. The work program covers about 20 areas of trade. The Round is also known semi-officially as the Doha Development Agenda, as a fundamental objective is to improve the trading prospects of developing countries." See WTO website, http://www.wto.org/english/tratop_e/dda_e/dda_e.htm (accessed 6 February 2014).
17. Sandra Smeltzer, "A Malaysia-United States Free Trade Agreement: Malaysian Media and Domestic Resistance," *Asia Pacific Viewpoint* 50, 1 (2009): 13–23, 14.

RETHINKING LAND AND NATURE: FOOD PRODUCTION, AGRARIAN REFORM, AND INDIGENOUS KNOWLEDGE

A series of food crises since 2007 resulting in almost one billion people living in a state of hunger and even more facing malnourishment raises important questions for advocates of a food sovereignty framework. In the face of ongoing demographic shifts in food consumption practices, population increases, and the threat of climate change to agricultural productivity, what does a shift from a large-scale, export-oriented, and global trade-based system need to look like? How can a system based on small-scale, family-led farming, as food sovereignty's proposed alternative, "feed the world"?

Globally since the 1960s, total area in agriculture has risen by about 11 percent but land concentration (including land-grabbing), urbanization, and environmental degradation have reduced access to productive land for small-scale farmers in developing countries. The FAO estimates that more than thirty million peasants lost access to land in the decade after the establishment of the WTO,[18] following a more extensive period of depeasantization in the second half of the twentieth century. Just under half of the world population now lives and works in rural areas, but in most industrialized countries, agricultural producers make up less than 5 percent of the population. For food sovereignty proponents, improving control over access to land for an increasing diversity of farmers worldwide is an essential step to implementing food sovereignty and challenging the consolidation of productive land evidenced in the corporate food regime. To this end, a number of recent articles and monographs summarize the case for redistributive land reform, highlighting its importance and implications for food sovereignty and for addressing the global "land grab" in which corporations and wealthy states secure land in the Global South to support their own domestic food supplies.

Sustainable agricultural intensification or "producing more food from the same area of land while reducing environmental impacts"[19] is a second area of concern for feeding the world under a food sovereignty framework. In its research on sustainable and ecologically sound production methods, the food sovereignty movement has sparked an increasing interest in agroecology, as a multifunctional approach to food production that incorporates livelihood provision, conservation of biodiversity, and ecosystem function and community well-being. A 2010 UN review of the literature on agroecology and the right to food suggests that small-scale farmers can double food production within a decade in critical regions by using agroecological production methods, and research consistently indicates that agrobiodiversity based on indigenous farmer knowledge contributes to food security.[20]

In addition to the potential of agroecological practices to reduce greenhouse gas emissions from agriculture and landscape contamination from agrochemicals and improve long-term soil fertility, food sovereignty has also been proposed as a new conservation paradigm involving "wildlife-friendly farming." This model of agricultural production depends on the maintenance of an agricultural matrix composed of small, agrobiodiverse farms that preserve a variety of complementary agricultural niches.

Advancing agroecology involves not just the promotion and maintenance of human-designed agroecosystems, but the recognition of the importance of preserving and utilizing local and indigenous seed and livestock varieties, indigenous food systems, and uncultivated foods. These plants and the local knowledge necessary to cultivate them play an important role in sustaining indigenous food sovereignty and are among the elements most threatened by encroachment of industrial agriculture. As indicated by the UN Special Rapporteur on the right to food, "agroecology is a knowledge-intensive approach. It requires public policies supporting

18. John Madeley, *Hungry for Trade: How the Poor Pay for Free Trade* (New York: Zed, 2000), cited in Philip McMichael, "A Food Regime Genealogy," *Journal of Peasant Studies* 36, 1 (2009): 139–69, 154.

19. Charles H. Godfray et al., "Food Security: The Challenge of Feeding 9 Billion People," *Science* 327, 5967 (2010): 812–18, 814.
20. E.g., Kanok Rerkasem et al., "Agrodiversity Lessons in Mountain Land Management" *Mountain Research and Development* 22 (2002): 14–19, cited in K. A. Kassam, "Viewing Change Through the Prism of Indigenous Human Ecology: Findings from the Afghan and Tajik Pamirs," *Human Ecology* 37, 6 (2010): 677–90.

agricultural research."[21] Food sovereignty practice and analysis has thus also focused on the practice of seed sovereignty and control over agricultural knowledge, technology, and genetic resources, with strong theoretical linkages to the rights-based approach to food sovereignty and intellectual property regimes.

UNITY IN DIVERSITY: GENDER, CLASS, AND IDEOLOGY

Since its inception, women within La Via Campesina have pushed the movement to address asymmetrical gender relations; this led to substantial structural changes within the movement in 2000 to ensure gender parity for regional and global representation. In 2008, La Via Campesina launched a world campaign "For an End to Violence Against Women," rearticulating its focus on gender as an integral component of strategic mobilization around food sovereignty. Food sovereignty activists frequently emphasize that although over half of the world's agriculture work is performed by women (60 to 80 percent in developing countries), women own less than 2 percent of the land.[22] But reshaping gender relations is not just about shifting property relations, but rather in challenging base inequalities in power that include sexism, patriarchy, racism, and class. For example, significant class and cultural differences exist between "small-scale" farmers in different world regions; bridging these differences has posed a challenge to consolidating a way forward on achieving a food sovereignty regime. However, a continued focus on eradicating class and gender inequality, in addition to resource inequality, forms part of the food sovereignty frames' particular attention to diversity and difference in the construction of an alternative food regime.

To what extent can the food sovereignty paradigm offer a "coherent political economy of an alternative global agrarianism" as either a reconfiguration of capitalism or a non-capitalist alternative? The food sovereignty movement is an expression of distinct political, ideological, and class-based interests, affecting both the experience of neoliberal globalization and the strategies and tactics to achieve food sovereignty. Organizations associated with La Via Campesina and other alternative food movements engage in active debate on how contradictions within the current global food system should be resolved. For example, although the food sovereignty movement as a whole expresses opposition to the use of genetically modified seeds, by 2007, 90 percent of the 13.3 million producers cultivating transgenic crops were small-scale farmers, mostly growing Bt cotton in China and India.[23] Debates about the relative merits of growing genetically modified crops among smallholders reflect a complex set of issues having to do with economic survival, available markets, property rights, values, and politics. Finally, Saturnino Borras notes that the shifting structures of global political economy have encouraged rural social movements to localize and internationalize at the same time, resulting in the emergence of "polycentric" rural social movements with different visions of development and demands for levels of integration within and among local, regional, and international food systems.[24]

As one former member of La Via Campesina's International Coordinating Commission argues,

> One of the principal characteristics of La Via Campesina is its social and cultural cohesion, within a comprehension of diversity. It is not a question of seeking out differences in order to synthesise or explain them. . . . We have achieved a sensibility of these diverse cultures, in a common base. This common base is that we understand that the crisis of rural family agriculture is the same all over the world. The causes are the same, whether it be in Wisconsin or São Paulo. The reality is the same, and the same neoliberal, or more plainly, capitalist policies have caused this crisis.[25]

In a similar vein, at the Nyéléni forum on food sovereignty, participants emphasized that

21. UNHCHR, "Eco-Farming Can Double Food Production in 10 Years, Says New UN Report," Geneva Press Release, 8 March 2011.

22. Raj Patel, "Transgressing Rights: La Via Campesina's Call for Food Sovereignty," *Feminist Economics* 13, 1 (2011): 87–116.

23. *Eds.*—Bt cotton is a genetically modified kind of cotton that produces insecticide.

24. Saturnino Borras, "The Politics of Transnational Agrarian Movements," *Development and Change* 41, 5 (2010): 771–803.

25. Paul Nicholson, cited in Hannah Wittman, "Interview: Paul Nicholson, La Vía Campesina," *Journal of Peasant Studies* 36, 3 (2010): 676–82, 678.

"while it is critical to have a common frame-work, there is no single path or prescription for achieving food sovereignty. It is the task of individual regions, nations, and communities to determine what food sovereignty means to them based on their own unique set of circumstances."[26] Thus, ongoing research into the framework of food sovereignty seeks to gain a richer and deeper understanding of that diversity as an element of niche complementarity leading to strong and resilient local food systems.

COMMUNITY-DRIVEN RESEARCH AND EMERGING RESEARCH DIRECTIONS

A key challenge of theorizing food sovereignty lies in the problem of understanding the "diversity in unity." Food sovereignty actions and movements are vibrant, regionally, geographically, politically, and practically diverse, making generalizations difficult about what food sovereignty is or will be in a definitional sense. . . . In addition, the conflation of the human right to food with other goals for reforming the food system, particularly in the Global North, can confuse "means, ends and complementary goals" related to food sovereignty as an element of, rather than framework for, overall food system reform. Thus it is important to note, as Annette Desmarais points out, that "the principles of food sovereignty are not a checklist of separate 'things to do' [but rather] integrative goals of a praxis that plays out differently from one organization, locale, region, country and transnational context to the next."[27]

The politics of scale pose a second theoretical conundrum to conceptualizing food sovereignty. Who "gets to be sovereign" and who is responsible for conceptualizing and enforcing rights to food policy is an important emerging area of inquiry. The food sovereignty movement focuses on local and regional autonomy in food system definition, but also depends on the enforcement of trade rules and supportive agricultural policy

at the national level. These intersections of scale provide for some interesting potential contradictions, especially in areas where food sovereignty is now formally emerging in national constitutions (e.g., Ecuador, Bolivia, and Nepal) and national and municipal-level agricultural policies (e.g., Brazil, Maine).

Finally, the vast majority of research on food sovereignty has been focused on the relations of production, following the rural, agrarian, and productivist orientation of the social movements that gave rise to the concept. Many of these same movements are making or strengthening connections with urban consumers through alternative marketing relationships, including community-supported agriculture projects, farmers' markets, institutional procurement programs, and direct marketing. Yet, as mentioned above, the extant, primarily North American and UK-based literature on the urban consumer in local food systems development and revitalization almost completely ignores the food sovereignty framework. In an important exception, in a case study of debates around sustainable agriculture in British Columbia, Patrick Condon et al.[28] advance the idea of "municipal enabled agriculture" as an opportunity to integrate issues of supply, the focus of food security, with control in municipal planning processes, as an element of food sovereignty in cities. Likewise, Moncayo[29] examines the potential of school-based food sovereignty programs in urban Bolivia to address the "nutrition transition," where traditional diets composed of healthy, indigenous foods have been replaced by the Western diet composed of "junk food." The community garden movement in New York City has also been referenced as a potential driver of urban food sovereignty, but much more research is needed in incorporating urban and consumer-driven elements into a food sovereignty framework.

In conclusion, the community-driven nature

26. Christina Schiavoni, "The Global Struggle for Food Sovereignty: From Nyéléni to New York," *Journal of Peasant Studies* 36, 3 (2009): 682–89, 685.
27. Cited in Jeff Boyer, "Food Security, Food Sovereignty, and Local Challenges for Transnational Agrarian Movements: The Honduras Case," *Journal of Peasant Studies* 37, 2 (2010): 319–51, 334.
28. Patrick M. Condon et al., "Agriculture on the Edge: Strategies to Abate Urban Encroachment onto Agricultural Lands by Promoting Viable Human-Scale Agriculture as an Integral Element of Urbanization," *International Journal of Agricultural Sustainability* 8, 1–2 (2010): 104–15.
29. Moncayo Márquez, Luis Carlos, "Advancing Towards Food Sovereignty in El Alto, Bolivia: Revitalizing the Consumption of Native, Nutritious and Agroecological food in Urban Centers" (MA thesis, Simon Fraser University, Vancouver, 2009).

of food sovereignty conceptualization, practice, and more recently, research, has allowed the transformation of knowledge and ways of knowing in new and important ways. By documenting innovative practices and conceptualizations around the way that food, ecology, citizenship, and social organization are connected, communities of social practitioners have led a research agenda that has only recently been "noticed" by university-based communities of inquirers, but one that is sure to expand exponentially in the face of urgent demands for alternative agricultural and food policy models that can address the imminent effects of global climate change.

QUESTIONS FOR REFLECTION AND DISCUSSION

1. Is there a human right to food? From which legal instruments is it drawn? What characteristics does it possess? What does it imply? What state duties exist with regard to the satisfaction of a human right to food? You will need to justify your answers by drawing on your own research and the sources you have been able to find. You might begin with footnote 6.

2. Is the human right to food enhanced by the discourse of "food sovereignty"? If so, in what respects? If not, why not?

3. What, precisely, is the difference between "food sovereignty" and "food security"? How might the two be interrelated? Is there any sense in which they could even be construed as interdependent? If so, how? If not, why not?

4. Wittman argues that "The food sovereignty approach can be distinguished as an 'epistemic shift' in which value relations, approaches to rights, and a shift from an economic to an ecological calculus concurrently challenge the rules and relations of a corporate or neoliberal food regime." How so? What, precisely, characterizes this "shift"? A shift from what to what?

5. Will a "shift" from the current corporate or neoliberal food regime to a food sovereignty approach occur? What factors do you think will contribute to a successful shift? What challenges do you think will inhibit a successful shift? In considering your answer, think about what the author considers is "wrong" with the current regime, but also think about whether the factors that created the current regime have changed or can change.

6. How does the way in which food security is framed have significant implications for how agricultural and food policy is developed and challenged? Does it implicate the right to food? If so, how? If not, why not?

7. Wittman quotes Farhad Mazhar's claim that

> The affirmation of individual rights to food, while a useful demand in the political environments of the North, has not been incorporated wholeheartedly into the food sovereignty discourse because it does not directly address the right of communities to produce food and to retain command and control over local food systems. From a food sovereignty perspective, a focus on egocentric rights diverts attention from concrete economic and political relations such as corporate control over agricultural inputs and knowledge and economic policies that structure the global food system. It also runs the risk of reducing the issue of hunger and malnutrition to a humanitarian problem for the rich countries to solve, a prospect unacceptable to societies with long and rich agrarian histories.

Do you accept this view? If so, why? If not, why not? What suppositions does it rest upon? What, if anything, might a human rights approach contribute to a food sovereignty movement? Which human rights, if any, are present or implicit in the food sovereignty movement, or could enhance it?

8. Wittman states that one of the areas of concern for the food sovereignty framework is sustainable agricultural intensification. The framework attempts to deal with problems like sustainability, environmental friendliness, wildlife preservation, conservation of biodiversity, and ecosystem functioning. Can the food sovereignty framework deal with these problems better than the current "neoliberal" regime? If so, how so? If not, why not? Consider the actors involved, their goals, and their capabilities.

9. Why does La Via Campesina focus on gender parity? What relevance does gender parity have, if any, to the achievement of food sovereignty? Do you think it a necessary focus for the achievement of La Via Campesina's aims? If so, why? If not, why not? What conception of the aims are you calling on, either explicitly or implicitly in the course of your argument? Is yours a fair or sustainable reading of the food sovereignty movement and discourse as promulgated by La Via Campesina? Why? Why not?

10. How might food sovereignty build local and regional climate resilience? What links can you see between food, climate, and resilience? Are there any examples you can think of (or find through research) where new local food movements are making a difference to resilience-related outcomes? If so, where? Does food sovereignty discourse add anything to such movements? If so, why? And what? If not, why not?

11. Wittman discusses the goals and concerns of the food sovereignty movement. Keeping in mind Kapur's essay on the dark side of human rights in Chapter 1, Reading 6, can you foresee any dark sides that may arise under the food sovereignty framework? For example, can a local producer approach like the food sovereignty framework still successfully keep the interests of the consumer in mind? Discuss any dark sides you can foresee and how they may be alleviated.

20. RICHARD PIERRE CLAUDE AND FELISA L. TIBBITTS *The Right to Education and to Human Rights Education*

Education is intrinsically valuable as humankind's most effective tool for personal empowerment. Education takes on the status of a human right because it is integral to and enhances human dignity through its fruits of knowledge, wisdom, and understanding. Moreover, for instrumental reasons education has the status of a multifaceted social, economic, and cultural human right. It is a social right because in the context of the community it promotes the full development of the human personality. It is an economic right because it facilitates economic self-sufficiency through employment or self-employment. It is a cultural right because the international community has directed education toward building a universal culture of human rights. In short, education is a prerequisite for individuals to function as fully human beings in modern society.

In positing a human right to education, the framers of the Universal Declaration of Human Rights (UDHR) axiomatically relied on the notion that education is not value-neutral. In this spirit, Article 26 lays out a set of educational goals analyzed in this essay along with discussion focusing on education about human rights in the light of Article 26.[1]

Human rights education (HRE) is a long-term strategy with sights set on the needs of coming generations. It is essential to construct innovative education programs to advance human development, peace, democracy, and respect for the rule of law. Reflecting these aspirations, the UN General Assembly proclaimed a UN Decade of Human Rights Education (1995–2004). In so doing, the international community referred to human rights education as a unique strategy for the "building of a universal culture of human rights."

THE RIGHT TO EDUCATION

In the wake of World War II, the globe lay in shambles, torn by international violence from

1. *Eds.*—The right to education is recognized also in Article 13 of the International Covenant on Economic, Social and Cultural Rights (ICESCR) and arguably implicitly in Article 19 of the International Covenant on Civil and Political Rights (ICCPR). For convenience, however, the author considers the right only as articulated in the UDHR.

Poland to the Philippines, from the tundra to the tropics. Discussion about the importance of education as indispensable for post-World War II reconstruction emerged in the earliest work of the UN Commission on Human Rights set up in 1946 by the UN Economic and Social Council (ECOSOC). ECOSOC was established to make recommendations for promoting the observance of human rights on the then untested theory that human rights-respecting regimes do not make war on other such regimes. Thus, to bring peace to the world, members began their work in 1947, electing Mrs. Eleanor Roosevelt to chair the Commission. The Commission's Rapporteur, Dr. Charles Malik (Lebanon), said that, from the beginning, all the Commission members knew that their task of composing a declaration of human rights was itself an educational undertaking. He said: "We must elaborate a general declaration of human rights defining in succinct terms the fundamental rights and freedoms of [everyone] which, according to the Charter, the United Nations must promote." He concluded: "This responsible setting forth of fundamental rights will exert a potent doctrinal and moral and educational influence" on the minds and behavior of people everywhere.[2] Malik's statement echoed the Preamble to the Universal Declaration proclaiming the instrument a common standard of achievement for all peoples and all nations who should "strive by teaching and education to promote respect for these rights and freedoms." This entirely new global "bottom up" program of educating people regarding their human rights marked a challenge to the "top down" strategies of diplomatic statecraft, balance of power manipulations, and realpolitik that were insufficient to forestall the calamity of two world wars.

FORMULATING THE RIGHT TO EDUCATION

The Universal Declaration of Human Rights shows its framers realized that education is not value-neutral, and in drafting the document, the Soviets, being most ideologically sensitive, were the first to speak on this point. Mr. Pavlov for the USSR argued that one of the fundamental factors in the development of fascism and Nazism was "the education of young people in a spirit of hatred and intolerance."[3] As it finally turned out, Article 26 took up Pavlov's point that education inescapably has political objectives, but ignored his ideologically rigid ideas, substituting several goals in positive terms. Thus Article 26, in its most contentiously debated section, says that the right to education should be linked to three specific educational goals: (1) the full development of the human personality and the strengthening of respect for human rights and fundamental freedoms; (2) the promotion of understanding, tolerance, and friendship among all nations, racial, or religious groups; and (3) the furthering of the activities of the UN for the maintenance of peace.

THE FIRST GOAL

This arresting notion of the development of the human being's full personality, while abstract, is important as a thematic thread running throughout the UDHR. Its significance in framing a holistic concept of human nature as essentially free, social, potentially educated, and entitled to participation in critical decision-making is bolstered by repetition at several points:

- Article 22 says everyone's rights to social, economic, and cultural rights are indispensable for the free development of his personality.
- Article 26 posits a right to education, and says "Education shall be directed to the full development of the human personality . . . ."
- Article 29 repeats the holistic vision of human rights, saying: "Everyone has duties to the community in which alone the free and full development of his personality is possible."

Given the goal of the full development of the human personality in the context of society, the only context in which this can occur, it follows that the right to education is a social right, a social good, and a responsibility of society as a whole.

Latin Americans took a leading role in framing the right to education. The Brazilian delegate

---

2. Charles Malik, *These Rights and Freedoms* (Lake Success, N.Y.: UN Department of Public Information, 1950), 4–5.

3. Commission on Human Rights, 3rd sess., Summary Record of the 69th Meeting (Lake Success) 11 June 1948, 13, UN Doc. E/CN.4/SR.67.

provided a keynote statement on the importance of value-based education and was the first to argue that education provides the individual with the wherewithal "to develop his [sic] personality, which was the aim of human life and the most solid foundation of society."[4] An Argentine proposal put substance on these abstractions, mimicking Article 12 of the American Declaration of the Rights and Duties of Man: "Every person has the right to an education that will prepare him [sic] to lead a decent life, to raise his standard of living, and to be a useful member of society."[5] Calling for greater conciseness, Mrs. Roosevelt cautioned against language that would overload the right to education. In this spirit, the framers settled on alternative simpler language: "education shall be directed to the full development of the human personality."[6]

The full development goal was intended to capture the enabling qualities of the right to education, and of education's potential as a foundation for a dignitarian, rights-respecting social order. This view follows from a close reading of the key phrase "full development of the human personality" which is immediately followed without so much as a comma by the phrase "and to the strengthening of human rights and fundamental freedoms." Using a standard canon legal interpretation, one might fairly conclude that the joining of the two elements was deliberate and meaningful, especially in view of Mrs. Roosevelt's injunction toward conciseness. The logic of the two ideas in combination tells us that education promoting the full development of the human personality and the dignity it entails also promotes human rights. And for such full development, education for dignity should take into account the total menu of human rights: personal rights like privacy; political rights like participation and the right to seek and disseminate information; civil rights like equality and non-discrimination; economic rights like a decent standard of living; and the right to participate in the community's cultural life. This analysis prefigures Brazilian Paulo

Freire's views advocated in his book, *The Pedagogy of the Oppressed*.[7] Freire emphasizes the connections between popular empowerment and self-realization as the consequence of people learning and exercising their human rights.

THE SECOND GOAL

Article 26 calls for education to *promote understanding, tolerance, and friendship among all nations, racial or religious groups*.[8] This idea started out under different language. Professor René Cassin, the influential French delegate and vice president of the Human Rights Commission, drew support for asserting that one goal of education should involve combating the spirit of intolerance and hatred against other nations and against racial and religious groups everywhere.[9] But again the Latin American delegations had the last word, showing their voting strength in supporting the view that educational goals should be framed in positive terms instead of negative goals such as combating hatred. Mr. Campos Ortiz of Mexico convincingly said that Article 26 should link the right to education with the positive goal of the promotion of understanding, tolerance, and friendship among all nations and racial and religious groups.[10]

THE THIRD GOAL

Article 26 says education should *further the activities of the United Nations for the maintenance of peace*.[11] In the final consideration of the Declaration before the General Assembly, the Mexican delegate said the right to education should be connected to the peaceful objectives of UN activities. Mr. Watt from Australia promptly objected and urged support for a broader reference to all the "purposes and principles of the United Nations."[12] Again, Mrs. Roosevelt expressed distaste for any formulation lacking conciseness and specificity, and said for that reason she associated

4. Official Record of the 3rd Session of the General Assembly, Part I, "Social Humanitarian and Cultural Questions," 3rd Committee, Summary Records of Meeting, 21 September–8 December 1948, reporting 147th Meeting of the Commission, held at the Palais de Chaillot, Paris, 19 November 1948, 597.
5. Ibid.
6. Cuban Amendment (UN Doc. A/C.3/261).

7. Paulo Freire, *Pedagogy of the Oppressed* (New York: Seabury, 1973).
8. Emphasis added.
9. Official Record, 587.
10. Ibid., 584.
11. Emphasis added.
12. Official Record, 594.

herself with the simpler Mexican proposition. She thought that *for educational purposes*, UN activities for the maintenance of peace should be recognized as "the chief goal of the United Nations."[13] True to pattern, other Latin American voices chimed in supporting the Mexican initiative. Mr. Carrera Andrade of Ecuador lyrically concluded that when the world's youth became imbued with "the guiding principles of the United Nations, then the future [would promise] . . . greater hope for all nations living in peace."[14]

Finally, the reference to UN peace activities was adopted and all dissent was swept away with the final version of Article 26 winning a unanimous 36 votes with 2 abstentions. As a result, Article 26, with three separate sections, now reads as it does.[15]

On 10 December 1948, the General Assembly solemnly adopted and proclaimed the UDHR. That body was alerted by several framers that the document could have little effect unless people everywhere knew about it and appreciated its significance for every human being. Therefore, the Assembly also passed Resolution 217 D urging that the widest possible publicity be given to the Declaration and inviting the Secretary-General and UN specialized agencies and nongovernmental organizations to do their utmost to bring the Declaration to the attention of their members.[16] One present-day result is that the Universal Declaration can be obtained from the UN in any of 300 languages.[17]

HUMAN RIGHTS EDUCATION (HRE) IN PRACTICE

HUMAN RIGHTS STANDARDS AND HRE

As evidenced in the preceding discussion concerning the centrality of education—especially HRE—to the UN goals and to the foundational values of the UDHR, states are expected to ensure that education is aimed at strengthening respect for human rights and fundamental free-

doms. Aimed at promoting awareness about the rights accorded by the UDHR and related human rights instruments, HRE may be understood as a direct expression of these goals, and likewise the procedures for redress of the violations of the rights that advance them. HRE is a deeply practical expression of the high-minded ideals of the UDHR—a deliberate attempt to foster a worldwide human rights culture. Indeed, HRE is formally defined as:

> all educational, training, information, awareness-raising and learning activities aimed at promoting universal respect for and observance of all human rights and fundamental freedoms and thus contributing, inter alia, to the prevention of human rights violations and abuses by providing persons with knowledge, skills and understanding and developing their attitudes and behaviors, to empower them to contribute to the building and promotion of a universal culture of human rights.[18]

An early UN instrument expressly supporting HRE as thus conceived was promulgated by UNESCO in 1974.[19]

It was the 1993 Vienna World Conference on Human Rights, however, that came to be considered the landmark, catalytic event for recognizing HRE. Two years later, it was followed by the above-noted UN Decade for Human Rights Education (1995–2004),[20] which in turn was followed in 2005 by the *permanent* World Programme for Human Rights Education.[21]

Most recently, in 2011, the UN General Assembly adopted the strongest policy instrument yet: the UN Declaration on Human Rights Education and Training (DHET).[22] While falling short of establishing a free-standing right to human rights education as such, Article 1(1) of the DHET declares that "Everyone has the right to know, seek and receive information about all human rights and fundamental freedoms and

---

13. Ibid.
14. Ibid., 589.
15. See UDHR, art. 26(1), (2), and (3).
16. GA Res. 217D, UN GAOR, 3d Sess., Pt. I, Resolutions, at 78, UN Doc. A/810 (1948).
17. See website of the Office of the High Commissioner for Human Rights, http://www.ohchr.org/en/udhr/pages/introduction.aspx [*Eds.*—accessed 11 June 2015].

18. UN Declaration on Human Rights Education and Training, art. 2, para. 1, GA 66/137 (19 December 2011).
19. UNESCO, Recommendation Concerning Education for International Understanding, Co-Operation and Peace and Education Relating to Human Rights and Fundamental Freedoms, GC (19 November 1974).
20. UN Decade for Human Rights Education, GA 49/184 (23 December 1994).
21. UN World Programme for Human Rights Education, GA 59/113 (10 December 2004).
22. Note 18.

should have access to human rights education and training." Additionally, the Declaration reaffirms that states bear the primary responsibility to promote and ensure HRE, though in practice it is civil society organizations that have engaged most enthusiastically in this regard.

Also noteworthy is the recognition given by regional human rights instruments, such as the African Charter on Human and People's Rights and the Council of Europe, which has a Charter on Education for Democratic Citizenship and Human Rights Education.[23] At the regional as well as global level, thus, HRE is a central element of broad programs aimed at establishing a culture of universally applicable, widely respected, human rights.

The Pedagogy of Human Rights Education

HRE and learning have components of knowledge, skills, and attitudes that are consistent with recognized human rights principles and thus empower individuals and groups to address oppression and injustice. The DHET highlights the centrality of pedagogy in HRE; it places explicit importance on how teaching and learning experiences themselves are organized. For this purpose, the Declaration draws a distinction between education *about* human rights (content), education *through* human rights (processes of learning), and education *for* human rights (learner outcomes that result in taking action to promote human rights). Article 2(2) provides:

Human rights education and training encompasses:
(a) Education about human rights, which includes providing knowledge and understanding of human rights norms and principles, the values that underpin them, and the mechanisms for their protection;
(b) Education through human rights, which includes learning and teaching in a way that respects the rights of both educators and learners;
(c) Education for human rights, which includes empowering persons to enjoy and exercise their rights and to respect and uphold the rights of others.

HRE may thus be seen as having legal as well as moral dimensions. The legal dimension incorporates sharing content about international human rights standards as embodied in the UDHR and other human rights instruments to which countries subscribe, embracing civil and political as well as social, economic, and cultural rights; and in recent years environmental and other group or collective rights have been added to this evolving framework. It is an incorporation that recognizes the importance of monitoring and accountability, of ensuring that governments uphold the letter and spirit of their human rights obligations.

At the same time, HRE is a cultural enterprise. The process of HRE is one that is intended to provide skills, knowledge, and motivation to individuals to transform their own lives and realities in ways that are more consistent with human rights norms and values. For this reason, interactive, learner-centered methods are widely promoted, with the following kinds of pedagogy being most representative of those promoted by HRE advocates (methods that are advocated across all kinds of HRE, but implemented most comprehensively in adult, popular education learning models):

- *Experiential and activity-centered*: involving the solicitation of learners' prior knowledge and offering activities that draw out learners' experiences and knowledge
- *Problem-posing*: challenging the learners' prior knowledge
- *Participative*: encouraging collective efforts in clarifying concepts, analyzing themes and engaging in activities
- *Dialectical*: requiring learners to compare their knowledge with knowledge gained from other sources
- *Analytical*: asking learners to think about why things are and how they came to be so
- *Healing*: promoting human rights in intrapersonal and interpersonal relations
- *Strategic thinking oriented*: directing learners to set their own goals and to think of strategic ways of achieving them
- *Goal and action oriented*: allowing learners to plan and organize actions in relation to their goals.[24]

23. CM/Rec(2010)7 (11 May 2010), adopted by Committee of Ministers, *Council of Europe Charter on Education for Democratic Citizenship and Human Rights Education*.

24. Asia-Pacific Regional Resource Center for Human Rights Education, "What Is Human Rights Education?" in *Human Rights Education Pack* (Bangkok: ARRC, 2003).

HRE in Schools

Perhaps the most popular HRE programming has been aimed at the schooling sector. Increasing numbers of countries report some degree of HRE in national curriculum frameworks (though the quality and depth of implementation is rarely known). Since the 1990s, international governmental organizations (IGOs) and nongovernmental organizations (NGOs) have engaged HRE in the schooling sector in collaboration with relevant national ministries. Further, nonformal HRE—through human rights clubs, for example—also takes place in the school environment.

HRE in school settings is adapted to the age of learners and to the conditions of national/local educational policies and schools, as seen in conceptual and developmental frameworks for HRE that have been developed by the United Nations and several NGOs. These frameworks assist in setting goals for HRE, illustrating both what it shares with, and what it adds to, other educational approaches that address such values as social justice. Table 1 efficiently communicates the dynamics of the methodologies involved:

The human rights themes and content of HRE in schools thus can be found as a cross-cultural theme within educational policy or integrated within existing subjects, such as history, civics/citizenship education, social studies, and humanities. HRE can be found also in the arts and in nonformal clubs and special events that take place in the school setting.

Regional and country-specific studies have attempted to identify the presence of human rights themes and approaches within educational standards and curricula. A sequence of

TABLE 1: METHODOLOGIES: HRE CONCEPTUAL AND DEVELOPMENTAL FRAMEWORK

LEVELS	GOALS	KEY CONCEPTS	SPECIFIC HUMAN RIGHTS PROBLEMS	EDUCATION STANDARDS AND INSTRUMENTS
Early childhood Preschool & lower primary Ages 3–7	Respect for self Respect for parents and teachers Respect for others	Self Community Responsibility	Racism Sexism Unfairness Hurting people (emotionally, physically)	Classroom rules Family life Convention on the Rights of the Child
Later childhood Upper primary Ages 8–11	Social responsibility Citizenship Distinguishing wants from needs from rights	Individual rights Group rights Freedom Equality Justice Rule of law Government Security Democracy	Discrimination/ prejudice Poverty/hunger Injustice Ethnocentrism Passivity	UDHR History of human rights Local, national legal systems Local and national history in human rights terms UNESCO, UNICEF
Adolescence Lower secondary Ages 12–14	Knowledge of specific human rights	International law World peace World development World political economy World ecology Legal rights Moral rights	Ignorance Apathy Cynicism Political repression Colonialism/ Imperialism Economic globalization/ neoliberalism Environmental degradation	Elimination of racism Elimination of sexism International Bill of Human Rights (UDHR, ICESCR, ICCPR) Regional human rights conventions UNHCHR/OHCHR UNHCR NGOs

Source: Adapted from Nancy Flowers, ed., *Human Rights Here and Now: Celebrating the Universal Declaration of Hum,an Rights* (Minneapolis: Amnesty International USA and University of Minnesota Homan Rights Resource Center, 1998).

comparative analyses of indicators of HRE principles and content in the text of constitutions and national education laws in nineteen countries in Latin America showed a quantitative and qualitative increase between 1990 and 2008. This analysis also involved an investigation of other mechanisms for promoting HRE, such as national plans of action, and specialized programs and educational units.[25]

As noted already, information on the actual implementation of HRE in schools is relatively scarce, though evidence-based research has expanded in recent years. National comparative studies on the implementation of HRE in schools have included Australia, Austria, Japan, and the United States. These studies have demonstrated the contextual factors in countries that have contributed to government support of HRE (such as pedagogical reforms and curricular spaces for HRE) as well as obstacles within the schooling sector (such as the testing culture, overcrowded curricula, and a lack of teacher training).[26] Stud-

ies have also exposed the ad hoc and nonsustainable nature of state support for HRE, with much of the real impetus for HRE coming from civil society. The Gerber study of Australia and the United States concluded that there was no apparent relationship between the governments' ratifications of international human rights treaties and domestic practices concerning human rights and HRE.[27]

In the United States, Dennis Banks's 2000 study revealed that less than half the fifty states had mandates for inclusion of human rights content in compulsory education, and that many of these mandates were linked to curriculum subtopics (for example, study of the Holocaust and genocides) that were more narrowly focused than the definition offered by the UN Office of the High Commissioner for Human Rights. It remained unclear how much time individual classroom teachers actually devoted to human rights instruction, or the degree to which such instruction is informed by accurate and current information on the topic.[28] In a subsequent study in the United States, Stone found that while the majority of states referenced human rights in their teaching standards, there was little evidence that systematic integration of human rights edu-

25. Inter-American Institute of Human Rights, *Inter-American Report on Human Rights Education, a Study of 19 Countries: Normative Development. Second Measurement* (San José, Costa Rica: Inter-American Institute of Human Rights, 2008). From 2002 through 2013, the IIDH (Instituto Interamericano de Derechos Humanos) produced annual reports on the status of HRE in relation to different aspects of schooling policies and practices. They can be found at http://www.iidh.ed.cr (accessed 12 April 2015).
26. Paula Gerber, *From Convention to Classroom: The Long Road to Human Rights Education: Measuring States' Compliance with International Law Obligations Mandating Human Rights Education* (Saarbrücken: VDM, 2008).

27. Ibid., 323.
28. Dennis Banks, "What Is the State of Human Rights Education in K-12 Schools in the United States in 2000? A Preliminary Look at the National Survey of Human Rights Education," paper presented at Annual Meeting of the American Educational Research Association, Seattle, Washington, 2001), ERIC Document ED 454 134.

TABLE 2: HRE IN SCHOOLS: PEOPLE'S WATCH IN INDIA

The Institute of Human Rights Education of People's Watch is the largest NGO working toward HRE in India and is actively engaged in training teachers in government schools throughout India. In Tamil Nadu alone, HRE is offered in over 2,000, primarily government-run schools. This NGO trains teachers in how to conduct HRE for children in grades 6, 7, and 8. There are lessons on the Indian Constitution and some United Nations documents in class six; children's rights and experiences in class seven; and discrimination—based on caste, religion, gender, ability, income, skin color, and language, among others—and the right to equal treatment in class eight. . . . The textbooks contain interactive features such as stories, participatory activities, and discussion questions to foster investigation into school and community realities. Since 1997, human rights educators have reached out to over 300,000 Indian school children. A study that examined impact of participation in the programming for 104 students showed that 56% of the students had reported that they had personally intervened or taken some kind of action when faced with a human rights violation. In addition, students indicated that they had educated others about human rights (20%), reported—or threatened to report—a human rights abuse (14%), and/or had experienced a personal change as a result of having participated in the HRE program.

Source: Monisha Bajaj, "From 'Time Pass' to Transformative Force: School-Based Human Rights Education in Tamil Nadu, India," *International Journal of Educational Development* 32 (2010): 72–80.

cation was occurring in the nation's classrooms.[29] Indeed, in school systems across the world, a lack of curricular space and teacher training in the content and pedagogy of HRE are consistently mentioned as being the primary barriers to implementing effective HRE in schools.

HRE IN NON-SCHOOL SETTINGS

UN standards call for HRE to be integrated within training programs for all government employees, including teachers, civil servants, law enforcement officials, prison officials, the military, social workers, diplomats, and state employees. These goals are largely aspirational though some progress has been made in recent years, including the elaboration of guidelines for integrating HRE within the training of law enforcement officials and civil servants.[30] The expansion of the presence of HR standards and values within the training of professional groups is a pressing priority for activists in HRE—and a fundamental component of creating a broad, effective human rights culture.

In contrast to the challenges of integrating HRE within training academies, the organization of nonformal HRE is much simpler. It is not surprising, therefore, that nonformal HRE with young people and with potentially vulnerable populations such as women and minorities is fairly widespread. HRE programming in the non-formal education sector can include clubs, study groups, short-term workshops and nonaccredited training courses. Women's human rights groups have been very active in nonformal HRE as a strategy for personal and social transformation.

A complement to programming oriented toward training a specific target group is the community-wide approach to HRE. "Human Rights Cities" is a project founded by the People's Movement for Human Rights Learning, aimed at developing sustainable, human rights friendly cities, which now exist in over twenty communities worldwide.[31] Relatedly, development organizations that provide programs adopting a rights-based approach also use HRE to foster community-wide respect for human rights and to empower communities in that respect. Such community-level initiatives, therefore, are fruitful contexts in which to appreciate the positive potential and empirical impact of HRE approaches.

THE FUTURE OF HRE

The HRE field shows signs of continuing development and evolution—this despite ongoing challenges in relation to political will and resources. At the international level, the United

29. Adam Stone, "Human Rights Education and Public Policy in the United States: Mapping the Road Ahead," *HRQ* 24, 2 (2002): 537–57.

30. Between 2011 and 2013, the Office for Democratic Institutions and Human Rights of the Organization for Security and Co-operation in Europe published four sets of HRE guidelines: for secondary school systems, law enforcement officials, civil servants (focusing on health workers), and human rights activists. See http://www.osce.org/resources (accessed 12 April 2015).

31. Details concerning the "Human Rights Cities" initiative of the People's Movement for Human Rights Learning (formerly known as the People's Decade for Human Rights Education) may be found in Stephen P. Marks, Kathleen A. Modrowski, and Walther Lichem, *Human Rights Cities: Civic Engagement for Societal Development* (New York: UN Habitat, 2008).

TABLE 3: HUMAN RIGHTS TRAINING OF POLICE IN VICTORIA, AUSTRALIA

In 1994, Victoria Police (Australia) conducted a raid on the Tasty Nightclub, a gay club in Melbourne. Four hundred and fifty-six patrons were strip-searched. Allegations of inappropriate searches and homophobic comments resulted in a class-action lawsuit against Victoria Police. Patrons received compensation.

In 2006, Victoria Police established the Human Rights Project. The Project monitors all aspects of policing and educates Victoria Police's 14,000 employees on human rights in the context of policing. These employees range from administrative staff, to investigative scientists to foot officers. International human rights law provides law enforcement officials with detailed standards for investigations, arrest and custody, use of force and firearms, and victims' assistance. On average, there was a 30% reduction in complaints about police conduct following the implementation of the HRE program.

Source: *A Path to Dignity: The Power of Human Rights Education*, documentary film, www.path-to-dinity.or (accessed 12 April 2014).

TABLE 4: NONFORMAL HRE WITH WOMEN IN TURKEY

Women for Women's Human Rights (WWHR)-New Ways in Turkey is a nongovernmental organization that organizes a life skills-legal literacy program for adult women through a partnership with the Turkey General Directorate of Social Services (GDSS) that began in 1999. WWHR trains and supports GDSS and additional NGO staff to deliver a 16-week Human Rights Education Program for women that focuses on awareness raising in legal literacy, self-empowerment, and building solidarity relationships among study group members and other HREP groups in the country. Since its pilot application phase in 1995–97, HREP has expanded to over 50 cities in all seven regions of Turkey, and nearly 9,300 women have participated. It is currently the most widespread, longest-running, and comprehensive non-formal adult human rights education program in the region, and a unique example of sustainable NGO-state partnership in the field of women's human rights in Turkey. A 2011 impact assessment found overwhelming evidence of impacts for learners in increased knowledge and awareness of women's rights and legal protections in Turkey; attitudes and feelings, including increased self-confidence, valuing of self, and courage; skills such as problem identification and problem solving; and taking action to improve their position, especially in family relations.

Source: Felisa Tibbitts, *Impact Assessment of the Human Rights Education Program for Women (HREP), 2005–2011*, prepared for Women for Women's Human Rights—New Ways (unpublished report, September 2012).

Nations, through its various agencies, continues to encourage governments to develop formal plans of action for HRE and to provide reports on their internal HRE activities as part of their regular treaty-based reports to the UN. The Office of the UN High Commissioner continues to publish technical resources to aid in the design, implementation, and evaluation of HRE programming in all sectors, so that growth in quantity and quality is possible. National human rights institutions have become increasingly engaged in HRE, and often have public awareness-raising as part of their mandate. Research in the field, though currently sparse, is beginning to increase. There is, therefore, both considerable expansion and room for more expansion in the HRE field.

International and national networks of educators, institutes, and organizations continue to dialogue and share resources on the content, standards, and methodology of HRE and learning. Two key international HRE organizations with ongoing HRE activities and numerous HRE resources that are publicly available are Amnesty International (www.amnesty.org) and Human Rights Education Associates (www.hrea.org).

Thousands of other national and subnational NGOs are actively engaged in carrying out HRE within their own environments.

Despite the visible expansion of HRE, however, continuing challenges facing the future concern opportunity, quality, and pedagogy. How can HRE become part of every school system and the training of professional groups? How can practitioners best design programming that is developmentally appropriate (e.g., for an adolescent or for an adult) and relevant to their concerns and needs? How can programming be designed so that it is not didactic but encourages critical thinking and analyses, even about the human rights framework itself? HRE has tremendous potential to facilitate processes of change that will result in a greater realization of human rights. As it grasps the hearts and minds of those who engage in it, we will see to what degree it will fulfill its wider potential as the foundation for a global order of respect, fulfilling the aspirations of the drafters of the UDHR whose vision for HRE as the "pedagogy of the oppressed" still resonates and expands despite the many challenges facing human rights realization in the contemporary world order.

QUESTIONS FOR REFLECTION AND DISCUSSION

1. Children in North America and Western Europe and increasingly in China, Japan, and South Korea typically have access to far greater educational opportunity (measured both in average length of education and in average per-pupil expenditures) than their counterparts elsewhere in the world where, in the poorest countries especially, children are often forced to work to enhance family income. Does such inequality constitute a per se abrogation of the right to education among the children of the poorer regions? If so, who is to blame, hold

accountable? Many states in the United States have attempted to combat town-by-town differences in education opportunity by requiring wealthier communities to send money to poorer communities for education. Does the fulfillment of the human right to education require a similar approach globally? What, in other words, does the human right to education have to say about equality of access to education?

2. Do parents violate the human right to education (and possibly other rights as well) by insisting that they have a right to the fruits of their children's labor? If it means denying their children access to formal education? If their children are unable to attend school for part of the year? If the children do so voluntarily, lovingly? What do the 1989 Convention on the Rights of the Child and 1999 ILO Convention (No. 182) Concerning the Prohibition and Immediate Elimination of the Worst Forms of Child Labour (each referenced in Documentary Appendix B) have to say about this issue? For keen insight, see Susan L. Bissell, "Earning and Learning: Tensions and Compatibility," in Burns H. Weston, ed., *Child Labor and Human Rights: Making Children Matter* (Boulder, Colo.: Lynne Rienner, 2005).

3. The famous U.S. Supreme Court decision of *Brown v. Board of Education*, 347 U.S. 483 (1954), overturning the doctrine of "separate but equal" in U.S. schools, is well over a half-century old. Yet U.S. schools continue to be more separate than equal when it comes to the education of African Americans. How, at least in theory, might this educational inequality be overcome via international human rights law? Does it matter that the United States is a party to the 1965 International Convention on the Elimination of All Forms of Racial Discrimination? How so? How not?

4. Similar inequalities exist between impoverished inner-city and well-funded suburban schools in the United States. Does it matter that the United States, in contrast to much of the rest of the world, is not a party to the 1966 International Covenant on Economic, Social and Cultural Rights? How so? How not?

5. Felisa Tibbitts suggests that education is a prerequisite for individual empowerment, echoing the "capabilities approach" to human rights pioneered by Martha Nussbaum (see Reading 3 in Chapter 1 of this book) and Nobel laureate Amartya Sen. Does this comport with your experience in the country in which you grew up? Can people be truly empowered without education? Does the answer differ in different societies?

6. Do you agree with the view expressed by a drafter of the UDHR that education is a preventive measure against "any attempt at a revival of fascism"? Does the very nature of totalitarian rule imply that the right to education has been abrogated? Is education inherently aligned with (or opposed to) particular ideologies? What is the difference between education and indoctrination?

7. In the course of fulfilling the human right to education, is it appropriate or desirable for governments to fund explicitly religious education? Why? Why not? How does funding religious education affect the freedom of religion?

8. Is the human right to education simply a means to expose people to Western values in the guise of providing values-neutral access to universal truths? What might a human rights activist interested in furthering access to education have to say to, for example, the governments and/or citizens of devoutly Islamic societies, deeply suspicious of Western intentions? Does the introduction of HRE from Western to non-Western cultures smack of cultural imperialism? If so, what is to be done about it? If not, why not? What would Richard Claude have said? Felisa Tibbitts?

9. Should human rights education receive the same emphasis as education in general? Less? More? Why? Why not? Consider the incentives states may have with regard to education in general and HRE in determining how much outside emphasis is required.

10. In his Declaration on the Human Right to Peace of 1 January 1997, http://unesdoc.unesco.org/images/0010/001055/105530e.pdf (reprinted in III Weston & Carlson III.S.3), former UNESCO Director-General Federico Mayor appealed to the world community as follows:

> At the dawn of the new millennium, our ideal must be to put [human rights] into practice, to add to them, to live and breathe them, to relive them, to revive them with every new day! . . . Human rights can neither be owned nor given, but must be won and deserved afresh with every passing day. Nor should they be regarded as an abstraction, but rather as practical guidelines for action which should be part of the lives of all men and women and enshrined in the laws of every country.

The statement suggests that human rights should be approached as *a way of life*. Should HRE reflect such an approach? What is the difference between HRE thus approached and indoctrination? Is there a difference? If so, why? If not, why not?

11. What challenges are unique to HRE for adults in comparison to younger persons? How do you think NGOs, states, and other actors in HRE can overcome these challenges? Consider the HRE Conceptual and Developmental Framework table in this reading when answering.

12. Consider Reading 4 in Chapter 1 where Weston discussed the universality of human rights in the face of differences between cultures. Do you foresee any challenges for HRE that may arise because of cultural differences? For example, will some paternalistic cultures emphasize all rights except women's rights? What are the challenges you foresee and how would you overcome them? Would Weston's respectful decision-making approach attempt to overcome the challenges you foresee? If so, how?

21. CINDY HOLDER *Culture as an Activity and Human Right*

Traditionally, culture has been treated as an object in international legal instruments. As a consequence, cultural rights in international human rights law have been conceived of as rights of access and consumption. This conception of cultural rights sets them up to appear less fundamental to human dignity than political, civil, and economic rights. However, much of the empirical evidence on human rights abuses suggests that the abuse of minorities' cultural rights and the abuse of other of their human rights are linked in ways that make it artificial to treat abuses of culture as less fundamental.

Recently, an alternative conception of culture has emerged from international legal instruments treating indigenous peoples. In these instruments culture is treated as an activity rather than a good. This activity is ascribed to peoples as well as persons; and protecting the capacity of both peoples and persons to engage in culture is taken to be as basic a component of human dignity as are freedom of movement, freedom of speech, and freedom from torture. However, the value of this treatment of culture extends beyond the human rights of indigenous peoples. Treating culture as an activity establishes an understanding of what cultural rights protect that clarifies the relationship between cultural rights and other mechanisms for protecting minorities and frames the role of cultural communities in the realization of human dignity as an important physical and political issue, not just a psychological one. This reveals a greater degree of coherence among international norms regarding the protection and preservation of minority cultures than is often recognized and defuses many of the standard worries about competition between human rights of peoples and human rights of individuals. In addition, it offers an account of what is wrong with violating cultural rights such that violations of a group's cultural rights are clearly and straightforwardly linked to violations of its rights to persist and flourish.

There is a long history among international human rights instruments and in the UN system of treating cultural integrity and access to cultural heritage as a constituent element of human dignity in its own right and not merely instrumentally necessary.[1] Cultural rights are widely acknowledged to be human rights, and the right to participate in culture appears as a matter of course in human rights declarations, treaties, and interpretive documents. For example, Article 27 of the Universal Declaration of Human Rights (UDHR) states: "Everyone has the right freely to participate in the cultural life of the community, to enjoy the arts and to share in scientific advancement and its benefits." And the

Excerpted with changes by permission of Sage Publications from Cindy Holder, "Culture as an Activity and Human Right: An Important Advance for Indigenous Peoples and International Law," *Alternatives: Global, Local, Political* 33, 1 (January–March 2008): 7–28. Copyright © 2008 Sage Publications.

1. On the difference between rights that protect basic constituents of dignity and rights that protect interests and activities because of their contribution to basic constituents, see James W. Nickel, *Making Sense of Human Rights*, 2nd ed. (New York: Blackwell, 2007); Cindy Holder, "Self-Determination as a Basic Human Right," in Avigail Eisenberg and Jeff Spinner-Halev, eds., *Minorities Within Minorities* (Cambridge: CUP, 2005), 294–316, 297.

Vienna Declaration of the 1993 World Conference on Human Rights reminds states (para. 19)
that "persons belonging to minorities have the
right to enjoy their own culture, to profess and
practice their own religion and to use their own
language in private and in public, freely and
without interference or any form of discrimination." In its General Comment 13: The Right to
Education, the Committee on Economic, Social
and Cultural Rights (CESCR, the monitoring
body for the 1966 International Covenant on
Economic, Social and Cultural Rights, ICESCR),
notes that the covenant obliges states to provide
education that is not only relevant and of good
quality in its form and content but also culturally
appropriate. The 1989 Convention on the Rights
of the Child (art. 30) states that a child belonging
to an ethnic, religious, linguistic, or indigenous
minority "shall not be denied the right, in community with other members of his or her group,
to enjoy his or her own culture, to profess and
practice his or her own religion, or to use his or
her own language." The 1988 Organization of
American States (OAS) Protocol of San Salvador
on economic, social, and cultural rights (art.
14.1(a)) commits the states party to it to recognize the right of everyone "to take part in the
cultural and artistic life of the community," including minority communities. And Article 5 of
the 1985 Declaration on the Human Rights of
Individuals Who Are Not Nationals of the Country in Which They Live includes the right of
aliens to retain their own language, culture, and
tradition alongside the rights to life, to protection
against arbitrary interference with their privacy,
to equality before the law, to freedom of conscience, and to found a family.[2]

To say that cultural rights are human rights is
to say that depriving an individual of her culture
wrongs her directly, over and above any wrong

done by undermining other aspects of her dignity. As the Human Rights Committee (HRC—
the treaty-monitoring body for the International
Covenant on Civil and Political Rights, ICCPR)
notes in connection with Article 27 of the ICCPR,
cultural rights are "distinct from and additional
to, all the other rights which, as individuals in
common with everyone else, [the members of a
group] are already entitled to enjoy under the
Covenant"; "the protection of these rights is directed towards ensuring the survival and continued development of the cultural, religious and
social identity of the minorities concerned" and
accordingly "these rights must be protected as
such and should not be confused with other personal rights."[3] This statement implies not only
that cultural rights do not depend on other rights
for their justification, but that they may themselves ground rights to conditions, objects, or
goods that are instrumentally necessary for a
people's culture.

This treatment of cultural rights has proved to
be an important resource for nonstate peoples.
In particular, the fact that cultural rights are
basic and universal has proved valuable in block-
ing certain kinds of arguments by states' representatives against the admissibility of complaints
arising from denials of access to or control over
ancestral land and resources. For example, in
Hopu and Bessert v. France the HRC was able to
accept the complainants' argument that building
a hotel on their ancestral burial grounds constituted a violation of their rights to privacy and to
family in part because the fundamental importance of cultural interests establishes an obligation to use the complainants' interpretation of
who counts as a member of their family when
determining whether a violation has occurred.[4]
In *Lansmann v. Finland*, the HRC rejected the
government's argument that state officials may
balance a culturally based claim to land or resources against national interests in economic
development on the grounds that insofar as the
interest in culture includes an interest in the persistence of the group's way of life, a group's cultural interest in being able to access or use

2. *Eds.*—In an accompanying footnote, the author additionally cites the following three instruments as "im-
portant documents in the historical development of
the international human right to culture": UNESCO
General Conference, Recommendation on Participa-
tion by the People at Large in Cultural Life and Their
Contribution to It, Nairobi, Kenya, 26 November 1976;
UNESCO Intergovernmental Conference on Cultural
Policies in Latin America and the Caribbean, Declara-
tion of Bogotá, 20 January 1978; and UN Human
Rights Committee (HRC), General Comment 23: The
Rights of Minorities (ICCPR art. 27), 8/4/94, UN Doc.
HRI/GEN/l/Rev.1 at 38 (1994).

3. UN Human Rights Committee (HRC), General Comment 23: The Rights of Minorities (ICCPR art. 27),
8/4/94, UN Doc. HRI/GEN/l/Rev.l at 38 (1994), 1, 9.
4. UN HRC, *Hopu and Bessert v. France*, ICCPR, Communication no. 549/1993: France 29/12/97, UN Doc.
CCPR/C/60/D/549/1993/Rev.1.

territory or resources may not be sacrificed for the sake of economic development.[5]

Nonetheless, the conception of culture at work in many international documents is problematic in several respects. In particular, there is a tendency to treat culture as a type of good—as an object or a state of affairs, valuable for its potential to be consumed, experienced, or used. For example, the 1966 UNESCO Declaration of the Principles of International Cultural Cooperation (art. 1) states: "Each *culture* has a dignity and value which must be respected and preserved" (emphasis added), and it describes cultures as "part of the common heritage belonging to all mankind." The 1995 UNIDROIT Convention on Stolen or Illegally Exported Cultural Objects (art. 2) defines cultural objects as those "of importance for archaeology, prehistory, history, literature, art or science." And the preamble to the 1992 European Charter for Regional or Minority Languages motivates and situates the cultural protections included in that document by noting that "the protection of the historical regional or minority languages of Europe, some of which are in danger of eventual extinction, contributes to the maintenance and development of Europe's cultural wealth and traditions."

This conception of culture encourages an understanding of what cultural rights protect that emphasizes objects, behaviors, and psychological states. So, the statements of cultural rights in many international documents have emphasized rights of access, preservation, and use. For example, in the 1995 European Framework Convention for the Protection of National Minorities (art. 5), states parties are directed to "promote the conditions necessary for persons belonging to national minorities to maintain and develop their culture, and to preserve the essential elements of their identity, namely their religion, language, traditions and cultural heritage." ICCPR Article 27 and Article 2(1) of the 1992

Declaration on the Rights of Persons Belonging to National, Ethnic, Religious and Linguistic Minorities describe persons belonging to minorities as having the right "to enjoy their own culture, to profess and practice their own religion, or to use their own language." And the Committee on the Elimination of Racial Discrimination (CERD) recommends that governments consider "vesting persons belonging to ethnic or linguistic groups . . . with the right to engage in activities that are particularly relevant to the preservation of the identity of such persons or groups." The ICESCR recognizes the right of everyone "to take part in cultural life." However, in its concluding observations regarding France's progress toward ICESCR compliance with the ICESCR in 2001, the CESCR-remedy recommended by the CESCR for concerns about inequalities in enjoyment of social and cultural rights by minorities is for the state party to "increase its efforts to preserve regional and minority cultures and languages, and that it undertake measures to improve education on, and education in, these languages."

This way of thinking about cultural rights places important limits on the extent to which nonstate groups can challenge state activities that threaten their continued ability to live as a people. For example, in the *Lansmann* complaint, the HRC rejected the government claim that cultural interests and economic interests could be treated on a par, but it left uncontested the Finnish government's framework for thinking about the kind of interest that Saami people have with respect to their culture. Within that framework, what the Saami have an interest in is a specific set of behaviors, symbols, self-understandings, and relations to objects and to one another, "the Saami way of life." Thus, although reindeer and the territory through which they move are a source of claims, they are considered objects on which symbols are projected and behaviors are enacted, not as part of a jurisdiction or domain with respect to which Saami decision making must be authoritative, and not as an extension of the Saami themselves. The Saami's right to culture protects that which is empirically necessary to *the* self-understandings and actions entailed by *the* way of life that distinguishes them from other peoples. Consequently, actions or activities that harm reindeer and the territory through which they move are ruled out by Saami cultural rights only when and to the extent that the harm makes it impossible for Saami to symbolize and

---

5. UN HRC, *Lansmann v. Finland and Lansmann et al. v. Finland*, communication no. 671/1995, UN Doc. CCPR/C/58/D/671/1995. The complainants in this case (a group of Saami reindeer breeders) argued that the Finnish government violated their Article 27 rights by granting logging concessions in areas that reindeer normally use for winter grazing. The decision ultimately went against the complainants because the committee found that the evidence did not permit them to conclude that the logging concessions constituted a pressing threat to the reindeer migration.

behave with respect to reindeer as prescribed by their way of life, understood as an identifiable set of behaviors, symbols, self-understandings, and relations to objects and people that is distinctive to them *as Saami.*

This view of what cultural rights protect sets a very high threshold for the impact that decision making must have on a group's way of life before it constitutes a human rights violation. The problem here, as Rosemary Coombe notes, is that culture is understood as a noun, not just grammatically but in its very essence. What cultural rights protect are "cultures"—objects or bundles of properties "that can be recognized, enjoyed, possessed, maintained, disseminated and preserved."[6] These objects or bundles of properties may be argued to merit protection either because they are of direct interest to individuals, or because accessing, consuming, exhibiting them, and so on are necessary conditions for something that is in the direct interest to individuals. What human rights are understood to protect are examples or tokens of a distinctive type of thing, "culture." These examples, "cultures," may be manifest either in individual human beings qua members of a specific group or in collections of objects, behaviors, rituals, and meanings that specific groups require or put to work in the course of maintaining their specificity.

Coombe remarks about these worrying features of how *culture* as a term is used in international legal instruments in the course of noting the ways usage lags behind changes in the way the term has come to be understood by academic anthropologists. However, Coombe continues, it is not obvious that the best response to this gap between how cultures are theorized academically and how they are described in international legal instruments is simply to substitute the former for the latter.[7] The purposes for which cultures are referred to in international documents are different from the purposes for such references in theoretical debates. Because of this, we must be careful to focus on the problems that conceiving of culture as a good poses from the perspective of the purposes international documents are intended to serve. From that perspec-

tive, the primary problem is that conceiving of culture as a good encourages adjudicators and policy-makers to think of cultures as static and external in origin both to individuals, who exhibit, wield, or consume cultures, and to those individuals' relations with one another, which manifest, express, reinforce, or undermine cultures. This frames questions about what cultural rights may and must protect in a way that emphasizes the potential for conflict between individual and collective right holders, and among interests in and across individuals.

For example, when culture is conceived of as a good, groups appear as producers of culture not in virtue of activities that reflect the distinctive relationships and persons that constitute them, but in virtue of mechanisms that ensure that a group's internal relations and persons carry "its" culture forward into the future. This sets up an inherent tension between individuals' interests in culture and their interests in self-expression and between the needs of cultural communities and those of the individuals that constitute them—a tension that limits both the kind and extent of moral claims that cultural rights may justify. When cultural rights are understood primarily as rights to access a good, "culture," those who make up cultural communities appear as little more than vessels within which culture is preserved and through which it is delivered, or, even worse, as material upon which communities express themselves.

The central issue here is how we are encouraged to think about what our human rights protect with respect to culture. From an individual perspective, when culture is conceived of as a good, what cultural rights appear to protect is access to or benefit from a specific kind of public good. As public goods, we may expect that cultures will be difficult to sustain, in part because of the contributions they require and in part because they are inevitably objects of divergent and incompatible plans. The necessity of a certain degree of coercion and repression thus appears to be built into cultural rights because of the nature of the interest at stake. Further, the intensity and moral difficulty of cultural rights appear to increase in direct proportion to increases in the degree of psychological significance with which a culture is vested. The more central cultural membership is made to personal well-being, the more important it is for individuals to be able to sustain and access it, and so

6. Rosemary Coombe, "Culture: Anthropology's Old Vice or International Law's New Virtue?" *ASIL Proceedings* 93 (1999): 261–70.
7. Ibid.

the greater the justification there seems to be for communities to enjoy wide powers for cultural preservation. However, the more important it is for individuals to access culture and put it to use in their personal psychology, the more problematic it becomes to allow communities to control the form and terms of cultural participation.

QUESTIONS FOR REFLECTION AND DISCUSSION

1. Holder argues that "Traditionally, culture has been treated as an object in international legal instruments. As a consequence, cultural rights in international human rights law have been conceived of as rights of access and consumption. This conception of cultural rights sets them up to appear less fundamental to human dignity than political, civil, and economic rights. However, much of the empirical evidence on human rights abuses suggests that the abuse of minorities' cultural rights and the abuse of other of their human rights are linked in ways that make it artificial to treat abuses of culture as less fundamental." Does revisiting the argument of Claudia Card (Chapter 2, Reading 8) on genocide yield any insights into the relationship between culture and human rights? If so, what?

2. What are the sources and meanings of cultural human rights? Be as specific and detailed as you can. If necessary, conduct further research to extend and strengthen your response to the question.

3. In what respects does Holder argue that the conception of culture at work in many international documents is problematic? Do you agree? Why? Why not?

4. Human Rights Education Associates (HREA) (http://www.hrea.org/index.php?base_id=157) argues that "The right to culture in human rights law is essentially about the celebration and protection of humankind's creativity and traditions. The right of an individual to enjoy culture and to advance culture and science without interference from the state is a human right. Under international human rights law governments also have an obligation to promote and conserve cultural activities and artifacts, particularly those of universal value. Culture is overwhelmingly applauded as positive in the vast majority of human rights instruments." Is this a convincing characterization of the human right to culture in the light of Holder's analysis? Why? Why not? What critique would Holder likely deliver in relation to this characterization of the right?

5. There is sometimes a tension between the right of a particular community to its traditional livelihood and culture (sometimes based on exploitation of particular animal and plant species) and environmental goals aimed at, for example, the preservation of biodiversity. Does Holder's analysis of the human right to culture assist in resolving such a tension? Why? Why not?

6. Holder argues that "The necessity of a certain degree of coercion and repression . . . appears to be built into cultural rights because of the nature of the interest at stake." What does this observation drive at? Can the tensions surrounding the right to culture be reconciled? Does the framework offered by Weston (Chapter 1, Reading 4) assist at all? Why and how so? Why not?

7. Culture is generally used to refer to a past or historical way of life. Artifacts, historical sites, and old traditions tend to capture the notion of culture as historic. How do the two approaches to the definition of culture deal with an understanding of culture that incorporates more recent or modern trends, values, and customs? Would either consider "new" or "modern" culture as protected under cultural rights? Are there any advantages or disadvantages to a more liberal or flexible understanding of culture that protects even newer values and customs?

8. How does the right to self-determination relate to cultural rights? Do both the majority and the minority of a state's population have the right to self-determination? Do both the majority and the minority of the state's population have the protections of cultural rights? What happens if the majority's right to self-determination conflicts with the minority's cultural rights?

9. Sometimes different cultures within a region or state can have conflicting claims over a historic site or resource. Consider the Hagia Sophia in Istanbul, Turkey. The Hagia Sophia was originally constructed as a church of the Byzantine Empire. Later, when the Ottoman

Turks conquered Istanbul (formerly known as Constantinople), they converted the Hagia Sophia into a mosque, a Muslim place of worship and community. Today, the Hagia Sophia is a museum. The Greek culture and the Turkish culture have conflicting claims over Hagia Sophia specifically and Istanbul generally. In fact, Greek and Turkish cultures have conflicting claims over many cultural things, sometimes as simple as who invented the baklava or the gyro. Does the understanding of cultural rights advanced by Holder provide any legal mechanism by which such conflicting cultural claims can be resolved or harmonized?

Chapter Five

Community or Group Rights— "Solidarity Rights"

IN this chapter, our focus turns toward human rights overtly understood (against the generally individualistic grain of traditional human rights understandings) to be community or group rights—often referred to as "solidarity" rights. As Burns Weston notes in Chapter 1, Reading 1 of this volume, these rights, whether considered justiciable or merely aspirational in character, are today understood to include the right to self-determination, the right to development, the right to a clean and healthy environment, the right to peace, and, arguably, the right to democracy (or to democratic governance).

The first of these rights to be recognized as binding in international law was the right to self-determination, as proclaimed in common Article 1 of the 1966 International Covenant on Economic, Social and Cultural Rights (ICESCR) and the 1966 International Covenant on Civil and Political Rights (ICCPR)—each stating that "all peoples have the right of self determination. By virtue of that right they freely determine their political status and freely pursue their economic, social and cultural development." Prior to these legally binding pronouncements, there were, as one would expect, numerous hortatory references to self-determination, as in many UN General Assembly (nonbinding) resolutions, for example. A noteworthy early reference, however, may be found in U.S. president Woodrow Wilson's famous "Fourteen Points" address to a 1918 joint session of the U.S. Congress outlining his proposals for a post-World War I peace settlement, including self-determination as an important postwar world order objective (resulting from the fragmentation of the old Austro-Hungarian and Ottoman empires and Russia's former Baltic territories into a number of new states). Another may be found in the 1941 Atlantic Charter signed by U.S. president Franklin D. Roosevelt and British prime minister Winston Churchill, who pledged the "Eight Principal points" of the Charter, a "pivotal policy statement" that defined the Allied goals for the post-World War II world, including the "right" of "all people . . . to self-determination"—in anticipation of its promotion under the auspices of the United Nations established roughly four years later. Hence the creation of the UN Trusteeship Council (one of the six main organs of the UN) to facilitate the transition of former colonial possessions into independent, self-governing states. Hence also the 1960 UN General Assembly Declaration 1514 (XV) on the Granting of Independence to Colonial Countries and Peoples, now part of customary international law. But the essential point of this brief history is that the right to self-determination, though rhetorically framed in terms of "people(s)," was understood in initial actual practice to mean a right of former colonial territories to political independence subject to the fulfillment of (contestable) preconditions determined and supervised by internationally authorized overseers. However, as the process of decolonization wound down and came ultimately to an official end when, in 1994, the Trusteeship Council suspended operation, the meaning of the right to determination began to shift. While a right to statehood continues to breathe life (for example, in Palestine and Kosovo), today the focus of the right to self-determination is closely aligned with the right to culture, in particular to the right of indigenous peoples to "determine their political status and freely pursue their economic, social and cultural development"—but *within*, not independent of, the legal framework of the territorial state within which they are situated—a circumstance fraught with controversy and complexity, as one should expect given the dynamics of the competing governing interests involved.

In light of the foregoing history, it is appropriate that Karen Engle should begin this chapter with a reflection on indigenous peoples and the rights of self-determination (and culture) central to their lives. She uses the 2007 UN Declaration on the Rights of Indigenous Peoples (UNDRIP), a landmark instrument, and an account of the historical relationship between indigenous rights advocacy and international human rights, to explore a question raised in several ways throughout her essay: "how might we explain the persistence of individual, liberal rights alongside the growing use and apparent acceptance of cultural and indigenous rights by indigenous peoples?" Engle notes that indigenous rights advocates were once skeptical concerning the value of putting their claims in human rights terms, but that even before the passage of the UNDRIP "the international indigenous rights movement had largely succeeded in achieving the recognition of cultural rights for indigenous peoples within various international and regional instruments and through the adjudicatory and quasi-adjudicatory mechanisms of international and regional institutions." Such successes were hard won, however, resulting from numerous compromises concerning "economic dependency, structural discrimination, and lack of indigenous autonomy." In other words, the "victories" were double-edged—and perhaps paradoxically (given Holder's arguments in preceding Chapter 4) because of, among other things, "the acceptance of a cultural rights framework by international institutions." Engle argues that "this right to culture, sometimes for individuals and sometimes for groups, fits quite comfortably with—and was perhaps even facilitated by—neoliberal development models." For her, the UNDRIP exemplifies just such kinds of tensions and uneasy alliances, presenting a challenge to the liberal civil and political rights paradigm through its embrace of self-determination and collective rights while simultaneously privileging such rights and resisting strong forms of indigenous self-determination. Often, revealingly, "indigenous rights advocates have . . . not been very successful in . . . gaining . . . recognition of rights that are in real tension with liberal, individual rights [such that] the former is nearly always subordinated to the latter." Engle argues that if we are willing to eschew comfortable interpretations of the UNDRIP and to engage in a critical examination of it, then the Declaration could provide an "important site for the ongoing struggle over the meaning of human rights, the dominance of human rights as the basis of justice, and the extent to which it might be mined or abandoned for alternative, transformative strategies."

Continuing with the theme of the ambivalence of human rights "progress" in relation to important community and solidarity rights, Bonny Ibhawoh explores the fractious narratives surrounding the human right to development. He draws out two main themes: first, the polemical nature of the debates concerning whether or not the right exists in the legal sense; second, the difficulty surrounding the practical implementation of the right to development. Ibhawoh argues that the debate concerning the legal existence of the right to development, rather than increasing understanding of the relationship between development and human rights, has merely underlined differences between the Global North and Global South. Significantly, in both regions, existing authority structures have deployed the right to development in service of "further[ing] their own interests through the legitimizing language of human rights." In particular, the "state-centric agenda that dominates Northern discourses on the right to development ignores the realities of a globalizing world where international factors increasingly affect the capacity of states to achieve development" and ignores the reality of an "inequitable political economy" within which Global North states "occupy privileged spaces." Echoing, to some extent, the conclusion of Marks (and Aristide) in concluding Reading 26 of this chapter, Ibhawoh points out that frequently "the human rights focus in the development discourse amounts to little more than the projection of power." The contradictions emerging from differing ideological deployments of the right to development explain, Ibhawoh suggests, the mixed prospects of the right itself. Yet, despite all this, the right to development discourse has changed the way we think about development by creating a new paradigm in which states have begun to respond to the need for development, and by providing at least "a reference point for demands for more equitable distribution of wealth and resources within and between states." Development, Ibhawoh concludes, provides an enlightening case study for reflection upon the uses and abuses of human rights language generally: "Although the ethical and humanistic ideals at the core of the international human rights regime are increasingly gaining universal acceptance. . . . The legitimizing language of human rights has been used to pursue goals that have more to do with the international politics of power and resistance, as well as the interests of ruling regimes, than with the welfare and empowerment of ordinary citizens." Human rights, as we have emphasized previously, retain a persistent vulnerability toward ideological deployments, even as their resistive, justice-sensitive energies rise time and again to critique the misuse to which human rights themselves can be put.

Further pursuing the theme of the ambivalence of human rights in relation to goals and outcomes with a distinctively collective dimension, Conor Gearty asks whether human rights are a "help" or a "hindrance" to environmental goals. He responds by saying that "for many detached observers, the immediate response to the question our title poses would be that of course human rights hinder environmental protection." The reasons for this turn on the fact that human rights exclusively address the needs of "the human"—not of other creatures or the environment itself—and that, in any case, the "human" of human rights has been predominantly understood as a distinctly "singular" being. Gearty argues that "[in] standard contemporary accounts of human rights from a philosophical perspective, the discussion is invariably about the self-fulfillment of the individual, his or her ability to set goals for leading a full life and then being free to go on to achieve those targets." He further observes: "The debate is about what are the necessary building blocks of such a successful life; it is not about what that life can or ought to do to make the world around it a better place, even for others to live in, much less simply for the planet's sake."

Where then, should we look for hope of change? Gearty, like other authors in this collection, turns to the power of social movements as a source of renewing human rights authorship. In the environmental social movement, he argues, there is a chance to bring the environmental and human rights movements together—itself an imperative task in light of the "impending climate change catastrophe." Human rights, for Gearty, bring to environmentalism a passion for the marginalized human being. He argues that "an approach to meeting the climate change challenge which is indifferent to human suffering will inevitably lead to decisions in which the world's poor are once again made to pay a price for the selfishness of others. The human rights approach can stop this happening." In return, however, the environmentalist offers human rights a new confidence in its own foundations:

> thinking hard about the embedded nature of humans in the world . . . reflecting upon our species as a part of the natural world . . . [promises] a renewed sense of the wonder of our existence and the beauty (as well as the immense productivity) of our seemingly innate propensity to think about others as well as solely about ourselves and our kin. . . . The survival of our species without the loss of our precarious commitment to goodness is surely enough of a foundation for human rights today.

Next, central to Gearty's survival concerns and an endorsement of his "precarious commitment to goodness," is Douglas Roche's focus on the human right to peace. Arguing that peace is the "major precondition for all human rights" and that "The time has come (in actuality, long past due) to emphasize that the peoples of the world have a sacred right to peace," he notes the countless deaths that have resulted from the violence of war in recent decades.[1] Yet, despite these savage betrayals of the right to peace, Roche underscores the intimacy—one could almost say codependency—between peace and human rights and its centrality in the international legal order, made explicit in the UDHR Preamble (recognizing that "the inherent dignity and the equal and inalienable rights of all members of the human family is the foundation of freedom, justice and peace in the world"). Citing UDHR Article 28 (proclaiming the human right to an international order necessary to the realization of peace and all other human rights), UN Charter Articles 1, 2(4), and 55 (designed to limit war-making), and 1984 UN Declaration on the Right of Peoples to Peace, Roche's argument frames the international human rights system as "a peace system" that should be put to serious work on behalf of peace-loving peoples everywhere as swiftly as possible. In this regard, he suggests that debate on the right to peace will "inevitably . . . center on the deeply controversial question of the future of nuclear weapons" and points to the International Court of Justice (ICJ) and its view on the matter. "It says," he concludes, that "nations have a legal obligation to get rid of them."[2] At the same time, Roche acknowledges that a peace system is never immune from danger and that, despite the entry of peace as a human right into UN discourse, the continuing risk of war, including nuclear war or war with other weapons of mass destruction, continues to cast a deep shadow over the future of humankind. He also acknowledges that "the abolition of nuclear weapons will not by itself guarantee peace" and that "the proponents of nuclear weapons . . . will use every argument they can think of, every political device they can find, and every form of intimidation they can invent to try to derail the [right to peace] debate." Roche adds: "They effectively disrupted the debate in UNESCO. They have rendered inoperative nuclear weapons abolition resolutions at the UN. They have used the tragedy of September 11 to scare the populace into believing that only gigantic amounts of weaponry can head off the terrorism of the future." But Roche is nonetheless optimistic. Despite the permanent state of national emergency in which we now live with the "war against terror," he argues, there still are hopeful signs—from grassroots civil society movements and actors in particular, who call for a meaningful peace and for governments to be held fully accountable to human rights standards. Such grassroots energies express new forms of community and solidarity over the

---

1. We could add to this, of course: deaths from other brutal realities such as genocide and toxic disasters (e.g., the Bhopal disaster in India that arose as a result of corporate negligence).

2. *Legality of the Threat or Use of Nuclear Weapons*, 1996 ICJ General List No. 95 (8 July 1996). For a somewhat less confident reading of this decision, see Burns H. Weston, "Nuclear Weapons and the World Court: Ambiguity's Consensus," *TLCP* 7 (1997): 371–99.

Internet, Roche observes, and thus, through emerging shared efforts at all levels bring new energies to bear in "the global quest for peace."

Finally, just as it was appropriate for Karen Engle's essay to begin this chapter with a discussion of the right to self-determination, the first claimed solidarity right on the international plane, so is it appropriate to end the chapter with Susan Marks's essay contemplating the human right to democracy, the most recent known candidate for membership in the third generation of international human rights. Engaging in an analysis equally aware of the ambivalence in her subject as the other authors in this chapter are of the ambivalence in theirs, she discusses the right to democracy—or "the right to democratic governance"—by addressing a germinal article published in 1992 by the late eminent legal scholar Thomas Franck and scholarly responses to it. Marks argues that Franck's article changed democracy from being perceived as a relatively neglected topic in international legal scholarship to one that quickly became a central focus of extensive debate in the field (and beyond). The Franck article having been little noted or discussed since, Marks then examines the right to democratic governance from four different perspectives to find out "what has become of" it—revealing, in the process, key facets of the right itself. Each of the analyses examined, Marks concedes, is limited, but the fourth and final analysis Marks pursues contains a strand that she suggests delivers a fascinating challenge to the previous three. This challenge centers on the point that it is not necessarily obvious that democracy as ideology should continue to carry our emancipatory aspirations, because the self-same democratic politics holding out the "promise of self-rule and equality" also "sustain[s] the conditions which privilege the wealthy and marginalize the poor." Perhaps, then, "democracy may be more of an impasse in liberatory politics than a signpost to them," she muses, and thus potentially challenges other existing accounts of the right to democratic governance. Accordingly, Marks concludes her analysis by turning to the words of democratically elected but now exiled President Jean-Bertrand Aristide of Haiti, speaking in exile. Aristide explains the history of Haiti, where the elite has "done everything in its power to keep the masses at bay." Turning to the fate of "any genuinely democratic project," Aristide concludes that the right to democracy is up against just this kind of challenge. For Aristide, Marks writes, "democracy is not just a matter of procedures and institutions, values and norms, transition and consolidation. It is a matter of struggle against determined, protracted, and highly organized resistance."

Each of the readings in this chapter emphasizes, in its own way, the observation that the true energies of human rights emerge in reactions to injustice and radical disrespect. Inevitably, human rights are entangled in the great political and ideological struggles of our time. They speak directly to the global situation in which humanity finds itself—staring into the face of great, potentially terminal threats (nuclear war, climate change, spiraling social unrest, and injustices in a rapidly consolidating pattern of privilege and oppression in the global order), and they speak just as directly to the most intimate aspirations of every human being on the planet for forms of respect, community, and solidarity with others. The struggle for their meaning remains as vital and precarious as it has ever been—if not more so.

22. KAREN ENGLE *On Fragile Architecture: The UN Declaration on the Rights of Indigenous Peoples in the Context of Human Rights*

In September 2007, after over two decades of preparatory work and many false starts, the UN General Assembly adopted the UN Declaration on the Rights of Indigenous Peoples (UNDRIP).[1] The document has been lauded by many for its understanding and expansion of collective rights, of the right to culture, and of self-determination. But however progressive the declaration may appear at some level, it also contains significant compromises. Embedded in it are serious limitations to the very rights it is praised for containing.

In this article, I use the declaration and indigenous rights advocacy more generally to consider the relationship between international indigenous rights and international human rights. I do so by tracing the development of movements that have advocated for both, with a particular eye toward their points of convergence and divergence and the extent to which each has influenced the other.

Once skeptical of international human rights, indigenous rights advocates in the 1980s and 1990s began to articulate their claims in human rights terms, particularly the human right to culture. I have argued elsewhere that, even before the passage of the UNDRIP, the international indigenous rights movement had largely succeeded in achieving the recognition of cultural rights for indigenous peoples in various international and regional instruments and through the adjudicatory and quasi-adjudicatory mechanisms of international and regional institutions.[2] These hard-fought successes, however, resulted from a number of compromises along the way and largely displaced or deferred many of the very issues that initially motivated much of the advocacy: issues of economic dependency, structural discrimination, and lack of indigenous autonomy. In other words, the victories have brought with them (often unintended) limitations and downsides, which I have largely pinned on the reification of indigenous culture, alongside the rejection of self-determination claims and the acceptance of a cultural rights framework by international institutions. This right to culture, sometimes for individuals and sometimes for groups, fits quite comfortably with—and was perhaps even facilitated by—neoliberal development models.

The UNDRIP offers a contemporary example of both the alliances and tensions that emerged from the use of the right-to-culture frame for indigenous advocacy. I would contend that, on the one hand, the UNDRIP challenges or at least pushes the liberal human rights paradigm by explicitly referring to the right to self-determination, embracing collective rights, and expressing an understanding of the interrelationship between rights to heritage, land, and development. On the other hand, it represents the continued power and persistence of an international human rights paradigm that eschews strong forms of indigenous self-determination[3] and privileges individual civil and political rights. In this sense, I contend that the UNDRIP signifies both the possible expansion and continued limitation of human rights and the perpetuation of certain biases, including the suggestion that cultural rights—particularly in their collective form—are outside the domain of human rights.

FINAL DRAFTING OF THE UNDRIP: COMPROMISES

BACKGROUND

When the UN General Assembly adopted the UNDRIP in 2007, it did so after over two decades

1. UN Declaration on the Rights of Indigenous Peoples, GA Res. 61/295, 13 September 2007, UN Doc. A/RES/61/295 (UNDRIP): 129 countries voted in favor, 4 opposed, and 11 abstained.
2. Karen Engle, *The Elusive Promise of Indigenous Development* (Durham, N.C.: Duke University Press, 2010).

3. By "strong forms," I mean both external self-determination models and forms of self-determination that provide for significant autonomy for indigenous groups vis-à-vis the state. I hope to distinguish these models, which do not rely on human rights concepts, from the human right to self-determination that has arguably been more broadly recognized for indigenous peoples, including in the UNDRIP.

of negotiation between and among indigenous peoples and states, dating back to 1982 when the Working Group on the Rights of Indigenous Populations was established to prepare the draft of a declaration. After a decade of annual meetings, the Working Group produced a draft for internal consideration in 1993. In 2006, after "a roller-coaster of hopes and disappointments," in an effort to facilitate the adoption of the declaration at the first session of the newly formed Human Rights Council, the chair of the Working Group suggested a list of changes to the 1993 draft. A new draft including those changes was presented to the Council, which adopted the declaration during its first session in June 2006.[4] The Council agreed to send the declaration to the General Assembly, in what was considered a moment of success both for the Council and for most indigenous peoples. Nevertheless, that version included key compromises that limited the right to self-determination as well as cultural and other collective rights.

These compromises, however, proved insufficient to guarantee the declaration's adoption by the General Assembly. In late November 2006, the Third Committee voted in favor of a non-action resolution on the declaration, deferring its consideration for a later date. The non-action resolution was formally proposed by Namibia on behalf of the African Union, in part on the ground that "the vast majority of the peoples of Africa are indigenous to the African Continent,"[5] and that "self-determination only applies to nations trying to free themselves from the yoke of colonialism."[6] In 2007, a number of additional compromises were made, the most significant of which were related to the right to self-determination.

4. Human Rights and Indigenous Issues, Report of the Working Group Established in Accordance with Commission on Human Rights Resolution 1995/32 of 3 March 1995 on its eleventh session, Annex I, UN Doc. E/CN.4/2006/79 of 22 March 2006.
5. Namibia: Amendments to Draft Resolution on Behalf of the African Union, UN Doc. A/C.3/61/L.57/ Rev.1 (21 November 2006).
6. "United Nations General Assembly Declines Vote on Declaration on Indigenous Rights" (8 December 2006), www.culturalsurvival.org/news/mark-cherrington/ united-nations-general-assembly-declines-vote -declaration-indigenous-rights [*Eds.*—accessed 20 June 2015].

RECOGNIZING AND LIMITING SELF-DETERMINATION

Much of the controversy throughout negotiations regarding the draft and the final declaration revolved around Article 3 of the 1993 draft, which was retained in the adopted declaration. It reads, "Indigenous peoples have the right of self-determination. By virtue of that right they freely determine their political status and freely pursue their economic, social and cultural development." This provision specifically applies common Article 1 of the two major covenants on human rights to indigenous peoples. Disagreements over the potential meaning of the term "self-determination" and over various attempts to limit it through addition of other language to the declaration were central to the failure of states and indigenous groups to agree on a text for the declaration for many years. They were also key to the African Union decision to oppose the declaration through the non-action resolution in 2006 and the opposition to the declaration by the four states that [at the time] voted against its final adoption—the United States, Canada, Australia, and New Zealand. These four states as well as many other countries along the way expressed concern that the right to self-determination might be read to include the right to statehood.

The 1993 draft of the declaration included an additional provision on the right to self-determination that listed the areas over which indigenous peoples would have control: "culture, religion, education, information, media, health, housing, employment, social welfare, economic activities, land and resources management, environment and entry by non-members."[7] A change that was made for the Human Rights Council consideration of the declaration and that remains in the adopted version arguably watered down that understanding of self-determination by instead stating that the right to self-determination guarantees "the right to autonomy or self-government in matters relating to their internal and local affairs, as well as ways and means for

7. Draft Declaration on the Rights of Indigenous Peoples, Report of the Working Group on Indigenous Populations on its Eleventh Session, in UN Commission on Human Rights, Subcommission on Prevention of Discrimination and Protection of Minorities, 45th Session, UN Doc. E/CN.4/Sub.2/1993/29/Annex I (23 August 1993), art. 31.

financing their autonomous functions."[8] [*Eds.*— However, as the author goes on to explain, this was not enough to win over the African states or other opponents of the Declaration as it stood.]

Ultimately, African states were swayed by a new compromise, including the addition of Article 46(1), which makes clear that the declaration does not support external forms of self-determination. It states that the declaration should not be "construed as authorizing or encouraging any action which would dismember or impair totally or in part, the territorial integrity or political unity of sovereign and independent States." This compromise language gave many indigenous peoples involved with the declaration significant pause, but most ultimately decided to support it with the assurance that other key provisions would remain intact, including those on land and resource rights and free and informed consent, which would in some sense protect "indigenous peoples' territorial integrity."[9]

While advocates largely backed the UNDRIP once it was passed, some admitted that the compromise was not a complete success. Indeed, the Indian Resource Center press release at the time embodies much of the ambivalence that was experienced in the moment. On one hand, it quotes Robert "Tim" Coulter, its executive director, stating that "for the first time, indigenous peoples' rights to self-determination and control over their land, resources, cultures and languages are being formally recognized," and concluding that the declaration "is a huge advance in the law of self-determination, the most important in 50 years. It is a tremendous advance in international human rights because collective rights of indigenous peoples are now recognized as human rights."[10] On the other hand, and without ever mentioning the last-minute compromise on self-determination, it quotes the director of its Washington, D.C., office, Armstrong Wiggins—a Miskito leader who had long argued for autonomous territory for the Miskito in Nic-

aragua—as stating, "It's not a perfect Declaration, but it is a good start. Our hope is that our children and our grandchildren will be able to make it better."[11]

As indigenous rights advocates both inside and outside international organizations have begun to encourage states and international institutions to take seriously the UNDRIP, they have attempted to make the most of the self-determination language. Yet, something has been lost in the compromise. The declaration seals the deal: external forms of self-determination are off the table for indigenous peoples, and human rights will largely provide the model for economic and political justice for indigenous peoples.

RECOGNIZING AND LIMITING COLLECTIVE RIGHTS

The UNDRIP has been praised by many for its broad recognition of collective rights. The UN Permanent Forum on Indigenous Issues states on its webpage that the UNDRIP gives "prominence to collective rights to a degree unprecedented in international human rights law. The adoption of this instrument is the clearest indication yet that the international community is committing itself to the protection of the individual and collective rights of indigenous peoples."[12]

What is rarely discussed, however, is that a number of provisions regarding collective rights, generally collective cultural rights, were dropped from the 1993 version of the draft in the series of compromises that led to the 2006 draft approved by the Human Rights Council. To the extent that these cultural rights appear in the adopted declaration, they are no longer explicitly stated as collective rights.

Moreover, Article 46 of the UNDRIP not only restricts the meaning of self-determination, but also potentially affects the meaning and application of all the rights contained in the declaration. Paragraph 2 reads in part: "The exercise of the rights set forth in this Declaration shall be subject only to such limitations as are determined by law and in accordance with international human

8. UNDRIP, art. 4.
9. Global Indigenous Peoples' Caucus, Steering Committee, "Report of the Global Indigenous Peoples' Caucus" (31 August 2007), www.hreoc.gov.au/social_Justice /declaration/ screport_070831.pdf [*Eds.*—accessed 11 June 2015].
10. Indian Law Resource Center, "UN Adopts Declaration on the Rights of Indigenous Peoples" (13 September 2007) [*Eds.*—accessed 14 February 2015].

11. Ibid.
12. UN Permanent Forum on Indigenous Issues, "About UNPFII and a Brief History of Indigenous Peoples and the International System" (2006), www.un-.org/esa/socdev/unpfii/en/history.html [*Eds.*—accessed 19 June 2015].

rights obligations."[13] Paragraph 3 calls for the interpretation of rights in the declaration "in accordance with the principles of justice, democracy, respect for human rights, equality, non-discrimination, good governance and good faith." In these provisions, what does the term "human rights" mean? If in fact the declaration intends to expand the recognition of human rights to include collective rights and the right to culture, could the declaration be limited by the same? Is the insistence on equality and non-discrimination a denial of rights that might be considered special or attach to a single culture? Are the provisions an acknowledgment or denial of conflict between human rights and indigenous rights, or are they productive of a distinction between the two?

LOOKING BACK: TWO DISCURSIVE AND LEGAL MOMENTS FOR INDIGENOUS RIGHTS ADVOCACY

The debates that led to the ultimate compromises to ensure the passage of the UNDRIP were not new. Indeed, these issues were not new to indigenous advocacy in general, which has long had a complex relationship with human rights law. Though by the time the UNDRIP was passed, human rights seemed to be the clearly appropriate avenue through which to pursue indigenous rights, it had not always been the preferred model.

REJECTION OF HUMAN RIGHTS IN THE 1970s AND 1980s

When, in the 1970s and early 1980s, indigenous peoples began to engage in pan-indigenous and transnational organization and eventually turn to international law, human rights was not an obvious forum for their struggles, even though it had become a significant tool for dissi-

13. A number of human rights instruments make clear that some or all of the rights they embody are subject "only to such limitations as are determined by law," but they do not, as in the UNDRIP, subject them to "international human rights obligations," given that the instruments themselves are meant to recognize or even create such obligations. See, e.g., Article 29 of the UDHR and Article 5 of the ICESCR.

dent political groups, especially in Latin America and Eastern Europe. For indigenous rights advocates, human rights was often seen as inseparable from the civilizing mission of colonial days or the globalizing or liberalizing mission of neocolonialism. As such, it was considered to offer little (but a site of resistance) to those whose aim was to reject assimilation.

The principal tactic indigenous rights advocates pursued at that time—at least in former British colonies—was external self-determination, which included the right of statehood. In North America, indigenous peoples began a "Fourth World movement," in which they both identified with and distinguished themselves from the decolonized or decolonizing Third World. They saw themselves as "nations" that maintain a distinct culture but are unrecognized, "deprived of the right to their own territories and its riches."[14] In Latin America, the focus was often on autonomy. Where indigenous peoples constituted the majority of the population (as in Bolivia), control of the nation—not secession—was sometimes the aim. As with the anticolonialist movement that had come before them, indigenous movements used an international legal frame that was distinct from human rights.

The right to self-determination in these forms constituted the dominant political and legal strategy for indigenous peoples through much of the 1980s.

MOVE TO HUMAN RIGHTS IN THE MID-1980s AND EARLY 1990s

In the late 1980s and early 1990s a number of indigenous rights advocates began to turn to human rights law as a site for legal and political struggle. In short, these indigenous rights advocates simultaneously softened their stance on self-determination and attempted to broaden the general, liberal model of human rights so as to incorporate a collective right to culture and allow for difference within an equality model. This move was both supported and encouraged by international and regional institutions that explicitly rejected attempts to conceive of indig-

14. George Manuel and Michael Posluns, *The Fourth World: An Indian Reality* (Toronto: Collier-Macmillan Canada, 1974), 40.

enous rights in the context of self-determination (external or internal), even while acknowledging the application of a human right to culture, if at times only for individuals.

A decision by the Inter-American Commission on Human Rights in 1983, the Human Rights Committee interpretation of the International Covenant on Civil and Political Rights (ICCPR) in its early years, and the language ultimately agreed on for International Labour Organization Convention No. 169 provide three examples of this double move. That is, each represents an explicit rejection of the applicability of the right to self-determination to indigenous peoples and sets the stage for a human rights-centered approach to indigenous rights.

THE INTER-AMERICAN SYSTEM OF HUMAN RIGHTS

In the early 1980s, conflicts arose in Nicaragua between Miskito Indians and the Sandinista government, in large part over the government's new agrarian reform program. The Miskito believed the program failed to take into account Indian ownership of many lands to be redistributed under the program. The Miskito brought a claim before the Inter-American Commission, arguing that the group should be guaranteed the right to the natural resources of the territory and the right to self-determination.

In response, the Commission acknowledged that international law recognizes the right of self-determination of peoples, but denied its applicability to the Miskito, insisting that "this does not mean . . . that it recognizes the right to self-determination of any ethnic group as such."[15] Nevertheless, the Commission made it clear that lack of rights to either political autonomy or self-determination did not mean that Nicaragua had "an unrestricted right to impose complete assimilation on those Indians."[16] Rather, using various rights under the American Convention on Human Rights and Article 27 of the ICCPR, to which Nicaragua was also a party, the Commission concluded that "special legal protection is recognized

for the use of their language, the observance of their religion, and in general, all those aspects related to the preservation of their cultural identity . . . which includes, among other things, the issue of the ancestral and communal lands."[17]

It was not altogether clear whether the Commission conceived of these rights as applying only to individuals (versus groups), but the human right to culture became the basis for the Commission's application of international human rights law to the Miskito. To the extent that it recognized that other rights were concerned, such rights were implicated in large part toward the aim of preserving culture. In more recent years, the Inter-American Court of Human Rights has continued to focus on the preservation of culture, though it has used the right to the "use and enjoyment" of property, found in Article 21 of the American Convention, as its principal rubric to protect culture in land claims.

THE HUMAN RIGHTS COMMITTEE

Although the Inter-American Commission used Article 27 of the ICCPR in its consideration of that convention's application to indigenous rights, the ICCPR does contain another arguably relevant provision. Article 1, which recognizes the right of "all peoples" to self-determination, has formed the basis of claims by some indigenous groups and individuals (on behalf of the group) before the Human Rights Committee (HRC).[18]

In a series of cases beginning in 1988, the Committee denied the admissibility of Article 1 claims on the grounds that the Optional Protocol under which complaints are brought recognizes only individual rights and that self-determination is a collective right, the violation of which individuals cannot be victims. Thus, in *Kitok v. Sweden*, the Committee never addressed the state's argument that the Saami did not constitute a people under Article 1,[19] in part because it found

15. OAS, Inter-American Commission on Human Rights, "Report on the Situation of Human Rights of a Segment of the Nicaraguan Population of Miskito Origin" (1983), at Part II, B(8) (describing the position articulated by Wiggins); Part II, B(9).
16. Ibid., Part II, B(11).

17. Ibid., Part II, B(15)
18. *Eds.*—The Human Rights Committee is the body of independent experts charged by the ICCPR to monitor implementation of the ICCPR by its states parties.
19. *Kitok v. Sweden*, Communication No. 197/1985, Views of the Human Rights Committee adopted on 10 August 1988, UN Doc. CCPR/ C/33/D/197/1985, at para. 4.1.

that Article 1 did not pertain to Kitok's individual application.[20] In the *Lubicon Lake Band* case, decided two years later, the Committee reiterated this position when it denied the applicability of Article 1 in a claim brought by an indigenous band in Canada on the grounds that the claim had been brought by the band's chief who, as an individual, "could not claim under the Optional Protocol to be a victim of a violation of the right of self-determination."[21]

At the same time, the HRC has been open to individual complaints under Article 27, beginning soon after the ICCPR entered into force. In 1977, Sandra Lovelace, born a Maliseet Indian, brought a complaint under the Optional Protocol against Canada because, after marrying a non-Indian man, she lost her tribal status under Canada's Indian Act. Though much of her claim focused on the fact that Indian men who married non-Indian women were entitled to keep their status, the Committee decided the case under Article 27, finding that the Act, which Canada claimed was in line with indigenous custom, violated Lovelace's right "to access to her native culture and language 'in community with the other members' of her group."[22] Thus the right to culture meant that she, as an individual, had a right to "her" culture.

Lovelace was the first in a series of cases to find Article 27 applicable to individual indigenous claims. In each of these cases, an individual right potentially trumped a potential collective right, even about membership of the collective. Many advocates have nevertheless seen the Committee approach to Article 27 as a positive application of the right to culture of indigenous people, if not peoples. They have been particularly encouraged by the Committee's indication in its General Comment 23 that the right to culture for indigenous peoples might support "a way of life which is closely associated with territory and use of resources."[23] That language in the recommendation,

however, follows a paragraph explicitly distinguishing the right to culture from the right to self-determination,[24] and a sentence foreshadowing Article 46(1) of the UNDRIP, indicating that the right to culture "does not prejudice the sovereignty and territorial integrity of a State party."[25]

INTERNATIONAL LABOUR ORGANIZATION (ILO)

In 1989, the ILO revised its 1957 Convention on Indigenous Peoples (Convention No. 107), which had largely been aimed at integrating indigenous people into industrialized, modern societies and had been highly criticized by indigenous rights advocates over the years. It did so through Convention No. 169, which provided new international standards meant to "remov[e] the assimilationist orientation of the earlier standards."[26]

A major source of controversy during the drafting of the convention was whether indigenous peoples were entitled to self-determination. The issue arose in part over whether to include the term "peoples" instead of either "people" or "populations," the latter of which had been used in Convention No. 107. Indigenous participants' insistence on the term "peoples" blocked the convention's adoption at one point, leading to two years of negotiation and an eventual compromise, after which the term "peoples" was finally included, but alongside a provision that disclaimed the attachment of any international rights to the term.

This explicit rejection of self-determination as recognized in international law received a negative response from many indigenous advocates at the time. As one commentator noted then:

> The indigenous peoples' representatives were furious that, of all the peoples of the world, they alone should be cut off from enjoying the same rights as other peoples as defined under international law. Cristobal Naikiai, a Shuar Indian from Ecuador and Vice-president of the Coordinator of Indigenous Organisations of the Amazon Basin, likened the process at the

20. Ibid., para. 6.3.
21. *Lubicon Lake Band v. Canada*, Communication No. 167/1984, Views of the Human Rights Committee adopted on 26 March 1990, UN Doc. Supp. No. 40 (A/45/40), at para. 6.3.
22. *Lovelace v. Canada*, Communication No. 24/1977, Views of the Human Rights Committee adopted on 30 July 1980, UN Doc. CCPR/C/13/D/24/1977, at para. 15.
23. UN Human Rights Committee, CCPR General Comment No. 23: The Rights of Minorities (art. 27), UN Doc. CCPR/C/21/Rev.1/Add.5 (1994), at para. 3.2.

24. Ibid., para. 3.1.
25. Ibid., para. 3.2.
26. International Labour Organization, Indigenous and Tribal Peoples Convention (No. 169), 27 June 1989, preamble.

International Labour Conference to the infamous conference in the 16th century when the church in Spain had debated on whether Indian people had souls or not.[27]

Other indigenous leaders protested as well. Leonard Crate, for example, the representative of the International Organization of Indigenous Resource Development, asked the Committee, "What is the difference between our claim and the claim of oppressed colonial peoples who want to live in their homelands?"[28]

Much of the memory of this early dissatisfaction with the rejection of the right to self-determination seems to have been lost over time. Many indigenous rights advocates, at least in states that have signed the convention, have embraced ILO Convention No. 169 as the only legally binding instrument specifically focused on indigenous rights. They have attempted, with mixed success, to compel states that have signed it to guarantee a wide range of indigenous rights, including the right to prior consultation by the state on development initiatives that affect lands they use or occupy.

THE HUMAN RIGHTS PARADIGM AFTER 1989

As the last section demonstrated, indigenous rights advocacy aimed at self-determination, particularly external forms of self-determination, had largely failed in terms of recognition by international instruments and the bodies that created and interpreted them. At the same time, those bodies proved to be open to some, particularly but not exclusively individually based, indigenous rights claims made under the rubric of the human right to culture. As advocates began to advocate and articulate human rights for indigenous peoples over the ensuing years, they did so within a new landscape for the development of human rights more generally. I consider this broad human rights landscape after 1989 to begin to understand how it both opened possibilities and posed limits for the articulation of indigenous peoples' claims.

Particularly since the end of the Cold War, human rights have become the lingua franca of both states and social movements, from the left to the right. With regard to the former, states claim to intervene—even militarily—in other states to protect human rights, and states resist such intervention in the name of human rights. Social movements of all stripes also frame their claims in human rights terms. Even arguments for significant redistribution of wealth and resources are largely made in the name of (economic and social) human rights. Moreover, states and social movements have participated in the expansion of both soft and hard international legal mechanisms for human rights, evidenced in part by the increase in number, scope, and power of regional and international instruments. In this sense, the developments in indigenous rights advocacy and jurisprudence described above simply present a microcosm of what has happened in human rights in the post-Cold War era. There are few legal and discursive spaces wholly outside the human rights framework.

Yet, like indigenous rights advocates who were skeptical of human rights for some time, the political left has a history of ambivalence toward human rights. Not unconnected to concerns about its civilizing mission, the left has long identified human rights as inextricably (and problematically) linked to capitalism and forms of liberal democracy that were seen to facilitate it. Arguably, the Cold War kept alive both the uneasiness with liberal, individualistic human rights and support for a different understanding of human rights that depended upon an active role for the state and emphasized redistribution over individual rights, especially individual property rights.

In the context of the drafting of the UDHR, for example, political theorist and past chair of the British Labour Party, Harold Laski, presented a Marxist-informed critique of rights. He warned that, even when proclaimed to be universal, declarations of rights had "in fact been attempts to give special sanctity to rights which some given ruling class at some given time in the life of a political society it controlled felt to be of peculiar importance to the members of that class."[29] Laski

27. Marcus Colchester, "Indigenous Peoples and the International Labour Organisation," *Interights Bulletin* 4 (1989): 43.
28. International Labour Conference, 76th Session, 1989, *Record of Proceedings*, 31/6.

29. Harold Laski, "Towards a Universal Declaration of Human Rights," in *Human Rights, Comments and Interpretations: A Symposium Edited by UNESCO* (1949), 78–92, 86.

was not necessarily opposed to a declaration on human rights, but he argued that such a declaration should attend to alternative formulations of human rights that were "struggling to be born."[30]

While many would disagree about the extent to which the alternative view of human rights suggested by Laski ever had significant traction in international law or institutions, I think most would agree that any reasonable prospect of it fell with the Berlin wall. As Wendy Brown puts it in her response to Michael Ignatieff's self-proclaimed "minimalist" argument in favor of "a defensible core of rights,"[31] Ignatieff's conception of human rights, rather than being minimalist, in fact provides a way to ensure that "individual rights especially those basic to free enterprise and free trade" are not limited.[32]

Although many disagree with Ignatieff's approach to human rights and would like to see greater attention given to economic and social rights and to collective rights, it seems difficult in the post-Cold War era to do little more than tame the (post-)neoliberal economic and political model that dominates the world. Neoliberalism has been "chastened," as David Kennedy puts it,[33] in part by human rights. And it has also arguably been legitimated by that same process.[34] Judging from the discourse of most states and international institutions since 1989, conceptions of rights that would challenge the liberal, individual, free-market model of human rights have had surprisingly little traction.

(RE)READING INDIGENOUS RIGHTS ADVOCACY AFTER 1989

I now return to the question I have raised in a number of ways throughout this essay: how might we explain the persistence of individual, liberal rights alongside the growing use and apparent acceptance of cultural and collective rights by indigenous peoples?

I hope the narrative I have woven has suggested some responses. As the resistance by international institutions to recognizing the right to self-determination of indigenous peoples demonstrates, human rights seems less threatening to states and international institutions than external forms of self-determination. Though states allowed the language of self-determination in the UNDRIP, they did so only by ensuring it would pose no threat to their territorial integrity.

The history of indigenous resistance also shows, however, that a simple application of individual civil and political rights to indigenous people (not peoples) would be insufficient. Thus, indigenous peoples argued early on for human rights that would ensure the group some forms of economic and political control; they largely did so through advocating for the right to culture or to collective property based on their cultural connection to it. As I hope to have demonstrated, indigenous rights advocates had some victories but also some losses with this strategy.

To the extent that they have been successful, I would contend (and have argued in detail elsewhere) that advocates have often aided in the production of indigenous subjectivities that are limited in terms of whom they actually cover and in terms of what rights they permit.[35] Perhaps more importantly, however, indigenous rights advocates have often not been very successful in terms of gaining the recognition of rights that are in real tension with liberal, individual rights. That is, the former is nearly always subordinated to the latter.

Examples of this subordination can be seen in the same forums we have already considered. Recall that the HRC, for example, has had a difficult time recognizing—or at least adjudicating

30. Ibid., 92.
31. Wendy Brown, "'The Most We Can Hope For': Human Rights and the Politics of Fatalism," *South Atlantic Quarterly* 103, 2–3 (2004): 451–63, 457.
32. Ibid.
33. See David Kennedy, "The 'Rule of Law,' Political Choices and Development Common Sense," in David M. Trubek and Alvaro Santos, eds., *The New Law and Economic Development: A Critical Appraisal* (Cambridge: CUP, 2006), 95.
34. Anthropologist Charles Hale demonstrates, in the context of Guatemala, that neoliberal modernization and indigenous cultural rights often fit quite comfortably together in what he terms "neoliberal multiculturalism": see Charles Hale, "Does Multiculturalism Menace? Governance, Cultural Rights and the Politics of Identity in Guatemala," *Journal of Latin American Studies* 34 (2002): 485–524.

35. I have discussed in detail the dark sides of the protection of culture as heritage, land, and development in Engle, *The Elusive Promise of Indigenous Development*, note 2, 148–61, 168–82, and 196–220.

on—anything more than an individual right to culture. Moreover, it has generally chosen the rights of individuals over groups when confronted with a conflict or even potential conflict between them.

Beyond subordinating collective rights to individual rights, the international law on indigenous rights has defined certain indigenous claims *out* of human rights. The HRC General Comment 23, for example, indicates that, for the most part, special provisions granted under ICCPR Article 27 "must respect the [non-discrimination] provisions of the Covenant both as regards the treatment between different minorities and the treatment between the persons belonging to them and the remaining part of the population."[36] Similarly, ILO Convention No. 169, after setting out indigenous peoples' right to culture, attaches a proviso in an Article dealing with indigenous custom by granting indigenous peoples "the right to retain their own customs and institutions, where these are not incompatible with fundamental rights defined by the national legal system and with internationally recognised human rights."[37]

Indigenous rights are thus defined, explicitly or implicitly, with what the literature on colonial law refers to as the "repugnancy clause." As Leon Sheleff explains, this clause was not presented "merely, or even mainly, as being some sort of compromise between conflicting value-systems and their normative rulings, but as being an expression of minimum standards being applied as a qualification to the toleration being accorded (by recognition) to the basically unacceptable norms of 'backward' communities."[38] Elizabeth Povinelli has discussed the contemporary resonances of this clause in Australian law's treatment of customary law, identifying an "invisible asterisk" that "hovers above every enunciation of indigenous customary law."[39]

Paragraphs (2) and (3) of Article 46 of the UNDRIP, as I suggest above, threaten to function in the same way as the repugnancy clause. By subjecting the rights contained in the declaration to the vague standards of "international human rights obligations" and "justice, democracy, respect for human rights, equality, non-discrimination, good governance and good faith," the provisions offer states a way to define certain indigenous claims out of these categories, and to deny them accordingly. In attempting to reconcile human rights and indigenous rights, they also reinforce the tensions between them.

CONCLUSION

It is not surprising that human rights for indigenous peoples had their ascendancy after 1989, and that the paradigm within which they were framed was both enormously popular—making it hard to resist, particularly with the lack of state support for a strong form of self-determination—and apparently constrained. But most of the work that has been done on the UNDRIP since its passage has been far from critical. It has attempted to bury old disagreements and focus on the implementation—through international legal and institutional mechanisms and domestic law—of the rights that it is seen to recognize. Relatedly, while some argue that the declaration goes beyond other international legal instruments in terms of recognizing indigenous rights, others insist that the declaration adds no new rights but rather is simply a statement of what already exists in customary international law.

I have on a number of occasions been encouraged to participate in the liberal interpretation project and to read the rights in the UNDRIP as broadly as possible, rather than recall the conflicts and tensions from the past. Indeed, one colleague told me directly that now is not the time for critique, as there is a need to shore up the "fragile architecture" of the UNDRIP. I think his analogy is apt, given that fragile architecture suggests a flawed foundation. But I would argue that now is the time to expose, not hide or reinforce, that foundation. If we are willing to examine it critically, the UNDRIP may have the potential to become an important site for the ongoing struggle over the meaning of human rights, the dominance of human rights as the basis of justice, and the extent to which it might be mined or abandoned for alternative, transformative strategies.

36. UN Human Rights Committee, CCPR General Comment No. 23, at para. 6.2.
37. International Labour Organization, Convention No. 169, art. 8(2).
38. Leon Sheleff, *The Future of Tradition* (London: Frank Cass, 1999), 123.
39. Elizabeth A. Povinelli, *The Cunning of Recognition* (Durham, N.C.: Duke University Press, 2002), 12.

QUESTIONS FOR REFLECTION AND DISCUSSION

1. What is Engle's key analytical concern in this reading?
2. Some argue that human rights already provide adequate protection to indigenous peoples without the right to culture or self-determination. How would advocates of indigenous rights, discussed above, counter that argument?
3. Engle writes: "the victories [won by indigenous rights advocates] have brought with them (often unintended) limitations and downsides, which I have largely pinned on the reification of indigenous culture, alongside the rejection of self-determination claims and the acceptance of a cultural rights framework by international institutions." What do you understand Engle to mean by this, and why? Can you draw on any additional evidence or sources to substantiate your response?
4. What, precisely, does Engle mean when she argues that the UNDRIP "signifies both the possible expansion and continued limitation of human rights and the perpetuation of certain biases"? To what is she referring? How does she substantiate her argument?
5. What *does* "indigenous self-determination" mean in international law? What sources are you drawing upon to substantiate your response? Why might your definition be more interpretively convincing than any other potential definitions you have discovered?
6. What *should* "indigenous self-determination" mean in international law? What normative frameworks or commitments inform your answer?
7. Engle poses the following question: "Is the insistence on equality and non-discrimination a denial of rights that might be considered special or attach to a single culture?" How do you answer the question? Why? Based upon what values? Based upon what evidence?
8. Engle also asks: "Are the provisions an acknowledgment or denial of conflict between human rights and indigenous rights, or are they productive of a distinction between the two?" How do you answer this question? Based on what reasons and reasoning?
9. What turns on distinctions between the terms term "people," "peoples," and "populations"? Which term(s) do you think should be employed when speaking of indigenous human rights and/or indigenous self-determination, and why?
10. How do you "explain the persistence of individual, liberal rights alongside the growing use and apparent acceptance of cultural and collective rights by indigenous peoples"? How does Engle explain it? Do you accept her explanation? Why? Why not?
11. In the conclusion, Engle argues that now is the time to examine the UNDRIP critically given its history of compromises instead of liberally interpreting it in an attempt to reinforce indigenous or cultural rights. Do you agree with Engle? Why? Why not?

23. BONNY IBHAWOH *The Right to Development: The Politics and Polemics of Power and Resistance*

Recent academic and policy debates on the right to development have focused on two main themes. First, since the early 1970s when the concept of a right to development first surfaced at the international level, a fierce and largely polemical debate among states, scholars, and practitioners has focused on whether there exists a right to development in the normative [i.e.,

Excerpted with changes by permission of Johns Hopkins University Press from Bonny Ibhawoh, "The Right to Development: The Politics and Polemics of Power and Resistance," *Human Rights Quarterly* 33 (2011): 76–104. Copyright © 2011 Johns Hopkins University Press.

legal] sense. The debate has served more to draw lines between the North and the South, rather than to increase understanding of the relationship between human rights and development.

The second and more current theme is the difficulty that has accompanied the implementation of the right to development. In spite of the broad acceptance of the right in the past two decades, critics continue to question its practical value for strengthening human rights generally. The defining document on the right to development, the UN Declaration on the Right to Development (DRD), is considered by many to be too vague to have any real impact on domestic and international development issues. Enforcement mechanisms are weak and there has been a lack of consensus and political will on the part of principal stakeholders to pursue the enforcement of this right as vigorously as other international human rights standards. The common conclusion is that the notion of a right to development has not and probably cannot deliver its promise.

Critics contend that the right to development is devoid of meaning and is unenforceable because of its scope and the inability of states to ever realize all of its components.[1] The right to development has been variously described as "catastrophic,"[2] and politically and practically a "total failure."[3] Even proponents concede that half a century of debates over the implications of the right to development and how it could make a meaningful practical contribution to the quest to link human rights and development has not produced a great deal.[4]

Such conclusions are often based on the assumption that the value of the discourse on the right to development can only truly be measured by its "tangible" outcomes such as the creation of binding international legal instruments and the emergence of effective enforcement mechanisms. Often overlooked are the intangible outcomes of the discourse in terms of clarifying concepts, mobilizing opinions, challenging orthodoxies, and building consensus on key issues. This essay argues that beyond the fuzziness and divisiveness that have characterized debates over the right to development, the discourse also manifests contradictions and paradoxes that raise pertinent questions about the normative objectivity of human rights talk.

In official Southern discourses, the right to development has mainly been advanced to rationalize and justify national priorities as well as legitimize statist political and economic agendas using the language of rights. In this sense, it is articulated not so much as a claim against the developed West, but as a means of maintaining the status quo and to counter domestic and international pressures for political liberalization. While the earlier phase of the discourses on the right to development tended to reflect a polemic of resistance, more recent debates increasingly reflect an international politics of power.

The paradox of right to development talk coming from the South is that it is at once deployed to demand radical change in the international economic order and to resist change in the national political order. When Chinese officials invoke the right to development to demand more favorable trade terms, the emphasis is often on challenging a hegemonic international economic system with a view to changing the status quo. Yet, when China invokes the right to development to deflect criticism of its human rights record, or to resist pressure to cap environmental emissions, the intent is clearly to maintain the domestic economic order and preserve the political status quo. South African officials can invoke the right to development in demanding radical changes in international pharmaceutical patent laws while at the same time using it to rationalize the failure to demand political reforms in Mugabe's Zimbabwe. The right to development has been used both as a sword and as a shield in the battle for high moral grounds on some of the most important human rights issues that confront our world today.

These contradictions are not limited to discourses from the South. The longstanding opposition to the right to development by some Northern states manifests similar paradoxes. Opposition to the right has come from some states which see the global redistributive justice framework of the right to development as incompatible with the free market and capitalist structures of the global economy. Even though the right to development as espoused in the DRD clearly places enforcement obligations on both states and the international community, many Northern states have conveniently focused more on the domestic responsibilities of developing countries rather than their own responsibility as key players in the global political economy. Rights-

1. See, e.g., Jack Donnelly, "In Search of the Unicorn: The Jurisprudence and Politics of the Right to Development," *California Western International Law Journal* 15 (1985): 473–509.
2. Peter Uvin, "From the Right to Development to the Rights-Based Approach: How 'Human Rights' Entered Development," *Development Practice* 17 (2007): 597–606.
3. Peter Uvin, *Human Rights and Development* (Bloomfield, Conn.: Kumarian Press, 2004), 42.
4. Philip Alston, "Ships Passing in the Night: The Current State of the Human Rights and Development Debate Seen Through the Lens of the Millennium Development Goals," *HRQ* 27 (2005): 755–829, 798; Makau Mutua, "Standard Setting in Human Rights: Critique and Prognosis," *HRQ* 29 (2007): 547–630, 564.

based development is narrowly interpreted in a manner that is essentially state-centric. While demanding structural economic and political changes within developing nations as a means of achieving the right to development, many Northern states continue to resist corresponding changes in the mechanisms of global trade and finance that are, in fact, central to the ability of developing states to enforce these rights.

This article argues that the basic problem that has bedeviled the elaboration and implementation of the right to development goes beyond the all-encompassing nature of the right or even the language in which it is embodied. Part of the problem is the political and ideological jockeying that underscores the discourse on the right to development. This holds larger implications for international human rights because the language of human rights has become a principal means of legitimizing complex and contradictory political and social agendas. It therefore is important that we pay as much attention to the tensions and contradictions of human rights as we have paid to the successes and triumphs. This requires examining how authoritarian structures co-opt and deploy the language of rights to legitimize power, maintain the status quo, and deflect pressures for reforms.

LINKING DEVELOPMENT AND HUMAN RIGHTS

For many years, academic and policy debates on human rights and development took place largely parallel to each other in spite of their obvious connections. There was little reference to development in the early debates at the United Nations leading to the adoption of the Universal Declaration of Human Rights (UDHR) in 1948, much of which focused on civil and political rights. Although the UDHR ultimately included provisions for economic, social, and cultural rights, these were not framed in terms of development. On the other hand, development studies that emerged as a self-defined field of academic and practical research in the 1960s were concerned mainly with how policy interventions or political action can change social orders. Coinciding with the era of decolonization and the emergence of new nations in many parts of the Global South, the goal of development studies was primarily economic growth rather

than human rights. The dominant thinking was that the agent of development was the state and that the means of development was national economic planning in the context of macro-commission and the International Monetary Fund. These taken-for-granted presumptions of development theories as they evolved from the 1950s onward set them apart from the discourse on international human rights.

This dichotomy between human rights and development fields began to change in the 1970s when the right to development was first articulated by developing countries in the context of a New International Economic Order (NIEO).[5] Throughout the 1970s, the international community repeatedly examined and debated the different aspects of the right to development. In 1979, a resolution of the UN Commission on Human Rights[6] expressly recognized the right to development as a human right and mandated the Secretary-General to study the conditions required for the effective enjoyment of the right by all individuals and peoples. Subsequently, various reports examining the right to development and extensive discussions in the Commission and the General Assembly led to the formulation of a Draft Declaration on the Right to Development, which was formally adopted by the General Assembly in December 1986.[7]

The DRD identified the right to development firmly within the framework of the emergent international human rights order. It defined the right to development as "an inalienable human right by virtue of which every human person and all peoples are entitled to participate in, contribute to, and enjoy economic, social, cultural and political development, in which all human rights and fundamental freedoms can be fully realized."[8] The DRD challenged states to focus more on human development in order to ensure

---

5. *Eds.*—See 1974 Declaration on the Establishment of a New International Economic Order.

6. *Eds.*—Replaced by the UN Human Rights Council in 2006.

7. *Eds.*—Art. 1(1). Development is defined in the DRD Preamble as a "comprehensive economic, social, cultural and political process, which aims at the constant improvement of the well-being of the entire population and of all individuals, on the basis of their active, free and meaningful participation in development and in the fair distribution of benefits resulting therefrom."

8. *Eds.*—Art. 1(1).

the realization of the right to development.[9] Although it made more explicit the links between international consensus in the realms of human rights and development, many of the DRD provisions were not entirely new. It included several elements of the two previous UN covenants— the Covenant on Civil and Political Rights (ICCPR) and the Covenant on Economic, Social and Cultural Rights (ICESCR). What was most significant about the DRD was that it brought together the development-oriented rights provisions of both covenants and in some cases, expanded them.

Since the adoption of the DRD in 1986, the United Nations Commission on Human Rights played a crucial role in developing the normative content of the notion through two significant events. First, the 1993 World Human Rights Conference leading to the Vienna Declaration affirmed that the right to development as established in the DRD is a "universal and inalienable right and an integral part of fundamental human rights." The second was through the appointment of an Independent Expert in 1999,[10] as well as a UN Working Group on the Right to Development. Besides these events, much of the intellectual initiative and advocacy for the right to development came from scholars from developing countries or, to use the term of the period, the "Third World." The discourse in this context was linked to the global political changes of the 1960s and 1970s starting with the decolonization movement, the recognition of the principle of self-determination, and the right of people to freely pursue economic, social, and cultural development.

The right to development as espoused in the DRD and related policy documents such as the reports of the UN Independent Expert and the Working Group on the Right to Development include four critical elements that are relevant to the discussion here. First, the conceptualization of development as a process facilitating the realization of human rights; second, recognition of the interrelatedness and interdependencies of all aspects of human rights; third, recognition that the right to development is both an individual and collective right; and finally, recognition that the duty bearers charged with the responsibility of fulfilling the right to development are not only states but also the international community.[11] The right to development approach, while incorporating elements of the other human rights approaches to development, is distinct in that it views "development," defined as a particular process of the improvement of well-being and expansion of freedoms, as a human right. It links development and human rights by placing the human person at the center of development and asserting that the elimination of violations of human rights is a necessary part of development.[12]

This linking of human rights and human development in policy and academic discourses has been done in two major ways.[13] The first is through the so-called rights-based approach to development, which affirms that human rights must be integrated into sustainable human development. The second approach to the right to

9. *Eds.*—Art. 2(3) stipulates: "States have the right *and duty* to formulate appropriate national development policies that aim at the constant improvement of the well-being of the entire population and of all individuals, on the basis of their active, free and meaningful participation in development and in the fair distribution of the benefits resulting therefrom" (emphasis added). Article 8 is more specific: "States should undertake, at the national level, all necessary measures for the realization of the right to development and shall ensure, *inter alia*, equality of opportunity for all in their access to basic resources, education, health services, food, housing, employment and the fair distribution of income. Effective measures should be undertaken to ensure that women have an active role in the development process. Appropriate economic and social reforms should be carried out with a view to eradicating all social injustices."

10. *Eds.*—The late Arjun Sengupta, one of India's most noted economists, former special secretary to the prime minister of India (Indira Gandhi), executive director and special adviser to the managing director of the International Monetary Fund, India's ambassador to the European Union, member secretary of the Indian Planning Commission, and member of the Rajya Sabha (upper house) of the Indian Parliament.

11. *Eds.*—Art. 4(2) of the DRD provides that "Sustained action is required to promote more rapid development of developing countries. As a complement to the efforts of developing countries, effective international cooperation is essential in providing these countries with appropriate means and facilities to foster their comprehensive development."

12. Arjun Sengupta, "On the Theory and Practice of the Right to Development," in Arjun Sengupta, Archna Negi, and Moushymi Basu, eds., *Reflections on the Right to Development* (London: Sage, 2005), 11.

13. Other writers have identified ways in which human rights are linked with development discourse. See, e.g., Stephen P. Marks, "The Human Rights Framework for Development: Seven Approaches," in ibid., 33.

development goes beyond conceptualizing a rights-based approach to development to considering development as a human right in and of itself. This flows from a holistic conception of human rights as interrelated and indivisible. One rather unique element of the DRD and the related reports of the UN Independent Experts is the recognition that the right to development is both an individual and collective entitlement. Beyond individual entitlements, the right to development is an entitlement that also pertains to communities, nations, and regions. This marks a departure from the individual-centered orientation of other international human rights instruments. In fact, the DRD is one of only a few international or regional human rights instruments that are premised as much on the rights of peoples as on those of individuals.

A related provision of the DRD that sets it apart from other international human rights instruments is the recognition that responsibility for ensuring the right to development rests not only with states, but also with the international community. In this context, human rights go beyond the traditional definition of being entitlements that individuals hold against the state. They are also construed as entitlements that states hold in relation to other states and the international community at large.

The notion that states and "peoples" can also claim development as a human rights entitlement against other states or the international community marked a major paradigm shift in human rights orthodoxy. It represented a challenge to and in some sense a repudiation of the dominant Western liberal egalitarian orientation of the international human rights system. Some saw the DRD as pushing into the international human rights regime a distinctly non-Western communitarian rights agenda. Thus, although the adoption of the DRD in 1986 and its reaffirmation in the Vienna Declaration and Programme of Action in 1993 have placed the right firmly within the international human rights corpus, the right to development remains one of the most contested and contentious facets of the international human rights regime.

CONTESTING THE RIGHT TO DEVELOPMENT

Since its adoption in 1986, the status of the DRD has remained a subject of an intensely divisive debate among diplomats, scholars, and practitioners, evincing a persisting North-South intellectual polarity. At the UN-sponsored "Global Consultation on the Right to Development as Human Rights" convened in Geneva in 1990, delegates were divided—pretty much along regional and hemispheric lines—over the implementation of the right to development. In spite of a conscious effort by the Global Consultation forum to avoid what it described as "sterile theoretical debates," the fault lines were evident. Participants from the North and South differed considerably in their perception of the global political economy. Regional difference also extended to the analysis of the best means of implementing the DRD with the main point of contention being the respective responsibilities of the developing and developed world.

Most Western participants argued for a basic needs approach, involving the prioritization of the achievement of certain economic and social rights, such as the right to food, shelter, and education. This argument was premised on the view that capitalism moderated by the distribution of income within the state is central to facilitating development in the South. Western participants also advocated an international regime based on concessional aid rather than the sharing of productive resources and technology. This position reflects an underlying concern among some Western nations about the rhetoric of the right to development, which emphasizes entitlements but tends to overlook the cost of providing them. In contrast, a coalition of participants from the developing world produced draft recommendations, which advocated giving priority in development policies to participation and political transformations, as opposed to basic needs. They also expressed a need for political transformation and democracy in international relations, rather than more aid or concessional resources.

The divisiveness that has characterized debates over the right to development can be attributed in part to the fact that unlike most other international human rights norms, the right to development has a distinctly international character—it resonates more in the interaction between states than within states. An individual-centered international human rights system, it seems, remains ill equipped to address resource-related human rights issues in which the state is not simply a duty bearer with enforcement obligations, but can also be a claimant. However, the North-South polarization over the right to development evident in most analyses tells only part of the story. Underlying the positions championed by both Northern and Southern states on the right to development are salient contradictions that complicate its elaboration and implementation.

THE RHETORIC OF OPPOSITION

For many advocates in the South, the discourse on the right to development has provided a fitting platform for challenging the orthodoxies and hegemonies of the global political economy. Their discourse, in essence, encapsulates a solidarity movement dating back to the NIEO seeking to change the rules of the game and thereby wrest a greater share of the world's wealth and income. It represents a political desire to restructure the international political economy and allow the developing societies of the South to participate more effectively in decision-making on international economic matters.

When ideas about restructuring the international economic order, which underscore the right to development, first emerged in the context of decolonization and the global political changes of the 1950s and 1960s, they were premised on legitimizing the principle of self-determination and the right of people to freely pursue their economic, social, and cultural development. The emphasis was on restructuring the world's economy to permit greater participation by and benefits to developing countries. By redressing the disadvantages of former colonized developing countries in the international economic system, the NIEO agenda aimed to further their economic advances by changing their economic relations with the developed countries.

Whether in the form of the NIEO agenda, the right to development, or the more recent emphasis on rights-based development, Southern discourses have focused on demanding radical change in the international economic order. The dominant Southern view is that the right to development requires wide-ranging changes in extant international economic regimes to ensure that they contribute to furthering the right to development in at least two ways. First, by encouraging rather than constraining conditions permitting the realization of the right to development within a country. Second, by ensuring

that intercountry inequalities, in terms of access to natural and other resources, are reduced as much as possible. This in turn requires an international economic system that provides greater flexibility of macroeconomic policy to individual countries, but also ensures that there is some international control.

It is in this context of international economic obligations and entitlements that the discourse on the right to development and development as a human right has been deployed both as a language of resistance and a strategy of opposition. The discourse becomes more than simply a debate about individual and collective economic empowerment, but also an extension of the polemics of power and resistance played out at both intellectual and diplomatic levels and shaped by historic and contemporary conditions. In the writings of principal "Third World" proponents of the right to development, the discourse assumes a tone that is profoundly critical of the global economic order and demands its fundamental reform.

The emphasis is on two main themes, the first of which is state sovereignty. According to Bedjaoui, "The 'right to development' flows from this right to self-determination and has the same nature."[14] This makes it much more a "right of the State or of the people, than a right of the individual." The second emphasis is on the obligations of rich countries to help poor countries. The discourse seeks to establish a claim on the assistance and cooperation of the developed world of the Northern hemisphere for accelerating the pace of economic development in the South. These positions implicitly reject the status quo in the international political economy and seek instead to resist its structural imbalance and inequities.

Yet, asserting the right to development solely in terms of the rights of states sells the concept short. Within the context of the DRD and related documents, right-holders are the collective individuals in a given state as well as groups within that collective, as in the case of minorities and indigenous people. States acting within the existing interstate system are the entities through which the international component of the right

14. Mohammed Bedjaoui, "The Right to Development," in Mohammed Bedjaoui, ed., *International Law: Achievements and Prospects* (Paris: Nijhoff, 1991), 1184.

to development is asserted. However, the role of developing states in asserting the right to development of their people internationally does not render the right an exclusively state one.

In other contexts, the discourse on the right to development also reflects a politics of resistance. In spite of the clear provisions of the DRD, dominant Southern discourses on the right to development seek to privilege states over local communities and individuals, promote economic rights at the expense of civil and political rights, and to demand radical change in the international economic system, while resisting domestic reforms that are equally crucial to fulfilling the right to development. However, this paradox is not limited to Southern discourses. If anything, similar contradictions are evident in Northern discourses of the right to development. Northern states and the powerful international financial institutions they control have been keen to link development in the South to liberal political and economic reforms at the domestic level. Yet, there has been a reluctance to extend these calls for reform to the workings of the international economic system within the framework of the rights of states and obligations of the international community espoused in the DRD.

A LANGUAGE OF POWER

Even though under international law states are considered the principal duty-bearer with respect to human rights of the people living within its jurisdiction, the right to development framework recognizes that the international community at large also has a responsibility to help realize universal human rights. The DRD also recognizes that states hold extraterritorial obligations regarding the enjoyment of the right to development. This is emphasized in Articles 3 and 4, which provide that states are required to create international conditions favorable to the realization of the right to development.[15] They have the duty to cooperate in order to achieve this right, and are required to act collectively to formulate development policies oriented to the fulfillment of this right.

These international dimensions of the right to development, which resonate deeply in Southern

discourses, have received less attention in Northern intellectual and diplomatic discourses. The opposition of Northern states, particularly the United States, to the right to development hinges on two main positions. First is the assumption that the global redistributive justice framework of the right to development is incompatible with the individual-centered free market and capitalist structure of the global economy. Second is the supposition that the very notion of framing development as a human right entitlement with binding obligations, even worse, binding extraterritorial obligations, is inherently flawed. This position is well captured in Jack Donnelly's arguments about the right to development and the limits of international "solidarity" obligations. While solidarity may require moral obligations to assist the developing world, Donnelly argues, solidarity does not establish a right to such assistance let alone a right to development.[16]

Also problematic from the point of view of some Northern states is that the right to development finds the right holder to be both the individual and the collective. Correspondingly, the duty bearer for these rights is seen as both the state (for individual rights) and the international community (for collective rights) through international assistance and cooperation. In rebuffing attempts to operationalize their legal obligations, many developed states have been particularly critical of the extraterritorial obligations under the right to development framework. To these states, right to development proponents seek to create binding legal obligations on what has traditionally been viewed as discretionary foreign aid. The concern here is not so much with the goals of development, but with the normative framework in which it is articulated. The right to development may be tolerable within a traditional state-centric human rights framework, but its explicit extraterritorial dimensions remain problematic for many Northern states. This may explain the growing preference for the language of "rights-based development" rather than the "right to development" by Northern states and the multilateral development and financial institutions that they control.

Although there are clear connections between the concepts of the right to development and rights-based development, some scholars and

---

15. *Eds.*—See notes 9 and 11.

16. Donnelly, "In Search of the Unicorn," 491.

practitioners find the latter more useful because it brings about a "root cause" approach to linking human rights and development, focusing primarily on matters of state policy and discrimination. The rights-based development approach is said to encourage the move from "needs to rights" from "charity to duties" and also implies "an increased focus on accountability."[17] This approach clearly complements and strengthens the core principles of the right to development. The problem, however, is that the emphasis in discourses of rights-based development, if not the actual practice, is almost always on state accountability rather than international obligations.

The appeal of a language of state-centered, rights-based development rather than one that stresses international obligations is obvious—the latter hints of entitlements and binding obligations which many Northern states and multilateral aid agencies would rather avoid. The international apparatus of human rights accountability makes it easier to deflect critical attention and questions of state responsibility from nonstate actors because that approach remains rigidly state-centric. This rights-based approach does little to empower the intended beneficiaries of development, be they people or the state. Northern discourses on the right to development do not espouse or even envision a fundamental reshuffling of cards of power, or redistribution of international resources worldwide.

In line with the provisions of the DRD, bilateral donors such as the UK Department for International Development (DFID), Norwegian Agency for Development Cooperation (NORAD), Danish International Development Agency (DANIDA), Swedish International Development Agency (SIDA), and Canadian International Development Agency (CIDA) have all adopted explicit mandates for human rights in development. United Nations agencies such as the UN Development Programme (UNDP) have also integrated human rights into their development mandates. Even international financial institutions such as the World Bank and the Monetary Fund that have long resisted bringing in "extraneous" non-economic indices into their operations, now give greater consideration to human

rights and good governance centered development in formulating lending policies. In all these, however, there remains an inclination toward the language of "rights-based approach" to aid, cooperation, and assistance rather than the language of the "right to development" and the international obligations it mandates.

This state-centered, rights-based approach serves more to affirm the status quo than to reform it. Huge ranges of rich-country behaviors that undermine the full realization of the right to development remain immune to criticism. "Northern over-consumption, a history of colonialism, lopsided environmental degradation, protectionism, the dumping of arms in the Third World, the history of shoring up past dictators, the wisdom of structural adjustment, and globalization—all are off the discussion table."[18] The inevitable conclusion is that there is a lot less in the state-centered rights-based approach to development than meets the eye. Much of it is about the quest for a moral high ground: draping oneself in the mantle of human rights to cover the fat belly of the development community, avoiding challenging the status quo, or questioning oneself or the international system.

This, in many ways, also mirrors the trend in Southern discourses of the right to development, which tend to privilege economic rights over civil and political rights and international responsibilities over domestic obligations. If the right to development has been co-opted by state structures in the South as a language for resisting a hegemonic international system while maintaining the domestic political status quo, Northern discourses have similarly been deployed as a language of power to maintain the international economic status quo while resisting Southern pressures for reform.

The state-centric agenda that dominates Northern discourses on the right to development ignores the realities of a globalizing world where international factors increasingly affect the capacity of states to achieve development. While Northern states and the multilateral organizations that they control profess commitment to human rights in their development aims and demand the same of Southern states, they have been less forthright in extending the same rights-

17. Benjamin Mason Meier and Ashley M. Fox, "Development as Health: Employing the Collective Right to Development to Achieve the Goals of the Individual Right to Health," *HRQ* 30 (2008): 259–355, 328.

18. Uvin, "From the Right to Development to the Rights-Based Approach," note 2, 601.

based reforms to their own actions and an inequitable global political economy within which they occupy privileged spaces. In the absence of such moves, the human rights focus in the development discourse amounts to little more than the projection of power.

CONCLUSION

The right to development has provided a means with which authority structures in both North and South have furthered their own interest through the legitimizing language of human rights. The contradictions arising therefrom partly explain why the status of the right to development has remained murky and the prospects of a binding treaty or mechanisms for enforcement remain dim.

Still, the right to development has been more than simply an instrument in the hands of Southern and Northern authority structures. The discourse on the right to development has brought about a significant substantive change in how we think about development, which has had real impact on the lives of many people around the world. The right to development approach has created a new paradigm in development thinking

that places human rights firmly within national and international development. Inspired by the vision of the DRD, many states have put in place constitutional provisions and enforcement mechanisms for the right to development. Thus, in spite of the formally nonbinding status of the DRD and other related resolutions, the right to development has had a salutary effect in the normative relations between states. It provides a reference point for demands for more equitable distribution of wealth and resources within and between states.

At the same time, the analysis presented here offers important lessons on the uses and misuses of human rights language. Although the ethical and humanistic ideals at the core of the international human rights regime are increasingly gaining universal acceptance, the legitimizing language of human rights has been used to pursue goals that have more to do with the international politics of power and resistance, as well as the interests of ruling regimes, than with the welfare and empowerment of ordinary citizens. We need to seriously consider the morally troubling outcomes that arise when human rights are co-opted by authority structures in ways that serve more to enhance their power than to alleviate human suffering.

QUESTIONS FOR REFLECTION AND DISCUSSION

1. Should a right to development exist in the normative sense? Why? Why not?
2. Ibhawoh states that the DRD defined the right to development as "an inalienable human right by virtue of which every human person and all peoples are entitled to participate in, contribute to, and enjoy economic, social, cultural and political development, in which all human rights and fundamental freedoms can be fully realized." Do you agree with this definition? Why? Why not? How would you define the right to development? In your answer, consider how your wording will lead to your desired application of the right in practice.
3. What is the difference between the individual right to development and the collective right to development? What are the implications of each? What duties and obligations does each create? Which does the North support and why? Which does the South support and why?
4. Ibhawoh argues that "the basic problem that has bedeviled the elaboration and implementation of the right to development goes beyond the all-encompassing nature of the right or even the language in which it is embodied. Part of the problem is the political and ideological jockeying that underscores the discourse on the right to development. This holds larger implications for international human rights because the language of human rights has become a principal means of legitimizing complex and contradictory political and social agendas." Do you agree with the conclusion that the language of human rights operates in the way Ibhawoh suggests? Why? Why not? What evidence and/or sources can you draw upon to support your position?
5. Are human rights merely politics by another name? Draw upon readings in this book and elsewhere to support your position. Then ask the same question about law. Would your answers differ? Why? Why not?

6. What characterized the dichotomy between development and human rights? How did this change, and why? What do you understand the relationship to be between development and human rights as a normative matter, and why?

7. What role does the global political economy play in the discursive tensions surrounding the right to development? What tensions can you identify with particular relevance to globalization and the shape of the international legal order? If you revisit the arguments of Dean and of Badiou drawn upon by Marks in Chapter 5, Reading 26, do you gain any insights into the relationships between democracy, development, globalization, and political economy? If so, what? Are they helpful? Why? Why not?

8. In your view, should development be understood primarily as a question of meeting basic needs? Should it be understood as the prioritization of realizing certain socioeconomic rights? What kind of regime is required for this approach? Is a "regime based on concessional aid rather than the sharing of productive resources and technology" adequate? Why? Why not? Upon what value commitments does your position rely?

9. In your view, should development be understood to demand "giving priority in development policies to participation and political transformations, as opposed to basic needs"? Why? Why not?

10. Should development be understood to necessitate "political transformation and democracy in international relations"? Why? Why not? And which conception of democracy is assumed in your response? Based on what?

11. What are the strengths and weaknesses of a rights-based approach to development? What does Ibhawoh say? What conception of rights is assumed by Ibhawoh's argument? Do you accept it? Why? Why not?

12. Ibhawoh concludes that the analysis of the tensions inhabiting the right to development highlights "important lessons on the uses and misuses of human rights language. Although the ethical and humanistic ideals at the core of the international human rights regime are increasingly gaining universal acceptance, the legitimizing language of human rights has been used to pursue goals that have more to do with the international politics of power and resistance, as well as the interests of ruling regimes, than with the welfare and empowerment of ordinary citizens. We need to seriously consider the morally troubling outcomes that arise when human rights are co-opted by authority structures in ways that serve more to enhance their power than to alleviate human suffering." Do you agree? Why? Why not?

13. Do you think Ibhawoh is right to accept the idea that the "ethical and humanistic ideals at the core of the international human rights regime are increasingly gaining universal acceptance"? Or is that too sweeping an assumption? Why? Why not?

24. CONOR GEARTY *Do Human Rights Help or Hinder Environmental Protection?*

THE CASE FOR HINDRANCE

For many detached observers, the immediate response to the question our title poses would be that of course human rights hinder environmental protection. The subject of human rights is, as it declares for all to see in the way that it describes itself, a field that is concerned not only with humans but also with the rights that flow from being human, rather than from being anything else: not an animal (even a Great Ape) or a fish for example, and certainly not a tree or a habitat or a lake, no matter how (objectively) magnificent. Indeed the subject of human rights is so focused on the singular human that it has historically had a great deal of trouble even with the fact of there being more than one human around. The origins of the subject in its modern form lie in the work of scholars like Thomas Hobbes, whose vision of the individual as an autonomous entity fighting to survive in a hostile state of nature has penetrated to the core of the

Reprinted with changes by permission of Edward Elgar Publishing from Conor Gearty, "Do Human Rights Help or Hinder Environmental Protection?" *Journal of Human Rights and the Environment* 1 (2010): 7–22. Copyright © Edward Elgar Publishing. Conor Gearty is professor of human rights law and former director of the Centre for the Study of Human Rights at the London School of Economics.

way the field is constructed today. In standard contemporary accounts of human rights from a philosophical perspective, the discussion is invariably about the self-fulfillment of the individual, his or her ability to set goals for leading a full life and then being free to go on to achieve those targets. The debate is about what are the necessary building blocks of such a successful life; it is not about what that life can or ought to do to make the world around it a better place, even for others to live in, much less simply for the planet's sake.

This separateness of each and every human, one from the other, has caused human rights to struggle to create a credible theory of how humans can sensibly get along together in a way that accords with their individualistically based human rights[1]—the arguments are still being gone over today, with their modern form being in the shape of questions about how you can reconcile democracy and human rights, majority rule with judicial oversight. One of the tricks employed by human rights activists in the past to get over this problem of individual self-absorption and therefore to secure support for marginalized people—native Americans, for example—has been to contrast their plight with that of animals, to the benefit of the human for sure but at a cost to the nonhuman living community, the whole point of insisting that you should not treat people like animals being that if they were animals it would be absolutely fine to exploit, beat, and treat them as you desired. If a subject has such trouble even with the idea of extending rights to all humans, and has needed the bad treatment of animals to make moral progress, how far is it from grasping that there are more than humans out there in need of support and protection, and that beyond even the nonhuman animals there are nonsentient living things capable of imposing moral demands even at a price to the achievement of the successful life to which so much human rights work is committed?

The law on human rights provides little relief from this philosophical speciesism. The idea of the world outside the human as being inherently capable of belonging to the individual, and

therefore as being something over which complete human mastery can be exercised, is one that is very deeply entrenched in the law in capitalist society in general and the English common law in particular. It took many struggles in the course of the nineteenth and early twentieth centuries to secure proper legal recognition of the humanity of slaves and of women, and therefore to see them as more than merely the property of their owners.[2] A subject in such difficulty with the simple question of what it means to be human is unlikely to have reached the point that it can accommodate serious challenges to the ownership of nonhuman property, and it is indeed the case that the history of human rights law is pockmarked by its deployment in defense of liberty against regulation, even where such regulation is manifestly in the public interest. With increased environmental awareness leading to proposals for legislation designed to protect the environment as such, predictable legal arguments have emerged emphasizing the human right to property and at very least the need for compensation before action can be taken. The property rights-based structure of our legal system has been a great inhibitor of action on the environmental front, and it is not unfair to characterize it as a position that is rooted in a human rights approach, not one progressives might like or share, but a human rights-based approach nonetheless. International law has made a different but in some ways also problematic contribution.

Of course, the human rights commitment shown by the international community, reflected in the deepening of the framework for the protection of international human rights standards, has been admirable. But it has come at a certain price, which has been the strengthening of the position of sovereign states, and in particular the integrity of the independence of governments over the geographic areas that states have been able to call their own. Human rights law is not responsible for this withdrawal of international engagement from internal affairs, of course, but it has been what has made it possible: respect for human rights has been the quid pro quo for national sovereignty in the

---

1. *Eds.*—For a pertinent though modest attempt in this struggle, see Burns H. Weston, "The Theoretical Foundations of Intergenerational Ecological Justice: An Overview," *HRQ* 34 (2012): 251–66.

2. The classic example with regard to race is the U.S. Supreme Court decision determining that slaves were in law the property of their masters, *Dred Scott v. Sandford*, 60 U.S. 393 (1856), 60 U.S. 393 (How).

global settlement achieved in the aftermath of the Second World War. Even the enforcement of human rights within member states has been slight, with the UN system not providing any real bite to back up the plethora of treaties that it has so enthusiastically endorsed, and outside the field of human rights (environmental protection for example) the problem of national sovereignty has been a very real one, hindering the emergence of the kind of global (or at least regional) solutions that many kinds of environmental challenges now clearly require.

This species-centered trend is exemplified by the Declaration on the Right to Development (DRD), proclaimed by the UN General Assembly in 1986. Here is a document which may have seemed like great progress when it was promulgated, but in these times of anxiety about climate change and the over-exploitation of the world's resources, its ringing phrases now have what can perhaps least unkindly be called a dated ring.

Article 1
1. The right to development is an inalienable human right by virtue of which every human person and all peoples are entitled to participate in, contribute to, and enjoy economic, social, cultural and political development, in which all human rights and fundamental freedoms can be fully realized.
2. The human right to development also implies the full realization of the right of peoples to self-determination, which includes, subject to the relevant provisions of both International Covenants on Human Rights, the exercise of their inalienable right to full sovereignty over all their natural wealth and resources.

Article 2
1.3. The human person is the central subject of development and should be the active participant and beneficiary of the right to development.

What is depressing for present purposes is that while this right to development has certainly been controversial in the human rights community, this has been mainly on account of its breadth and the degree of the obligation it places, if any, on developed countries to assist developing nations. The issue has not been about the potential damage that is done by such a profoundly human-oriented approach to the world's resources—explicable perhaps in human rights terms, but worryingly narrow nevertheless. The human rights-respecting nations began this destruction of the world just around the same time they were adopting their various rights charters, the argument runs, so why should these states be allowed now to slow down the growth of nations whose only "fault" has been to have their own progress stymied by colonial domination?

We can conclude this section by acknowledging that the debit side of the human rights account clearly stacks up against its value in the field of environmental protection. But this is by no means the end of the story; the subject of human rights did not achieve the transdisciplinary power it enjoys today by being easily tied down. The phrase oozes with multiple meanings, of which we have so far only referred to three (those rooted in philosophy, constitutional law, and international law). There are international relations approaches which see human rights as a tool of diplomacy and as such are neither here nor there from an environmental point of view—unless they underpin military invasions with all the astonishing environmental damage that such marauding entails (among its many other excesses). Anthropological perspectives are more benign but similarly off-center so far as the environment is concerned, save insofar as they have assisted in the emergence of the concept of the rights of indigenous peoples, a point of important convergence between our two subject areas. There is one approach, however, that fits more comfortably than these, and that suggests we should be careful before we write off entirely the possibility of effective support between our two fields.

HELP AT HAND

The discipline of sociology is often thought of as inimical to human rights, but in its subversion of the established fields we can detect a possible route to effective mutual reciprocity as between our two areas of enquiry. The sociological attitude to human rights is relaxed about finding truth and happy to delink itself from the certainties of law and philosophy. It sees human rights as a term whose meaning is constructed, not discovered, and which is therefore capable of change, indeed has changed over the generations, and will alter again in the future—is constantly on the move, in fact. A core feature of this approach is concern about the abuse of power. It sees human rights as a subject which has a long and noble tradition as a galvanizer of resistance to oppression. Its heroes are not just the American and French revolutionaries who overthrew external and internal domination in the name of human rights but also the abolitionists and universal suffragists of the nineteenth century, with a special place of honor being reserved for the rebellious slaves whose courageous uprising led to the foundation of Haiti in 1804. This brand of human rights sees the term as a phrase around which positions of opposition to power can be articulated, new bonds of solidarity can be garnered, and fresh versions of right and justice can be launched on a disbelieving world.

Proponents of this vibrant, fluctuating, intentionally indefinable approach to human rights are always at risk of veering into cynicism. They acknowledge that revolutions go wrong, that human rights victories can turn to defeat in the hands of human-rights-warriors-turned-despots. They recognize that the powerful are often better equipped to deploy the language to suit themselves, that law and philosophy can be turned against them to justify human rights abuses in the name of human rights, so they are always quick (and often right) to view state action in negative terms. But what keeps them going is a belief in the power of the language of human rights to achieve radical change, to challenge real injustice and to build a new and better world. With the eclipse of socialism as the dominant progressive ideology of our time, standing up for human rights has become all the more appealing such that human rights has somehow managed to grow in prestige while all around it other progressive projects have been knocked back.

Expressed in these terms, the link between human rights and environmental activism is much easier to make. In their commitment to change, their attitude to power and in their mode of organizing, human rights groups resemble the green and environmental activists who have done so much to bring the need for environmental protection to public attention. Indeed, the human rights movement could learn a great deal from the environmentalists in this regard, not least how to think about human rights. For one of the interesting aspects of comparing

these two social movements is to see quite how imaginatively and in tactical terms astutely the environmentalists have used the language of rights. They have been much better—more creative—than the human rights people themselves. As Neil Stammers puts it in his excellent study of human rights and social movements, "activists from a wide variety of social movements have been . . . showing us how to think about human rights for a very long time [and that] the green movement . . . has generated a range of claims to environmental rights and environmental justice."[3]

This is where we begin to see the first indicators of a convergence between human rights and environmental protection. The link between human and environmental rights was first made in 1972 at the Stockholm Conference on the Human Environment [as reflected in its influential, ground-breaking declaration[4]]—the first phase of the environmental movement, which was largely dissipated by the economic recession that began in 1973 and continued through much of the 1970s, so that it was not until the 1992 Earth Summit in Rio de Janeiro that a framework for environmental and human rights emerged, in the form of the Rio Declaration and the Agenda 21 Plan of Action.[5] Buoyed by this new interest, the UN Special Rapporteur on Human Rights and the Environment for the Sub-Commission on the Prevention of Discrimination and Protection of Minorities released an important account of the relationship between human rights and the environment, making the link between human rights abuses and environmental damage more explicitly than had ever previously been done at an official level.[6] So far as the NGO sector is concerned, this being our primary interest at this juncture, the major breakthrough was the publication in 2004 of

3. Neil Stammers, *Human Rights and Social Movements* (London: Pluto, 2009), 145.
4. See 1972 Stockholm Declaration on the Human Environment.
5. Rio Declaration on Environment and Development, 13 June 1992; Agenda 21, 13 June 1992.
6. Commission on Human Rights, Sub-Commission on Prevention of Discrimination and Protection of Minorities, Review of Further Developments in Fields with Which the Sub-Commission Has Been Concerned: Human Rights and the Environment, Final Report Prepared by Special Rapporteur General, Fatma Zohra Ksentini, UN Doc. E/CN.4/Sub.2/1994/9.

Friends of the Earth International's *Our Environment, Our Rights: Standing Up for People and the Planet* (the FoEI Report).[7]

There are a number of points of real interest about this report from a social movement perspective. They show us a method of "doing human rights" that works from an environmental point of view.

First, there is the way in which the authors cleverly link the delivery of human rights to environmental protection: it is "access to . . . unspoiled natural resources that enable survival, including land, shelter, food, water and air."[8] Thus can pollution control and environmental integrity be recast as mechanisms of enforcement of human rights, standing not behind human rights as informing meta-values explaining why human rights matter (which would be impossible) but rather functioning as sine qua non conditions of existence for the realization of much of the human rights agenda. The Universal Declaration of Human Rights (UDHR) presupposes a functioning, human-friendly planet when it asserts the various rights to which (rather blithely we can now see) it declares all humanity to be entitled. The more fleshed-out provisions of the Covenant on Economic, Social and Cultural Rights precede the emergence of the modern environmental movement but its ambitious road map to a better world, including many of the rights highlighted in the FoEI Report, are made contingent as a matter of practicality on each state party undertaking "to take steps, individually and through international assistance and co-operation, especially economical and technical, to the maximum of its available resources, with a view to achieving progressively the full realization of the rights recognized in the present Covenant by all appropriate means."[9] The phrase specifically emphasized here is the door through which concerns about the environment can enter the human rights calculus. But it is a small opening compared to the seemingly authorized plunder of the first sentence of Article 1.2 declaring that "All peoples may, for their own ends, freely dispose of their natural wealth and resources without prejudice to any obligations arising out of international economic co-operation, based upon the principle of mutual benefit, and international law." The FoEI report is right to point to the premise of a functioning planet that underpins all human rights, but (a feature . . . of the historical moment when the core international human rights law was being formed) it is an unspoken one, we might say today somewhat recklessly assumed. The FoEI Report reminds us that it is one of the challenges facing the social movements—of both environmental and human rights complexions—namely to force it farther into the open.

The second observation to make about the Report is that it is impressively aware that "Environmental rights go hand-in-hand with civil and political rights."[10] The point is easy to miss: in the world of human rights there are these so-called "first-generation" rights which underpin the commitment of proponents of human rights to the principles of democratic government and the rule of law. Together with respect for human dignity, these two principles make up the three foundations of the modern human rights movement. It is tempting in the environmental context to move directly to the economic and social, bypassing the civil and political as being concerned with a different set of issues. But access to courts, the ability to protest, and the capacity to obtain information are all central features of the struggle to achieve better environmental protection. This has been more obvious now than ever before, this being a time when those who care about the environment have needed to work hard, take risks, and sometimes profoundly annoy and aggravate in order to grab the world's attention. Even in democratic countries guided by the rule of law and informed by respect for human dignity, this has not been an easy matter: protest has been prohibited and then disrupted, protesters beaten, arrested, often jailed. In non-democratic countries matters have been of course much worse.

Third, there is the FoEI Report's healthily pragmatic approach to human rights, its understanding that "the existing human rights declarations and covenants do carry significant moral weight, and can be used to bring global attention to violations happening in the most remote corners of the earth"[11] and that this strength can be turned to good environmental effect. Successful

7. See www.foei.org/en/publications/pdfs/climate . . . /human_rights.pdf [*Eds.*—accessed 12 June 2015].
8. Ibid., 5.
9. Art. 2.1.
10. Note 6, 6.
11. Ibid.

social movements are absolutists in the pursuit of their interests but invariably open-minded about how they can be realized. Their attitude to human rights therefore is different from that of the human rights activists: these human entitlements are more a better set of tools with which to do the job in hand than they are the job itself. Protecting human rights is the point of departure for where you want to be, not the place where you hope to arrive. It is part of the consequence of the success of the human rights movement that its minders spend so much time fighting hijackers, but there are surely worse usurpers around than the environmental movement. Like the sociologist, environmental activists see human rights as fluid and (in a good way) volatile and unstable. Unlike the lawyers they roam beyond the documentation to find new rights. Unlike the philosophers they do not pass their projects through a test rooted in historical or rational consistency. What matters is what works and what can be achieved. Thus having rehearsed the litany of standard rights, the FoEI report continues, "We also believe in the right to claim reparations for violated rights, including rights for climate refugees and others displaced by environmental destruction, the right to claim ecological debt, and the right to environmental justice."[12] And then there is the following:

> Many of these rights, particularly the political ones, are well-established and enshrined in various conventions and agreements. We can credit the establishment of some of these rights, as well as the acceptance of others that are not yet legally recognized, to the ongoing struggles of communities and indigenous peoples around the world. Other "new" rights, including rights for climate refugees, have arisen over recent years due to the acceleration of economic globalization and the accompanying environmental destruction and social disruption. Still others, like the right to claim ecological debt, have emerged as the result of years of campaigning by Friends of the Earth and others for the recognition of the impacts of northern resource depletion and natural destruction in southern countries. All of these rights are equally important, and they are all interdependent. Environmental rights are human rights, as

> people's livelihoods, their health and sometimes their very existence depend upon the quality of and their access to the surrounding environment as well as the recognition of their rights to information, participation, security and redress.[13]

The extract stands as a classic exposition of the positive effect of combining human rights and environmental activism. In particular the idea of rights already (as it were) in the legal womb, waiting to be born, breaks the grip that the old documents have on the subject, opening it up to respond to the need for "new rights" to reflect not changes in human nature exactly but rather alterations in the habitat in which that nature has to exist. There is also the understanding that rights flow not from the discovery of some hitherto inaccessible truth but rather from struggle and the fighting of political battles, a classic sociological insight. Once we see human rights and environmental protection as forms of activism driven by a desire to make the world a better place both for its own sake and for the sake of all who live on it (animals [including humans] among them), we can see that there are in fact close bonds between the two fields, and that human rights are a help rather than a hindrance to progress in the environmental field.

AN INTERNATIONAL RIGHT TO ENVIRONMENTAL PROTECTION?

Agenda 21, the Rio Declaration on Environment and Development, and the Statement of Principles for the Sustainable Management of Forests were adopted by the United Nations Conference on Environment and Development, the famous Rio Conference referred to earlier, held in 1992.[14] The first principle declared that "Human beings are at the centre of concerns for sustainable development. They are entitled to a healthy and productive life in harmony with nature." Much of the Declaration is concerned with controlling the impact of sovereign power and the right to development so as to build in some environmental sensitivity into their mode of operation. Principle 5 has a strong human rights dimension: "All States and all people shall coop-

12. Ibid., 5.

13. Ibid.
14. See text following note 4.

erate in the essential task of eradicating poverty as an indispensable requirement for sustainable development, in order to decrease the disparities in standards of living and better meet the needs of the majority of the people of the world." In terms of explicit human rights, however, the closest the document gets is when it asserts entitlements to information in Principle 10. There is also this anticipation of a strong future human rights trend in Principle 22:

> Indigenous people and their communities and other local communities have a vital role in environmental management and development because of their knowledge and traditional practices. States should recognize and duly support their identity, culture and interests and enable their effective participation in the achievement of sustainable development.

It is perhaps understandable that the finalized declaration did not include any generalized "right to a good environment"—it is hard to see what credibility such an assertion would have enjoyed and its appearance may well have added little to what was already being addressed. The report of the Special Rapporteur on Human Rights and the Environment, Mrs. Fatma Zohra Ksentini, in July 1994, did include a draft Principle to the effect that "All persons have the right to a secure, healthy and ecologically sound environment" and that "This right and other human rights, including civil, cultural, economic, political and social rights, are universal, interdependent and indivisible" (Principle 2 in Annex 1).[15] The report also asserted that "All persons have the right to an environment adequate to meet equitably the needs of present generations and that does not impair the rights of future generations to meet equitably their needs" (Principle 4).

Viewed overall, however, less progress in this generalized field has been achieved than might perhaps have been first thought possible in the early 1990s. It is true that Article 24 of the African Charter on Human and Peoples' Rights states that "All people shall have the right to a general satisfactory environment favourable to their development." The Additional Protocol to the American Convention on Human Rights (San José, 1969), which relates to economic, social and cultural rights, adopted at San Salvador in

1988, also contains a clause concerning the right to an environment, Article 11 providing that "everyone shall have the right to live in a healthy environment and to have access to basic public services," the states parties then being required to promote the protection, preservation, and improvement of the environment. The Convention on the Rights of the Child, dated 20 November 1989, explicitly refers to the need for the education of the child to be directed, inter alia, to "the development of respect for the natural environment" (Article 29, para. (e)). But this hardly amounts to a strong momentum toward a new legal framework.

The UN Declaration on the Rights of Indigenous Peoples, adopted by the General Assembly in September 2007, provides protection for the environment in the time-honored human rights way of looking at habitat through people. One of the driving forces behind this declaration was the realization, acknowledged in its preamble, "that respect for indigenous knowledge, cultures and traditional practices contributes to sustainable and equitable development and proper management of the environment." The document itself has plenty of good things to say about fostering these communities, seeking to protect them before destruction becomes their way of life as well. Article 29 is most specific about the linkage between the two:

> 1. Indigenous peoples have the right to the conservation and protection of the environment and the productive capacity of their lands or territories and resources. States shall establish and implement assistance programmes for indigenous peoples for such conservation and protection, without discrimination.
>
> 2. States shall take effective measures to ensure that no storage or disposal of hazardous materials shall take place in the lands or territories of indigenous peoples without their free, prior and informed consent.
>
> 3. States shall also take effective measures to ensure, as needed, that programmes for monitoring, maintaining and restoring the health of indigenous peoples, as developed and implemented by the peoples affected by such materials, are duly implemented.

We may conclude that the overall international human rights law record in this field is pretty modest. This is not necessarily a bad thing in it-

15. Note 5.

self. The risk in too much apparent success in this sphere is that the right to environmental protection joins the ranks of those other human rights guarantees which are more honored in the breach than in the observance, with weak governmental commitment and ineffective enforcement structures combining to make the supposed advance worse than useless.[16]

16. [*Eds.*—Two leading essays on the right to environment appear to share a perspective more sanguine than the author's "pretty modest" assessment. The first, by Luis E. Rodriguez-Rivera, contends that a human right to environment may be said to exist based on "hard law" sources backed by the voluminous "soft law" expressions of environmental protection that have emerged worldwide in recent years. Luis E. Rodriguez-Rivera, "Is the Human Right to Environment Recognized Under International Law?" *Colorado Journal of International Environmental Law and Policy* 12 (2001): 1–45. The second, by Dinah Shelton, observes the existence of the right to environment in three different formulations around the world based principally on treaties and national case law: (1) as an entitlement derived from other substantive rights, (2) as a substantive right autonomous unto itself, and (3) as a cluster of procedural entitlements. Dinah Shelton, "Human Rights and the Environment: What Specific Environmental Rights Have Been Recognized?" *Denver Journal of International Law and Policy* 35 (2006): 129–71.

In a more recent essay on the right to environment, however, Burns Weston corroborates the author's precedent conclusion and the perceived risk he identified. See Burns H. Weston, "The International Legal Status of the Human Right to a Clean and Healthy Environment," addendum to Burns H. Weston and David Bollier, *Green Governance: Ecological Survival, Human Rights, and the Law of the Commons* (New York: CUP, 2013), 285–336. His essential arguments are: *first*, that the international policy- and decision-making elites who define the substance and procedure of human rights simply have yet to recognize the combined hard and soft law authority on which the right is said to stand sufficiently to count as law universally or, indeed, as international law at all; *second*, that, in any event, and regardless of formulation, the right's standing in the current state sovereignty system is essentially limited in official jurisdictional reach. None of this, Weston and Bollier argue in a companion essay, should surprise: "In our highly decentralized and far too voluntarist international legal order, it is the commercial and statist imperatives of the contemporary global political-economy that repeatedly trump human rights and environmental values." Burns H. Weston and David Bollier, "Toward a Recalibrated Human Right to A Clean and Healthy Environment: Making the Conceptual Transition," *JHRE* 4 (2013): 116–42. Indeed, they continue, "as long as ecological governance remains in the grip of essentially unregulated (liberal or neoliberal) capitalism—responsible for most of the plunder and theft of our ecological wealth over the last century and a

CONCLUSION: MUTUAL RECIPROCITY AS A NECESSARY FUTURE

The need to bring the environmental and human rights movements together has been rendered both urgent and vital by the impending climate change catastrophe. For just as the human rights protagonist has often given the impression that he or she does not care about the natural world, so too have some environmentalists seemed at times to despise people. There is in such activists a potential casualness about humankind which may be understandable emotionally (it is our reckless species which has brought us to the verge of collapse) but which when worked through into policies and positions will—if left unchallenged—invariably involve the poor and the vulnerable (whose personal responsibility for environmental change is nonexistent) paying a heavy price for the polluting and destructive recklessness of others. It will be the

half—there never will be a human right to environment widely honoured across the globe in any official sense, least of all an autonomous one as currently, essentially loosely, conceived" (118). Accordingly, they propose a "recalibrated" human right to environment "anchored in a cognizably well-defined, rich history of both substantive and procedural justice" (119)—to wit, *a human right to commons- and rights-based ecological governance* (or "Green Governance," as they call it): "it is important," they urge, "to reimagine and establish the human right to environment in a form and substance different from current incarnations" (120). The inclusive human right to commons- and rights-based ecological governance constitutes such a right, they assert, "embracing as it does structural and procedural issues equally with normative ones, thereby better integrating with people's everyday social and production experiences and practices. Moreover, it does not privilege any right or cluster of rights (liberty, equality, or solidarity rights) over another except as a particular fact or context warrants" (120). The proposed right also affirms, they assert, what Sam Adelman might call a "meta right"—a foundational right that would, where necessary, take precedence over other rights notwithstanding the problematic of "a hierarchy at odds with the assertion that all rights are equal and indivisible"—or, in Adelman's alternative words, "a 'species right' (a new category of . . . right which transcends traditional categorizations, highlights the truly universal nature of the threat, and which we hold not simply as individual human beings but rather by virtue of our membership [in] the species homo sapiens" (ibid.), quoting originally from Sam Adelman, "Rethinking Human Rights: The Impact of Climate Change on the Dominant Discourse," in Stephen Humphreys, ed., *Human Rights and Climate Change* (Cambridge: CUP, 2010), 159–80, 159.

Maldives that disappears, the Bangladeshi millions who will find their homes inundated, and the Inuit whose habitats will be destroyed. To put this another way, an approach to meeting the climate change challenge which is indifferent to human suffering will inevitably lead to decisions in which the world's poor are once again made to pay a price for the selfishness of others. The human rights approach can stop this happening. By focusing on equality and respect for individual dignity, an insistence on attention to human rights has the effect of forcing all decision-makers to look outside their own circle, to see the human as well as the global consequences of their actions. It is an essential ethical component of a proper response to climate change.

And what can the environmentalist offer human rights in return? The problem with all branches of human rights is lack of confidence in the foundations of the subject. There are historical reasons for this: a commitment to equal dignity made sense when the field was dominated by an explicitly Judeo-Christian ethic, but in the postreligious world (where most human rights activism is to be found) this theological basis for belief in equality is much harder to sustain. Why are we all equal? Why should not one be favored over the other? What is so wrong about abusing power if you are lucky enough to have it? Human rights thinkers are far from being able to answer these questions effectively, but thinking hard about the embedded nature of humans in the world around them at least points the enquiry in the right direction. It is only through reflecting upon our species as a part of the natural world that we can come to a renewed sense of the wonder of our existence and the beauty (as well as the immense productivity) of our seemingly innate propensity to think about others as well as solely about ourselves and our kin. And if we can expand our horizons to include an imaginative leap beyond the living into the realm of the billions of as yet unborn (indeed not yet conceived) humans of the future, we will be able to see that here is a vast category of the powerless who demand our attention. Our empathy with the other is one of our finest attributes and it is through the language of human rights that it finds a highly effective because universal form of contemporary expression. But its innateness does not mean that its manifestation cannot be greatly reduced by the social situation in which it finds itself. The survival of our species without the loss of our precarious commitment to goodness is surely enough of a foundation for human rights today.

QUESTIONS FOR REFLECTION AND DISCUSSION

1. According to Gearty, what implications do the origins of human rights bear for the ability of human rights to respond adequately to environmental challenges? Do you agree with Gearty on this point? Why? Why not? Do human rights amount to "philosophical speciesism"? Is it possible to imagine the "human" subject at the heart of human rights in ecologically oriented ways? What theories might you call on to defend your position on these questions?

2. Gearty suggests that "The sociological attitude to human rights is relaxed about finding truth and happy to delink itself from the certainties of law and philosophy. It sees human rights as a term whose meaning is constructed, not discovered, and which is therefore capable of change, indeed has changed over the generations, and will alter again in the future—is constantly on the move in fact." Is this a helpful approach? Or is it too destabilizing? If you think it is the latter, what precisely does it destabilize? How, in general, might an emphasis upon the social construction of meaning assist—or reduce—the impact of human rights? Substantiate your answer as carefully as you can.

3. How have the languages of environmental protection and human rights converged? What sources can you draw upon to demonstrate this? What sources does Gearty draw upon? Can you supplement them? If so, how? In what senses have the languages failed to converge? Can you find evidence to support the idea that there is still a gap between human rights and environmental protection regimes? If so, what?

4. How do environmental rights go "hand in hand" with civil and political rights?

5. Does a human right to the environment exist? If so, based on what? And in which form(s)?

6. Gearty argues that "an approach to meeting the climate change challenge which is indifferent to human suffering will inevitably lead to decisions in which the world's poor are once again made to pay a price for the selfishness of others." The human rights approach can stop this happening, he argues. "By focusing on equality and respect for individual dignity, an insistence on attention to human rights has the effect of forcing all decision-makers to look outside their own circle, to see the human as well as the global consequences of their actions. It is an essential ethical component of a proper response to climate change." Do you agree? If so, why? If not, why not?

7. Do you think that human rights are an adequate response to the complexities of the climate crisis? Or are they too flawed to assist? Substantiate your response as carefully as you can.

8. How can human rights law, discourse, and imagination be expanded so as to be adequate to the climate crisis? What values or theories do you draw upon in order to answer this question?

9. What is Green Governance? How does it address the current issues of environmental rights? What would Gearty think about Green Governance? Is Green Governance focused on the individual human, like the other human rights approaches to environmental rights that Gearty previously criticized, or not?

10. As the editors note below (n 16), Weston and Bollier assert that the human right to commons- and rights-based ecological governance is a meta right or a species right. Given that, in theory, all human rights are deemed equal and interdependent, is this appropriate? Risky? Are civil and political rights meta rights in the industrialized Global North? If so, should they be? If not, why not? Are there objective criteria according to which one may legitimately designate meta human rights? If yes, what are they? If no, why not?

11. In his conclusion, Gearty argues that in the post-religious world (without, for example, a Judeo-Christian theological basis for equal dignity), human rights thinkers and activists can find spiritual satisfaction in the environment and the survival of the human race. Do you agree with Gearty? Why? Why not? Where do you think the basis for equal dignity can be found?

25. DOUGLAS ROCHE *Peace: A Sacred Right*

The work already accomplished in the UN system to develop the concept of the human right to peace is one of the world's best-kept secrets. The culture of war so pervades public opinion that it has drowned out voices asserting that the human right to peace is a fundamental right of every human being and is, in fact, the major precondition for all human rights. The time has come to emphasize that the peoples of the world have a sacred right to peace.

That very concept—"the peoples of our planet have a sacred right to peace"—was inserted into

the first operative paragraph in the Declaration on the Right of Peoples to Peace, adopted by the UN General Assembly on 12 November 1984.[1] One does not need to be reminded of the countless deaths in wars that have occurred in the [three] decades following. Such a recounting does not invalidate the UN Declaration, it only underlines the point that this right needs to be better understood before procedures are developed to enforce it under the rule of law.

The intimate linkage between human rights and peace was first recognized in the Preamble and in Articles 1 and 55 of the UN Charter; in

Excerpted with changes by permission of Novalis, Saint Paul University, from Douglas Roche, *The Human Right to Peace* (Toronto: Novalis, 2003), 122–44. Copyright © 2003 Novalis, Saint Paul University, Ottawa.

1. United Nations General Assembly Declaration on the Right of Peoples to Peace, 12 November 1984.

Article 28 of the Universal Declaration of Human Rights (UDHR); and in the Covenant on Civil and Political Rights (ICCPR), and the Covenant on Economic, Cultural and Social Rights (ICESCR). The Preamble to the Charter, in stirring language evoked by the ashes of World War II, affirms that the peoples of the UN are determined "to practice tolerance and live together in peace with one another as good neighbours." Article 1 proclaims as the first purpose of the UN the maintenance of international peace and security. Written a few years later, the Preamble to the UDHR states: "The recognition of the inherent dignity and the equal and inalienable rights of all members of the human family is the foundation of freedom, justice and peace in the world." These documents affirm the right of states to peace through a "peace system" with the primary goal being the preservation of peace and a respect for human rights as essential to the development of friendly relations among nations.

Taken together, these documents provide a basis for the human right to peace, but it was not until 1978, when the UN General Assembly adopted the Declaration on the Preparation of Societies for Life in Peace, that the right to peace began to take shape in a more formal way. The Declaration states:

> every human being, regardless of race, conscience, language or sex, has the inherent right to life in peace. Respect for that right, as well as for the other human rights, is in the common interest of all mankind and an indispensable condition of advancement of all nations, large and small, in all fields.

The Declaration calls on countries to ensure that their international and national policies are directed toward achieving life in peace, especially with regard to younger generations. This emphasis on national duty and youth would become the central element in later elaborations of the right to peace.

The Declaration was given a boost with the 1981 African Charter on Human and Peoples' Rights, which proclaimed that all peoples have the right to national and international peace and security. Article 3 declared firmly: "Human beings are inviolable. Every human being shall be entitled to respect for his life and the integrity of his person. No one may be arbitrarily deprived of this right."

Like its 1978 counterpart adopted by the General Assembly, the African Charter places the onus for ensuring the right to peace on governments, but also emphasizes the individual citizen's duty to work toward the right to peace.

Subsequently, the UN General Assembly adopted the Declaration on the Right of Peoples to Peace in 1984.[2] After affirming the principle that "the peoples of our planet have a sacred right to peace," the resolution "declares that the preservation of the right of peoples to peace constitute[s] a fundamental obligation of each State." The Declaration went on to state that the exercise of this right demands "the elimination of the threat of war," particularly nuclear war. (It was undoubtedly this reference to the elimination of the threat of nuclear war that caused multiple abstentions by Western states. Although the vote was 92 in favor and none opposed, there were 34 abstentions and the Declaration could not be implemented.) Although the Declaration does not explicitly declare the right to peace as a "human right," it can be argued that its intent was just that. This is clear in the assertion that "life without war serves as the primary international prerequisite for the material well-being, development and progress of countries, and for the full implementation of the rights and fundamental human freedoms proclaimed by the United Nations." In this statement, the right to peace is considered the fundamental prerequisite for the fulfillment of other basic rights. For instance, the Declaration understands that economic development is only possible in the presence of peace. It links human rights, development, and peace as three conditions that cannot exist in isolation from one another. Simply stated, without peace, every other right is illusory. Thus—and in retrospect—even in 1984 the UN was responding to a changing international environment with the kind of innovative thinking needed to lift up humanity to confront the challenges of globalization.

A MAJOR DIPLOMATIC EFFORT

Only with the end of the Cold War in the 1990s did work toward the right to peace grow from a few sentences in international agree-

2. UN GA Res. 39/11 (12 November 1984).

ments into a major diplomatic effort. This new push was, in part, a product of the hopeful climate surrounding the end of the superpower rivalry. However, the 1997 Declaration of a Human Right to Peace by UNESCO Director-General Federico Mayor[3] was very much a response to the many conflicts that had consumed one society after another earlier in the decade. The wars in Iraq, Somalia, Yugoslavia, Rwanda, and elsewhere left a sense that the international community had taken a wrong turn after the end of the Cold War and was missing a golden opportunity to build a better foundation for peace. This window of opportunity was the driving force behind the UNESCO Director-General's call to get back on track and build the lasting conditions for peace within two or three years.

Mayor's Declaration was different from past elaborations of the right to peace in that it not only confirmed the importance of peace as the precursor of all other rights, but also laid out a strategy to achieve it. The plan called for energies to be refocused on the systemic and root causes of conflict so that conflicts can be tackled in the early stages and the kind of out-of-control bloodletting that had characterized recent conflicts may be avoided.

Of course, to achieve the right to peace, it is first necessary to make the transition from a culture of war to a culture of peace. Mayor's Declaration realizes that the international community cannot simultaneously absorb the cost of war and the cost of peace. The Declaration is thus a wake-up call of sorts in that it puts the spotlight on a dangerously flawed international order and calls upon us to do what is necessary to build a more peaceful one. Not only is this necessary for our very survival, but since peace is "a prerequisite for the exercise of all human rights and duties," it is also our right.

The means to achieve this right are divided in the Declaration into two concurrent strategies. First, the Declaration calls for immediate action on urgent issues such as poverty, environmental destruction, and international justice, and it calls upon the international community to provide the UN system with the necessary resources and power to tackle these challenges. In other words, countries need to reduce their investment in arms and militarism and reinvest in the con-

3. Issued 1 January 1997.

struction of peace. The second strategy involves a massive education campaign focused on youth and designed to foster an understanding and tolerance of other cultures as well as an understanding of the value of peace and justice.

In hindsight, and especially in the wake of September 11, these goals and their suggested time line seem perhaps overly optimistic. But the Declaration nonetheless ignited a flurry of interest and activity among governments and civil society. It was quickly followed in 1997 by a meeting of experts organized by the University of Las Palmas, the Tricontinental Institute of Parliamentary Democracy and Human Rights, and UNESCO that was held in Las Palmas, Spain. The participants included Mohammed Bedjaoui, president of the International Court of Justice. The meeting recognized the intimate link between peace and human rights and called for a formal Declaration on the Human Right to Peace, which would be ready for the fiftieth anniversary of the UDHR in 1998.

THE OSLO DECLARATION

In 1997, the Norwegian Institute of Human Rights convened a meeting in Oslo to prepare a draft Declaration for UNESCO's General Conference later that year. The aim of the Declaration was to broaden the human dimension of peace and to divide the right to peace into three interrelated components. The first defines peace as a human right, understanding that all human beings have a right to peace inherent to their humanity. War and violence of any kind, including insecurity, are considered "intrinsically incompatible" with the human right to peace. The section calls on states and members of the international community to ensure its implementation without discrimination.

The second section elaborates on this task by making it a "duty" for all global actors, including individuals, to "contribute to the maintenance and construction of peace" and to prevent armed conflicts and prevent violence in all its manifestations.

The third section elaborates the "Culture of Peace"—the means by which the right to peace is to be achieved. As we have seen, the culture of peace is a strategy that seeks to root peace in people's minds through education, communication, and a set of ethical and democratic ideals.

DRAFT OSLO DECLARATION ON THE HUMAN RIGHT TO PEACE

Article 1: Peace as a human right

- Every human being has the right to peace, which is inherent in the dignity of the human person. War and all other armed conflicts, violence in all its forms and whatever its origin, and insecurity also are intrinsically incompatible with the human right to peace;
- The human right to peace must be guaranteed, respected and implemented without any discrimination in either internal or international contexts by all states and other members of the international community;

Article 2: Peace as a duty

- Every human being, all states and other members of the international community and all peoples have the duty to contribute to the maintenance and construction of peace, and to the prevention of armed conflicts and of violence in all its forms. It is incumbent upon them notably to favour disarmament and to oppose by all legitimate means acts of aggression and systematic, massive and flagrant violations of human rights which constitute a threat to peace;
- As inequalities, exclusion and poverty can result in the disruption of peace both at the international level and internally, it is the duty of states to promote and encourage social justice both on their own territory and at the international level, in particular through an appropriate policy aimed at sustainable human development;

Article 3: Peace through the culture of peace

- The culture of peace, whose aim is to build the defenses of peace in the minds of human beings every day through education, science and communication, must constitute the means of achieving the global implementation of the human right to peace;
- The culture of peace requires recognition and respect for—and the daily practice of—a set of ethical values and democratic ideals which are based on the intellectual and moral solidarity of humanity.

In essence, the right to peace is a global ethic of nonviolence and reverence for all life and offers a blueprint for identifying the roots of global problems and for addressing conflicts early. It is an attempt to move beyond the day-to-day crises that make the headline news and to address their deep-seated causes.

The power of this draft declaration is in its challenge to the hypocrisy dominating the world order today and it was here that the codification of the right to peace came to a temporary halt. A remarkable debate on the Oslo Draft Declaration took place in UNESCO's General Conference on 6 November 1997. One European country after another either attacked or expressed reservations about the right to peace and accused Mayor of overstepping his mandate. Countries from the South struck back, accusing the North of wanting to protect their arms industries. At the end, Paraguay stated, "This rich discussion shows that the culture of peace is the central issue . . . and that the Human Right to Peace is needed for individuals and states." Noting that the debate split North and South, Paraguay added, "Perhaps peace is a greater concern in the South where scarce resources are being diverted to war."

Failing to achieve a consensus, Mayor did not press further with the issue. Skepticism about the human right to peace continued to echo for years after. In the informal discussions at the UN in 1999 that concerned the Draft Declaration and Programme of Action on a Culture of Peace,[4] the U.S. delegate stated: "Peace should not be elevated to the category of human right, otherwise it will be very difficult to start a war." Whether the speaker was aware of the irony of this statement or not, he had put his finger precisely on why a human right to peace is needed.

Efforts are continuing at the UN, but they still lack the necessary Western backing. In 2002 the UN Social, Humanitarian and Cultural Committee adopted a resolution calling for the promotion of the right to peace. The resolution would have the UN affirm that the peoples of the planet have a sacred right to peace, and resources released through disarmament measures should be devoted to the economic and social development of all peoples, particularly those in developing countries. Although the resolution had 90 votes

---

4. See Consolidated Report Containing a Draft Declaration and Programme of Action on a Culture of Peace, 53rd Sess., Provisional Agenda Item 31, UN Doc. A/53/370 (2 September 1998).

in favor, a hefty 50 votes (mostly Western countries and the new East European members of NATO) were cast against it, and 14 abstentions were registered. Such division renders the resolution practically inoperable.[5]

Some states are still arguing that the "right to peace" has not been negotiated at a sufficiently high level of international relations. Denmark, speaking for the EU, said the issue should be dealt with in other forums (the same argument that was used in UNESCO meetings). Canada—speaking on behalf of the United States, New Zealand, and Australia—expressed opposition because the resolution focused more on relations between states, as opposed to states' obligations to their peoples. The fact that Cuba was the main sponsor alienated many Western states. Nonetheless, an objective reading of the text does not provide any reason for rejection—unless a state wants to keep its options for warfare open. If the peoples of the states that voted against the resolution knew what their governments were doing, the governments would not be able to slide away so easily from their responsibility to build the structural basis for the right to peace.

When language is softer, the idea of moving away from war as a means of resolving conflict meets less resistance. For example, in 2003, the UN General Assembly concluded five months of negotiations by adopting by consensus a resolution on the prevention of armed conflict.[6] The resolution called on parties to a dispute threatening international peace to make the most effective use of existing and new methods for peacefully settling disputes, including arbitration, mediation, other treaty-based arrangements, and the International Criminal Court, thus promoting the role of international law in international relations. It reaffirmed the primary responsibility of the Security Council for maintenance of international peace and security. And it called on Member States to support poverty eradication measures and enhance the capacity of developing countries to comply with treaties on arms control, nonproliferation, and disarmament; and to strengthen their international verification instruments and eradicate illicit trade in

small arms and light weapons. The resolution was hailed as a landmark in efforts to move the world body from a culture of reacting to crises to one of preventing them reaching critical mass.

Though shying away from any implication that the prevention of armed conflict sets the stage for a full-scale discussion of the "right to peace," the resolution contains important elements of the culture of peace. Far from being an anodyne or just another resolution, it is infused with an obligation to the victims of violence and challenges states to move from rhetoric to reality in preventing violence. It is a significant step forward by the UN in preparing the way for the right to peace.

Meanwhile, attention in UNESCO has shifted back from a right to peace to the culture of peace. This was easier to digest for those who did not want their right to make war impeded. Everyone, after all, could be for peace in general, and especially in the abstract. UNESCO showed its wisdom by treading slowly. It developed the concept of the culture of peace into a series of programs that would, at least in the minds of those who truly understood the dimensions of the culture of peace, prepare the groundwork for later acceptance of the human right to peace.

A THIRD GENERATION OF RIGHTS

To fully grasp the potential of the human right to peace to change human conduct, it is necessary to consider the evolving nature of human rights.

[*Eds.*—The author summarizes the more extensive treatment of the evolution of first, second, and third generation of human rights, recounted in Reading 1 (Weston) in Chapter 1. He then elaborates on third-generation rights.]

Essentially, third-generation rights call for the redistribution of power and resources, and consider the current international system ineffective in its attempts to resolve contemporary issues. Third-generation rights include the right to political, economic, and cultural self-determination; the right to economic and social development; the right to participate in and benefit from the common heritage of mankind; the right to a healthy environment; the right to humanitarian

---

5. The resolution was nevertheless subsequently adopted by the UN GA Res. 57/216 on the Promotion of the Right of Peoples to Peace.
6. UN GA Res. 57/337, adopted 2 July 2003.

relief, and the right to peace. The key characteristic of these rights is that they are fundamentally collective in nature and require international cooperation for their achievement. A clean environment cannot be achieved by the actions of one country since pollution does not recognize national frontiers. Likewise, it is difficult for a country to raise its gross national product when other countries' tariffs prevent it from selling its goods to raise revenue that could be put toward social services.

More generally third-generation rights provide an essential ingredient lacking in first- and second-generation rights. Largely based on the individual, first- and second-generation rights are permeated by an atmosphere of selfishness that sees the individual as the primary concern. But this focus neglects the fact that, more than ever, society is a system of competing groups and individuals and that, for society to achieve its full potential, it is necessary to participate cooperatively, within the community. Achieving this demands major changes from the individualistic attitude that prevails in Western democracies.

The challenges inherent in globalization make such an approach vitally necessary. The very nature of the dilemmas the third generation of rights seeks to address—namely the right to a clean environment, development, and peace—are issues that today pertain to humanity's very survival. The world has rapidly compressed through a breathtaking combination of population growth, technological and economic advancement, and interdependence. Combining these with a readily available supply of deadly weapons and easily transmitted contagion of hatred and incitement to violence makes it essential and urgent to find ways to prevent disputes from turning massively violent.

In reality more than a new generation, third-generation rights are perhaps better thought of as an awakening. World problems can no longer be solved by the actions of one state alone. Keeping the peace, protecting the environment, and fostering sustained and equitable development require cooperative and determined action at the international level. Lacking this, states cannot fulfill their first- and second-generation obligations.

Human rights are thus indivisible and interdependent. One set of human rights cannot be realized in a world where others are absent or violated. Framed this way, the metaphor for successive "generations" of rights is somewhat misleading since, although they coexist, generations actually succeed each other in the true sense of the term. In reality, the international community has approached human rights in a top-down fashion. Just as it was realized that taking the first generation of human rights seriously necessitated fulfilling the second, achieving the first and second generations of human rights in a globalized world requires realizing the third set of rights. Although at a nascent stage and thus not as established as its "ancestors," this new generation of rights offers a blueprint for confronting and managing the pressing challenges posed by globalization.

The most important among these newly emerging rights is the human right to peace. Often regarded as just another third generation right in the human rights literature, the right to peace is unique. It transcends all other rights, enables their exercise, and offers the innovation needed to lift up society and allow it to achieve its full potential in an interconnected world. Indeed, without basic security of the person, other human rights are but an illusion. What use is the right to vote, or the right to medical care, in a society torn apart by armed conflict?

[*Eds.*—The author next notes that some human rights scholars have argued that the human right to peace and other third-generation rights do not rise to the level of "rights" since they have "no specific meaning" and impose no "specific duties." In riposte, the author notes that first- and second-generation rights may at one time have suffered the same defect, but over time evolved to have very specific content and consequences. Third-generation rights, the author contends, must be given the same opportunity to evolve. He then continues:]

Human rights are a product of their times, and such is the case with first- and second-generation rights. One group of rights is not meant to outdate or ascend another, but rather to expand upon and supplement others. This is clear in the international community's continually expanding conception of what it considers to be human rights and the strides that have been made to formalize them. New aspects of life, new situations, and new types of conflict that cannot be foreseen are continually pushing the definition of human rights beyond old limits. This is a normal legal process that has been adopted by national legal systems the world over, and it should be no surprise that the same process is becoming evident in an increasingly interconnected world.

Such is the case with the right to peace, which is the product of a paradigm shift at the international level. Rights that focus solely on the relationship between the state and the individual are not sufficient in responding to a globalized world in which problems are no longer defined purely in national terms. The same global circuitry that fuels transportation, information, finance, and organization has also increased the power of the arms trader, the warlord, the religious fanatic, the deranged political leader, the human trafficker, and the terrorist. There is, thus, a technological burden with which the other two generations of human rights were never designed to cope, and the right to peace is an attempt to respond to the perils of the modern interconnected world. Dismissing the right to peace as vague and declaring that it offers nothing new is an exercise that misses the mark. The right to peace is innovative and addresses a whole swath of new and interconnected global challenges.

Obviously, the world community has much work to do before the "right to peace" is codified in the same way that political, civil, economic, and social rights have been codified in the covenants to the UDHR. But the fact that so much progress has been made in recognizing, defining, and implementing the right to peace is a sign of the advance of civilization. Those who wish to maintain the war culture and divert yet more precious resources to prosecute wars must not be permitted to use the terrorist attacks of September 11 as an excuse. This will not get at the systemic causes of the problems faced by the international community today.

Only when we fully understand our own potential to make the human right to peace the ruling norm in society will the international community have fulfilled the promise it made in 1945. This promise was to construct the defenses of peace in the minds of all the peoples of the Earth and finally "save succeeding generations from the scourge of war."

HUMAN RIGHTS HAVE COME A LONG WAY

In considering to what the child is entitled so that he or she can live in minimum economic and social standards, is it too much of a leap to state that the first thing the child needs to grow up safely is a peaceful environment? Children must have peace in order to develop in a way that is consistent with the inherent human rights they possess. Peace is their right. But it cannot yet be formally articulated in ways that guarantee that the processes of sustainable development will not be destroyed by the ravages of war. The political system has not yet sufficiently matured.

Nonetheless, the subject of the human right to peace has clearly entered circles of discussion at the UN. Some hold that it is already a component of developing international law. This is a signal moment because a full discussion of the right to peace puts a new spotlight on the age-old question of the abolition of war itself. In the new era of weapons of mass destruction, the viability of war as a legal means to resolve disputes is clearly over. War today can lead to the obliteration of humanity. Unfortunately, the world community, held in check by the forces of the culture of war, is a long way from outlawing war. The debate on the human right to peace, therefore, is a step forward. As it is pursued, it will force the political system to face up to its responsibility to at least avoid war.

The debate inevitably will center on the deeply controversial question of the future of nuclear weapons. The International Court of Justice has already given its view on this matter: it says nations have a legal obligation to get rid of them.[7] While the abolition of nuclear weapons will not by itself guarantee peace, it is an elementary fact of the twenty-first century that as long as nations brandish nuclear weapons there can be no peace. Indeed, P. N. Bhagwati, former chief justice of the Supreme Court of India, argues that "the main function of the right to peace is the promotion and protection of the right to life through peaceful settlement of disputes, by the prohibition of the threat or use of force in international relations, by the prohibition of the manufacture, use and deployment of nuclear weapons, and by total disarmament."[8]

7. *Legality of the Threat or Use of Nuclear Weapons*, 1996 ICJ General List No. 95 (8 July 1996). For a less sanguine reading of this decision, see Burns H. Weston, "Nuclear Weapons and the World Court: Ambiguity's Consensus," *TLCP* 7 (1997): 371–99.
8. *Eds.*—The author provides no reference for this quotation.

The proponents of nuclear weapons do indeed know which way the debate on the human right to peace is headed. That is why they will use every argument they can think of, every political device they can find, and every form of intimidation they can invent to try to derail the debate. They effectively disrupted the debate in UNESCO. They have rendered inoperative nuclear weapons abolition resolutions at the UN. They have used the tragedy of September 11 to scare the populace into believing that only gigantic amounts of weaponry can head off the terrorism of the future. They have already caused an erosion of civil liberties in the guise of combating terrorism.

These proponents of militarism as the route to peace appear to operate today from the commanding heights of public opinion. But against this insidious thinking that war equals peace is rising a new army, not of soldiers but of highly informed, dedicated, and courageous citizens of all countries who do see the perils ahead. There is a blossoming of both understanding and action in the new phenomenon of an alert civil society calling governments to account for paying only lip service to their human rights commitments. Buttressed by the dynamic means of electronic communication, they are bringing new energy to the global quest for peace.

QUESTIONS FOR REFLECTION AND DISCUSSION

1. A principal purpose of the United Nations, as stated in UN Charter Article 1(1), is "To maintain international peace and security" and, to this end, "to bring about by peaceful means . . . adjustment or settlement of international disputes or situations which might lead to a breach of the peace." But what does "peace" mean? On what conceptions and/or values do you draw in forming your answer?

2. In "Nonterritorial Actors and the Problem of Peace," in Saul H. Mendlovitz, ed., *The Creation of a Just World Order* (New York: Free Press, 1975), 151–88, 151–52, political scientist Johan Galtung defines "peace" as the absence of "structural" as well as "direct" violence. "reproduced in the agricultural, industrial, commercial, and administrative sectors of society," Galtung writes, structural violence is the "way that surplus is extracted from the lower levels [of society] and transferred upwards, making the higher levels richer at the expense of the lower levels, producing the famous 'gaps' in development [and resulting in] often highly differential morbidity and mortality rates between rich and poor countries, districts, and individuals." Clearly the UN Charter use of the word "peace" addresses *direct* violence. Does it also address *structural* violence? Should it? Why? Why not?

3. For the purpose of defining the right to peace, is it helpful or unhelpful to define "peace" to mean not only the absence of hostilities ("negative peace") but also the presence of social justice ("positive peace")? Should the human right to peace encompass both meanings? Why? Why not? Note in this connection that the English word "peace" has two Arabic counterparts: *sulah*, meaning the end of hostilities or a truce; and *salaam*, meaning an enduring nonviolent relationship based on mutual respect. Is *sulah* possible without *salaam*? Why? Why not? How would Roche answer these questions? For pertinent discussion, see Burns H. Weston, "The Role of Law in Promoting Peace and Violence: A Matter of Definition, Social Values, and Individual Responsibility," in W. Michael Reisman and Burns H. Weston, eds., *Toward World Order and Human Dignity: Essays in Honor of Myres S. McDougal* (New York: Free Press, 1976), 114–31.

4. The many armed conflicts since the UN's founding—now including the U.S. military invasion of Afghanistan in 2001 and Iraq in 2003; the 2011 military intervention of Belgium, Canada, Denmark, France, Italy, Norway, Qatar, Spain, UK, and United States into Libya; Russia's 2014 military incursion in Ukraine; and the currently ongoing hostilities of and against the Islamic State of Iraq and the Levant (ISIS) in Iraq and Syria—bear witness that the UN has been largely unable to achieve the goal of "international peace and security" for which, in major part, it was established. Why? Who is responsible for this violent state of affairs?

5. Have UN member states, especially the major powers, made it impossible for the UN to achieve its goals? Do your answers to these questions affect your judgment about the existence of the right to peace? Are you persuaded by Roche that a right to peace exists? Why? Why not?

6. Are there economic barriers to peace? Who profits from a lack of peace? Consider the question John Somerville posed in his classic *The Peace Revolution: Ethos and Social Process* (Westport, Conn.: Greenwood Press, 1975), 150:

> What would be the probable effect of a law which provided that whenever the government waged war, and drafted the youth, all industry and capital would become public property for the duration, that private profit and private dividends would cease (be socialized), and all salaries would be limited to the scale of military pay? What proportion of the public would accept the moral principle that, if lives are drafted, property should also be drafted?

Can you think of any wars that would not have been waged if Somerville's moral principle had been accepted at the time? If so, should this principle be viewed as integral to the right to peace?

6. Are the growing national debts of high social spending states around the world a contradiction to the call of the right to peace for state policies to be directed toward achieving life in peace with special regard for younger (future) generations? Why? Why not? Would your answer be the same if the question were framed relative to bloated military spending? Why? Why not?

7. In "Peace as a Human Right," *Bulletin of Peace Proposals Journal* 11, 4 (1980): 319–30, Philip Alston contended that absent "drastic transformation of the existing international system" it is highly unlikely that an effective mechanism for peace enforcement will ever exist. Do you agree? Disagree? Is Alston's contention tantamount to saying there is no human right to peace? Why? Why not?

8. Do you agree with Roche that the international political process has not yet sufficiently matured to formally articulate the right to peace "in ways that guarantee that the processes of sustainable development will not be destroyed by the ravages of war"? Do you think that the right to peace will ever be so completely achieved as to "guarantee" anything? Why? Why not? On what evidence or research does your response rely?

9. If the United States eliminated its nuclear arsenal, as the author proposes all states do, would the world actually be any closer to peace? Why? Why not? How might your answer be greeted by Ambassador Roche and others like him who have worked hard to negotiate nuclear and other arms reductions worldwide?

26. SUSAN MARKS *What Has Become of the Emerging Right to Democratic Governance?*

In 1992, the *American Journal of International Law* published an article by Tom Franck[1] entitled "The Emerging Right to Democratic Gover-

Excerpted with changes by permission of Susan Marks from Susan Marks, "What Has Become of the Emerging Right to Democratic Governance?" *European Journal of International Law* 22, 2 (2011): 507–24. Copyright © 2011 Susan Marks. This essay is a revised version of the author's paper presented at the conference "Remembering Tom Franck: The Man and His Legacy," held in May 2010 at the School of Oriental and African Studies in London.

1. *Eds.*—The author writes: "I could not bring myself to change the affectionate use of Tom Franck's first name which characterized my original presentation, and ask readers to forgive this lapse from academic formality."

nance."[2] When you type Tom's name in conjunction with "democratic governance" into Google, you get 116,000 hits. HeinOnline lists 313 articles in U.S. law reviews citing the piece, and to that list could be added a hundred further texts, and perhaps substantially more, in non-U.S. journals and in reports and other policy documents. But far be it from me to endorse such crude measures of academic impact; what are really striking are the epithets that have come routinely to be attached to this article: "seminal," "pioneering," "path-breaking." This is plainly a contribution to international legal scholarship which has inspired and provoked many people.

2. Thomas M. Franck, "The Emerging Right to Democratic Governance," *AJIL* 86 (1992): 46.

I am among those who were inspired and provoked by it during the decade of its appearance, and here I revisit the topic for the first time since then, asking "What has become of the emerging right to democratic governance?"

Before suggesting some possible answers, let me recall the main lines of Tom's argument. He began by highlighting two events that had recently occurred at the time he was writing. In Russia, the attempted coup of August 1991, aimed at putting a stop to Gorbachev's reforms and preventing the break-up of the Soviet Union, was foiled. Then, the next month in Haiti, the successful overthrow of elected president Jean-Bertrand Aristide elicited an unprecedented response in international organizations. The UN General Assembly demanded that Aristide be returned to office, while the OAS recommended that its members impose sanctions on Haiti "to bring about the isolation of those who hold power [there] illegally."[3] In both these cases, Tom remarked, "the leaders of states constituting the international community vigorously asserted that *only* democracy validates governance."[4] He went on: "This dramatic statement attains even more potency if, as in the Haitian case, it is transposed from political philosophy, where it is 'mere' moral prescription, to law, where a newly recognized 'democratic entitlement' was used in both the OAS and the UN General Assembly to impose new and important legal obligations on states."[5]

As this already makes clear, Tom's thesis had to do with validation (and, with that, legitimacy), democracy, and entitlement. He claimed that the legitimacy of governments was becoming a matter not just of national arrangements, but of international law. Furthermore, under international law democracy was becoming the basis of governmental legitimacy. Indeed, democratic governance was becoming an enforceable entitlement. "We are not quite there," he wrote, "but we can see the outlines of this new world in which the citizens of each state will look to international law and organization to guarantee their democratic entitlement."[6] What made the development so dramatic—such a "sea change"[7]—was, of course, that international law had previously been understood as strictly agnostic with regard to the forms of government.

But if the post-Cold War turn to liberal democracy was the watershed in Tom's account, he considered that the democratic norm had not suddenly materialized from nothing. He identified three key "building blocks" which had helped toward its construction. The first, going back to the interwar period, was the principle of self-determination. On his account, self-determination "postulates the right of a people organized in an established territory to determine its collective political destiny in a democratic fashion." It is linked to a "long-evolving tradition of maintaining observers . . . at elections in colonies and trust territories."[8] The second, originating in the "anti-totalitarianism born of World War II," was the right to "free political expression."[9] Protected through a multiplicity of international and regional regimes, rights to freedom of expression, assembly, and opinion constitute "the essential preconditions for an open electoral process."[10] The third, and newest, building block was the emerging entitlement to periodic elections which are free and fair. As Tom explained, with a "substantial new majority of states [now] actually practicing a reasonably credible version of electoral democracy," stipulations in human rights treaties for a right to genuine periodic elections begin "to approximate prevailing practice and thus may be said to be stating what is becoming a customary legal norm applicable to all."[11]

Although Tom well recognized that democracy is not synonymous with elections, his analysis placed considerable emphasis on this third and newest building block as the capstone of the edifice, and the latter part of his discussion was given over to the question of how to implement and enforce the democratic entitlement conceived as a right to free and fair elections. He was impressed with the election-monitoring activities and institutions which had burgeoned in the early 1990s, again highlighting Haiti as a case in point. The UN mission to oversee the elections in Haiti in 1990 "may be understood," he wrote,

3. OEA/Ser.F/V.1/MRE/RES.1/91, corr.1 (1991).
4. Franck, "The Emerging Right to Democratic Governance," 47.
5. Ibid.
6. Ibid., 50.
7. Ibid.
8. Ibid., 52.
9. Ibid., 61.
10. Ibid.
11. Ibid., 64.

"as the first instance in which the United Nations, acting at the request of a national government, intervened in the electoral process solely to validate the legitimacy of the outcome."[12] At the same time, he noted the way "Monitoring by governmental and nongovernmental observers became an important ad hoc part of the post-1989 transition from Communist to democratic regimes in Eastern Europe."[13] He expected international monitoring of national elections to become increasingly routine with time.

In bringing his article to a conclusion, Tom made reference to the well-known claim that liberal democracy is conducive to peace, not generally, but with other liberal democracies—the so-called "liberal peace." It follows from this, he wrote, that "one way to promote universal and perpetual nonaggression—probably the best and, perhaps, the only way—is to make democracy an entitlement of all peoples."[14] At the same time, he pointed to the links between democracy and human rights, the sense in which democracy supports the protection of human rights and hence also the restoration and maintenance of civil peace in postconflict societies. Finally, in one of the article's most quoted passages, he highlighted the connection to economic liberalization: "The entitlement now aborning is widely enough understood to be almost universally celebrated. It is welcomed from Malagache to Mongolia, in the streets, the universities and the legislatures, not only because it portends a new, global political culture but also because it opens the stagnant political economies of states to economic, social and cultural, as well as political, development."[15] "as even the Chinese leadership must be discovering," he commented, economic development is "linked inextricably with political freedom. An economic free market cannot long flourish without creating pressure for a free market of ideas."[16]

That, then, was the emerging right to democratic governance, as conceptualized by Tom in 1992. In turning now to the present, I want to examine four different ways of answering the question what has become of it today—four different accounts of its contemporary significance

and fate—and also to discuss Haiti, one of the countries that interested Tom most. What can we reveal with hindsight about the democratic norm and in particular, about its place within that phase of capitalist consolidation we now call neoliberalism?

LEGITIMACY

An initial way of answering the question "What has become of the emerging right to democratic governance?" is to say that the idea of such a right has become accepted, even if still as a proposition about emerging international law, rather than as a settled norm. Greg Fox is among those who have written along these lines. In the *Max Planck Encyclopaedia of Public International Law* on the "right to democracy," he highlights the developments since the early 1990s that lend further weight to the arguments Tom adduced.[17] International and regional organizations have created a range of mechanisms to promote and secure democratic governance in member states. Within the UN, there is now an Electoral Assistance Division, and democracy promotion is also part of the Organization's activities in the fields of postconflict reconstruction, the rule of law, and conflict resolution. In the EU, the existence of stable institutions for guaranteeing democracy is among the criteria for admission to membership, while the Organization of American States explicitly proclaims democracy as an internationally guaranteed right and allows for suspension of member states in which a democratically elected government is overthrown. In various forms, democracy promotion is likewise a feature of the work of the Organization for Security and Cooperation in Europe, the African Union, the Commonwealth, and Mercosur.

For Fox, these developments show strong support for the emergent norm of democratic governance, but they also make clear that it must continue to be regarded as emergent. As he sees it, two principal constraints have limited the progress of the democratic entitlement. First, there is a lack of consensus about the definition of democracy involved. Second, there is signifi-

12. Ibid., 72–73.
13. Ibid., 74.
14. Ibid., 88.
15. Ibid., 90.
16. Ibid.

17. Gregory H. Fox, "Democracy, Right to International Protection," *Max Planck Encyclopaedia of Public International Law*, www.mpepil.com [*Eds.*—accessed 20 June 2015].

cant variation in the extent to which a democratic norm is recognized across different regions of the world. European and Inter-American practice stands in sharp contrast to the absence of any regional framework for democracy promotion in Asia and the Middle East. . . . Fox comments that "This wide spectrum of commitment to democratic governance provides an uncertain foundation for a global norm."[18] That said, his overall conclusion is that (as he puts it elsewhere) "the legal door is now open to determined efforts to spur democratization, and . . . the failure to do good everywhere should not be seen as a bar to doing good anywhere."[19]

For those doubtful about the emerging norm, a key concern has always been enforcement. What action is legitimated in the name of enforcement? Inasmuch as the democratic entitlement has been linked with a right of "pro-democratic intervention," the worry has been expressed that it dangerously weakens the legal prohibition on the use of force. A new right of unilateral pro-democratic intervention drapes the "arbitrary exercise of power . . . in the robes of dubious legality."[20] But the misgivings also go farther, and have to do with the question of what it means to license "pro-democratic" interference, whether in the form of military or nonmilitary action, and whether unilaterally or collectively. As one author observes, in a "typical case, all sides of a political struggle claim the democratic high ground."[21] A right to democratic governance makes it possible for powerful outsiders to overrule that struggle and claim legal justification for doing so. If such a right "has any determinacy, [it] entails what amounts to a liberal-democratic *jihad*, a drive to impose a specific liberal-democratic world view that has yet to find general acceptance."[22] For the writer of these words, there is no evidence that international law endorses this, and nor should it. "Until such time as

a genuine consensus emerges as to the criteria of governmental legitimacy," he maintains that "the principle of nonintervention will remain an enlightened one."[23]

SECURITY

A second way of answering the question "What has become of the emerging right to democratic governance?" takes up and refocuses that last concern. On this analysis, far from carrying on in the direction Tom pointed, the democratic entitlement has collapsed under the weight of the post-9/11 security agenda. The impact of the "war on terror" on activities in the field of democracy promotion is discussed by Thomas Carothers, long-standing head of the Democracy and Rule of Law program at the Carnegie Endowment for International Peace and a leading practitioner of democracy promotion in the United States, in two articles in *Foreign Affairs*.[24] In the first, published in 2003, Carothers writes of the "tradeoffs" between security and democracy which characterized prevailing U.S. foreign policy. By 2006, when the second article appeared, Carothers was clear things were going badly wrong. Western democracy assistance was being publicly denounced as "illegitimate political meddling."[25] Carothers explains that this can be understood, in part, as a consequence of changes in the nature and context of democracy promotion. Many of the countries that had welcomed democracy assistance in the early post-Cold War years had evolved into "semiauthoritarian" states with the trappings of democracy but no serious commitment to electoral competition. This initially stymied pro-democratic organizations, but with time it led them to change the way they worked. They began to focus on building the capacity of local civic groups and political parties to challenge the government in elections. The results were evident in the various "color revolutions" of the former Eastern bloc. In this regard, Carothers comments that the motives of U.S. and other foreign agencies range "from the principled to the

18. Ibid., para. 36.
19. Gregory H. Fox and Brad R. Roth, "Democracy and International Law," *Review of International Studies* 27, 3 (2001): 327–52, 338.
20. Michael Byers and Simon Chesterman, " 'You the People': Pro-Democratic Intervention in International Law," in Gregory H. Fox and Brad R. Roth, eds., *Democratic Governance and International Law* (Cambridge: CUP, 2000), 259–92.
21. Brad R. Roth, "Popular Sovereignty: The Elusive Norm," *ASIL Proceedings* 91 (1997): 362–72, 367.
22. Ibid., 368.

23. Ibid., 370.
24. Thomas Carothers, "Promoting Democracy and Fighting Terror," *Foreign Affairs* 82 (2003): 84–97; Carothers, "The Backlash Against Democracy Promotion," *Foreign Affairs* 85 (2006): 55–68.
25. Ibid.

instrumental," though these "subtleties are generally lost on the targets . . . who tend to view such efforts as concerted campaigns to oust them."[26]

But while Carothers concedes that the backlash may be partly a matter of democracy promotion becoming a victim of its own success—"autocrats feeling the heat"[27]—he emphasizes that there is also a wider unease. Autocrats are able to portray democracy assistance as illegitimate political meddling because, in many countries of the world, "Washington's use of the term 'democracy promotion' has come to be seen . . . as a code word for 'regime change,'" that is to say, "the replacement of bothersome governments by military force or other means."[28] At the same time, Carothers points to the way counterterrorism laws and practices instituted by the administration further undermine the work of U.S. democracy advocates. Detention without trial, unwarranted interception of communications, and torture by or with the collusion of U.S. officials made it "all too easy for foreign autocrats to resist U.S. democracy promotion by providing them with an easy riposte: 'How can a country that tortures people abroad and abuses rights at home tell other countries how to behave?'"[29]

Carothers's analysis is not specifically directed to the emerging right to democratic governance, but it is plain that, as a potential basis for democracy promotion, that right is implicated in his discussion. On issues ranging from arbitrary detention to infringement of privacy, and from restrictions on public protest to racial discrimination, security fears have been invoked to legitimate deep incursions into established democratic practice. This has not just been a matter of national policy; through action of the UN Security Council, it has drawn support from international law. The result has been to reverse the trends that supposedly underpin the emergent democratic entitlement.

DEVELOPMENT

A third way of answering the question "What has become of the emerging right to democratic governance?" differs again. Here what is proposed is that Tom's thesis has been neither accepted, nor undermined. Rather, the democratic norm he had in mind has mutated into something else. Whereas his vision was of a universal entitlement backed up by an institutionalized and ideally worldwide system of election monitoring, today democracy promotion is a dimension of development work. In 2002 the UN Development Programme *Human Development Report* took as its theme "Deepening Democracy in a Fragmented World."[30] Referring to the "new consensus" that "governance matters for development,"[31] the report emphasizes that what matters for human development is not just effective governance—important though that is—but democratic governance. This is in part because political freedoms are aspects of human development in their own right, but also because democracy can trigger a virtuous cycle of development, as political freedoms empower people to press for policies and priorities which expand the well-being of all. At the same time, democratic governance contributes to defusing or resolving social tensions, helps to prevent crises such as famines, and promotes the dissemination of information about critical health-related and other issues.

In highlighting the links between human development and democratic governance, the report notes the "sombre realities of 21st century politics."[32] Although recent decades have seen a worldwide shift from authoritarian to democratic politics, "Most attempts at democratization are fragmented, involving small steps and large, forward and back."[33] As Carothers also observes, countries that held democratic elections for the first time in the 1980s and early 1990s in many cases either have returned to more authoritarian forms of rule or are "stalled" between democracy and authoritarianism. Others still are blighted by extremism and persistent or recurrent conflict. This shows that democracy "means more than elections. It requires the consolidation of democratic institutions and the strengthening of democratic practices, with democratic values and

30. UNDP, *Human Development Report 2002: Deepening Democracy in a Fragmented World* (New York: OUP, 2002).
31. Ibid., 51.
32. Ibid., 1.
33. Ibid., 15.

26. Ibid., 62.
27. Ibid., 63.
28. Ibid., 64.
29. Ibid., 65.

norms embedded in all parts of society."[34] In particular, the report underlines the need for democratic values and norms to be embedded in the work of the military and police. Human development depends on personal security and civil peace, and, in turn, personal security and civil peace depend on bringing the security sector under democratic civilian control.

This recharacterization of democracy as a development issue is reflected institutionally in the fact that the UNDP is currently the lead agency on democratic governance in the UN system. According to the UNDP website, a third of the Programme's annual budget goes to projects, programmes, and initiatives relating to democratic governance, and more than 130 UNDP offices around the world promote democratic governance as part of the activities they undertake at the request of governments. This work is said to support efforts to advance democratic governance in four main areas: expanding participation in political decision-making, particularly by women and the poor; fostering the rule of law and making public institutions more transparent, accountable, and responsive; promoting anti-corruption, equal opportunity, and empowerment of marginalized groups; and facilitating country-led assessments of democratic governance.

Considered from this angle, democratic governance is not so much a criterion of governmental legitimacy or an enforceable entitlement as a part of the project of international development. It names the form of "good governance" which is today promoted alike by development agencies, aid workers, and peace-building authorities. At issue, for scholars of development, is the difference between "democratic transition" and "democratic consolidation."

IDEOLOGY

I have discussed the idea that Tom's claim has moved, respectively, forward, backward, and sideways, so to speak. Logically, of course, there is only one further possibility. So let me turn now to a fourth and final way of answering the question "What has become of the emerging right to democratic governance?" in which the

focus is not on what has changed, but instead on what has stayed the same, what has remained in place. Here, then, the question of the right's current significance and fate becomes a question about what it is and always was. In the writings we have considered so far, the general assumption is that our political hopes are appropriately expressed as aspirations to democracy, even if the consolidation of democracy is difficult to achieve, even if democratic practice has come under pressure from the "prevention of terrorism," and even if there is no agreement on how democracy should be defined in the context of a democratic entitlement. For the political theorist Jodi Dean, however, it is not at all clear that we should continue to treat democracy as the cure for contemporary political problems, rather than "symptomatic of them."[35] Of course, we may treat it as both, but what is important for Dean is the elementary point that democracy as we know it *sustains* inequality. While the concept of democracy brings with it ideas of self-rule and political equality, "Real existing constitutional democracies privilege the wealthy. As they install, extend, and protect neoliberal capitalism, they exclude, exploit, and oppress the poor, all the while promising that everybody wins."[36]

To highlight the contradiction between reproducing social inequality and promising mutual gain is to assert the ideological character of democracy. In Dean's analysis, moreover, the ideology of democracy goes hand in hand with the ideology of neoliberal capitalism. She wants us to see how democracy sets parameters which place "growth, investment, and profit . . . politically off-limits,"[37] and how in process alternative ways of organizing collective life are systematically occluded. The appeal to democracy absorbs transformative energies by lodging politics "in a field of already given possibilities."[38] If she calls that field neoliberal capitalism, the name given to it in Tom's article is "the economic free market," and it is evoked too in the language of "investment," "ownership," and "pacts" used in connection with the mutation—the third account of the democratic norm as an aspect of development work—I have just described. Under

34. Ibid., 14.

35. Jodi Dean, *Democracy and Other Neoliberal Fantasies* (Durham, N.C.: Duke University Press, 2009), 76.
36. Ibid.
37. Ibid.
38. Ibid., 76.

these conditions, Dean maintains that democracy is less a signpost than an impasse. Since the key ideological move is not to conceal the contradictory character of democratic politics but instead to acknowledge and deflect it ("Look, democracy isn't perfect"), there is, on the one hand, an evasion of responsibility for "current failures"; on the other hand, there is also an evasion of responsibility "for envisioning [a different] politics in the future."[39]

Liberal democracy is a system of representation, and in another recent intervention in debates about democracy the philosopher Alain Badiou reflects on what it is that gets represented.[40] To be sure, liberal democracy represents—in the sense of registering and measuring—the variety of opinions electors have about candidates, parties, policies, and programmes. But at a deeper level it also represents—in the sense of instantiating and upholding—a particular form of society and politics. In his words, democracy is "first of all the representation of the general system that bears its forms . . . [that is to say, it is] the consensual representation of capitalism, or of what today has been renamed the 'market economy.'"[41] This state of affairs was evident, for example, in the UK 2010 general election campaign, where democracy had become meaningless in the sense that all the really important questions were out of contention; all that was on offer was, with (major and minor) variations, "more of the same"[42]—more transparency, more accountability, more diversity, more inclusion in the current framework that was not itself in question.

Like Carothers and the UNDP, Dean and Badiou are not specifically concerned in their writing with the emerging right to democratic governance. Yet, again, their assessments have implications for that right, suggesting a different kind of critique from the one that focuses on the dangers of pro-democratic intervention. From their perspective, the issue is the character of democracy as part of the ideology of neoliberalism. The institutions of democratic governance have indeed spread around the world. But—so these critics invite us to ask—have those phenomena brought emancipation to the world's exploited and oppressed? Have they contributed positively to the reduction of poverty and helped efforts to redress the massive disparities of wealth and opportunity within and between countries? Have they improved the lives of the vast majority of the inhabitants of this planet to any significant extent at all? The fourth and final way of responding to the question "What has become of the emerging right to democratic governance?" returns not with an answer, but with these questions.

HAITI

The idea of the emerging right to democratic governance drew its immediate inspiration, as we have seen, from events which occurred in the late 1980s and early 1990s. One of the countries on which Tom particularly focused was Haiti, and it will be instructive, before concluding, to consider the more recent history of that country. How does the Haitian case stand with respect to the analyses we have just reviewed? What can we learn from it about the new departure in political and legal affairs it once seemed to epitomize? The starting point for Tom's analysis is the international response to the military coup which occurred in the country in 1991. Noting the "sudden and violent interruption of the democratic process" in Haiti, the UN General Assembly "strongly [condemned] the illegal replacement of the constitutional president," affirmed "as unacceptable any entity resulting from that illegal situation," and demanded the "immediate restoration of the legitimate Government of President Jean-Bertrand Aristide."[43] By way of enforcement, sanctions were imposed by the OAS and later also by the UN. The two organizations brokered an agreement for Aristide's return in 1993. After enlisting U.S. military assistance, he was finally able to resume office under the terms of this agreement the following year.

For periodization purposes, let us treat this as a first phase of international efforts to "promote democratic governance" in Haiti. A second phase relates to the period after Aristide was reelected president in 2000. Again his presidency was violently challenged, but this time the international "pro-democratic" intervention was to remove

39. Ibid., 94.
40. Alain Badiou, *The Meaning of Sarkozy*, trans. David Fernbach (London: Verso, 2008).
41. Ibid., 91.
42. Dean, *Democracy and Other Neoliberal Fantasies*, note 35, 93.
43. UN GA Res. 46/7, 11 October 1991.

rather than reinstate him. His rule was replaced by the deployment to Haiti of a "multinational interim force" led by the United States and France to restore order, facilitate humanitarian assistance, and "promote the rebuilding of democratic institutions" in the country.[44] The interim force was replaced shortly afterwards by the UN Stabilization Mission in Haiti (MINUSTAH), still in place today [with a democracy-building mandate].[45]

A third phase of this history differs from the first two, in that it was initiated not by a political insurgency, but by the catastrophic earthquake that struck Haiti in January 2010. Within days U.S. forces were again deployed to the country, and, alongside emergency relief, the discussion was again of security, humanitarian assistance, and promotion of democratic governance.

Returning now to the question of the emerging right to democratic governance, the most obvious conclusion we can draw from these events is that democracy promotion has remained vivid in the work of the UN and other international organizations, and that it continues to be associated with elections, even if it is also closely linked to security, development, and reconstruction. The removal of Aristide in 2004, after U.S. support for him had evaporated, likewise confirms the idea that regime change and democracy promotion may not be so far apart. Beyond those points, however, Haiti helps to bring into focus some further important aspects, to do with the context, effect, and premise of democracy promotion. Let us begin with the *context* in which democracy promotion occurs. The Secretary-General referred in his remarks after the 2010 earthquake to Haiti's extreme poverty, and emphasized the responsibility of the international community to help the local authorities in overcoming it. In welcoming the government's commitment to a new social contract, he also stressed the country's immediate need for food, water, and shelter. But why was there that need? Why was there that poverty? If international intervention belongs with the solution to Haiti's troubles, what is missing here is any sense that it may also be part of their cause.

Take the moment in 1994 when Aristide won the U.S. military support on which his reinstate-

ment depended. The condition for that support was structural adjustment. Aristide was forced, when he returned to Haiti, to reduce government spending, privatize public services, and remove import tariffs. Haiti had previously been self-sufficient in its staple of rice, but opening the market to subsidized American grain meant that local production virtually ceased. And while the country's agricultural collapse was supposed to be offset by an expansion in manufacturing, the new factories did not last long, and the slums just grew and grew. This prompts reflection on the *effect* of democracy promotion. As Peter Hallward observes in a thoughtful study of recent Haitian history, "Rather than strengthen Haiti's capacity to resist the [long-standing] foreign manipulation of its economy," international initiatives undertaken within the framework of democratic governance programmes have tended to weaken the prospects for democratic control of economic life. These initiatives "combine with IMF-driven structural adjustment to enhance U.S. penetration of the local market."[46]

In turn, this directs attention to the *premise* of democracy promotion. For all the talk of democratic governance, the [true] thrust [of intervention and its motivating ideology], [Hallward] writes, is to reaffirm "perhaps the most consistent theme of Western commentary on the island: that poor black people remain incapable of governing themselves."[47]

CONCLUSION

It is common among those writing about democracy from an international legal perspective to begin with the observation that this has been a neglected topic. Tom Franck altered that. With his article on the emerging right to democratic governance, he inaugurated a large and wide-ranging debate on the relationship between democracy and international law. We have considered that debate from four different standpoints. These do not, of course, enable us to capture the entirety of what has been, or might be, said, but they do reveal some notable facets of

44. UN SC Res. 1529 (2004), 29 February 2004.
45. See UN SC Res. 1542 (2004), 30 April 2004. [*Eds.*— See also http://www.un.org/en/peacekeeping/missions/minustah (accessed 20 June 2015).]

46. Peter Hallward, *Damming the Flood: Haiti, Aristide and the Politics of Containment* (London: Verso, 2007), 179.
47. Peter Hallward, "Option Zero in Haiti," *New Left Review* 27 (2004): 23–47, 25.

the emerging right to democratic governance as it may appear today.

According to the first analysis, the emerging right to democratic governance is supported by developments within international organizations, though still as an entitlement which is emergent rather than fully established. The norm's further progress is hampered by the variations that exist in regional practice, and also by a lack of consensus over how democracy should be defined. In this regard, Greg Fox distinguishes between procedural definitions and substantive ones, and explains that the problem with the latter is that they are so broad as to become almost useless as standards of measurement capable of meaningfully evaluating conduct. What he does not explain, however, is why we should be more interested in meaningful evaluation than meaningful democracy. He assumes that the democratic entitlement is a matter of "doing good," but puts measurement before the improvement of social conditions.

To note this is not to suggest that Fox's analysis is wrong, just that it is limited. The same applies to the other analyses. According to the second, the emerging right to democratic governance has been seriously undermined by the counterterrorist agenda of the period since 9/11. Thomas Carothers lays particular blame at the feet of George W. Bush, arguing that his administration is responsible for fuelling anti-Americanism and producing a backlash against efforts to promote democratic governance abroad. But Carothers does not consider the possibility that what is at stake may not be a simple matter of anti-Americanism; equally, it may not be a "backlash," in the sense of a reflex motion in reverse. He wants us to think of the work of democracy promotion as an essential good, sometimes travestied though "instrumentalism," and puts to one side the idea that there may be sound reasons for questioning that.

According to the third analysis, the emerging right to democratic governance has been neither supported by recent history, nor undermined by it. Rather, the most significant change affecting it is that it has become part of the project of international development. And in this context, the focus has shifted from democratic transition to democratic consolidation. On the other hand, this is not a linear path. Most attempts at democratization are "fragmented, involving small steps and large, forward and back." The UNDP directs valuable attention here to the complexity of democratic processes. Yet again, something important may be missed. For to speak in those terms is to make the problems seem endogenous to the country concerned, rather than also caught up in the dynamics of a larger system that needs itself to be placed under scrutiny.

The fourth and final analysis sidesteps the issue of changes affecting the emerging right to democratic governance, to concentrate instead on its historical significance and future potential. Central to this analysis is a critique of democracy as ideology. If democratic politics hold out the promise of self-rule and equality, they also sustain the conditions which privilege the wealthy and marginalize the poor. One way they currently do that is by fostering resignation to democracy's "imperfection." Another way is by absorbing and neutralizing transformative energies. What follows from this critique? To Jodi Dean, it is not obvious that we should continue to express our emancipatory aspirations in democratic terms; democracy may be more of an impasse in liberatory politics than a signpost to them. And what holds for democracy presumably holds too for the emerging right to democratic governance. That delivers a fascinating challenge to all three of the other analyses. But in contemplating it, there is one further perspective we will do well to take into account.

In an interview conducted in 2006, Jean-Bertrand Aristide speaks from his South African exile about democracy in Haiti.[48] His country is characterized by dramatic inequality, with power and wealth concentrated in the hands of a tiny elite and the vast majority of the population surviving on less than US$2 a day. He explains that, throughout Haitian history, the elite has "done everything in its power to keep the masses at bay, on the other side of the walls that protect their privilege." "This is what any genuinely democratic project is up against," he says.[49] A "hollow version of democracy" has been instituted by this privileged class, and is maintained inasmuch as they control the means of repression. To Aristide, democracy is not just a matter of procedures and institutions, values and norms, transition and consolidation. It is a matter of struggle against determined, protracted, and highly organized resistance.

48. Jean-Bertrand Aristide, "One Step at a Time," trans. and ed. Peter Hallward, in Hallward, *Damming the Flood*, note 46, 317.
49. Ibid., 321.

QUESTIONS FOR REFLECTION AND DISCUSSION

1. What, according to Susan Marks, is the "emerging right to democratic governance" as conceptualized by Thomas Franck in 1992? Be as specific, precise, and accurate as you can. What is the structure of Marks's analysis of Franck's argument? What key characteristics of Franck's conception of the right does Marks draw out?

2. According to Gregory Fox, what has become of "the emerging right to democratic governance"? How does Fox, according to Marks's analysis of his work at least, support his view? What critique is offered by Marks and others to Fox's position? Do you agree with Fox? Or with his critics? Why? Why not?

3. Has democratic entitlement collapsed under the weight of the post-9/11 security agenda? Upon what do you base your conclusion? What implications does your answer have for Franck's analysis? What implications does it have for Fox's?

4. Can the quest for security be reconciled with a right to democracy?

5. Do you agree with the analysis offered by Carothers? Why? Why not?

6. What do you think are the advantages and/or disadvantages of recharacterizing democracy as a development issue?

7. Does democracy as we know it sustain inequality? How? How not? What would Jodi Dean argue?

8. When Alain Badiou argues that democracy is the "consensual representation of capitalism," what do you understand him to mean? Do you agree? Why? Why not?

9. When Marks writes that "The fourth and final way of responding to the question 'What has become of the emerging right to democratic governance?' returns not with an answer, but with these questions," to what questions does she refer? And how do you answer those questions? Based upon what value commitments?

10. Marks argues that the example of "Haiti helps to bring into focus some further important aspects, to do with the context, effect, and premise of democracy promotion." What are they? Do you think the Haiti example is helpful? Why? Why not?

11. In concluding, and characterizing the position of Aristide, Marks writes that a "hollow version of democracy" has been instituted by a privileged elite "and is maintained inasmuch as they control the means of repression." What evidence is there to support this claim relative to the contemporary dilemmas of democracy and relations between state and market in the globalized age? What evidence contradicts it?

12. Is the "hollow version of democracy" referred to by Aristide democracy at all? Does this Haitian form of governance take anything away from the pro-democracy arguments presented?

13. What do you understand "true" democracy to be? Is contemporary democracy democratic enough? Why not and according to which conception of democracy? Why and according to which conception of democracy?

14. What do you believe has become of the emerging right to democratic governance? Feel free to advocate for one of the positions presented in the article, or present your own.

Part II
ACTION

Chapter Six

International Human Rights: Action Overviews

IN this chapter, we move beyond the many human rights issues introduced in Part I of this volume to discuss the essential elements of human rights action, focusing primarily on the enforcement or implementation of international human rights. To provide context for understanding some of the many forms of human rights action evident in our modern era and their guiding principles, the chapter begins with Burns Weston's panoramic historical review of human rights institution building. His presentation, ranging over several centuries, ultimately confronts us with distinctively contemporary efforts to take action against needless inhumanity and to grapple with human suffering in its many human-made forms.

Weston's essay, "Human Rights: Prescription and Enforcement," begins by referencing some of the historical antecedents of modern human rights law,[1] revealing a long line of humanitarian ethical concern, which, even if it has found imperfect expression, predates modern international humanitarian and human rights law and reveals a certain continuity of international moral focus upon the conduct of hostilities between states. He notes that the "laws of war" traverse many decades of the modern era, becoming formalized first in the Geneva and Hague conventions of the mid- to late nineteenth century and currently defined by the four Geneva conventions of 1949, their two additional protocols of 1977, the statutes for the ad hoc war crimes tribunals for the former Yugoslavia and Rwanda, and the Statute of the newly established International Criminal Court (whose jurisdiction the United States has so far refused to accept). While the term "laws of war" seems ironic because war is the ultimate form of social violence, these specific rules seek to restrain violent activities precisely in the field of battle. The fundamental principles of action underlying "humanitarian law" (as the humanitarian rules of armed conflict are today called) are essentially the same as those undergirding international human rights law. They express a foundational concern with basic levels of respect and human decency.

Weston's exposition draws out the links between humanitarian legal impulses, the centrality of peace to the UN Charter and to the role of international human rights law in a

---

1. The essay, Reading 27, is a continuation of Reading 1 (Weston) in Chapter 1. The reader may wish to review Reading 1 before taking on Reading 27, in particular its preliminary pre-World War II history of human rights ("Historical Development").

way that supplements the arguments of Roche in Reading 25 in Chapter 5 by providing a detailed account of the institutional and non-institutional dynamics implicated in the international framework. Human rights emerge from Weston's account as an influential component of the international legal order and intimately linked to legal accountability for human violation—focally, in this case, in time of war—in an analytic narrative drawing a clear trajectory from the Nazi war trials to the International Criminal Court.

Weston also draws out complexities surrounding the ambivalent role of state sovereignty in the international human rights system. He notes that a proposal to ensure the protection (that is, the *enforcement*) of human rights was "explicitly rejected" at the San Francisco conference that drafted the UN Charter: human rights were to be "promoted" rather than enforced. Thus, unlike the goal of maintaining international peace and security, human rights were given a qualified status. Weston argues that "the Charter is conspicuously given to generality and vagueness in its human rights clauses, among others." This means, he suggests, that, for some, human rights commitments can appear "nebulous promotional obligation[s]." At the same time, however, he points out that human rights possess a powerful normative traction: "human rights can no longer be considered a matter 'essentially within the domestic jurisdiction' of states."

Weston's account surveys the multiple layered and interlocking systems that currently exist for human rights protection, suggesting, as do so many readings in this book, the rich and complex normativity of international human rights and their intimate and challenging relationships with peace and war, respect and violation, justice and injustice. It is particularly useful to read Weston's account of humanitarian and human rights law against the background of his understanding of law itself—especially apt for apprehending the dynamics of human rights law as it flows through and from social movement energies, political structures, and institutional arrangements alike. For Weston, it is important to "to think upon law in functional rather than institutional terms, and from this perspective to acknowledge its invention, its application, and its appraisal both within and beyond the formal corridors of power"[2]—and not just international law, but law generally. He writes:

> Law does not live by executives and legislators and judges alone. It lives also by individual human beings such as ourselves, pushing and pulling through reciprocal claim and mutual tolerance in our daily competition for power, wealth, respect, and other cherished values. To turn a phrase, law is legitimized politics—a Hydra-headed process of social decision, involving persons at all levels and from all walks of public and private life who, with authority derived both explicitly and implicitly from community consensus or expectation, and supported by formal and informal sanction, effect those codes or standards of everyday conduct by which we plan and go about our lives.[3]

Law, then, is a rich product of community dynamics and interactions. And human rights law is no different, emerging and being positioned in multiple ways that reflect the dispersed nature of the forms of "ownership" taken of them. Human rights law is caught, just as all law is, in the crosscurrents of human aspiration and manipulations of power. It is simultaneously inspiring *and* imperfect.

The imperfection of law and its enforcement—particularly of international human rights law—is a theme directly addressed by Harold Koh's contribution to this chapter, which

---

2. Burns H. Weston, "The Role of Law in Promoting Peace and Violence: A Matter of Definition, Social Values, and Individual Responsibility," in W. Michael Reisman and Burns H. Weston, eds., *Toward World Order and Human Dignity* (New York: Free Press, 1976), 114–31, 116.
3. Ibid., 116–17.

poses the deceptively simple question "How Is International Human Rights Law Enforced?" Koh begins his analysis with the following frank statement:

> I wouldn't be surprised if many were to give a pessimistic answer [to the question]: international human rights law is not enforced, you might say. Just take a look at the massive human rights violations in Bosnia [and Syria and elsewhere]. . . . Look, you might say, at the world's willingness to overlook human rights violations committed by more powerful nations. . . . International human rights law is not enforced, you might say, because human rights norms are vague and aspirational, because enforcement mechanisms are toothless, because treaty regimes are notoriously weak, and because national governments lack the economic self-interest or the political will to restrain their own human rights violations.

Koh responds to this familiar response by pointing to the imperfect enforcement of domestic law. Drawing an account of dynamic, multilayered sets of responses in domestic law similar to Weston's account of law generally, Koh argues that "norms of international human rights law . . . are imperfectly enforced" but enforced nonetheless "through a complex, little-understood legal process that I call transnational legal process"—an "international-to-national" or "vertical" legal process as Koh describes it. This transnational legal process is made up primarily of interactions between a variety of groups and entities whose programs and initiatives are addressed to human rights enforcement in ways that are not consistent with a model of centralized, coercive governmental or intergovernmental policing. Echoing Weston's definition of legal process generally, Koh describes an array of "values entrepreneurs" operating in this "vertical" sense to shape behavior consistent with human rights doctrines, principles, and norms—for example, the International Committee of the Red Cross (ICRC) fostering humanitarian law since the nineteenth century, and the World Medical Association inserting human rights norms into their code of professional ethics exemplified by the torture provisions of the Association's 1975 Declaration of Tokyo.[4] Thus, according to Koh, the "vertical" strain to norm-consistency among diverse nongovernmental groups is an important component of human rights enforcement in world affairs. He paints a rich picture of a complex field of action contributing to human rights enforcement, though seldom recognized as such by those who assume law enforcement to be restricted to governmental policing bureaucracies according to some conceptually narrow model of domestic law, which Koh characterizes as "state-to-state" or "horizontal" enforcement institutions.

As we turn to this state-to-state field of action, the enforcement or implementation picture emerges as all too disappointing—and examples are legion. As Koh asserts, "the overall picture of this standard enforcement story is one of impotence, ineffectiveness, of a horizontal system where the key actors are nation-states and intergovernmental organizations, the key forums are governmental forums, and the key transactions are transactions between states and other states." Koh argues that it is through the vertical "repeated cycle of interaction, interpretation, and internalization—this transnational legal process—that international law acquires its 'stickiness,' and that nations come to 'obey' international human rights law out of a perceived self-interest that becomes institutional habit." Fundamentally, the state-to-state paradigm fails to account adequately for the multiple ways in which international human rights norms percolate and circulate through the international system. Fundamentally, as Koh tells us, it is a transnational process of essentially

---

4. http://www.wma.net/en/30publications/10policies/c18 (accessed 20 June 2014).

nongovernmental energies in a complex array of interacting circumstances, motives, institutional and non-institutional dynamics, and actors—vectors of effect that are complicated to trace yet powerfully influential—that emerge ultimately to put legal and nonlegal feet on the human rights ground.

The final essay in this chapter looks at the complexities and lack of uniformity characterizing human rights enforcement through a distinctively empirical, sociological lens. Sociologist Wade Cole presents an analysis of treaty compliance and the effects of treaties on human rights outcomes. His central claim is that "too often, scholars assume that the mechanisms established to monitor and enforce human rights treaties are ineffectual without actually evaluating whether this claim has empirical merit." Cole argues that, in reality, such a claim is susceptible to detailed empirical evaluation—that it is, in short, "eminently verifiable." Accordingly, he postulates a series of hypotheses concerning the effectiveness of human rights treaties, and analyzes their veracity in the light of a detailed analysis of data concerning a particular set of human rights treaties. His analysis leads him to conclude that, far from being completely ineffective—indeed, far from the implications of the phrase "myth and ceremony" in his chosen title—the best available evidence suggests that treaties do positively affect the human rights practices of states, even if not uniformly—a conclusion compatible with Harvard University political scientist Beth Simmons's extensive empirical studies of human rights treaty compliance.[5] Cole argues, for example, that "enhanced monitoring and enforcement provisions are reasonably effective in improving the human rights practices of states," and that interstate complaints procedures can produce better human rights outcomes than situations without such procedures. Likewise, he contends, individual complaints procedures produce a positive effect—but not always (as in the case of the 1966 International Convention on the Elimination of All Forms of Racial Discrimination (ICERD) where the use of such procedures appears to have exacerbated racial discrimination). Meanwhile, the effects of "straightforward ratification" of human rights treaties show that "rights-abusing countries join human rights treaties at rates equal to rights-affirming countries."

Cole's analysis reiterates the message delivered by Weston and Koh concerning the complex flow and eddy of different motivational factors operating at multiple levels in international legal process. In Cole's study, these factors do not produce predictable outcomes in many cases, and the correlation between treaty ratification and improved outcomes is revealed to be far from uniform. "Ratification," argues Cole, "is not an all-or-nothing enterprise," and the flexibility in the international human rights system relative to conditional or qualified ratifications has inconsistent effects. Some countries use reservations to make more "precise and sincere treaty commitments" while other countries use them to "enervate the treaties." In any case, on the basis of Cole's findings, it is clear that human rights treaty membership is not merely myth or ceremony. On the contrary, under particular conditions, human rights treaties have a positive and beneficial effect on state practices regarding human rights. However, what Cole's analysis ultimately reveals is that despite the international proclamation that all human rights are "universal, indivisible and interdependent and interrelated," in reality "different categories of right do not respond uniformly to treaty membership."

Arguably most provocative, however, is Cole's final observation that picks up on themes now familiar to the reader from Chapter 1 onward in this book and reiterated hereinafter: that treaties aiming to protect "subaltern" or marginalized groups of humans reveal the

5. See, e.g., Beth A. Simmons, *Mobilizing for Human Rights: International Law in Domestic Politics* (New York: CUP, 2009).

strongest points of resistance—or worse, they exacerbate the original human rights problem (as just noted vis-à-vis ICERD, for example). This is an empirical finding that exposes, yet again, the persistence of historical and contemporaneous ideological dynamics concerning differential power relations, and points again to the central sense in which human rights themselves remain fraught with ambiguity in both theory and practice.

27. BURNS H. WESTON *Human Rights: Prescription and Enforcement*

DEVELOPMENTS BEFORE WORLD WAR II

Ever since ancient times, but especially since the emergence of the modern state system, the Age of Discovery, and the accompanying spread of industrialization and European culture throughout the world, there has developed, for economic and other reasons, a unique set of customs and conventions regarding the humane treatment of foreigners. This evolving International Law of State Responsibility for Injuries to Aliens, as these customs and conventions came to be called, represents the beginning of active concern—however much they served the interests of colonial expansion—for human rights on the international plane. The founding fathers of international law—particularly Francisco de Vitoria, Grotius, and Emmerich de Vattel—were quick to observe that all persons, outlander as well as the Other, were entitled to certain natural rights, and they emphasized, consequently, the importance of according aliens fair treatment.

With the exception of occasional treaties to secure the protection of Christian denominations, it was not until the start of the nineteenth century, however, that active international concern for the rights of nationals began to make itself felt. Then, in the century and a half before World War II, several noteworthy efforts to encourage respect for nationals by international means began to shape what today is called the International Law of Human Rights (which for historical but no theoretically convincing reasons was treated separately from the International Law of State Responsibility for Injuries to Aliens).

Throughout the nineteenth and early twentieth centuries, numerous military operations and

diplomatic representations, not all of them with the purest of motives but performed nonetheless in the name of "humanitarian intervention" (a customary international law doctrine), undertook to protect oppressed and persecuted minorities in the Ottoman Empire, Syria, Crete, various Balkan countries, Romania, and Russia. Paralleling these actions, first at the Congress of Vienna (1814–15) and later between the two World Wars, a series of treaties and international declarations sought the protection of certain racial, religious, and linguistic minorities in Central and Eastern Europe and the Middle East. During the same period, the movement to combat and suppress slavery and the slave trade found expression in treaties sooner or later involving the major commercial powers, beginning with the Treaty of Paris (1814) and culminating in the International Slavery Convention (1926).

In addition, beginning in the late nineteenth century and continuing well beyond World War II, the community of nations, inspired largely by persons associated with what is now the International Committee of the Red Cross, concluded a series of multilateral declarations and agreements designed to temper the conduct of hostilities, protect the victims of war, and otherwise elaborate the humanitarian law of war (now commonly referred to as International Humanitarian Law). At about the same time, first with two multilateral labor conventions concluded in 1906 and subsequently at the initiative of the International Labour Organization (established in 1919), a reformist-minded international community embarked upon a variety of collaborative measures directed at the promotion of human rights. These measures addressed not only concerns traditionally associated with labor law and labor relations (e.g., industrial health and safety, hours of work, and annual paid holidays), but also—mainly after World War II—such core human rights concerns as forced labor, discrimination in employment and occupation, freedom of association for collective bargaining, and equal pay for equal work.

Finally, during the interwar period, the covenant establishing the League of Nations (1919)—though not formally recognizing "the rights of Man" and failing to lay down a principle of racial non-discrimination as requested by Japan (mainly because of the resistance of Great Britain and the United States)—nevertheless committed its members to several human rights goals: fair and humane working conditions, the execution of agreements regarding trafficking of women and children, the prevention and control of disease in matters of international concern, and the just treatment of indigenous colonial peoples. Also, the victorious powers—who as "mandatories" were entrusted by the League of Nations with the tutelage of colonies formerly governed by Germany and Turkey—accepted responsibility for the well-being and development of the inhabitants of those territories as "a sacred trust of civilization." This arrangement was later carried over into the trusteeship system of the United Nations.

As important as these efforts were, however, it was not until after the war—and the Nazi atrocities accompanying it—that active concern for human rights truly came of age internationally. In the proceedings of the International Military Tribunal at Nürnberg in 1945–46 (the Nürnberg trials), German high officials were tried not only for "crimes against peace" and "war crimes" but also for "crimes against humanity" committed against civilian populations, even if the crimes were in accordance with the laws of the country in which they were perpetrated. Although the Tribunal, whose establishment and rulings subsequently were endorsed by the UN General Assembly, applied a cautious approach to allegations of crimes against humanity, it nonetheless made the treatment by a state of its own citizens the subject of international criminal process. The ad hoc international criminal tribunals established in 1993–94 for the prosecution of serious violations of International Humanitarian Law in the former Yugoslavia and in Rwanda were its first heirs on the international plane. Both courts were empowered to impose sentences of life imprisonment (though not the death penalty), and both focused their efforts, with some success, on political leaders who had authorized human rights abuses. Most conspicuous was the arrest and detention in June 2001 of former Yugoslav president Slobodan Milošević by the International Criminal Tribunal for Yugoslavia, representing the first time a former head of state was placed in the physical custody of an international judicial authority. The Tribunal charged him with war crimes and crimes against humanity allegedly committed by Serbian forces in Kosovo in 1999 and subsequently with the crime of genocide allegedly committed by Serbian forces during the war in Bosnia and Herzegovina in 1992–95. His trial ended with his death in March 2006.

Also heir to the Nürnberg tribunal is the International Criminal Court (ICC), authorized by the adoption by 120 countries of the Rome Statute of the International Criminal Court in July 1998.[1] The statute created an independent, permanent international criminal court with legal personality separate from the United Nations and whose substantive jurisdiction includes crimes against humanity, crimes of genocide, war crimes, and crimes of "aggression" (pending the adoption of an acceptable definition of that term). However, the creation of the court, which depended on the ratification of the statute by at least 60 signatory states, was resisted by some countries, notably the United States, on the ground that it would unduly infringe upon their national sovereignty. Indeed, during the administration of President George W. Bush (2001–9), the United States not only refused to ratify the statute but also took the unusual step of withdrawing its signature from it. Given the sway of the United States in world affairs, this rendered the long-term future of the court uncertain. Despite some initial operational problems and uneven support from states party to the Rome Statute, the ICC subsequently made notable progress in prosecuting perpetrators of the world's most heinous crimes and thus bolstered its near-term future.

HUMAN RIGHTS IN THE UNITED NATIONS

The United Nations, founded in 1945 after World War II and the Holocaust, was created principally to maintain international peace and

1. Rome Statute of the International Criminal Court, 17 July 1998.

security and to encourage and promote respect for human rights and fundamental freedoms. The Charter of the United Nations confirms these two purposes and begins its recognition of the second by reaffirming a

> faith in fundamental human rights, in the dignity and worth of the human person, in the equal rights of men and women and of nations large and small.

It states that the purposes of the UN are, among other things:

> to develop friendly relations among nations based on respect for the principle of equal rights and self-determination of peoples . . . [and] to achieve international co-operation . . . in promoting and encouraging respect for human rights and for fundamental freedoms for all without distinction as to race, sex, language, or religion.

In addition, in two key articles, "all members pledge themselves to take joint and separate action in co-operation with the Organization for the achievement of" these and related purposes.

It must be noted, however, that a proposal to ensure the protection (i.e., enforcement) of human rights as distinct from their promotion (i.e., advocacy) was explicitly rejected at the Charter-drafting San Francisco conference establishing the UN. Accordingly, while providing for the UN Security Council to enforce the UN's first primary purpose (maintaining international peace and security), the drafters did not specify a comparable body to give teeth to its second primary purpose (promoting human rights and fundamental freedoms). Also, the Charter expressly provides that nothing in it "shall authorize the United Nations to intervene in matters which are essentially within the domestic jurisdiction of any state," except upon a Security Council finding of a "threat to the peace, breach of the peace, or act of aggression." Furthermore, though typical of major constitutive instruments, the Charter is conspicuously given to generality and vagueness in its human rights clauses, among others.

Thus, not surprisingly, the reconciliation of the Charter's human rights provisions with the history of its drafting and its "domestic jurisdiction" clause has given rise to legal and political controversy. Some authorities have argued that, in becoming parties to the Charter, states accept

no more than a nebulous promotional obligation toward human rights and that, in any event, the UN has no standing to insist on human rights safeguards in member states. Others have insisted that the Charter's human rights provisions, being part of a legally binding treaty, clearly involve some element of legal obligation; that the "pledge" made by states upon becoming party to the Charter consequently represents more than a moral statement; and that the domestic jurisdiction clause does not apply, because human rights can be considered no longer a matter "essentially within the domestic jurisdiction" of states.

When all is said and done, however, it is clear from the actual practice of the UN that the problem of resolving these opposing contentions has proved less formidable than the statements of governments and the opinions of scholars would suggest. Neither the Charter's drafting history nor its domestic jurisdiction clause—nor, indeed, its generality and vagueness in respect of human rights—has prevented the UN from investigating, discussing, and evaluating specific human rights situations. Nor have they prevented it from taking concrete action in relation to them—at least not in the case of "a consistent pattern of gross violations," as in the Security Council's imposition of a mandatory arms embargo against South Africa in 1977 and its authorization of the use of military force to end human rights abuses in Somalia and Haiti in the early 1990s.

In 2003 the Security Council intervened in a civil war in Côte d'Ivoire by authorizing a military peacekeeping force—an action that, with the help of the Economic Community of West African States (ECOWAS), led ultimately to the ouster of an electorally defeated presidential incumbent (Laurent Gbagbo) and the reestablishment of public order under a newly elected president (Alassane Ouattara). Additionally, during the Libya Revolt of 2011, a civil war fought between forces loyal to Colonel Muammar al-Qaddafi and those seeking to oust his government, the Security Council authorized UN member states to establish and enforce a no-fly zone over Libya and to use "all necessary measures" to prevent attacks on civilians.

In 2005 the member states of the United Nations recognized the principle of the "responsibility to protect" (often called R2P). Under this principle, states have a responsibility to protect their civilian populations against genocide and other mass human rights atrocities. If they fail to do so, according to the R2P principle, states forfeit their sovereign immunity, and the international community is responsible for using appropriate diplomatic, humanitarian, and other means to protect the populations being victimized—and to this end, in accordance with the UN Charter, to be prepared to take collective action in their defense.

The R2P principle was controversial because it contradicted the long-established principle of state sovereignty. It was invoked by the UN Security Council to authorize military interventions in a second civil war in Côte d'Ivoire (2010), Libya (2011), and other countries. However, in 2013 the international community's resistance to U.S. plans to launch missile strikes against Syria in retaliation for that country's alleged use of internationally prohibited chemical weapons against its own population added significant doubt to the already controversial assertion that the R2P principle, however warranted morally, is a legally binding principle.

Of course, governments usually are protective of their sovereignty, or domestic jurisdiction. Also, the UN organs responsible for the promotion and protection of human rights suffer from most of the same disabilities that afflict the UN as a whole, in particular, the absence of supranational authority, the presence of divisive power politics, and the imposition of crippling financial constraints by member states (most notably the United States). Hence, it cannot be expected that UN actions in defense of human rights will be, normally, either swift or categorically effective. Indeed, many serious UN efforts at human rights implementation have been deliberately thwarted by the major powers. In 1999, for example, opposition by China and Russia prevented the Security Council from agreeing on forceful measures to end ethnic cleansing by Yugoslav and Serbian forces in Kosovo, prompting the United States and other members of the North Atlantic Treaty Organization (NATO) to take matters into their own hands through a massive bombing campaign against Serbian targets. Assuming some political will, however, the legal obstacles to UN enforcement of human rights are not insurmountable.

From the beginning, four of the six principal organs of the United Nations (the General Assembly, the Economic and Social Council [ECOSOC], the Trusteeship Council, and the Secretariat) shared responsibility for the encouragement and promotion of human rights—although, as the UN's history bears witness, the Security Council and the International Court of Justice (World Court) have been called into protective human rights service in special circumstances from time to time. Primary responsibility for the advancement of human rights under the UN Charter rests, however, in the General Assembly (the UN's main deliberative body) and, under its authority, in its Social, Humanitarian and Cultural Affairs Committee (commonly referred to as the "Third Committee"), the Human Rights Council (which replaced the former Commission on Human Rights in 2006), and the UN High Commissioner for Human Rights. ECOSOC's responsibility for human rights (though diminished when the former Commission on Human Rights under its authority was replaced by the Human Rights Council under the jurisdiction of the General Assembly) extends to several other commissions, such as the Commission on the Status of Women, the Commission for Social Development, and the Commission on Crime Prevention and Criminal Justice, as well as UN specialized agencies such as the International Labour Organization and the World Health Organization. The Trusteeship Council suspended operations in November 1994 following the independence of Palau, the last remaining UN trust territory. The Secretariat facilitates and administers many human rights policies and programs by virtue of its multifaceted day-to-day work on behalf of the United Nations as a whole, including working closely with each of the UN's principal organs.

THE UN COMMISSION ON HUMAN RIGHTS (1946–2006) AND THE UN HUMAN RIGHTS COUNCIL

THE UN COMMISSION ON HUMAN RIGHTS AND ITS INSTRUMENTS

Between 1946 and 2006 the UN Commission on Human Rights, created as a subsidiary body of ECOSOC, served as the UN's central policy organ in the human rights field. For the first twenty years of its existence, however, the Commission believed itself to be unauthorized to deal with human rights complaints. During its first two decades, therefore, and together with other

UN bodies such as the ILO, UNESCO (the United Nations Educational, Scientific and Cultural Organization), the UN Commission on the Status of Women, and the Commission on Human Rights Crime Prevention and Criminal Justice, it concentrated on setting human rights standards and drafting a number of historically vital international human rights instruments. Among the most important of these were the Universal Declaration of Human Rights, the International Covenant on Economic, Social and Cultural Rights, and the International Covenant on Civil and Political Rights and its two Optional Protocols (1966 and 1989). Together, these three instruments and the Optional Protocols constitute what has come to be known as the International Bill of Human Rights, serving as touchstones for interpreting the human rights provisions of the UN Charter. Also central in this regard were the International Convention on the Elimination of All Forms of Racial Discrimination (1965), the Convention on the Elimination of All Forms of Discrimination against Women (1979), the Convention against Torture and Other Cruel, Inhuman or Degrading Treatment or Punishment (1984), and the Convention on the Rights of the Child (1989), each of which elaborated on provisions of the International Bill of Human Rights.

Beginning in 1967, the Commission was explicitly authorized to deal with violations of human rights, and shortly thereafter it set up elaborate mechanisms and procedures to investigate alleged human rights violations and otherwise monitor compliance by states with international human rights law. Thus, much of the work of the Commission became investigatory, evaluative, and advisory in character. Each year it established a working group to consider and make recommendations concerning alleged "gross violations" of human rights, reports of which were referred to the Commission by its Sub-Commission on Prevention of Discrimination and Protection of Minorities—later known as the Sub-Commission on the Promotion and Protection of Human Rights—on the basis of both "communications" from individuals and groups and investigations by the subcommission or one of its working groups. Also, on an ad hoc basis, the Commission appointed special rapporteurs, special representatives, special committees, and other envoys to examine human rights situations—both country-oriented and thematic—and to report back to it on the basis of trustworthy evidence. These fact-finding and implementation mechanisms and procedures were the focus of the Commission's attention during the 1970s and '80s. In the 1990s the Commission turned increasingly to economic, social, and cultural rights, including the right to development and the right to an adequate standard of living. Increased attention was paid also to the rights of minorities, indigenous peoples, women, and children.

In the early twenty-first century the Commission on Human Rights came to be viewed as ineffective, in part because its membership included countries with poor human rights records. It therefore was replaced by the UN Human Rights Council in 2006.

THE UN HUMAN RIGHTS COUNCIL AND ITS INSTRUMENTS

The UN Human Rights Council was created as a subsidiary intergovernmental body of the UN General Assembly and initially comprised nearly 50 UN member states. The Council was charged with strengthening the promotion and protection of human rights worldwide. To this end, it was mandated to address and make recommendations regarding human rights violations wherever found and to discuss all human rights issues and situations that require its attention throughout the year, including, but not limited to, violence against women and children, sexual violence in conflict, genocide, the human rights of indigenous peoples and the disabled, child soldiers, and human trafficking.

One year after its founding, the Council adopted an "institution-building package" to guide its work and to establish its mechanisms and procedures. Among them were the universal periodic review mechanism, by which the Council assesses the human rights records of every UN member state, including members of the council itself during their terms of membership; the Advisory Committee, the council's "think tank" for advice on thematic human rights issues, superseding the Sub-Commission on the Promotion and Protection of Human Rights, established under the former UN Commission on Human Rights; and the complaint procedure, giving standing to individuals and civil-society organizations to bring human rights violations to the Council's attention.

Like its predecessor, the Council also works with special rapporteurs, special representatives, independent experts, and working groups that monitor, examine, advise, and report publicly on human rights issues and on particular human rights situations in specific countries.

OFFICE OF THE UN HIGH COMMISSIONER FOR HUMAN RIGHTS

The Office of the High Commissioner for Human Rights (OHCHR), established by the UN General Assembly in 1993, is the UN bureau mandated to promote and protect human rights guaranteed under international law. To this end, it focuses on standard setting, monitoring, and implementation and serves as a secretariat providing administrative, logistical, and substantive support to the Human Rights Council and other UN bodies concerned with human rights. It was consolidated with the former UN Centre for Human Rights in 1997.

The UN High Commissioner for Human Rights is the official within the OHCHR principally responsible for implementing and coordinating UN human rights programs and projects around the world. Appointed by the Secretary-General in a regular rotation of geographic regions and approved by the General Assembly, the UN High Commissioner serves a fixed term of four years with the possibility of renewal for an additional four-year term. The first High Commissioner, José Ayala Lasso of Ecuador, held office from 1994 to 1997. He was succeeded by the former president of Ireland, Mary Robinson (1997–2002); the Brazilian diplomat Sergio Vieira de Mello (2002–3), who was tragically killed by terrorists; the former Deputy High Commissioner for Human Rights and Assistant Secretary-General Bertrand Ramcharan (interim 2003–4); the Canadian judge Louise Arbour (2004–8); and the South African jurist Navanethem Pillay, whose four-year mandate (beginning in 2008) was renewed for two years in 2012.

Among other duties, the High Commissioner is charged by the General Assembly to promote and protect all civil, political, economic, social, and cultural rights; to provide advisory services and technical and financial assistance in the field of human rights to states that request them; to coordinate human rights promotion and protection activities throughout the UN system, including education and public-information programs; and otherwise to enhance international cooperation for the promotion and protection of human rights—all within the framework of the International Bill of Human Rights. The office of the High Commissioner for Human Rights won increasing praise and support for the work it has done over the years, and many observers ascribed these successes to the high calibre of its successive High Commissioners.

THE UNIVERSAL DECLARATION OF HUMAN RIGHTS

The Universal Declaration of Human Rights (UDHR) was adopted without dissent by the UN General Assembly on 10 December 1948. The catalogue of rights set out in it is scarcely less than the sum of most of the important traditional political and civil rights of national constitutions and legal systems, including equality before the law; protection against arbitrary arrest; the right to a fair trial; freedom from ex post facto criminal laws; the right to own property; freedom of thought, conscience, and religion; freedom of opinion and expression; and freedom of peaceful assembly and association. Also enumerated are such economic, social, and cultural rights as the right to work, the right to form and join trade unions, the right to rest and leisure, the right to a standard of living adequate for health and well-being, and the right to education.

The UDHR, it should be noted, is not a treaty. It was meant to proclaim "a common standard of achievement for all peoples and all nations" rather than enforceable legal obligations. Nevertheless, a number of its provisions have acquired a status juridically more important than originally intended, a reflection of its wide use, even by national courts, as a means of judging compliance with human rights obligations under the UN Charter. It is also one of the instruments constituting the International Bill of Human Rights.

THE INTERNATIONAL COVENANT ON ECONOMIC, SOCIAL AND CULTURAL RIGHTS

The International Covenant on Economic, Social and Cultural Rights (ICESCR) was opened for signature on 16 December 1966, and entered into force on 3 January 1976. Also part of the International Bill of Human Rights, it elaborates upon most of the economic, social, and cultural rights set forth in the Universal Declaration of Human Rights, including, among others, the right to work, the right to form and join trade unions, the right to health, and the right to education. Unlike its companion agreement, the International Covenant on Civil and Political Rights, however, generally this covenant, sometimes called a "promotional convention," was not intended for immediate implementation, the state parties having agreed only "to take steps" toward "achieving progressively the full realization of the rights recognized in the . . . Covenant," and then subject to "the maximum of [their] available resources." One obligation, however, was subject to immediate application: the prohibition of discrimination in the enjoyment of the rights enumerated on grounds of race, color, sex, language, religion, political or other opinion, national or social origin, property, and birth or other status. Also, the international supervisory measures that apply to the ICESCR oblige the state parties to report to the UN Economic and Social Council on the steps they have adopted and on the progress they have made in achieving the realization of the enumerated rights. In 2008 the adoption of an Optional Protocol led to the creation of an individual-complaints mechanism for the ICESCR—the Committee on Economic, Social and Cultural Rights—which was comparable to the Human Rights Committee of the International Covenant on Civil and Political Rights.

The International Covenant on Civil and Political Rights and Its Optional Protocols

The International Covenant on Civil and Political Rights (ICCPR), likewise a part of the International Bill of Human Rights, was opened for signature 19 December 1966, and entered into force 23 March 1976. Just as the International Covenant on Economic, Social and Cultural Rights elaborates upon most of the economic, social, and cultural rights enumerated in the Universal Declaration of Human Rights, so the ICCPR elaborates upon most of the civil and political rights set forth in the Universal Declaration of Human Rights, including the right to non-discrimination but excluding the right to own property and the right to asylum. The covenant also designates several rights not listed in

the UDHR, among them the right of all peoples to self-determination and the right of ethnic, religious, and linguistic minorities to enjoy their own culture, to profess and practice their own religion, and to use their own language. To the extent that the UDHR and the covenant overlap, however, the latter is understood to explicate and help interpret the former.

In addition, the Covenant calls for the establishment of a Human Rights Committee, comprising persons serving in their individual expert capacities, to study reports submitted by the state parties on measures they have adopted to give effect to the rights recognized in the Covenant. For state parties that have expressly recognized the competence of the committee in this regard, the committee also may respond to allegations by one state party that another state party is not fulfilling its obligations under the Covenant. If the committee is unable to resolve the problem, the matter is referred to an ad hoc conciliation commission, which eventually reports its findings on all questions of fact, plus its views on the possibilities of an amicable solution. State parties that become party to the Covenant's First Optional Protocol further recognize the competence of the Human Rights Committee to consider and act upon communications from individuals claiming to be victims of Covenant violations, provided that the respondent state has recognized the competence of the Committee in this regard and that domestic remedies have been exhausted—emulating the legal standing given to individuals before the UN Commission on Human Rights after 1967.

Other treaty-based organs within the UN system that are similarly empowered to consider grievances from individuals in a quasi-judicial manner are the Committee on Economic, Social and Cultural Rights, the Committee on the Elimination of Racial Discrimination, the Committee on Torture, the Committee on the Elimination of Discrimination against Women, the Committee on the Rights of Persons with Disabilities, and the Committee on Enforced Disappearances. Additionally, the 1990 International Convention on the Protection of the Rights of All Migrant Workers and Members of their Families and the Optional Protocol to the Convention on the Rights of the Child contain provisions for individual complaints that are not yet operational.

The Second Optional Protocol of the International Covenant on Civil and Political Rights, which is aimed at abolishing the death penalty worldwide, was adopted in 1989 and entered into force in 1991. The Protocol has been favorably received in most of the countries of Western Europe and in many countries in the Americas, though not in the United States.

Numerous other human rights treaties drafted under UN auspices address a broad range of concerns. Supplementing the ICCPR and ICESCR considered above, the Office of the High Commissioner for Human Rights lists several other "core international human rights instruments," including the 1965 International Convention on the Elimination of All Forms of Racial Discrimination; the 1979 Convention on the Elimination of All Forms of Discrimination against Women; the 2002 Optional Protocol of the 1984 Convention against Torture and Other Cruel, Inhuman or Degrading Treatment or Punishment; and the 2006 Convention on the Rights of Persons with Disabilities. The OHCHR also details a nonexhaustive list of "other universal instruments relating to human rights" (although including the core instruments just noted). The list is nonetheless long and diverse and embraces declarations, principles, guidelines, standard rules, and recommendations which, according to the OHCHR, "have no binding legal effect," as well as covenants, statutes, protocols, and conventions that, it asserts, "are legally binding." The wide scope of topical categories includes the right of self-determination, the rights of indigenous peoples and minorities, social welfare, and humanitarian law (i.e., the humanitarian rules of armed conflict).

Thus, across a wide range of issues and themes and in addition to overseeing human rights treaties deemed legally binding in theory, the UN has adopted human rights instruments that are presumptively not legally binding, as is, in contrast, a treaty or a resolution of the Security Council. Such instruments—particularly when they enunciate principles of great and solemn importance—may nevertheless create strong expectations about authority and control. Perhaps the best-known examples subsequent to the Universal Declaration of Human Rights are the Declaration on the Granting of Independence to Colonial Countries and Peoples (1960) and the Declaration on Principles of International Law concerning Friendly Relations and Co-operation among States in accordance with the Charter of the United Nations (1970) which affirms, among other things, "the duty of all states to refrain from organizing, instigating, assisting or participating in . . . terrorist acts."

HUMAN RIGHTS AND THE HELSINKI PROCESS

After World War II, international concern for human rights was evident at the global level outside the UN as well as within it, most notably in the proceedings and aftermath of the Conference on Security and Co-operation in Europe (CSCE), convened in Helsinki, Finland, on 3 July 1973, and concluded there (after continuing deliberations in Geneva) on 1 August 1975. Attended by representatives of 35 governments—including the NATO countries, Warsaw Pact nations, and 13 neutral and nonaligned European states—the conference had as its principal purpose a mutually satisfactory definition of peace and stability between East and West, previously made impossible by the Cold War. In particular, the Soviet Union wished to gain recognition of its western frontiers as established at the end of World War II (which ended without conclusion of an omnibus peace treaty). The West, with no realistic territorial claims of its own, sought concessions primarily on security requirements and human rights, largely in that order.

The Final Act of the Conference, also known as the Helsinki Accords, begins with a Declaration on Principles Guiding Relations between Participating States, in which the participating states solemnly declare "their determination to respect and put into practice," alongside other "guiding" principles, "respect [for] human rights and fundamental freedoms, including the freedom of thought, conscience, religion or belief" and "respect [for] the equal rights of peoples and their right to self-determination." It was hoped that this declaration, the importance of which is reflected in its having been signed by almost all the principal governmental leaders of the day, would mark the beginning of a liberalization of authoritarian regimes.

From the earliest discussions, however, it was

clear that the Helsinki Final Act was not intended as a legally binding instrument. The expressions "determination to respect" and "put into practice" were seen to represent moral commitments only, the Declaration of Principles was said not to prescribe international law, and nowhere did the participants provide for enforcement machinery. On the other hand, the Declaration of Principles, including its human rights principles, was always viewed as being at least consistent with international law; and, in providing for periodic follow-up conferences, it made possible a unique negotiating process (the "Helsinki process") to review compliance with its terms, thus creating normative expectations concerning the conduct of the participating states. In these ways, the declaration, ergo the Helsinki Final Act, proved to be an important force in the fall of the Iron Curtain and the transformation of Eastern Europe in 1989–90.

The Helsinki process, involving long-running "follow-up," "summit," and other meetings, served also to establish a mechanism for the evolution of the CSCE from a forum for discussion to an operational institution, beginning with the adoption of the Charter of Paris for a New Europe in 1990. In 1994 the CSCE was renamed the Organization for Security and Co-operation in Europe, and its principal organs and bureaus eventually included an Office for Democratic Institutions and Human Rights (in Warsaw), a Conflict Prevention Centre (in Vienna), a High Commissioner on National Minorities (in The Hague), and a Court of Conciliation and Arbitration (in Geneva). These offices were increasingly pressed into service to alleviate major deprivations of human rights, particularly those arising from ethnic conflicts. In addition, the Vienna Human Dimension Mechanism and the Moscow Human Dimension Mechanism provide a preliminary formal means of raising and seeking to resolve disputes about violations of human rights commitments, including the possibility of on-site investigation by independent experts. All these mechanisms bespeak, however, an essentially interstate process; neither individuals nor nongovernmental organizations (NGOs) have access to them except indirectly as suppliers of information and conveyors of political pressure. They thus contrast markedly with the individual-complaint procedures that are available within the UN system and in regional human rights systems.

REGIONAL HUMAN RIGHTS SYSTEMS AND DEVELOPMENTS

Action for the international promotion and protection of human rights has proceeded at the regional level in Europe, the Americas, Africa, Southeast Asia, and the Middle East. By the first decade of the twenty-first century, however, only the first four of these regions had created enforcement mechanisms within the framework of a human rights charter.

Human Rights in Europe

On 4 November 1950, the Council of Europe agreed to the European Convention for the Protection of Human Rights and Fundamental Freedoms, the substantive provisions of which were based on a draft of what is now the International Covenant on Civil and Political Rights. Together with its 11 additional protocols, this convention, which entered into force on 3 September 1953, represents the most advanced and successful international experiment in the field to date. Over the years, the enforcement mechanisms created by the convention have developed a considerable body of case law on questions regulated by the Convention, which the state parties typically have honored and respected. In some European states the provisions of the Convention are deemed to be part of domestic constitutional or statutory law. Where this is not the case, the state parties have taken other measures to make their domestic laws conform with their obligations under the Convention.

Notwithstanding these successes, a significant streamlining of the European human rights regime took place on 1 November 1998, when Protocol No. 11 to the Convention entered into force. Pursuant to the Protocol, two of the enforcement mechanisms created by the Convention—the European Commission of Human Rights and the European Court of Human Rights—were merged into a reconstituted court, which now is empowered to hear individual (as opposed to interstate) petitions or complaints without the prior approval of the local government. The decisions of the court are final and binding on the state parties to the convention.

A companion instrument to the European Convention—similar to but preceding the International Covenant on Economic, Social and Cultural Rights—is the European Social Charter (1961) and its additional protocol (1988). In contrast to the adjudicatory enforcement procedures of the European Convention, the Charter's provisions are implemented through an elaborate system of control based on progress reports to the various committees and organs of the Council of Europe. The revised European Social Charter, which was intended gradually to replace the 1961 Charter and entered into force in 1999, modernizes its forebear's substantive provisions and strengthens its enforcement capabilities. The basic rights set forth in the revised Charter concern housing; health; education; labor rights, employment, and parental leave; protection from poverty and social exclusion; free movement of persons and non-discrimination; migrant worker rights; and non-discrimination of persons with disabilities.

HUMAN RIGHTS IN THE AMERICAS

In 1948, concurrent with its establishment of the Organization of American States (OAS), the Ninth Pan-American Conference adopted the American Declaration on the Rights and Duties of Man, which, unlike the Universal Declaration of the UN adopted seven months later, set out the duties as well as the rights of individual citizens. Subsequently, in 1959, a meeting of the American Ministers for Foreign Affairs created the Inter-American Commission on Human Rights, which has since undertaken important investigative activities in the region. Finally, in 1969, the Inter-American Specialized Conference on Human Rights adopted the American Convention on Human Rights, which, among other things, after entering into force in July 1978, made the existing Inter-American Commission an organ of the Convention and established the Inter-American Court of Human Rights, which sits in San José, Costa Rica. In November 1988, the OAS adopted the Additional Protocol to the American Convention on Human Rights in the Area of Economic, Social and Cultural Rights. Of the 26 Western Hemispheric states that so far have signed the Convention, only the United States has yet to ratify it. Nor is the United States a party to the additional protocol, which entered into force in November 1999.

The core structure of the Inter-American human rights system is similar to that of its Eu-

ropean counterpart. Nevertheless, some noteworthy differences exist, and three stand out in particular. First, the American Convention, reflecting the influence of the American Declaration, acknowledges the relationship between individual duties and individual rights. Second, the American Convention reverses the priorities of the European Convention prior to Protocol No. 11 by guaranteeing individual petitions while making interstate complaints optional. Finally, both the Inter-American Commission on Human Rights and the Inter-American Court of Human Rights operate beyond the framework of the American Convention. The Commission is as much an organ of the OAS Charter as of the American Convention, with powers and procedures that differ significantly depending on the source of the Commission's authority. The court, while primarily an organ of the Convention, nonetheless has jurisdiction to interpret the human rights provisions of other treaties, including those of the OAS Charter.

HUMAN RIGHTS IN AFRICA

In 1981 the Eighteenth Assembly of Heads of State and Government of the Organization of African Unity (replaced by the African Union [AU] in 2002) adopted the African Charter on Human and Peoples' Rights. Also known as the "Banjul Charter" for having been drafted in Banjul, Gambia, it entered into force on 21 October 1986, and boasts the vast majority of the states of Africa as parties.

Like its American and early European counterparts, the African Charter provides for a human rights commission (the African Commission on Human and Peoples' Rights), which has both promotional and protective functions. There is no restriction on who may file a complaint with it. In contrast to the European and American procedures, however, concerned states are encouraged to reach a friendly settlement without formally involving the investigative or conciliatory mechanisms of the Commission. Also, the African Charter did not, at the beginning, call for a human rights court. African customs and traditions, it has been said, have long emphasized mediation, conciliation, and consensus rather than the adversarial and adjudicative procedures that are common to Western legal systems.

Nevertheless, owing largely to political

changes wrought by the end of the Cold War, an African Court of Human and Peoples' Rights (ACHPR) was created in January 2004 to render judgments on the compliance by AU states with the African charter. The Court did not replace the Commission.

A year earlier, however, in 2003, there came into being the African Court of Justice (ACJ), intended to serve as the AU's principal judicial body and, in this capacity, to rule on disputes over the interpretation of AU treaties. Concern for rising costs in the face of little forward movement on the part of the ACJ, however, led to proposals for the creation of a new court, the African Court of Justice and Human Rights (ACJHR). Designed to have two chambers—one for general legal matters that would supersede the ACJ, the other for judgments on the interpretation and application of human rights treaties—the ACJHR came into being when, in 2008, a merger protocol was adopted uniting the ACJ and the ACHPR. It was believed that the ACJHR had the potential to be progressively influential in the protection of human rights in Africa. It was also recognized, however, that this prospect—above all the ACJHR's legitimacy—depended on the independence and moral character of its judges and on the training and effectiveness of its staff.

It is, in any event, fair to say that the African human rights system was still in its infancy at the beginning of the twenty-first century, given especially the turmoil and violence that beset northern and sub-Saharan Africa during this time. But four distinctive features of the African Charter—and thus, the African human rights system—are noteworthy and give reason for hope. First, the Charter provides for economic, social, and cultural rights as well as civil and political rights. In this respect it resembles the American Convention and differs from the European Convention. Second, in contrast to both the European and American Conventions, it recognizes the rights of groups in addition to the family, women, and children. The aged and the infirm are accorded special protection also, and the right of peoples to self-determination is elaborated in the right to existence, equality, and nondomination. Third, it uniquely embraces two third-generation, or "solidarity," rights: the right to economic, social, and cultural development and the right to national and international peace and security. It differs from other treaties also by

detailing individual duties as well as individual rights—to the family, society, the state, and the international African community.

Human Rights in the Arab World

In September 1968 the Council of the League of Arab States created the Arab Commission on Human Rights. Its main purposes were to inform the Arab public about and otherwise promote human rights, not to monitor the human rights practices of the Arab states or to challenge their violations of human rights when found. Primarily the Commission has been preoccupied with the rights of Arabs living in Israeli-occupied territories.

On 22 May 2004, however, the Arab League adopted the Arab Charter on Human Rights, which entered into force on 15 March 2008. The Charter affirms the principles set forth in the International Bill of Human Rights—including, for example, the right to liberty and security of persons, equality of persons before the law, protection of persons from torture, the right to own private property, freedom to practice religion, and freedom of peaceful assembly and association.

At the same time, the Charter does not prohibit cruel, inhuman, or degrading punishments, fails to extend rights to noncitizens in many areas, and authorizes restrictions on freedom of thought, conscience, and religion that exceed what is deemed permissible under international human rights law. Furthermore, the Charter relegates many important rights issues to the discretion of national legislation—e.g., the death penalty against children and the rights of men and women in marriage.

Additionally, the Charter affirms the principles set forth in the 1990 Cairo Declaration on Human Rights in Islam, a declaration of the member states of the Organisation of the Islamic Conference that provides an Islamic perspective on human rights and affirms that all the rights and freedoms mentioned in the Declaration are subject to Shari'a, or Islamic law, stated in Article 25 to be "the only source of reference for the explanation or clarification of any of the articles of [the] Declaration." Accordingly, though using universalist language akin to that found in the International Bill of Human Rights, the Arab charter is imbued with an "Islamic particularity." It also expresses Arab concern regarding territorial disputes between Israel and the Palestinians. Thus, its controversial Article 2(3) provides that

> all forms of racism, Zionism and foreign occupation and domination constitute an impediment to human dignity and a major barrier to the exercise of the fundamental rights of peoples; all such practices must be condemned and efforts must be deployed for their elimination.

The Charter also provides for the election of a seven-person Committee of Experts on Human Rights, which is empowered to request and study reports and to submit its own findings to the Commission. No other institutions or procedures for monitoring human rights are specified in the Charter, however. In this sense as well as others, the Arab human rights system compares unfavorably with its European, Inter-American, and African counterparts.

Human Rights in Asia

Despite efforts by NGOs and the United Nations, Asian states were at best ambivalent—and at worst hostile—to human rights concerns over many years, thus precluding agreement on almost all regional human rights initiatives. But in early 1993, anticipating the World Conference on Human Rights held in Vienna later that year, a conference of Asia-Pacific NGOs adopted an Asia-Pacific Declaration of Human Rights, and in 1998 another meeting of NGOs adopted an Asian Human Rights Charter. Both of these initiatives supported the universality and indivisibility of human rights. However, while the first initiative called for the creation of a regional human rights regime, the second urged instead the establishment of national human rights commissions and so-called "People's Tribunals," which would be based more on moral and spiritual foundations rather than on legal ones.

The states of Asia were slow to respond to these initiatives. Their positions were indicated at a UN-sponsored workshop in 1996, where the 30 participating states concluded that "it was premature . . . to discuss specific arrangements relating to the setting up of a formal human rights mechanism in the Asian and Pacific region." The same states agreed, however, to "[explore] the options available and the process necessary for establishing a regional mecha-

nism"—a promise that echoed a similar pledge made by ASEAN (the Association of Southeast Asian Nations) following the 1993 UN World Conference on Human Rights.

More than fourteen years later, in November 2007, ASEAN's 10 member states adopted the ASEAN Charter, which, following its entry into force in December 2008, gave ASEAN legal personality, established its organizational framework and procedures, and provided for a human rights body that would promote and protect human rights as signaled in the Charter's preamble, purposes, and principles. In October 2009 ASEAN's member states formally established the ASEAN Intergovernmental Commission on Human Rights, and in November 2012 they adopted ASEAN's first-ever Human Rights Declaration.

In Southeast Asia and around the world, however, ASEAN's Declaration has been greeted with skepticism. Many respected rights groups, including Amnesty International, criticized the Declaration for being an unhappy compromise between ASEAN's communist and noncommunist member states; for containing language both too broad and too restrictive to guarantee people's rights; and for otherwise falling short of international human rights standards. Of particular concern were provisions that called for rights to be enjoyed in a "balanced" way, subject to "national and regional contexts" and deferential to "different cultural, religious and historical backgrounds," thus challenging the quintessential universality of human rights. Additionally, critics challenged the Declaration for having been drafted in a noninclusive, nontransparent manner, and they faulted ASEAN's charter for failing to mandate powers sufficient for its enforcement. Accordingly, they called on ASEAN leaders to return the declaration to the ASEAN Intergovernmental Commission on Human Rights explicitly to redraft the Declaration in an inclusive and transparent manner and in keeping with internationally recognized human rights law and standards.

Not to be overlooked, however, are other developments bearing upon human rights instruments and mechanisms in Southeast Asia, specifically in relation to particular groups of people. In January 2007 members of ASEAN adopted a common declaration in which they recognized the need for a new instrument to protect and promote the rights of migrant workers. In April 2010, the ASEAN Commission for the Promotion and Protection of the Rights of Women and Children was inaugurated in Hanoi.

INTERNATIONAL HUMAN RIGHTS IN DOMESTIC COURTS

Using domestic courts to clarify and safeguard international human rights is a relatively new and still evolving approach to human rights advocacy, particularly when civil as distinct from criminal litigation is called into play. In addition to the inevitable interpretative problems involved in applying norms fashioned in multicultural settings, controversial theories about the interrelation of national and international law, as well as many procedural difficulties, burden the human rights claimant in this setting. To be sure, significant progress has been made, as is perhaps best evidenced, at least insofar as the United States is concerned, in the far-reaching decision handed down by the U.S. Court of Appeals for the Second Circuit in *Filártiga v. Peña-Irala* (1980). In that celebrated case, the court interpreted a theretofore obscure provision of the Judiciary Act of 1789 known as the Alien Tort Statute (ATS) as allowing foreign victims of human rights abuses by foreign wrongdoers in foreign countries to seek civil remedies in the U.S. judicial system, holding that the "well-established universal" prohibition of torture under customary international law, which applies regardless of the nationality of the victim or the perpetrator (at least in the case of private litigants), must be honored in U.S. courts—an outcome akin to an assertion of universal criminal jurisdiction, as confirmed by sympathetic rulings following *Filártiga*.

In 1998–99, in keeping with *Filártiga*, the UK's highest tribunal, the Law Lords of the British House of Lords, captured international attention when, in response to an extradition request by a Spanish court, it upheld the arrest in England of former Chilean president Augusto Pinochet on charges of torture and conspiracy to commit torture in violation of international treaty law. Although Pinochet was later returned to Chile for reasons of ill health and declared by a Chilean court to be mentally unfit to stand trial, the Law Lords' ruling established the precedent that former heads of state do not enjoy immunity from prosecution, at least for systematic human rights crimes—a principle now en-

shrined in the workings of the International Criminal Court. In addition, a considerable number of British cases, decided in the absence of national legislation expressly enabling claims for extraterritorial human rights abuses and therefore based on principles of common law tort, have revealed a willingness to hold corporations liable for human rights violations perpetrated abroad. European Union (EU) regulations and civil law cases within EU member states, assisted by broadened EU and member-state laws regulating tort cases, are similarly inclined, even to the point of referencing customary international law to reinforce legislative intent and allow for universal civil jurisdiction on a "necessity basis."

Yet, in two prominent human rights cases in the United States, *Sosa v. Álvarez-Machain* (2004) and *Kiobel v. Royal Dutch Petroleum* (2013), the U.S. Supreme Court moved in the opposite direction, limiting the jurisdictional foundation upon which *Filártiga* and its progeny rest. *Kiobel*, the more unfriendly of the two, was a class-action suit on behalf of Nigerian residents who had peacefully protested devastating health and environmental harms resulting from unregulated oil drilling by Royal Dutch Petroleum (RDP; now Royal Dutch Shell PLC) in their homeland, the Ogoniland region of the Niger Delta. The plaintiffs alleged that RDP—which was incorporated in the UK and headquartered in the Netherlands—had armed, financed, and conspired with Nigeria's then military dictatorship to suppress the protests and accused the Nigerian authorities of having committed between 1992 and 1995, with RDP's assistance and complicity, crimes against humanity (including torture and extrajudicial executions), false arrests, and other violations of international law against the Ogoni people. Refusing, however, to follow the *Filártiga* precedent by invoking a canon of statutory interpretation known as the "presumption against extraterritorial application" (when legislation gives no clear contrary mandate), the Supreme Court, in a splintered decision, held that, because "all the . . . conduct took place outside the United States," the ATS did not apply, and it therefore decided in favor of RDP. Accordingly, the court paid no heed to customary international law as authorized in the ATS. Additionally, but without explanation, it rejected a universal-jurisdiction reading of the ATS, seemingly even in suits claiming exceptionally heinous human rights crimes.

Informed observers responding to *Kiobel* appear generally to have agreed upon at least four implications of the court's reasoning in the case: (1) that foreign corporations would thenceforth be largely, if not completely, insulated from U.S. prosecution under the ATS for human rights violations committed against foreign nationals in foreign countries; (2) that U.S. corporations would not be so insulated; (3) that the development of litigation in Europe and elsewhere outside the United States would be affected by *Kiobel* only slightly, if at all; and (4) that the applicability of *Kiobel* to foreign natural persons, never addressed by the court, was uncertain. There also was substantial agreement that the court's stated rationales for its decision—the minimization of "international friction" and related separation-of-powers concerns—were insufficient to justify eliding more than three decades of established ATS precedent. Consequently, other rationales have since been advanced, as have also credible proposals for circumventing *Kiobel*'s actual and potential rationales in favor of laws protecting against at least severe human rights violations anywhere in the world—as the United States already has done to some extent with respect to genocide and war crimes. In these lights, it is not unreasonable to suggest that, with creative and persistent effort, human rights advocacy via domestic courts, supplementing other domestic law processes and focused especially on severe human rights abuses, is within reach in the United States as well as beyond. If this be so, then human rights can be made to respond more effectively to the mutiple ways in which vulnerability is enacted and entrenched in a world with a long and savage record of human abuse.

HUMAN RIGHTS IN THE EARLY TWENTY-FIRST CENTURY

Whatever the current attitudes and policies of governments, the reality of popular demands for human rights, including both greater economic justice and greater political freedom, is beyond debate. A deepening and widening concern for the promotion and protection of human rights on all fronts, hastened by the ideal of self-determination in a postcolonial era, is now unmistakably woven into the fabric of contemporary world affairs.

Substantially responsible for this progressive development has been the work of the UN, its allied agencies, and such regional organizations as the Council of Europe, the OAS, and the AU. Also contributing to this development, particularly since the 1970s and '80s, have been six other salient factors: (1) the emergence of nationalism and rising expectations in the developing world following the post-World War II dismantling of colonial empires, (2) the public advocacy of human rights as a key aspect of national foreign policies, made initially legitimate by the example of U.S. president Jimmy Carter, (3) the emergence and spread of civil society on a transnational basis, primarily in the form of activist nongovernmental human rights organizations, (4) a worldwide profusion of teaching and research devoted to the study of human rights in both formal and informal settings, (5) the proliferation of large UN conferences in areas such as children's rights, population, social development, women's rights, human settlements, and food production and distribution, and (6) a feminist intellectual and political challenge regarding not only the rights of women worldwide but also what feminists consider to be the paternalistic myths and mythic structures that purport to define humane governance generally.

To be sure, because the application of international human rights law depends for the most part on the voluntary consent of nations, formidable obstacles attend the endeavors of human rights policy makers, activists, and scholars. Human rights Conventions continue to be undermined by the failure of states to ratify them, by emasculating reservations and derogations, by self-serving reporting systems that outnumber objective complaint procedures, and by poor financing for the implementation of human rights prescriptions. In short, the mechanisms for the enforcement of human rights are still in their infancy, a situation due in no small measure to the post-Cold War dominance of neoliberalism in world affairs, which is strongly resistant to state and market regulation of the economy. In this context, the vexing question of corporate accountability for human rights abuses, and the dangers to human rights values and capabilities posed by overbearing corporate power, also present complex contemporary challenges for the future of human rights. Nevertheless, it is certain that, out of necessity no less than out of realism, a palpable concern for the advancement of human rights is here to stay.

QUESTIONS FOR REFLECTION AND DISCUSSION

1. Weston discusses the institutionalization of human rights on the international plane in the years preceding World War II. What principal human rights developments took place prior to World War II? Did any of them survive? Did any of them foreshadow events to come? If so, how?

2. Weston briefly discusses the UN and regional approaches to protecting human rights, as well as the Helsinki process. Which type of system is more effective in addressing human rights? And why? What do you draw upon to substantiate your response?

3. What are the pros and cons of engaging in human rights development through regional organizations rather than through the broader, universal level of the United Nations?

4. What challenges face the institutionalization of international human rights in Asia and the Middle East? What deeper issues does this question invoke?

5. Given the enforcement inadequacies identified by Weston in this reading, what use are human rights? Are they important? How? How not? And why?

6. Weston claims that human rights are "here to stay." What justifies this conclusion? How does Weston establish it? Do you agree that human rights will, as an empirical matter, survive? Why? Why not?

7. *Should* human rights be here to stay? What are the arguments in their favor? Against? What values do your answers draw upon?

8. In "The International Human Rights Movement: Part of the Problem?" *HHRJ* 15 (2002): 101–25, David Kennedy writes:

> The strong attachment of the human rights movement to the legal formalization of rights and the establishment of legal machinery for their implementation makes the achievement of these forms an end in itself. Elites in a political system—international, national—which has adopted the rules and set up the institutions will often themselves have the impression and insist persuasively to others that they have addressed the problem of violations with an elaborate, internationally respected and "state of the art" response. This is analogous to the way in which holding elections can come to substitute for popular engagement in the political process. These are the traditional problems of form: form can hamper peaceful adjustment and necessary change, can be over- or under-inclusive. Is the right to vote a floor—or can it become a ceiling? The human rights movement ties its own hands on progressive development.

Do you think Kennedy is right to argue that elites in the human rights movement have made the achievement of legal forms an end in itself? Why? Why not? On what evidence does your response draw?

9. What role should countries with poor human rights records play within the UN human rights system? Weston notes that the UN Commission on Human Rights fell out of favor in part because its membership included countries with poor human rights records. The UN Human Rights Council (UNHRC), its successor, was established in part to overcome this problem. Do you agree that countries with poor human rights records should not serve in the UN human rights system generally? On the UNHRC specifically? In each case, why? Why not? Do you agree that the United States, given its dubious human rights record since 2000 especially, should be refused membership on the UNHRC? Why? Why not? Has it ever been?

28. HAROLD HONGJU KOH *How Is International Human Rights Law Enforced?*

I wouldn't be surprised if many were to give a pessimistic answer to the question that is the title of this lecture: international human rights law is not enforced, you might say. Just take a look at the massive human rights violations in Bosnia; violations that have gone unredressed in Cambodia; the crises in the Congo, Sierra Leone, Algeria, Burundi, and elsewhere. Look, you might say, at the world's willingness to overlook human rights violations committed by more powerful nations. International human rights law is not enforced, you might say, because human rights norms are vague and aspirational, because enforcement mechanisms are toothless, because treaty regimes are notoriously weak, and because national governments lack the economic self-interest or the political will to restrain their own human rights violations. So if the question is "how is international human rights law enforced?" many of you might answer "not at all, or hardly at all," or that international human rights law is only occasionally "complied with" by nation-states acting out of transparent convenience or self-interest.

Let me take a somewhat different tack, asking first, "What do we mean when we say that any laws are enforced?" Are any laws perfectly enforced? Even here in Bloomington, Indiana, the height of civilization, are the parking laws or burglary laws perfectly enforced? Of course, you would concede, parking violations occur here in Bloomington, and burglaries occur, perhaps even daily, sometimes egregiously. But those facts alone hardly mean that there is no enforcement of laws against parking violations or burglary. Here in Indiana, the laws against burglary may be underenforced, they may be imperfectly enforced, but they are enforced, through a well-understood domestic legal process of legislation, adjudication, and executive action. That process involves prosecutors, statutes, judges, police officers, and penalties that interact, interpret legal norms, and work to internalize those norms into the value sets of citizens like ourselves.

But if we are willing to give that answer to the question "how is domestic law enforced?" why not similarly answer the question whether international human rights law is enforced? In much the same way, these norms of international human rights law are underenforced, imperfectly enforced, but they are enforced through a complex, little-understood legal process that I call transnational legal process. As I have elaborated in other writing, transnational legal process can be thought of in three phases: the institutional interaction whereby global norms of international human rights law are debated, interpreted, and ultimately internalized by domestic legal systems. To claim that this complex transnational legal process of enforcing international human rights law via interaction, interpretation, and internalization exists is not to say that it always works or even that it works very well. As I will be the first to concede, this process works sporadically, and that we often most clearly see its spectacular failures, as in Cambodia, Bosnia, and Rwanda. But the process of enforcing international human rights law also sometimes has its successes, which gives us reason not to ignore that process, but to try to develop and nurture it. Just as doctors used early successes in addressing polio to push our understanding of how the prevention and healing process works, lawyers can try to globalize the lessons of human rights enforcement. So if the question is "how is international human rights law enforced?" my short answer is through a transnational legal process of institutional interaction, interpretation of legal norms, and attempts to internalize those norms into domestic legal systems.

With that introduction, let me divide the balance of these remarks into two parts: First, how, in theory, does transnational legal process promote national obedience of international human rights law? Second, how does transnational legal process (this process that I call "interaction, interpretation, and internalization") work in real cases?

THE THEORY OF TRANSNATIONAL LEGAL PROCESS

The first question, why do nations obey international human rights law, is really a subset of a much broader question: why do nations obey international law of any kind? That timeless question has troubled thinkers over historical eras dating back to the Roman Empire.

From Compliance to Obedience

Let us start by asking what it means to "obey" international law at all. Imagine four kinds of relationships between rules and conduct: coincidence, conformity, compliance, and obedience. For example, I have lived my whole life in the United States; but a few years ago, I took a sabbatical year in England. While there, I noticed that everybody drives on the left side of the road, as a matter of both practice and law. Yet what is the relationship between the law and the observed practice?

One remote possibility is coincidence. It could be coincidence that the law is that everyone must drive on the left and that in practice everybody does so. Yet coincidence might explain why one person's external practical behavior conforms to a rule, but not why millions of people throughout the country do the same. That suggests a second possibility: conformity. If people know of the rule that you must drive on the left, they may well choose to conform their conduct to that rule when convenient, but feel no obligation to do so when inconvenient. (Perhaps some Scots, for example, swerve over and drive on the right, in remote unpopulated areas of the Hebrides.) But, is there a third possibility, compliance? Perhaps people are both aware of the rule and accept the rule for a variety of external reasons, for example, to get specific rewards, to receive insurance benefits, or to avoid certain kinds of bad results, such as traffic tickets, or getting hit by an oncoming car. These are instrumental reasons why someone might decide to comply with a rule even if they felt no normative obligation to obey it. Finally, there is a fourth possibility, obedience: the notion that a person or an organization adopts the behavior that is prescribed by the rule because he or it has somehow internalized that rule and made it a part of their internal value system.

Notice that as we move down this scale from coincidence to conformity to compliance to obedience, we see an increase of what I will call "norm-internalization." As you move from grudgingly accepting a rule one time only to habitually obeying it, the rule transforms from being some kind of external sanction to becoming an internal imperative. We see this evolutionary process regularly in our daily lives: when you put on a bicycle helmet; when you snap on your seatbelt; when you recycle a steel can; when you do not smoke in the cafeteria. All these are examples of people moving from conformity with a rule to compliance and gradually to obedience, which is driven by a sense of an internalized norm. There is a further point as well: the most effective form of law enforcement is not the imposition of external sanction, but the inculcation of internal obedience. Most traffic laws, litter laws, tax laws, and the like are enforced primarily not by enforcement officers, but by the social internalization of norms of obedience! Indeed, enforcement is maximized when a norm is so widely obeyed that external sanctions become virtually unnecessary.

The Relationship Between Enforcement and Obedience

Five distinct explanations have emerged to answer the question "why do nations obey?": power; self-interest or rational choice; liberal explanations based on rule legitimacy or political identity; communitarian explanations; and legal process explanations at the state-to-state level ("horizontal" or "international legal process" explanations) and from the international-to-national level ("vertical" or "transnational legal process explanations").

In their current form, each of these five approaches gives their own short answer to the question "how is international human rights law enforced?" Let me start with the realists, who date back to Thomas Hobbes, but include such modern-day theorists as George Kennan, Hans Morgenthau, and Henry Kissinger. To the question "why do nations obey international law?" their short answer is power: nations never truly "obey" international law, they only comply with it, because someone else makes them. Why, for example, did Iraq ultimately respect the borders of Kuwait? In the end, because the other nations of the world came in and drove Saddam out! Under this view, nations can be coerced or bribed to follow certain rules, or even induced to bargain in the shadow of such incentives. But in the end, the critical factor is neither altruistic nor normative, only the realist values of power and coercion. Thus, the familiar power explanation traces back to Thucydides: the strong states do what they can, the weak states suffer what they must, but in the end there is no real "obedience" of international law, only such coincidence between national conduct and international rules that results from power and coercion.

There is a second, kinder and gentler explanation, based on the self-interest rationales favored by the vibrant school of "rational choice" theory. Under this explanation, nations may choose rationally to follow certain global rules out of a sense of self-interest. This rationale helps explain why, for example, complex global rules have emerged in a whole variety of international areas in which nations have established regimes structured around legal rules born of self-interested cooperation. Under the rationalist account, participants in a given issue area will develop a set of governing arrangements, along with a set of expectations, rules, and decision-making procedures (in other words, a regime) both to restrain the participants and to provide means for achieving their common aims. Within these regimes, international law stabilizes expectations and promotes compliance by reducing transaction costs, providing dispute resolution procedures, performing signaling functions, triggering negative responses, and promoting information disclosure.

My major complaint about the self-interest explanation is that it does not take account of what I consider to be an important factor (the "vertical" internalization of international norms into domestic legal systems). For the rationalists, the decision to obey the law remains perpetually calculated, never internally felt. Compliance always remains an instrumental computation, never an internalized normative imperative.

This brings me to a third possible explanation for why international human rights laws are enforced, so-called "liberal" theories, which I divide into those scholars who follow principles of "rule legitimacy" and those who focus on national "political identity." Both sets of theorists derive their analysis from Immanuel Kant's pamphlet in 1795, *Perpetual Peace*. Rule-legitimacy theorists, led by the late Thomas Franck of NYU, argue that nations do feel some sort of internal "compliance pull" toward certain rules that they feel are legitimate, for example, the rules against genocide or the rules favoring diplomatic immunity. When nations perceive that rules are legitimate, either because they meet some procedural standard of legitimacy or some substantive notion of due process or distributive justice, they will obey that rule because they are "normatively pulled" toward that rule by its legitimacy.[1] In my view, this rule-legitimacy approach is problematic because it claims to draw its power from the legitimacy of rules themselves, rather than from communitarian and legal process pressures. In fact, most of us do not litter when others are watching, not because the no littering rule itself has such compliance pull, but because of a combination of internal impulse and felt peer pressure. In the same way, Franck's rule-legitimacy ends up being another way of saying that a state obeys a norm because it has been both internalized, and is being enforced by "communitarian peer pressure" (which, I will argue below, is really a form of transnational legal process).

A second view, pressed strongly by other members of this liberal school, argues that whether or not nations comply with international law depends crucially on the extent to which their political identity is based on liberal democracy. This approach derives from a branch of international relations literature known as the "Democratic Peace" literature, pioneered by Michael Doyle, Bruce Russett, and many others who have sought to verify a basic tenet of Kant's writing that liberal democracies do not go to war with each other.

Transposing this basic maxim to international law, two former Harvard theorists, Anne-Marie Slaughter and Andrew Moravcsik, have flipped this maxim, arguing not so much that democracies do not fight each other, but, rather, that democracies are more inclined to "do law" with one another. For these analysts, the key variable for whether a nation will or will not obey international law is whether they can be characterized as "liberal" in identity, that is, having certain democratic attributes such as a form of representative government, civil and political rights, and an independent judicial system dedicated to the rule of law. Not surprisingly, many liberal scholars focus on European Union law, noting that the European system of human rights works be-

---

1. Franck calls this the "compliance pull" of particular international legal rules. See generally Thomas M. Franck, *The Power of Legitimacy Among Nations* (New York: OUP, 1990)

cause it is largely composed of liberal democracies, who share reasons for collective obedience. This helps explain why, for example, the embryonic African human rights system (a collection of democracies and authoritarian systems) does not work nearly as well.

What is troubling about this view is that it suggests that liberal states interact mainly in a zone of law while nonliberal states interact in a zone of politics. But in my view, any analysis that treats a state's identity as somehow exogenously or permanently given is overly essentialist. National identities, like national interests, are socially constructed products of culture, ideology, learning, and knowledge. As we have witnessed, nations transition back and forth from dictatorship to democracy; and what is more, democratization has powerful international dimensions, potentially spreading from one country to another by contagion, control, or consent. Liberal identity analysis does not directly address the impact of compliance on democratization, and thus leaves unanswered a critical, constructivist question: to what extent does compliance with international law itself help constitute the identity of a state as law-abiding, and hence, as "liberal" or not? The notion that "only liberal states do law with one another" can be empirically falsified, particularly in such areas as international commercial law, where even rogue states tend to abide fastidiously by private international law rules on letters of credit without regard to whether they are representative democracies. Finally, like the "cultural relativist" argument in human rights, the claim that nonliberal states somehow do not participate in a zone of law denies the universalism of international law and effectively condones dealing with nonliberal states within a realist world of power politics.

A fourth possible explanation ("communitarian" reasons) can be found in the English "International Society" school of international relations, particularly in the work of Martin Wight and Hedley Bull, who traced their international origins back to the Dutch international law scholar Grotius. These theorists argue that nations obey international law because of the values of the international society of which they are a part. The idea is that one's membership in a community helps to define how one views the obligations of that community. When someone becomes a member of a church, they decide they will conduct their lives differently because they now view themselves as Catholic, Jewish, or Muslim. Similarly, the governments of Russia, Ukraine, and Turkey should all feel communitarian pressure to obey the European Convention on Human Rights (the "rules of their church") because they have all now become members of the Council of Europe.

Unlike a liberal approach, this communitarian, constructivist approach at least recognizes the positive transformational effects of a state's repeated participation in the legal process. At the same time, however, the approach gives too little study to the vertical "transmission belt" whereby the norms created by international society infiltrate into domestic society. The existence of international community may explain the horizontal pressures to compliance generated among nation-states on the global plane, but it does not clarify the vertical process whereby transnational actors interact in various fora, generate and interpret international norms, and then seek to internalize those norms domestically, as future determinants of why nations obey.

Fifth and finally, there are so-called "legal process" explanations for why nations obey international law. Let me distinguish here between what I call "international legal process" or horizontal reasons for compliance, which tend to function at a government-to-government level, and the so-called "vertical" explanation, which focuses on the relationship between the international and the domestic legal systems. Suppose, for example, that [Country X] wishes to urge [Country Y] to join the global land mine treaty. Initially, the two governments will engage in government-to-government discussions at the "horizontal" nation-state level within an intergovernmental process organized by the United Nations. But at the same time, there is also a "vertical," transnational process whereby governments, intergovernmental organizations, nongovernmental organizations, and private citizens argue together about why nations should obey international human rights law. Through this vertical dynamic, international rules that are developed at a government-to-government level gradually work their way down and become internalized into domestic legal structure.

My broader point, simply speaking, is that all five explanations (power, self-interest, liberal theories, communitarian theories, and legal process explanations) work together to help explain why nations obey international law. These five explanatory strands work together as complementary conceptual lenses to give a richer explanation of why compliance with international law does, or does not, occur in particular cases.

To clarify, let me ask the parallel question, how is domestic law enforced? What is the explanation, for example, for why we now buckle our seat belts, even though nobody wore seat belts a quarter of a century or so ago? First, because after the seat belt rule was issued, a lot of tickets were given out and I felt coerced to comply: a power explanation. A second factor: self-interest. People calculated that it is more rational to wear your seat belt to avoid injury, sanction, or to gain insurance benefits. Third, the seatbelt rule acquired "rule legitimacy" and over time developed a compliance pull. Over time, this became part of one's sense of personal identity. Individuals calculated: "If I am a law-abiding person, I ought to obey the seat-belt laws." Partly, the rationale was communitarian. Authorities exhorted people with slogans such as "Seat Belts Save Lives." And fifth and finally, the seatbelt rule was inculcated via legal process. Seat belts were required by state laws, required by federal highway standards, incorporated into federal automotive standards and became part of the way the automobiles were made.

So in short, how are seat belt laws enforced? Not by any one of these factors acting alone, but by all of them acting in combination. As we move through the five explanations (from power to legal process), we also move from external enforcement of legal rules to internal obedience with legal rules. True compliance is not so much the result of externally imposed sanctions so much as internally felt norms. In other words, as we move from external to internal factors, we also move from coercive to constitutive behavior. As always, the best way to enforce legal norms is not to coerce action, not to impose sanctions, but to change the way that people think about themselves: whether as teetotalers, safe drivers, or regular taxpayers. In short, our prime way to enforce the law is to encourage people to bring rules home, to internalize rules inside themselves, to transform themselves from lawless into law-abiding individuals.

What does this have to do with international human rights law? I would argue that in the international arena, we are seeing the exact same process at work: a process by which norms and rules are generated and internalized and become internal rules, normative rules, and rules that constitute new nations. The best example we have is South Africa; a country that for many years was an outlaw was subjected to tremendous international pressure and coercive mechanisms [such as international sanctions] over a long period of time. Through a gradual process, South Africa has converted itself into a country that has undergone a fundamental political transformation. It has now reconstituted itself and through its constitutional processes has begun to internalize new norms of international human rights law as domestic law.

In the same way, if the United States is attempting to encourage China to follow norms of international human rights law, the analysis above suggests the need to utilize all five of the persuasive strategies noted: power, self-interest, liberal theories, communitarian theories, and legal process explanations. As with the seat belt example, our goal is not simply to coerce conduct. More fundamentally, we seek to encourage a change in the nature of the Chinese political identity to reconstitute China as a nation that abides by core norms of international human rights law.

In short, a theory of transnational legal process seeks to enforce international norms by motivating states to obey international human rights law—out of a sense of internal acceptance of international law—as opposed to merely conforming to or complying with specific international legal rules when the state finds it convenient.

HOW IS INTERNATIONAL HUMAN RIGHTS LAW ENFORCED?

Against this background, how should we now understand the recent history of international human rights enforcement? Let me contrast what I will call the horizontal story of enforcement with what I prefer: the vertical, transnational story of human rights enforcement.

The "Horizontal" Story

The conventional "horizontal" story about international human rights law enforcement is that international human rights law was born about fifty years ago, the product of the 1945 UN Charter, the Nuremberg and Tokyo war crimes trials (in 1945–46 and 1946–48 respectively), and the 1948 Universal Declaration of Human Rights (UDHR). Under this view, the principal enforcers of human rights law have always been nation-states, who have always interacted with one another on an interstate, government-to-government level. The UN Charter introduced into this picture UN organizations and UN norms, which soon led to regional human rights systems as well:[2] in Europe, the Strasbourg Council of Europe and Helsinki Organization of Security and Cooperation in Europe processes; in the Americas, the Inter-American Commission and Court of Human Rights; in Africa, the African Commission on Human and Peoples' Rights and Court of Human and Peoples' Rights; and far less well-developed regional human rights systems in Asia and the Middle East.

In this postwar order, an international regime developed in which governments and intergovernmental organizations began to put pressure on each other (always at a horizontal, intergovernmental level) to comply with human rights, invoking such universal treaty norms as the international covenants on civil and political and economic, social, and cultural rights. UN-based organizations such as the UN Human Rights Council and treaty-based organizations such as the UN Human Rights Committee participated as intergovernmental actors in this horizontal international regime which addressed all manner of global issues: worker rights, racial discrimination, the rights of children, women, and indigenous peoples. As we soon saw, the difficulties of this horizontal, state-to-state enforcement mechanism were legion: the rules were largely declaratory and precatory, and the few mechanisms created had virtually no enforcement. Occasionally new mechanisms would be created: judicial fora, such as the Yugoslav and Rwandan War Crimes Tribunals, or new executive actors, such as the UN High Commissioner on Human Rights, or new quasi-legislative fora, such as the 1993 Vienna Conference on Human Rights or the 1995 Beijing Women's Conference. Despite these occasional advances, the overall picture of this standard enforcement story is one of impotence, ineffectiveness, of a horizontal system where the key actors are nation-states and intergovernmental organizations, the key forums are governmental forums, and the key transactions are transactions between states and other states.

The "Vertical" Story

If one accepts the horizontal story as the entire picture of human rights enforcement, then the glass is indeed more than half-empty. But what is the vertical picture? The "vertical" story of human rights enforcement, I would argue, is a much richer picture: one that focuses on a transnational legal process that includes a different set of actors, fora, and transactions. The key agents in this transnational legal process are transnational norm entrepreneurs, governmental norm sponsors, transnational issue networks, interpretive communities and law-declaring fora, bureaucratic compliance procedures, and issue linkages among issue areas.

Many efforts at human rights norm-internalization are begun not by nation-states but by "transnational norm entrepreneurs," private transnational organizations or individuals who mobilize popular opinion and political support within their host country and abroad for the development of a universal human rights norm. Such norm entrepreneurs first became prominent in the nineteenth century, when activists such as Lord William Wilberforce and the British and Foreign Anti-Slavery Society pressed for treaties prohibiting the slave trade, Jean-Henri Dunant founded the International Committee of the Red Cross, and Christian peace activists, such as America's William Ladd and Elihu Burritt promoted public international arbitration and permanent international criminal courts. Modern-day entrepreneurs have included individuals as diverse as Eleanor Roosevelt, Jesse Jackson, the Dalai Lama, Aung Sang Suu Kyi, and Princess Diana. These nongovernmental actors seek to develop transnational issue networks to discuss and generate political solutions among concerned individuals at the domestic, regional, and international levels, among government agencies, intergovernmental organizations (international and domestic), academics, and private foundations. Moreover, these norm entrepreneurs seek national government officials and bureaucracies concerned with the same issue

2. See Reading 31 (Shelton) in Chapter 7.

areas and seek to enlist them as allies in their transnational cause. These governmental norm sponsors—for example, UN Human Rights Commissioner Mary Robinson, Presidents Oscar Arias Sánchez of Costa Rica, Jimmy Carter of the United States, and the Pope, to take just a few prominent ones—use their official positions to promote normative positions. These transnational actors then seek governmental and nongovernmental fora competent to declare both general norms of international law (e.g., treaties) and specific interpretation of those norms in particular circumstances (e.g., particular interpretations of treaties and customary international law rules). Such law-declaring fora thus include treaty regimes; domestic, regional, and international courts; ad hoc tribunals; domestic and regional legislatures; executive entities; international publicists; and nongovernmental organizations: law-declaring fora that create an "interpretive community" that is capable of defining, elaborating, and testing the definition of particular norms and their violation.

The next vertical step is for national governments to internalize norm-interpretations issued by the global interpretive community into their domestic bureaucratic and political structures. Within national governments and intergovernmental organizations, for example, in-house lawyers and legal advisers acquire institutional mandates to ensure that the government's policies conform to international legal standards that have become imbedded in domestic law. Such institutional mandates to justify noncompliance with international legal norms may be found within the legal advising apparatus of national governments . . . as well as in intergovernmental organizations (the UN, OAS, etc.).

In the same way as corporations develop standard operating procedures to address new domestic mandates regarding corporate sentencing guidelines, occupational health and safety, and sexual harassment, domestic institutions adopt standard operating procedures, and other internal mechanisms to maintain habitual compliance with the internalized international norms. These institutions evolve in path-dependent routes that avoid conflict with the internalized norms. Thus, over time, domestic decision-making structures become "enmeshed" with international legal norms, so that institutional arrangements for the making and maintenance of an international commitment become entrenched in domestic

legal and political processes. Gradually, legal ideologies come to prevail among domestic decision-makers so that they seek to avoid perceptions that their actions will be perceived as domestically unlawful. Finally, strong process linkages exist across issue areas. Thus, when the United States adopts a twelve-mile limit in the ocean law area, for example, it is bound by it when dealing with refugees sailing toward U.S. shores. These institutional habits soon lead nations into default patterns of compliance. These patterns act like riverbeds, which channel conduct along compliant pathways. When a nation deviates from that pattern of presumptive compliance, frictions are created.

By so saying, I do not mean to suggest that international legal violations never occur. I merely suggest viewing human rights enforcement through vertical, "transnational legal process" lenses can help explain why, in Louis Henkin's famous phrase, "almost all nations observe almost all principles of international law almost all of the time."[3] To avoid such frictions in its continuing interactions, a nation's bureaucracies or interest groups may press their leaders to shift over time from a policy of violation into one of compliance. Thus it is through this repeated cycle of interaction, interpretation, and internalization (this transnational legal process) that international law acquires its "stickiness," and that nations come to "obey" international human rights law out of a perceived self-interest that becomes institutional habit. I am not saying that the "horizontal" is wrong, only that it is incomplete. A state-to-state process account simply does not capture the full picture of how international human rights norms are currently generated, brought into domestic systems, and then brought back up to the international level.

CONCLUSION

Let me close with two thoughts. First, the foregoing analysis teaches something about our duty, as citizens, to participate in transnational legal process. Once one comes to understand the process by which international human rights norms can be generated and internalized into

3. Louis Henkin, *How Nations Behave*, 2nd ed. (New York: Praeger, 1979), 47.

domestic legal systems, one acquires a concomitant duty, I believe, to try to influence that process, to try to change the feelings of that body politic to promote greater obedience with international human rights norms.

In that effort, every citizen counts. To this, many might say, "What can one person really do? Isn't such influence beyond the capacity of any one person?" But could not Martin Luther King, Jr., Aung Sun Suu Kyi, Nelson Mandela, and Jody Williams have said the same thing? In response, many might say: "But surely, I am not such a world historical figure," to which I would answer, "You don't need to be a Nobel Prize winner to make a difference. Just look at Fred Korematsu, Linda Brown, and Rosa Parks, ordinary people who simply said that they would not live in a Japanese internment camp, or attend a segregated school, or go to the back of the bus." In short, we need look no further than those individuals who have triggered these legal processes in our own lifetime to promote the enforcement of human rights norms.

The struggle of these individuals reminds us again of the remarkable words of Robert Kennedy, which are etched on his grave in Arlington Cemetery:

Each time a man stands up for an ideal, or acts to improve the lot of others, or strikes out against injustice, he sends forth a tiny ripple of hope, and crossing each other from a million different centers of energy and daring, those ripples build a current that can sweep down the mightiest walls of oppression and resistance.

What Kennedy was talking about is the need for individuals to activate transnational legal process. As proof that what he says is indeed possible, one need look only at the country in which he said those words: South Africa in 1966, a country which only three decades later has now been transformed by international human rights law.

So, in closing, if my question is "how is international human rights law enforced?" my answer is simple. International human rights law is enforced not just by nation-states, not just by government officials, not just by world historical figures, but by people like us, by people with the courage and commitment to bring international human rights law home through a transnational legal process of interaction, interpretation, and internalization.

QUESTIONS FOR REFLECTION AND DISCUSSION

1. Koh offers five explanations as to why states obey international law. What are they? Which is the most convincing? Why? What does Koh say?

2. What is Koh's theory of transnational legal process? How does he use this theory to explain what it means to "obey" international law? Is his analysis convincing? Why? Why not?

3. Koh describes four kinds of relationships between rules and conduct. What are they? How do these relationships interplay in the enforcement of law?

4. Harold Koh asks: "How is international human rights law enforced?" He answers: "not just by nation-states, not just by government officials, not just by world historical figures, but by people like us." He identifies these two patterns as, respectively, "horizontal" legal process and "vertical" legal process. Are you persuaded by these distinctions or, more precisely, Koh's use of them? Would they not be more accurate in reverse, with "nation-states," "government officials," and "world historical figures" populating vertical legal process and "people like us" populating horizontal legal process? Why? Why not? Consider that legal theorists ordinarily associate "vertical" legal processes with centralized, hierarchical law-making and law-enforcing mechanisms and structures (as in the case, generally, of national law systems, for example), and "horizontal" legal processes with the reverse (as in the case, generally, of much of international law which, as some put it, lacks a city hall. Might not an altogether different terminology or typology facilitate better understanding, e.g., "official legal process" and "unofficial legal process" or "top-down legal process" and "bottom-up legal process"—or other equivalents? Your opinion and why?

5. Who are "people like us"? How is it possible for "people like us" (most of "us" being without official position or significant legal standing) to *enforce* international human rights

law? And just how well do "people like us" (and government officials and world historical figures and others) enforce international human rights law? Is anyone likely to be excluded by the term "people like us"? Is it possible that different assumptions could be in play in constructing the "us," and not all of them benign?

6. Koh states: "the best way to enforce legal norms is not to coerce action, not to impose sanctions, but to change the way that people think about themselves." Do you agree? Why? Why not? In light of human rights crises in places such as North Korea and Syria, would you say that sanctions are futile? Why? Why not?

7. Koh focuses on two key questions. First, how, in theory, does transnational legal process promote national obedience of international human rights law? Second, how does transnational legal process (the process he calls "interaction, interpretation, and internalization") work in real cases? What are Koh's answers to these two questions? Do you agree with him? Disagree? Why? And what does he mean by the "interaction, interpretation, and internalization" of international human rights law—"internalization" in particular?

9. If there is no "internalization" of a human rights doctrine, principle, or rule, does this mean that persons living in a country where "internalization" does not take place have no rights in respect of such norm? No enforceable rights? Which? Does the distinction matter? Is a claimed human right without a domestic remedy a human right at all—for example, China in respect of various civil and political rights (e.g., the right to speak freely or to vote in national elections)? Or the United States in respect of various economic, social, and cultural rights (e.g., the right to education or the right to health)? What about a claimed human right without *any* remedy anywhere? What does Koh say? What does Weston say in Reading 1 of Chapter 1? What do you say? Why?

10. In conclusion, Koh states: "once one comes to understand the process by which international human rights norms can be generated and internalized into domestic legal systems, one acquires a concomitant duty . . . to try to influence that process, to try to change the feelings of that body politic to promote greater obedience with international human rights norms." In contrast, in "The International Human Rights Movement: Part of the Problem?" *HHRJ* 15 (2002): 101–25, 117–18, Harvard law professor David Kennedy writes:

> human rights offers itself as the measure of emancipation. This is its most striking (and misleading) promise. Human rights narrates itself as a universal/eternal/human truth and as a pragmatic response to injustice (there was the Holocaust and then there was the genocide convention, women everywhere were subject to discrimination and then there was CEDAW). This posture makes the human rights movement itself seem redemptive "as if doing something for human rights was, in and of itself, doing something against evil. . . . But there are bad consequences when people of good will mistake work on the discipline for work on the problem. . . . We routinely underestimate the extent to which the human rights movement develops in response to political conflict and discursive fashion among international elites, thereby overestimating the field's pragmatic potential and obscuring the field's international dynamics and will to power.

Do you share Koh's or Kennedy's worldview? Why? Is there a way to reconcile the two? How?

11. Do you believe that you, personally, have a duty to participate in the making of international human rights law? In the enforcement of it? Definitely? Probably? Possibly? Not at all? Does it depend on your intended profession? Other reasons? Why?

29. WADE M. COLE *Human Rights as Myth and Ceremony? Reevaluating the Effectiveness of Human Rights Treaties, 1981–2007*

More than three decades ago, John W. Meyer and Brian Rowan argued that many features of modern organizations derive not from their internal task demands but rather from an institutional environment that furnishes basic structural templates and action scripts.[1] Subsequent work extended this line of thought to nation-states as organizations writ large. States, in this view, are constituted by and operate within a broader "world society." This shared external environment propels states to become increasingly isomorphic in terms of their ministerial structures, constitutional provisions, education systems, school curricula, and a host of policies regarding citizenship rights, science, rape, the environment, and population control.

Since the Second World War, human rights have become a core normative element of world society. Human rights are putatively universal standards, principles, and values that regulate the relationship between states and individuals by investing the latter with basic sets of rights claims against the former. A state's legitimacy is increasingly pegged to its support of human rights principles; however, scholars from the world society approach routinely acknowledge that many states endorse human rights principles—for example, by ratifying human rights treaties—without putting those principles into practice. Human rights principles, that is, are "decoupled" from everyday practices. In 2005, Hafner-Burton and Tsutsui published an analysis in which they used world society theory to explain why human rights treaties fail to have their intended effects on the countries that ratify them.[2] Not only that, they reported that levels of abuse worsened fol-

lowing ratification of several core human rights treaties, a phenomenon they dubbed "radical decoupling." Others have also found that the treaties often exacerbate rather than attenuate human rights abuse.[3]

Recent analyses give reason to be more optimistic, but only slightly so. Using more sophisticated methodological techniques than previously employed, scholars began to uncover positive but highly contingent treaty effects. These studies found that human rights treaties had their intended impact on practices when mediated by domestic factors such as level of democracy and judicial effectiveness. This means, however, that human rights treaties have largely failed to matter where they are needed most.

There is little consensus as to the causal mechanisms driving the perverse association between ratification and repression. For some, human rights treaty ratification amounts to little more than cheap talk. Others posit that countries ratify as a tactical concession, either to placate domestic opposition groups or to mollify the international community. Yet others view ratification as "window dressing," a way for countries to align themselves with externally legitimated models of statehood. Treaties, in this view, function as "myths" that are "taken for granted as legitimate, apart from evaluations of their impact on . . . outcomes."[4] Despite (or perhaps because of) the limited impact of human rights treaties on practices, states continue to ratify them; it is in this sense that ratification has been described as ceremonial.

I argue that this view of human rights treaties, although widely held, misses a core insight of Meyer and Rowan's original statement, which holds that decoupling and face work are sustain-

Excerpted with changes by permission of the University of Chicago Press from Wade M. Cole, "Human Rights as Myth and Ceremony? Reevaluating the Effectiveness of Human Rights Treaties, 1981–2007," *American Journal of Sociology* 117, 4 (2012): 1131–71. Copyright © University of Chicago Press.

1. John W. Meyer and Brian Rowan, "Institutionalized Organizations: Formal Structure as Myth and Ceremony," *American Journal of Sociology* 83 (1977): 340–63.
2. Emilie Hafner-Burton and Kiyoteru Tsutsui, "Human Rights in a Globalizing World: The Paradox of Empty Promises," *American Journal of Sociology* 110 (2005): 1373–1411.

3. Linda C. Keith, "The United Nations International Covenant on Civil and Political Rights: Does It Make a Difference in Human Rights Behavior?" *Journal of Peace Research* 36 (1999): 95–118; Oona Hathaway, "Do Human Rights Treaties Make a Difference?" *Yale Law Journal* 111 (2002): 1935–2042; Emilie Hafner-Burton and Kiyoteru Tsutsui, "Justice Lost! The Failure of International Human Rights Law to Matter Where Needed Most," *Journal of Peace Research* 44, 4 (2007): 407–25.
4. Meyer and Rowan, "Institutionalized Organizations," note 1, 344.

able only to the extent that organizational activities and outcomes are shielded from rigorous scrutiny. "Inspection and evaluation," after all, "can uncover events and deviations that undermine legitimacy."[5] By implication, if human rights violations are effectively monitored or enforced, the legitimacy that accrues to disingenuous treaty ratification evaporates. An even stronger prediction—one that has yet to be analyzed in the empirical literature—is that "*deceremonialized*" monitoring and enforcement will render human rights treaties more efficacious, resulting in improved country-level practices.

I evaluate this prediction using data for up to 148 countries between 1981 and 2007. I analyze the effects of four core human rights instruments on measures that correspond as closely as possible with the substance of each. These instruments are the International Convention on the Elimination of All Forms of Racial Discrimination (ICERD), the International Covenant on Civil and Political Rights (ICCPR), the Convention against Torture and Other Cruel, Inhuman or Degrading Treatment or Punishment (CAT), and the Convention on the Elimination of All Forms of Discrimination against Women (CEDAW), adopted respectively in 1965, 1966, 1984, and 1989. The ICCPR and CAT focus on different categories of rights *protections*—civil and political rights on the one hand, personal integrity rights on the other—that apply equally to all individuals, whereas the ICERD and CEDAW seek to eradicate discrimination vis-à-vis distinct categories of rights *holders*—namely, racial minorities and women. When evaluating the effect of these treaties on outcomes, I take different levels of monitoring and enforcement into consideration. As a result, I find, in contrast with existing research, that human rights treaties often have direct salutary effects on the practices of states that join them.

My analysis uncovers positive effects where others have not because I address two primary limitations of previous studies. First, scholars tend to view treaty membership as a binary variable—either a country ratified a treaty or not—that fails to consider *different levels of treaty commitment*. I take a more nuanced approach to treaty membership by analyzing whether compliance varies with a country's decision to (1)

sign rather than ratify; (2) enter reservations, understandings, or declarations that qualify or evade specific treaty provisions; or (3) accede to more stringent monitoring and enforcement than is required. Second, my analysis includes a *broader range of outcomes* than most previous studies have employed and tailors outcome measures to treaty content, thus making it easier to detect treaty effects.

ACCOUNTING FOR THE (IN)EFFECTIVENESS OF HUMAN RIGHTS TREATIES

THEORIZING THE "THREE PILLARS" OF COMPLIANCE

Why—or under what conditions—do states comply with human rights treaties? The answer to this question depends largely on one's view of the international system in which states operate. If we take seriously the notion that states are organizations writ large and if we approach the study of states qua organizations using an open-system perspective that emphasizes how "environments shape, support, and infiltrate organizations,"[6] then what kind of environment is the international system? Richard Scott describes three kinds of environments: regulative, normative, and cultural-cognitive.[7] In a regulative international system, the behavior of states would be rooted in the logic of instrumentality and structured by formal rules and laws. Because states' fundamental interests are not easily revised, behaviors must be manipulated by incentives or sanctions. Regulative systems, that is, must coerce behavioral change. Viewing human rights treaty regimes in this fashion is consistent with "realist approaches [that] focus on the material incentives for certain behaviors."[8]

Human rights treaty regimes, of course, lack the mechanisms for imposing costs on contumacy or dispensing rewards for compliance; as such, behaviors must be incentivized by third

5. Ibid., 359.

6. Richard W. Scott, *Organizations: Rational, Natural, and Open Systems*, 5th ed. (Upper Saddle River, N.J.: Prentice Hall, 2003), 29.
7. Richard W. Scott, *Institutions and Organizations*, 2nd ed. (Thousand Oaks, Calif.: Sage, 2001).
8. Beth A. Simmons, "International Law and International Relations," in Keith E. Whittington, R. Daniel Keleman, and Gregory A. Caldeira, eds., *The Oxford Handbook of Law and Politics* (Oxford: OUP, 2008), 187–208, 191.

parties such as other states. For example, human rights agendas can be advanced by withholding economic aid to abusive regimes or by entering into preferential trade agreements with countries that improve their practices. In the absence of this kind of enforcement and given the non-self-enforcing nature of human rights agreements, states in regulative systems are expected to flout their commitments whenever expediency or raison d'état dictates. But then, realists also expect that states, as rational actors, will assess the costs and benefits of treaty membership ex ante before joining. If the expected costs of joining a human rights treaty outweigh the anticipated benefit of membership, countries will self-select out of the regime.

Contrasting starkly with regulative systems, in which action is governed above all else by considerations of costs and benefits, normative systems are grounded in the imperatives of appropriateness and obligation. Morals and values, rather than inducements and sanctions, constitute the driving forces of compliance. Behaviors change because actors' fundamental beliefs about right and wrong change. Binding expectations—in the form, for example, of treaty commitments—are the glue that holds normative systems together. The assumption is "that when nations enter into an international agreement they alter their behavior, their relationships, and the expectations of one another in accordance with its terms," even in the absence of material rewards or sanctions.[9]

Thus, normative systems seek to change the internal interests and preferences of actors rather than the external incentives or disincentives for action. In this view, states must be convinced that human rights norms are relevant, appropriate, and valid before meaningful and lasting change will occur. They must, in other words, be socialized to accept the norms embodied in human rights treaties.

Finally, in cognitive-cultural systems, behavior is shaped by taken-for-granted understandings, schemata, and symbols that mediate between the external world and the internal mental states of socially constructed actors. Patterns of behavior reflect not only what is mate-

rially advantageous or morally appropriate but also what is "thinkable" in a given cultural and institutional context.

Sociological institutionalists argue that states frequently adopt globally promulgated policy scripts and structural models based on considerations of legitimacy, quite apart from moral evaluations and regardless of practical utility or sincere commitment. The same principle applies to the adoption of human rights treaties. Put simply, "ratification of human rights treaties increases the legitimacy of the state," but "states may ratify human rights treaties without being convinced of the value of ideas codified in the treaties."[10] Indeed, countries often express a purely rhetorical commitment to human rights treaties without modifying their underlying preferences or existing behaviors. Human rights practices, in other words, are frequently decoupled from human rights treaty commitments.

In this respect, sociological institutionalism predicts the same behavioral outcome— noncompliance—as realism, even if the motives producing that outcome differ. But institutionalists, unlike realists, view legitimacy as a worthwhile and valuable resource. To be sure, the quest for legitimacy is what motivates abusive regimes to join human rights treaties in the first place. It follows that the loss of legitimacy represents a real cost that countries wish to avoid. Inasmuch as the legitimacy conferred by perfunctory commitments is premised on the illusion of compliance, factors that compromise this illusion are costly. Consequently, although the monitoring and enforcement provisions of human rights treaties may not impose tangible costs on recalcitrant states in terms of material sanctions, they nevertheless make it difficult for states to derive legitimacy from insincere commitments.

This final point brings me to the core arguments undergirding my analysis. Too often, scholars assume that the mechanisms established to monitor and enforce human rights treaties are ineffectual, without actually evaluating whether this claim has empirical merit. Hafner-Burton et al., for example, blame rampant decoupling on the "very low level of enforcement mechanisms

9. Abram Chayes and Antonia Handler Chayes, "On Compliance," *International Organization* 47 (1993): 175–205, 176.

10. Emilie Hafner-Burton, Kiyoteru Tsutsui, and John W. Meyer, "International Human Rights Law and the Politics of Legitimation: Repressive States and Human Rights Treaties," *International Sociology* 23 (2008): 115–41, 121–22.

for most human rights treaties,"[11] but they did not probe deeper to determine if enhanced surveillance or implementation provisions improve compliance rates. Likewise, Neumayer notes that the "monitoring, compliance, and enforcement provisions [of human rights treaties] are nonexistent, voluntary, or weak and deficient."[12] All international human rights treaties provide for some kind of monitoring, even if only self-reporting requirements. However, the allegation that enforcement mechanisms are universally "weak and deficient" has yet to be analyzed. The question is eminently verifiable, given the existence of different monitoring and enforcement mechanisms of varying strength.

Strength of Commitment

Are some treaty commitments and mechanisms more effective than others in terms of their impact on human rights outcomes? To address this question, I analyze four levels of commitment to human rights treaties—signature, qualified ratification, ratification in general, and ratification with enhanced monitoring and enforcement—for their effect on countries' human rights performance. These modalities of treaty membership range in strength from shallow nonbinding endorsements to deep legal obligations that delegate oversight to external treaty bodies.

Signature Versus Ratification

The most fundamental distinction with respect to treaty commitments is between signature and ratification. Signing a treaty incurs a weaker obligation under international law than ratification does. According to the UN *Treaty Handbook* "a signing State does not undertake positive legal obligations under the treaty upon signature."[13] Rather, signature "allows States time . . . to enact any legislation necessary to implement the treaty domestically, prior to under-

taking the legal obligations under the treaty at the international level." Unlike signature, ratification ipso facto binds a country legally to the terms of a treaty. Ratification refers "to the act undertaken on the international plane, whereby a State establishes its consent to be bound by a treaty. Once a State has ratified a treaty at the international level, it must give effect to the treaty domestically."[14] Because signature does not create a legally binding obligation to comply, it is presumably less costly than ratification. Therefore, in a purely regulative system, ratification should have a stronger effect on practices than signature.

In contrast, Article 18 of the Vienna Convention on the Law of Treaties (1969) declares that signature imposes an obligation "to refrain in good faith from acts that would defeat the object and purpose of the treaty." For this reason, Goodman and Jinks argue that "ratification is not the 'magic moment' of acceptance of human rights norms. As a matter of international law, core treaty obligations attach earlier in the incorporation process—that is, upon *signature* of the treaty."[15] In a normative system, then, signature as well as ratification should have a beneficial effect on practices. These contrasting views lead to the following hypotheses:

Hypothesis 1a (the legal commitment hypothesis). Human rights treaties will be more effective for countries that ratify rather than [merely] sign them.

Hypothesis 1b (the moral commitment hypothesis). Human rights treaties will be effective for countries that sign or ratify them.

Conditional Ratification

Countries that ratify human rights treaties need not commit to them wholesale. Countries can exempt themselves from specific treaty provisions or clarify their interpretation of the treaty by entering reservations, understandings, and declarations (RUDs). According to Neumayer, RUDs "allow a country to become a state party to an international treaty in a qualified and con-

---

11. Ibid., 121.
12. Eric Neumayer, "Do International Human Rights Treaties Improve Respect for Human Rights?" *Journal of Conflict Resolution* 49, 6 (2005): 925–53, 926.
13. United Nations, *Treaty Handbook* (New York: UN, 2001), 3.

14. Ibid., 6, 60.
15. Ryan Goodman and Derek Jinks, "Measuring the Effects of Human Rights Treaties," *EJIL* 14, 1 (2003): 171–83, 173.

tingent manner."[16] Reservations function as line-item vetoes, rendering specified portions of a treaty nonbinding while leaving the remainder of it intact.

Declarations and understandings allow countries to articulate their position on a treaty without modifying or nullifying its legal effect. Legal scholars debate the legitimacy of RUDs. One view holds that such qualifications facilitate broader participation but at the expense of a treaty's core objectives, thus sacrificing depth (unconditional membership) for breadth (universal membership). According to Lijnzaad, reservations "turn a human rights instrument into a moth-eaten guarantee" by "restrict[ing] the potential domestic effect of a human rights treaty."[17] An opposing view suggests that RUDs actually "permit agreement on deeper commitments than would otherwise be possible."[18] If countries were not permitted to enter exemptions or interpretations, they might simply negotiate weaker treaties. Moreover, the very act of depositing a RUD signals a country's respect for international law. Less scrupulous states tend to ratify treaties unconditionally but disingenuously, regardless of their intention to comply.

These competing perspectives on RUDs imply two hypotheses. The first perspective contends that rights-abusing states use reservations to evade treaty provisions with which they cannot or will not comply. Although normative pressures lead repressive governments to ratify human rights treaties at rates equal to rights-affirming countries, RUDs permit abusers to blunt the impact of their commitments. Countries that ratify unconditionally, then, are expected to show a greater respect for human rights when compared with conditional ratifiers. Hypothesis 2a states this formally.

Hypothesis 2a (the unqualified commitment hypothesis). Human rights treaties will be more effective for countries that unconditionally ratify than for countries that ratify with RUDs.

Others have suggested that RUDs are used primarily by countries that take their treaty commitments seriously. Countries that adhere to the rule of law, in particular, are inclined to enter carefully worded exemptions or interpretations at the time of ratification while faithfully honoring the unreserved portions of a treaty. . . . Thus, an alternative to the unqualified commitment hypothesis can be proposed.

Hypothesis 2b (the precise commitment hypothesis). Human rights treaties will be more effective for countries that modify or interpret their treaty commitments by entering RUDs than for countries that ratify unconditionally but disingenuously.

RATIFICATION WITH ENHANCED MONITORING

One final dimension of treaty commitment concerns the extent to which countries submit to enhanced monitoring and enforcement provisions. All four treaties under consideration provide for interstate complaints, whereby a state party formally alleges that another state party has violated its treaty obligations. In theory, these complaints are submitted to and evaluated by independent oversight bodies established under each treaty; to date, however, no such complaints have ever been lodged. Two of the treaties—the ICCPR and CAT—require states to make formal declarations under specific treaty provisions (articles 14 and 21 respectively) before complaints can be filed against them by other state parties (and, in turn, before they can file complaints against other state parties). Acceding to interstate complaints under these treaties therefore requires an additional step, over and above ratification. In contrast, interstate complaints procedures form an integral part of the ICERD and CEDAW (under articles 11 and 29 respectively), so that accession to those procedures is subsumed within ratification. Countries wishing to exempt themselves from interstate complaints under these treaties must enter a reservation to that effect.

In addition to interstate complaints procedures, three of the treaties—CAT, ICCPR, and ICERD—contain further provisions that, if acceded to by states, permit oversight bodies to receive complaints of abuse from individuals. For ICERD and CAT, states authorize individuals

16. Eric Neumayer, "Qualified Ratification: Explaining Reservations to International Human Rights Treaties," *Journal of Legal Studies* 36, 2 (2007): 397–429, 397.
17. Liesbeth Lijnzaad, *Reservations to UN Human Rights Treaties: Ratify or Ruin?* (Dordrecht: Nijhoff, 1995), 3.
18. Edward T. Swaine, "Reserving," *YJIL* 31 (2006): 307–66, 311.

within their jurisdiction to submit complaints by making a declaration under articles 14 and 22, respectively, whereas for the ICCPR states must join the First Optional Protocol, which itself can be signed or ratified with or without RUDs.

It bears reiterating that countries need not recognize the competence of oversight committees to receive interstate or individual complaints. Those opting not to do so are required only to submit periodic reports detailing the measures they have taken to implement treaty provisions. These reports, when they are submitted at all, often exaggerate the degree of compliance. For these reasons, I expect that the following hypothesis holds.

Hypothesis 3 (the deep commitment hypothesis). Human rights treaties will be more effective for countries that accede to optional monitoring and enforcement provisions than for countries that do not.

This hypothesis can be further refined to predict different levels of compliance for each type of optional commitment. I expect that individual complaints procedures will have a larger impact on human rights practices when compared with interstate complaints mechanisms. This expectation arises from the simple fact that the interstate complaints procedures have never been used and hence do not pose a credible threat to rights-abusing countries. It is likely that the generalized "sovereignty costs" of mechanisms that allow states to complain about the internal behaviors and practices of other states are simply too great, which discourages their use.

Individuals, less concerned than states with upholding sovereignty norms, are much more apt to complain about human rights abuses. However, the frequency with which individuals file complaints varies considerably across treaties.

Despite variation in the use of individual complaints mechanisms across treaties, as a whole these provisions should have a greater impact on human rights practices relative to interstate complaints procedures. Although treaty bodies lack the capacity to enforce their decisions regarding allegations of abuse, Jack Donnelly has concluded that the individual complaints procedure "provides a genuine, if limited, instance of international monitoring, which in at least a few cases has altered state

practice."[19] Accordingly, I offer the following revision to Hypothesis 3.

Hypothesis 3a (the individual complaints hypothesis). Human rights treaties will be more effective for countries that submit to individual complaints provisions than for countries that submit only to interstate complaints provisions.

[*Eds.*—Next, in lengthy detail, the author elucidates his "research design" pursuant to which he tests his hypotheses—"Dependent Variables: Human Rights Practices," "Independent Variables: Treaty Membership," and "Control Variables"—and his "method' of doing so. He then turns to the results of his findings.]

RESULTS

In contrast with previous research, which found that "the CAT does not have unconditional effects" on levels of torture, my results show that two levels of treaty membership had a direct positive effect on human rights outcomes: consistent with the deep commitment hypothesis (Hypothesis 3), countries that authorized the Committee against Torture to receive interstate and individual complaints evinced higher levels of respect for physical integrity rights relative to countries that merely signed or ratified the CAT.

In addition to the effect of optional commitments, periods of civil war substantially curtailed respect for physical integrity rights whereas democracy was associated with greater levels of respect. These findings are intuitively sensible. Democratic countries respect due process, the rule of law, and the fundamental rights of life and liberty, whereas regimes in battle-torn countries resort to practices such as torture and political imprisonment in order to neutralize political competitors, rivals, and recusants.

As with the CAT, my findings regarding the ICCPR show that enhanced monitoring and enforcement resulted in improved human rights performance. These findings once again support Hypothesis 3. Conversely, states that modified

19. Jack Donnelly, "International Human Rights: A Regime Analysis," *International Organization* 40 (1986): 599–642, 611.

their ratification of the ICCPR and First Optional Protocol by entering RUDs had lower levels of respect for empowerment rights. Rather than using RUDs to increase the precision of their commitments, it would appear that countries modified or interpreted their commitments in ways that undermined the treaties. This finding contradicts the precise commitment hypothesis (Hypothesis 2b).

Signatories to the ICCPR had better empowerment rights practices than other countries even though ratification—a stronger, legally binding commitment—had no appreciable effect. How could this be? The dynamics of treaty commitment points to a possible answer. Most countries that signed human rights treaties did so early, immediately after the treaties were adopted, and these "first-mover" countries were generally respectful of human rights. Average empowerment rights scores for countries that *signed* the ICCPR prior to 1985 were more than a full point higher (on an 11-point scale) relative to countries that *ratified* the ICCPR during the same period; after 1985, empowerment rights scores were higher among ratifiers than among signatories. Although rights-affirming countries are deeply committed to human rights norms, they undertake treaty commitments cautiously because of their respect for the rule of law. Given uncertainty over the legal and political ramifications of the ICCPR—which was, after all, one of the first and most far-reaching human rights treaties—these countries expressed their moral support by signing but delayed the incursion of legal commitments through ratification. As more countries bound themselves legally to the covenant, the level of uncertainty surrounding it declined and countries began to ratify in greater numbers. In any event, the results run contrary to the legal commitment hypothesis (Hypothesis 1a) and provide at least partial support to the moral commitment hypothesis (Hypothesis 1b).

The effect of CEDAW membership on women's rights differs fundamentally from the CAT and ICCPR/First Optional Protocol. In contrast to these treaties, conditional CEDAW ratifications (i.e., those in which countries enter RUDs) resulted in improved women's rights performance, lending support to the precise commitment hypothesis (Hypothesis 2b). This finding is somewhat unexpected given that "CEDAW has attracted the greatest number of reservations with the potential to modify or exclude most, if not all, of the terms of the treaty."[20] In fact, CEDAW is one of the most heavily reserved human rights treaties, and the number of RUDs a country enters increases significantly as the percentage of its population that is Muslim increases. Predominantly Muslim countries have entered sweeping reservations to CEDAW, such as one by Oman that purports to exempt it from "all provisions of the Convention not in accordance with the provisions of the Islamic Sharia." To determine whether such modifications undermine the treaty's efficacy, I analyzed the effect of conditional CEDAW ratification among Islamic and non-Islamic countries.

The findings show that ratification with RUDs is associated with a statistically significant decline in women's rights scores among Islamic countries, whereas the effect remains significantly positive for non-Islamic countries. Even such rights-affirming countries as Australia, Canada, and Switzerland have entered RUDs to CEDAW. For these countries, reservations are designed primarily to harmonize CEDAW with domestic legislation, so the precise commitment hypothesis (Hypothesis 2b) holds. Conversely, reservations entered by predominantly Muslim countries would appear to defeat the purpose of CEDAW by immunizing discriminatory practices and legal provisions from the treaty's reach.

Aside from the effects of conditional ratification, CEDAW membership was statistically unrelated to respect for women's rights. Neither signature nor ratification, by itself, predicted women's rights outcomes, nor did accession to interstate complaints procedures. Women's rights tended to improve as a function of population density and the share of parliamentary seats held by women, but the effects of other control variables were much less stable or significant.

States that signed and ratified the ICERD were less likely than nonsignatories and nonparties to discriminate. Thus, Hypothesis 1b (the moral commitment hypothesis) finds support. One additional mode of commitment—accession to interstate complaints provisions—was also associated with an improvement in the treatment of minorities. Hypothesis 3, the deep commit-

20. Belinda Clark, "The Vienna Convention Reservations Regime and the Convention on Discrimination Against Women," *AJIL* 85 (1991): 281–321, 317.

ment hypothesis, is therefore partially supported. However, individual complaints provisions led to increased levels of discrimination with respect to countries' most disadvantaged minority groups, in direct opposition to the individual complaints hypothesis (Hypothesis 3a).

What might account for the ineffectiveness of the ICERD's individual complaints procedure relative to those established under the ICCPR and CAT? Recall that fewer than 50 petitions have been submitted under the ICERD, compared with more than 400 under the CAT and nearly 2,000 under the ICCPR. On the basis of these figures, it appears that the effectiveness of individual complaints procedures depends on the frequency of their use.

DISCUSSION AND CONCLUSION

Taken as a whole, the evidence shows that enhanced monitoring and enforcement provisions are reasonably effective in improving the human rights practices of states. In three of the four treaties under investigation, countries that acceded to interstate complaints procedures experienced better human rights outcomes as a result. Moreover, for two of the three treaties that allowed individual complaints, accession to these provisions had a positive effect on human rights outcomes.

These findings suggest that, for many human rights treaties, optional interstate and individual complaints provisions contribute to improved practices. Because states can reasonably assume that they will never be targeted by an interstate complaint, the procedure does not pose a credible threat and therefore has no direct impact on the costs of treaty abrogation. Rather, acceding to interstate complaints provisions is a purely ceremonial commitment that nevertheless has tangible consequences in most cases. The effect of interstate complaints provisions would therefore seem to flow from a "logic of appropriateness," suggesting that international human rights treaty regimes operate as normative rather than regulative systems.

Unlike states, individuals have demonstrated a much greater propensity to complain about human rights violations, although the number of complaints filed under the ICCPR and CAT greatly outnumbered the number submitted under the ICERD. This variation, in turn, ap-

pears to be linked to human rights outcomes, and for good reason: individual complaints play an important role in monitoring and publicizing rights violations. Complaints are reviewed and decided on their merits by committees of independent experts, whose decisions are compiled, published, and scrutinized. Therefore, as the volume of individual complaints increases, the ability of countries to conceal their human rights violations declines, thus undermining the logic of confidence that sustains decoupling. Consistent with Meyer and Rowan's oft-overlooked contention that routine surveillance and evaluation make it difficult for organizations to decouple symbolic structures from core activities, individual complaints procedures deceremonialize treaty monitoring and, to the extent that they are used, contribute to improved practices.

But what about the effects of straightforward ratification? Studies of treaty ratification consistently demonstrate that rights-abusing countries join human rights treaties at rates equal to rights-affirming countries. Neglecting to adjust for this pattern of ratification can bias treaty effects downward, obscuring an otherwise positive (or, at least, neutral) relationship between ratification and practices.

To be sure, in the one case in which ratification exerted a statistically significant effect on practices in this analysis, the effect was positive: ICERD ratification led to reduced levels of political discrimination against minorities.

Compared with interstate and individual complaints provisions, findings for other levels of commitment were much less robust. Signing the ICERD and ICCPR was associated with improved human rights practices, even though signature does not bind a country legally to the terms of a treaty. Yet signing the CAT and CEDAW had no appreciable effect on human rights outcomes. It would appear that the aforementioned tendency for rights-affirming countries to sign rather than ratify human rights treaties—a tendency that produces positive signature effects—weakens as the collective human rights regime strengthens.

We have seen, however, that ratification is not an all-or-nothing enterprise, as countries can modify or interpret their treaty commitments using RUDs. Conditional or qualified ratifications of this sort had inconsistent effects on human rights outcomes. On average, women's rights scores increased among non-Islamic countries that ratified the CEDAW conditionally, suggesting that they used RUDs to make more precise and sincere treaty commitments. Conversely, the negative effect of conditional CEDAW ratification on women's rights among predominantly Muslim countries, as well as the general negative effect of conditional ICCPR ratification on empowerment rights, suggests that RUDs were used in these cases to enervate the treaties.

On the basis of these findings, it is evident that human rights treaty membership is not always predicated on myth and ceremony. Under some conditions, human rights treaties have a beneficial impact on practices.

However much the international community may emphasize that "all human rights are universal, indivisible and interdependent and interrelated" in theory, different categories of rights do not respond uniformly to treaty membership in practice. Indeed, it is instructive that the two "anomalous" findings in the analysis—the exacerbating effect of (1) the ICERD's individual complaints mechanism on racial discrimination and (2) conditional ratification of CEDAW on gender discrimination in Islamic countries—pertain to treaties that protect "subaltern" groups. These treaties exist precisely because the human rights standards already in place were deemed inadequate to protect vulnerable or historically marginalized groups from discrimination. Extending rights to these groups, however, has been contentious: despite significant improvements in the status of women and minorities since World War II, racial and gender discrimination persists in many regions of the world, reinforced in part by refractory cultural understandings and deep-seated religious worldviews that assign different roles, statuses, or aptitudes to individuals on the basis of their ascribed identities.

These findings suggest that similar patterns of compliance and contumacy might characterize efforts to protect other historically disadvantaged groups.

QUESTIONS FOR REFLECTION AND DISCUSSION

1. Wade Cole suggests that human rights treaty ratifications are often seen as cheap talk, tactical concessions, or "window dressing," and that seen from these perspectives, human rights treaties function as "myths" that are "taken for granted as legitimate, . . . apart from evaluations of their impact . . . on outcomes," and that despite (or because of) the "limited impact of human rights treaties on practices, states continue to ratify them; it is in this sense that ratification has been described as ceremonial." How does Cole respond to the myth-and-ceremony critics? What conclusions does he reach? Do you agree with him, and, if so, does his response confirm or change your viewpoint about treaty interpretation and enforcement? And on what evidence do you base your viewpoint?

2. Cole uses the term "radical decoupling." What does this term mean? How does decoupling affect a state's legitimacy?

3. According to Cole, what "core insight of Meyer and Rowan's original statement" do such views of human rights treaty ratification miss?

4. Cole argues that his "analysis uncovers positive effects where others have not because I address two primary limitations of previous studies." What are these limitations? Is his claim convincing? Why? Why not?

5. In your view, is the international legal order a regulative, normative, or cultural-cognitive environment? A mixture of all three? Find and present evidence to support your views.

6. What are the different levels of treaty commitment? What are the pros and cons of each level?

7. Are some treaty commitments and mechanisms more effective than others in terms of their impact on human rights outcomes?

8. How does Cole approach Question 7 in methodological terms? And what answers does Cole's analysis yield? Cole asserts that individual complaint procedures are more effective than interstate complaint procedures. Do you agree? If so, how? If not, why not?

9. Cole concludes that "however much the international community may emphasize that 'all human rights are universal, indivisible and interdependent and interrelated' in theory, different categories of rights do not respond uniformly to treaty membership in

practice." He furthermore notes that "it is instructive that the two 'anomalous' findings in the analysis—the exacerbating effect of (1) the ICERD individual complaints mechanism on racial discrimination and (2) conditional ratification of CEDAW on gender discrimination in Islamic countries—pertain to treaties that protect 'subaltern' groups." How does this empirical finding relate to other readings in the book thus far—in particular Readings 2 (Grear) and 6 (Kapur) in Chapter 1 and 14 (Beveridge-Mullally) in Chapter 3? What continuities and discontinuities can you identify, if any, between the empirical evidence presented by Cole and the accounts by the other readings?

Chapter Seven

Public Sector Approaches to International Human Rights Implementation

IN this chapter, we consider "public" sector approaches to the implementation of international human rights. The readings selected consider first the role of the United Nations and its various elements, actors, and institutions; second, an analysis of the role and future of regional human rights regimes; third, an examination of dilemmas facing international criminal accountability and humanitarian intervention; and—finally—the thorny issue of extraterritorial legal accountability for corporate entities in domestic courts where corporations commonly seek the advantages of "forum shopping" or "jurisdictional arbitrage" to evade liability. Throughout the chapter's readings are critical questions of institutional design and reflections upon the configuration of relationships between legal regimes and the politics dedicated to human rights implementation strategies.

The chapter's exploration begins with "The United Nations and Human Rights." Stephen Marks carefully explores and analyzes the role of the UN as "The principal institutional framework for furthering human rights in the world community." The UN, he explains, is unique in the international legal system: the "only intergovernmental structure with a general mandate for realizing all human rights in all countries." However, as might be expected, the subject of the UN and its role in the implementation of human rights is both contestable and contested. For some commentators, the organization is merely a tool of realpolitik, a geopolitical implement deployed by the most powerful states in their own favor. For others, the UN presents a genuine attempt to establish a normative order responsive to the deep challenges facing humanity.

Marks locates his analysis against an introductory framing of the UN Charter and its relationship with human rights to "set the stage for explaining the UN's strengths and weaknesses as a force for the realization of human rights in the global community." He examines the UN membership's fragile consensus on the content of human rights; the UN promotion and protection of human rights norms, institutions, and procedures—both Charter- and treaty-based; the role of peace operations; and the emergence of the "responsibility to protect" (R2P) doctrine. Concluding his analysis, Marks draws attention to the significant fact that "state sovereignty is less than ever an insurmountable obstacle to UN action to pursue the Charter objective of universal respect for human rights." The UN, he observes, has evolved, expanding its role in various ways; and at the same time there is a growing potential for civil society participation in "transformative processes of governance" in countries transitioning from formerly communist positions or escaping the strictures of dictatorship. These developments, he asserts, hold out hope for human rights progress—a trajectory made particularly visible in human rights institution building. But Marks is no naïve dreamer. He draws the reader's attention to the savage contradictions of ongoing practical realities, including the brute fact of "massive violations [that] continue to occur in the course of internal armed conflict, especially when fed by xenophobic nationalism and religious fanaticism." In the light of Marks's analysis, there is no doubt that the challenges facing the UN human rights program are multiple and complex. However, it is fair to conclude, with Marks, that, however contingently in some cases, the UN has made and continues to seek a meaningful contribution to the pursuit of human rights for all.

The UN system is of course but one component of a wider set of international institutions and procedures currently and systematically dedicated to promoting and protecting human rights. Dinah Shelton turns the reader's attention to regional initiatives in this regard, and about which she asks, in the light of "breakthroughs, burdens, and backlash," the straightforward question: "What future for regional human rights?" Positioning regional human rights institutions and procedures as "systems" (the analytical construct that in her judgment best encompasses the interdependence, complexity, and punctuated equilibrium that characterize these arrangements), she details what a human rights system looks like: (1) a list or lists of internationally guaranteed human rights, (2) permanent institutions, and (3) compliance or enforcement procedures. In addition, each system is composed of various subsystems. At the global level, the UN system consists in large part of numerous interacting organs and specialized agencies concerned with human rights. Regional human rights systems contribute to the global system, as well as forming their own interdependent systems. Subsystems of actors also exist: states, intergovernmental organizations, nongovernmental organizations, corporations and other business entities, and networks of individuals often referred to as civil society.

It is with this understanding that Shelton evaluates the promise of, and challenges to, regional human rights systems, both established and emergent. Tracing the origins of the regional systems in historical and political context, beginning with the end of World War II and continuing as progressive impulses have emerged in different regions of the world, she offers a comprehensive overview of the regional human rights systems presently existing in Europe, the Americas, and Africa, and emerging in the Middle East and Southeast Asia. Additionally, she explores and illuminates the tensions between universal norms and regional values; the nuances of the normative, procedural, and institutional evolution of the systems; and finally, the burdens placed on the systems and the sobering realities of state backlash and noncompliance. Ultimately Shelton concludes that regional systems are indispensable for the achievement of effective compliance with international human rights law, but that they face "unprecedented challenges that threaten their future." While their nature as systems means that regional systems are "strengthened by the variety of subsystems that interact and even compete as parts of them. . . . They are also [engaged] in constant exchanges with their environments and thus never reach equilibrium. As a result," Shelton argues, "their operations will never be completely consistent with their goals; there will almost always be some malfunction or inefficiency in the process." It is, Shelton affirms, "nonetheless possible to seek reform and greater efficiency to achieve the aim of promoting and protecting international human rights."

Next, Richard Falk explores "two dilemmas in the search for humane governance." First, he introduces the "struggle to make political leaders and military commanders accountable under international law whether or not they happen to be on the winning side in a major war or occupy the upper layers of the global political hierarchy." Second, he explores "humanitarian intervention"—often a highly contestable dimension of state action taken in the name of human rights implementation in other jurisdictions, or, in Falk's words "ostensibly . . . to prevent extensive human rights violations."

Falk's analysis reveals certain troublesome discrepancies in the international legal order—discrepancies that go to the heart of the questions of legitimacy and normative acceptability. With respect to the establishment of criminal accountability for human rights violations, Falk underlines the discernible sense in which the structures of such accountability are blemished by "victor's justice." With respect to practices of humanitarian intervention, he identifies patterns reflecting the divisiveness and contestability of so-called "humanitarian" intervention.

In respect of the issue of victor's justice, Falk's central concern is on the "split form of accountability" that manifests itself in the uneven attribution of culpability as between "winners" and "losers"—central examples being the absence of international criminal accountability for the Allied firebombings of major German and Japanese cities and the U.S. atomic bombings of Hiroshima and Nagasaki during the Second World War. It is comforting to assume that matters of accountability have improved or that the lack of it is a thing of the past, but Falk allows no such comfortable assumption to stand. He leaves a strong impression of an uneven, differentially applied jurisprudence closer to a jurisprudence of legitimation than to one of conscience.

Turning to "humanitarian intervention," Falk sees this being related to globalization "and [to] an accompanying heightened sense of human solidarity combined with human rights activism." He traces the rise of "humanitarian diplomacy," pointing to its contested status and to conflicting explanations of its meaning: is it a natural outcome of attention being paid to human rights, or is it an attempt to sustain military budgets and retain geopolitical dominance? In the 1990s, was it a result of "the CNN factor" and pressure to respond to humanitarian disasters? Or was it a way of deflecting "growing criticism of neoliberal globalization in the 1990s as a heartless, capital-driven restructuring of global economic relations"?

Additionally, Falk traces the rise of "humanitarian intervention" and the development of the "responsibility to protect" (R2P) doctrine, briefly explained by Stephen Marks (Reading 30) in this chapter. Placing particular significance on civil movement activism and on the role of civil society, Falk suggests that the "responsibility to protect norm" may be emerging as part of customary international law. At the same time, he observes, it remains dependent upon the will of the dominant states—a reality that runs the risk that humanitarian intervention will be overly dependent upon its coincidence with the strategic political or military objectives of the major powers. Hope, he asserts, lies in the ethical and political acuity of civil society.

Finally, this chapter turns to one of the most challenging questions facing the future of human rights implementation: the question of state imposition (through international and national strategies) of meaningful corporate accountability for human rights violations by them committed extraterritorially. The question, argue Anna Grear and Burns Weston, "is one of increasing contemporary significance in the struggle for global justice." Grear and Weston point to the growing international conviction that the traditional state-centric logics limiting responsibility for extraterritorial human rights abuses are increasingly counterproductive in the face of the "dense, entangled, and rights-violating realities of contemporary globalization." Grear and Weston focus directly upon the most controversial issue facing the implementation of international human rights law—"the challenge of holding powerful corporate actors to account for human rights abuses committed beyond a state's recognized jurisdiction." This is a longstanding challenge, most recently addressed by the 2013 U.S. Supreme Court holding in *Kiobel v. Royal Dutch Petroleum Co.*—a case regarded by some commentators and by human rights activists as having brought a hopeful line of cases deploying the U.S. Alien Tort Claims Act (ATCA) to a disappointing end, disregarding ATCA's instruction to apply a doctrine of universal jurisdiction to establish tortious liability for corporate human rights abuses committed abroad.

While not *Kiobel* enthusiasts, Grear and Weston question the extent to which the *Kiobel* 2013 judgment is truly a death knell for such strategies. They tend to agree with the proposition of a British legal scholar that, after a preceding U.S. Court of Appeals judgment ruling against the plaintiff complainants, "ATCA was a thin thread on which to hang legal accountability for [TNC] violations." Grear and Weston likewise argue that ATCA cases, for all the welcome publicity they manage to bring to gross corporate violations of human rights around the world, ultimately divert attention from the more fundamental reforms needed. At any rate, they conclude that *Kiobel* 2013 has not totally closed the door on imaginative transnational litigation strategies under ATCA because there is sufficient jurisprudential uncertainty remaining to ensure future interpretive engagement in the courts. The implications of the *Kiobel* 2013 judgment in other parts of the world, especially in the EU, which is developing its own jurisprudential trajectory, is likely to be very limited—and in any case, a host of alternative strategies (including legislative approaches) remain available. Ultimately, however, neither the existing litigation strategies nor the alternatives so far proffered are entirely satisfying as a mode of holding powerful transnational corporations to account. What is required is genuine, direct international human rights accountability for corporations. Such accountability can be truly effective, Grear and Weston insist, only in a context where the values used to interpret such accountability are suitably sensitive to the plight of the most disadvantaged. There thus would remain a need for constant critical engagement with the question of human rights meanings, even if and when direct accountability for corporations is established in international human rights law.

This chapter, just as much as those preceding and following it, reveals the complexity, tensions, and countervailing pressures facing enforcement of human rights in a globalized age.

30. STEPHEN P. MARKS *The United Nations and Human Rights*

The principal institutional framework for furthering human rights in the world community is the United Nations, the only intergovernmental structure with a general mandate for realizing all human rights in all countries. The UN is a tool of geopolitics for some and a beacon of hope for others. We begin with some preliminary observations

Excerpted with changes by permission of Stephen P. Marks from Stephen P. Marks, "The United Nations and Human Rights" (unpublished manuscript on file with the author, 2014). Copyright © 2014 Stephen P. Marks. The author gratefully acknowledges the research assistance of Erin James.

on the place and promise of human rights in and under the UN Charter to set the stage for explaining the UN's strengths and weaknesses as a force for human rights in the global community.

HUMAN RIGHTS IN THE UN CHARTER

The founders of the UN, not content to treat human rights as merely one among many shared objectives of UN member governments, implicitly articulated a theory of peace according to which respect for human rights and fundamental freedoms is a necessary condition for peace within and among nations. The Charter's Preamble places "faith in fundamental human rights" immediately after its aim "to save succeeding generations from the scourge of war." Yet the Charter does not apply this theory to the relative powers of the UN main organs. Instead, the human rights provisions are relegated, in the chapter on the purposes of the UN, to achieving international cooperation (art. 1(3)) and, in the chapter on international economic and social cooperation, to promoting "universal respect for, and observance of, human rights and fundamental freedoms for all without distinction as to race, sex, language, or religion" (art. 55). The UN General Assembly (UNGA) may initiate studies and make recommendations for the purpose of "assisting in the realization of human rights" (art. 13(1)) and the Economic and Social Council (ECOSOC) may make recommendations and draft conventions on human rights (art. 62(2), (3)) as well as set up commissions, including to promote human rights (art. 68), which it did in 1946 by establishing the UN Commission on Human Rights (replaced in 2006 by the UN Human Rights Council or HRC). The Charter language was deliberately weak, emphasizing "promotion" rather than "protection" by the General Assembly and ECOSOC, while granting to the UN Security Council (UNSC) sole authority to render binding decisions and require states, under the threat of economic, military, or other sanction, to modify their aggressive behaviors.

Articles 55 and 56 of the Charter stipulate that the member states pledge themselves to take joint and separate action in cooperation with the Organization to "promote . . . universal respect for and observance of human rights." This "pledge" (a legally ambiguous term) remains the core human rights obligation of member states. In practice it has meant mainly promotion rather than protection but has nonetheless resulted in an impressive body of international human rights law, as well as studies and public information on a wide range of human rights and related issues. However, the widely recognized principles of territorial sovereignty and non-intervention into "matters which are essentially within the domestic jurisdiction of any state" (art. 2(7)), have prevented the UN from taking decisive action to stop governments from mistreating their populations in violation of their Article 56 pledge.

FRAGILE CONSENSUS ON THE CONTENT OF HUMAN RIGHTS

The Commission on Human Rights was tasked to draft the Universal Declaration of Human Rights (UDHR), adopted by the UNGA on 10 December 1948 and stating in its Preamble that "a common understanding of these rights and freedoms is of the greatest importance for the full realization of [the Charter Article 56] pledge." But this "common understanding" proved a fragile consensus that was challenged throughout the Cold War when the UN became a debating forum of opposing ideologies. Delegates from Western countries denounced the lack of democracy, freedom, and human rights in the Eastern bloc, and Soviet bloc countries and members of the Non-Aligned Movement criticized the West for its racial discrimination, support of apartheid, and domination in the global economy in ways that drastically curtailed economic, social, and cultural rights. With the end of the Cold War and a seeming delinking of human rights and ideology, words took on new meaning and a new, at least partially restored, consensus became possible. Symbolic of this moment was the World Conference on Human Rights, convened by the UN in Vienna in 1993, which adopted the Vienna Declaration and Programme of Action (VDPA), confirming the universality of human rights standards as defined by the UN and largely rejecting the counterclaims of cultural relativism.[1] The consensus reached was a fragile bridging of the very real divide between perceptions of human rights by different governments and peoples' movements. The governments assembled in Vienna nonetheless agreed that

> All human rights are universal, indivisible and interdependent and interrelated. The international community must treat human rights globally in a fair and equal manner, on the same footing, and with the same emphasis. While the significance of national and regional particularities and various historical, cultural and religious backgrounds must be borne in mind, it is the duty of States, regardless of their political, economic and cultural systems, to

---

1. On the tension between the universality of human rights and cultural relativism, see Reading 4 (Weston) in Chapter 1.

promote and protect all human rights and fundamental freedoms.[2]

The claim of universality, indivisibility, interdependence, and interrelatedness of human rights is repeated like a mantra in UN instruments, masking many real tensions that still challenge this consensus. Deeply cultural antinomies, disguised as "particularities" and "backgrounds" to be "borne in mind," translate into political wrangling in UN debates over issues of religious intolerance, freedom of expression, sexual orientation and gender identity, and reproductive rights, among others. Meanwhile, some perceive the idea of human rights as a Western cause or as a tool of Western imperialism. Whatever political interpretations countries or groups of countries may wish to give to a particular human rights issue under debate, there is little disagreement that the UN is the forum where the legitimacy of claims of universality of human rights are tested.

PROMOTING AND PROTECTING HUMAN RIGHTS THROUGH THE UNITED NATIONS

The space for UN action in a wide range of human rights concerns has opened over the last thirty years owing to a political willingness to limit the scope of Charter Article 2(7) (domestic jurisdiction) and expand that of the Article 56 (cooperation with the UN to achieve human rights). The UN does much today that would have been deemed "intervention" by most states a few decades ago—e.g., investigation of abuse, adoption of UNGA and UNHRC resolutions explicitly denouncing countries by name, sending special envoys and rapporteurs, receiving complaints from individuals, addressing urgent appeals to governments, and conducting inquiries. Indeed, the range of UN human rights action allowed now covers at least three means of preventing harm (education and information, standard setting and interpretation, and institution building within member states) and five tools to respond to human rights situations and protect human rights (monitoring through reporting and fact finding, adjudication, political supervision, humanitarian action, and coercive action). Taken together, these means and methods for promoting and protecting human rights describe what the

2. Vienna Declaration (VDPA).

UN can do to move from the lofty words of the UDHR to action that affects people's lives.

PROMOTION AND PROTECTION THROUGH UN HUMAN RIGHTS MECHANISMS

Originally, the principal body responsible for human rights in the UN was the Commission on Human Rights. It carried out the bulk of the standard-setting activity of the early years following the adoption of the UDHR. In the 1950s and early 1960s, the first human rights treaties adopted by the UN related to trafficking and prostitution, the political rights of women, the nationality of married women, and consent to marriage, minimum age for marriage, and registration of marriages. A major milestone was the adoption in 1966 of the two international covenants—International Covenant on Economic, Social and Cultural Rights (ICESCR) and the International Covenant on Civil and Political Rights (ICCPR)—which together transformed the aspirational rights of the UDHR into binding treaty law. A second milestone was the systematic advancement of women's rights in the Declaration on the Elimination of Discrimination against Women of 1967, followed by the 1979 Convention on the Elimination of All Forms of Discrimination against Women (CEDAW). In the 1970s and 1980s the UN adopted other core human rights treaties on racial discrimination, torture, children's rights, and, in the 1990s and 2000s, rights of migrant workers and persons with disabilities. For all their shortcomings, the expansion of the thirty UDHR articles into a considerable body of treaty law, with an impressive amount of interpretative work by nine treaty-monitoring bodies, is an undeniable UN accomplishment.

The Commission, consisting of 53 governments elected by ECOSOC to which it reported, was replaced in 2006 by the Human Rights Council, consisting of 47 governments elected by the UNGA, to which it reports. Before and following the 2006 reform, an array of mechanisms have evolved, based either on the Charter (applicable to all UN member states) or on treaties (binding only the states that have ratified them) which are administered by the Office of the High Commissioner for Human Rights (OHCHR). It thus is now common to distinguish between Charter-based and treaty-based procedures.

PROMOTING AND PROTECTING HUMAN RIGHTS THROUGH
CHARTER-BASED PROCEDURES

Most Charter-based procedures relate to the principal UN organs with responsibility over human rights—the UNGA (especially its subsidiary body the UNHRC), ECOSOC, and the Secretariat (principally the OHCHR). However, other units of the UN Secretariat have significant human rights responsibilities, such as Office for the Coordination of Humanitarian Affairs (OCHA), Department of Political Affairs (DPA), and Department of Peacekeeping Operations (DPKO). Moreover, other main organs of the UN occasionally address human rights, such as the International Court of Justice (ICJ) and the Security Council (UNSC). In addition, there are funds and programs of ECOSOC and the UNGA, which engage in human rights work, such as the UN Development Programme (UNDP), the UN Children's Fund (UNICEF), the UN Fund for Population Activities (UNFPA), the UN High Commissioner for Refugees (UNHCR), and the UN Entity for Gender Equality and the Empowerment of Women (UN-Women). Among the 14 Specialized Agencies, autonomous organizations coordinated by ECOSOC and UNGA, the International Labour Organization (ILO), Food and Agriculture Organization (FAO), UN Educational, Scientific and Cultural Organization (UNESCO), and World Health Organization (WHO) contribute in various ways to human rights. OHCHR and six other agencies (UNDP, UNICEF, UNFPA, UNESCO, WHO, and FAO) adopted in 2003 the "Common Understanding among UN Agencies on a Human Rights-Based Approach to Development Cooperation," which defined a number of criteria for a UN standard Human Rights-Based Approach (HRBA).[3] Owing to space limitations, however, these agencies are not further reviewed here.

The High Commissioner for Human Rights

The post of UN High Commissioner for Human Rights (UNHCHR), whose origins may be traced to a proposal from René Cassin of France to create a position of Attorney-General for Human Rights, was established as recommended by the VDPA in 1993. UNGA Resolution 48/141 of 20 December 1993 creating the post stipulates that the High Commissioner be appointed for four years (renewable once) by the Secretary-General, approved by the UNGA, and tasked with promoting and protecting the effective enjoyment by all people of all civil, cultural, economic, political, and social rights, including the right to development. The first High Commissioner functioned as a senior official promoting human rights alongside the Secretariat's Centre for Human Rights in Geneva. The second High Commissioner, former president of Ireland Mary Robinson, merged the Centre into the OHCHR and considerably expanded its role. Four others have served in this capacity as of this writing, with a seventh to be selected in 2014.[4]

The stature of the OHCHR has grown, as has its size. Half the staff of over 1,100 is located in the Geneva Headquarters, 2 percent in the New York Office, and the rest deployed in 58 field offices (12 country or stand-alone offices, 13 regional offices or centers, 15 human rights components of UN peace missions and 18 human rights advisers to UN Country Teams). The country offices engage in monitoring, public reporting, and technical assistance.[5] In humanitarian or other crises, OHCHR staff may be deployed in the field by the Rapid Response Unit for fact-finding missions and commissions of inquiry.[6]

---

3. UNDP, Report from the Second Interagency Workshop on Implementing a Human Rights-Based Approach in the Context of UN Reform, Stamford, Conn., 5–7 May 2003.

4. Chronologically, the High Commissioners have been Mr. José Ayala Lasso (1994–97), Ms. Mary Robinson (1997–2002), Mr. Sergio Vieira de Mello (2002–3), Mr. Bertrand G. Ramcharan (Acting High Commissioner from 2003 to 2004), Ms. Louise Arbour (2004–8), and Ms. Navanethem Pillay, South Africa (2008–14).
5. This information is available as of September 2011 in OHCHR, *OHCHR Management Plan 2012–2013: Working for Results* (Geneva: OHCHR, 2011), 11–15.
6. Since 2006, the Rapid Response Unit has deployed for these purposes in Timor-Leste, Western Sahara, Sudan, Liberia, Lebanon, Beit-Hanoun, (the Occupied Palestinian Territories), Kenya, Togo, Guinea, three times in the OPT (Goldstone, Committee of high level expert to follow Goldstone and Israeli attack on humanitarian flotilla. It has also conducted human rights assessment missions in Togo, Sierra Leone, Bolivia, Somalia, and Madagascar, http://www.ohchr.org/EN/Countries/Pages/WorkInField.aspx [*Eds.*—accessed 14 June 2015].

The Human Rights Council (UNHRC)

As explained above, the UNHRC was created by UNGA resolution 60/251 in 2006 to replace the Charter-based Commission on Human Rights. After a review, its working methods were set out in Council Resolution 16/21 of 25 March 2011. It meets in regular session at least three times a year, for a total of at least ten weeks, and can meet at any time in special session to address human rights violations and emergencies if one-third of the member states so request. By early 2014, it had held 20 special sessions, dealing with such issues as the Palestinian Occupied Territories, the war in Lebanon, the situations in Darfur, Myanmar, Sri Lanka, the Democratic Republic of Congo, Haiti, Côte d'Ivoire, Libya, Syria, and the Central African Republic, as well as food and financial crises. The major innovations of the reform are the Council Advisory Committee (18 experts, functioning as a think tank for the Council) and Universal Periodic Review (UPR).

Complaints Procedures

Since the late 1960s, the UN has had two non-treaty procedures for receiving complaints ("petitions") to review alleged human rights violations. The first is the so-called "public" procedure, established in 1967 by ECOSOC Resolution 1235 (XLII), according to which the former Commission could "make a study of situations which reveal a consistent pattern of violations of human rights, as exemplified by the policy of apartheid . . . and racial discrimination . . . and report, with recommendations thereon, to the Economic and Social Council."[7] Although conceived as a means of attracting attention to apartheid in South Africa and other situations characterized by colonialism and racism, the "1235 procedure" was used to examine all types of situations and usually involved appointing a Special Rapporteur to visit the country under scrutiny. The political willingness of the UNHRC to create thematic and country mandates described in the next section and that of the mandate holders to receive complaints and take urgent actions has made the 1235 procedure unnecessary.

In 1970, ECOSOC adopted a confidential complaints procedure—called the "1503 procedure" after the ECOSOC resolution number—under which the Commission examined in closed session complaints alleging "a consistent pattern of gross and reliably attested violations of human rights."[8] Although it was a cumbersome procedure (involving closed meetings of a working group in a subcommission, then a working group of the Commission before reaching the Commission), the possibility of the situation being placed on a public list or transferred to a public procedure was a source of pressure on governments complained against. Such pressure does not change a regime but contributes to efforts to alter abusive practices. On 18 June 2007, the UNHRC, in its resolution 5/1 on institution building, replaced the 1503 procedure with a new confidential complaint procedure to address consistent patterns of gross and reliably attested violations of all human rights and all fundamental freedoms occurring in any part of the world and under any circumstance. These complaints—between 11,000 and 15,000 annually[9]—may be submitted by individuals, groups, or nongovernmental organizations that claim to be victims of human rights violations or have direct, reliable knowledge of such violations. It has been claimed that 94 percent of countries respond to complaints relating to human rights situations.[10] Of course, a response does not mean the situation is corrected, only that the government sees fit to provide its views and explanations and may—while not necessarily admitting that it has been prodded by the procedure—correct the situation to avoid a Council or UNGA resolution denouncing its violations. Communications are screened by a Working Group on Communications, which may decide to submit them for further action to the Working Group on Situations, which then may dismiss the communication, keep it under consideration, or report to the Council with recommendations. Since 2006 the Council has taken up and eventually discontinued consideration of human rights situations in Kyrgyzstan, Iran, Uzbekistan, Turkmenistan, the

7. Adopted 6 June 1967.

8. Adopted 27 May 1970.
9. Jane Connors and Markus Schmidt, "United Nations," in Daniel Moeckli, Sangeeta Shah, and Sandesh Sivakumaran, eds., *Textbook on International Human Rights Law*, 2nd ed. (Oxford: OUP, 2014), 371.
10. Ibid.

Maldives, the DRC, Guinea, Tajikistan, and Iraq. In 2012, it decided to take up public consideration of the situation in Eritrea. A more meaningful and public form of scrutiny of human rights violations and other issues is provided by the "special procedures" described next.

Special Procedures of Thematic and Country Rapporteurs

Beginning in 1980, the Commission on Human Rights appointed numerous working groups or Special Rapporteurs, Representatives, and Experts, either through "thematic mandates," which examine a general problem of particular significance to ensuring respect for human rights, or through "country mandates," focused on a country whose human rights performance has convinced the Council that monitoring is necessary.

As of 2014, there were some thirty-seven "thematic mandates" covering a litany of contemporary human rights issues, including housing, child prostitution, involuntary disappearances, extreme poverty, food, freedom of opinion and expression, the independence of judges and lawyers, migrants, environmentally sound management and disposal of hazardous substances and wastes, contemporary forms of racism, safe drinking water and sanitation, transnational corporations, older persons, foreign debt, terrorism, violence against women, and health. The thematic mechanisms include special procedures to collect information directly from victims and to communicate with governments. Dialogue with governments serves not only to request a clarification of the situation concerning the alleged victim but also to apply an "urgent action" or "prompt intervention" procedure when necessary to protect the victim, her or his family, witnesses, or NGOs involved, and to facilitate on-site visits. The reports of the special rapporteurs constitute a mode of accountability that many governments take quite seriously.

In the case of "country mandates," the country rapporteurs communicate with victims, their representatives, NGOs, and governments. In 2014 a total of 14 countries were under scrutiny by Special Rapporteurs or Independent Experts (Belarus, Cambodia, Central African Republic, Côte d'Ivoire, Eritrea, North Korea, Haiti, Iran, Mali, Myanmar, OPT, Somalia, Sudan, and Syria).

The effectiveness of these special procedures has been enhanced since 1993 by annual meetings of the special rapporteurs, representatives, experts, and chairpersons of working groups and the recommendations they adopt. A legitimate concern with efficiency and effectiveness was reflected in a major 2007 reform in which the UNHRC defined the following general criteria of "paramount importance while nominating, selecting and appointing mandate-holders," namely: "(a) expertise; (b) experience in the field of the mandate; (c) independence; (d) impartiality; (e) personal integrity; and (f) objectivity."[11] The process has become more transparent as a result of a review of the procedures completed in 2011. In particular, the Council affirmed that "The integrity and independence of the special procedures and the principles of cooperation, transparency and accountability are integral to ensuring a robust system of the special procedures that would enhance the capacity of the Council to address human rights situations on the ground."[12] It also stated that it "strongly rejects any act of intimidation or reprisal against individuals and groups who cooperate or have cooperated with the United Nations, its representatives and mechanisms in the field of human rights, and urges States to prevent and ensure adequate protection against such acts."[13]

The innovation of the special procedures stands as one of the most valuable human rights achievements of the UN political organs and the NGOs that lobby them. Equally innovative in the 2007 reform was the Universal Periodic Review, next.

Universal Periodic Review (UPR)

The UPR was created at the same time as the Human Rights Council, which adopted its modalities in 2007.[14] It allows the Council to review the human rights records of all the UN member states (193 as of this writing) on the basis of in-

11. Human Rights Council Resolution 5/1 of 18 June 2007, Institution-Building of the United Nations Human Rights Council, annex, para. 39
12. Human Rights Council Resolution 16/21, of 25 March 2011, annex, 24.
13. I 30.
14. UNGA Resolution 60/251 of 15 Mar 2006, para. 5(e).

formation provided by the reporting government, UN treaty bodies and special procedures, and stakeholders (including nongovernmental organizations, national human rights institutions, human rights defenders, academic institutions, research institutes, and regional organizations). The process got off to a disappointing start, however, as governments would line up friendly countries to make positive comments on the reports, taking up the available time for discussion. The process has become much more probing, and the recommendations that emerge from the consideration of country reports are supposed to be implemented by the state concerned, with capacity-building and technical assistance, as needed. Failure to implement the recommendations made during the first review is taken up during the second review, and, if necessary, the Council may address cases where states are not cooperating. All countries having been reviewed once by October 2011, a second cycle, begun in 2012, is to be completed in 2016.

Members of the Council address recommendations to the government, often specific and penetrating. The 2010 UPR of the United States, for example, resulted in 228 recommendations, including such issues as torture and the closing of the Guantanamo Bay facility.[15] Recent setbacks include Israel's refusal to attend its own UPR and the successful effort by the Russian Federation to remove two recommendations by Georgia and have them relegated to footnotes. These are dangerous precedents for an otherwise positive evolution of the UPR process.

PROMOTING AND PROTECTING HUMAN RIGHTS THROUGH TREATY-BASED PROCEDURES

Nine of the UN human rights treaties have functioning monitoring committees, called "treaty bodies," that examine states parties' reports on progress made and problems encountered, and formulate observations on what needs to be done to comply with the obligations of the treaty in question: the 1966 ICESCR and ICCPR, the 1965 International Convention on the Elim-

ination of All Forms of Racial Discrimination (ICERD), the 1979 Convention on the Elimination of All Forms of Discrimination against Women (CEDAW), the 1984 Convention against Torture and Other Cruel, Inhuman or Degrading Treatment or Punishment (CAT), the 1989 Convention on the Rights of the Child (CRC), the 1990 International Convention on the Protection of the Rights of All Migrant Workers and Members of Their Families (ICMW), the 2006 International Convention on the Rights of Persons with Disabilities (ICRPD), and the 2006 International Convention for the Protection of All Persons from Enforced Disappearance (ICPPED). A tenth treaty body, the Subcommittee on Prevention of Torture, monitors places of detention under CAT.

The effectiveness of the treaty system depends on (1) universal ratification without crippling reservations, (2) timely presentation and proper consideration of reports with follow-up on recommendations, (3) judicious use of the capacity to issue general comments, and (4) availability of complaints and inquiry procedures. Endorsed as a major objective of the High Commissioner, universal ratification would mean convincing all countries to ratify or accede[16] to the current 9 core human rights treaties and 3 optional protocols. One of the problems is that some countries, such as the United States, insist on reservations, understandings, and declarations to weaken the obligations so as not to contradict domestic law, or as many Islamic countries do, to interpret respect for equality of men and women so as not to contradict Islamic law. Others ratify for public relations purposes without the intent to implement the provisions of the treaty. On final analysis, the effectiveness of the treaty system depends on what use the ratifying countries make of the treaty, if any, to make genuine progress in human rights. Social science research shows that, under certain conditions, once a treaty has been ratified, improvements in human rights performance tend to occur even "where there is a minimal incentive for local actors to mobilize, where national courts are minimally competent to render independent judgments, and where the state has at

15. Report of the Working Group on the Universal Periodic Review, United States of America, UN Doc. A/HRC/16/11, 4 January 2011.

16. Accession is the process of joining for countries that did not sign when a treaty was first opened for signature.

least some capacity to address the rights issues at stake."[17]

On the second issue of the effectiveness of the reporting process,[18] the High Commissioner reported in 2012 that only 16 percent of the reports are received on time, although that proportion is one-third after the one-year grace period.[19] She described the problems faced by the treaty body system and proposed a series of changes to strengthen it, including a comprehensive reporting calendar; a simplified and aligned reporting process; strengthening the individual communications procedures, inquiries, and country visits; strengthening the independence and expertise of treaty body members; strengthening the capacity to implement the treaties; and enhancing the visibility and accessibility of the treaty bodies.[20] An intergovernmental process considered reform of the treaty body system in 2012–14 without achieving radical reform. The process called for a simplified reporting procedure and use of common core documents, as well as capacity building for reporting states, and the General Assembly approved these modest reforms in a 2014 resolution, in which it encouraged treaty bodies to achieve "greater efficiency, transparency, effectiveness and harmonization through their working methods," and urged states to eliminate "all acts of intimidation and reprisals against individuals and groups for their contribution to the work of the human rights treaty bodies."[21] Meanwhile, however, the treaty bodies have demonstrated willingness to draw on the expertise of their members and "shadow reports" from civil society, typically revealing major human rights deficiencies. After considering state reports, civil society inputs, and engaging dialogue with reporting government representatives, the treaty body issues "concluding observations" that often raise concerns and make recommendations touching on the real human rights problems faced by the states parties.

The third feature of the human rights treaty system is the capacity of the treaty bodies to issue general comments judiciously clarifying the normative content of their respective treaties and providing guidance to states and civil society as to what is expected to fulfill their obligations. While general comments and concluding observations are not technically binding on the states parties, many of these statements have acquired considerable interpretive authority.[22]

The fourth dimension is the complaints and inquiry procedures. Seven of the human rights treaties (or optional protocols to them) provide for individuals to bring complaints alleging a violation, namely, ICCPR, ICERD, CAT, CEDAW, ICRPD, ICPPED, ICMW, ICESCR, and CRC. As of 2014, the individual complaint mechanisms had not yet entered into force for the ICMW and the CRC. For the others, a considerable body of case law is emerging, including numerous findings of violations (a stronger outcome than the expression of "concern" in the concluding observations under the reporting procedure).[23] Complaints from one state party that another state party is not giving effect to the provisions of the treaty may be considered under CAT, ICMW, ICPPED, ICESCR and the CRC. However, this provision for state-to-state complaints has never been used. In addition, ICERD and ICCPR provide for an interstate dispute settlement procedure. Six of the treaty bodies (CAT, CED, CEDAW, CESCR, CRC, and CRPD, once the relevant protocol is in force for the latter) may, on their own, initiate confidential inquiries if they have received reliable information containing well-founded indi-

17. Beth A. Simmons, *Mobilizing for Human Rights: International Law in Domestic Politics* (Cambridge: CUP, 2009), 363.

18. See Reading 29 (Cole) in Chapter 6, which explores this subject matter in detail.

19. United Nations Reform: Measures and Proposals, Note by the Secretary-General, UN Doc. A/66/860 (26 June 2012), 21. See also http://www.ohchr.org/EN/HRBodies/HRTD/Pages/ TBStrengthening.aspx [Eds.—accessed 14 June 2015].

20. United Nations Reform, 37–95.

21. UN General Assembly Resolution 68/268, adopted 9 April 2014, UN Doc. A/RES/68/268.

22. All the general comments of all the treaty bodies are available at http://www2.ohchr.org/english/bodies/ treaty/comments.htm (accessed 25 April 2015).

23. Since its inception in 1976, the HRC established under the ICCPR has examined over 2,000 complaints pursuant to the ICCPR's first protocol. See Jakob Th. Möller and Alfred de Zayas, *The United Nations Human Rights Committee Case Law 1977–2008: A Handbook* (Kehl am Rhein: Engel, 2009). For the emerging jurisprudence of the general comments and state-specific concluding observations of the CESCR, see Malcolm Langford and Jeff A. King, "Committee on Economic, Social and Cultural Rights: Past, Present and Future," in Malcolm Langford, ed., *Social Rights Jurisprudence: Emerging Trends in International and Comparative Law* (New York: CUP, 2008), 477–516.

cations of serious or systematic violations of the conventions in a state party that has recognized the competence of the committee to initiate inquiries. Such inquiries have been conducted in eight states by CAT and one by CERD. Under the optional protocol to CAT, the Subcommittee on Prevention of Torture (SPT) makes regular visits to places of detention, recommends action to improve the treatment of detainees, and may provide assistance for that purpose.

In sum, the Charter-based and treaty-based procedures have evolved to the point of forcing governments to address a remarkable range of human rights problems, sometimes with real results. The prospects of making real progress through the UN diminish as governments face national security emergencies or engage in massive human rights violations, each of which call for the UN to use other mechanisms—primarily through the Security Council—to seek human rights conforming behavior.

PROMOTING AND PROTECTING HUMAN RIGHTS THROUGH PEACE OPERATIONS

A humanitarian emergency and intense diplomatic pressure is required before the UN Security Council will use its enforcement powers, and occasionally has used those powers for human rights purposes. The UNSC is much more willing to support deployment of UN personnel in the context of a comprehensive political settlement to a long-festering conflict, and the doctrine applicable in such cases has been called "second generation" or "expanded" peacekeeping. Setting up and running peacekeeping operations (PKOs) is the responsibility of the Department of Peacekeeping Operations (DPKO), which functions out of UN headquarters in New York. Human rights components have been part of PKOs in Angola, Burundi, Cambodia, Central African Republic, El Salvador, Guinea Bissau, Haiti, Kosovo, Iraq, Rwanda, Sierra Leone, Somalia, and Timor-Leste. As of this writing, there are human rights components in most UN peacekeeping operations, including the Democratic Republic of the Congo (MONUSCO), Darfur (UNAMID), South Sudan (UNMISS), Liberia (UNMIL), Côte d'Ivoire (UNOCI), Haiti (MINUSTAH), and Afghanistan (UNAMA). The OHCHR provides expertise and support to the human rights components of

PKOs and the component head is OHCHR representative in-country.

When consent is given by the territorial state to a multicomponent peace operation, the UN role is couched in terms of "cooperation" (with whatever is left of a sovereign state) rather than of "intervention." But the form of action, despite consent to the agreement and to the international military and civilian presence, is clearly an intrusive one. The potential impact of the UN efforts is considerable, whether through an explicit human rights program or through the promotion of the rule of law and good governance. At the same time, however, the UN itself has been accused of human rights violations[24] and of responsibility for major public health disasters.[25]

Thus, "intervention" by the UN in human rights situations, where normal rules of state sovereignty would otherwise preclude it, has been resorted to, and in such a manner, as Richard Falk put it a generation ago, that the "basic social contract between States and the United Nations is . . . being rewritten."[26] Acceptance by the international community of these encroachments constitutes a major shift in international relations that enhances considerably opportunities for the UN to investigate and improve human rights situations inside member states.

Beyond the investigative and educational tasks of human rights components of peacekeeping, UN field operations are called upon to contribute to the institutionalization of key democratic institutions, without which progress to ensure human rights during a peace operation will be short-lived. Judicial reform, constitution drafting, professionalization and demilitarization of the police—all are tasks that the UN has been

24. Frédéric Mégret and Florian Hoffmann, "The UN as a Human Rights Violator? Some Reflections on the United Nations Changing Human Rights Responsibilities," *HRQ* 25 (2003): 314–42.
25. *Final Report of the Independent Panel of Experts on the Cholera Outbreak in Haiti,* 29. The independent expert on the situation of human rights in Haiti, noting the rejection by the UN of responsibility for the outbreak as accused in a class action law suit filed with a court in New York in October 2013, recommended that full reparation for damages be provided and that "those responsible for the tragedy should be punished." Report of Independent Expert on the Situation of Human Rights in Haiti, Gustavo Gallón, UN Doc. A /HRC/25/71 (7 February 2014), para. 77.
26. Richard A. Falk, "The United Nations and the Rule of Law," *TLCP* 4 (1994): 611–42, 630.

given and in respect of which its capacity to produce lasting results has not been adequately tested.

The UN role in this area has to be seen also in a broader context of trends toward democratization, during the window of opportunity provided by UN multicomponent peace operations. Since the mid-1990s, many of these human rights tasks have been pursued by field operations under the responsibility of OHCHR, whose field offices operate under difficult conditions with inadequate resources. In other situations democratization is rendered impossible by acts of aggression, genocide, crimes against humanity, and other mass violations of human rights. Only coercive economic and/or military action, preferably multilateral, can make a difference under such circumstances.

CORRECTIVE ACTION THROUGH PEACE ENFORCEMENT AND THE RESPONSIBILITY TO PROTECT

If and only if the Security Council, acting under Chapter VII of the UN Charter, determines by nine votes out of fifteen, including a concurring vote of all five permanent members (art. 27), that there is a "threat to the peace, breach of the peace, or act of aggression" (art. 39) may it adopt economic sanctions or authorize military force to restore peace. The practice of the UNSC has been uncertain about using this power for human rights purposes. For example, under Resolution 688 (1991),[27] it demanded the end of repression and respect for human rights of the Kurds in Northern Iraq, followed by the UK and the United States establishing no-fly zones to protect humanitarian operations, although not specifically authorized by the resolution. Acting explicitly under Chapter VII in Resolution 940 (1994),[28] the UNSC declared that "the situation in Haiti continues to constitute a threat to peace and security in the region" and authorized the use of military force to restore the legitimately elected president and government of Haiti following the overthrow of Aristide, but felt the need to refer to the "unique character of the present situation in Haiti . . . requiring an exceptional response."

However, in 1994, the UN failed to act to halt the genocide perpetrated in Rwanda, resulting in 800,000 deaths. The UN Force Commander concluded, "the only solution to this unacceptable apathy and selective attention is a revitalized and reformed international institution charged with maintaining the world's peace and security, supported by the international community and guided by the founding principles of its Charter and the Universal Declaration of Human Rights."[29] Efforts to obtain Chapter VII authorization for military intervention also failed in Kosovo in 1999, resulting in NATO military intervention without Security Council authorization to protect Kosovar Albanians against Serbian atrocities.[30] Echoing the view of the UN Secretary-General, the Independent International Commission on Kosovo concluded that the NATO military intervention was illegal but legitimate.[31] In response to the Kosovo intervention, the International Commission on Intervention and State Sovereignty (ICISS) was created in 2000 to address this gap between legality and legitimacy, and sought "to strengthen the prospects for obtaining action, on a collective and principled basis, with a minimum of double standards, in response to conscience-shocking situations of great humanitarian need crying out for that action" and recommended "That the General Assembly adopt a draft declaratory resolution embodying the basic principles of the responsibility to protect."[32] By the time of the 2005 UN World Summit meeting, which brought

---

29. Roméo Dallaire, *Shake Hands with the Devil* (Toronto: Random House, 2004), 520.
30. It has also been argued that "The Kosovo Liberation Army committed human rights abuses against Serbian civilians and personnel in order to trigger reprisals, which would in turn force the international community to intervene on their behalf." Michael Ignatieff, "I. Human Rights as Politics," Tanner Lectures on Human Values, Delivered at Princeton University 4–7 April 2000, 317.
31. Independent International Commission on Kosovo, *The Kosovo Report: Conflict, International Response, Lessons Learned* (Oxford: OUP, 2000). For further discussion on the Kosovo intervention, see Reading 32 (Falk).
32. International Commission on Intervention and State Sovereignty, *The Responsibility to Protect: Report of the International Commission on Intervention and State Sovereignty* (Ottawa: International Development Research Centre, 2001), 74.

---

27. SC Res. 688, UN SCOR, 46th Sess., 2082nd mtg., at 31, UN Doc. S/INF/47 (1991).
28. SC Res. 940, UN SCOR, 49th Sess., Supp. No. 49, at 51, UN Doc. S/INF/50 (1994).

together heads of state and government to take stock five years after the UN Millennium Declaration, the moment seemed ripe for the international community to address the conclusion of the ICISS by committing to the doctrine of the responsibility to protect ("R2P"), by which they seek to ensure that their populations are shielded from genocide, war crimes, crimes against humanity, and ethnic cleansing.[33]

The need for such a new doctrine is based also on the unacceptability for many states of the nineteenth century doctrine of "humanitarian intervention," which was a controversial exception to the prohibition of intervention in the domestic affairs of states used primarily by the European powers to intervene in the Ottoman Empire to protect Christian populations.[34] By stressing prevention and rebuilding, with military intervention being a last resort requiring UNSC approval, R2P shifts the debate from the conventional "right to intervene" to the needs of those seeking or needing support and to the primary role of states in guaranteeing the protection of the rights of their own population.[35] Yet, after accepting it in 2005, the UN has been reluctant to invoke R2P in recent conflicts, in spite of the commitment of states "to take collective action, in a timely and decisive manner, through the Security Council, in accordance with the Charter, including Chapter VII, on a case-by-case basis and in cooperation with relevant regional organizations as appropriate, should peaceful means be inadequate and national authorities are manifestly failing to protect their populations from genocide, war crimes, ethnic cleansing and crimes against humanity."[36] The doctrine has been referred to in Security Council Resolutions concerning the Great Lakes region, Sudan, Libya, Côte d'Ivoire, Yemen, Mali, South Sudan, Central African Republic, and Syria,[37] but only in Darfur and Libya was it used to authorize enforcement action. The way R2P was applied in Libya explains in part the reluctance to use it for enforcement action in the civil war in Syria.[38]

A final observation on the human rights dimensions of the UN mandate in international peace and security is the use of enforcement powers for the prosecution of individuals responsible for genocide, crimes against humanity, and war crimes. Using the authority of Chapter VII, the Security Council innovated in the 1990s by establishing a mechanism for trying those accused of genocide, war crimes, and crimes against humanity, through two ad hoc UN criminal tribunals, the International Criminal Tribunal for the Former Yugoslavia (ICTY) in 1991 and the International Criminal Tribunal for Rwanda (ICTR) in 1994. In 1998, governments adopted the Rome Statute creating the International Criminal Court (ICC), which came into force in 2002, establishing a permanent tribunal, independent of the UN, with jurisdiction to investigate and bring to justice individuals who commit the most serious crimes of international concern, specifically genocide, war crimes, and crimes against humanity.

CONCLUSIONS

This essay only scratches the surface of the complex web of UN institutions and bodies and their vast potential to contribute, through multilateral diplomacy and action, to the realization of human rights. It should be clear that state sovereignty is less than ever an insurmountable obstacle to UN action to pursue the Charter objective of universal respect for human rights. The traditional limitations based on Article 2(7) are receding. As a result, the margin for action by the UN has expanded. Treaty bodies have demonstrated considerable vigor by drawing governments' attention to failures to meet human rights obliga-

---

33. GA Res. 60/1, UN Doc. A/RES/60/1 (15 September 2005) [hereinafter 2005 World Summit Outcome], paras. 138 and 139. The doctrine was endorsed by the Security Council in its unanimous Resolution 1674 of 28 April 2006 on the Protection of Civilians in Armed Conflict. The question of genocide is addressed in Reading 8 (Card) in Chapter 2 of this volume.
34. The question of humanitarian intervention is addressed by Richard Falk in Reading 32.
35. See Implementing the Responsibility to Protect, Report of the Secretary-General, 12 January 2009, UN Doc. A/63/677.
36. 2005 World Summit Outcome, para. 139.

37. References to Responsibility to Protect (RtoP or R2P) in Security Council Resolutions, http://www.responsibilitytoprotect.org/index.php/component/content/article/136-latest-news/5221-references-to-the-responsibility-to-protect-in-security-council-resolutions [*Eds.*—accessed 25 April 2015].
38. See Spencer Zifcak, "The Responsibility to Protect After Libya and Syria," *Melbourne Journal of International Law* 13 (2012): 2–35.

tions and expanding the power to respond to individual complaints. Mandate holders in special procedures have enhanced their independence and expertise. They have provided extensive documentation of thematic and country problems, addressing specific recommendations to governments and political bodies (specifically, the Human Rights Council and the General Assembly).

Transitions to democracy in former communist-party states and in existing and former dictatorships across the Middle East have released the potential for the participation of civil society in transformative processes of governance. The UN human rights institutions, principally the OHCHR, have been supportive and have provided technical assistance for building human rights institutions. However, massive violations continue to occur in the course of internal armed conflict, especially when fed by xenophobic nationalism and religious fanaticism. The UN provides support to the ICC and other prosecutorial mechanisms to hold perpetrators and their commanders criminally responsible. Preventive diplomacy, peacemaking, and peacekeeping functions have demonstrated the value of integrating the human rights dimension into comprehensive peace agreements, with the support of OHCHR.

These are but a few of many challenges facing the UN in its human rights program. Despite frustrations with the UN as a large bureaucracy that moves slowly and sometimes is unresponsive to urgent human rights problems, or is constrained by the conflicting interests of the member states that provide political supervision, the UN has sought to promote and protect human rights in ways that increasingly redefine the pledge of member states "to take joint and separate action in co-operation with the Organization for the achievement of . . . universal respect for, and observance of, human rights and fundamental freedoms for all without distinction as to race, sex, language, or religion."

QUESTIONS FOR REFLECTION AND DISCUSSION

1. Stephen Marks states that "The founders of the United Nations, not content merely to add human rights as one among many shared objectives of UN member governments, implicitly articulated a theory of peace according to which respect for human rights and fundamental freedoms is a necessary condition for peace within and among nations. Yet the Charter does not apply this theory to the relative powers of the main organs of the UN." Why do you think human rights was delegated only a promotional role in the UN Charter? Does this undercut the importance of human rights in the UN's mission to secure peace and security in the state system? Why? Why not? And why only a "pledge" by member states to promote human rights? Is this the language of obligation, aspiration, or something else? Do you think the role of human rights in the UN has evolved since the Charter? If so, has this evolution been for the better or worse? Why?

2. Marks states that the "pledge" member states make is a "legally ambiguous term." What does he mean? Do you agree? Why or why not?

3. Marks cites the "fragile consensus on the content of human rights" as one of the limits on UN ability to act on human rights issues. This discussion hearkens back to the debate between universalism and cultural relativism; see Reading 4 (Weston) in Chapter 1 of this volume. Do you think there needs to be one, universally shared understanding of what constitutes human rights? Are there any advantages to not having one shared definition? Does a universal understanding necessarily have to be a Western understanding? If so, why? If not, why not?

4. Despite the long-term UN contribution to promotion and protection of human rights via the preparation and adoption of many standard-setting human rights treaties that, by definition, are intended to be binding on the states parties to them, widespread violations of even the most fundamental human rights continue more or less unabated. To minimize further damage to the UN's already fragile authority and prestige, might it be better for the UN to propose, instead, model laws that can be later enacted into national legislation? Indeed, might not a model-laws approach serve the cause of human rights more effectively because it would obviate the need for ratifications and because it could adapt to local idiosyncrasies from the highest to the lowest of domestic jurisdictions? What arguments might weigh against this idea?

5. Of the four principal concerns for the effectiveness of UN human rights treaties, universal ratification without crippling reservations; timely presentation and proper consideration of reports with follow-up recommendations; general comments; and availability of a complaints procedure for individual cases, which one do you consider to be the most pressing? The most feasible? The most likely? Why?

6. Marks discusses the desire for universal ratification of human rights treaties and how reservations, understandings, and declarations made by ratifying states often undercut the purpose of these treaties. Is a push for universal ratification desirable? Practical? What are the benefits? Do reservations have any beneficial use in promoting human rights or do they merely provide ratifying states a means to derogate from their treaty obligations? Draw on Readings 29 (Cole) and 37 (Ignatieff) to inform your discussion.

7. Is there anything to prevent the incorporation into local law of the substantive provisions of UN-adopted human rights treaties? Precisely such an approach has been adopted in the state of Iowa where city councils, first in Burlington and later in Iowa City, made the substantive provisions of the 1965 International Convention on the Elimination of All Forms of Racial Discrimination (ICERD) part of the human rights ordinances of the two cities. Following the first such initiative in Burlington in 1986, the *Burlington Hawkeye* editorial suggested that "The idea of turning international conventions in to local ordinances will constitute a national endorsement which the [U.S.] Senate will be under pressure to recognize" ("City Shows Local Issues Have Global Roots," *Burlington Hawkeye*, 1 September 1986). The editorial quotes Burns Weston, who helped to inspire the movement, as saying that "This will force judges in local jurisdictions to pay attention to international justice. . . . it is a case of thinking globally and acting locally." Would the UN be well advised to reconsider the uses to which its many proposed or minimally ratified human rights treaties might be put? Are you prepared to work for the same approach in your home town? If not, why not?

8. What is the role of the UN Human Rights Council? Of its Advisory Committee? Are these organs effective? How might they be improved?

9. Marks describes the "complaints procedures." What are these? What functions do they serve? How useful are they to advocates for victims of human rights violations?

10. Marks identifies two types of "special procedures" for monitoring human rights compliance. What are they and how do they compare to each other? Is one more effective than the other? What are the pros and cons of these special procedures?

11. The Human Rights Council reviews "the human rights records of all the UN member states," and makes recommendations of how the governments can redress human rights violations. Because these recommendations are not obligatory, how effective are they? What can the Council do to ensure compliance?

12. Marks also discusses "treaty bodies." What are they and what do they do? Which are the most effective? Least effective? How do they compare to the "Charter-based bodies"?

13. What, according to Marks, are the ways in which the UN has moved away from the nonintervention principle? Has this been a positive or negative development? Why? Under what human rights scenario do you believe the UN should be authorized to intervene into a sovereign state's affairs? Using what type of intervention? Diplomatic? Military? Economic? Reactive? Preemptive? Preventive? Is a state's prevention of a minority group from going to school or owning property sufficient? What about a military coup that results in the death and disappearance of thousands?

14. Given the mixed record of UN peacekeeping missions, should the UN be involved in them? If not the UN, then who? Or should anyone? If you were an adviser to your nation's representative to the United Nations, what changes would you suggest the UN undertake to strengthen peacekeeping missions? Should the UN put its efforts only into democratic institution building and let its member states, or other international organizations (e.g., NATO), use force to respond to human rights abuses?

15. One of the biggest complaints about human rights treaties is the failure of states to meet their reporting requirements. Given the lack of compliance by states in submitting timely reports, do you think the idea of the reporting system is a good one or is it time to develop a new scheme to monitor state compliance with treaty obligations? Also, how reliable are state reports when they come from the state itself? Are the inputs from civil society adequate to balance the sources of information or would it be more beneficial and

reliable to have independent observers compile these reports? Why? Why not? How might this be accomplished? Are there alternatives?

16. After reading Marks's essay, what in your view is the biggest challenge facing the UN relative to promotion and protection of human rights? How would you propose that the UN meet this challenge?

17. On balance, has the United Nations done a good or a bad job in *promoting* human rights? In *protecting* human rights? What are your reasons for concluding as you do? What does Marks say?

31. DINAH L. SHELTON *Breakthroughs, Burdens, and Backlash: What Future for Regional Human Rights Systems?*

A human rights system embraces a list or lists of internationally guaranteed human rights and obligations; permanent institutions; and compliance or enforcement procedures. At the global level, for example, the UN system consists in large part of numerous interacting organs and specialized agencies concerned with human rights.[1] Regional human rights systems contribute to the global system, as well as forming their own interdependent systems. Subsystems of actors also exist: states, intergovernmental organizations, nongovernmental organizations, corporations, other business entities, and networks of individuals.

The following essay evaluates the contributions of and challenges to existing and emerging regional human rights systems. Its conclusion asserts that regional systems are indispensable to achieving effective compliance with international human rights law, but that they are facing unprecedented challenges that threaten their future. The flexibility to evolve is particularly important: systems analysis suggests that those systems that can balance stasis and change, stability and chaos, are the most successful in maintaining themselves in the long run, however much they are challenged by unforeseen developments in the short run.

THE ORIGINS OF REGIONAL SYSTEMS

Provoked by the pre-World War II and wartime Holocaust, the global concern with human rights that emerged during and after the war brought regional systems into being. Given this widespread concern it is thus no surprise that regional organizations created or reformed after the war should have added human rights to their agendas.

Historical and political factors have encouraged each major region of the world to support the promotion and protection of human rights. And each has done so inspired by the human rights provisions of the 1945 UN Charter and the 1948 Universal Declaration of Human Rights (UDHR).

The Americas, however, had a tradition of regional approaches to international issues, including human rights, growing out of regional solidarity developed during the movements for independence in the nineteenth and twentieth centuries. Pan American Conferences, for example, acted on human rights matters well before the creation of the United Nations. This history of concern led the OAS to refer to human rights in its Charter (although only in general and in a single provision) and also to adopt the 1948 Inter-American Declaration of the Rights and Duties of Man, the world's first international human rights instrument of a general nature, predating the UDHR by over six months.

Europe had been the theater of the greatest atrocities of the Second World War and felt compelled to press for international human rights guarantees as part of European reconstruction. Faith in Western European traditions of democracy, the rule of law, and individual rights inspired belief that a regional system could be

1. For details about the UN system, see Reading 30 (Marks) in this chapter.

successful in avoiding future conflict and in stemming postwar revolutionary impulses supported by the Soviet Union.

Somewhat later, African states emerged from colonization, with self-determination an early focus of their human rights agendas. Struggles for national cohesion and against human rights abuses in South Africa encouraged the emergence of regional action in Africa, as did the early efforts of the International Labour Organization (ILO) to end the abuse of African workers during the colonial period. Further stimulus came in the late 1970s when the UN General Assembly, reversing its earlier skepticism about regional human rights systems, adopted, in 1977, its first resolution in support of the regional promotion and protection of human rights, and actively began to promote the creation of an African regional system.[2]

More recently, to sanction human rights violations in Libya and Syria, the "Arab Spring" encouraged stronger action within the Arab League to implement and apply the human rights norms that were adopted in the 2004 Arab Charter of Human Rights. Some states in the region and civil society organizations have initiated discussions about the feasibility of creating a human rights court to further develop this regional system. At present, the League has a human rights commission and the Charter a human rights committee—neither of which, however, accepts petitions or communications.

In 2007, the Association of Southeast Asian Nations (ASEAN), operating for more than three decades on the basis of periodic conferences, concluded an organizational treaty that incorporated concern for human rights. Based on this treaty (or charter), ASEAN created an intergovernmental human rights commission and adopted an ASEAN Declaration of Human Rights. These developments occurred after major armed conflicts in the region ended, leading to efforts to deal with atrocities that had taken place, especially the "killing fields" of Cambodia. The strong leadership of a few ASEAN countries and support from the UN, coupled with a political thaw-

ing in Burma and concerns about China's assertiveness in the region, stimulated ASEAN to join other regions in beginning to develop norms and institutions to promote and protect human rights. A similar discussion has been initiated in the South Asian Association for Regional Cooperation (SAARC).[3]

One early impulse to regionalism came from frustration during the two-decades-long effort of the UN to transform the UDHR into a binding human rights treaty to complete the international bill of rights, a process that resulted not with one treaty but two covenants, the International Covenant on Economic, Social and Cultural Rights (ICESCR) and International Covenant on Civil and Political Rights (ICCPR). During the process, however, it became clear that the compliance mechanisms at the global level would not be strong and any judicial procedures to enforce human rights would have to be at the regional level. As a result, beginning with Europe, regional systems focused on the creation of procedures of redress, establishing control machinery to supervise the implementation and enforcement of the guaranteed rights. The functioning of the three regional courts is one of the great contributions of these systems to international human rights law.

In sum, regional systems have elements of uniformity and diversity in their origins. All of them have been inspired by agreed universal norms and UN institutions concerned with human rights. At the same time, each region has its own issues, concerns, and priorities. As the systems have evolved, the universal framework within which they began and their own interactions have had reciprocal influence, leading to many convergent norms and procedures in an overarching, interdependent, and dynamic system. In many respects the regions are thinking globally and acting regionally, each using the jurisprudence of the others and amending its

2. GA Res. 32/127 of 16 December 1977. For a discussion of the UN's earlier negative attitude, see Burns H. Weston et al., "Regional Human Rights Regimes: A Comparison and Appraisal," *Vanderbilt Journal of Transnational Law* 20 (1987): 585–638, 586.

3. SAARC was established in 1985 to promote regional cooperation between its member states (Bangladesh, Bhutan, India, Maldives, Nepal, Pakistan, and Sri Lanka). But local conflicts limited its ability to act. However, a SAARC representative attended the UN 2012 workshop on regional arrangements for promotion and protection of human rights (Geneva, 12–13 December 2012) and the first meeting on focal points for cooperation between the UN and regional human rights mechanisms (Geneva, 14 December 2012).

procedures by reference to the experience of others.

THE REGIONAL HUMAN RIGHTS SYSTEMS NOW EXISTING

Five regional human rights systems now exist fully or partially developed in Europe, the Americas, Africa, the Middle East, and Southeast Asia, and in that sequence chronologically.

THE EUROPEAN SYSTEM

The European system, the first to be fully operational, began with the creation of the Council of Europe by ten Western European states in 1949 and the adoption in 1950 of the European Convention on Human Rights (ECHR).[4] Since the end of the Cold War, it has expanded to include Central and Eastern European countries, bringing the total membership to forty-seven; regardless of their date of entry, all the member states are bound by the ECHR, which defines the system's substantive mandate—consisting initially of a short list of civil and political rights, but over time lengthened by further guarantees.

The European system was the first to create an international court for the protection of human rights and to create a procedure for individual denunciations of human rights violations, but the role of the victim was initially very limited and admissibility requirements were stringent. As the system has matured, however, the institutional structures and normative guarantees have gradually and substantially strengthened, although access to the European Court of Human Rights (ECtHR) has been curtailed with recent amendments to the Convention enacted in the face of an overwhelming caseload. Most of the system's evolution has been the result of efforts to improve its effectiveness and add to its guarantees, but some changes have been responsive to the activities of other regional organizations within and outside Europe. Moreover, a few recent changes can be attributed to the impact of expanding member-

ship in the Council of Europe and backlash from some member states unhappy with the court's jurisprudence. In fact, the European system is characterized by its evolution through the adoption of human rights treaties strengthened by protocols, and the most significant texts form a network of mutually reinforcing human rights protections in Europe.

THE INTER-AMERICAN SYSTEM

The Inter-American system as it exists today began with the transformation of the Pan American Union into the OAS. The OAS Charter proclaims the "fundamental rights of the individual" as one of the Organization's basic principles. The 1948 American Declaration of the Rights and Duties of Man gives definition to the Charter's general commitment to human rights. Over a decade later, in 1959, the OAS created a seven-member Inter-American Commission on Human Rights with a mandate of furthering respect for human rights among member states. And in 1969, the American Convention on Human Rights conferred additional competence on the Commission to oversee compliance with the Convention (in addition to the 1948 Declaration). The Convention, which entered into force in 1978, also created the Inter-American Court of Human Rights, based in San José, Costa Rica. The Court has jurisdiction over contentious cases submitted by the Commission against states that accept its jurisdiction; the Court also may issue advisory opinions at the request of the Commission or any OAS member state. Additionally, the Commission prepares country reports and conducts on-site visits to individual countries, examining the human rights situation in the particular country and making recommendations to the government.

The twenty-five states that have ratified the American Convention are bound by its provisions, while other member states are held to the standards of the American Declaration. Notably, nearly all the nonratifying states are the English-speaking common law countries of North America (including Canada and the United States) and the Caribbean. Communications may be filed against any state; the optional clause applies only to interstate cases. Standing for nonstate actors to file communications is broad. Like the

4. Formally the Convention for the Protection of Human Rights and Fundamental Freedoms.

European system, the Inter-American system has expanded its protections over time through adoption of additional human rights norms. In addition to the 1948 Declaration and 1969 Convention, six additional major instruments help to define the Inter-American system.[5]

THE AFRICAN SYSTEM

In Africa, the regional promotion and protection of human rights is established by the African Charter on Human and Peoples' Rights (Banjul or African Charter), designed to function within the framework of the African Union (AU), which in 2001 replaced the original regional Organization for African Unity (OAU) founded in 1963. The African Charter differs from other regional treaties in its inclusion of "peoples' rights." It also includes economic, social, and cultural rights to a greater extent than either the European or American conventions.

The Charter establishes an African Commission on Human and Peoples' Rights of eleven independent members elected for a renewable period of six years. Unlike the other systems, the African system envisages not only interstate and individual communications procedures, but a special procedure for situations of gross and systematic human rights abuse, and like the Council of Europe and the OAS, the OAU/African Union has continued to engage in standard setting.

THE ARAB LEAGUE

On 12 September 1966, the Council of the League of Arab States adopted its first resolution on human rights, calling for the establishment of a steering committee to elaborate a program for

---

5. Namely, the 1985 Inter-American Convention to Prevent and Punish Torture; the 1988 Additional Protocol to the American Convention on Human Rights in the Area of Economic, Social and Cultural Rights; the 1990 Second Additional Protocol to the American Convention on Human Rights to Abolish the Death Penalty; the 1994 Inter-American Convention on the Prevention, Punishment, and Eradication of Violence against Women; the 1994 Inter-American Convention on Forced Disappearance of Persons; and the 1999 Proposed American Declaration on the Rights of Indigenous Populations.

the celebration of Human Rights Year in 1968. The Committee recommended the creation of a permanent Arab Committee on Human Rights and the convening of an Arab Conference on Human Rights. The latter was held in December 1968 in Beirut. That same year, the Council of the League created the Arab Commission for Human Rights with the limited mandate of promoting and providing information about human rights. Twenty-five years later, on 15 September 1994, the League approved an Arab Charter on Human Rights, building on earlier texts adopted by regional nongovernmental and intergovernmental organizations. Notwithstanding, the Charter was highly criticized for falling below international standards and never entered into force.

In May 2004, however, the League adopted a revised Arab Charter on Human Rights, which entered into force on 15 March 2008. The 2004 Charter includes many provisions based on, and consistent with, the standards found in global instruments, and it also reflects developments in international human rights jurisprudence. Nonetheless, the Charter has been criticized for its continued condemnation of Zionism, some of its omissions, and lack of a complaints mechanism. The emerging Middle East system is marked by the great divergence among its states in their willingness to accept and give effect to international human rights law.

ASIA

In Asia as a whole, no human rights system exists. Many hurdles hamper creation of an Asia-Pacific regional system. First, there is far greater diversity of language, culture, legal systems, religious traditions, and history in the Asia-Pacific region than exists in other regions of the world. Second, the geographical limits of the region are both unclear and vast. These two factors suggest that the region may be better served by "subregional" mechanisms that may develop more quickly and easily among states in smaller areas of geographic proximity. But a third factor hindering the development of a regional system has been the unwillingness of governments in the region in general to ratify human rights instruments. This general reluctance to accept human rights treaty obligations, invoking so-called "Asian values" to prioritize Asian culture over the universality of human rights, makes it unlikely that an effective regional system can garner widespread support in the near future.[6]

On the other hand, these problems have diminished with increased democratization, the recent worldwide economic crisis, and concern for human rights in a growing number of countries in the region. ASEAN has shown the potential for subregional arrangements to develop. Similar to other regional organizations, the 2007 ASEAN Charter, implemented through the creation of the ASEAN Intergovernmental Commission on Human Rights (AICHR), declares ASEAN's purposes to include strengthening democracy, promoting rule of law, and protecting human rights and fundamental freedoms; and Article 14 of the Charter calls for establishing an ASEAN human rights body.

On 18 November 2012, the Heads of State of ASEAN adopted the ASEAN Human Rights Declaration, further clarifying the mandate of the AICHR. While the AICHR was responsible for drafting the Declaration, the actual drafting was done by a group of human rights experts it appointed. The Working Group's terms of reference were not made public and drafts of the Declaration remained confidential, although some versions were leaked. Overall, the UN High Commissioner for Human Rights criticized the process as "not the hallmark of the democratic global governance to which ASEAN aspires" and rued that the process would undermine respect for the declaration.[7] Importantly, the ASEAN Declaration is seen as a precursor to a formal treaty for the region, as has happened with human rights declarations at the UN and in other regional systems.

UNIVERSALITY AND REGIONAL DIVERSITY

The seemingly endless debate over universality and diversity in human rights law is inescapable when evaluating regional systems. The issue of normative diversity is complex. Virtually all the legal instruments creating the various regional systems refer to the UDHR and the UN Charter, providing a measure of uniformity

in the fundamental guarantees and a reinforcement of the universal character of the Declaration. The rights contained in the treaties also reflect the human rights norms set forth in other global human rights declarations and conventions. In addition, as each successive system has been created it has looked to normative instruments and the jurisprudence of those systems founded earlier, in some instances inviting experts from other regional bodies to participate in drafting the normative instruments. Yet, there are clear differences in the regional instruments within the framework of the universal norms. The differences may be less pronounced than appears at first reading, however, because of provisions regarding choice of law and canons of interpretation contained in the regional instruments. The application of these provisions has led to cross-referencing and mutual influence in jurisprudence that is producing some convergence in fundamental human rights principles.

UNIVERSAL NORMS

The European system, "considering the Universal Declaration of Human Rights,"[8] provides that the "like-minded" governments of Europe have resolved "to take the first steps for the collective enforcement of certain of the rights stated in the Universal Declaration."[9] The Preamble to the American Convention also cites the UDHR, as well as referring to the OAS Charter, the Inter-American Declaration of the Rights and Duties of Man, and other international and regional instruments not referred to by name. The drafting history of the American Convention shows that the states involved utilized the European Convention, the UDHR, and the Covenants in deciding on the Convention guarantees and institutional structure. The African Charter mentions the Charter of the United Nations and the UDHR in connection with the pledge made by the African states to promote international cooperation. In the Charter's Preamble, the African states also reaffirm in sweeping fashion "their adherence to the principles of human and peoples' rights and freedoms contained in the decla-

6. For discussion of "cultural relativism" and human rights, see Reading 4 (Weston) in Chapter 1 of this volume.
7. OHCHR, Press Release, 8 November 2012.

8. European Convention, Preamble.
9. Ibid.

rations, conventions and other international instruments adopted by the Organization of African Unity, the Movement of Non Aligned Countries and the United Nations."

The Preamble to the Arab Charter is similarly explicit in reaffirming the principles of the UN Charter, the Universal Declaration of Human Rights, the provisions of the two UN International Covenants, on Civil and Political Rights and on Economic, Social and Cultural Rights, and the Cairo Declaration on Human Rights in Islam.

The Arab Charter further expresses the belief of the participating states in the rule of law and "that mankind's enjoyment of freedom, justice and equal opportunity is the hallmark of the profound essence of any society."

Despite defects in its drafting process, the content of the ASEAN Declaration also is rooted in universal norms. The Preamble reaffirms adherence to the ASEAN Charter, in particular respect for the promotion and protection of human rights and fundamental freedoms, "as well as in the principles of democracy, the rule of law and good governance"; also a "commitment to the Universal Declaration of Human Rights, the Charter of the United Nations, the Vienna Declaration and Programme of Action (VDPA), and other international human rights instruments to which ASEAN Member States are parties." The reference to the Vienna Declaration is significant in that the Declaration reaffirmed the universality of human rights as contained in the UDHR, rejecting the arguments for cultural relativism that had been mounted in some of the preparatory meetings, especially those within Asia.

The various regional instruments not only mention the global instruments, they contain similar guarantees and in many instances use language identical to that contained in other instruments. The economic, social, and cultural rights contained in the UDHR are also found in the American Declaration, the African and Arab Charters, and the ASEAN Declaration. The Arab Charter and the African Charter include the principle of self-determination from Article 1 of the Covenants, a right perhaps understandably omitted from the European and American systems. In the Arab Charter, virtually all the rights contained in the ICCPR are included, in some cases with more or less detail.

REGIONAL DIVERSITY

While basing themselves on universal norms, regional instruments nevertheless contain different guarantees and emphases; indeed the preambles of all the regional instruments refer to their regional heritages. The European Convention focuses on civil rights, especially due process, although economic and social rights are guaranteed by the later adopted European Social Charter. The American system is strongly concerned with democracy and the rule of law, having experienced repeated military coups in the region. The preamble to the American Convention begins with a reference to democratic institutions and to guarantees emphasizing the right to participate in government and the right to judicial protection. The Arab Charter is deistic, taking religion as its starting point, referring in its preamble to God, monotheistic religions, the Islamic Shari'a, and other divine religions. It refers both in its preamble and in Article 1 to rejecting racism and Zionism and to the close link between human rights and world peace. The preamble to the African Charter contains similar language on Zionism and racism. The African Charter focuses on economic development, calling it essential to pay particular attention to the right to development. It also is unique in including peoples' rights, but the preamble indicates that they are viewed as instrumental; it recognizes "that the reality and respect of peoples'" rights should necessarily guarantee human rights.

Among the pronounced differences, the Arab Charter is unique in omitting explicit mention of slavery, although it prohibits forced labor, which could be intended to include slavery. The Arab Charter has few guarantees of political rights, leaving out the right to free and fair elections. It specifies only the right of citizens to occupy public office. The Arab Charter is also less protective of the rights of aliens.

The ASEAN Declaration is notable in not mentioning freedom of association and the African Charter does not include the right to privacy. Yet, like the African and Arab instruments, it includes rights not mentioned in the earlier global and regional texts. The newer instruments have provisions on the right to development, environmental rights, freedom from human trafficking, rights of the elderly and, in the case of the Arab and ASEAN instruments, the rights of persons with disabilities. The ASEAN Declaration adds mention of migrant workers, as well. The African Charter is unique in its section on peoples' rights, including therein self-determination, permanent sovereignty over natural resources, the right to development, the right to peace and security, and the right to "a general satisfactory environment favourable to their development." The Arab Charter prohibits trafficking in human organs and the exploitation of children in armed conflict. Article 25 also guarantees cultural rights, including those of language and religion, to persons belonging to minorities.

Most regional systems have added to the catalogue of rights over time. In the European system, even before the signing of the Convention, the Assembly proposed the inclusion of additional rights by Protocol 1. The evolutionary character of the European system, reflected in its numerous protocols and related human rights treaties, is not unique. Regional systems seem to add new rights in a kind of feedback process of mutual inspiration, including such specific guarantees as abolition of the death penalty, prohibition of violence against women, right to a satisfactory environment, and strengthened guarantees in regard to economic, social, and cultural rights. In almost all instances, regional action has preceded UN instruments on the same topic.

It is notable that in no case has a right been limited or withdrawn by a later instrument, though all the regional instruments contain limitations clauses whose language is often similar, based on the UDHR. They also contain "clawback" clauses that limit certain rights to the extent provided in national law. The European Convention, for example, provides that the right to marry and to found a family is "according to the national laws governing the exercise of this right" (art. 12). The African and Arab Charters contain extensive clawback clauses that could undermine the effectiveness of both systems, although the developing jurisprudence of the African system is encouraging in insisting on effective enforcement of the rights.

Some of the greatest differences among the regional instruments are found in the derogations provisions. The bases for derogating differ as well as the lists of nonderogable rights. In the American system, states may suspend guarantees "in times of war, public danger, or other emergency that threatens the independence or security" of the state. In contrast, the European

Convention limits the grounds for suspending rights to "time of war or other public emergency threatening the life of the nation" making it harder to justify a suspension of rights. On the other hand, the list of nonderogable rights is much longer in the Inter-American system, so ease of derogation is balanced by greater human rights protections in periods of emergency. Africa has no general derogation clause, but the clawback provisions may make it unnecessary. Article 4 of the Arab Charter is close to the language of the ICCPR, referring to public emergencies which threaten the life of the nation and requiring that the measures be "strictly required by the circumstances."

In sum, there is diversity about diversity. The basic texts of each regional system reaffirm universal norms, but there are sufficient references to regional specificities that the states and the supervisory organs of each system could choose to focus on their differences instead of their similarities. Thus it is important to study the normative evolution of the systems as reflected in the jurisprudence of the regional commissions and courts.

NORMATIVE EVOLUTION

The regional human rights systems have evolved through a complex interplay of environmental pressures, institutional changes, and interregional contacts. Perhaps most importantly, the dynamic reading given human rights guarantees by the regional supervisory organs has prevented a rigid formalism from reducing the relevance of regional systems as circumstances change and new problems arise. Judges and commissioners have used their monitoring powers to apply and creatively interpret the often general terms of the treaties. The ECtHR has confirmed that "the Convention is a living instrument which . . . must be interpreted in the light of the present-day conditions."[10] The Inter-American Court has similarly emphasized the notion of "evolving American law."[11]

---

10. *Tyrer v. United Kingdom*, 26 Eur. Ct. H.R. (ser. A) (1978), at 10.
11. See Interpretation of the American Declaration of the Rights and Duties of Man within the Framework of Article 64 of the American Convention, Advisory Opinion OC-10/89, 14 July 1989, Inter-Am. Ct. H.R. (Ser. A) No. 10 (1989), at paras. 37–38.

The three systems that accept complaints have a growing case law detailing the rights and duties enunciated in the basic instruments. The jurisprudence of the regional human rights bodies has thus become a major source of human rights law. In many instances this case law reflects a convergence of the different substantive protections in favor of broad human rights protections. In other instances, differences in treaty terms or approach have resulted in a rejection of precedent from other systems. In general, the judges and commissioners have been willing to substantiate or give greater authority to their interpretations of the rights guaranteed by referencing not only their own prior case law but the decisions of other global and regional bodies.

To the extent there is a progressive convergence of human rights norms, it is in large part stimulated by victims and their lawyers. They submit memorials that draw attention to the relevant case law of other systems and help to expand human rights protections by obtaining a progressive ruling in one system, then invoking it in another. This tendency is enhanced by the liberal standing rules of the Inter-American and African Commissions. Many complaints are filed by nongovernmental organizations familiar with and operating in more than one system. In the European system, briefs submitted amicus curiae by NGOs similarly draw attention to regional and global norms and jurisprudence. The epistemic community of NGOs has its parallel in the regular meetings of the commissioners and judges of the regional systems, now supplemented by meetings organized to discuss cooperation between the UN and the regional systems. The resulting progressive development of regional human rights law strongly suggests that no human rights lawyer should rely solely on the jurisprudence of a single system in pleading a case.

PROCEDURAL AND INSTITUTIONAL EVOLUTION

Regional human rights procedures and institutions have evolved perhaps to an even greater extent than have substantive human rights guarantees. While some changes result from amendments to the basic legal instruments, other changes are due to regional bodies developing their own implied powers.

INDIVIDUAL COMPLAINTS PROCEDURES

One of the greatest contributions of the regional systems is the establishment of complaint mechanisms for judicial or quasi-judicial redress of human rights violations. Europe was the first to create a commission and court that could hear complaints, followed by the Americas and Africa. The Inter-American Commission on Human Rights, from its creation in 1960, interpreted its powers broadly to include the ability "to make general recommendations to each individual state as well as to all of them."[12] This was deemed to include the power to take cognizance of individual petitions and use them to assess the human rights situation in a particular country. The Inter-American system was thus the first to make the complaints procedure mandatory against all member states.

The regional commissions and courts have gradually strengthened their procedures for handling complaints. In the European system, a slow evolution toward individual standing first allowed individuals to appear before the court in the guise of assistants to the Commission. A protocol later permitted them to appear by right. With the entry into force of Protocol 11, complainants gained sole standing and the Commission ceased to exist as the ECtHR became a full-time body.

The African system evolved quickly through the African Commission's interpretation of its powers and revision of its rules of procedure. The major institutional change in the African regional human rights system came with the establishment of the African Court on Human and Peoples' Rights on 2 July 2006. The African Court's jurisdiction extends to cases alleging any violation of a right guaranteed by the African Charter on Human and Peoples' Rights, the Charter on the Rights and Welfare of the Child, the Protocol to the African Charter on Human and Peoples' Rights on the Rights of Women in Africa, or "any other legal instrument relating to human rights ratified by the States Parties concerned." Unlike other courts, the jurisdiction of the African Court does not seem to require exhaustion of local remedies or proceedings before

---

12. Inter-American Commission on Human Rights, First Report 1960, OAS Doc. OEA/Ser.L/V/II.1, Doc. 32 (1961).

the Commission as a prerequisite to filing a case with the court. At the conclusion of proceedings, Article 45, entitled "Compensation," indicates that the Court has broad remedial powers.

The monitoring of the 2004 Arab Charter on Human Rights, indicated in the various paragraphs of Article 48, is done through periodic reports of states parties submitted to the Secretary General of the League of Arab States, who, in his turn, refers them to the Arab Human Rights Committee. The Committee studies the reports and makes its remarks, in the presence of a state representative. The Arab Human Rights Committee may request from a state party "additional information relating to the implementation of the Charter" (Article 48(2)).

There are obviously some commonalities but also differences in the composition, functions, and procedures of the existing commissions, committees, and courts. The commonalities stem from the fact that member states of the organization create the bodies and the states decide how much scrutiny they are willing to accept of their human rights practices, including through allowing victims to bring petitions or complaints against them. Compliance is a concern in every human rights system; without the peer pressure of states in the organization, human rights bodies have little ability to ensure that their recommendations and decisions are implemented. Several factors are relevant.

First, the work of a human rights body is only as good as its membership. If decisions must be taken by consensus, it will be only as good as its weakest member.

Second, human rights bodies should have adequate meeting time to carry out their functions. Currently, the only full-time human rights body is the ECtHR. All other commissions and courts are organized as part-time bodies whose members are employed elsewhere. As long as membership on human rights bodies is a part-time occupation, some delegation of functions to the secretariats will be necessary, but this will therefore require oversight and accountability.

Linked to the foregoing second factor, the secretariat for each human rights body is supplied by the parent organization. In practice the head of the organization will often take into account the views of the human rights body, but there is always a risk of political appointments or other interference if the human rights body does not control the hiring and tenure of its staff. This is a matter of urgency and even crisis in nearly all human rights systems, as are the common problems of short-term employment contracts, limited financing, and budgetary shortfalls.

Ultimately, the commitment to human rights of the member states is determinative. If the level of respect for human rights norms on the domestic level is low, and domestic institutions are not effective, the workload of human rights bodies becomes unmanageable and their decisions ineffective.

ON-SITE VISITS AND COUNTRY STUDIES

The trust and cooperation that develops in regional systems can lead to highly effective mechanisms apart from the individual communications procedures. The technique of the on-site visit is an invaluable instrument in human rights protection and promotion, enabling regional bodies to gather information and verify the information they have received. At the same time, governments can clarify the context and complexities of situations. On-site visits allow officials and private persons to be heard and increase public knowledge of the regional system. Finally, on-site visits can deter violations by the mere presence of an outside human rights group. As such, a principal advantage to on-site visits is preventive. Unlike communications procedures, which begin only *after* a violation has occurred and local remedies have been exhausted, on-site visits can occur whenever indications are received that violations may take place, or where a state seeks assistance in evaluating and improving its human rights performance. Visits can be cooperative rather than confrontational, offering the same advantages as the "constructive dialogue" entered into through UN reporting mechanisms, but with better information.

BURDEN AND BACKLASH

All the regional systems have seen dramatic changes in their environments, from democratic transitions in South Africa, Central and Eastern Europe, and much of Latin America to backsliding, armed conflicts, and other emergencies that have challenged the regional institutions. Also, when new member states have joined, as has happened to all the regional systems, they bring with them new possibilities and problems. Countries in transition face enormous challenges in building democratic institutions that go beyond elections, such as independent judicial systems, professional police and military, a free press, and accountability for violations, and as a consequence regional bodies are increasingly occupied with issues of democracy, armed conflict, transnational crime, environmental protection, economic development, science and technology, and, indeed, the full range of human activities. Regional systems also face unprecedented problems from the resurgence of minority nationalism and ethnic tensions, often leading to massive violations of human rights by nonstate actors.

In response, regional systems are attempting to broaden their activities without reducing their emphasis on the individual complaint procedures that have been their major contribution to the development of human rights law. Unfortunately, limited time and resources mean that key functions cannot always be fulfilled expeditiously or, in some instances, at all. The promise of regional systems is conditioned on the willingness of member states to increase support and resources for regional institutions in the future.

CHANGES IN MEMBERSHIP

Efforts to strengthen human rights protections on the regional level have succeeded in large part because of the cultural, geographic, economic, and historical proximity of the original member states in the region. The relative homogeneity fostered a sense of trust among the member states that made them less sensitive to criticism of their human rights performance.

Changes in membership in all the regional systems have been significant and influential. The Inter-American and African systems have benefited from the recent adherence of large and important states in the region. The transition to democracy in South Africa brought it into the African system where its resources and example of peaceful change have been important. In Europe, in contrast, the post-Cold War admission of Central and Eastern Europe states into the Council of Europe has caused a previous attitudinal like-mindedness defined by Western Europe to dissipate. Over half the member states of the Council (24 of the 47) have joined since 1990, nearly all of them from Central and East-

ern Europe, and this change in membership has affected the culture of the system and the nature of cases that are brought, as well as the burden of cases and problems of compliance with judgments. The Court faces unprecedented situations of widespread violations where factual determinations of responsibility are often difficult and compliance uncertain. Many European cases have become comparable to those found in the Inter-American and the African systems, challenging the effectiveness of the system, especially in situations of armed conflict.

OVERBURDENING

All human rights bodies are struggling with rising caseloads. Without additional resources, which have not been forthcoming, they face an ever-increasing backlog of petitions, increasing the time applicants must wait for a decision. The European system has been particularly hard-hit by the exponential growth in complaints, a tribute to its success but also the result of admitting new member states with little historical commitment to human rights. The ECtHR compulsory jurisdiction over all forty-seven member states allows some 800 million individuals to complain of human rights violations. More than 100,000 of them do so each year.

The Inter-American Commission's caseload is also expanding, as is its mandate. The Commission's monitoring functions grow with each new treaty adopted in the system, because unlike the UN, the OAS does not create a new treaty body for each new instrument. In addition, each OAS General Assembly adopts resolutions requesting IACHR action on new issues and priorities.

BACKLASH

Regional systems have faced growing problems of noncompliance and backlash from states, which sometimes seek to "reform" the institutions in response to criticism of governments' human rights records. Three high-level conferences on the future of the ECtHR have met since 2010 and parliamentary debates have been held in the British Parliament and the Netherlands Senate. The UK government has been a strong critic of what it views as "judicial activism" on the part of the Court; it has objected in particular to judgments on voting rights for convicted felons. The Court's decisions on asylum-seekers have also produced intense and widespread criticisms, particularly when coupled with extension of economic and social rights to those seeking entry. Critics complain that the decisions interfere with national immigration policies, especially in the light of anti-terrorism efforts.

Regarding the Inter-American system, objection to jurisprudence of the human rights bodies has led to significant changes. The Caribbean states of Barbados, Guyana, Jamaica, and Trinidad established a Caribbean Court of Justice in 1999 in large part out of disagreement with Inter-American standards on due process in death penalty cases. On 26 May 1998, Trinidad and Tobago denounced the American Convention on Human Rights, followed by Venezuela in September 2013. More recently, the IACHR spent more than two years defending itself against efforts to weaken its autonomy and its mandate. While the Convention and the IACHR Statute remained intact after this period, a chilling effect can be seen in some of the new rules adopted and subsequent decisions of the Commission. Some states also shifted from direct attacks to lobbying for election of their candidates for the Commission or Court or against the renewal of mandate holders deemed too active.

The African system also has been the target of criticism and suggestions for reform. It faces many of the same problems that have arisen in other regional systems. The Commission is chronically hampered by a lack of resources from the African Union, resulting in poor terms of service and conditions of work for the staff of the Secretariat, with consequent low morale among the staff and lack of resources to publish its reports, which has diminished the Commission's visibility and public awareness of its work. Commentators have criticized also the low level of compliance with Commission decisions.

CONCLUSIONS

All systems are strengthened by the variety of subsystems that interact and even compete as parts of them. The adaptive moves by each further modify the problems, stimulating additional coevolution. The variety of responses leads to overall sustainability and resistance to threats, just as a diverse ecosystem is more resilient to challenge than a monocultural system because each component can respond as it is differently adapted. Each subsystem benefits from the response of the others, learning and evolving in an ongoing interdependent process.

Human rights law has thus been enhanced through the developing jurisprudence and evolution of regional human rights systems. The various systems reinforce global norms while responding to the particular problems of each region. Through the participation of NGOs and their own interactions, they learn from each other, enhancing the legitimacy of their decisions by relying on precedents from other systems. They are engaged also in constant exchanges with their environments and thus never reach equilibrium. As a result, their operations will never be completely consistent with their goals; there will almost always be some malfunction or inefficiency in the process. It is nonetheless possible to seek reform and greater efficiency to achieve the aim of promoting and protecting international human rights at the regional level.

QUESTIONS FOR REFLECTION AND DISCUSSION

1. What if any advantages might regional human rights systems have over the UN system? And vice versa? What are the relative strengths and vulnerabilities of the UN and regional systems?

2. What role, if any, should the UN play in the development of regional human rights systems?

3. How are the European, Inter-American, and African human rights systems the same? How do they differ? What explains the similarities? The differences? What are their comparative strengths? What are their comparative weaknesses?

4. Based on Shelton's analysis, would you consider it preferable to expend the money currently spent on a global enforcement system rather than regional human rights systems? Why? Why not?

5. Shelton argues that "While basing themselves on universal norms, regional

instruments nevertheless contain different guarantees and emphases; indeed the preambles of all the regional instruments refer to their regional heritages." Conduct a comparative analysis of these differing references to heritage in the respective preambles. How are these regional heritages signaled by the documents? What language is particularly significant? What cultural concepts are either explicit or implicit in the preambles?

6. Do you think that any particular regional heritage is more, or less, conducive to respect for human rights? On what basis? Deploying which definition of human rights? And why that particular definition? What does your choice of definition privilege and/or overlook/devalue? What commitments inform your perception of the issues?

7. Shelton concludes that "Human rights law has . . . been enhanced through the developing jurisprudence and evolution of regional human rights systems. The various systems reinforce global norms while responding to the particular problems of each region." Do you agree? Is this an overly positive assessment? Why not? Why?

8. Are the norms in the UN system, in any case, "global" in the sense of being universally accepted? Is there another way to see the relationship between the UN's global norms and the role of the regional systems? What is it?

9. Shelton points out that the UN tried for two decades to make the UDHR binding and, instead, created the ICESCR and ICCPR as a result of the failed effort. Why do you think the UN failed to make the UDHR binding? What are the major differences between the ICESCR and the ICCPR?

10. Identify obstacles to overcome to improve the effectiveness of regional human rights enforcement mechanisms (treaties and court systems). Should regional human rights enforcement mechanisms eventually move toward a unified international mechanism? Why? Why not? In what ways would centralizing authority for enforcing human rights be better than the current arrangement? Worse?

32. RICHARD A. FALK *Searching for a Jurisprudence of Conscience: International Criminal Accountability and Humanitarian Intervention*

I here address two vital aspects of the broad endeavor to promote humane global governance: first, the struggle to make political leaders and military commanders accountable under international law whether or not they are on the winning side in a major war or occupy the upper layers of the global political hierarchy; the second is humanitarian intervention, purportedly undertaken to protect against extensive human rights violations. Both the search for accountability and the uses of humanitarian intervention reveal certain core discrepancies in the international legal order. These are reflected, in the first instance, by a lurking practice of "victor's justice," and, in the second instance, by patterns associated with commonly self-serving, therefore divisive and contestable, geopolitical interests.

Excerpted with changes by permission of Richard Falk from Richard Falk, "Humanitarian Intervention and Legitimacy Wars: Seeking Peace and Justice in the 21st Century" (unpublished manuscript on file with the author, 2013). Copyright © 2013 Richard Falk.

INTERNATIONAL CRIMINAL ACCOUNTABILITY

Ever since the Allied Powers prosecuted, convicted, and punished German and Japanese leaders at Nuremberg and Tokyo,[1] there has been a wide split at the core of the global effort to impose criminal accountability on those who commit crimes against peace, crimes against humanity, war crimes, and genocide on behalf of a sovereign state. The law is always expected to

1. The original Nuremberg Judgment of 1 October 1946, including a dissenting opinion by the Soviet judge, may be found in International Military Tribunal, *Trial of the Major War Criminals* (Nuremberg, 1947), 171–343. The Tokyo Judgment of 4 November 1948 may be found in Bernard Röling and C. Rüter, eds., *The Tokyo Judgment: The International Military Tribunal for the Far East* (Amsterdam: APA University Press, 1977), III-Annex nos. A-4 and A-5. Additionally, the Nuremberg Judgment is available online at http://avalon.law.yale.edu/subject_menus/judcont.asp [*Eds.*—accessed 27 June 2015], and the Tokyo Judgment at http://werle.rewi.hu-berlin.de/tokio.pdf [*Eds.*—accessed 27 June 2015].

push toward consistency of application as a condition of its legitimacy. In the setting of international criminality, however, the global pattern of enforcement to date has been one in which comparatively petty criminals are increasingly held to account while the Mafia bosses escape existing mechanisms of international accountability almost altogether. Such double standards are too rarely acknowledged in discussions of international criminal law; likewise their corrosive effects. But once understood, it becomes clear that this pattern seriously compromises the claim that international criminal law as now applied is capable of achieving global justice.

NUREMBERG AND TOKYO WAR CRIMES TRIBUNALS

A pattern of double standards was encoded immediately after World War II in the seminal undertakings at Nuremberg and Tokyo that assumed the form of "victors' justice" in the weak sense of the term. The strong sense of victors' justice involves imposing punishment on those who are innocent of substantive wrongdoing beyond the misfortune of being on the losing side in a war. The weak sense is that the implementation of international criminal law is undertaken only against individuals on the losing side who are indeed responsible for substantive wrongdoing, while exempting seemingly guilty individuals on the winning side.

THE ATOMIC BOMB ATTACKS

Yet even a weak sense of victors' justice may act to exempt even the most severe and harmful forms of criminal behavior from legal scrutiny, and thereby badly confuse our understanding of the distinction between criminal and noncriminal activity. Surely the indiscriminate "saturation" bombings of German and Japanese cities by Allied bomber fleets—no less than German and Japanese indiscriminate bombing of Britain and China—and the dropping of atomic bombs on Hiroshima and Nagasaki were "crimes" that should have been investigated and prosecuted if the tribunals had been truly "legal" in the sense of imposing individual accountability on both victors and vanquished for their combat operations.

What is more, by refusing to prosecute victors, their substantive "crimes" attained a kind of perverse de facto legality. There is little doubt that if Germany or Japan had developed the atomic bomb first, and then alone used it but nevertheless lost the war, the individuals responsible would have been charged with and convicted of crimes against humanity and war crimes by the victorious Allied powers, and their behavior stigmatized in the annals of customary international law.

The only judicial body to pass judgment on the atomic bomb attacks on Japanese cities was a lower Tokyo court in the *Shimoda* case handed down 7 December 1963—that is, with a subtle touch of Japanese humility, the exact day of the twenty-second anniversary of the Pearl Harbor attacks.[2] Relying on expert testimony by respected Japanese specialists in international law, the court concluded that the attacks on large Japanese cities violated existing international law because of their indiscriminate and toxic characteristics. The case was initiated by survivors of Hiroshima and Nagasaki who sought nominal damages and were held to lack legal standing to put forward criminal allegations.

As might have been expected, Japan, as a defeated state and one that remained subordinate to American military power and diplomatic influence, was not inclined to pursue the matter any further, and seemed precluded from doing so by the peace treaty with the United States in which it waived all claims arising from the war. Not surprisingly the *Shimoda* judgment virtually disappeared down the memory hole of atomic diplomacy. In 1996 the International Court of Justice in an Advisory Opinion responding to a question put to it by the UN General Assembly narrowly defined the conditions under which it might possibly be lawful to resort to nuclear weapons in situations of extreme self-defense that if applied to the 1945 atomic attacks would definitely result in their criminalization.[3] As far

2. See *The Shimoda Case* (judgment of 7 December 1963), District Court of Tokyo, reprinted in *Japanese Annual of International Law*, 1964, 212 (English translation).
3. See Legality of the Threat or Use of Nuclear Weapons (Advisory Opinion of 8 July 1996), UN Doc. A/511218 (1996). The opinion is available at http://www.icj-cij .org/docket/index.php?p1=3&p2=4&k=e1&p3=4&case =95 [*Eds.*—accessed 22 June 2015]. For a simultaneously sympathetic and circumspect response to this opinion, see Burns H. Weston, "Nuclear Weapons and the World Court: Ambiguity's Consensus," *TLCP* 7 (1997): 371–99.

as is known no effort has been made by any nuclear weapons state to alter its doctrine governing threat and use, including the threat of nuclear annihilation, in light of this most authoritative assessment by the World Court.

Had the defeated states used an atomic bomb and the perpetrators been charged and convicted, this might have made it somewhat more difficult for the victors to rely upon nuclear weaponry in the future, and might have encouraged them to work diligently and reasonably to negotiate a treaty regime of unconditional prohibition. Instead, the victorious United States government has never been willing to express formally even remorse for these wartime atrocities that completely lacked the partially redeeming feature of military necessity. It has retained, developed, possessed, deployed, and threatened other nations with the use of nuclear weapons on numerous occasions, including the possibility of using weaponry with payloads many times the magnitude of those first bombs dropped on Japan. As well, having opened this ultimate Pandora's Box, others have acquired the weaponry and relied on its ultrahazardous energy technology to produce nuclear power.

It is not just the inherent unfairness of victors' justice, but its tendency to normalize unacceptable wartime behavior if done by the winning side in a major war, which nullifies the very possibility of a jurisprudence of conscience. The closest that the U.S. government has come to acknowledge officially its culpability in relation to Hiroshima and Nagasaki was in a single line in Barack Obama's speech of 5 April 2009 in Prague that envisioned a world without nuclear weapons: "as the only nuclear power to have used a nuclear weapon, the United States has a moral responsibility to act." Unfortunately, this sentiment was neither a belated apology nor repeated in Obama's Nobel Peace Prize acceptance speech a few months later. Further, no concrete steps have been taken by the Obama administration to initiate a nuclear disarmament process, not to be confused with managerial arms control measures that have been endorsed.

This split notion of accountability as between winners and losers remains descriptive of how international criminal law is currently implemented. Indeed, the gap has widened over time, or at least become more evident. This awareness is partly a result of increasing efforts by the intergovernmental system of states to hold losers and vulnerable political actors accountable while holding firm the impunity of the powerful and their friends. The NGO community has by and large been opportunistic, supporting efforts to hold officials accountable for their criminality without worrying too much about double standards and selective implementation, seeming to reason that a glass half-full is to be preferred to an empty glass. This has had the unfortunate effect of appearing to legitimate the hierarchical character of world order. By ignoring the crimes of the powerful political actors on the world stage while validating the criminal prosecution of weaker political actors, an attitude of normalcy or indifference becomes associated with double standards in international criminal law.

Encouragingly, the recent trend has exhibited a gradual increase in the availability of international mechanisms to hold leaders accountable, including the establishment of a variety of special or ad hoc international tribunals, including those constituted by civil society initiatives, to address serious criminal allegations (former Yugoslavia and Rwanda, Japanese comfort women, indigenous peoples) relating to genocide and crimes against humanity. The big institutional step forward was, of course, the establishment in 2002 of the International Criminal Court (ICC), a permanent institutional venue within which to fight state crime—but so far in practice not to disturb the impunity enjoyed by those with geopolitical muscle at their disposal.

CRIMES AGAINST PEACE

For reasons relevant to the argument made here, the negotiations of the ICC had to stop short of incorporating crimes against peace into its claim of jurisdictional authority, reflecting the interest of major states in not acknowledging restrictions on their use of what geopolitically oriented diplomats call "the military option." This reflects a thinly disguised insistence on discretion to use force as an instrument of foreign policy despite the unconditional prohibition of threats or uses of force in Article 2(4) of the UN Charter. The repeated Israeli, American, and British military threats directed at Iran throughout the last decade are a flagrant instance of relying on a nondefensive threat to use force against a sovereign state. By Nuremberg or Charter standards such threat diplomacy would appear to be a naked example of a crime against peace.

Again the issue of victors' justice lurks in the background, but this time in a reverse relationship to that pertaining to the atomic bomb. The World War II tribunals were most intent at the time on criminalizing recourse to aggressive war. At Nuremberg, the judgment went out of its way to declare that crimes against peace are the worst possible offense against the law of nations, encompassing the lesser realities of crimes against humanity and war crimes—and, except for Indian Justice Pal, the judges in both tribunals had little trouble reaching such a legal conclusion. It was this conclusion that underlay the original conception of the UN as being a war prevention institution ("to save succeeding generations from the scourge of war" per the UN Charter preamble) whose charter restricted valid claims to use force to situations of self-defense against a prior armed attack and to occasions on which the UN Security Council (UNSC) mandated a use of force for the sake of international peace and security.

Despite such legal foregrounding of this war prevention priority, however, the UNSC veto given to the World War II winners conferred a permanent exemption from accountability of a sort that continued and widened the failure to hold the winners criminally accountable at Nuremberg or Tokyo. The practice of the UN has confirmed the refusal of these five permanent members of the UNSC, along with a few other states, to live according to the precepts of the Charter. Indeed, they would bring geopolitical pressures to bear so that the UNSC, as it did in March 2011, would mandate an interventionary use of force in Libya that was neither defensive nor necessary for the sake of international peace and security.[4] Because of its challenge to milita-

rism and geopolitical reliance on force, the prohibition of crimes against peace has been basically marginalized as an international crime, supposedly because there was no agreement among governments as to a definition of aggression, but more genuinely because geopolitical actors refused to accede to any formal challenge to their discretion to threaten and use force to resolve international conflicts, pursue their interests, and impose their political will. Here the leverage of geopolitical pressure keeps the legal precedent set at Nuremberg and Tokyo after World War II from becoming a behavioral norm. That is, it was appropriate to criminalize the aggression of Germany and Japan, but not acceptable to hamper the activities of geopolitical "peacekeepers" by the application of such a restrictive norm to their behavior.

The Nuremberg Promise

Sensitive to the precariousness of its legitimacy, the Nuremberg Tribunal made an attempt to overcome the flaw of double standards. This gesture to remove criminal accountability from the domain of geopolitics can be labelled "the Nuremberg promise," and involves a commitment by the victors *in the future* to abide by the norms and procedures used to punish the German and Japanese surviving military and political leaders—in effect, promising to correct this flaw associated with victors' justice by converting criminal accountability from rule of power to rule of law applicable to all rather than a consequence of the outcome of wars or a reflection of geopolitical hierarchy.

The chief prosecutor at Nuremberg, Justice Robert Jackson of the U.S. Supreme Court, gave this promise an enduring relevance in his official statement to the court: "If certain acts and violations of treaties are crimes, they are crimes whether the United States does them or whether Germany does them. We are not prepared to lay down a rule of criminal conduct against others which we would not be willing to have invoked against us." Peace activists frequently quote Jackson's words, yet political leaders who take no notice of either the original flaw at Nuremberg or the obligation to remove it consistently ignore them, suggesting that Jackson's rhetoric at the time, seemingly made in good faith, was not sufficient to generate a sense of obligation on

---

4. The authorizing resolution of the UNSC seemed limited to providing humanitarian protection to the civilian population of the Libyan city of Benghazi, but was operationally expanded by NATO to include a full-scale military air effort to tip the balance in an internal civil war in favor of the anti-Qaddafi forces. UNSC Resolution 1973 of 17 March 2011 was officially delimited as establishing a "No-Fly-Zone" over Libya, although there was accompanying language that should never have been accepted by the five abstaining states to the effect that "all necessary measures" were approved. In Qaddafi's case he was brutally killed by the rebel military forces that captured him in his hometown of Sirte on 20 October 2011.

the part of American leaders who subsequently have acted on behalf of the United States.

A parallel issue arises in relation to the willingness of a defeated country to accept the criminalization of its leadership. The German philosopher Karl Jaspers, in his *The Question of German Guilt* (1946), argued that the psychopolitical acceptability of these convictions and punishments of German leaders would have to wait until it becomes clear in the future whether the Nuremberg promise was going to be kept by the victors. If the promise was broken, then in retrospect the Nuremberg process should be properly interpreted as a legal form of vengeance rather than an expression of criminal justice. Taking Jaspers seriously in this respect would raise questions about the liberal embrace of international criminal law despite its incorporation of double standards.

INSTITUTIONALIZING INTERNATIONAL CRIMINAL LAW

This dual pattern of criminal accountability that cannot be fully reconciled with law or legitimacy has given rise to several reformist efforts, both progressive and regressive. By extraordinary efforts, a global coalition of NGOs and the commitment of a group of middle powers have raised liberal hopes by establishing the ICC at The Hague despite the opposition of geopolitical heavyweights. On the other hand, fearful of losing or compromising their impunity, such heavyweights as the United States, China, India, and Russia have refused to ratify the ICC, and the United States has gone farther, pressuring over one hundred countries to sign statements agreeing not to hand over to the ICC Americans accused at The Hague of international crimes.

The result is that this and other formal and informal initiatives have not yet seriously impinged on the hierarchal realities of world politics, which continue to exhibit an embrace of the Melian ethos when it comes to criminal accountability: "the strong do what they will, the weak do what they must." Such an ethos marked, for Thucydides, unmistakable evidence of Athenian decline, but for contemporary realists a different reading has been prevalent. Underpinning political realism has been the premise that hard power calls the shots in history, and the losers have no choice but to cope as best they can. Double standards persist: those who are enemies

of the West or evildoers in Africa are targets of global prosecutorial zeal, while those in the West who wage aggressive war or mandate torture as national policies continue to enjoy impunity as far as formal legal proceedings are concerned.

The veto in the UNSC both complements the "naturalness" of victors' justice and is a prime instance of constitutionalizing double standards. The veto power, while sounding the death knell for the UN in its assigned role of ensuring war prevention based on law rather than geopolitics, is not without providing certain benefits to world order. This availability of the veto is probably responsible for allowing the Organization to achieve and maintain universality of membership even during times of intense geopolitical conflict. Without the veto, the West would have likely pushed the Soviet Union and China out the door during the Cold War years, and the UN would have lost its inclusive and universalist character in a manner similar to the discrediting of the League of Nations, an experience after the end of World War I that transformed Woodrow Wilson's dream into an enfeebled nightmare. Arguably the veto and victors' justice are examples of Faustian bargains that enable a semblance of law and justice to be present in international life, and to convey the impression that there is a morally evolutionary process at work that introduces a gradually increasing measure of civility into the conduct of world politics. The question is whether this appearance of civility is to be treated as a form of moral progress, however slow or halting, or rather as the prostitution of law and institutions to geopolitical abuses and ambitions. There is no assurance that the evolution of international criminal law has any prospect of overcoming the current pattern of an open-ended geopolitical right of exception.

Yet this realist world of unequal states has been embodied imperfectly even within the UN. So conceived, the anachronistic character of the 1945 UNSC persists as a remnant of the colonial era. This is delegitimizing. The year 2015 is not 1945, but the difficulty of achieving constitutional reform within the UN means that India, Brazil, Turkey, Indonesia, Germany, Japan, and South Africa seem destined to remain indefinitely as ladies-in-waiting while the UN goes about its serious geopolitical business. What this means for UN authority, including its sponsorship of the politics of individual criminal accountability, is that all that is "legal" is more often than not "illegitimate," and lacking in moral force.

My argument seeks to make two main points: first, double standards pervade the treatment of war crimes eroding the authority and legitimacy of international criminal law; second, those geopolitical hierarchies that are embedded in the UN framework lose their authority and legitimacy by not adapting to changing times and conditions, especially the collapse of the colonial order and the rise of non-Western centers of soft and hard power. In this latter instance, it is the inability to reflect the geopolitical ratio of power that partially hampers the legitimacy of the UN, not its realist tendency to express its legitimacy by exhibiting in its procedures and structures the relative strength of political actors. Of course, even if the UN enhanced its *geopolitical* legitimacy by taking account of global shifts in capabilities and influence, this would not necessarily pose a challenge to hierarchy and double standards.

UNIVERSAL JURISDICTION

There are different kinds of initiatives taken to close this gap between the legal and the legitimate in relation to the criminality of political leaders and military commanders. One move is at the level of the sovereign state, which is to encourage domestic criminal law to extend its reach to cover international crimes. Such authority is known as Universal Jurisdiction (UJ), a hallowed effort by states to overcome the enforcement weaknesses of international law, initially developed to deal with the crime of piracy, which being interpreted as a crime against the whole world could be prosecuted anywhere regardless of where and on whose behalf the pirate operated. Many liberal democracies in particular have regarded themselves to varying degrees as agents of the international legal order as well as providing for the rule of law for relations within their national boundaries. This has led governments to endow their judicial system with some authority to apprehend and prosecute those viewed as criminally responsible for state crimes even if the criminal acts were performed outside of geographic boundaries. The legislating of UJ represented a strong tendency during the latter half of the twentieth century in the liberal democracies, especially in Western Europe, to be proactive with respect to the im-

plementation of international criminal law by escaping to some extent from the constraints of geography.

This development reached public awareness in relation to the dramatic 1998 detention in Britain of Augusto Pinochet, former ruler of Chile, in response to an extradition request from Spain where criminal charges had been judicially approved. The ambit of UJ is wider than its formal implementation as its mere threat is intimidating, leading those prominent individuals who might be detained and charged to avoid visits to countries where such claims might be plausibly made. In late 2011, George W. Bush canceled a speaking engagement in Switzerland because of indications that he might be arrested and charged with international crimes if he ventured across the Swiss borders. Similar reports have suggested that high Israeli officials have changed travel plans in response to warnings that they could face arrest, detention, or extradition for alleged crimes, especially in recent years those associated with either the Lebanon War of 2006 or the 2008–9 Israeli military attack on Gaza. In other words, the possibility of an assertion of UJ may have a behavioral and psychological impact even if the defendant is not brought physically before the court to stand trial.

As might be expected, UJ gave rise to a vigorous geopolitical campaign of pushback, especially by the governments of the United States and Israel,[5] which exhibited the most anxiety that their leaders might be subject to criminal apprehension by foreign national courts even in countries that were political friends. As a result and consequent intense pressure from both countries, several of the European UJ states were forced to roll back their UJ legislation, thereby calming somewhat the worries of travellers with records of public service on behalf of their countries that was potentially vulnerable to criminal prosecutions in foreign courts!

CIVIL SOCIETY TRIBUNALS

There is another approach to spreading the net of criminal accountability, and while it re-

5. *Eds.*—In this regard, see Reading 33 (Grear and Weston) next in this chapter discussing the 2013 U.S. Supreme Court decision in *Kiobel v. Royal Dutch Petroleum Co.*, 133 S. Ct. 1659 (2013).

mains controversial, it seems responsive to the current global atmosphere of populist discontent. It involves claims by civil society, by the peoples of the world, to establish institutions and procedures designed to close the gap between law and legitimacy in relation to the application of international criminal law. Such initiatives can be traced back to the 1966–67 establishment of the Bertrand Russell International Criminal Tribunal that examined charges of aggression and war crimes associated with the American role in the Vietnam War. The charges were weighed by a distinguished jury of private citizens composed of persons of moral and cultural authority headed by Jean-Paul Sartre. The Russell Tribunal was derided by critics at the time as a "kangaroo court" or a "circus" because its legal conclusions were predetermined, one-sided, and amounted to foregone assessments of guilt; because its authority was self-proclaimed and without governmental approval; because it had no control over those accused; and because its capabilities fell far short of enforcement.

What was overlooked in such criticism was the degree to which this dismissal of the Russell experiment reflected the monopolistic and self-serving claims of the state and state system to control the administration of law, ignoring the contrary claims of society to have law administered fairly in accord with justice, or at least to expose its distortions and double standards. Also ignored by the critics was the fact that only such spontaneous initiatives of concerned persons and groups could overcome the blackout of truth on the matters of criminality achieved by the geopolitics of impunity. The Russell Tribunal may not have been "legal" if law is understood in the sense of deriving its authority from the state or from international organizations, but it was "legitimate" in responding to double standards, by calling attention to massive crimes and dangerous criminals who otherwise might enjoy a free pass, and by producing a generally reliable and comprehensive narrative account of criminal patterns of wrongdoing and flagrant violations of international law that destroy or disrupt the lives of entire societies and millions of people. Such societal initiatives require a great effort that lacks the benefit of public funding, and only occur where the criminality being legally condemned seems severe and extreme, and where

geopolitical forces effectively preclude systematic inquiry by established institutions of criminal law.[6]

It is against this background that a steady stream of initiatives have built on the Russell experience in the 1960s. Starting in 1979, the Basso Foundation in Rome sponsored a series of such proceedings, under the rubric of the Permanent Peoples Tribunal, that explored a wide variety of unattended criminal wrongs, including dispossession of indigenous peoples, the Marcos dictatorship in the Philippines, massacres of Armenians, and self-determination claims of oppressed peoples in Central America and elsewhere. In 2005, the Istanbul World Tribunal on Iraq examined contentions of aggression and crimes against peace, crimes against humanity, and war crimes associated with the 2003 U.S./UK invasion and occupation of Iraq, causing as many as one million Iraqis to lose their lives, and several million to be permanently displaced from home and country.

In November 2011 the Russell Tribunal on Palestine, a direct institutional descendant of the original Russell undertaking, held a session in South Africa to investigate charges of apartheid (as a crime against humanity) being made against Israel. A few days later, the Kuala Lumpur War Crimes Tribunal launched an inquiry into charges of criminality made against George W. Bush and Tony Blair for their roles in planning, initiating, and prosecuting the Iraq War, to be followed a year later by a subsequent inquiry into torture charges made against former Vice President Dick Cheney, former Secretary of Defense Donald Rumsfeld, and Attorney General Alberto Gonzales.

Without doubt, such societal efforts to bring at large war criminals to symbolic justice should become a feature of the growing demand around the world for real global democracy sustained by a rule of law, a jurisprudence of conscience that does not exempt from criminal accountability

---

6. Investigative journalism does act as a partial complement to the efforts of citizens' tribunals. See, e.g., Seymour M. Hersh, *Mylai 4: A Report on the Massacre and Its Aftermath* (New York: Random House, 1970), which made a notable contribution by exposing the execution by American military personnel of Vietnamese villagers.

the rich and powerful whether they are acting internally or internationally.[7]

Meanwhile, the problems of victors' justice and double standards pervade and subvert the proper application of international law. As long as power, influence, and diplomatic skills are unevenly divided, there will be some tendency for this to happen, as we may see vividly as we turn next to so-called "humanitarian intervention."

HUMANITARIAN INTERVENTION

The opportunistic reliance on law when it serves the interests of the powerful and victorious has permeated also interventionary diplomacy, specifically humanitarian intervention, invoked principally in the context of large-scale violations of international human rights law and purportedly to prevent or minimize such violations. Indeed, due largely to this self-serving opportunism, no issue in global civil society since the end of the Cold War has been more divisive than the morality, legality, and politics of humanitarian intervention; and as consequence global civil society has not been able in the most difficult instances to serve effectively as the global voice of conscience relative to it.

In some instances, however, especially where the facts of extreme humanitarian crisis have been stark and uncontested, or where the grand strategy goals of the intervening actors have been plain, civil society actors have managed sufficient agreement to act as either a force for intervention or opposition—as in the 1990s, for example. During these years, the peoples of East Europe, the Soviet Union, and South Africa were unexpectedly liberated from oppressive rule without significant accompanying violence (a near political miracle), the ideological tensions that underpinned the Cold War disappeared, and an ethos of neoliberal globalization took command of political consciousness. It was a histori-

cal moment when the building blocks for a hopeful future based on the rule of law, global justice, and the absence of international warfare seemed to provide the world community with many of the ingredients of such a future, applied with high drama against such dictators as Augusto Pinochet and Slobodan Milošević and driving an unexpectedly successful campaign that, in 2002, established the permanent ICC.

It was largely during this immediate post-Cold War period that, as a by-product of globalization and an accompanying heightened sense of human solidarity combined with human rights activism, there emerged what its supporters described as "humanitarian diplomacy," the contested centerpiece of which was the use of force. Viewed mainly as a natural incident of the rising attention given to the protection of human rights, this emergence gave rise to several humanitarian interventions each of which, fraught with controversy, generated sharp debate in civil society circles and widely divergent academic commentary. This was especially so in connection with Somalia, Rwanda, Bosnia, East Timor, and particularly, Kosovo, and later Iraq. The debate focused on three kinds of core concerns: was the intervention under discussion legally, morally, and politically justified and feasible? Did a refusal to intervene in the face of a humanitarian catastrophe expose a serious weakness in the structure of world order and the quality of global leadership? Were the most convincing explanations of particular instances of intervention and nonintervention associated with strategic, not humanitarian, concerns?

The voices of civil society were discordant. They clashed on the interpretation of facts, norms, and motives pertaining to each instance of humanitarian intervention, first in a serious way after the high-profile reversal of the American approach to Somalia in 1993–94, particularly the refusal of the Clinton presidency to sustain its dominant role in peacekeeping efforts due to armed resistance in Somalia producing American casualties, a retreat that led to a reassessment of humanitarian diplomacy by the United States.

The Somalia failure spilled over in tragic ways to discourage in 1994 an international response by the United Nations to an unfolding massive genocide in Rwanda—particularly lamentable in relation to Rwanda as most reliable observers be-

---

7. There is a need to distinguish what I mean by "a jurisprudence of conscience," (the claim that law should treat equally *all* offenders of norms of international criminal law) from those who act on the basis of their conscience to justify behaviors that from other societal perspectives constitute crimes—for one instance, the assassination by right to life advocates of doctors who perform abortions.

lieved that a small international commitment by way of humanitarian intervention could almost certainly have saved several hundred thousand Tutsi lives. This same attitude of reluctance accounted also for the shallow early commitment to oppose Serbian ethnic cleansing in Bosnia, a horrifying process that culminated in the 1995 Srebrenica massacre of several thousand Muslim males. In relation to Somalia and these other two humanitarian challenges, the UN had formally acknowledged some level of a responsibility to protect, as in each situation there existed a demonstrated and imminent humanitarian emergency. The failures to protect effectively arose from the weakness of political will on the part of major states, especially the United States, exhibited by the unwillingness to take the risks and pay the costs of intervention by making sufficient troops available and committing the necessary resources to get the job done.

Kosovo

These cross-cutting issues of impulse and restraint assumed a much more contested form in relation to Kosovo in the late 1990s. On the one side, Kosovo was technically subject to the sovereignty of the Belgrade government of former Yugoslavia. Russia and China were geopolitical opponents of any UNSC authorization of humanitarian intervention, and therefore no basis existed in international law to use force to protect the Albanians in Kosovo from a gathering threat of ethnic cleansing. On the other side, the United States, in conjunction with the countries of Western Europe, possessed the political will and the logistical means to act effectively on behalf of the threatened Albanian Kosovars who made up about 85 percent of the population. The strength of this political will, however, was not primarily an expression of a deeper humanitarian commitment in one instance rather than another. Instead, it seemed mainly to reflect an American geopolitical motivation to reestablish Atlanticist solidarity in the aftermath of the Cold War. The United States was also eager to convey to Europe its continuing hegemony on the continent, especially in light of tensions arising in relation to foreign trade and investment. Additionally, Washington was eager to convince Europeans that NATO, then approaching its fiftieth anniversary, was still a viable and useful alliance,

and that it could have a new rationale that took account of the collapse of the Soviet Union. The European locus of the humanitarian crisis was also a factor. European governments, with their memories of the Holocaust rekindled, exhibited a guilty conscience about their earlier failures to prevent violence in Bosnia, and did not want to reinforce this impression by acting passively in face of the worsening situation in Kosovo.

The complex Kosovo circumstances thus exposed deep divisions in civil society, brought to the surface before, during, and after the Kosovo War. *On the interventionist side* were those who primarily identified with the endangered civilian population in Kosovo, and accorded highest priority to the humanitarian imperative of providing security for these potential victims along with the invalidation and criminalization of the Serbian leadership in Belgrade, considerations of auspices and legality being distinctly secondary. Charter norms governing the use of force had long since partially broken down and consequently lost some of their authoritative status, it was argued, allowing "a coalition of the willing" to be treated as adequate legal grounding for humanitarian intervention. *On the anti-interventionist side*, civil society actors advanced two often overlapping arguments: that any international use of nondefensive force without a UNSC mandate would establish a bad and dangerous precedent threatening to the sovereignty and independence of weaker states in the future; and that entrusting NATO with such an undertaking was to embrace "military humanism" of a highly questionable variety, concealing a series of nonhumanitarian goals (ranging from the establishment of military bases to a show of U.S. readiness to use force to uphold its strategic interests), and thereby extending NATO's writ beyond what was permissible by reference to the UN Charter or even to the NATO treaty itself—in effect, endorsing a new instrument of hegemonic geopolitics. It was on this basis that China and Russia let it be known that they would make use of their UNSC veto and why the United States reacted to this eventuality by circumventing the Council, thereby avoiding the need to defy UN authority.

The problematic character of the Kosovo War encouraged assessments that were intended to influence future responses to unfolding humanitarian emergencies. The most influential assessments were made by independent groups of

prominent individuals who investigated the issues in controversy, preparing reports offering
detailed analysis of the events, summarizing
conclusions and recommendations. Such groups
performed as "independent commissions," consisting of prominent citizens appointed on the
initiative of governments that funded the exercise. The goal of these exercises was to present a
report to the Secretary-General of the United
Nations and to influence public opinion by encouraging media coverage. The main intellectual
objective was to provide a normative framework
for humanitarian intervention in the future that
would combine the effectiveness of Kosovo
without generating so much controversy.

The first of these commissions was the Independent International Commission on Kosovo.
Chaired by Richard Goldstone, a member of the
South African Constitutional Court and the first
prosecutor at the International Criminal Tribunal for the former Yugoslavia (ICTY), it was
funded by several governments, principally Sweden, and its final report was submitted to the
Secretary-General.[8] The Commission was to find
an adequate way to address the controversy surrounding an intervention that was irreconcilable
with the international law of the UN Charter.
The report relied on a distinction between the
"legality" and the "legitimacy" of humanitarian
interventions in particular instances. The argument made was that the facts relating to Kosovo
justified the apprehension of an impending humanitarian catastrophe, but that there existed no
legal means to intervene without obtaining a
prior Chapter VII mandate from the UNSC. At
the same time, the urgency of the situation combined with the availability of an effective means
to protect the endangered Kosovar population
meant that the moral and political grounds for
intervention were present, making the operation
legitimate.

The second effort to learn from Kosovo resulted from an initiative of the Canadian government in the form of the International
Commission on Intervention and State Sovereignty, chaired by Gareth Evans, a former foreign minister of Australia and by Mohamed
Sahnoun, a prominent diplomat and interna-

tional civil servant from Algeria. The report of
the Evans/Sahnoun Commission,[9] focusing
more on the generic problems posed by Kosovo
than on the Kosovo experience itself, advocated
a creative linguistic move to minimize the seeming inconsistency between humanitarian intervention and the idea and reality of state
sovereignty by shifting the emphasis from the
right of the intervener to the duty of the international community to protect those who are
threatened with imminent catastrophe. This
duty was called "the responsibility to protect"
(now popularly known as "R2P"), a responsibility that takes precedence when, in the face of an
impending humanitarian catastrophe, a permanent member of the UNSC nonetheless with-
holds its consent. Such a normative shift makes
sovereignty conditional on protecting people
within territorial boundaries, and is associated
with efforts to achieve so-called "responsible
sovereignty." It repudiates classical views of sovereignty as unconditional, which, over the centuries, has provided states with an autonomous
zone for the perpetration of "human wrongs."
The UNSC has been influenced by this report,
accepting the normative reorientation as a part
of a peacekeeping reform package recommended
by the Secretary-General's High-Level Panel on
Threats, Challenges and Change, and formally
endorsed by UNSC resolutions, including UNSC
Resolution 1706 enunciating a new approach at
the time to the Darfur crisis.[10]

POST-KOSOVO: 9/11, IRAQ, DARFUR

Even before the 9/11 attacks, the neoconservative turn in American political life, especially
foreign policy, meant that the dynamics of normative (moral and legal) globalization, so prominent in the 1990s, would no longer have the
contested benefit of American leadership. The
Bush presidency from its outset in January 2001,
defined by an entourage of neoconservative ad-

8. For the text of the final report, see Independent In-
ternational Commission on Kosovo, *The Kosovo Report:
Conflict, International Response, Lessons Learned* (Oxford:
OUP, 2000).

9. See the report by the International Commission on
Intervention and State Sovereignty, *The Responsibility to
Protect* (Ottawa: International Development Research
Centre, 2001).
10. See UN, High-Level Panel on Threats, Challenges
and Change, *A More Secure World: Our Shared Responsibility: Report of the Secretary-General's High-Level Panel on
Threats, Challenges and Change* (New York: UN, 2004),
59–74.

visors, indicated its strong opposition to humanitarian diplomacy, as well as its skepticism about the usefulness of international law and international institutions. It voiced particular doubts about funding UN peacekeeping operations. The new emphasis was to be on strategic priorities: an increased defense budget, an unwillingness to constrain national security policy by arms control treaties, a preoccupation with the future of the Middle East, and a definite swing toward relying on unilateral initiatives and avoiding multilateral entanglements. These features of American foreign policy greatly shaped the U.S. response to the 9/11 attacks; and what followed upon them dramatically altered the global setting and heavily influenced both the diplomacy relevant to humanitarian intervention and the ongoing civil society debate about it.

There was some support among liberal hawks for extending the Kosovo precedent to Iraq in the lead-up to the invasion of March 2003. Most notably, Michael Ignatieff, Christopher Hitchens, and Anne-Marie Slaughter supported the invasion of Iraq on the partially humanitarian grounds of deposing a cruel tyrant, and were willing to overlook the absence of UNSC endorsement. The official American emphasis prior to the invasion was on the strategic threat posed by Iraq due to its alleged possession of weapons of mass destruction, its supposed links to international terrorism, and, only incidentally, its dictatorial and brutal governing process. After the invasion, as it became clear that there were no WMDs to be found in Iraq and no credible evidence of significant links to transnational terrorism, the official rationale in Washington shifted rather unconvincingly to the promotion of democracy and human rights by way of military intervention and occupation. In November 2006, after years of denial, President Bush finally acknowledged that oil was a factor, that if the United States were to withdraw from Iraq it would lose control over Iraqi oil pricing, which could drive the world price up to $300–$400 per barrel.

This attempted legal/moral rationalization for the Kosovo War in the context of the Iraq War was generally repudiated by civil society actors throughout the world. On 15 February 2003, a few weeks before the invasion, there took place the largest expression of globalized antiwar sentiment in world history, with some 12 million demonstrators assembled in 80 countries and some 600 cities. Even in countries whose leaders were prepared to ignore their domestic public opinion and give support to American policy, such as the UK and Spain, the citizenry was opposed from the outset.

Of course, there was an abstract humanitarian justification for seeking regime change in Iraq, but the means chosen illustrate the dangers of humanitarian intervention being used as a pretext for aggressive warfare. Furthermore, even if UN authorization for the use of force had been obtained, military action of a nondefensive sort in the absence of any immediate threat of humanitarian catastrophe would have resulted in an outcome not very dissimilar from what has occurred. Humanitarian intervention may be effective as an emergency measure to protect a vulnerable population, but it is rarely able to impose a new political structure on a country. The Iraq experience is therefore best interpreted as follows: in the absence of a humanitarian emergency, intervention is unlikely to achieve humanitarian goals at an acceptable cost, and especially so if the main goal is to restructure the political life of the target country. Of course, Iraq was an extreme case, given the relative stability of political rule at the time of the invasion, the unwillingness of the UN to give its blessings, and the unified and widespread opposition to the proposed war throughout global civil society.

This opposition of course continued during the long and bloody occupation of Iraq, and took several forms, perhaps most notably a world tribunal process. In at least twenty countries, civil society initiatives organized an informal tribunal composed of citizens who passed legal judgment on the invasion and occupation, concluding that the American and British leaders were criminally responsible for violating international law, and should be held personally accountable. The culminating expression of this global initiative was the World Tribunal on Iraq (WTI) held in Istanbul in June 2005. The juridical inquiry was conducted by a distinguished panel of world citizens, presided over by the Indian novelist, Arundhati Roy. The panel, without pretending professional competence or governmental authority, issued a Declaration of Conscience that expressed the judgment that the Iraq War was a war of aggression and that its perpetrators were indictable under international criminal law.

If Iraq shows that political will is insufficient to liberate an oppressed people, the anguishing

humanitarian crisis in Darfur, accounting for between 300,000 and 400,000 deaths, with more
than two million others displaced and at risk,
shows that a requisite political will and an
aroused public opinion is necessary to fashion an
effective response. UNSC Resolution 1706[11] accepts the mandate of "the responsibility to protect" norm, but absent the consent of the
government of Sudan and without the deep
commitment of the United States and other important states, the deepening ordeal endured by
the people of Darfur resembles the experience of
Rwanda in 1994, except that in Darfur the mass
lethality is exhibited in a more gradual, less coordinated process. Civil society is almost as unified as in relation to Iraq, but is unable to
transform the clear moral and legal commitment
into a political project without the participation
of the main geopolitical forces on a sufficient
basis. As the case of East Timor shows, where
consent is present, and a regional actor with requisite capabilities is deeply engaged, the humanitarian mission can be effectively implemented.

In conclusion, it seems clear that "the responsibility to protect" is an emergent norm of customary international law, but its implementation
in specific instances is not yet a reflection of its
status in law. It remains primarily dependent on
mobilizing the political will of states, especially
dominant states, which can be pushed just so far
by an aroused public opinion calling for protective action. At present, such a political will is not
likely to be supportive of humanitarian intervention unless it coincides with significant strategic interests. Also, where the territorial
sovereign refuses consent, even geopolitical actors often cannot translate their interventionary
commitment into viable political projects, and
the attempt to do so can be exceedingly costly.
However, civil society actors can play significant
roles in shaping public attitudes, especially before and after the event, mobilizing support for
intervention (e.g., George Clooney pleading the

11. *Eds.*—UN Doc. S/RES/1706 (2006); and see note
10.

case of Darfur at the UNSC) and building opposition to the use of force and subsequent military
occupation as in the case of Iraq.

A CONCLUDING NOTE

In seeking accountability for gross violations
of human rights through the existing international legal mechanisms, the role of geopolitics
and the uneven distribution of global power persist as vexing. Problems of victors' justice and
double standards continue, therefore, to undermine a consistent application of international
law. Meanwhile, however, civil society is seeking
to increase the ethical and political relevance of
international law by illuminating its geopolitical
manipulation and by forming its own parallel
institutions that focus on the criminality of the
strong and the victimization of the weak. There
remain many obstacles on the long road to global
justice, but beginning to take place is at least
some clearing of the geopolitical debris, by which
I mean the opportunistic reliance on law when
it serves the interests of the powerful and victorious, and its determined avoidance and suppression whenever it restrains or censures their
behavior. Until international law has the capacity to treat equals equally the corrective checks
of progressive civil society are a vital ingredient
of a jurisprudence of conscience despite their
lack of governmental legitimacy. The tragedy of
Syria since 2011 illuminates all of these disquiet-
ing features of world order: political paralysis
due to antagonistic regional and international
alignments; contradictory perceptions of the legality, feasibility, and effects of intervention; distrust among leading states arising from the
experience of prior humanitarian interventions.
To be incapable of stopping such atrocities as
have been repeatedly committed in Syria exposes the toxic side of the Westphalian framework of world order and the urgent need to
affirm the premises of a jurisprudence of conscience in support of humane and sustainable
planetary governance.

QUESTIONS FOR REFLECTION AND DISCUSSION

1. What does Falk mean by "Jurisprudence of Conscience"? How and why does the "Jurisprudence of Conscience" supported by Falk differ from the current state of affairs in international law?

2. Falk argues that "Both the search for accountability and the uses of humanitarian intervention reveal certain core discrepancies in the international legal order." What are they and how are they signaled?

3. To what extent do you agree that "law is always expected to push toward consistency of application as a condition of its legitimacy"? Do you think that there is any principled justification for the application of "double standards" as between nations with differing ideologies in international law? What might such justifications be? What do such justifications assume? What do they undermine?

4. Do you agree with Falk that "the dropping of atomic bombs on Hiroshima and Nagasaki were 'crimes' that should have been investigated and prosecuted if the tribunals had been truly 'legal' in the sense of imposing individual accountability on both victors and vanquished for their combat operations"? Why? Why not?

5. What, in your view, has more power on the international legal plane, law or politics? What would Falk say?

6. What does Falk mean by his claim that the "split notion of accountability as between winners and losers" remains descriptive of the current implementation of international criminal law? What evidence does Falk adduce in support of this claim? Can you think of any further evidence that either supports or undermines his contention?

7. Falk argues that the "dual pattern of criminal accountability that cannot be fully reconciled with law or legitimacy has given rise to several reformist efforts, both progressive and regressive." To what does he refer?

8. Falk argues that "no issue in global civil society since the end of the Cold War has been more divisive than the morality, legality, and politics of humanitarian intervention." What dilemmas and challenges does such a situation give rise to? How might these be addressed?

9. What, in your view, constitutes humanitarian intervention? A speech in the UN critical of another country's treatment of its own or other citizens? A transboundary radio or television broadcast for the same purpose? The termination of diplomatic relations in protest of mistreatment of citizens or others? A trade embargo? Deployment of armed forces to the nation's border? Where do you draw the definitional line, and why?

10. Does the requirement for UN Security Council Resolutions to be unanimous hinder the UN mission? According to the UN Charter, under what circumstances is the use of force legal? Was the U.S.- and British-led intervention into Kosovo legal? Was it legitimate? Was it justified? Why not? Why and on what basis?

11. Is a legal system in which an action is simultaneously legal yet illegitimate a coherent one? Why? Why not? What does your answer imply about the relationships between law and morality, or law and justice? Is your answer theoretically coherent? And with which theory of the relationship between law and justice/law and morality or law, justice, and morality?

12. What is the current status of the "responsibility to protect" doctrine?

13. What, if anything, in your view, do civil society initiatives, such as the 2005 World Tribunal on Iraq, contribute to respect for human rights? And how? What evidence can you offer in support of your views?

33. ANNA GREAR AND BURNS H. WESTON *Human Rights Accountability in Domestic Courts: Corporations and Extraterritoriality*

The universalism at the heart of International Human Rights Law (IHRL) is, in aspiration at least, well known and much vaunted. However, the concept of universalism (quite apart from critiques of its insufficient inclusivity in both theory and practice) suffers from a key and problematic imbalance: the concept recognizes individual and group claims to the universal enjoyment of human rights (albeit in limited fashion), but scarcely at all the imposition of meaningful corresponding obligations to honor human rights and be held accountable for their violation. This imbalance is especially troubling in the contemporary neoliberal world order in which powerful "private actors"—transnational corporations (TNCs)[1]—violate individual and group rights, often extensively, but with relative impunity because the state, especially the industrialized state, now often tends to diminish its historically assumed role as human rights duty bearer par excellence to favor *realpolitik* corporate agendas that typically are beyond the capacity of the vast majority of human rights claimants to influence, let alone countermand.

Human rights observance and accountability is in any case extremely precarious. As Costas Douzinas puts it, the "age of human rights" has been marked by "more violations of [human rights] principles than any of the previous and less 'enlightened' epochs."[2] Thus, while human rights principles are celebrated as a globally triumphant meta-ethic[3]—the "world-wide secular religion"

(Elie Wiesel[4]); "the essential . . . touchstone, the creed of humanity that surely sums up all other creeds directing human behavior" (Nadine Gordimer[5])—the last almost seventy-five years reveal unprecedented levels of human brutality and precarity and unevenly imposed risk and vulnerability—painfully marked, it must be emphasized, by massacres, genocides, and ethnic cleansings, unprecedented levels of excoriating poverty and stark inequalities between the Global North and Global South (due in no small measure to the historically rapacious colonial empires of the North). Meanwhile, climate change intensifies pressures upon even the most widely recognized human rights as the state increasingly imposes security measures on its own populations in response to messianic terrorism and projected climate-related social instabilities (actual and projected), while systemic and systematically produced inequalities in the foundations of world order generate food insecurity and mass privation.

The state, it is clear, is often complicit in one or more of these radical and uneven impositions of suffering. But it is also clear that the international human rights system design is itself a contributory factor, providing the state with easily manipulated levels of obligation, turning on the nature of the rights at stake, the identities of the alleged violator and claimed victim (including but not limited to their nationalities), the place of violation, and other such variables. Typically, these considerations are said to be neutral as between plaintiffs and defendants. In reality, however, they tend to serve more the interests of the rich and powerful than they do the "ordinary" person—often, indeed, to the harsh detriment of vast numbers of people.

That these manipulable levels of state obligation can be and often are used to block human rights accountability for extraterritorial violations

Excerpted with changes by permission of Oxford University Press from Anna Grear and Burns H. Weston, "The Betrayal of Human Rights and the Urgency of Universal Corporate Accountability: Reflections on a Post-*Kiobel* Lawscape," *Human Rights Law Review* (2015): 1–24. Copyright © 2015 Anna Grear and Burns H. Weston. The authors gratefully acknowledge Damian F. Bakula, research assistant to Professor Weston, for invaluable help at the outset of this initiative.

1. Also called "multinational corporations" (MNCs).
2. Costas Douzinas, *The End of Human Rights: Critical Legal Thought at the Turn of the Century* (Oxford: Hart, 2000).
3. See Michael Ignatieff, *Human Rights as Politics and Idolatry* (Princeton, N.J.: PUP, 2001).

4. Elie Wiesel, "A Tribute to Human Rights," in Yael Danieli et al., eds., *The Universal Declaration of Human Rights: Fifty Years and Beyond* (Amityville, N.Y.: Baywood, 1999), 3, cited by Ignatieff, *Human Rights as Politics and Idolatry*, note 3, 53.
5. Nadine Gordimer, "Reflections by Nobel Laureates" in Danieli et al., eds., *The Universal Declaration of Human Rights*, cited by Ignatieff, *Human Rights as Politics and Idolatry*, note 3, 53.

of human rights comes, therefore, as no surprise—a matter of pivotal importance in a globalized world order dominated by state/market interests. It is incontrovertible that the state, with diverse bases of power at its disposal, not only can impact significantly the rights of individuals and groups far beyond its territorial borders but also via agile doctrinal maneuvering, can escape legal responsibility beyond those limits, both for itself and for favored others who, but for that maneuvering, should be held accountable for human rights violations abroad. Unsurprisingly, in academic circles, in a growing number of national and international decision-making bodies, and elsewhere in the worldwide struggle for global justice, the conviction is mounting that the logics limiting responsibility for extraterritorial human rights abuses are no longer apt—that they are, indeed, *subversive* of the quintessential claim that human rights are universal in character and to be treated as such whenever and wherever they are threatened or denied. Increasingly it is being asked why national citizenship should have anything to do with limiting the enjoyment of *universal* human rights. The question is acute: since when and by whom has it been determined that *citizens'* rights are the equivalent of, or substitute for, *human* rights?

In this short space, we cannot hope to capture all the conditions and permutations that bear upon the implementation of universal human rights in domestic decision-making settings. We can and do challenge, however, the use of "procedural" issues to exempt powerful corporate actors from accountability for human rights abuses committed beyond a state's recognized jurisdiction—a use made especially prominent by the 2013 U.S. Supreme Court holding in *Kiobel v. Royal Dutch Petroleum Co.* pursuant to which, by most interpretations, foreign corporations were largely if not completely accorded immunity from U.S. pursuit of human rights violations against foreign nationals in foreign countries.[6] In so ruling, it seems to many, the Court closed down, prima facie at least, a much favored strategy of human rights litigation aimed at establishing extraterritorial human rights accountability.[7]

Thus we ask, what is the relationship between human rights betrayal and human rights accountability in the post-*Kiobel* "lawscape"? Has the time now arrived for the imposition of mandatory, universal human rights accountability for TNCs ? We argue that it has, and not least because human rights themselves are being narrowly re-interpreted in national fora as values dependent for their meaning and realization upon a corporate global order. At the same time, however, given the nature of TNC juridical dominance and the ideological hegemony of neoliberal capitalism, we remain deeply aware of the contingent nature of our project, and therefore urge continuous vigilance of those forces that would seek to prevent its realization.

TRANSNATIONAL CORPORATIONS (TNCS) AND EXTRATERRITORIALITY

TNCs—despite, or perhaps even because of, their identification as private sector actors—possess immense and increasing levels of state-like power in the national and international political economies of the present world order. Propelled by the ideological ascendency of neoliberalism, they dominate virtually the entire international legal order, influencing key international institutions and gaining inordinate structural control.[8] It is well known that the power of some TNCs has for some time exceeded the power of many states, and that it includes a complex interaction with the neoliberal state, particularly in the Global North, and which in any case is profoundly implicated in the genesis of this extensive TNC control. Indeed, as Ellen Woods rightly points out, state power is *indispensible* to the conditions of accumulation for capital and that it is the state itself that has provided the "conditions enabling global capital to survive and navigate the world."[9]

6. *Kiobel v. Royal Dutch Petroleum Co.*, 133 S.Ct. 1659 (2013).
7. See, e.g., "Agora: Reflections on *Kiobel*: Excerpts from the *American Journal of International Law* and *AJIL Unbound*," AJIL 107 (2013): 601–863.

8. That corporations dominate the entire global order is widely accepted by theorists of globalization as the defining phenomenon of the global age. See, e.g., Ronen Shamir, "Corporate Social Responsibility: A Case of Hegemony and Counter-Hegemony," in Boaventura de Sousa Santos and César A. Rodríguez-Garavito, eds., *Law and Globalisation from Below: Towards a Cosmopolitan Legality* (Cambridge: Cambridge University Press 2005), 92.
9. Ellen Meiksins Woods, *Empire of Capital* (London: Verso, 2005), 139.

TNCs, then, exercise immense influence over the material, economic, and political lives of millions of human beings, and over the life chances of other species and ecosystems generally—a reality sharply etched in the the 1984 Bhopal disaster in India, where the negligence of a U.S. company, Union Carbide, resulted in the deaths of thousands of people, injury of hundreds of thousands of people and animals, and extensive environmental damage. In light of this haunting tragedy and of widespread human and environmental abuse at the hands of TNCs and other corporate actors, the need of individuals, groups, and states to be able to assert extraterritorial jurisdiction to hold globally powerful corporate human rights violators to account is now incontrovertible. It also is urgent. As Upendra Baxi has observed, there is a pressing need for the tragedy of Bhopal (and of other rights-violating disasters resulting from corporate malfeasance or negligence) to provoke law into responding directly[10] and for law to follow a deeply ethical impulse by offering a supportive response to the increasingly vocal social movements emerging from the ashes of such violations. Baxi puts the challenge succinctly and with great poignancy: "the continuing movement of the Bhopal-violated beckons a new jurisprudence of human solidarity in a runaway globalizing world."[11] Whether, in domestic courts and elsewhere, IHRL will now develop as Baxi urges—and thereby help to redress the imbalances generated by "predatory globalization" (to borrow from Richard Falk[12])—is precisely the question haunting this present reflection.

The contemporary globalized world challenges multiple, settled assumptions of the existing Westphalian international legal order—among them, to significant degree, an almost sacred commitment to the core Westphalian principle of state territorial sovereignty which, among other things, assumes that any particular state is capable of controlling the activities of entities operating from within its jurisdictional boundaries. The problem is, however, that the contemporary realities of globalization directly refute this assumption. Multiple powerful corporate entities are quite simply capable of operating across borders in ways that transcend the regulatory control of any one state. The fundamental discrepancy between the transnational nature of these powerful entities and the territorially limited assumptions of the traditional state-centric international human rights system has therefore provoked a growing number of scholars and others to argue that the discrepancy presents a profound impediment to effective human rights accountability in the corporate sector. Indeed, as Janet Dine points out, multiple studies now suggest that TNCs should be subject to direct human rights and environmental duties—that is, "they should have responsibilities towards the planet and to stakeholders other than shareholders."[13] We share this conviction.

Despite the cogency of such arguments, however, and despite the egregious nature of some of the corporate human rights violations inspiring them, TNCs are at present under no direct, formally binding human rights obligations under international law except insofar as a TNC act might constitute an international crime. Nor does international law explicitly impose obligations on home states to regulate the extraterritorial conduct of TNCs headquartered within their territory. Under IHRL, the obligation of the state is to respect, protect, and fulfill the human rights of individuals within its territorial jurisdiction; and while the obligation to *protect* includes the obligation to exercise due diligence to prevent or mitigate the acts of private actors (including corporations) from violating the human rights of individuals, this obligation, too, is limited by territorial jurisdictional limits. In short, but for some essentially voluntarist and self-monitoring standards for TNCs and other business enterprises which sometimes are held out as solutions, there is in IHRL an almost complete absence of any effective way of holding corporations directly accountable for human rights abuses, or of preventing such abuses or even of ensuring redress for the victims of such abuses.

This lack of a clear, direct international law obligation to regulate the overseas activities of TNCs and other business enterprises is at least

10. Upendra Baxi, "Writing About Impunity and Environment: The 'Silver Jubilee' of the Bhopal Catastrophe," *JHRE* 1, 1 (2010): 23–44, 44.
11. Ibid.
12. Richard Falk, *Predatory Globalization: A Critique* (Cambridge: Polity, 1999).

13. Janet Dine, "Jurisdictional Arbitrage by Multinational Companies: A National Law Solution?" *JHRE* 3, 1 (2012): 44–69, 45.

partially responsible for a collection of alternative legal strategies and standards intent on corporate good behavior: the due diligence requirements of export credit agencies, corporate and securities disclosure regulations, whistleblowing laws, contractual duties, tort and criminal laws, sanctions legislation, and the like. However, none of these options are directed specifically at the problem of transnational corporate accountability for human rights abuse; and in any case, as we shall see, the extraterritorial dimension of state responsibility to protect human rights, even deploying such alternative strategies, remains abundantly contested—and unsatisfying.

Straightforwardly put, the current situation is this: the regulation of TNCs (as well as other business enterprises) operating abroad is left largely to the legal systems of the states in which they operate, not the law of their "home" state or *siège social*. Highly problematic, however, is the plain fact that the states in which TNCs operate are frequently developing states which, for lack of effective administrative, judicial, and policing institutions and mechanisms or because of a widespread culture of corruption (frequently encouraged by TNC management), are commonly unable or unwilling to regulate TNC conduct effectively. Also problematic are complex "conditionality" packages issued by international financial institutions such as the International Monetary Fund (IMF) and World Bank and favoring a trading partner from the Global North in a way that effectively lowers human rights and environmental protection standards. Indeed, the few countries in the Global South that have attempted to reject neoliberal strictures have been effectively forced by Western funding bodies to relent. Further, the IMF and World Bank have most pressured precisely those marginalized societies where poverty is most rife—insisting upon such "structural adjustments" as deregulation, privatization, and the removal of protective policies difficult if not impossible for the affected populations to endure. Structural patterns and practices such as these raise troubling questions about the degree to which the IMF, World Bank, and also the World Trade Organization (WTO) and other international trade organizations, have become "midwives" to the neoliberal order of power (the WTO rules having been extensively influenced by corporations and thus described by some as a formalization of global corporate power).

In short, there exists at present a severe accountability gap when it comes to holding corporate entities legally responsible for human rights abuses they commit or facilitate. Leaving TNC regulation to the legal systems of states in which TNCs operate is no guarantee of human rights protection whatsoever or even of respect for basic human rights standards. Mainstream strategies remain overwhelmingly voluntaristic and over-friendly to corporate interests, and globally no adequate accountability structure yet exists.

What is more, the accountability gap is compounded by the sheer complexity and elusiveness of the transnational corporate form itself. It is well known that corporations are fictions invented by national law, "legal persons" granted a juridical existence separate from their executives and shareholders who, as a result, enjoy "limited liability" shielded by a "corporate veil." In the case of the TNC, however, new levels of complexity emerge. TNCs are complicated interlocking layers of corporate entities which present a structural complexity that makes accountability extremely difficult to construct, granting TNCs a juridical elusiveness jealously guarded by those who gain from TNC privileging in the global order. TNCs gain their immense power not only from the law's failure to take into account the material distinctions between kinds of persons, but also from the law's failure to "account [for] the reality of the accumulation of power represented by a large number of companies related by interlocking shareholdings."[14]

When such corporate complexity combines with the international law doctrine of sovereign state equality and overblown assumptions about the power of the state to hold corporations to account, the problem of extraterritorial accountability emerges with a particular *rigueur*. The juridical complexity of the TNC and its protean ability to evade jurisdictional accountability, in a complex and densely interwoven global order especially, clearly limits the state's ability to hold TNCs accountable and profoundly reduces the possibilities of redress for corporate human rights violations.

In the post-*Kiobel* lawscape, what hope, then, can still be found in the doctrine of universal jurisdiction and under the U.S. Alien Tort Claims Act?

14. Ibid., 46.

THE DOCTRINE OF UNIVERSAL
JURISDICTION AND THE U.S. ALIEN TORT
CLAIMS ACT (ATCA)

Despite the sanctity of state sovereignty under international law and consequent limitations on extraterritorial liability, it has long been recognized that certain international crimes can give rise to "universal jurisdiction," a grant to every state of legal authority to apply international law to certain violations of the "law of nations" even if the state in question had no connection to the violation when it occurred. This point is important for present purposes. The original—and archetypal—universal jurisdiction offense is piracy, the prime example of a violation of the law of nations.[15] All states can enforce the prohibition against piracy as a matter of universal jurisdiction. In the words of eighteenth-century common law scholar William Blackstone, piracy is incontestably "an offence against the universal law of society."[16] It is via this relatively narrow aperture of legal doctrine that human rights advocates have sought to deploy creative arguments for extraterritorial accountability.

Fundamentally, universal jurisdiction operates today as it did at its origin: as an authoritative mandate to enforce existing international law against an act deemed offensive to the law of nations—an offence so profound that the offender is rendered *hostis humani generis*: "an enemy of all mankind."[17] The exercise of universal jurisdiction, it should be understood, is not the same as a state applying its own law to another state, but the limitations hindering the extraterritorial application of IHRL have led to creative approaches using *national* law, not IHRL, to establish liability for human rights harms extraterritorially inflicted. There exists, however, one notable albeit indirect and unique excep-

tion: when the national legislation authorizes resort to "the law of nations" as a source of law for decision, then human rights norms accepted as customary international law, part of the law of nations (as well as core components of IHRL), may be invoked for the rule of decision. The paradigmatic example of this exception is of course the well-known statute unique to the United States known as the Alien Tort Claims Act (ATCA),[18] also called the Alien Tort Statute (ATS). Originally enacted during the first session of the First U.S. Congress as section 9 of the Judiciary Act of 1789 (establishing the Federal Judiciary) primarily to protect against piracy, it has for more than three decades been deployed by litigants to overcome the limitations burdening the extraterritorial application of universal human rights doctrines, principles, and rules, beginning in 1980 when, in *Filártiga v. Peña-Irala*,[19] the U.S. Second Circuit Court of Appeals decided—for the first time in modern times—in favor of foreign human rights claimants based on the ACTA.

THE ALIEN TORT CLAIMS ACT (ATCA)

Since *Filártiga*, the United States has proved magnetically attractive to foreign litigants, although not least because of important procedural advantages in using U.S. courts—for example, the possibility of contingency fees. Providing that "The district courts [of the United States] shall have original jurisdiction of any civil action by an alien for a tort only, committed in violation of the law of nations or a treaty of the United States," this statute, for many years after *Filártiga*, has been judicially interpreted to allow foreign citizens to seek civil (tort) remedies in U.S. courts for human rights violations committed outside the Unites States, thus enabling non-U.S. litigants to present "unique substantive causes of action against [TNCs] that . . . breached their human rights."[20] Particularly noteworthy is the language used in the Second Circuit judgment, echoing the early development of the doctrine of universal jurisdiction in the context of piracy. The court famously stated: "for purposes of civil liability, the torturer has become—like

15. See, e.g., *The Paquete Habana, The Lola*, 175 U.S. 677 (1900).
16. William Blackstone, *Commentaries on the Laws and Constitution of England* 4 (Oxford: Clarendon, 1769), Ch. 5, III/71.
17. A legal term of art that originated in admiralty law, such that maritime pirates and slave traders were held to be beyond legal protection, subject to arrest, prosecution, conviction, and punishment by any state even if that state had not been directly attacked. Under contemporary public international law, the doctrine of universal jurisdiction now applies also to torturers and perpetrators of other crimes against humanity.

18. 28 U.S.C. § 1350.
19. *Filártiga v. Peña-Irala*, 603 F 2d 876 (2d Cir. 1980).
20. Sarah Joseph, *Corporations and Transnational Human Rights Litigation* (Oxford: Hart, 2004), 16.

the pirate and slave trader before him—*hostis humani generis,* an enemy of all mankind."[21]

Filártiga concerned, as is well known, not a corporation but a former Paraguayan police inspector-general who had tortured and killed a member of the Filártiga family. But the authority that issued from *Filártiga* was widely celebrated among human rights activists—heralded as a "beacon of hope"[22] by those who welcomed the ATCA "revival" as a powerful way of challenging corporate human rights abuses. Indeed, the vast majority of TNC human rights litigation has arisen in U.S. courts pursuant to this domestic legislation. Over time, particularly in the 1990s, numerous cases involving corporate human rights abuses began to come before the U.S. courts, gradually evolving into an application of the universal jurisdiction doctrine enabling U.S. courts to hold corporate actors accountable in tort for human rights abuses committed far beyond U.S. jurisdictional borders.

Perhaps predictably, however, this was a trajectory that, at the hands of a more conservative ideology and politics (and therefore the appointment of more conservative jurists) was ultimately to be significantly challenged—as indeed it was in *Kiobel* 2010 by the U.S. Second Circuit Court of Appeals (the same though differently composed court that decided *Filártiga*)—and later in *Kiobel* 2013 by the U.S. Supreme Court in what many commentators have regarded as a particularly retrogressive ruling. It is to these two decisions in *Kiobel v. Royal Dutch Petroleum Co.*[23] that we now turn.

KIOBEL IN 2010: A DEAD END FOR HUMAN RIGHTS ACTIVISTS?

The facts of *Kiobel* fully reflect the fundamental concerns of the litigation trend that took off under ATCA in the 1990s against claimed TNC human rights abuses. The case exemplifies the widespread visceral sense of injustice that instances of corporate human rights violation evoke the world over.

The relevant events took place in Ogoniland, Nigeria, an oil-rich region of the Niger Delta intensively exploited for its oil reserves by Shell Oil (a subsidiary of Royal Dutch Shell) beginning in 1956, now a location synonymous with corporate human rights violations epitomizing the "justice problem which arises when a repressive regime, extractable natural resources, transnational corporate interests, and a vulnerable population collide."[24] Between 1990 and 1993, in light of extensive environmental damage, including the negative health effects of gas flaring and damage wreaked by repeated oil spills (reportedly 2,976, or 2.1 million barrels in 1976–1991), Ogoniland residents rose up in nonviolent protest. The Nigerian government, however, reacted violently. Several Ogoni leaders were murdered—nine in particular, known as the "Ogoni 9" (including now world-famous Ken Saro-Wiwa). All were arrested on trumped up charges, brought to trial, sentenced to death, and, in 1995, executed. The trial, widely considered a travesty of justice, exposed not only the repressive nature of the Nigerian regime at the time, but the extensive and rights-violating complicity of the TNCs operating in Ogoniland—particularly Shell. Ken Saro-Wiwa's death, deemed by many to be a judicial murder, also gained rapid and widespread international condemnation.

Several lawsuits were initiated in the U.S. against individuals and entities related to Royal Dutch Shell. *Kiobel,* brought under the ATCA, was one of them. The complaint alleged that the Royal Dutch Petroleum Company (incorporated in the Netherlands), Shell Transport and Trading Company (incorporated in England), and Shell Petroleum Development Company of Nigeria (incorporated in Nigeria) aided and abetted extrajudicial killings, torture, and commission of crimes against humanity and other human rights violations by the Nigerian military. The corporate defendants, it was alleged,

> provided logistical support, transportation and weapons to Nigerian authorities to attack Ogoni villages and stifle opposition to Shell's oil-excavation activities. Ogoni residents were beaten, raped, shot and/or killed during

21. *Filártiga,* 890.
22. Earthrights, Press Release, 29 June 2004, cited by Dine, "Jurisdictional Arbitrage," 52.
23. The is available at 621 F.3d 111, 123–24 (2d Cir. 2010). The Supreme Court decision of 17 April 2013 is available at 133 S.Ct. 1659 (2013).

24. Hari M. Osofsky, "Climate Change and Environmental Justice: Reflections on Litigation Over Oil Extraction and Rights Violations in Nigeria," *JHRE* 2, 1 (2010): 189–210, 192.

these raids. In 1995, Ken Saro-Wiwa and John Kpuinen were notoriously hanged after being convicted of murder by a special tribunal in the course of which Royal Dutch Shell allegedly bribed witnesses, conspired with Nigerian authorities to orchestrate the trial, and offered to free Ken Saro-Wiwa in return for an end to [his organization's] international protests against Shell. During the trial, members of Ken Saro-Wiwa's family, including his elderly mother, were beaten.[25]

Esther Kiobel was one of the plaintiffs—her husband, Dr. Barinem Kiobel, having been executed in 1995 for his nonviolent protest alongside Ken Saro-Wiwa.

In 2010, a majority of the U.S. Second Circuit Court of Appeals ruled that, because the scope of liability in an ATCA suit is determined by customary international law and because "no corporation has ever been subject to any form of liability (whether civil or criminal) under the customary international law of human rights," corporate liability "is not a discernable—much less universally recognized—norm of customary international law that we may apply pursuant to [ATCA]."[26] The plaintiffs' claims were accordingly dismissed for lack of subject matter jurisdiction. The grounds for optimism about an ATCA revival vis-à-vis TNC accountability had reached, it seemed, something of a dead end.

Dine, however, argues that much of the hubris surrounding the ATCA "revival" was misplaced in the first place, despite its value in revealing "how complex extraterritorial claims are, how difficult it is to sue TNCs and the fact that no matter how 'common sense' the solution appears to outraged human rights and environmental activists, legal solutions remain elusive."[27] She observes that some of the claims advanced by NGOs concerning ATCA at its high point were of doubtful reliability and unduly optimistic. Most of the cases were in any event settled out of court—and the settlements thus obtained under the ATCA were, for Dine, simply a way for TNCs to avoid any formal admission of liability. She writes: "I would argue that it is wrong to call such settlements *victories* because

the law has not been thereby developed to cover the instances of abuse forming the substance of the claim: there is no precedent for the future."[28]

In addition to being critical of the hype surrounding the ATCA as a cause célèbre for human rights progress, Dine is critical of the legislation itself. For her, the ATCA invited an excessively restrictive standard for the substantive ground of a complaint raised under it. In *Kiobel*, the Second Circuit Court found that only very restrictive grounds could be allowed—relying on the U.S. Supreme Court ruling in *Sosa v. Álvarez-Machaín*,[29] a precedent in which the Supreme Court held that claims must be founded on "a norm of international character accepted by the civilized world and defined with a specificity comparable to the features of the 18th Century paradigms we have recognized."[30] Thus, although the ATCA revival did achieve an intensification of TNC reputational risk (as well as some compensation for victims of corporate abuse), *Kiobel* 2010, without overruling *Filártiga*, but by adhering to a restrictive reading of the basis for universal jurisdiction, did appear—to some at least—to narrow the potential cause of action to eighteenth-century standards and thereby produce something of a full stop for twenty-first-century human rights activists long before the Supreme Court ruling of 2013.

Dine's view has considerable resonance when the facts are as clearly pernicious as they were in *Kiobel*. Unmistakably, *Kiobel* 2010 implicated the public-private divide that traditionally has sheltered corporate violations of human rights; a company can be held liable under the ATCA, it appears, if its activity amounts to "state action" in breach of international law. But as Dine argues, *Kiobel* 2010 also reveals "the extent to which the ATCA was a thin thread on which to hang legal accountability for [TNC] violations."[31] Despite the benefit of ATCA cases bringing gross corporate violations of human rights to public attention, she observes, ultimately the litigation strategy centering upon the ATCA diverted attention from the kind of fundamental reforms necessary to change legal regimes comprehensively. Diverting attention from such reforms

---

25. Dine, "Jurisdictional Arbitrage," 54.
26. Judgment of 17 September 2010, note 43, headnote.
27. Dine, "Jurisdictional Arbitrage," 53.

28. Ibid.
29. 542 U.S. 692 (2004).
30. Ibid., 725.
31. Dine, "Jurisdictional Arbitrage," 55.

has, moreover, proved beneficial to the violating TNCs, as human rights activists have spent energy fighting on a difficult and somewhat flimsy platform rather than concentrating on changing the rules of IHRL to establish that companies can be human rights violators and to provide mechanisms for holding them to account.[32]

At any rate, despite the apparent disappointment presented by *Kiobel* 2010, the possibility of extraterritorial liability under the ATCA has continued to inspire an industry of argument and commentary. As Ingrid Wuerth recently noted, "After more than thirty years of extensive high-profile litigation along with sustained academic commentary, a large and seemingly ever-growing number of basic questions about [the ATCA] remained unanswered. . . . As lower courts and litigants hacked their way through a thickening jungle of unresolved [ATCA] issues, clarification from Congress or the Supreme Court felt long overdue."[33] That clarification was attempted in 2013 when the U.S. Supreme Court delivered the final *Kiobel* judgment.

KIOBEL IN 2013: CONFIRMING DISAPPOINTMENT?

In 2013, in *Kiobel v. Royal Dutch Petroleum Co.*,[34] the U.S. Supreme Court, in a splintered decision and invoking a canon of statutory interpretation known as the "presumption against extraterritorial application" (when legislation gives no clear contrary mandate), held that "the presumption against extraterritoriality applies to claims under the [ATCA], and that nothing in the statute rebuts that presumption"[35]—a conclusion reached apparently without heed to the ACTA's express directive to apply "the law of nations" (including such IHRL norms as are accepted as customary international law). At the same time, the Court suggested that claims arising from conduct outside the United States could be actionable under the ATCA "where the claims touch and concern the territory of the United States . . . with suffi-

cient force to displace the presumption against extraterritorial application."[36]

According to Burns Weston, "informed observers responding to *Kiobel* [2013] appear generally to have agreed upon at least four implications of the Court's reasoning:"[37]

(1) that foreign corporations would . . . be largely, if not completely, insulated from [U.S.] "prosecution" under the [ATCA] for human rights violations committed against foreign nationals in foreign countries, (2) that [U.S.] corporations would not be so insulated, (3) that the development of litigation in Europe and elsewhere outside the United States would be affected by [*Kiobel*] only slightly, if at all; and (4) that the applicability of [*Kiobel*] to foreign natural persons, never addressed by the court, was uncertain.[38]

The Supreme Court's decision was definitive in one centrally important respect: that the presumption against extraterritoriality applies to the ATCA. On the facts presented to it, the Supreme Court held that the presumption was not overcome because the relevant conduct took place within the territory of a foreign sovereign and because the claims did not sufficiently "touch and concern" U.S. territory; the foreign defendants (Dutch Shell Petroleum) had no more than a "corporate presence" in the United States. For Vivian Grosswald Curran and David Sloss, the decision "apparently [sounded] the death knell for 'foreign-cubed' human rights claims under the [ATCA]—that is, cases in which foreign defendants committed human rights abuses against foreign plaintiffs in foreign countries [and that] the Court's decision overrules, *sub silentio*, a line of cases that originated with *Filártiga v. Peña-Irala*."[39] In the words of Julian G. Ku, "All nine justices rejected decades of lower-court precedent and widespread scholarly opinion when they held that [the ATCA] excluded cases involving purely extraterritorial conduct, even if the alleged conduct constituted acts that are uni-

32. Ibid.
33. Ingrid Wuerth, *"Kiobel v. Royal Dutch Petroleum Co.: The Supreme Court and the Alien Tort Statute," AJIL* 107 (2014): 601–21, 602.
34. Second Circuit ruling of 17 September 2010.
35. Ibid., 1669.
36. Ibid.
37. Burns H. Weston, "Human Rights: International Human Rights in Domestic Courts," *Encyclopaedia Britannica Online* (2013) (accessed 20 September 2014).
38. Ibid.
39. Vivian Grosswald Curran & David Sloss, "Reviving Human Rights Litigation After *Kiobel*," 107 *AJIL* 107 (2014): 858–63, 858.

versally proscribed under international law."[40] For Ku, this amounted to nothing short of the unanimous rejection in *Kiobel* of universal jurisdiction, a conclusion which, while possibly overstated, drives at the importance of the decision for the hopes (misplaced hopes, Dine would argue) of human rights activists and litigants seeking to use the ATCA as a strategic route toward extraterritorial corporate human rights accountability and, ultimately, universal jurisdiction over at least gross human rights violations committed by corporations abroad.

Not surprisingly, given the enormity of the stakes at hand, the issue of corporate liability attracted a range of submissions from multiple *amici*. The Court received statements from governments (Argentina, Germany, the Netherlands, the UK, and the United States), the European Commission, NGOs, scholars, and—of course—corporations. Since the Court's central holding was that alleged corporate malfeasance must "touch and concern the territory of the United States" with "sufficient force" in order to displace the presumption against extraterritoriality, logically the Court had to address that issue directly if it was to do justice to the question of corporate liability at all. Protective of corporate functioning among other interests, one may assume, the Court reasoned that, since corporations are often "present" in many countries, "corporate presence" alone is insufficient to displace the presumption.

Perhaps from a corporate perspective the implications of *Kiobel* concerning extraterritorial corporate liability may seem clear. But this would be misleading. First, the Court did not address the question of corporate liability under the ATCA directly, and notwithstanding that it was because of this concern that it granted *certiorari* in the first place. Second, the Court's stated rationales for its decision—the minimization of "international friction" and related separation-of-powers concerns—have been judged unpersuasive by informed legal scholars or, in any event, as insufficient to justify eliding more than three decades of established ATCA precedent. Third, as Wuerth argues, the "opinions arguably assume the viability of [the ATCA] suits against

corporations,"[41] thus leaving the door open to such actions albeit in an ambivalent manner. Wuerth comments: "Not surprisingly, [the] ambiguities in the majority opinion have already generated spirited commentary on what *Kiobel* will mean for future ATS cases. The blogospheric spin is well under way."[42]

There are many other aspects to the *Kiobel* 2013 holding. Prominently exposed and debated from a range of perspectives under the auspices of the *American Journal of International Law* published in 2013,[43] they reflect, among other things, the inevitable complexities implicated by the position of the ATCA at the nexus of profoundly competitive political concerns—a fractious space between impulses of outrage concerning extraterritorial corporate human rights violations and political anxieties concerning the foreign policy costs accruing to an overly "interventionist" U.S. in a world of ostensibly juridically equal sovereign states. In any case, *Kiobel* 2013 appears to have generated as much intense debate as that which preceded it. It seems, therefore, that it would be overly simplistic and premature to claim that *Kiobel* has definitively settled matters.

Does *Kiobel* signal (and entrench) a disappointing death knell for such transnational human rights litigation strategies? And if it does, does it matter as much as some human rights activists and scholars appear to think?

ASSESSING *KIOBEL* AND ATCA IN GLOBAL CONTEXT

First, it is not at all clear that *Kiobel* signals the death knell for ATCA litigation for corporate human rights abuses outside the territorial jurisdiction of the United States. Ralph Steinhardt, for example, argues that, appearances to the contrary, the 2013 judgment "adopts a rhetoric of caution without foreclosing litigation that fits the *Filártiga* model."[44] Indeed, the case invites more ATCA litigation precisely *because* so many issues remain unresolved and because "what is

---

40. Julian G. Ku, "*Kiobel* and the Surprising Death of Universal Jurisdiction Under the Alien Tort Statute," *AJIL* 107 (2014): 835–41, 835.

41. Wuerth, "*Kiobel v. Royal Dutch Petroleum Co.,*" 609.
42. Ibid.
43. "Agora: Reflections on *Kiobel.*"
44. Ralph G. Steinhardt, "*Kiobel* and the Weakening of Precedent: A Long Walk for a Short Drink," *AJIL* 107 (2014): 841–45, 841.

law in *Kiobel* isn't clear and what is clear in *Kiobel* isn't law."[45] In short, *Kiobel* 2013 fails to offer solid precedent, and additionally breaks with precedent by forging (on dubious doctrinal grounds) a "new presumption" of uncertain application. The answer to our first question, then—whether *Kiobel* signals a disappointing death knell for transnational ATCA litigation strategies—surely must be "not necessarily." The door is left ajar. But, as noted above, the ATCA route may be, in any case, a distraction from more direct and productive modes of corporate human rights accountability. Although we can see the symbolic, rhetorical, and juridical potency of the ATCA despite its falling short of delivering meaningful corporate accountability, we share the increasingly widespread conviction that direct corporate liability for human rights violations is now overdue, especially in the light of the pervasive structural dominance of TNCs and the present-day ideological hegemony of neoliberalism.

Second, to assess *Kiobel* accurately, in particular its ambiguity relative to remedies for extraterritorial corporate human rights abuse, it is important that it and the ATCA be viewed in comparative law perspective—particularly since, as Robert McCorquodale points out, "the case law in the rest of the world is unlikely to be greatly affected by the ruling."[46] McCorquodale reaches this conclusion based largely on his analysis of European Union regulations and civil law cases and on the fact that the vast majority of non-U.S. TNCs are based in Europe—a fact that alone suggests that U.S. legislation and jurisprudence is unlikely to be the last word for Europeans, least of all on so important an issue. Indeed, a range of approaches has been taken across the EU, enabling litigants to bring corporations before national courts for extraterritorial human rights violations. Like the ATCA litigation, however, these cases do not put such violations directly in human rights terms. Instead, like the ATCA, they tend to deploy other causes of action (including tort) to drive at the harms caused.

EU approaches to corporate accountability for human rights violations in the EU, McCorquodale explains, are affected by two European regulations binding on all EU member states: first, the Brussels I Regulation, which provides that "national courts within the EU have jurisdiction over all who are domiciled in their national jurisdiction" (which for corporations is defined as "the location of a corporation's 'statutory seat,' 'central administration' or 'principal place of business'"[47]); second, the Rome II Regulation, which imposes a uniform rule dictating that the applicable law of a claim shall be the law of the state where the damage occurred, irrespective of where the claim is brought. The implication is that, subject to limited exceptions (which include cases where the law of the state of harm does not effectively protect human rights), the courts in the EU must apply the law of the state where the harm was caused. This means that the court hearing the case imposes neither its own law nor international law on claims that have arisen in the territory of another state—which in turn means that EU states simply do not face the anxieties implied in *Kiobel* relative to the principle of state sovereignty.[48]

Also noteworthy, as McCorquodale points out, is the UK case of *Chandler v. Cape*,[49] which, in a country with long experience in extraterritorial liability questions, establishes the principle that the law can impose upon a parent corporation

> a duty of care in relation to the health and safety of its subsidiary's employees . . . [a ruling that suggests] an increased likelihood that UK courts will consider, in contrast to the *Kiobel* [2013] decision, that a parent corporation domiciled in that state has assumed a duty of care towards third parties affected by the operations of subsidiaries located elsewhere, at least where the parent corporation has developed and implemented group-wide policies and practices.[50]

---

45. Ibid.
46. Robert McCorquodale, "Waving Not Drowning: *Kiobel* Outside the United States," *AJIL* 107 (2014): 846–51, 846.

47. Ibid.
48. Of course, the EU approach is not without its own anxieties. From the standpoint of ensuring genuine human rights protection, relying on the law of the state of harm can be risky. Success depends on the sufficiency of that state's commitment to human rights law and practice and on the adequacy of its legal mechanisms to ensure meaningful accountability. It is possible EU courts would end up applying a low standard of protection.
49. *Chandler v. Cape PLC*, [2012] EWCA (Civ) 525 (Eng.).
50. McCorquodale, "Waving Not Drowning," 848.

McCorquodale emphasizes, additionally, that the UK development of a legal basis for bringing and deciding claims by victims of extraterritorial corporate human rights violations have not relied on cases under the ATCA, a fact rendering *Kiobel* of unlikely relevance for cases brought in the UK.

On final analysis, however, McCorquodale determines that, though the ATCA cases are largely irrelevant to the case law "elsewhere in the world," their human rights aspect retains a submerged relevance.[51] He writes: "none of the violations has been cast directly in human rights terms," but instead "as . . . a claim in tort for negligence or a breach of contract. Even a case involving the alleged torture and mistreatment of indigenous people was brought as a claim in tort for negligent management and as instigating trespass to the persons."[52] This position, like the ATCA case law, simply re-emphasizes the problematic nature of the gap in IHRL concerning direct corporate liability for human rights abuses. Transnational litigation strategies, whether in the United States or beyond, leave certain kinds of human rights abuses unaccounted for.

Perhaps, therefore, in light of this failure, *Kiobel* 2013 reveals its greatest impact in a paradoxically positive way: the ATCA cases signaled that a national court was prepared at least to consider claims against corporations for violations of IHRL. By placing an apparent but ambiguous limit on ATCA-based litigation, *Kiobel* 2013 strengthens the rationales for paying attention to non-ATCA strategies—including non-ATCA litigation strategies. For McCorquodale, "the strength and breadth" of the EU cases might initiate claims outside the United States—including against U.S. corporations—and inspire non-ATCA based actions in the United States also—but non-U.S. litigation will not be significantly affected by the *Kiobel* decision, and the EU trajectory will continue to develop.

This paradoxical circumstance, however, still leaves the problem of the accountability gap in IHRL. Even EU litigation strategies do not address corporate human rights abuses in human rights terms directly. Perhaps, then, *Kiobel* usefully draws attention to the limitations of litiga-

tion strategies *in toto*, and invites fresh engagement with a wide range of nonlitigation strategies—a possibility related to Dine's critique, noted above, of the ATCA as a distraction from more productive, system-critical modes of engagement with the central problem.

A novel and imaginative litigation-related strategy that addresses directly a systemic gap highlighted for a post-*Kiobel* lawscape is offered by Maya Steinitz, who proposes the establishment of an International Court of Civil Justice (ICCJ) with jurisdiction over cross-border torts.[53] This solution, Steinitz suggests, would directly address what she calls the " 'problem of the missing forum."[54] The strategy thus directly responds to the perceived post-*Kiobel* "loss of forum" but leaves unanswered the fundamental gap in IHRL accountability structures that *Kiobel* 2013 so usefully, in our view, reemphasizes.

Various nonlitigation strategies have been proposed as well. Curran and Sloss propose, for example, a legislative response, drawing in part upon pending French legislation and existing German and Belgian law.[55] Their proposed legislative model, they contend, balances the fractious political concerns reflected in the debate surrounding *Kiobel*, because the statutes in Germany and Belgium and the pending legislation in France not only establish the right of victims of genocide, war crimes, and crimes against humanity to initiate judicial proceedings against perpetrators who commit such crimes extraterritorially, but also allow public prosecutors to block such proceedings if they consider that the case would impair the state's foreign policy objectives. In a sense, the Curran and Sloss proposal revives the *Filártiga* approach, but—like that case—does not address human rights violations falling short of the level of action required to trigger universal jurisdiction. Accordingly, their approach cannot embrace a wide range of contemporary and important modes of corporate human rights abuse.

Similarly, Justine Nolan, Michael Posner, and Sarah Labowitz argue that courts are only one among a growing number of routes to remedy

51. Ibid., 850 (emphasis added).
52. *Guerrero v. Monterrico Metals PLC*, [2009] EWHC 2475 (QB) (Eng.).

53. Maya Steinitz, "The Case for an International Court of Civil Justice," *Stanford Law Review Online* 67 (2014): 75–83.
54. Ibid., 77.
55. Curran and Sloss, "Reviving Human Rights Litigation After *Kiobel*," 859.

corporate human rights abuses.[56] They rightly argue that "the role of the U.S. and other courts is only part of an expanding set of remedies and accountability measures that are helping to shape the rules of the road for global companies with respect to human rights."[57] The authors make the case for greater enforcement of stronger labor and workplace health and safety laws and other forms of robust accountability structure in countries where TNCs operate—although also acknowledging, importantly, that this particular strategy is directly affected by "chronic failures in developing a governmental order based on the rule of law."[58] Other strategies listed by the authors include standard-setting by intergovernmental organizations; provisioning of resources by the World Bank; home country reporting requirements and sanctions; and voluntary multi-stakeholder initiatives. From a critical perspective, however, all such approaches would likely share fundamental systemic weaknesses. For example, standard-setting, while desirable, relies on adequate enforcement to become meaningful. Provisioning of international financial resources risks burdensome conditionality measures. Home country approaches (reporting requirements and sanctions) rely entirely for their effectiveness upon adequate degrees of commitment to human rights-based law and practice and upon relevant legal machinery to guarantee meaningful accountability. And voluntary multi-stakeholder initiatives can do much to raise awareness, but run a serious risk, as a wide range of scholarship reveals, of amounting to little more than "corporate blue washing" exercises: when it comes to corporate human rights accountability, voluntarism is, we submit, an insufficiently compelling route towards corporate human rights respect.[59]

TOWARD DIRECT, MANDATORY ACCOUNTABILITY?

Our analysis thus far has suggested that in the post-*Kiobel* 2013 lawscape—just as before it—human rights are inadequately protected in the face of TNC complexity, power and global influence. The various legal strategies deployed to protect human rights by recruiting alternative legal avenues and forms of accountability are ultimately unsatisfying. So we share Dine's fundamental conviction that the time has now come for direct corporate answerability for human rights abuses. And Dine is by no means alone in her conviction. Indeed, pressure is now building for a meaningful intervention under the auspices of the United Nations. On 26 June 2014, at the 26th session of the UN Human Rights Council, a resolution supporting the "elaboration of an international legally binding instrument on Transnational Corporations and Other Business Enterprises with respect to Human Rights" was formally adopted.[60]

However, even as we welcome such an important initiative, we retain a caution, already noted, that suspects the nature of global corporate power and the neoliberal ideological hegemony of the global juridical order. It is by no means certain that mandatory accountability will deliver all that human rights activists and violated communities and individuals might hope for. Since the 1970s at least, TNCs have successfully resisted all UN-based efforts to hold them accountable to human rights standards, including in relation to the draft UN Norms on the Responsibility of Transnational Corporations and other Business Enterprises with Regard to Human Rights.[61] State complicity in the process of TNC resistance is also clearly discernible. In our view, the global juridical order is simply too ideologically skewed to guarantee the kind and level of human rights justice that is so viscerally hoped for across the planet. At the same time, however, we strongly believe that direct human

56. Justine Nolan, Michael Posner, and Sarah Labowitz, "Beyond *Kiobel*: Alternative Remedies for Sustained Human Rights Protection," *AJIL Unbound* e-48, at e-50, 4.
57. Ibid.
58. Ibid.
59. See, e.g., Penelope Simons, "Corporate Voluntarism and Human Rights: The Adequacy and Effectiveness of Voluntary Self-Regulation Regimes," *Relations Industrielles/Industrial Relations* 59 (2004): 101; Simons, "International Law's Invisible Hand and the Future of Corporate Accountability for Violations of Human Rights," *JHRE* 3, 1 (2012): 5–43.

60. UNHRC, Elaboration of an International Legally Binding Instrument on Transnational Corporations and Other Business Enterprises with Respect to Human Rights (A/HRC/26/L.22) adopted 26 June 2014.
61. UNESCOR, Norms on the Responsibilities of Transnational Corporations and Other Business Enterprises with Regard to Human Rights (2003), UN Doc. E/EN 4/Sub. 2/2003/12/Rev. 2.

rights accountability under IHRL, if allowed, would provide an important juridical advance towards fraying corporate human rights *impunity*.

Here we return to a central problem that haunts this analysis: the traditionally state-centered nature of the Westphalian international legal order—including, of course, the traditional state-centric orientation of IHRL—and this suggests that IHRL is ill equipped in structural and ideological terms to hold TNCs directly accountable for human rights abuses. As De Sousa Santos has argued, "the continuation of a state-centric logic in the field of human rights will represent a growing impediment to an efficient and morally decent human rights policy."[62] This challenge becomes even more acute in a situation where states are reconstituted as complexly complicit agents of global neoliberal capitalism. Tony Evans and Alison Ayers argue that the state is now effectively an administrative unit for managing the global economy,[63] whereas Panitch suggests that states should be understood as "the *authors* of a regime that defines and guarantees, through international treaties and constitutional effect, the global and domestic rights of capital."[64]

There is, thus, a genuine risk that TNCs will continue to engineer international human rights norms in their own favor while still largely evading attempts to hold them liable in an IHRL framework; and, in any case, that framework is structurally and ideologically ill suited to the task at this point in time, and therefore unlikely to deliver—even with the important development of a directly applicable duty—sufficiently rigorous forms of corporate human rights accountability. What such a mechanism *could* achieve, however, is an important contribution to the dissolution of corporate human rights impunity by introducing a direct mandatory standard that they have long resisted having imposed upon them. This, in turn, holds out a hope—albeit a

contingent one—of addressing at least some of the structural disadvantages placed upon vulnerable human beings and communities by the public/private divide—a key juridical mechanism of corporate responsibility evasion that would be punctured, at last, by the direct imposition of corporate human rights accountability under IHRL—no matter how imperfectly.

CONCLUSION

Globalization presents a pressing context in which to address the challenges of extraterritoriality and the related complexities of holding TNCs accountable for human rights abuses. Given the fact that a wide range of responses to this urgent challenge is visible beyond the U.S., and given that a range of non-court options is available in both national and international law, it is arguable that the fundamental predicament in the post-*Kiobel* order is, in some ways, no more negative than it was beforehand. There existed, pre-*Kiobel*, a deeply problematic lack of direct, effective corporate accountability for extraterritorial human rights violations. And there remains, post-*Kiobel*, a deeply problematic lack of direct, effective corporate accountability for extraterritorial human rights violations.

So, if it is right to conclude that ATCA litigation was always an over-hyped distraction standing in the way of the search for more useful alternatives, perhaps the greatest virtue of the post-*Kiobel* international order is that this, at least, is now conspicuously apparent. Hopefully the highly contingent and ambiguous "dead end" presented by *Kiobel* offers a vital impetus for continued engagement with the various doctrinal and other issues implicated by the case. Continued engagement in what may be, thanks to *Kiobel*, a fresh opportunity to step beyond the current limitations of national and international legal imagination to challenge the state and corporate sensibilities of a globalized neoliberal world order must be taken very seriously, placed high on global agenda with "the urgency of now." Perhaps then we can move toward the achievement of universal jurisdiction for human rights protection directly.

However, if our analysis is correct, this alone will not be sufficient. Ongoing critical vigilance will be required. When all is said and done—and despite the importance and urgency of achieving

62. Boaventura de Sousa Santos, *Toward a New Legal Common Sense: Law, Globalization and Emancipation* (London: Butterworths, 2002), 267.
63. Tony Evans and Alison J. Ayers, "In the Service of Power: The Global Political Economy of Citizenship and Human Rights," *Citizenship Studies* 10, 3 (Special Issue, January 2006): 289–308, 294.
64. Leo Panitch, *"Rethinking the Role of the State,"* in James H. Mittelman, ed., *Globalization: Critical Reflections* (Boulder, Colo.: Lynne Reiner, 1995), 95 (emphasis added).

direct corporate human rights accountability, there still is reason to doubt that the global community—even when such accountability is established—will ultimately make good on its promise to address human rights violations with true compassion and justice. Although the post-Kiobel lawscape presents an ideal space in which to achieve mandatory corporate accountability under IHRL as a strategic move against contemporary corporate impunity, little real progress is guaranteed until the ideological hegemony currently dominating the international order is overcome. Not until then, we suspect, will the voices of the Bhopal-violated for a "new jurisprudence of human solidarity in a runaway globalizing world" be truly heard.

QUESTIONS FOR REFLECTION AND DISCUSSION

1. Why are TNCs a particularly complex target for international human rights accountability? What factors bear on the problem relative to (a) the nature of TNCs, (b) the characteristics of the international legal order, and (c) international human rights laws and norms? Substantiate your answers as fully and carefully as you can.

2. Grear and Weston's argument clearly implies that human rights are not as universal as they aspire to be. Do you agree? Can you find evidence, in this or in other readings, that supports such a claim? What patterns can you discern in relation to the enforcement and non-enforcement of international human rights? How might such patterns relate to the complexity of holding corporate actors to account for human rights violations? Substantiate your answers as fully and carefully as you can.

3. How do you understand Baxi's phrase, "a new jurisprudence of human solidarity in a runaway globalizing world"? Why might such a movement of human solidarity be particularly timely in the context of globalization? Might globalization itself be seen as a manifestation of such solidarity? Why or why not? Provide evidence/sources in support of your answers.

4. Janet Dine (cited by Grear and Weston) argues that TNCs should be placed under direct human rights and environmental duties—that is, "that they should have responsibilities towards the planet and to stakeholders other than shareholders." Do you agree? Why or why not?

5. What key features of the international legal order explain the "problem of extraterritoriality"?

6. Was *Kiobel* in 2010 a "dead end" for human rights activists? Why? Why not?

7. What, if anything, does the final judgment in *Kiobel* "clarify"? What is left unresolved? Does the lack of resolution matter? Why or why not? And in what sense?

8. Does *Kiobel* signal (and entrench) a disappointing death-knell for transnational human rights litigation strategies? What do Grear and Weston say?

9. Why is the ATCA so important for human rights litigation in the United States?

10. Should states have an obligation to police the activity of TNCs domiciled in their state for conduct occurring outside their state?

11. Is an international approach to human rights enforcement necessary? Is it sufficient to rely on each state to monitor and enforce human rights within their domestic jurisdiction? Why or why not? What do Grear and Weston say?

12. What are the strengths and weaknesses of the EU approach to corporate extraterritorial liability for human rights abuses?

13. What are the relative strengths and weaknesses of corporate accountability approaches based on (a) litigation strategies; (b) legislative approaches identified by Vivien Curran and David Sloss; and (c) the alternatives offered by Justine Nolan, Michael Posner, and Sarah Labowitz? Are you satisfied with any of these approaches (a) singly or (b) taken together? Why? Why not?

14. How would you protect human rights from violation by powerful TNCs? What is the best strategy and why?

Chapter Eight

Private Sector Approaches to International Human Rights Implementation

ADDRESSING the enforcement of human rights, the late international legal scholar Louis Henkin wrote in 1980 that it was "the early assumption [of the founders of the United Nations] that states might be prepared to scrutinize other states and be scrutinized by them."[1] This optimism has not stood the test of time in any sustained way. There is a discernible lack of commitment on the part of many governments, including the U.S. government, to protect human rights in their own countries and, through international institutions, at the global level as well. Even when it takes place, human rights implementation, as made apparent by the readings in Chapter 7, is accompanied by suspicion and contestation concerning less than altruistic state motivations. Add to this the sheer systemic complexities facing human rights as central normative elements of the international legal order, and it is clear that there is little if anything visible to warrant human rights optimism. What is more, as also was made evident in the last chapter, the passionate and powerful defense of human rights has typically emerged not from governments but from private individuals and groups at the grassroots—the dispersed sets of energies, collaborations, and networks known as "civil society" (or "global civil society") in our increasingly digitalized Internet Age).

The Internet has become a dynamic, powerful, and endlessly communicative medium for human rights critiques of powerful actors, be they states, corporations, other organizations, or even powerful individuals. Anyone regularly using social media will daily encounter petitions, awareness-raising films, and numerous other imaginative modes of "speaking truth to power": the plight of ordinary people oppressed by dictatorial governments; disturbing governmental encroachments on privacy; police brutality; corporate criminal activities; the trafficking of children; racial, religious, and sexual intolerance and discrimination; the gang rape of women and girls; the exploitation of laborers; the despoliation of ecosystems; climate change injustices; and a host of other contemporary sources of outrage are

---

1. Louis Henkin, *The Rights of Man Today* (Boulder, Colo.: Westview, 1980), 94.

vividly carried by a multitude of communications media into every home well-resourced enough to be part of a global digital citizenship.

Such expressions of grassroots popular concern for human rights have multiplied as time has passed. The trends that are now so central to daily digital life and so present in mainstream and "subversive" media alike were described, as early as 1987, as "social patterns of non-statist political participation in international affairs." These participatory patterns fed the nascent "worldwide human rights movement"—and even in 1987 it was clear that these trends were on the rise:

> In our time political life has been marked by a renewed resurgence of social movements . . . , peace movements, human rights movements, environmental movements, urban movements, movements of indigenous people and movements for alternative forms of economic life. Massive popular movements have challenged authoritarian regimes and demonstrated opposition to specific policies. . . . Grass-roots movements have sprung up everywhere. . . . While it is possible to interpret their character and significance in different ways, it is not possible to ignore them: no analysis of modern political life can leave them out. [2]

The late Richard Pierre Claude's contribution to this chapter addresses a powerful strand in the unfolding of this global participatory story: the development and role of nongovernmental organizations (NGOs) as significant catalysts for the promotion and protection of internationally recognized human rights. This is a crucial reflection. NGOs were foundational to the entire international human rights law enterprise; their development germinated in the origins of the Universal Declaration of Human Rights (UDHR) when, according to the late William Korey,[3] NGOs played an important role in the formulation of international human rights norms.[4]

In his essay, Claude answers the question "What Do Human Rights NGOs Do?" by presenting historical examples to explain the roles NGOs have played—and continue to play—in the energetic and oftentimes fractious national and international politics concerning the promotion and protection of one or more internationally recognized human rights. The power of such actors should not be underestimated. Perhaps the most famous such group is Amnesty International (AI), winner of the 1977 Nobel Peace Prize. In 2005, AI claimed more than 1.8 million members in over 150 countries,[5] the work of which is now well known worldwide.[6]

What, then, do NGOs ultimately do? Claude's answer is, in essence, that they do battle against human rights ignorance and abuse, particularly when governments and other public authorities ignore or violate human rights standards, typically when overcome by alleged national security imperatives or by the seductive forces of realpolitik. Human rights-violating forces within "our global political economy," Claude argues, "will not change on

---

2. Saul H. Mendlovitz and R. B. J. Walker, *Towards a Just World Peace: Perspectives from Social Movements* (London: Butterworths, 1987), 9.

3. Historian, lobbyist on international issues for B'nai B'rith, and director of the Anti-Defamation League.

4. William Korey, *NGOs and the Universal Declaration of Human Rights: A Curious Grapevine* (New York: St. Martin's, 1998), 48. The subtitle of Korey's book derives from Eleanor Roosevelt's reference to NGOs when she presciently told the *New York Times* two days before the adoption of the UDHR that a "curious grapevine" would carry word of the Declaration throughout the world so that information "may seep in even when governments are not so anxious for it." *New York Times,* 8 December 1948, 3.

5. See AI website at http://www.amnesty.org.

6. For an extensive but by no means exhaustive list of mostly international human rights NGOs, see http://en.wikipedia.org/wiki/List_of_human_rights_organisations (accessed 1 January 2015).

the basis of mere appeals to conscience or excessive trust in new international rules and institutions. To keep such negative forces in check, people must organize to pursue common objectives, fashion new modes of humane governance, and work out human rights respecting accommodations to conflicting interests." For Claude, NGOs are central to this necessity. NGOs persist in presenting challenges to power, and commonly emerge from potent grass root network activisms to press for social justice and human rights fulfillment at the highest levels—as well as by awakening global public awareness of human violation. NGOs, he argues, can be understood to be part of the "authorship" of human rights claims emerging from struggle, from the experiential pain of injustice, disrespect, and the failure of fundamental decencies so critical to human rights aspirations.

In this and other ways, NGOs, like other networks and communities worldwide, address also—of necessity—the deepening power and control exercised by corporations, for in the twenty-first century it is abundantly clear that the "private" sector presents a powerful threat to human rights futures. There is widespread evidence of global human rights abuses deep within the global economic order, and enacted by corporations in the pursuit of profit and larger market share—sometimes in partnership with complicit state elites. Of course, corporations can be a force for human rights progress as well—especially when forced by social movement energies to be "human rights aware." NGOs and other forms of organized—sometimes even disorganized—resistance to human rights violations can succeed in bringing the business community face to face with consumer and other demands for human rights compliance. Other corporate actors may have a strong ethical mandate. However, despite these possibilities, the record of corporate human rights and environmental abuse is extremely long and well supported by a heart-rending litany of evidence.

Indeed, in her contribution to this chapter, Penelope Simons argues that something very fundamental is amiss in the current global legal order—that the global political economy, and the international legal system that purport to manage it for "we the peoples of the United Nations" (i.e., most of the world's population), themselves reveal a fundamental dynamic that facilitates the aggregation of power and for decades, has defied attempts—including UN attempts— to build corporate accountability into meaningful international legal human rights structures. Simons writes: "There is something very wrong with our global economic system, which takes little, if any, account of the environmental and human rights costs of business activity. Such costs are neither internalized by markets nor adequately able to restrain market actors as 'external' norms or standards." She also notes that, corporate rhetoric to the contrary notwithstanding, "any discussion of binding international human rights obligations still meets with strong resistance, if not vehement opposition."

But Simons's central analytical concern in her essay is with the latest rehearsal of the struggle to build corporate human rights accountability into the international legal system—the mandate of Harvard political science professor John Ruggie, former UN special representative of the Secretary-General on the Issue of Human Rights and Transnational Corporations and Other Business Enterprises (SRSG). The core problem with Ruggie's analysis, Simons argues, is that Ruggie perceives the fundamental problem to be one of "governance gaps" while failing to address the underlying realities of the flawed international legal order itself. Drawing on "third world" and feminist scholarship, Simons builds a powerfully persuasive case in support of her view, concluding that "by limiting his recommendations to the clarification of legal norms applicable to business where they engage in behavior that violates international criminal law norms, while at the same time cautioning against the adoption of a more general international treaty [to regulate transnational corporate behavior], Ruggie missed the opportunity to push states and business actors out of their comfort zone." Simons unquestionably accepts that "the problem of corporate impunity for extra-territorial human rights violations is deeply complex." But that is precisely the reason, she maintains, that the problem "needs to be tackled creatively and intelligently at a variety of jurisdictional and normative levels." She concludes: "Without engaging international law as an integral part of the strategy to address corporate human rights impacts and account-ability . . . we will more or less continue business as usual."

Arguably the most invidious flaw of the international legal order is that, in practice, it does not keep sufficient faith with its pledge to honor the interdependent but often com-peting principles of "equal rights" of peoples and the "the sovereign equality" of states—each principles of customary international law now enshrined in the UN Charter.[7] This much criticized flaw, as is made clear in Simons's analysis, relates as much to a history of colonial oppression as it does to ongoing forms of the neocolonial dynamics of neoliberal globalization. This theme, it may be recalled, was identified in the first chapter of this book—and has emerged since. The persistence of identifiable patterns suggests factors re-sistant to the search for a just global order and for the full and fair realization of human rights—patterns turning on the construction of relative degrees of privilege and oppression, inclusion and exclusion. These patterns reveal, in a very real sense, a central and problem-atic inequality of access to "the system." In turn, this concern is fundamental to the degree of participation and agency within national polities also.

The powerful question, raised by Jordan Paust's contribution to this chapter, is whether—in the face of elite dominance and the exercise of systematic exclusion—there is a human right to revolution. An even more provocative application of his question po-tentially circles around whether or not there ever could be a human right to a globalized revolution. Paust's essay, however, is confined to the right to revolution within the terri-torial state, a central dynamic of which Paust identifies as the oppressive nature of the denial by state elites of "a relatively full and free sharing of power" within the body politic. For Paust, a key concern in this setting must be the role of violence in changing the reign-ing political order, and the ways in which violence could be a legitimate or illegitimate means of protest. Paust is careful to argue that permissible revolution is a right "not vested in some minority of an identifiable society," but, rather, in "the people" as a whole to mount resistance against the structures of state power—"a right of the people" to political agency and participation. It is, he contends, "one of the strategies available to a people for the securing of authority, national self-determination, and a relatively free and equal en-joyment of the human right of all persons to participate in the political processes of their society." But Paust is also very clear that in all situations where exercise of the right to revolution—especially violent revolution—may be contemplated, "an adequate analysis of strategies or tactics of revolution or 'civil disobedience' demands consideration of all rele-vant features of context, including, of course, an examination of the larger social process in which such strategies or tactics operate." A "realistic and policy-serving jurisprudence," he argues, "would integrate relevant principles of international law into appropriate anal-ysis and choice about the permissibility of a particular method or means of violence in a given social context, using tools of phase and value analysis for empirical inquiry and choice."

Paust reserves an important and sobering thought for those who are, in his words, "rightly concerned about the evils of any form of violence and the threat that domestic violence can pose to human dignity and international peace." To such people, he extends

---

7. UN Charter Articles 1(2) and 2(1) respectively.

an invitation to consider the salutary words of President John F. Kennedy: "those who make peaceful evolution impossible make violent revolution inevitable."[8] It is a thought-provoking point to place next to the evidence of increasingly undemocratic propensities that at this writing accompany the rapid accumulation of economic and political power by a powerful transnational elite in the contemporary political economy and legal order of our world community. What developments, one wonders, might yet attend the future evolution of a human right to revolution?

8. Address by John F. Kennedy at Punta del Este, quoted in M. Cherif Bassiouni, ed., *The Law of Dissent and Riots* (Springfield, Ill.: Thomas, 1971), vii. President Kennedy also declared, "Is not peace, in the last analysis, basically a matter of human rights?" Address by John F. Kennedy at American University (10 June 1963), quoted in Myres S. McDougal, Harold D. Lasswell, and Lung-chu Chen, *Human Rights and World Public Order: The Basic Policies of an International Law of Human Dignity* (New Haven, Conn.: YUP, 1980), 236n229.

34. RICHARD PIERRE CLAUDE *What Do Human Rights NGOs Do?*

"Non-governmental organizations" are referenced in Article 1 of the UN Charter, and "unlike much UN jargon, the term, NGOs passed quickly into popular usage, particularly from the early 1970s onwards."[1] Human rights NGOs are generally not-for-profit private associations devoted to promoting and protecting human rights. They pursue these goals at multiple levels: international, regional, national, and local. They also have attracted the attention of many political scientists and lawyers.[2]

"The NGO population has grown dramatically in recent years," writes Ann Marie Clark of Purdue University.[3] "In 2003," she continues, "1,046 (44 percent) of the NGOs holding consultative

status at ECOSOC listed human rights as one of their concerns, although that includes groups not solely focused on human rights, [and this] growth in . . . NGOs concerned with human rights at the UN can be considered a fair reflection of the growth of all kinds of human rights NGOs globally."[4] The files of the Human Rights Internet (Ottawa) indicate that, counting part-time and strictly national groups (e.g., the Cambodian Project Against Domestic Violence or the Chad Association for Human Rights), human rights NGOs number over 11,000, many of them local and regional.[5]

Those NGOs that specialize in human rights are able to maximize the free flow of information across borders, spreading the word on human rights violations around the globe. They all use the politics of information gathering and advocacy, and they perform many other tasks as well. They also have a good reputation and are widely trusted, according to a 2001 international survey conducted by Strategy One in Australia, France, Germany, the United Kingdom, and the United States, canvassing 1,100 opinion leaders.[6]

NGOs come from a wide range of political, social, cultural, and financial environments. Some operate in relative freedom and enjoy high

Excerpted with changes by permission of the University of Pennsylvania Press from Richard Pierre Claude, "NGO Activism in Science, Technology, and Health," in Claude, *Science in the Service of Human Rights* (Philadelphia: University of Pennsylvania Press, 2002), 146–61. Copyright © 2002 University of Pennsylvania Press.

1. Peter Willetts, "Non-Governmental Organizations," in Gabriela Maria Kutting, ed., *Institutional and Infrastructure Resource Issues: Conventions, Treaties, and Other Responses to Global Issues*, vol. 3 (Paris: UNESCO-EOLSS, 2001), 229.
2. See, e.g., Ann Marie Clark, "Nongovernmental Organizations: Overview," in David P. Forsythe et al., eds., *Encyclopedia of Human Rights* (Oxford: OUP, 2009), 4: 87–96. See also Julie A. Mertus, "Human Rights and the Promise of Transnational Civil Society," in Burns H. Weston and Stephen P. Marks, eds., *The Future of International Human Rights* (Ardsley, N.Y.: Transnational, 1999), 433–56.
3. Clark, "Nongovernmental Organizations," 87.

4. Ibid.
5. See the Human Rights Internet website at http://www.hri.ca [*Eds.*—accessed 22 June 2015].
6. Strategy One, *Institutional Trust: A Five Country Survey* (New York: Edelman Public Relations, 2001).

prestige, others are brutally repressed. All are independent of the state and seek no political power for themselves. They play an important role in the growth of civil society in virtually every country in the world. Their myriad functions become clear when we answer the question: what do NGOs do?

- they *monitor* human rights violations
- they undertake programs of information sharing and *public education*
- they sponsor programs of *technical training*
- they undertake and demonstrate the utility of rigorous *technical analysis*
- they engage in *lobbying* activities to influence public policy
- they organize *advocacy campaigns* to promote rights and redress wrongs
- they build *solidarity* with other domestic and international NGOs
- they perform *service functions* and provide humanitarian support
- they protect and vindicate human rights in *litigation*

MONITORING VIOLATIONS

The tragic case of Joelito Filártiga, the seventeen-year-old son of Paraguay's most famous physician, illustrates the work of Amnesty International (AI) in monitoring human rights violations, including the right not to suffer government-sponsored torture.

For decades, Dr. Joel Filártiga ran a clinic for the 50,000 impoverished people in the Ybycuí Valley of Paraguay. Because Dr. Filártiga was an outspoken critic of General Alfredo Stroessner's dictatorship and its derelict public health policy, and because he gave free medical care to the *campesinos*, the police suspected him of leftist sympathies and subversive activities. In 1976, his teenage son Joelito Filártiga was abducted by police inspector Américo Peña-Irala, who assumed the boy could be forced to betray his father. Instead, he died of cardiac arrest during a hideous torture interrogation. Thereafter, Dr. Filártiga and his family cooperated with AI human rights workers in Paraguay. Richard Alan White, a historian visiting from UCLA, documented the case in Asunción and transmitted information about the politically motivated torture-murder to AI research headquarters in Lon-

don.[7] The Amnesty Secretariat took an interest in the murdered boy's case because AI is dedicated to acting on behalf of those prisoners of conscience who suffer torture in violation of the Universal Declaration of Human Rights.

As in all cases, AI double-checked the facts, making sure that the Filártigas were not advocates of violence, that the boy was taken as a prisoner of conscience and tortured for political reasons. They then organized a worldwide campaign, issuing reports and urgent action memos calling on members to pressure the Paraguayan and other governments to take action. Soon the dictator buckled under the intense international outcry and suspended Peña-Irala, who, while visiting the United States, was tracked down by Dr. Filártiga and his daughter Dolly in New York and subsequently apprehended by U.S. immigration authorities.

Thereafter, Dolly Filártiga and her father filed a wrongful death action in the Federal District Court for the Eastern District of New York under the 1789 Alien Tort Statute alleging that in 1976 Police Inspector Peña-Irala kidnaped and tortured Joelito Filártiga to death. The district court dismissed the Filártigas' complaint for lack of subject matter jurisdiction.

In 1980, however, the U.S. Court of Appeals for the Second Circuit reversed, recognizing the emergence of a universal consensus that international law affords substantive rights to individuals and places limits on a state's treatment of its citizens. From these circumstances emerged the landmark decision of *Filártiga v. Peña-Irala*,[8] marking the first time a U.S. federal court accepted jurisdiction in a civil suit against torture committed in a foreign country. Peña-Irala's responsibility for the human rights offense supplied the basis on which the court ruled that officially sanctioned torture is a violation of international law. "Like the pirate and slave trader before him," the Court said, "the torturer has become the enemy of all mankind." In 1984, on remand to the District Court and on the basis of expert testimony from four medical specialists, Judge Eugene Nickerson announced a total

---

7. Richard Alan White, *Breaking Silence: The Case That Changed the Face of Human Rights* (Washington, D.C.: Georgetown University Press, 2004), providing a unique participant-observer's account of *Filártiga v. Peña-Irala*, 630 F. 2d 876 (2d Cir.,1980).
8. *Filártiga v. Peña-Irala.*

judgment against Peña-Irala amounting to $10,385 million. The *Filártiga* case became important as a precedent, having many progeny including some directed at corporations for human rights violations.[9]

PUBLIC EDUCATION AND INFORMATION SHARING

B'Tselem is the Hebrew name popularly used by the Israeli Center for Human Rights in the Occupied Territories. It was established in 1989 by a group of prominent academics, attorneys, journalists, and Knesset members. The Hebrew word means "in the image of," and is used also as a synonym for human dignity as reflected in Genesis 1:27: "And God created humans in his image. In the image of God did He create him." The group seeks to document and educate the Israeli public and policy-makers about human rights violations in the Occupied Territories and to combat the phenomenon of denial they say is prevalent among the Israeli public. Ultimately the educational objective is to create a human rights culture in Israel in compliance with Israel's obligations under international law.

In 1989 in Atlanta, the Carter-Menil Award for Human Rights was presented to B'Tselem in recognition of its important work and its consistent and careful accuracy in reporting. They ensure the reliability of information by conducting their own fieldwork and research and thoroughly cross-checking with relevant documents, official government sources, and information from other sources, among them Israeli, Palestinian, and other human rights organizations. The scores of B'Tselem reports, called "Information Sheets," cover most kinds of human rights violations that have occurred in the Occupied Territories at the hands of the Israeli government, e.g., torture, fatal shootings by security forces, restriction on movement, expropriation of land, discrimination in planning and building in East Jerusalem, administrative detention, and settler violence. Reports are supplemented by press conferences and educational outreach programs in Israel relying on volunteers who set up information stands, distribute printed material, and participate in protests in the Occupied Territories. This educational sharing information is designed to provide the Israeli public with a basis for taking action and making choices. Their regularly published Information Sheets proclaim that readers of their publications may decide to do nothing, but they cannot say "We didn't know."

TECHNICAL TRAINING

Training, as distinct from the broader field of education, is directed at teaching others to become proficient in a particular task or field of technical operations. Illustrative is a program of technical training to implement the International Labour Organization (ILO) Convention No. 169 concerning the rights of "tribal peoples in independent countries." The Convention stresses as vital to the human rights of "tribal peoples" the ownership and possession of the lands they traditionally occupy and their right to participate in the management and conservation of these resources. Such participatory rights play an important role in the work of the Center for the Support of Native Lands, working in Central and South America and responsible for remarkable examples of technology transfer promoted by the nonprofit conservation group.[10] The NGO responds to initiatives by the indigenous peoples themselves seeking to gain social and political advantage from detailed and long-standing knowledge of their environmental heritage. Professional ethnocartographers lend a technical helping hand to train Indian community workers. As a result, the Bolivian indigenous "people of the Izozog" learned the methodologies of mapping techniques, which they used effectively in an area encompassing over 19,000 square kilometers as of 2001.[11]

With the support of the Bolivian Ministry of Sustainable Development and with training by Native Lands ethnocartographers, surveyors, and draftsmen, Indian leaders enthusiastically took on responsibility to handle the mapping project,

9. But see Chapter 7, Reading 33 (Grear and Weston) in this volume, describing the U.S. Supreme Court decision in *Kiobel v. Royal Dutch Petroleum Co.*, 133 S. Ct. 1659 (2013), substantially if not completely limiting *Filártiga*'s impact.

10. See the Center's website at http://www.native-lands.org [*Eds.*—accessed 22 June 2015].
11. Mac Chapin and William Threlkeld, *Indigenous Landscapes: A Study in Ethnocartography* (Alexandria, Va.: Center for the Support of Native Lands, 2001).

managing all the field activities. The "para-cartographers" meticulously documented the locations of their traditional homeland, settlements, temporary structures, soils, trees, water, forests, and other treasured natural resources such as sites where honey and medicinal plants can be found. Displacing official maps that showed enormous swaths of land as "uninhabited," the new map resulted in naming many physical features and renaming some landmarks from Spanish back to the original Guarani names.

In addition to the empowerment objectives of the project, a major outcome was the national development of a plan to establish the Gran Chaco National Park and Integrated Management Area, a 3.4 million hectare tract extending to the Paraguayan border. To be administered by the Izoceos, it is the largest territorial protected area in tropical America. In September 1995, the area was legally established by presidential decree, and a year later an agreement was signed giving the Indian Assembly administrative control over the area.

TECHNICAL ANALYSIS

Each violation of human rights and fundamental freedoms deserves individual attention and universal condemnation. No one seriously interested in applying statistical science to monitoring human rights violations would argue that "if you can't count them they don't count." However, those who work in the field of human rights know that fixing the responsibility for violations requires an assessment of how, how much, and why human freedoms are curtailed or endangered.

The Science and Human Rights Program of the American Association for the Advancement of Science (AAAS) has a distinguished history of initiating helpful and technically cutting-edge methods for the promotion, analysis, and implementation of internationally defined human rights. A model of excellence in analyzing large-scale human rights violations is the AAAS report titled *State Violence in Guatemala, 1960–1996*.[12] The report combined historical analysis with statistics from the International Center for Human Rights

Investigations (CIDH) to present a compelling history of the deliberate and sustained violence committed by state forces during Guatemala's domestic armed conflict. Subtitled "A Quantitative Reflection," it relied on a database meticulously assembled covering 43,070 violations against 16,265 victims, of whom 13,527 were victims whose full identity was known. The statistics present a clear picture of the period 1959–94, decades of unrelenting Guatemalan state reliance on extrajudicial violence to maintain political control in a divided nation. Data analysis by the authors credibly supported the view that state terror over time expanded in both intensity and in the scope of its victims, from selective assassinations of militants in the armed insurgency to an ever-widening attack on members of the political opposition. The report also inquired into the methods and agents of violence, including the government's use of civilians to attack other civilians, a policy that contributed to the long-term militarization of Guatemalan society. Analysis of data-based information showed how violence rose and fell across all presidential regimes, military and civilian. Human rights violations were analyzed by the gender, ethnicity, and age of the victims, and regional differences showed the ever-increasing penetration of violence into rural areas.

The statistical profile of such violence showed that a record number of over 800 killings and disappearances per month took place during 17 months of President José Efraín Ríos Montt's incumbency (1978–82). Nevertheless, because of increased state censorship and intimidation of the media by killings of journalists and attacks on media offices and equipment at that time, fewer government killings were reported during his regime. The press blackout coincided with the Reagan administration lobbying to restore military aid to Guatemala cut off by the U.S. Congress in 1977. Thus, the question how people do or do not get timely information about human rights violations has a strong bearing on how they can respond to such abuses, both where the violations take place and among attentive groups in other countries as well.

LOBBYING

Sometimes human rights NGOs influence public policy through the standard methods of

12. Patrick Ball, Paul Kobrak, and Herbert F. Spirer, *State Violence in Guatemala, 1960–1996: A Quantitative Reflection* (Washington, D.C.: AAAS, 1999).

political lobbying. An example of such work under the sponsorship of Physicians for Human Rights (USA) took place when, in July 2000, over 75 activists from 26 states gathered in Washington, D.C., to participate in the first U.S. Campaign to Ban Landmines (USCBL).[13] As a grassroots and legislative action coalition (including medical school students, health professionals, and others), they met with hundreds of members of Congress or their aides, gaining the immediate support of over 40 percent, and actively urged the president to join the 1997 Ottawa Convention Banning Land Mines.[14] Calling for a total ban on the use, manufacture, stockpiling, and transfer of antipersonnel landmines, it was ratified by 162 countries as of 16 February 2015, including all NATO nations except the United States. The treaty seeks to reduce needless human suffering by increasing resources for mine clearance, mine awareness, and mine assistance.

In 2000, U.S. Representative Jim McGovern from Maine and others circulated a "Dear Colleague" sign-on letter in the House that urged President Clinton to take steps toward joining the treaty. Physicians for Human Rights, the coordinator of the USCBL, also organized an action- and information-packed conference with over 200 participants. In turn, growing out of the USCBL, the young people who attended launched their own initiative, "Students Against Landmines." To motivate the participants, Nobel Laureate Jody Williams spoke at the event, and USCBL distributed a new Human Rights Watch report, "Clinton's Landmine Legacy," along with the Watch Committee website address. Further solidarity came from representatives of the Bahá'í, Buddhist, Catholic, Jewish, Lutheran, Methodist, and Muslim communities who participated in an interfaith prayer service to remind everyone that the heart and soul behind the ban betokened the tens of thousands of innocent civilians killed and maimed by landmines.

The failure of the Clinton administration to sign on to the landmine treaty did not deter PHR from its lobbying activities under the succeeding

Bush Administration. Since lobbying involves the effort to influence decision-making elites, PHR wisely added a professional elite component to their campaign, asking prominent health professionals (deans of medical schools, hospital heads, directors of health-related organizations, etc.) to endorse a letter to all the 2004 presidential candidates urging them to support the landmine treaty and associate themselves with the campaign and PHR's "sign-on" letter accessible on the Internet. Most did so. However, as of this writing, the United States, though a signatory, has yet to ratify the treaty.

ADVOCACY

Advocacy by NGOs in the form of campaigns of persuasion and pressure is conventionally directed at units of government, but also sometimes at private groups and corporations. Advocacy campaigns have become a routine concern of ever more public interest groups. The work of French-based Médecins Sans Frontières (Doctors Without Borders), an NGO monitoring and reporting on pharmaceutical companies and their response to the AIDS pandemic, is illustrative. It has undertaken heroic work in Africa and played an important role in raising international consciousness about the need there for HIV/AIDS treatment where very few can afford the drugs that have enabled richer countries to convert the malady from a killer to a manageable illness.

In the United States, sympathetic NGOs, including gay and lesbian organizations and human rights groups, have pressured pharmaceutical companies to cease all efforts to block access to generic drugs where branded medications are not available or are priced out of the reach of people with HIV/AIDS. In a remarkable 2003 essay, Dr. William Prusoff explained that, in a Yale University pharmacology laboratory, he and his late colleague, Dr. Tai-shun Lin, developed d4T, an important antiretroviral drug that forms a critical part of a "cocktail" used beneficially by people with HIV and AIDS.[15] As the patent holder, Yale leased usage to the Bristol-Myers Squibb drug company for clinical trials, develop-

13. Physicians for Human Rights (USA), "PHR Steps Up Efforts to Get U.S. to Join Mine Ban Treaty," *Record* 13 (April 2000), 1–4, 4.
14. Officially known as the Convention on the Prohibition of the Use, Stockpiling, Production and Transfer of Anti-Personnel Mines and on Their Destruction, concluded 18 September 1997.

15. William Prusoff, "The Scientist's Story," *New York Times*, 6 March 2001, 4.

ment, and marketing. But, according to Prusoff, Médecins sans Frontières made all the difference, having played the critical role of convincing Bristol-Myers Squibb to cut the cost of the antiretroviral drug. The NGO demands on the drug company convinced the Yale administration, pressured by law students and the school newspaper, to join the cause. Forgoing substantial profits, the company, through its vice president, announced its cooperation "to energize a groundswell of action" to fight AIDS in Africa. Bristol-Myers Squibb reduced the cost of the Yale-patented drug Zerit to 15 cents for a daily dose, 1.5 percent of the cost to an American patient. On the basis of his experience, Prusoff concluded, nothing less would do than a well-organized international advocacy effort.

BUILDING SOLIDARITY

Building solidarity distinctively calls for an explicit manifesting of sympathetic concern for the causes and concerns of others. In our global society, it is an ever more important function for nongovernmental organizations to mobilize moral and material transnational political support across national boundaries among themselves and others to achieve human rights for the marginalized and oppressed. Efforts at solidarity building necessarily involve interaction and networking. In *Activists Beyond Borders*, Margaret E. Keck and Kathryn Sikkink ably analyzed the development of networks of environmental NGOs.[16] The "common advocacy position," they say, is more likely to produce mutually supportive concrete results. Moreover, the very process of networking promotes a search for common ground and solidarity.

Consider the case of Alexandr Nikitin, a nuclear safety inspector, former Soviet navy submarine captain, and environmental activist. In February 1996, he was arrested by Russian authorities and charged with divulging "state secrets" to the Bellona Foundation, a Norwegian environmental organization that exposed dangers of nuclear waste disposal practices posed by deteriorating nuclear submarines of the Russian

navy in the Barents Sea region in and near Murmansk. Captain Nikitin was held in pretrial detention for ten months, and then released only under condition that he not leave St. Petersburg. In 1998, after several attempts by the St. Petersburg Procuracy and Russian security services to produce a viable indictment, Nikitin's first trial ended inconclusively, with the judge sending the case back for further investigation. He was finally acquitted in December 1999, and the decision was upheld by the Russian Supreme Court in April 2000. It noted that the Russian Constitution clearly states that "everyone has the right to a favorable environment, reliable information about its state, and compensation for damages inflicted on his health and property by ecological violations." Further, the Constitution prohibits employing unpublished laws in prosecuting citizens, a tactic the Russian Federal Security Service tried to use against Nikitin. The Supreme Court Presidium of the Russian Federation finally closed the case by rejecting the General Prosecutors' protest against the St. Petersburg verdict.[17]

These developments were monitored by the Commission on Security and Cooperation in Europe (the Helsinki Commission) before which Captain Nikitin testified in 2000 that, as the Russian people have increasingly become aware of their rights, environmental NGOs have emerged as among the strongest and most popular of organized groups, albeit not to the liking of President Vladimir Putin who ominously singled out environmental groups as fronts for international espionage. Nikitin is the founder of the Environmental Rights Center in St. Petersburg, which addresses issues at the intersection of environmental and human rights and, in turn, works with the Coalition for Environment and Human Rights consisting of over forty grassroots NGOs in Russia. Nikitin freely acknowledged that, as a defensive measure, the groups with which he is linked work cooperatively and in solidarity with others, networking their efforts at national and international levels to enhance their efficacy (and security). Moreover, the Norwegian Bellona Foundation enjoys international solidarity links fostered by the Sierra Club, which in 2000

16. Margaret E. Keck and Kathryn Sikkink, "Environmental Advocacy Networks," in *Activists Beyond Borders: Advocacy Networks in International Politics* (Ithaca, N.Y.: Cornell University Press, 1998), 121–63.

17. See Case Number 476p2000pr. *Decision of the Supreme Court Presidium of the Russian Federation*, 13 September 2000, examining the General Prosecutor Deputy's protest against the verdict of the St. Petersburg City Court, 29 December 1999.

awarded Nikitin and the Bellona Foundation its highest international honor, the Earthcare Award in defense of the survival of a livable global environment.

SERVICE AND HUMANITARIAN RELIEF

By the start of the millennium, nearly 39 million people worldwide had been uprooted from their homes by war, including seven million displaced in 1999 alone. Medical assistance is frequently critically important to persons victimized by armed conflict, torture, cruel, inhumane treatment and punishment, and other egregious human rights deprivations.

Forensic medicine used for legal investigations is a uniquely pertinent humanitarian service valuable in modern human rights cases, as was dramatically illustrated relative to the Balkan wars of the 1990s in the former Yugoslavia, which brought terrible suffering to East Central Europe and caused enormous human carnage and dislocations. War, ethnic cleansing, persecution of minorities, indiscriminate attacks on civilians, lack of respect for humanitarian principles, and deliberate targeting of aid workers were some of the trademarks of the conflict in Bosnia. That catastrophe exacted a substantial cost in lives and human health, and in the aftermath of hostilities, forensic work was critically important.

The story of its most tragic episode, involving the Muslim enclave of Srebrenica, is brilliantly recounted from a physician's point of view by Dr. Sheri Fink, in *War Hospital*, a gripping account of medical service, surgery, and survival.[18] For almost the entire month of April 1993, Serbian forces surrounding the town obstructed all convoys of humanitarian supplies. Members of the armed militia violated standards of humanitarian law with a medical blockade excluding health professionals from entering. During the siege, denial of humanitarian assistance meant that Srebrenica was left with a single doctor for over 40,000 people, of whom some 30,000 were refugees, and the deaths of thousands of civilians. In the years that followed, the surviving women of Srebrenica joined together to find out what happened to their families, and in 2000, at

a new morgue facility in the northern Bosnian town of Tuzla, investigators tried to uncover the answer. Dozens of international experts worked for months, digging up 2,028 bodies and finding another 2,500, spread over more than a score of sites. In their cold storage facilities, they assembled the disinterred remains.

The International Commission for Missing Persons, in coordination with Physicians for Human Rights (USA), provided state of the art technology for the forensic pathologists identifying the remains. The mitochondrial DNA sequencers donated by the California-based "PE Biosystems" made possible matching DNA from the victims' bones with blood samples from a relative. Appropriately, the fit served two purposes. The process informed the surviving families of the fate of their missing loved ones. It also established evidence useful in proceedings at the International Criminal Tribunal for the former Yugoslavia (ICTY) in The Hague, making it possible for the court—along with the International Criminal Tribunal established to judge the 1994 genocide in Rwanda (ICTR) which likewise has made use of such forensic evidence, though less so, to cross an historic threshold because such evidence was not produced during the trials in Nuremberg and Tokyo following World War II.

On 2 August 2001, the ICTY found former general Radislav Krstić guilty of genocide for his role in the systematic execution of more than 7,000 unarmed Muslim men and boys near Srebrenica in 1995.[19] He was sentenced to forty-six years imprisonment. Prosecutors said that the Krstić trial was the first international trial where forensic evidence played such a crucial role. Presiding Judge Almiro Rodriques said: "By deciding to kill all the men of fighting age, a decision was taken to make it impossible for the Muslim people of Srebrenica to survive." He concluded: "What was ethnic cleansing became genocide."[20]

LITIGATION

Perhaps because the United States has developed what some call "the most litigious society

---

18. Sheri Fink, *War Hospital: A True Story of Surgery and Survival* (New York: Public Affairs, 2003).

19. *Prosecutor v. Radislav Krstić*, IT-98-33 (2 August 2001).
20. As quoted in Marlise Simons, "Tribunal in Hague Finds Bosnia Serb Guilty of Genocide," *New York Times*, 3 August 2001, 1, 8.

on earth,"[21] it is ardently litigious NGOs in the United States that lead the world in reliance on litigation for the protection and vindication of human rights. Such groups include the Center for Constitutional Rights (CCR, New York), Global Rights-Partners for Justice (Washington, D.C.), Human Rights First (HRF, New York and Washington, D.C.), the Southern Center for Human Rights (SCHR, Atlanta) and, focused primarily on U.S. domestic law cases, the Southern Poverty Law Center (SPLC, Montgomery, Ala.).

An NGO such as the SCHR which, like the CCR, HRF, and SPLC, operates like a law firm must wait to receive grievances from potential plaintiffs because, under traditional standards of legal ethics, they cannot initiate lawsuits on their own. In 1999, the SCHR acted on serious complaints they received, suing the Fulton County jail on behalf of HIV-positive jail inmates. Many of these unfortunate people in Georgia's largest jail were awaiting trial on minor charges and had not been convicted of any crime. They said that 23 inmates died in the Fulton County jail for lack of proper medical care in the preceding two years. Defendants in the suit included Correctional Healthcare Solutions, Inc., the contractor responsible for inmates' health and medical care. Filed in Federal District Court in Atlanta in early 2000, the suit alleged that the contractor withheld timely medication and was otherwise careless, causing hundreds of inmates infected with HIV and AIDS to suffer excruciating and unnecessary pain, develop resistance to life-saving medication, and risk premature death.

The District Court found for the plaintiffs and ordered the Fulton County officials to rectify "a criminal justice system . . . rife with errors, waste, and delay."[22] Judge Marvin Shoob ordered, inter alia, that inmates be screened for HIV, TB, and other diseases upon admission to the jail, and that a new health care contractor provide an HIV specialist at the jail to diagnose, prescribe, and provide medication for and monitor those who are HIV positive. Additionally, the judge appointed Dr. Robert Greifinger, former chief medical officer of the New York Department of Corrections, to evaluate improvements over time. On the occasion of his first visit, Dr. Greifinger found dental equipment dumped in a

sink and hardly cleaned before being used on the next patient. His general conclusion was that "the medical staff at the County Jail had not learned the basic hygienic lessons of the nineteenth century." Under Judge Shoob's orders, however, Dr. Greifinger soon found conditions "remarkably better," but insisted after ten months that "they still [were] not at a point . . . where these new systems [could] continue without, quite frankly, the supervision of the court."[23]

Such judicial oversight is critically important in the United States, which leads the world in the number of prison inmates. Litigation on behalf of their human rights is essential because they otherwise have little or no influence through conventional political processes to assure minimal humane living conditions.

CONCLUSIONS

Throughout the world, the recognition of internationally defined human rights and the need for adherence by public authority to domestic and international law are acknowledged. They are also often ignored as governments give higher priority to perceived national security needs, economic gain, and political advantage. These perennial forces within our global political economy will not change on the basis of mere appeals to conscience or excessive trust in new international rules and institutions. To keep such negative forces in check, people must organize to pursue common objectives, fashion new modes of humane governance, and work out human rights respecting accommodations to conflicting interests. This means, among other actions, vindicating human rights via NGOs persistently speaking truth to power; heroic grassroots level action by individuals advocating social justice and asserting their human rights; the vigilance of professionals demanding the political space necessary to exercise their commitments to professional responsibility; and the willingness of technically trained people to offer their expertise when needed in the service of human rights wherever they are endangered. Increasingly, NGOs serve as catalysts in the promotion and protection of internationally recognized human rights.

21. "We Are the World's Most Litigious Society," *Telegraph*, 1 September 2013.
22. *Ruben Foster v. Fulton County, Georgia*, No. 1:99-CV-900-MHS, Atlanta Division (12 July 2002), 1301.
23. See http://www.schr.org [*Eds.*—accessed 22 June 2015].

QUESTIONS FOR REFLECTION AND DISCUSSION

1. Why are human rights NGOs important actors in the international human rights movement? What purpose or purposes do they serve? Are they more effective than states or intergovernmental organizations in promoting and protecting human rights? What are their comparative advantages? Their comparative weaknesses? What does Claude say?

2. Of the nine NGO functions discussed by Claude, which does Claude think are the most important? Which do you think are most important? Why?

3. For maximum effectiveness in promoting and protecting human rights, is it better for human rights NGOs to concentrate on influencing a target country's domestic policy or the foreign policies of their home countries? Why? Suppose the target country were Afghanistan, China, Colombia, Congo, Cuba, Egypt, Indonesia, Iran, Iraq, Myanmar (Burma), North Korea, Saudi Arabia, Sudan, Syria, Ukraine, or Zimbabwe. Does your answer depend on the country selected? Why? Why not?

4. Often it is difficult for human rights NGOs to resolve whether it is useful or not to take action in a particular country or on a particular issue. As observed in David Weissbrodt, "The Contribution of International Nongovernmental Organizations to the Promotion and Protection of Human Rights," in Theodor Meron, ed., *Human Rights in International Law* (Oxford: Clarendon, 1984), 403–29, 409, a human rights NGO must answer several key questions each time: Might intervention help or hurt the victims? What sort of intervention would be most effective? Have interventions in the target country or with respect to the given type of problem been successful in the past? Are the officials of the country receptive to initiatives from outsiders? Are the facts sufficiently well established to permit diplomatic intervention or publicity? Which NGO would be most effective in raising the issues? How would/should one answer these questions? How would Claude?

5. Similarly, how does an NGO decide whether to accept a case or file a complaint on behalf of a victim of a human rights abuse? What criteria would aid the NGO in determining whether it would be the best organization to handle the case? Should the choice be based on political judgments or strictly legal ones? Why? Why not?

6. What are the moral/ethical responsibilities of professionals and professional associations relative to international human rights? How should professional associations in, say, law, medicine, or journalism operate in relation to human rights abuses in their areas of specialization? Should they undertake human rights missions? In fields unrelated to their areas of expertise? How might they have the most impact in promoting and protecting human rights?

7. Some people argue that professionals sometimes have a duty to be or appear to be neutral in the face of human rights abuse—for example, journalists who may need access to authoritative information. Do you accept this argument? Can you think of situations in which it might be made by lawyers? Doctors? Is there a danger of cooptation? What are the limits beyond which professionals should not go? For example, a doctor or lawyer administering to a tortured prisoner at the behest of the torturing authorities? See, e.g., Jacobo Timmerman, *Prisoner Without a Name, Cell Without a Number*, trans. Toby Talbot (New York: Knopf, 1981).

8. Given that most NGOs operate to advance specific human rights interests, is there any danger that they may offer information skewed toward their specific interest? Is there a reliability issue with NGOs? Are there other dangers that might be posed by overreliance on NGOs?

9. How, if at all, are NGOs monitored and controlled? How, if at all, should they be?

10. Human rights NGOs have at various times been criticized for being fragmented, inadequately coordinated, redundant, and the like. Is this a problem and, if so, is there a solution to it? Should the UN and/or regional human institutions play a coordinating role? If you were charged to recommend a central body to coordinate NGOs, what would you propose to ensure that no human rights complaint gets overlooked and that minimal overlap in cases or complaints is the rule rather than the exception? Should these be priority goals? Why? Why not?

11. Typically NGOs are financially strapped, making it difficult for them to carry out their important functions. Mostly they are funded via private charitable contributions and project-oriented foundation grants. Are there other means of financial support that

should be considered? For example, should states and/or intergovernmental organizations, regional as well as global, be required to make, say, annual contributions? Why? Why not?

12. Should the role of human rights NGOs be strengthened? Why and how? Why not? Should they be represented in UN and/or regional bodies? If so, given that not all NGOs can participate, by what criteria would they be chosen and by whom? Might a global peoples' assembly, representing global civil society, within or independent of the UN, prove beneficial? Along these lines, see Richard Falk and Andrew Strauss, "On the Creation of a Global Peoples Assembly: Legitimacy and the Power of Popular Sovereignty," *Stanford Journal of International Law* 36 (2000): 191–220.

13. Upendra Baxi argues in *The Future of Human Rights* (Oxford: OUP, 2006), 219, that at various UN social summits it has been emphasized that corporations should be "equal partners to human rights realization." Noting the effects of this tilt toward market actors and economic entities on the UN, Baxi argues that the NGO movement "remains exposed to the new grammar of market rationality. The very production of human rights goods and services now entails new, often onerous, patterns of social cooperation (working together) between the efficient causes of human and human rights violation and progressive social human rights movements that must persuade the violators, in cost-efficient ways, to reduce the nature and scope of the violation. In the process, some degree of commodification of human suffering and human rights becomes ineluctable." Do you agree with Baxi? Disagree? Either way, why?

14. Do you think that the record of multinational corporations in developing countries and the general ascendancy of neoliberal economic priorities hold out hope for the realization of human rights? Or do you think that human rights—including the NGO actors seeking to support them—are in certain forms of danger from the dominance of market values and rationality? Support your answers with examples and evidence.

35. PENELOPE SIMONS *International Law's Invisible Hand and the Future of Corporate Accountability for Violations of Human Rights*

[T]here is no long-term future outside of a radical cultural shift banning the self-serving Western perspective . . . the beginning is necessary of a process aimed at the development of a legal system that is much less about creating an efficient backbone for an exploitative economy and much more about a vision of civilization, justice and respect.
— International University College of Turin (IUC) Global Legal Standards Research Group, 2009

Excerpted with changes by permission of Edward Elgar Publishing from Penelope Simons, "International Law's Invisible Hand and the Future of Corporate Accountability for Violations of Human Rights," *Journal of Human Rights and the Environment* 3 (March 2012): 5–43, Copyright © 2012 Edward Elgar Publishing. Epigraphs: Executive Summary, (IUC) Global Legal Standards Research Group, 2009, https://hal.archives-ouvertes.fr/hal-00405054/document?; Susan Marks, "Empire's Law," *Indiana Journal of Global Legal Studies* 10, 1 (2003): 449–66.

Those studying globalization must begin to consider the ways in which globalizing processes intersect with and reproduce pre-existing forms of exploitation and exclusion.
—Susan Marks, "Empire's Law," 2007

There is something very wrong with our global economic system, which takes little, if any, account of the environmental and human rights costs of business activity. Such costs are neither internalized by markets nor adequately able to restrain market actors as "external" norms or standards. As Paul Hawken notes, "the single most damaging aspect of the present economic system is that the expense of destroying the earth is largely absent from the prices set in the marketplace."[1] Meanwhile, Upendra Baxi has remarked that "The suffering of impoverished people is irrelevant to the ruling standards

1. Paul Hawken, *The Ecology of Commerce: A Declaration of Sustainability* (New York: Harper Business, 1993), 13.

of the global capital, which must measure excellence of economic entrepreneurship by standards other than those provided by endless human rights normativity."[2] Moreover, there is a considerable unevenness of treatment between human rights and environmental concerns. While it may be possible to discern at least a rhetorical willingness among powerful corporate actors to consider binding legal obligations to address some of the environmental impacts of commerce that contribute to climate change, any discussion of binding international human rights obligations still meets strong resistance, if not vehement opposition. This resistance has characterized the debate on business and human rights for decades.

The current iteration of this debate now occupies a central place in global politics and has been focused around the [former] mandate of Harvard professor John Ruggie as UN Special Representative of the Secretary-General (SRSG) on the Issue of Human Rights and Transnational Corporations and Other Business Enterprises.[3] This new UN special procedure emerged out of the controversy created by the draft UN Norms on the Responsibility of Transnational Corporations and Other Business Enterprises with Regard to Human Rights (the Norms),[4] unanimously adopted in 2003 by the former Sub-Commission on Promotion and Protection of Human Rights. Their submission to the Human Rights Commission (now the Human Rights Council, UNHRC) sparked a heated controversy and propelled the issue to the forefront of global debate. Unlike other codes of conduct and multi-stakeholder initiatives such as the Global Compact, the Organization for Economic Cooperation and Development (OECD) Guidelines for Multinational Enterprises, or the Voluntary Principles on Security and Human

Rights, the Norms were drafted in mandatory language, were designed as a basis from which a treaty could be negotiated, and if adopted would have imposed binding human rights obligations directly on corporate actors. Indeed, one of the most contested and polarizing characteristics of the Norms was "their apparent attempt to impose obligations directly on companies, in addition to parallel obligations on states."[5]

Throughout his tenure as SRSG, Ruggie skillfully avoided the controversy created by the Norms. He made the decision early in his first mandate to leave them behind, dismissing them as a "distraction."[6] Adopting an approach he termed "principled pragmatism,"[7] he trod a careful and strategic path, consulting with a wide range of stakeholders and keeping business and government "on side."

In May 2011, at the end of his second mandate, Ruggie submitted his Guiding Principles on Business and Human Rights.[8] These principles are intended to implement his Protect, Respect and Remedy policy framework and subsequent related reports. The policy framework and Guiding Principles focus on addressing the regulatory gaps in relation to the human rights impacts of business activity, and, in particular, business activity in so-called "Third World" states.

One cannot dispute the significance of Ruggie's contribution to the global dialogue on corporate accountability. However, beyond recommending to the UNHRC the establishment of an international process to clarify legal standards relating to egregious violations of human rights that amount to international crimes—already widely accepted as applicable to business

2. Upendra Baxi, *The Future of Human Rights* (New Delhi: OUP, 2006), 252.
3. UNHRCOR, Business and Human Rights: Towards Operationalizing the "Protect, Respect and Remedy" Framework, Report of the Special Representative of the Secretary-General [SRSG] on the Issue of Human Rights and Transnational Corporations and Other Business Enterprises, (2009) UN Doc. A/HRC/11/13, 3–5, where the SRSG discusses how the framework is beginning to be used by governments, business, and civil society.
4. UNESCOR, Norms on the Responsibilities of Transnational Corporations and Other Business Enterprises with Regard to Human Rights (2003) UN Doc. E/CN.4/Sub.2/2003/12/Rev.2.

5. David Kinley, Justine Nolan, and Natalie Zerial, "The Politics of Corporate Social Responsibility: Reflections on the United Nations Human Rights Norms for Corporations," *Company and Securities Law Journal* 25 (2007): 30–42, 35.
6. UNESCOR, Interim Report of the Special Representative of the Secretary-General [SRSG] on the Issue of Human Rights and Transnational Corporations and Other Business Enterprises (2006) UN Doc. E/CN.4/2006/97, at 69.
7. Ibid., 81.
8. UNHRCOR, Guiding Principles on Business and Human Rights: Implementing the United Nations "Protect, Respect and Remedy" Framework, Report of the Special Representative of the Secretary-General [SRSG] on the Issue of Human Rights and Transnational Corporations and Other Business Enterprises, John Ruggie (2011), UN Doc. A/HRC/17/31.

entities—neither Ruggie's policy framework nor his Guiding Principles recommend that, going forward, the UN strategy for addressing corporate human rights impunity should include the goal of developing international legal obligations for business entities. According to Ruggie, "The root cause of the business and human rights predicament today lies in the governance gaps created by globalization—between the scope and impact of economic forces and actors and the capacity of societies to manage their adverse consequences." These gaps, he has argued, create a "permissive environment for the wrongful acts by companies of all kinds without adequate sanctioning or reparation."[9]

It is argued here, however, that, to address corporate impunity effectively, one simply cannot deal with the governance gaps alone. One must also identify and address the root causes of those gaps. This article thus seeks to demonstrate the problems with the SRSG's approach by arguing that, along with the interventions of international financial institutions in the economies of developing states, one of the most significant impediments to corporate human rights accountability is the structure of the international legal system itself.

BINDING OBLIGATIONS FOR CORPORATE ACTORS AND THE APPROACH OF THE SRSG

Throughout his mandate, SRSG Ruggie implied that binding international obligations for corporate actors might be included in his strategy to address corporate human rights impunity. Making reference to the Norms and to his decision that they were unhelpful to the advancement of the mandate, he maintained that he had not ruled out the possibility that international obligations could have a place in his recommendations: "nothing that has been said here should be taken to imply that innovative solutions to the challenges of business and human rights are not necessary or that the further evolution of international and domestic legal principles in relation to corporations will not form part of those solutions."[10] Yet, despite his contention, neither the final report of the SRSG's first mandate nor the first two reports of his second mandate (his

2009 and 2010 reports) which build on this framework, nor the Guiding Principles, outline any concrete role for international legal obligations for corporations.

THE "PROTECT, RESPECT, AND REMEDY" POLICY FRAMEWORK, THE GUIDING PRINCIPLES, AND GOVERNANCE CAPACITY

For Ruggie, an important first step in addressing corporate human rights impunity was the further elucidation and codification of the state "duty to protect." This exercise, he argued, would help to clarify where direct legal obligations for corporations might be needed. Accordingly, aiming to provide a coherent approach to the "Protect, Respect and Remedy" framework by addressing governance gaps and a means to develop the normative content of corporate responsibility for human rights, the framework focuses on three pillars: the further development of the state duty to protect under international human rights law; the clarification of the moral responsibility of corporate actors to respect human rights; and the development of remedies for victims of corporate violations of human rights.[11] The framework and its further development or "operationalization" in the 2009 and 2010 reports, along with the "Guiding Principles," goes some way to addressing aspects of the problem of corporate human rights impunity. This includes: disentangling and clarifying the respective human rights obligations of states under international human rights law and the moral responsibility of corporations to respect human rights (to do no harm); suggesting a range of important policy areas on which both home and host states should focus to ensure that corporate actors respect human rights in their business activities; providing ideas for grievance mechanisms for victims of human rights abuses, and guidance to states and business on how to implement these policies.

[*Eds.*—The author proceeds then to consider proposals put forward by SRSG Ruggie for safeguarding state capacity to protect international human rights by way of Bilateral Investment Treaties (BITs) and host state government agree-

---

9. Ibid., 3.
10. Ibid.

11. Ibid., 17.

ments (HGAs). The author concludes that, in the end, these proposals "appear to ignore or to gloss over the power relations reflected in, and created by, these types of agreements, as well as the long history of exploitation of Third World states and facilitation of foreign corporate activity." She continues:] BITs and HGAs are only the tip of the iceberg. The human rights governance capacity of many Third World states has been undermined by years of economic intervention by international financial institutions and is deeply embedded in the structure of the international system. The history and current iteration of this process is examined next relative to the work of Third World Approaches to International Law (TWAIL) scholars.

GOVERNANCE CAPACITY: INTERNATIONAL LAW AND INSTITUTIONS

TWAIL scholarship considers and critiques the power relationships entrenched in the structure of international law from the perspective of Third World peoples and states. While by no means homogeneous in their critiques, TWAIL scholars (or "TWAILers") articulate certain common concerns. According to O. C. Okafor, the "TWAIL movement within the discipline of international legal studies is best viewed as a broad dialectic (or large umbrella) of opposition to the generally unequal, unfair, and unjust character of an international legal regime that all too often (but not always) helps subject the Third World to domination, subordination, and serious disadvantage."[12] For Makau Mutua, TWAIL scholarship:

is driven by three basic, interrelated and purposeful objectives. The first is to understand and deconstruct and unpack the uses of international law as a medium for the creation and perpetuation of a racialized hierarchy of international norms and institutions that subordinate non-Europeans to Europeans. Second it seeks to construct and present an alternative normative legal edifice for international governance. Finally, TWAIL seeks

through scholarship, policy, and politics to eradicate the conditions of underdevelopment in the Third World.[13]

In an increasingly globalized world "national governments, even the most powerful among them, face growing difficulty in controlling the activities of business."[14] However, it is the Third World states that face the greatest challenges in this regard. In addition, a significant proportion of corporate violations of human rights or complicity in such abuses take place within these states. TWAIL scholarship therefore provides an indispensable critical lens for examining the problem of corporate human rights impunity and governance capacity.

The Postcolonial Era and Economic Governance

In his monograph *Imperialism, Sovereignty and the Making of International Law*, Antony Anghie undertakes an historical analysis of colonialism and international law. In doing so he unpacks and demonstrates the ways in which international law has been used from colonial times to the present to subjugate and suppress the peoples of the Third World. Unsurprisingly, the economic interests of European and other Northern states (and their corporate actors) have played a central role in this history. The desire to gain control of natural resources was the driving force behind the conquest of non-European peoples and establishment of colonies.[15] International legal rules were developed in relation to colonialism to justify and protect those interests. The underlying purpose of international law that was developed in the context of the colonial and postcolonial eras was precisely the promotion and protection of economic interests of the North. Thus, as newly independent states emerged from colonial rule as sovereign entities and attempted to assert their sovereignty and establish control over their natu-

---

12. See Obiora C. Okafor, "Newness, Imperialism, and International Legal Reform in Our Time: A TWAIL Perspective," *Osgoode Hall Law Journal* 43 (2005): 171–91, 176.

13. Makau Mutua, "What Is TWAIL?" *American Society of International Law, Proceedings of the Annual Meeting* 94 (2000): 31–40.
14. Susan Marks, "Empire's Law," 461. Marks goes on to say that "The question of the significance of this development for nation-state based systems of power is considered by many to be one of the most important political questions of our age."
15. Antony Anghie, *Imperialism, Sovereignty and the Making of International Law* (Cambridge: CUP, 2005), 211.

ral resources, Northern states responded using legal doctrines such as state succession, acquired rights, contracts, and consent to protect the interests of their corporate nationals in these states and to resist the attempt by these new sovereign actors to establish a new international economic order which included their own sovereignty over their natural resources.

Anghie notes, for example, that former colonial powers sought new ways to justify the protection of concession agreements which often had been acquired through coercion or through dubious legal agreements based on the ostensible "consent" of colonial peoples. According to Anghie, this protectionism was accomplished through early arbitral decisions concerning disputes between Third World states and transnational oil and gas corporations such as two key decisions, the Abu Dhabi arbitration[16] and the Qatar case,[17] which were among those cases instrumental in developing international law relative to state contracts. These cases, he states, explicitly demonstrate the techniques used by arbitrators to extend the protections for corporate investors and which had the effect of diminishing host state sovereignty, and thereby host state governance capacity.

This was accomplished in a number of ways. First, such contracts were removed from the purview of the domestic law of the host state on the basis that (in the case of Abu Dhabi) no domestic law existed or that (in the case of Qatar) such law that did exist was not sufficient for the purpose of interpreting the investment contract in question. In these and subsequent cases, arbitrators drew on the doctrine of sources to apply "general principles of law" to extend the laws, legal doctrines, and principles of the home state (including acquired rights and unjust enrichment) to the contract. Second, arbitrators began to treat these agreements as having been "internationalized." This conclusion, Anghie notes, was based on the asserted "unique nature" of such agreements and on the fact that they were governed not by domestic law but by an "international law of contracts" drawn from general

principles of law.[18] Thus, Anghie notes, by the time the *Texaco v. Libya Award*[19] was decided in the late 1970s these developments had "enabled the effortless transposition of Western concepts of law that provided for the comprehensive protection of private property."[20]

In disputes over these contracts, international law and legal argumentation were used also to alter the relative bargaining power of the corporate actors involved by bringing them onto the same plane as the sovereign states. On the one hand, the agreements were held to be "quasi-treaties" between a sovereign state and a private actor. By contracting with a private actor, it was argued, the states in these situations elevated the corporate actors to a quasi-sovereign entity. On the other hand, such agreements were characterized as private contracts, not between a sovereign state and a private actor, but between two private parties, thus negating the sovereign status of the state and removing its bargaining power as a sovereign entity. As Anghie puts it: "Whether a quasi-treaty between a sovereign and a quasi-sovereign entity, or a contract between two private parties, what is common to both characterizations is the real reduction of the powers of the sovereign Third-World state with respect to the Western corporation."[21]

What Anghie's research makes clear is that a diminished economic governance capacity has been a reality for Third World states since their emergence as states into the international community. Put another way, these states began their life as new subjects of international law with significantly less control over foreign investment than their Northern counterparts.

International Financial Institutions and Human Rights Governance

One recurring theme that emerges in the TWAIL scholarship is how this history of Third World states and international law is replicated

16. *Petroleum Development Ltd v. The Sheikh of Abu Dhabi* (1951) ILR 144.
17. *Qatar (Ruler of) v. International Marine Oil Company* (1953) ILR 534.

18. Anghie, *Imperialism, Sovereignty and the Making of International Law*, 229–30.
19. *Texaco Overseas Petroleum Co. and Cal. Asiatic Oil Co. v. The Gov't of the Libyan Arab Republic*, 53 ILR 389 (1977).
20. Anghie, *Imperialism, Sovereignty and the Making of International Law*, 230.
21. Ibid., 235.

in the contemporary international legal system. As Okafor notes, "despite the discontinuities that exist in the exact forms and techniques that were deployed, there is indeed a historical continuity from at least the sixteenth century onward in international law's tolerance of, if not active support for, the negation and/or erasure of Third World . . . agency."[22]

For Chimni, what distinguishes more recent developments in international law from the colonial period are the means and manner through which this is accomplished. He writes:

> The colonial period saw the complete and open negation of the autonomy of the colonized countries. In the era of globalization, the reality of dominance is best conceptualized as a more stealthy, complex and cumulative process. A growing assemblage of international laws, institutions and practices coalesce to erode the independence of third world countries in favour of transnational capital and powerful States. The ruling elite of the third world, on the other hand, has been unable and/or unwilling to devise, deploy, and sustain effective political and legal strategies to protect the interests of third world peoples.[23]

This assemblage of international laws, institutions, and practices, which has transformed the relationship between Third World states and international law, refers to, among other things, the lending practices and policies of the World Bank and the IMF as well as the growth of international trade and investment rules over the past two decades. Both of these have had significant implications with respect to Third World states' authority and ability to comply with their international human rights obligations [because, as is well known,] recipient states of IMF and World Bank loans were required by these institutions to implement a particular set of economic policies to restructure their economies and reduce government intervention. Voting structure in these institutions, as Chimni observes, has given Northern states "a dominant voice in the decision-making process, with the result that third world countries and peoples [have been] unable to influence in any way the content of conditionalities imposed upon them."[24] These conditionalities required, among other things, the liberalization of domestic markets (including the lowering of tariffs, the deregulation of labor markets, privatization, and deregulation of business activity), on the basis that such measures would stabilize their economies and enhance economic growth. In addition, the IMF and the World Bank often provided the technical support to reform legal regimes in a manner that would accomplish these objectives, tending "to concentrate on improving policies and institutions in favor of investors, mainly foreign, without commensurately strengthening policies and institutions for the poor and environment and thereby creating an imbalance."[25]

The structural adjustment programs, development policies, and good governance policies were premised on addressing poverty and the needs of Third World states. TWAIL scholars, among others, have argued that the development and good governance policies allowed the World Bank to increase its intervention in these states and to give the appearance of protecting human rights while continuing the pursuit of their neoliberal policies. Thus, James Gathii observes that

> The good governance agenda recasts the neoliberal economic policies of the World Bank in the guise of a new lingo compatible with, rather than opposed to, human rights. This conception gives preference to economic policy over human rights, unless these rights can be conceptualized within this economic logic,

22. Obiora C. Okafor, "Poverty, Agency and Resistance in the Future of International Law: An African Perspective," in Richard Falk, Balakrishnan Rajagopal, and Jacqueline Stevens, eds., *International Law and the Third World: Reshaping Justice* (New York: Routledge-Cavandish, 2008), 100–101.
23. B. S. Chimni, "Third World Approaches to International Law: A Manifesto," in Antony Anghie et al., eds., *The Third World and International Order: Law, Politics and Globalization* (Boston: Nijhoff, 2003), 72.

24. B. S. Chimni, "International Institutions Today: An Imperial Global State in the Making," *EJIL* 15 (2001): 1–37, 20.
25. Heike Mainhardt-Gibbs, "The World Bank Extractive Industries Review: The Role of Structural Reform Programs Towards Sustainable Development Outcomes," in *Striking a Better Balance: The Final Report of the Extractive Industries Review* (Washington, D.C.: World Bank, 2003), 6: 6.

such as openness in international trade, finance, commerce, and reduced social spending in education and health, for example. The World Bank has, therefore, tended to support only those rights that fit within its ascendant laissez-faire commitments. Ultimately then, it is civil and political rights—those most compatible with neo-liberal economic reform, such as private property and freedom of contract—that have received the most support in the good governance agenda.[26]

The measures prescribed also served the interests of foreign investors of the states that control the World Bank and the IMF. The effect of these conditionalities was to relocate the economic governance of these states to the international financial institutions, while at the same time weakening or undermining the ability of these states to undertake social reform, including measures to respect, protect, and fulfil the human rights of those subject to their jurisdiction. Moreover, these programs have played a significant role in increasing poverty in these states and causing violations of human rights. As Salomon observes, "Disaggregated into its component parts, poverty reflects a range of violated human rights and the violation of many human rights is, in turn, a cause of poverty."[27]

INTERNATIONAL TRADE AND INVESTMENT LAW: ENTRENCHING LIBERALIZATION MEASURES

International trade and investment laws are also implicated in this deterritorialization of economic governance and the facilitation of corporate activity. An increasingly sophisticated regime of direct and indirect corporate rights has been entrenched under the various free trade agreements such as North American Free Trade Agreement (NAFTA), the World Trade Organization (WTO) agreements, as well as the large number of bilateral free trade agreements and investment treaties between developed and Third World states.

An examination of WTO law, policy, practice, and its impacts is essential to understanding the current state of human rights governance incapacity, particularly in Third World states. First, the relationship between the WTO, the World Bank, and the IMF is entrenched in the Marrakesh Agreement establishing the WTO.[28] The WTO has an obligation to cooperate with the Bank, the IMF, and other related agencies with the aim of "achieving greater coherence in global economic policy-making."[29] Second, these agreements have had much the same effect on governance capacity as the World Bank and IMF interventions have had. As William Tabb observes: "the thrust of international agreements on trade and investment has been almost uniformly to extend TNC freedom to operate with fewer impediments globally. It is the freedom of sovereign states to regulate economic activity which has been restricted."[30] Studies have shown that the liberalization requirements imposed by the trade agreements—which WTO member states are required to adopt as a complete package—can and do have an impact on the ability of states to comply with their international human rights obligations.

The WTO Agreement on Agriculture (AoA)[31] is a case in point. Agriculture plays a vital role in the economies of many Third World states. According to the Food and Agriculture Organisation (FAO), "Some 70 per cent of the poor in developing countries live in rural areas and depend on agriculture for their livelihoods, either directly or indirectly. In the poorest of countries, agricultural growth is the driving force of the rural economy. Particularly, in the most food-insecure countries, agriculture is crucial for income and employment generation."[32]

For Third World states—particularly those in

26. James T. Gathii, "Good Governance as a Counter Insurgency Agenda to Oppositional and Transformative Social Projects in International Law," *Buffalo Human Rights Law Review* 5 (1999): 107–74, 121–22.
27. Margot Salomon, "International Economic Governance and Human Rights Accountability," LSE Law, Society and Economy Working Papers 9/2007, 19, www.lse.ac.uk/collections/law/wps/wps.htm [Eds.— accessed 22 June 2015].

28. Marrakesh Agreement Establishing the World Trade Organization (15 April 1994), 1867 UNTS 154.
29. Ibid., arts. 111, 5.
30. William K. Tabb, *Economic Governance in the Age of Globalization* (New York: Columbia University Press, 2004), 272.
31. Agreement on Agriculture (15 April 1994), 1867 UNTS 410.
32. Food and Agriculture Organization of the United Nations (FAO), *The State of Food Insecurity in the World 2006: Eradicating World Hunger—Taking Stock Ten Years After the World Food Summit* (Rome: FAO, 2006), 28.

the early stages of economic development—state intervention in the agricultural sector is critical to ensuring agricultural growth. Historically, states have protected their agriculture sectors as they move from early to middle stages of economic development. They have done so by using a wide range of policy mechanisms, including state trading and export monopolies; a variety of nontariff barriers; state marketing boards to ensure price stability for both producers and consumers; subsidies for producer inputs and credit; and government investment in rural infrastructure and agricultural research, most of which are now prohibited under the AoA.

The AoA requires WTO members to liberalize their agricultural markets by eliminating farm subsidies (although certain minimum levels are allowed), reducing export subsidies, changing all non-tariff barriers to tariffs (a process known as "tarification"), and reducing their tariffs on agricultural products. Many Third World states had already liberalized their agricultural markets under the structural reform programs of the World Bank and IMF. Many of them therefore had few, if any, subsidy programs in place, and are now prohibited from reintroducing them. At the same time, the AoA rules allowed certain industrialized states to keep particular subsidy programs intact and, through the tarification process, to set high initial tariffs on many products crucial to the economies of Third World states "in terms of food supply, employment, economic growth and poverty reduction."[33]

The impact of the AoA rules is compounded by corporate activity in global agricultural markets. These markets are dominated by small groups of corporations that control almost every sector of the agricultural industry—from farm inputs such as seeds, pesticides, and fertilizers, to exporting, shipping, processing, and food retailing. There are no provisions in the AoA or in any other WTO agreement to deal with market structure and concentration of corporate power. Nor does the AoA, or any other relevant WTO agreement, adequately regulate the practice of selling goods at below-production costs—a practice known as dumping. Transnational corporate actors, mainly from industrialized states that control the markets, have been able to benefit from, among other things, protected subsidies and then from selling onto the world market at below the cost of production, with the result that many Third World states have been unable to compete globally against such commodities with their exports. Nor have these states been able to prevent cheaper subsidized goods from undercutting the price of locally produced agricultural products in domestic markets. In both cases, the livelihoods of farmers and farm laborers are placed at risk.

In this way, the AoA has contributed to undermining the ability of these states to protect important economic and social rights, including, significantly, the right to food. The FAO has noted that "Opening national agricultural markets to international competition—especially from subsidized competitors—before basic market institutions and infrastructure are in place can undermine the agriculture sector, with long-term negative consequences for poverty and food security."[34]

FEMINIST INSIGHTS: CORPORATE ACTORS AND THE STRUCTURE OF INTERNATIONAL LAW

The preceding sections illustrate some of the ways in which international law and international financial institutions can be understood to have undermined the ability of states to regulate foreign economic activity in compliance with their human rights obligations. This section engages in a closer study of the structure of international law and its implications for corporate human rights accountability, and does so by drawing on feminist insights.

Feminist structural bias critiques, in particular, provide a useful approach to exploring the power dynamics and partiality embedded in the structure of international law, premised upon the notion that international law protects male

---

33. FAO, "Synthesis of Country Case Studies," *Agriculture, Trade and Food Security: Issues and Options in the WTO Negotiations from the Perspective of Developing Countries: Report and Papers of an FAO Symposium Held at Geneva on 23–24 September 1999*, Paper 3, 19. Also available at www.fao.org/docrep/meeting/X3065E.htm [*Eds.*— accessed 22 June 2015].

34. FAO, *State of Food and Agriculture 2005: Agricultural Trade and Poverty—Can Trade Work for the Poor?* (Rome: FAO, 2005), 6, 140.

interests and that therefore its structure is biased against women. In their monograph, *The Boundaries of International Law*,[35] Hilary Charlesworth and Christine Chinkin, show how, through "silences [as well as] positive rules and structures,"[36] the gendered structure of international law marginalizes or excludes women—a phenomenon that "does not emerge as a simple gap or vacuum that . . . might be remedied by some rapid construction work, [but] rather [as] an integral part of the structure of the international legal order, a critical element of its stability."[37] International legal discourse, they observe, is founded on "a variety of distinctions, ostensibly between 'public' and 'private' [that] shape international law and . . . have gendered consequences."[38] For example, while international law "formally removes 'private' concerns from its sphere, the international legal system nevertheless strongly influences them. One form of influence is the fact that 'private' issues are left to national, rather than international, regulation."[39] Certain concerns that may have an impact on women, therefore, may be left to be dealt with by the domestic law of the state, even where this may result in, or allow for, the subjugation of women. Thus, these public/private distinctions, they argue, not only "characterise the reality of the international community . . . they are also connected with political choices of whether or not to intervene legally."[40]

In a similar way, international law generally leaves the regulation of corporate actors (private capital) to the domestic sphere. International human rights law speaks to the actions of states and does not directly address the activities of non-state actors. It also imposes no clear obligations on states to regulate the extraterritorial human rights conduct of their corporate nationals. Nor does it clearly require states to deal with corporate groups in a way that protects the human rights of individuals outside the state's jurisdiction. International law itself views transnational corporate actors as disaggregated entities—each parent, subsidiary, and affiliate as a separate legal entity—each subject to the laws of the state within which they are incorporated or operate, even though these entities may, and often do, act as an integrated whole. This lack of direct international oversight has an important impact on how the domestic sphere deals with these actors.

Moreover, in domestic law, the integrated nature of the corporate group generally remains legally unrecognized, a factor that has significant implications for human rights accountability. Under domestic corporate/company laws, corporate actors may legitimately use a subsidiary to shelter the parent company and other members of a corporate group from activities that may attract legal liability. Even in cases where a subsidiary is found liable for egregious human rights abuses, "the liability will not necessarily attach to related companies and therefore it will not necessarily be the case that a successful claimant can access the assets of the corporate group . . . or the assets of its members and directors."[41] Domestic courts are reticent to "pierce the veil" of corporate groups to impose liability on parent companies for the acts of their subsidiaries. This reticence becomes all the more problematic in cases where the subsidiary (which allegedly committed, or was complicit in, the impugned acts in the host state) is held by the parent corporation in the home state through a number of subsidiaries, each one incorporated in a different national jurisdiction.

Feminist theoretical insight suggests that the structure of international law is such that these entities can exploit its silences, remaining on the margins and navigating between two dichotomously constructed regulatory spheres. In this way corporate entities avoid both international and domestic oversight, while at the same time gaining robust legal protections for their trade and investment activities. Karen Engle draws an interesting comparison in this

35. Hilary Charlesworth and Christine Chinkin, *The Boundaries of International Law: A Feminist Analysis* (Manchester: Manchester University Press, 2000).
36. Ibid., 49.
37. Ibid.
38. Ibid., 57.
39. Ibid., 56.
40. Ibid.

41. Rachel Nicolson and Emily Howie, "The Impact of the Corporate Form on Corporate Liability for International Crimes: Separate Legal Personality, Limited Liability and the Corporate Veil—An Australian Law Perspective," Paper for ICJ Expert Legal Panel on Corporate Complicity in International Crimes (2007), 11.1.160, http://www.hrlrc.org.au/files/ icj-paper-e-howie-and-r-nicolson-final-0207.pdf [*Eds.*—accessed 22 June 2015].

regard between women and market actors. Both, she argues, inhabit the margins of international law. But unlike women who seek to be included and protected by international law, corporations and other business entities, operating from a position of power, have chosen to remain on the unregulated periphery, seeking precisely to avoid public international law's interference in their activities.[42]

However, contrary to Engle's conclusion that global business actors operate solely in the private or unregulated sphere, it is clear that these powerful actors are able to play on both sides of the public/private fence. Thus, the regulation of trade and investment—which addresses and circumscribes governmental conduct to facilitate and protect the activities of private capital—is deemed an appropriate matter for international law to address. Unlike women, transnational corporate actors are the privileged insiders of the international legal system, playing key roles in the promotion, negotiation, and drafting of these trade and investment regimes and enjoying remarkable success in resisting and avoiding the "imposition of new human rights norms on their structure and operations."[43] The public/private, international/domestic, regulated/unregulated distinctions are interdependent and operate to facilitate rather than restrain corporate activity.

Charlesworth and Chinkin as well as others have also pointed to the gendered consequences of the distinction in international law between binding/nonbinding obligations. Matters of concern to women such as the environment and human rights, for example, are treated as "soft" issues, that are deemed appropriately regulated by "soft" nonbinding instruments. As Charlesworth and Chinkin state:

> States use "soft" law structures for matters that are not regarded as essential to their interests ("soft" issues in international law) or where they are reluctant to incur binding obligations. Many of the issues that concern women thus suffer a double marginalization in terms of traditional international law-making: they are

seen as the "soft" issues of human rights and are developed through "soft" modalities of law-making that allow states to appear to accept such principles while minimizing their legal commitments.[44]

A consistent feature of the business and human rights debate has been the insistence by states and corporations on "soft" or "voluntary" forms of regulation, and this approach has characterized the work of the SRSG. In the same way, therefore, the human rights of those subject to corporate abuses (or business complicity in such abuses) are doubly marginalized by being treated as a soft issue and by the regulation of extraterritorial corporate activity by "soft" law. In the end, this soft-law approach becomes binding in its result on the victims of human rights abuses.

INTERNATIONAL LAW'S INVISIBLE HAND AND THE FUTURE OF CORPORATE HUMAN RIGHTS ACCOUNTABILITY

The preceding sections suggest that the root causes of corporate impunity for violations of human rights are deeply embedded in the international legal system. International law has been used progressively since colonial times to protect and facilitate foreign investment and trade activity while at the same time undermining the ability of Third World states to control and regulate transnational corporate actors. The policies and practices of international financial institutions have played a central role in this process. In addition, the structure of international law itself and international law's relationship with domestic law are also implicated.

During his tenure, SRSG Ruggie identified certain aspects of this reality but failed to examine the deep structural roots of this problem.

CONCLUSION

Ruggie amassed significant goodwill among states and the business community during his tenure. His normative framework had been

42. Karen Engle, "Views from the Margins: A Response to David Kennedy," *Utah Law Review* 105–18 (1994): 108–9.
43. Baxi, *The Future of Human Rights*, note 2, 258.
44. Charlesworth and Chinkin, *The Boundaries of International Law*, note 35, 66.

widely endorsed by these two powerful constituencies, but by limiting his recommendations to the clarification of legal norms applicable to business where they engage in behavior that violates international criminal law norms, while at the same time cautioning against the adoption of a more general international treaty, Ruggie missed the opportunity to push states and business actors out of their comfort zone.

The problem of corporate impunity for extraterritorial human rights violations is deeply complex and needs to be tackled creatively and intelligently at a variety of jurisdictional and normative levels. The SRSG has made significant inroads on a number of fronts. Nevertheless, binding international human rights obligations for transnational human rights actors must form a part of the global strategy going forward. Without engaging international law as an integral part of the strategy to address corporate human rights impacts and accountability, as well as state governance capacity, there remains the fear that, despite some changes in state policies, business policy, due diligence and reporting, we will more or less continue business as usual.

QUESTIONS FOR REFLECTION AND DISCUSSION

1. Should multinational corporations and other transnational business enterprises be involved in promoting and protecting internationally recognized human rights, or should they stick to that for which they are constituted: producing goods and services, expanding markets, and making profits? Why? Why not?

2. Do multinational corporations and other transnational business enterprises have any comparative advantages relative to other entities or groups in promoting and protecting internationally recognized human rights? If so, what are they? If not, why not?

3. To what extent, if at all, is it appropriate or just to stretch institutions (such as business enterprises) created for one purpose to perform another (such as the promotion and protection of human rights)? Is that, in any case, what advocating for corporate human rights responsibility amounts to? Give reasons for your answers.

4. Simons notes that one of the most divisive characteristics of the draft UN Norms on the Responsibility of Transnational Corporations and Other Business Enterprises with Regard to Human Rights (the Norms) "was their apparent attempt to impose obligations directly on companies, in addition to parallel obligations on states." Do you think there is a case for multinational corporations and other transnational enterprises to bear mandatory human rights duties, analogous to those of the state? Why? Why not?

5. Of what would such a duty consist? Would the nature of the duty likely to be constructed affect your argument as to whether such a duty should be imposed on corporations or not? Is there a case to be made for the systematic regulation of multinational corporations and other business enterprises relative to the promotion and protection of human rights? If so, what is it? If not, why not?

6. Do you think SRSG Ruggie's approach, which he calls "principled pragmatism" and which is intended to keep business and government "on side," is adequate? Is it merely an accommodation to the existing distribution of power, or is it something more? Why? Is Ruggie's approach, which addresses "governance gaps," adequate? Why? Why not? What does Simons say? Do you agree with her? Why? Why not?

7. Ruggie's "protect, respect, and remedy" approach "focuses on three pillars: the further development of the state duty to protect under international human rights law; the clarification of the moral responsibility of corporate actors to respect human rights; and the development of remedies for victims of corporate violations of human rights." Analyze the differences, and the potential relationships between, the state's claimed legal duty to protect and the corporation's claimed moral duty to respect human rights. What are the strengths and weaknesses of this formulation? Is it adequate in the context of the current neoliberal, globalized world order? Why? Why not? For possible assistance, see Reading 38 (Grear) and Reading 39 (Evans) in this volume.

8. As Simons notes, Antony Anghie has argued that "The desire to gain control of natural resources was the driving force behind the conquest of non-European peoples and establishment of colonies." Can you see any analogues to these motives and trajectories of

engagement in the contemporary world? Where? What explains the observed continuities between colonialism and neoliberal globalization in the international legal order? Do you think this continuity is a positive or negative phenomenon? Support your position as fully and carefully as you can.

9. Simons cites approvingly James Gathii's argument that "The good governance agenda recasts the neo-liberal economic policies of the World Bank in the guise of a new lingo compatible with, rather than opposed to, human rights." Gathii argues, however, that this new rhetoric—e.g., openness in international trade, finance, commerce, and reduced social spending in education and health—"gives preference to economic policy over human rights [and that] The World Bank has [therefore] tended to support only those rights that fit within its ascendant laissez-faire commitments. Ultimately then," Gathii concludes, "it is civil and political rights—those most compatible with neoliberal economic reform, such as private property and freedom of contract—that have received the most support in the good governance agenda." How, if at all, do this view and the arguments on which it rests tie in with earlier readings in Chapter 4 of this volume on the status of socioeconomic rights? What commonalities and distinctions emerge between the positions of the writers in question, and what do any commonalities or distinctions you can find imply concerning the relationships between all of these issues? Support your argument as fully and precisely as you can, being careful to analyze with contextual accuracy.

10. What, if anything, do feminist critiques add to an account of the underlying structural assumptions of international law? What implications might this have, if any, for human rights and for the nature of the "human rights subject"? For possible assistance, see Chapter 1, Reading 2 (Grear) and Chapter 3, Reading 14 (Beveridge and Mullally). Do you think that the feminist critique of international law is helpful? Pointless? Why? Why not? Does it bear any relation to other critiques of international law based on other identity perspectives? Consider, for example, TWAIL scholarship: what is it and what are its central concerns? How does it tie into feminist critiques? Or with other readings in this volume? Can you discern any common themes? If so, what are they, where are they to be found, and what is their relationship, if any, with each other? Support your answer as fully and carefully as you can.

11. As historically conceived, human rights law is, in theory, about the relationship between human beings and the state. See, e.g., Reading 1 (Weston) in Chapter 1 of this volume. By what theory or logic, then, is it possible, if at all, to cause nonhuman corporate and other business entities to be accountable to the legal regime of public international human rights law? Indeed, by what theory or logic is it possible to hold legally accountable to public international human rights law private actors of any kind that have, at least in theory, little or no standing in the public international law order? Is it, in the end, a matter of only *moral* corporate responsibility, not *legal*? Why? Why not? What would Simons say? What might the U.S. Supreme Court say in light of its decision in *Citizens United v. Federal Election Commission*, 557 U.S. 952 (17 August 2009)(Docket No 8-205)? For that matter, what might the so-called "war on terrorism" tell us given that nonstate actors called terrorists are daily accused by Washington, London, and other capitals of violating virtually all the most fundamental international human rights doctrines, principles, and rules, not to mention the public international laws of war?

12. What worldview position do your answers to the foregoing eleven questions assume? In relation to what overall conception of life or set of values are your answers formulated?

36. JORDAN J. PAUST *The Human Right to Revolution*

This country, with its institutions, belongs to the people who inhabit it. Whenever they shall grow weary of the existing government, they can exercise their constitutional right of amending it or their revolutionary right to dismember or overthrow it.

—Abraham Lincoln, First Inaugural
Address, 4 March 1861

These are the words not of a twentieth-century revolutionary or even an eighteenth-century founder of our republic, but of a nineteenth-century Republican president at the beginning of a long and destructive civil war in the United States. What Abraham Lincoln recognized was the fundamental democratic precept that authority comes ultimately from the people of the United States, and that with this authority there is retained a "revolutionary right to dismember or overthrow" any governmental institution that is unresponsive to the needs and wishes of the people.[1]

Excerpted with changes by permission of Emory University School of Law and Jordan J. Paust, "The Human Right to Participate in Armed Revolution and Related Forms of Social Violence: Testing the Limits of Permissibility," *Emory Law Journal* 32 (1983): 545–81. Copyright © 1983 Emory University School of Law and Jordan J. Paust.

1. In this essay, the right of "revolution" refers to the right fundamentally to change a governmental structure or process within a particular nation-state, thus including the right to replace governmental elites or overthrow a particular government. Thus defined, one might distinguish "revolution" from claims for minority protection, claims to be free from external oppression, and claims to secession. It is worth emphasizing that this paper is concerned with the legal propriety (under domestic and international law) of revolutionary social violence and does not address moral propriety or "justness" as such. However, in contrast to some writers, it does recognize that civil disobedience might, in a given case, involve a repudiation of the general authority of a constituted government. But "civil disobedience" can, under certain circumstances, involve revolutionary claims, strategies, or effects. One author argues realistically that disobedience limited to particular matters, which "does not, in fact, challenge the existence of the larger society, only its authority in this or that case," is "not revolution but civil disobedience," adding that "unlimited and uncivil disobedience" is "revolution." Michael Walzer, "The Obligation to Disobey," in Edward Kent, ed., *Revolution and the Rule of Law* (Englewood Cliffs, N.J.: Prentice-Hall, 1971), 111, 119, 125.

The right of revolution recognized by President Lincoln has, of course, an early foundation in American history. Both the Declaration of Independence (1776) and the Declaration of the Causes and Necessity of Taking Up Arms (1775) contain recognitions of this right, and several state constitutions within the United States consistently recognized the right of the people "to reform, alter, or abolish government" at their convenience. Indeed, the American Republic was founded on revolution.

The American Revolution served as a precursor for numerous others in the Americas, Europe, and elsewhere, even into the twentieth century. Today, it is common to recognize that all peoples have a right to self-determination[2] and, as a necessary concomitant of national self-determination, a right to engage in revolution. Yet it is not as widely understood that, under international law, there are limits to the permissibility of armed revolution and the participation of individuals in revolutionary social violence.

The purpose of this essay is to clarify the nature and scope of the right of revolution. In doing so, it is necessary to identify the relationship between the right of revolution and the international legal precepts of authority, self-determination, and more general norms of human rights. With these interrelations in mind, one can also identify and clarify relevant legal constraints on armed revolution and the participation of individuals in such a process.

Such a focus should inform choice with regard to permissibility, but a realistic and policy-serving decision about the legality of any particular strategy of armed revolution (or of social violence in general) must also hinge upon adequate inquiry into the actualities of circumstance or contextual analysis. Such decisions must be guided by an awareness of community expectations about the process of authority as well as an awareness of all relevant domestic and international legal policies at stake, actual trends in authoritative decision, relevant features of past and present context, and probable future

2. For discussion of the right to self-determination relative to indigenous peoples, see Reading 22 (Engle) in Chapter 5.

effects that might condition the serving or thwarting of legal policies in the future.

With such a focus, one should discover that private individuals and groups can and do engage in numerous forms of permissible violence. It is too simplistic to say, therefore, that authoritative violence can only be engaged in by "the government" or by governmental elites and functionaries. The useful question is not whether private violence is permissible, but what forms of private violence are permissible, when, in what social context, and why. As Professor Reisman argues: "insistence on non-violence and deference to all established institutions in a global system with many injustices can be tantamount to confirmation and reinforcement of those injustices. In certain circumstances, violence may be the last appeal or the first expression of demand of a group or unorganized stratum for some measure of human dignity."[3] Of course, such an injunction can also have particular relevance concerning the question of revolutionary social violence. Here, as elsewhere, no facile "rule" or simplistic prohibition will do.

GENERAL LEGAL POLICIES AT STAKE

Natural Law, Authority of the People, and the American Revolution

Two historic declarations provide an inventory of the forms of oppression thought to justify armed revolution. The American Declaration of Independence proclaimed to the world the expectation that all governments are properly constituted "to secure" the inalienable rights of man, that governments derive "their just powers from the consent of the governed," and that "it is the Right of the People to alter or abolish any form of government which" becomes destructive of these ends. More specifically, the American people denounced the king of England as a tyrant who was "unfit to be the ruler of a free People" because, among other things, he invaded "the rights of the people, dissolved representative governmental bodies, obstructed the administration of justice, failed to control the depredations

of the military, and engaged in numerous other strategies of tyranny and oppression." The Declaration of the Causes and Necessity of Taking Up Arms had also denounced Parliament's "cruel and impolitic purpose of enslaving the colonial Americans . . . by violence, the British government's intemperate rage for unlimited domination, acts of cruel aggression, and numerous oppressive measures that had reduced our ancestors to the alternative of choosing an unconditional submission to the tyranny of irritated ministers, or resistance by force."

It is important to note two primary aspects of the right of revolution claimed in these two Declarations. First, the claim was made in a situation in which a ruler and a government sought to subject a people to despotism through various forms of political and economic oppression. Second, and most important, the Declaration of Independence was proclaimed "in the Name, and by authority of the . . . People." Thus, although the framers of these Declarations appealed to natural law and inalienable rights, including the right to be free from government oppression and to alter or abolish oppressive forms of government, the primary justifying criterion was the proclaimed authority of the people.

Since the dawn of U.S. constitutional history, the U.S. Supreme Court has consistently recognized that the primary source of authority in the United States is the people of the United States. As the Court early declared, "their will alone is to decide."[4] Thus, necessarily, any criterion of permissibility under U.S. domestic law must ultimately be compatible with the will of the people of the United States. The authority of the people is the peremptory criterion, and, under domestic law, their will alone is to decide.

For this reason, the right of revolution is in the nation as a whole and is not a right of some minority of an identifiable people. In Locke's view, the right of revolution was a right of the majority of a community. This view was shared by many of the founders of the American Republic as well as many others, and is reflected in early U.S. state constitutions.

In view of the above, one can also recognize the propriety of a claim by the government, when representing the authority of the people,

---

3. W. Michael Reisman, "Private Armies in a Global War System: Prologue to Decision," *VJIL* 14 (1973): 1–55, 32–33.

4. *Ware v. Hylton*, 3 U.S. (3 Dall.) 199, 237 (1796); see also 236.

to regulate certain forms of revolutionary violence or, when reasonably necessary, incitement to violence engaged in by a minority of the people of the United States and without their general approval. Indeed, several Supreme Court cases document the permissibility of such a claim, although a few others seem to go too far. If, however, the right of revolutionary violence is engaged in by the predominant majority of the people, or with their general approval, the government (or a part thereof) would necessarily lack authority, and governmental controls of such violence or incitements to violence would be impermissible. Thus, for example, it would be constitutionally improper to allege that incitement to violence is always a justification for government suppression of such conduct even if violence is imminent. Permissibility does not hinge on violence as such, but ultimately on the peremptory criterion of authority—i.e., the will of the people generally shared in the community.

In the United States, loyalty is owed to the Constitution as such and not to any particular government. Even some of the earlier cases that affirmed a broad power to regulate the advocacy of social violence mentioned a "danger to organized government," "existing Government," or "representative government" and thus, implicitly, to the American form of constitutional government. Also of primary concern was the need for the government to "be responsive to the will of the people . . . so that changes, if desired, may be obtained by peaceful means."[5]

Cases such as *Dennis v. United States, Yates v. United States*, and *Scales v. United States*[6] addressed the advocacy of violent revolution by members of the Communist Party of the United States who, as a small and disfavored minority, were hardly representing the general will and authority of the people of the United States at those periods in time. Thus, although mere advocacy is permissible today, the Communist Party, if it still represents a disfavored minority, would not have a right to initiate an armed revolution against the government of the United States.

In an unusual case, a United States circuit court responded to an alien's claim that the right of revolution is inherent in every individual by remarking: "That right, if it exists, depends upon where such individual attempts to operate," adding that "revolution presupposes an antagonism between a government and its nationals, not between a government and aliens. As a citizen of Denmark, appellant has no right of revolution as against the United States."[7] It is certainly not the point of the circuit court that all forms of outside participation in revolution are unlawful, especially in view of the well-known assistance of foreign participants to the American colonials during the Revolutionary War. Rather, the court held that foreign persons do not have a right of revolution against the government of the United States. In that sense, the decision was consistent with the view that a right of revolution can be exercised by a majority of the people of the United States, but not by a mere minority of the people or by nonresident aliens who are considered to form no part of the people of this nation.

In summary, numerous cases either affirm or are consistent with a distinction between permissible forms of violence approved by the authority of the people and unlawful violence, especially violence engaged in contrary to the authority of the people. Perhaps in recognition of such a distinction, Justice Black has stated:

> Since the beginning of history there have been governments that have engaged in practices against the people so bad, so cruel, so unjust and so destructive of the individual dignity of men and women that the right of revolution was all the people had left to free themselves. . . . I venture the suggestion that there are countless multitudes in this country, and all over the world, who would join [the] belief in the right of the people to resist by force tyrannical governments like those.[8]

As the next section demonstrates, there are apparently countless multitudes . . . all over the world who would recognize the permissibility of such a right of revolution by a people.

5. *Keyishian v. Board of Regents*, 385 U.S., at 602 (quoting *De Jonge v. Oregon*, 299 U.S. 353, 365 [1937]).
6. *Dennis*: 341 U.S. 494 (1951); *Yates*: 354 U.S. 298 (1957); *Scales*: 367 U.S. 203 (1961).

7. *Kjar v. Doak*, 61 F.2d 566, 569 (7th Cir. 1932).
8. *In re Anastaplo*, 366 U.S. 82, 113 (Black, J., dissenting).

PERMISSIBILITY UNDER INTERNATIONAL LAW

It is doubtful whether Justice Black had in mind specific portions of the 1948 Universal Declaration of Human Rights (UDHR) when he recognized the seemingly wide approval of a general right of revolution, but he could have. The preamble to the Universal Declaration declares, for instance, that "it is essential, if man is not to be compelled to have recourse, as a last resort, to rebellion against tyranny and oppression, that human rights should be protected by the rule of law." As one commentator has noted, the UDHR preamble actually supports the right of revolution or rebellion, and it reflects the growth of acceptance of that right at least from the time of the American Declaration of Independence, an acceptance so pervasive as to allow text writers to conclude that "the right of a people to revolt against tyranny is now a recognized principle of international law."[9] Indeed, prior to the American and French Revolutions of the eighteenth century, the right of revolution had been accepted in several human societies. Scholars have identified related expectations, for example, among the early Greeks and Romans; in Germanic folk law; among naturalist theorists such as Thomas Aquinas in medieval Western Europe; and in the writings of early international scholars such as Grotius and Vattel.

Today, the right of revolution is an important international precept and a part of available strategies for the assurance both of the authority of the people as the lawful basis of any government and of the process of national self-determination. Under international law, the permissibility of armed revolution is necessarily interrelated with legal precepts of authority and self-determination, as well as with more specific sets of human rights. For example, the right to change a governmental structure is necessarily interrelated with the question of the legitimacy of that structure in terms of the accepted standard of authority in international law and with the precept of self-determination, both of which are interrelated and are also interconnected with the human rights of individuals to participate in the political processes of their society." As recognized in numerous international instruments and by the International Court of Justice, all peoples have the right to self-determination and, by virtue of that right, to freely determine their political status."[10] Similarly it is recognized "that the application of the right of self-determination requires a free and genuine expression of the will of the peoples concerned."[11] Political self-determination, in fact, is a dynamic process involving the genuine, full, and freely expressed will of a given people, that is, a dynamic aggregate will of individuals. The "will of the people" is actually the dynamic outcome of such a process and reflects an equal and aggregate participation by individuals and groups in a process of authority.

Furthermore, there is a significant consistency among the precept of self-determination, the human right to individual participation in the political process, and the only standard of authority recognized in international law. Self-determination and human rights both demand that the only legitimate basis of the authority of any government is the dynamic process of self-determination and authority noted above.

The first two paragraphs of Article 21 of the Universal Declaration recognize the rights of every person "to take part in" the governmental processes of one's country and to "equal access to public service." The more significant content of Article 21, however, is set forth in paragraph 3 that states: "The will of the people shall be the basis of the authority of government; this will shall be expressed in periodic and genuine elections which shall be held by secret vote or by equivalent free voting procedures." A legitimate government, the Declaration affirms, is one in which the "will of the people" is the basis of authority. The authority of a government exists lawfully on no other basis, in no other form. Indeed, the only specific formal reference to the concept of authority that one finds among all of the major international legal documents is the reference to the authority of the people of a given community.

9. Gerald Sumida, "The Right of Revolution: Implications for International Law and Order," in Charles A. Barker, ed., *Power and Law: American Dilemma in World Affairs* (Baltimore: Johns Hopkins University Press, 1971), 130, 134.

10. Western Sahara Advisory Opinion, 1975 ICJ 12, 31 33, 36, citing several international instruments including the authoritative Declaration on Principles of International Law, GA Res. 2625, 25 U.N. GAOR Supp. (No. 28), at 121, UN Doc. A/8082 (1970).
11. Ibid., 32, 55.

Many interrelated norms from the Universal Declaration, when taken together, tend to confirm the clear and unswerving criterion of authority contained in the third paragraph of Article 21. When one considers how individuals acting within a political process are to exercise their rights, affirmed in the Declaration, to take part in governmental processes and to obtain equal access to public service in a manner that is consistent with the rights of each and every person to equality, dignity, and the equal protection and enjoyment of law, it seems clear that participation should be on the basis of one person, one voice. Stated differently, an equally weighted "will" of each individual conjoined in a so-called "will of the people" or common expression is the only formula that allows equal individual participation in a political process. Having this in mind, it is understandable why Article 21 contains other references to what one might term the related aspects of a process of authority. There is a great deal of illuminating consistency within the Article, evidencing that the people of a given community have the right to alter, abolish, or overthrow any form of government that becomes destructive to the process of self-determination and the right of individual participation. Such a government, of course, would also lack authority and, as a government representing merely some minority of the political participants, it could be overthrown by the majority in an effort to ensure authoritative government, political self-determination, and the human rights of all members of the community equally and freely to participate.

Thus, as mentioned, the right of revolution supported by the preamble to the Universal Declaration and accepted by text writers as a principle of international law is a concomitant precept and a part of available strategies for the securing of the authority of the people and national self-determination. Importantly also, the international precepts of authority and self-determination provide criteria relevant to our inquiry into the permissibility of individual participation in armed revolution. As in the case of domestic standards, the right of revolution is necessarily a right of the majority against, for example, an oppressive governmental elite. Furthermore, the authority of the people is the only legitimate standard. Although the process of authority is dynamic and individuals might engage in violence with the approval of the people, the right of revolution is not a right of only some minority of the people or to be utilized in an effort to oppress the authority of the people. Indeed, in view of the many interrelated international legal precepts noted above, an oppression of the authority of the people is a form of political slavery that is not only violative of human rights but also constitutes a treason against humanity.

THE CONCEPT OF REVOLUTION AND
CRITERIA OF PERMISSIBILITY

When one considers further the use of the concept of revolution in American legal history, one is struck by the fact that many conceptual categorizations have been utilized. The right of revolution has been described variously as "the great and fundamental right of every people to change their institutions at will"; a "legal right" of the people; "the reserved right" of a people; "an original right" of the people; a "natural right"; "a most sacred right"; "an indubitable, inalienable, and indefeasible right" of the community; and a "revolutionary right."

Perhaps some of these are useful, but they seem merely to supplement the general points noted above that this right is that of the people, it is their right to change their institutions at will, and the peremptory criterion of permissibility remains the authority of the people. Even the U.S. Supreme Court has added little to clarify the criteria or the policies at stake in differing social contexts.

Although some have recognized that armed revolution is a form of "self-defense" for an oppressed people and others seek to limit the right of revolution to cases of a reasonably necessary defense against political oppression, the principles of necessity and proportionality should apply only to the strategies of violence utilized during revolution and are not needed for the justification of a revolution. Indeed, according to Lincoln, Jefferson, and so many of the founders, revolution is justified whenever the people generally so desire.

The "necessity" test endorsed by some writers might actually relate to another question, the question of when a defense of right arises because of oppression of an individual's right to participate in the political process. It might be argued that an individual or group has a right to use strategies of violence when reasonably necessary and proportionate to the effectuation of a human right to participate. If so, such a use of violence is not to be engaged in to deny participation by others or to oppress others politically, and such a use of violence might not have as its aim the achievement of an authoritative revolution by the people as a whole. Nevertheless, permissible revolution might be stimulated by such a strategy, and governmental elites that deny a relatively full and free sharing of power might themselves be denied some form of participation temporarily in order to effectuate the fuller and freer sharing and shaping of power by all participants.

It is important to reiterate here that the right of revolution as such is not vested in some minority of an identifiable society. Violence as a right of political failures is incompatible with any objective conception of self-determination of a people and contravenes domestic and international standards of authority as well as the human right of other persons to participate. In the turbulent 1960s, Professor Charles Black identified a related question—whether disobedience of state laws is compatible with the authority of a federal constitutive process.[12] He argued that a revolutionary movement using massive "civil disobedience" mounted against "the very structure of state power" is not necessarily unconstitutional or "incompatible with federal allegiance." He also suggested that we are not "bound to hold up the wax hand of the effigy of state law" in such a circumstance where state power "cannot and will not fulfill its basic obligations to federal law and human justice." Thus, he argues that certain forms of revolutionary activity can result in revolutionary change within a part of the overall constitutive process and that a higher, overall authority reflected in "federal law and human justice" can provide a useful criterion for choice about permissibility. Actually, as Black noted, such a movement within a federal union can be supported by federal authority and constitute "a mere claim of legal right, asserted against what only seems to be law." Others seem to agree that such a claim is permissible and go so far as to suggest that it is not a claim to engage in civil "disobedience," but is actually an

appeal to supreme federal law within a federal union. It is, at least, a claim to disobey one set of putative laws under a claim of deference to another.

Even in times of relative tranquility, the decisions of official elites are constantly subject to a process of review. All persons are participants in such a process whether or not they are aware of that fact, even if they participate through an apathetic or hostile inaction that can function as a form of passive acceptance of official elite decisions or allow more active participants to play a more effective role in the review of decisions. As McDougal, Lasswell, and Reisman remarked in another context:

> Most of us are performing these roles without being fully aware of the scope and consequences of our acts. Because of this, our participation is often considerably less effective than it might be. Every individual cannot, of course, realistically expect or demand to be a decisive factor in every major decision. Yet the converse feeling of pawnlike political impotence, of being locked out of effective decision, is an equally unwarranted orientation. The limits of the individual's role are as much a function of his passive acquiescence and ignorance of the potentialities of his participation as of the structures of the complex human organizations of the contemporary world.[13]

Such a recognition is profound. It can redirect attention to the fact of private participation in the creation, shaping, and termination of law as well as private participation in the overall process of authority. Whether actively or passively, individuals do play a role even in a revolutionary process during which other participants make contending claims about authority and even clash in arms.

There is an unavoidable need, therefore, to address the question of the legality of various forms of private participation. Since the declarations of even authoritatively constituted official elites are not determinative, what jurisprudential orientations offer the most useful guidance concerning the permissibility of various forms of

---

12. See Charles Black, "The Problem of the Compatibility of Civil Disobedience with American Institutions of Government," *Texas Law Review* 43 (1965): 492–506.

13. Myres S. McDougal, Harold D. Lasswell, and W. Michael Reisman, "Theories About International Law: Prologue to a Configurative Jurisprudence," *VJIL* 8 (1968): 188–299, 193.

private participation? As noted above, only a jur-isprudential orientation that is sufficiently real-istic and policy serving will suffice. Such an orientation must be sufficiently contextual and attentive to all relevant legal policies at stake, including awareness of actual trends in decision, relevant features of past and present context, and probable future effects.

For this reason, no easy, mechanistic test of permissibility concerning strategies or tactics of private violence will suffice. As several writers recognize, an adequate analysis of strategies or tactics of revolution or "civil disobedience" de-mands consideration of all relevant features of context, including, of course, an examination of the larger social process in which such strategies or tactics operate.

One of the more involved contextual ap-proaches to the ethics of revolution generally is that offered by philosopher Herbert Marcuse.[14] Marcuse noted that "violence per se has never been made a revolutionary value by the leaders of historical revolutions." What should be con-sidered, he argued, are the goals sought to be achieved and predictable social outcomes. Ratio-nal criteria can aid in what he termed an "histor-ical calculus" of the "chances of a future society as against the chances of the existing society with respect to human progress." For Marcuse, a rational historical calculus

must, on the one side, take into account the sacrifices exacted from the living generations on behalf of the established society, the estab-lished law and order, the number of victims made in defense of this society in war and peace, in the struggle for existence, individual and national. The calculus would further have to take into account the intellectual and material resources available to the society and the manner in which they are actually used with respect to their full capacity of satisfying vital human needs and pacifying the struggle for existence. On the other side, the historical calculus would have to project the chances of the contesting revolutionary movement of improving the prevailing conditions, namely,

whether the revolutionary plan or program demonstrates the technical, material, and mental possibility of reducing the sacrifices and the number of victims.[15]

At the same time, Marcuse was quick to identify a peremptory limit to revolutionary "means." As he explained,

No matter how rationally one may justify revolutionary means in terms of the demon-strable chance of obtaining freedom and hap-piness for future generations, and thereby justify violating existing rights and liberties and life itself, there are forms of violence and suppression which no revolutionary situation can justify because they negate the very end for which the revolution is a means. Such are arbitrary violence, cruelty, and indiscriminate terror.[16]

From a legal perspective, Marcuse's statement about the means of violence is equally relevant. Under international law, including the law of human rights, there are certain forms of violence that are impermissible per se. Included here are strategies and tactics of arbitrary violence, cru-elty, and indiscriminate terror. International law also prohibits the use of violence against certain targets, and permissible uses of force are condi-tioned generally by the principles of necessity and proportionality.

Thus, with regard to questions of legality con-cerning targets, tactics, and strategies of social violence, international law already provides nor-mative guidance. A realistic and policy-serving jurisprudence would integrate relevant princi-ples of international law into appropriate analy-sis and choice about the permissibility of a particular method or means of violence in a given social context, using tools of phase and value analysis for empirical inquiry and choice.

CONCLUSION

Here, an effort has been made to identify and clarify the nature and scope of the right to revo-lution in both U.S. domestic and international law. As noted, the right of revolution is a right of the people. It is to be exercised in accordance

14. See, e.g., Herbert Marcuse, "Ethics and Revolu-tion," in Richard T. DeGeorge, ed., *Ethics and Society* (New York: Doubleday, 1966), 133–47. This is, of course, a different focus from one addressing the legal-ity of revolution.

15. Ibid., 52.
16. Ibid., 53.

with a peremptory precept of authority documentable in both U.S. constitutional and international law, the will of the people expressed through a dynamic process involving an aggregate will of individuals. Revolution is actually one of the strategies available to a people for the securing of authority, national self-determination, and a relatively free and equal enjoyment of the human right of all persons to participate in the political processes of their society.

With regard to the separate question of the legality of various means of furthering revolution, numerous sets of domestic and international law already proscribe certain forms of social violence. For example, international law, including human rights law, prohibits tactics of arbitrary violence, cruelty, and indiscriminate terror; the targeting of certain persons (such as children) and certain things; and generally any unnecessary death, injury, or suffering.

Accordingly, normative guidance exists concerning the permissibility of strategies and tactics, but refined, realistic, and policy-serving inquiry or choice concerning such methods of social violence must be guided by a jurisprudential orientation that is sufficiently contextual and policy-attentive for such a task.

Finally, those who are rightly concerned about the evils of any form of violence and the threat that domestic violence can pose to human dignity and international peace might also consider the warning of President John F. Kennedy: "those who make peaceful evolution impossible make violent revolution inevitable."[17]

17. Address by John F. Kennedy at Punta del Este, in M. Cherif Bassiouni, ed., *The Law of Dissent and Riots* (Springfield, Ill.: Thomas, 1971), vii. President Kennedy also declared, "Is not peace, in the last analysis, basically a matter of human rights?" Address by John F. Kennedy at American University (10 June 1963), quoted in Myres S. McDougal, Harold D. Lasswell, and Lung-Chu Chen, *Human Rights and World Public Order: The Basic Policies of an International Law of Human Dignity* (New Haven, Conn.: YUP, 1980), 236n229.

QUESTIONS FOR REFLECTION AND DISCUSSION

1. Why is Jordan Paust's essay the last in this chapter? Is it that violence is the ultimate weapon of the disenfranchised or otherwise marginalized? Perhaps of both? Either way, do you agree with these two propositions? Why? Why not?

2. Is resort to violence in defense of human rights inherently contradictory? However much or little the right to revolution may be legally sanctioned, what about the proposition that the taking of life, if not also the large-scale destruction of property (as in New York City on 11 September 2001, for example), never can be morally justified no matter what the purpose? What would Paust say?

3. In *Why Men Rebel* (Princeton, N.J.: PUP, 1970), Ted Robert Gurr reasons that "Relative deprivation, defined as perceived discrepancy between value expectations and value capabilities," is among the prime explanations of collective violence. Gurr goes on to consider "three other concepts frequently employed in the analysis of disruptive collective behavior that are not directly analogous [to relative deprivation] but that appear to be alternatives to it: dissonance, anomie, and conflict." *Dissonance*, he says, is "a concept widely used in individual psychology" that refers to "inconsistency between two cognitive elements or clusters of elements . . . that people . . . are motivated to reduce or eliminate." *Anomie*, he explains, is "specifically a sociological concept" that refers to "a breakdown of social standards governing social behavior," which, in turn, can lead to "widespread deviant behavior and the establishment of alternative norms." And *conflict* he defines as a condition in which "the source of [relative deprivation] is another group competing for the same values" or as a process of "interaction between groups in their respective attempts to alleviate [relative deprivation]." What bearing does this theorizing have on the revolutionary use of force in defense of human rights? Do social systems that produce relative deprivation, dissonance, anomie, and/or conflict forfeit legitimacy, and, instead, legitimate such use of force?

4. Is there a human right to revolution? Note that the Preamble to the UDHR says that "it is essential, if man [sic] is not to be compelled to have recourse as a last resort to rebellion against tyranny and oppression, that human rights should be protected by the rule of law." Does this clause represent recognition of the principle that people have a right to revolt

against tyranny and oppression? Or is it meant simply to warn states how best to avoid rebellion?

5. If there is a right to revolution, when is it permissible? Impermissible? Paust argues that two standards must be met: first, the resistance or revolution must be taken up on the authority and interest of the majority of the people, not simply an aggrieved minority; second, it must be taken up against a state that oppresses its citizenry by political or economic means. Do you agree with Paust? Disagree? Why?

6. Does the right to revolution depend on the type of government that is the target of revolt? Does it apply equally to citizens of democratic states and nondemocratic states? Or is it "merely" the exercise of the right that is at stake? If so, what status does the right then have in theory?

7. Paust emphasizes that the right to revolution belongs to the people generally and not to a minority. However, sometimes, arguably oftentimes, revolutions are backed by substantial but not majority populations, or sometimes a revolution may involve many different groups of rival revolutionaries combating each other and the government. What does the right to revolution say about these types of circumstances where there is not one single revolutionary group representing the overwhelming majority of the people?

8. If there is a right to armed rebellion, what level of violence is permissible? Do human rights proponents have any legal or moral obligation to use only that proportion of violence that is necessary to defend their interests? If so, how do you measure proportionality?

9. Is it possible that violence or the threat of violence is an important element in maintaining democratic forms of governance? If so, what does this signify for Paust's view that the right to resistance or revolution should not be available to an aggrieved minority? Is it possible that Paust's formulation, presupposing individual rights and liberal democracy, is too Western to be universally applicable? Or can it be universally applied?

10. If there is a right to violent revolution, then what role may individuals from other states or the international community generally play in that violent revolution? May others help the revolutionaries? May others help the government fighting the revolution? May still others choose to help neither? May others choose to intervene when neither side wants outside intervention? Beyond permissible conduct, what duties does international law impose on others? Support your answer with the norms and doctrines of international law.

11. In "The Right to Rebel," *Oxford Journal of Legal Studies* 8 (1988): 34–54, 46, Tony Honoré suggests that if there is a right to revolution it should be conditioned on the exhaustion of nonviolent remedies, e.g., constitutional methods, recourse to the legal system, political propaganda, peaceful protests, civil disobedience, passive resistance, and so forth. Do you agree? Are there instances when it is not possible to exhaust peaceful remedies or when the exhaustion of peaceful remedies would be known to be futile? Can you provide examples?

12. Herbert Marcuse has argued that violence is incorporated in oppressive institutions and that it is possible that logic and language will not suffice to reform, transform, or eliminate them. In *Counterrevolution and Revolt* (Boston: Beacon, 1972), 132–33, Marcuse writes:

> The slogan "let's sit down and reason together" has rightly become a joke. Can you reason with the Pentagon on any other thing than the relative effectiveness of killing machines—and their price? The Secretary of State can reason with the Secretary of the Treasury, and the latter with another Secretary and his [sic] advisers, and they all can reason with Members of the Board of the great corporations. This is incestuous reasoning; they are all in agreement about the basic issue: the strengthening of the established power structure. Reasoning "from without" the power structure is a naive idea. They will listen only to the extent to which the voices can be translated into votes, which may perhaps bring into office another set of the same power structure within the same ultimate concern.
>
> The argument is overwhelming. Bertolt Brecht noted that we live at a time where it seems a crime to talk about a tree. Since then, things have become worse. Today, it seems a crime merely to *talk* about change while one's society is transformed into an institution of violence, terminating in Asia [and now Africa] the genocide which began with the liquidation of the American Indians. Is not the sheer power of this brutality immune against the spoken and written word which indicts it? And is not the word which is directed against the practitioners of this power the same they use to defend their power?

Is there a level on which even incautious and reckless action against oppressive and/or tyrannical social structures seems justified?

13. In *Young India*, New Delhi Newspaper, 27 July 1924, Mohandas K. Gandhi made the following assertion:

> They say "means are after all [just] means." I would say "means are after all everything." As the means, so the end. Violent means will give violent [results]. . . . There is no wall of separation between means and ends. . . . I have been endeavoring to keep the country [India] to means that are purely peaceful and legitimate.

Does Gandhi's view supply a workable axiom applicable to the pursuit of human rights? Why does he link "peaceful" means with "legitimate" means? Do you agree with Gandhi's objection to violence? Why? Why not?

14. If human rights are captured by mainstream neoliberal political discourse such that corporations now win human rights arguments on their own behalf and human rights are invoked to provide legitimation for waging war in countries of which the United States and its allies disapprove, does this undermine the right to revolution or make it more important? What are the reasons for your answer?

15. If the state gains complete access to all your personal records (through the kind of super-"snooping" technology revealed by the leaks concerning the development of PRISM in the United States in 2013) and has the technology, in the form of microdrones, to control every aspect of your behavior, then what implications would this have for the human right to revolution? Would the right, in real terms, have any meaning? Provide reasons for your answer.

Chapter Nine

Global Trajectories, Global Futures

THROUGHOUT this book, certain themes have been recurrent. This is so because in human rights—in both theory and action—certain historical and contemporary patterns, visible to scholars, policy makers, practitioners, and activists alike even if not to everyone, form part of the "seamless web" that makes it possible to call human rights an intellectual discipline, a standard of behavior, a policy agenda, a course of action, a preferred system of governance. At any rate, these patterns point to certain core features of the international human rights law landscape that are likely to affect global futures. The essays draw on some of the most significant contemporary themes and trends of human rights discourse within the global order, and raise troubling implications concerning the tenability and security of human rights futures.

A recurring, critical theme in international human rights literature is that of "U.S. exceptionalism." It has long been argued that the United States, as the world's principal (if now declining) superpower, has long resisted the application to itself of the international human rights law standards it urges upon other nations. In "American Exceptionalism and Human Rights," Canadian Michael Ignatieff looks more closely at the issue, arguing that what is exceptional about the United States is not its inconsistency, hypocrisy, or arrogance (given that many nations exhibit these traits), but the particular "combination of leadership and resistance that defines American human rights behaviour . . . [and which presents] a complex, ambivalent paradox of being simultaneously a leader and an outlier."

Ignatieff poses a three-part typology of U.S. exceptionalism: *exemptionalism* (carefully distinguished from isolationism), *double standards*, and "*legal isolationism,*" and then grapples with the centrally important question of what price the United States pays for its exceptionalism and whether it can practice less exceptionalist modes of engagement with human rights in the future. Ignatieff also evaluates the four types of explanation commonly offered for U.S. exceptionalism: the *realist argument*, based on the exceptional power of the United States in the world order; the *cultural argument*, related to a North American sense of "Providential destiny"; the *institutional argument*, based in "America's specific institutional organization"; and finally, the *political argument*, related to the "supposedly distinctive conservatism and individualism of American political culture."

Ignatieff concludes that, as a language of universalist claims, human rights "has gone global by going local, by establishing its universal appeal in local languages of dignity and freedom." This overlooked "vernacularism" has decisive significance for Ignatieff's evaluation of U.S. exceptionalism, for he argues that "We need to think through the relation between national rights traditions and international standards, to see that these are not in the antithetical relation we suppose. American attachment to its own values is the condition and possibility of its attachment to the universal, and it is only as the universal receives a national expression that it catches the heart and the conviction of citizens."

Thus, according to Ignatieff, U.S. exceptionalism "lays bare the relation between the national and the universal in the rights cultures of all states that have constitutional regimes of liberty." In an increasingly interdependent global order, the United States surely stands increasingly to lose unless it applies the logic of its own national rights culture—and the logic of its international human rights interventions—to itself, and also learns to engage more openly with the international community. The nature of global power is shifting, and the United States, for as long as it remains the world's sole (declining) superpower, could only gain, it would seem, by transforming its fundamental stance and relating in new, more respectful ways to other nations. Potentially the international order of human rights would benefit as well. Of course, matters are complex and the future is uncertain.

Human rights futures are, without doubt, deeply at stake in the geopolitical shifts of power taking place in our present world order—for example, with the rise of China's ambition and reach which poses for the United States and, indeed, the entire global order, an uncertain future for which new maps are not yet available. This point strengthens Ignatieff's conclusion. But power is an especially complex matter in the contemporary neoliberal order where the power of the state is densely interwoven with the power of international financial institutions and transnational corporations as private sector quasi-states. If traditional imperial power leaves a decisively influential structural trace in the international legal order (as Simons argues in preceding Chapter 8), "new" forms of imperialism—and reconstituted modes of national and international influence—appear to be working their way out through the highly uneven, marketized relations of an increasingly networked world.

This particular shift in the nature of global power is a central concern of Anna Grear's contribution to this chapter. Grear argues that "contemporary economic globalization provides the general structural context in which [transnational corporations or TNCs] have emerged as the dominant actors of the entire international legal order. They possess, in some cases, more economic clout and political influence than do many nation-states." This development, she suggests, is one that should be understood to be particularly perilous for human rights because globalization has been demonstrated to "generate unprecedented levels of peril and risk . . . and has been linked to emergent new forms of systemic violence and deepening human vulnerability, as well as to extensive environmental degradation." Nevertheless, given that human rights are the global lingua franca of human aspiration and form the dominant ethical language of the global order, human rights themselves, Grear observes, have become "a target for global corporate desire." Her concern is not just with corporate accountability for human rights abuses; she is interested in the implications of corporations themselves being increasingly conceptualized as human rights beneficiaries—or even as human rights victims. "Is it possible," Grear asks, "that TNCs are in the process of accumulating rights and deploying *human rights* arguments and thereby gaining a complex form of legal humanity that endangers human beings and communities?" The question goes to the heart of her concern: "if human rights *are* colonized by corporations—if powerful economic entities are "insiders" to human rights—what language and concept of human rights will survive to protect vulnerable human beings *from* these powerful global economic actors? Is the genesis of a corporation-friendly human rights legal sensibility a danger to the very future of human rights?"

Setting her analysis unambiguously against the uneven material conditions of the global order, Grear highlights the complex shifts in the nature of power that have enabled the corporation to emerge, in effect, as a "private sector *quasi-state*" without the duties or forms of democratic accountability traditionally placed upon the state by international human rights law. She argues that "the overall picture of the relationship between corporations and human rights in the context of contemporary globalization gives much cause for anxiety concerning the future of human rights" and that "the contemporary role of the state in the prioritization of corporate interests is decisive, especially in the context of a state-centric framework of international human rights law constructed with a public-private divide that makes it ill-equipped to hold powerful private entities to account."

For Grear, however, it is not just human rights law and policy that are at stake because of "the imperatives of economic globalization" and their "distorting effects." It is also human lives. Coupled with the rights-threatening and progressively more coercive state in the post-9/11 world order, where repression is practiced precisely in the name of national security and national interests, the imperatives of economic globalization as currently conceived portend an Orwellian future. This is a regressive trend, Grear asserts, likely to deepen as the climate crisis becomes more securitized and "presents ever more extreme exigencies, shortages, disasters, and mass destabilizing movements of climate refugees." For her, the question of whether or not human rights can survive to protect vulnerable human beings and communities is an open one as we look into the future of the twenty-first century and beyond.

The closing essay by Tony Evans in this chapter and book revisits the fundamental nature of human rights in our globalized age and in so doing engages in a sense with Grear's concerns and broadly supports her account of the distortion of the international legal order under the imperatives of neoliberal globalization. Evans argues that "At the heart of the historical struggle over legitimate universal human rights are two questions: What kind of right? And whom do they benefit?" He records the standard response to both questions: first, "that lists of legitimate universal human rights can be found within the pages of international law"; second, "that these rights offer protection to the disempowered, the vulnerable, and the weak from governments and other powerful actors." Evans then subjects these standard answers to an evaluation drawn from an international political economy perspective. Ultimately his analysis reveals that human rights are no longer subversive categories aimed at the protection of human beings but are "used to lend legitimacy to the practices of powerful global economic actors," a conclusion that confirms Grear's account of the distortion of international human rights law by powerful corporate interests.

Evans, however, places particular emphasis on the idea that "the [neoliberal] emphasis on individualism and limited government, which civil and political freedoms support, has seen the rich accumulate an even greater share of wealth and resources and offered a justification for withdrawing welfare and social entitlements from the poor." In other words, his analysis unambiguously points, as do so many in this book and across the human rights field generally, to the globalized trends so clear in the patterns and trajectories emerging from sociological and empirical evidence concerning the material realities of the globalized world order. For his part, Evans takes us first to the end of the Cold War, for it was at this critical historical juncture that neoliberalism gained ascendancy. Communism (in Russia and Eastern Europe at least) collapsed, and civil and political rights gained an explicit, openly celebrated and unmatched form of superiority. While many argue that civil and political rights (particularly the right to property) and freedom of individual action combined with laissez-faire economics to ensure socioeconomic rights, it is relatively clear from Evan's argument (and from broader evidence throughout the relevant literatures) that this has not been the reality. Indeed, Evans argues that "in the absence of any champion for economic and social rights, the neoliberal consensus upon which the practices of globalization are built has succeeded in establishing the language of civil and political rights as the acceptable voice—indeed the only legitimate voice—of human rights talk." The material conditions accompanying such a mutation in the balance between rights have demonstrated a marked decline in state support for those most in need, while social and economic programs have been dramatically eviscerated as neoliberal orthodoxy has predominated.

Evans draws upon the literature of citizenship and international citizenship to offer insight into the shift away from human rights as forms of protection for the vulnerable toward human rights as modes of "legitimating the practices of globalization." The criticisms emerging from reflection upon such literature suggests, concludes Evans, "that the attempt to secure universal civil, political, and economic rights through the medium of citizenship may, in fact, reinforce a set of values that support current exclusionary practices found in globalization." As regards the notion of the international citizen itself, far from offering a "satisfactory response to globalization, the idea of the international citizen lends further support to neoliberal assertions that economic and social claims are aspirations, not universal human rights." Thus, while it is tempting to think that the gaps left by the decline in the role of the state as the main political actor in the global order might be filled by civil society—a hope supported by other readings in this book—for Evans, civil society itself is changing to "reflect the narrow self-interests of those in a structural position to take full advantage of the conditions of globalization, to the exclusion of the many." Evans argues, in short, that "the idea of universal human rights [has been] co-opted by the prevailing neoliberal consensus" and that "those who stand in the way of the 'imperatives' of globalization risk violations of their rights—civil and political, economic and social."

Thus the question returns: what future is there for human rights? As we stand here at this historical twenty-first-century juncture, facing climate change pressures, a burgeoning national security discourse, expanding surveillance, and deepening trends of difference between the global elite and the masses of ordinary people struggling with deepening poverty, draconian working conditions, and a sense of profound political exhaustion—what hope remains in human rights futures? It is just possible that the answer turns upon which kind of civil society will prevail: a narrow, self-serving elitist one or the rapidly energizing set of global citizens' and peoples' movements now experimenting with alternative forms of social order and seeking an eco-humane future in which human rights can emerge reenergized as modes of justice and passionate commitment to shared and fundamental forms of respect.

37. MICHAEL IGNATIEFF *American Exceptionalism and Human Rights*

DEFINING EXCEPTIONALISM

Since 1945, America has displayed exceptional leadership in promoting international human rights. Thanks to Eleanor and Franklin Roosevelt, the United States took a leading role in the creation of the United Nations and the drafting of the

Universal Declaration of Human Rights in 1948. Throughout the Cold War and afterward, few nations placed more emphasis in their foreign policy on the promotion of human rights, market freedom, and political democracy. At the same time, however, the same U.S. government has resisted complying with human rights standards at home or aligning its foreign policy with these standards abroad. It has supported rights-abusing regimes from Pinochet's Chile to Suharto's Indonesia; sought to scuttle the International Criminal Court, the capstone of an enforceable global human rights regime; maintained practices—like capital punishment—at variance with the human rights standards of other democracies; engaged in unilateral preemptive military actions that other states believe violate the UN Charter; failed to ratify the Convention on the Rights of the Child and the Convention on the Elimination of Discrimination against Women; and ignored UN bodies when they criticized U.S. domestic rights practices. What is exceptional here is not that the United States is inconsistent, hypocritical, or arrogant. Many other nations, including leading democracies, could be accused of the same things. It is, rather, the combination of leadership and resistance that defines American human rights behavior that is exceptional, a complex and ambivalent paradox of being simultaneously a leader and an outlier, and it raises a fundamental question about the very place of the world's most powerful nation in the network of international laws and conventions that regulate a globalizing world. To what extent does the United States accept constraints on its sovereignty through the international human rights regime, international humanitarian law, and the UN Charter rules on the use of force? To what degree does America play by the rules it itself has helped to create?

In this essay, I set out a three-part typology of American exceptionalism; identify and examine four central explanations offered by commentators; and finally raise two questions about policy: what price does the United States pay for exceptionalism in human rights? What can be done to exercise human rights leadership in a less exceptional way?

DISTINGUISHING TYPES OF AMERICAN EXCEPTIONALISM

American exceptionalism has at least three separate elements. First, the United States signs on to international human rights and humanitarian law conventions and treaties and then exempts itself from their provisions by explicit reservation, nonratification, or noncompliance. Second, the United States maintains double standards: judging itself and its friends by more permissive criteria than it does its enemies. Third, the United States denies jurisdiction to international human rights law in its own domestic law, insisting on the self-contained authority of its own domestic rights tradition. No other democratic state engages in all three of these practices to the same extent, and

none combine these practices with claims to global leadership in the field of human rights.

Exemptionalism

The first variant of exceptionalism is *exemptionalism*. America supports multilateral agreements and regimes, but only if they permit exemptions for American citizens or U.S. practices. In 1998, the United States took part in the negotiations for the ICC but secured guarantees that its military, diplomats, and politicians would never come before that court. The Clinton administration signed the treaty before leaving office, only to have the incoming Bush administration unsign it. The Bush administration went on to negotiate agreements with allied countries requiring them to guarantee that they would not hand over U.S. nationals to the ICC.

Exemptionalism, of course, is not confined to the domains of human rights-related treaties. U.S. withdrawal from the Kyoto Protocol on Climate Change fits into the same pattern. Exemptionalism has also been on display in the war on terror in the U.S. insistence that while conditions of detention at Guantánamo and elsewhere will comply with Geneva Convention standards, interrogation procedures and determination of status will be determined by executive order of the president.

Exemptionalism is not the same as isolationism. The same administration that will have nothing to do with the ICC is heavily engaged in the defense and promotion of religious freedom abroad, the abolition of slavery, the funding of HIV/AIDS relief, and the protection of victims of ethnic and religious intolerance in Sudan. Nor is exceptionalism a synonym for unilateralism. An administration that will not engage on the ICC is insistently engaged with the UN and other allies on the issue of HIV/AIDS.

Exemptionalism also involves the practice of negotiating and signing human rights conventions but with reservations. Thus the United States ratified the International Covenant on Civil and Political Rights (ICCPR) in 1991 while exempting itself from the provisions banning inflicting the death penalty on juveniles.[1] America is

---

1. See U.S. reservations to the ICCPR at https://treaties.un.org/Pages/ViewDetails.aspx?src=TREATY&mtdsg_no=IV-4&chapter=4&lang=en [*Eds.*—accessed 22 June 2015].

not the only country to insist on this type of exemption. Saudi Arabia, for example, insists that international human rights convention language relating to free marriage choice and freedom of belief remain without effect in its domestic law.

These exemptions are simply the price that any universal rights regime has to pay for country-by-country ratification. Indeed, it is doubtful that the framework would exist at all if it did not allow latitude for countries to protect the specificity of their legal and national traditions.

While European states also ratify with reservations and exceptions, they question whether a U.S. exemption on the right to life—a core human rights principle—can be justified. Allowing a state to pick and choose how it adheres to such a central principle threatens to empty international conventions of their universal status. Moreover, exemptionalism turns the United States into an outlier. The United States now stands outside an abolitionist consensus vis-à-vis capital punishment that applies to all democratic states and most nondemocratic ones, with the exception of China.

Even when the United States ratifies international rights conventions, it usually does so with a stipulation that the provisions cannot supersede U.S. domestic law. Thus, with a few exceptions, American ratification renders U.S. participation in international human rights symbolic, since adopting treaties does not actually improve the statutory rights protections of U.S. citizens in domestic law.

Exemptionalism also takes the form of signing on to international rights conventions and then failing to abide by their requirements. The U.S. record of treaty compliance is no worse than that of other democracies, but because of the superpower's exceptional political importance, U.S. forms of noncompliance have more impact than those of less powerful states.

A third element of exemptionalism is the practice of negotiating treaties and then refusing to ratify them altogether or ratifying them only after extended delays. For example, the Senate refused to ratify the Convention on the Rights of the Child, leaving the United States the only nation besides Somalia not to do so. The United States took nearly forty years to ratify the Genocide Convention. Failure to ratify does not mean that the United States fails to comply. Nonratification simply means that U.S. advocates cannot use international standards in domestic U.S. litigation. Nonratification means that UN instruments and standards have no legal standing in U.S. courts. How serious this is depends on the extent of the gap between current U.S. federal and state standards and international norms. Where this gap is large, Americans may lack rights and remedies available in other democratic states.

Double Standards

The second feature of American exceptionalism is *double standards*. The United States judges itself by standards different from those it uses to judge other countries, and judges its friends by standards different from those it uses for its enemies. This is the feature Harold Koh identifies as the most costly and problematic aspect of American exceptionalism. The United States criticizes other states for ignoring the reports of UN rights bodies, while refusing to accept criticism of its own domestic rights performance from the same UN bodies. This is especially the case in relation to capital punishment in general and the execution of juveniles in particular, as well as conditions of detention in U.S. prisons. Overseas, the United States condemns abuses by hostile regimes—Iran and North Korea, for example—while excusing abuses by such allies as Israel, Egypt, Morocco, Jordan, and Uzbekistan. It has been condemned for arming, training, and funding death squads in Latin America in the 1980s, while condemning the guerrillas as terrorists. Hence when the United States called for a global war on all forms of terrorism after September 11, it faced accusations that its own policies toward attacks on civilians had been guilty of double standards.

Legal Isolationism

The third form of exceptionalism—*legal isolationism*—characterizes the attitude of U.S. courts toward the rights jurisprudence of other liberal democratic countries. The claim here is that American judges are exceptionally resistant to using foreign human rights precedents to guide them in their domestic opinions. This American judicial self-sufficiency is exceptional when compared to other judiciaries, with judges in Israel inspecting Canadian precedents on minority rights cases, and judges in the South African Constitutional Court studying German cases to interpret social and economic rights claims.[2]

The American legal profession in general, however, has not ignored global human rights developments, and American academic experts have played key roles in international rights institutions. American constitutional scholars assisted their Eastern European and South African counterparts in drafting constitutions, and U.S. programs of democracy development abroad have an increasingly important rule-of-law component. But the trade in legal understanding continues to be mostly one-way, with the U.S. legal tradition teaching others but not learning much itself.

American mainstream values are more than just the artifact of American conservatism since the 1960s. These values are structured legally by a rights tradition that has always been different from those of other democratic states and increasingly diverges from international human rights norms.

International human rights laws allow more infringements of private liberty, in the name of public order, than do U.S. laws. The ICCPR mandates specific overrides of free speech if the free speech involves a threat to public order, the defamation of a religious or ethnic group, or the promotion of war propaganda. When the United States ratified the ICCPR, it specifically exempted itself from these provisions, just as it exempted itself from the ICCPR prohibition on juvenile execution. The European Human Rights Convention permits states to suspend political and civil rights in times of national emergency, while the U.S. Constitution has no provision for the declaration of national emergencies and only a single reference to presidential power to suspend habeas corpus.[3]

The U.S. Constitution makes no reference to socioeconomic and welfare rights—entitlements to food, shelter, health care, and unemployment insurance—that are standard features of both international rights regimes and the constitutions of European states. Certain U.S. constitutional rights like the right to bear arms do not feature

in other democratic systems. While the West presents an appearance of a common rights identity to the non-Western world, its leader—the United States—increasingly stands apart.

Changes in European law have widened the legal gulf that now divides the North Atlantic states. The U.S. legal tradition once shared a great deal with British common law. Thanks to the UK's incorporation of European Human Rights Convention into its domestic law, the British rights system now shares more with the Europeans than with the Americans. The British have accepted the jurisdiction of the European Court of Human Rights; whenever that court hands down a ruling requiring legislative or administrative change, Parliament obliges. Such deference to a transnational legal authority would be unthinkable in the United States. All of this helps to reduce the commonality of the common law tradition and to increase the degree to which American rights culture has become an outlier among the other liberal democracies.

EXPLAINING AMERICAN EXCEPTIONALISM

Four types of explanation for American exceptionalism have been offered by scholars: a *realist* one, based in America's exceptional power; a *cultural* one, related to an American sense of Providential destiny; an *institutional* one, based in America's specific institutional organization; and finally a *political* one, related to the supposedly distinctive conservatism and individualism of American political culture.

REALISM

A *realist* explanation of American exceptionalism would begin with America's exceptional global power since 1945. Exceptionally powerful countries get away with exemptions in their multilateral commitments simply because they can. Human rights and humanitarian law instruments are weakly enforced in any event. The United States can exempt itself from the ICC—and try to block its operation—because no other country or group of countries has the power to stop it. No other state has the capacity to sanction the United States if it ducks compliance with the Vienna Convention on the Law of Treaties, ignores the derogation procedures of human

2. Anne-Marie Slaughter, "Judicial Globalization," *VJIL* 40 (2000): 1103–24.
3. For an extended discussion of this point, see Michael Ignatieff, *The Lesser Evil: Political Ethics in an Age of Terror* (Princeton, N.J.: PUP, 2004), chap. 2.

rights conventions, and delays ratification of other treaties for decades.

On a realist account, support for international law and willingness to submit to its constraints would be in inverse relation to a state's power. The less powerful a state, the more reason it would have to support international norms that would constrain its more powerful neighbors. The more powerful a state, the more reluctant it would be to submit to multilateral constraint. Support for international law is bound to be strongest among middling powers like France, Germany, and Canada, democratic states that already comply with multilateral rights norms in their own domestic rights regimes, and that want to use international law to constrain the United States. As Joseph Nye, Jr., has put it, "multilateralism can be used as a strategy by smaller states to tie the United States down like Gulliver among the Lilliputians."[4] Thus for middling powers the cost of their own compliance with human rights and humanitarian law instruments is offset by the advantages they believe they will derive from international law regimes that constrain larger powers. For the United States the calculus is reversed.

A realist would argue that the United States seeks to maintain its power in a global order of states at the lowest possible cost to its sovereignty. In this, it behaves just like other states. The problem with realist explanations is that the United States has wanted to do much more than this. It has promoted the very system of multilateral engagements—human rights treaties, Geneva Conventions, UN Charter rules on the use of force and the resolution of disputes—that abridge and constrain its sovereignty. Realism alone cannot account for the paradox of American investment in a system that constrains its power.

CULTURE

What realism fails to explain is why multilateral engagements that do constrain American power have appealed to American leaders as different as Roosevelt and Reagan. It seems impossible to explain this paradox without some

analysis of culture—specifically, of the way in which American leaders have understood the relation between American constitutional values and human rights. Across the political spectrum since 1945, American presidents have articulated a strongly messianic vision of the American role in promoting rights abroad. This messianic cultural tradition has a long history, from the vision of the Massachusetts Bay Colony as a "City upon a Hill" in the sermons of the Puritan John Winthrop, through the rhetoric of Manifest Destiny that accompanied westward expansion in the nineteenth century, the Wilsonian vision of U.S. power making the world safe for democracy after World War I, and Roosevelt's crusade for the "four freedoms" in World War II. The global spread of human rights has coincided with the American ascendancy in global politics and has been driven by the missionary conviction that American values have universal significance and application. What is important here is the conflict between national interest and messianic mission. Messianism has propelled America into multilateral engagements that a more realist calculation of interest might have led the nation to avoid. In American domestic politics, this sense of mission has refigured the ideal of a multilateral order of international law, not as a system of constraints on U.S. power, but as a forum in which U.S. leadership can be exercised and American intuitions about freedom and government can be spread across the world.

This desire for moral leadership is something more than the ordinary narcissism and nationalism that all powerful states display. It is rooted in the particular achievements of a successful history of liberty that U.S. leaders have believed is of universal significance, even the work of Providential design. For most Americans, human rights are American values writ large, the export version of its own Bill of Rights.

But if human rights are American values writ large, then, paradoxically, Americans have nothing to learn from international human rights. In the messianic American moral project, America teaches the meaning of liberty to the world; it does not learn from others. U.S. policy, across administrations both Republican and Democrat, has been designed both to promote American values abroad and to safeguard them from foreign interference at home.

This concern to ward off foreign influence is more than just a powerful state's attempt to

4. Joseph S. Nye, "Seven Tests: Between Concert and Unilateralism," *National Interest* 66 (2001): 9–13.

make the rules and exempt itself from them. The United States defends these exemptions in terms of the democratic legitimacy of its distinctive rights culture. A realist account would explain exceptionalism as an attempt to defend U.S. sovereignty and power. The messianic account adds to this the idea that the United States is defending a mission, an identity, and a distinctive destiny as a free people. From an American perspective, rights cannot be separated from the democratic community they serve; they are enforced by that community, and their interpretation must therefore depend solely on the institutions of that community.

America is not the only powerful state that has articulated its identity in terms of its rights and believed in a special mission to export its vision of government. From Napoleon onward, France sought to export its legal culture to neighbors and colonies as part of a civilizing mission. The British Empire was sustained by the conceit that the British had a special talent for government that entitled them to spread the rule of law to Kipling's "lesser breeds."[5] In the twentieth century, the Soviet Union advanced missionary claims about the superiority of Soviet rule, backed by Marxist pseudoscience. Indeed the United States and the Soviet Union each battled for the allegiance of developing nations by advancing messianic claims about the universal validity of their own rights systems. The Soviets sought to convince newly independent countries in Africa and Asia of the superiority of Soviet social and economic guarantees, while the Americans insisted that civil and political rights, guaranteeing property and political participation, were the sine qua non of development. It was not until a faltering Soviet regime signed the Helsinki Final Accord in 1976, allowing the formation of human rights NGOs in the Eastern Bloc, that the Soviets effectively admitted that there were not two human rights cultures in the world but one, in which social and economic rights enjoyed equality of status with civil and political ones.

Viewed against this historical perspective, what is exceptional about American messianism is that it is the last imperial ideology left standing

in the world, the sole survivor of imperial claims to universal significance.

INSTITUTIONS

A third explanation would get at the fine-grained and contingent features of American exceptionalism by stressing the distinctiveness of American institutions. The U.S. system devolves significant powers to the states, meaning that key dimensions of human rights behavior—like punishment—remain beyond the legislative purview of the central state, as they are in many European countries. Even if it wanted to do so, the United States lacks a central instrument to harmonize domestic law in the light of international standards. Next, the U.S. Senate requires two-thirds majorities for ratification of international treaties, imposing a significantly higher bar to incorporation of international law than do other liberal democracies. These institutional features, created by the founders to protect citizens from big government or from foreign treaties threatening their liberties, impose exceptional institutional barriers to statutory and nationwide compliance with international human rights.

What drove the Western Europeans to create the European Convention on Human Rights was the catastrophe of two world wars, followed by the vulnerability of their postwar democracies. A common human rights framework, enforced by a supranational court, was accepted by sovereign states because it was held to "lock in" the stability of the new democratic regimes in Italy, Germany, and France, against both communist subversion and the resurgence of fascism. The United States had no such incentive to surrender its sovereign prerogatives as a state and has continued to regard transnational international law regimes as potential violations of its democratic sovereignty.

POLITICS

The historical strength of American conservatism might qualify as a fourth factor explaining American exceptionalism. It is worth adding, however, that conservatism is not a synonym for isolationism.

Evangelical conservatism has been a driving force behind the cause of religious freedom in

5. Niall Ferguson, *Empire: The Rise and Demise of the British World Order and the Lessons for Global Power* (London: Basic, 2002), chap. 3 ("The Mission").

China and Sudan. Evangelical conservatism also helped to inspire the intervention in Iraq, configuring it for American domestic consumption as a campaign to bring democracy to the oppressed and unfree.

If America has been more conservative on key human rights issues than Europe, and more inclined toward engagement in issues of religious freedom than more secular Europeans, the next question is whether this conservative orientation is a permanent or passing difference. The conservative ascendancy in American politics since the late 1960s makes it easy to forget just how strong its ideological competitor—social liberalism and liberal internationalism—used to be. Beginning with Roosevelt's speech to the 1944 Democratic Convention, calling for a second bill of rights, guaranteeing rights to work, food, housing, and medical care, a liberal political consensus in Congress and in the courts drove toward statutory creation of social and economic entitlements, culminating in the social reform legislation of Lyndon Johnson's Great Society and the momentous decisions of the Warren Court. At the high-water mark of American liberalism in the mid-1960s, America would not have looked exceptional. The attitudes of its courts and legislatures toward welfare rights and entitlements would have seemed consistent with the European social democratic consensus of the period. In the international sphere, at least until the Vietnam debacle, there were relatively few criticisms of American exceptionalism among its allies. The United States exercised global leadership through multilateral alliances and treaties. However, in international politics, the conservative ascendancy in American politics has been marked, since Ronald Reagan, by a reassertion of nationalist and exceptionalist rhetoric and policy.

The conservative counterrevolution in American politics does help to explain why America's human rights performance, at home and abroad, has diverged from those of its democratic allies since the 1960s. But there remains a question of whether this is a permanent or a passing phenomenon. Already, one key explanatory factor driving American exceptionalism in human rights—America's particular experience of slavery and racism—may be passing into history. Slavery and segregation made America exceptional among liberal democratic states, and southern politicians led the opposition to American adoption of international rights regimes from

the late 1940s to the 1960s. The same politicians who wielded states' rights arguments against the use of federal power to desegregate the South invoked national sovereignty arguments to resist adoption or implementation of international rights regimes. Conservative southern hostility to the use of federal power to promote civil rights at home extended to the use of international human rights to promote racial equality.

[While this dire historical experience may now be over,] Southern conservatives are still bastions of opposition to international law. Jesse Helms and other southern senators have fought measures like the International Criminal Court while they also oppose conventions on the rights of the child and the elimination of discrimination against women because these appear to impose secular and liberal doctrines about family discipline. The United States is thus alone among liberal democracies in having a strong domestic political constituency opposed to international human rights law on issues of family and sexual morality.

For the moment at least, the domestic conservative forces that have made America exceptional remain in the ascendant.

EVALUATING AMERICAN EXCEPTIONALISM

If the previous analysis is correct, then current American exceptionalism is therefore fundamentally explained by the weakness of American liberalism. American commitment to international human rights has always depended on the political fortunes of a liberal political constituency, and as these fortunes have waxed and waned, so has American policy toward international law.

Whether exceptionalism is an enduring or a passing phenomenon, it remains to determine whether it is a good or a bad thing. From the 1950s through the 1970s, the liberal academic consensus held American exceptionalism to be a very bad thing indeed. Yet this liberal consensus never went unchallenged. It always faced opposition from an influential strand of conservative and nationalist legal thinking, represented in the American Bar Association, some of whose chief members, suspicious of international law and of international organizations, led the opposition to the Genocide Convention and other international agreements. Beginning in the 1980s, a conservative legal counterattack gained ground, taking a strongly Americanist or nationalist view of international law. By 2000, the conservative nationalist consensus had influential support inside the George W. Bush administration, and their influence helped to drive the administration's fierce opposition to the ICC, its withdrawal from Kyoto, and even its insistence that the United States had the right to interpret the Geneva Conventions and Torture Convention as it pleased. For conservative nationalists, the most powerful state cannot be tied down, like Gulliver, by international human rights norms. Its effectiveness as a world leader depends on being free of such constraints. Besides, its rights performance at home does not stand in need of lessons from abroad. The conservatives did more than defend American national pride and national interest. They raised a key argument of principle: why should a republic, based in the rule of law, be constrained by international agreements that do not have the same element of democratic legitimacy?

In addition to a "nationalist" justification for exceptionalism, conservatives offer a "realist" argument as well. Far from being a problem, exceptionalism might be a solution. By signing on to international human rights, with reservations and exemptions, by refusing to be bound by agreements that would constrain its sovereignty, the United States manages to maintain leadership in global human rights at the lowest possible cost to its own margin of maneuver as the world's sole superpower.

Exceptionalism, therefore, achieves a balance: the United States remains within the framework of international human rights law, but on its own terms. Exceptionalism is the functional compromise, therefore, that enables America to be a multilateral partner in the human rights enterprise.

A liberal internationalist would reply that if America wants to be a human rights leader, it must be consistent. It must obey the rules it seeks to champion. Leadership depends on legitimacy and legitimacy requires consistency. Certainly double standards increase resistance to American leadership, whether the issue is Palestine or Iraq. Double standards also diminish the lure of American example. But the argument that American exceptionalism is a costly mistake cannot be pushed too far. The fact that the United States exempts itself from some international norms does not diminish its capacity to enforce others.

Nor has American exceptionalism prevented the development of international human rights and humanitarian law. Other states have taken the lead in developing the ICC statute, and the Land Mines Treaty is in existence despite U.S. opposition. The European Convention on Human Rights did not wait for American inspiration. Of course, there are limits to what other states can achieve when the world's most powerful state opposes or refuses to engage. But equally, American leadership has not proven as crucial, nor its opposition as damaging, to international law as either American internationalists or their European allies are prone to believe. Exceptionalism can also directly damage U.S. national security interests. America's unilateral arrogance in Iraq has alienated friends, made needless enemies, forced the United States to go it alone, and increased the cost of its projection of power overseas. To this might be added the evidence from Abu Ghraib prison. A country that thinks it is too virtuous, too exceptional, to pay respect to the Geneva Conventions and begins to write its own rules about detention, interrogation, and special status can end up violating every value it holds dear.

Human rights exceptionalism, especially double standards, may also end up endangering U.S. security. America's Iraq policy over the past twenty years demonstrates that when the United States supports authoritarian regimes, ignoring their human rights performance, these authoritarian rulers can metamorphose into a national security threat. Ignoring the rights behavior of Saddam Hussein in the 1980s turned out to be a disaster for U.S. interests in the Gulf region, as did turning a blind eye to the abuses of Sukarno of Indonesia. Pressuring them, before it was too late, to make changes, or quarantining them as a future danger, would have paid better dividends to U.S. security than keeping quiet about their abuses. Reducing double standards requires rethinking the supposed conflict between human rights and security interests. If U.S. policy consistently used human rights standards as a predictor of internal stability and external dangerousness, it would make better national security judgments about whom to trust and whom it can rely on. If it used its security relationships to pressure regimes toward better human rights performance, it would contribute something to stabilizing the regions where U.S. security interests are at stake.

This complementarity between human rights

and national security interests is acknowledged, at least at the rhetorical level, in the national security policy of the George W. Bush administration. President Bush's 2003 speech to the National Endowment for Democracy contended that America's national security interests in the Arab world depended on the promotion of women's rights, political participation, and market reforms. It is by no means certain that this rhetoric will ever be transformed into practice, or even whether it can be. What is certain is that turning a blind eye to the human rights abuses rampant in the Arab regimes has eroded U.S. influence by rendering the United States complicit with regimes that have lost the confidence of their people.

Finally, any evaluation of American exceptionalism fundamentally expresses a certain preference for a certain type of America. Those who wish America were less exceptional are actually expressing the desire for it to be a certain kind of good international citizen, one bound, despite its exceptional power, by multilateral definitions of appropriate state responsibility toward its citizens and rules relating to the use of force against other states. The virtue of this multilateral identity is that it would make America more attractive to itself, a benevolent superpower voluntarily restricting its sovereignty for the sake of the greater global good.

The question to ask of this benevolent liberal internationalism is whether it has any sustained electoral appeal among the American public. Under Franklin Roosevelt's leadership, this image was briefly anchored in a constituency of political support. But the fate of this image of American identity has been tied to the fortunes of American liberalism, and these fortunes have not fared well in the past thirty years. For now a liberal multilateralism is more liberal than most Americans would be comfortable to be: against the death penalty, in favor of allowing American citizens to be tried in international courts, and in favor of surrendering some freedom of maneuver to the United Nations. The country that is often called the last fully sovereign nation on earth has yet to be convinced that it stands to gain from this identity.

CONCLUSION

As a language of moral claims, human rights has gone global by going local, by establishing its universal appeal in local languages of dignity and freedom. As international human rights has developed and come of age, not much attention has been paid to this process of vernacularization. We must ask whether any of us would care much about rights if they were articulated only in universalist documents like the Universal Declaration, and whether, in fact, our attachment to these universals depends critically on our prior attachment to rights that are national, rooted in the traditions of a flag, a constitution, a set of founders, and a set of national narratives, religious and secular, that give point and meaning to rights. We need to think through the relation between national rights traditions and international standards, to see that these are not in the antithetical relation we suppose. American attachment to its own values is the condition and possibility of its attachment to the universal, and it is only as the universal receives a national expression that it catches the heart and the conviction of citizens.

American exceptionalism lays bare the relation between the national and the universal in the rights cultures of all states that have constitutional regimes of liberty. The question is what margin of interpretation should be allowed these nations in their human rights performance, and what margin shades into a permissive surrender of those values that should be universal for all nations. If all nations are, at least to their own citizens, exceptional, we want an international rights culture that welcomes, rather than suppresses, authentic national expressions of universal values. Americans will not believe any truths to be self-evident that have not been authored by their own men and women of greatness, by Jefferson and Lincoln, Martin Luther King, Jr., and Sojourner Truth. The American creed itself—because it speaks so eloquently of the equality of all peoples—enjoins Americans to deliberate, to listen, to engage with other citizens of other cultures. This is what a modern culture of rights entails, even for an exceptional nation: to listen, to deliberate with others, and if persuasive reasons are offered them, to alter and improve their own inheritance in the light of other nations' example. The critical cost that America pays for exceptionalism is that this stance gives the country convincing reasons not to listen and learn. Nations that find reasons not to listen and learn end up losing.

QUESTIONS FOR REFLECTION AND DISCUSSION

1. If "exemptions are simply the price that any universal rights regime has to pay for country-by-country ratification" and if "it is doubtful that the framework would exist at all if it did not allow latitude for countries to protect the specificity of their legal and national traditions," is U.S. exemptionalism exceptional? Why? Why not? What does Ignatieff say?

2. Ignatieff argues that "the United States judges itself by standards different from those it uses to judge other countries, and judges its friends by standards different from those it uses for its enemies." How is this consistent with the rule of law values that the United States uses as a justification, in some cases, for its exceptionalism? Can you reconcile U.S. double standards with the rule of law? If so, how? If not, why not?

3. Is U.S. "legal isolationism" an intelligent response to a globalizing world—including a globalizing juridical order? Why? Why not? Is there a consistent and acceptable explanation for U.S. legal isolationism? If so, what is it? If not, why not? If the latter, what alternative approach would be preferable? And why?

4. Ignatieff offers four different explanations for U.S. exceptionalism: a realist one; a cultural one; an institutional one; and a political one. Which, if any, of these, do you find compelling justifications for U.S. exceptionalism? Which is the most convincing? And why? Which is the least convincing? And why?

5. Are there particular agreements or instances in which you think American *exemptionalism* is justified? If so, what are they? If not, why not?

6. Ignatieff argues that "From an American perspective, rights cannot be separated from the democratic community they serve; they are enforced by that community, and their interpretation must therefore depend solely on the institutions of that community." Does the United States respect the right of other nations in the international order to honor their own conception of human rights? *Should* it? Why? Why not?

7. Ignatieff makes the point that "At the high-water mark of American liberalism in the mid-1960s, America would not have looked exceptional." Why does the United States look so exceptional now, in relation to socioeconomic entitlements? Is this a positive or negative state of affairs? Why? How do you explain it?

8. How does the U.S. valorization of its own virtue and version of the rule of law sit with the radical extension of corporate power in the U.S. legal system? Do you see this as consistent with, or antithetical to, a strong rule of law? Why?

9. Ignatieff canvasses the arguments of the conservatives and the liberal internationalists concerning the nature of U.S. exceptionalism. Which side do you agree with, and why? What deeper value commitments does your position reflect? Are these deeper value commitments defensible? Why? Why not?

10. What price, if any, does the United States pay for exceptionalism in human rights?

11. What can be done to exercise human rights leadership in a less exceptional way? Should it be exercised in a less exceptional way? Why? Why not? Can exceptionalism, in any case, be described as "human rights leadership" worthy of the name? Why? Why not?

12. What is the best explanation (not necessarily justification) for U.S. policy that promotes adherence to widely agreed upon international agreements to which it does not consider itself bound? Is there a persuasive one? If so, what is it? If not, why not?

13. Ignatieff concludes that "The American creed itself—because it speaks so eloquently of the equality of all peoples—enjoins Americans to deliberate, to listen, to engage with other citizens of other cultures. This is what a modern culture of rights entails, even for an exceptional nation: to listen, to deliberate with others, and if persuasive reasons are offered them, to alter and improve their own inheritance in the light of other nations' example. The critical cost that America pays for exceptionalism is that this stance gives the country convincing reasons not to listen and learn. Nations that find reasons not to listen and learn end up losing." In the light of this argument, is U.S. exceptionalism ultimately compatible with U.S. democratic values? If so, why? If not, why not?

14. It is possible to argue that U.S. exceptionalism is unexceptional, since the EU and developing states as well as a range of other nations routinely seek exceptional accommodation in international law. As Sabrina Safrin asks in "The Un-Exceptionalism of U.S. Exceptionalism," *Vanderbilt Journal of Transnational Law* 41 (2008): 1307–54, 1351: "[Is the]

present rhetoric and emphasis on U.S. exceptionalism . . . overstated at best and misguided and even dangerous at worst?" Or does the United States have a case to answer?

15. Does global justice require a less exceptionalist United States? Why? Why not?

16. Ignatieff describes American participation in international human rights agreements as symbolic because it stipulates its participation upon the provision that the human rights agreement cannot supersede domestic U.S. law. How does this kind of behavior compare with states that accept a human rights agreement on paper but do not abide by its terms, possibly ignore it altogether?

38. ANNA GREAR *Corporations, Human Rights, and the Age of Globalization: Another Look at the "Dark Side" in the Twenty-First Century*

SETTING THE SCENE

Corporations have been described as *the* dominant social actors of our age. It is unsurprising, therefore, that they have a significant impact on human rights, oftentimes negative; and it is also, therefore, unsurprising that there has emerged a burgeoning body of scholarship that addresses the well-known difficulties of holding corporations accountable for the abuses they inflict upon human beings and the environment, and the fact that the transnational corporation (TNC), in particular,[1] is capable of evading accountability for the wrongs it commits by virtue of its diffuse legal form and consequent ability to elude jurisdictional controls.[2] A wide range of scholarship, numerous legal actions, consumer campaigns, and community testimonies point to an extensive list of corporate human rights violations: acts of negligence, state-corporate complicity in driving indigenous populations off

lands plundered for their natural resources, the exploitation of low-paid workers, the failure to clean up industrial disasters that negatively affect human and animal populations, ecosystems, and entire regions, and so forth.

Less well canvassed in discussions of corporations and human rights, however, is the idea that corporations *as corporations* can claim human rights as beneficiaries of human rights law, and make claims as "victims" of human rights abuses. The trend, however, is clear—and is especially marked within the jurisprudence of the European Court of Human Rights (ECtHR), as Marius Emberland's careful analysis in the *Human Rights of Companies* reveals.[3] To many, such a legal reality seems startling; the idea of corporate human rights seems inherently contradictory—an oxymoron—because a corporation is not a human being and because human rights, it is assumed, are for human beings, not corporations. The idea of corporate human rights becomes even more puzzling, indeed, when considered in relation to TNCs. How is it possible that a structurally diffuse multinational corporation can invoke—*even discursively*—a category of rights designed for the protection of living human beings and their communities? The question is important. Yet, for

1. Paragraph 20 of UN Document E/CN.4/Sub.2/2003/12/Rev.2, Norms on the Responsibilities of Transnational Corporations and Other Business Enterprises with Regard to Human Rights, defines a TNC as "an economic entity operating in more than one country or a cluster of economic entities operating in two or more countries—whatever their legal form, whether in their home country or country of activity, and whether taken individually or collectively."
2. See Janet Dine, "Jurisdictional Arbitrage by Multinational Companies: A National Law Solution?" *JHRE* 3, 1 (2012): 44–69.

3. Marius Emberland, *The Human Rights of Companies: Exploring the Structure of ECHR Protection* (Oxford: OUP, 2006): "protagonists of for-profit business activity have sought refuge under Convention guarantees normally conceived in relation to the needs of the natural person, and as such far removed from a business context" (7). One particularly striking example is that of the application of Article 8(1) of the European Convention on Human Rights to a corporation in *Colas Est SA and Others v. France* Reports 2002-III: "Everyone has the right to respect for his private and family life, his home and his correspondence."

some lawyers in particular, the concept of corporate human rights is unproblematic. Corporations are, after all, legal persons, they argue. They represent human interests and there is no reason in principle why they ought not to have human rights as well as contractual, proprietary, and constitutional rights. Law, as such lawyers understand, has an almost limitless facility for the production of new forms of personification, new forms of legal subjectivity. The extension of human rights to corporations is in this light merely another unremarkable development reflecting law's systemic facility for populating and categorizing its own universe. Indeed, it has been noted that where companies have been granted "victim status" in respect of certain human rights, "the basis for that protection appears to have been the status of the company as a legal person."[4]

There is another important question concerning the extension of human rights to corporate entities, namely, whether the grant of corporate human rights is a good or a bad thing for human rights themselves. To reflect on this pivotal question, we must necessarily place our reflections on corporations and human rights firmly within the materialities of the globalized age, for it is in the context of globalization (and in particular, the unprecedented power of TNCs) that this question must be answered. Indeed, globalization is a context (along with the climate crisis) that lends pressing urgency to reflection on the relationship between corporations and the potential future of human rights and, relatedly, the question whether or not human rights as originally imagined by the drafters of the Universal Declaration of Human Rights can even survive.

Two major contemporary realities converge in the subject of globalization and human rights. The first is the phenomenon of contemporary economic globalization as the dominant form of globalization. The second is the globalization and discursive ascendancy of rights discourse itself. The convergence between these two realities suggests further questions. Could it be that human rights discourse is somehow implicated in the complex inequalities and rights violations vis-

ible in the globalized economic order? Could it be the case that international human rights law and corporate dominance reflect common ideological commitments at work in globalization?

Contemporary economic globalization provides the general structural context in which TNCs have emerged as the dominant actors of the entire international legal order. They possess, in some cases, more economic clout and political influence than do many states. At the same time, globalization, in which corporations are the dominant actors, has been shown to generate unprecedented levels of peril and risk for human beings and their communities, linked to emergent new forms of systemic violence and deepening human vulnerability as well as to extensive environmental degradation. Human rights, meanwhile, provide *the* ascendant ethical language of contemporary global law and politics. It is unsurprising, therefore, that human rights should become a target for global corporate desire. Indeed, various scholars have pointed out that the very meaning of human rights is now thoroughly open to a globalized neoliberal ideology profoundly implicated in the production of intense human suffering, particularly in the Global South. In this process, moreover, powerful economic actors have somehow "acquired new or fuller legal identities as rights-holders, in turn influencing the character of legal systems and legal process." Is it possible that TNCs are in the process of accumulating rights and deploying *human rights* arguments and thereby gaining a complex form of legal humanity that endangers human beings and communities? Does such a possibility effect a mutation in the very meaning and potential of human rights? And if human rights *are* colonized by corporations—if powerful economic entities are "insiders" to human rights— what language and concept of human rights will survive to protect vulnerable human beings *from* these powerful global economic actors? Is the genesis of a corporation-friendly human rights legal sensibility a danger to the very future of human rights?

Let us begin our reflection by locating corporate human rights discourse unambiguously within the matrix of contemporary globalization and its relationship with the past. We can trace contemporary processes of globalization to well-established transnational flows of people, goods, and religious ideas, from at least the sixteenth century, and perhaps even earlier to the thirteenth-century emergence of the Mongol Empire.

---

4. Christopher Harding, Uta Kohl, and Naomi Salmon, *Human Rights in the Market Place: The Exploitation of Rights Protection by Economic Actors* (Aldershot: Ashgate, 2008), 2. The authors also emphasize (footnote 30) that this basis for the extension of human rights subjectivity to corporations is not limited to Europe.

What is different in our age is the marked intensification of transnational flows, which have led many commentators to describe a *qualitative departure* from earlier forms of global interaction.[5] The contemporary phase of globalization, which (revealingly) began with European colonial domination in the nineteenth century, is characterized by an exponential shift in the sheer scale, speed, density, and content of its transnational flows.

Contemporary globalization is thus a multifaceted phenomenon characterized by "economic, social, political, cultural, religious and legal dimensions intertwined in most complex ways,"[6] and the term "globalization" points to a complicated "range of diverse and even contradictory processes, events and developments."[7] Yet, for all globalization's complexities, certain trends have become unambiguous—and bleak. Contemporary globalization is increasingly characterized by a widening, savage gap between rich and poor; the looming threat of anthropogenic climate change; the emergence of pervasive state anxieties about global security post-9/11; the privatization of organized violence; apocalyptic misgivings about the future survival of the human race in the face of likely future global pandemics, water shortages, and other exigencies; the threat presented by the unprecedented mass movement of populations fleeing environmental disaster, and so forth. Globalization has also been convincingly linked to escalating global violence.[8] The news for human rights realization, in this light, is far from encouraging.

UNDERSTANDING TNC DOMINANCE

To help us grasp the degree of corporate dominance reflected by contemporary globalization, it is helpful to think of familiar images when we reflect upon the materialities of twenty-first-century life. The contemporary range and pace of global interactions is reflected in an increasingly tumultuous "rush of products, ideas, persons and money [stimulated by] jet transportation, electronic telecommunication . . . and extensive computerization."[9] Corporate influence is further reflected in the monopolistic control, in many cases, of technoscientific developments technologies, including biotechnologies and nanotechnology—indeed, with the power irrevocably to change nature itself. When we add to this picture the commercialized globalization of popular culture, and the pervasive reach of global commodity brands, then what emerges is a clear sense of the ubiquitous influence of TNCs as *the defining phenomenon* of contemporary globalization.

TNCs function in highly significant respects as the "key agents of the new world economy."[10] Their dominance is supported, moreover, by the International Monetary Fund (IMF), the World Trade Organization (WTO), and other international economic institutions, themselves "both a symptom of and a stimulus for globalization,"[11] widely understood to be (especially after the 2008 financial crash) a *global economic elite*, guardians of the existing world order, essentially committed to an ideology of privatization, deregulation, and the pursuit of financial profit above all else. This neoliberal ideology, however, has had demonstrably destructive societal results, a fact borne out by the apology of the IMF itself in June 2013 for the socioeconomic and political devastation caused in Greece by its austerity demands.[12] Austerity ideology, in the hands of the IMF, the European Central Bank, and the European Union (EU), is seen by many as being a

5. Boaventura de Sousa Santos, *Toward a New Legal Common Sense: Law, Globalization and Emancipation* (London: Butterworths, 2002), 165. De Sousa Santos refers to a range of commentators committed to such a view. See also Michael Featherstone, ed., *Global Culture: Nationalism, Globalization and Modernity* (London: Sage, 1990); Anthony Giddens, *Sociology* (Oxford: Polity, 1990); Martin Albrow and Elizabeth King, eds., *Globalization, Knowledge and Society* (London: Sage, 1990).
6. De Sousa Santos, *Toward a New Legal Commonsense Law*, note 5, 166.
7. Upendra Baxi, *The Future of Human Rights* (Oxford: OUP, 2006), 235.
8. Paedar Kirby, *Vulnerability and Violence: The Impact of Globalisation* (London: Pluto, 2006).

9. Timothy W. Luke, "New World Order or Neo-World Orders: Power, Politics and Ideology in Informationalizing Glocalities," in Mike Featherstone, Scott Lash, and Roland Robertson, eds., *Global Modernities* (London: Sage, 1995), 91–108, 99–100, cited in Robert McCorquodale and Richard Fairbrother, "Globalization and Human Rights," *HRQ* 21 (1999): 735–66, 738.
10. De Sousa Santos, *Toward a New Legal Common Sense*, note 5, 167.
11. McCorquodale and Fairbrother, "Globalization and Human Rights," note 9, 737.
12. See http://www.reuters.com/article/2013/06/06/us-imf-greece-idUSBRE9550M320130606 (accessed 21 June 2015).

form of redistribution in favor of capitalism's dominant institutions by "socializing" the cost of the financial crisis—a process in which the private risks of the owners of capital are underwritten by the state as the losses of corporations and banks were (and are) mitigated while the ordinary taxpayer has been left holding future debts that pass the worst impacts of the crisis to hard-pressed citizens, most recently in the form of devastating austerity programs. Meanwhile, IMF-EU austerity rhetoric has been linked to spiraling rates of social deprivation and mass instabilities in crisis-struck nations (such as Greece). The globalized economic institutions widely regarded as the engines of the neoliberal world order (particularly the IMF and the World Bank) continue to insist, in the main, despite recent IMF concessions concerning the need for a "rebalancing,"[13] upon an ideologically constructed institutional separation between politics and economics in the service of the agenda of global capitalism in which the state increasingly plays a facilitating role.

What implications do these developments have for the power of corporations in the global age—and for the future of human rights? Stephen Gill has argued that the worldwide amendment of old constitutions and the formation of new ones under the influence of the IMF, the World Bank, and other institutional agencies of global capitalism, amounts to the construction of a "*de facto* constitution for global capital," operative in a range of contexts: international, regional, and national.[14] Pointing to the collapse of the Eastern bloc and the emergence of arguments about the "end of history," Gill suggests that "To a greater or lesser extent new forms of possessive individualism re-emerged worldwide and social institutions were re-defined to create an emergent market civilization—a monoculture of both social development and mind that is as-

sociated with a new political economy of disciplinary neoliberalism."[15] Ulrich Beck argues that the power of global business is engaged in a meta-struggle with states in the form of "a creeping, post-revolutionary, epochal transformation of the national and international state-dominated system governing the balance of power and the rules of power"—a reality in the light of which "globalization needs to be decoded."[16] Beck characterizes contemporary globalization as "one of the most important changes there has been in the history of power,"[17] a complex set of shifts and struggles in which TNCs emerge as "private sector *quasi-states*."[18]

It is against this background that we need to position the question of the relationship between human rights and the corporation. Scholars argue that global corporate dominance has now produced a situation in which human rights discourse is thoroughly colonized by powerful formations of global capital. Some go further, and accuse human rights of being, in effect, a Trojan horse for neoliberal values.[19] Such accounts point, as do post-colonial critiques, to the "dark side" of the international human rights project—to its continuities with nineteenth-century practices of colonial power and the "othering" of certain nondominant modes of being human.[20] These discriminatory patterns continue to be visible in the twenty-first century, even while, as Tony Evans and Alison Ayers argue, the idea of universal human rights is currently forced to serve a hegemonic neoliberal approach to rights that has effectively "co-opted" human rights "in support of processes associated with capitalist globalization."[21]

In short, TNCs wield *unprecedented* and almost

---

13. Madame Christine Lagarde, Managing Director of IMF, recently announced a modest shift (or "rebalancing" as she prefers) in IMF policy by backing off "collective action clauses" (CACs) in sovereign debt negotiations relative to struggling economies such as Greece which have been severely—and unnecessarily— harmed by the IMF (and EU) heretofore. See http://www.imf.org/external/np/tr/2014/tr041014.htm (accessed 21 June 2015).

14. Stephen Gill, "Constitutionalizing Inequality and the Clash of Globalizations," *International Studies Review* 4 (2002): 47–65, 49.

15. Ibid., 50.
16. Ulrich Beck, *Power in the Global Age* (Cambridge: Polity, 2005/2006), 52.
17. Ibid.
18. Ibid., 75.
19. Costas Douzinas, *Human Rights and Empire: The Political Philosophy of Cosmopolitanism* (Abingdon: Routledge-Cavendish, 2007), for example, 190–92. See also Anne Orford, "Beyond Harmonisation: Trade, Human Rights and the Economy of Sacrifice," *Leiden Journal of International Law* 18, 2 (2005): 179–213.
20. See Chapter 1, Reading 6 (Kapur).
21. Tony Evans and Alison J. Ayers, "In the Service of Power: The Global Political Economy of Citizenship and Human Rights," *Citizenship Studies* 10, 3 (2006): 289–308 (abstract). See also Reading 39 (Evans), next in this chapter.

unimaginable levels of power and influence, such that scholars of the global political economy agree, "regardless of their disciplinary, analytic or ideological inclinations . . . [that] corporate global rule is already here."[22] This global corporate rule, moreover, extends increasingly into the semantically overstretched, but ethically ascendant language of human rights, and is reflected likewise in modern and evolving neoliberal formations of international human rights law.

TNCS AND HUMAN RIGHTS DISCOURSE: THE EFFECTS OF CORPORATE DOMINANCE IN THE HUMAN RIGHTS AGE

Such is the decisive influence of TNCs on international human rights law and discourse that Upendra Baxi has argued that the entire UDHR paradigm stands imperiled by the development of a new paradigm of "trade-related, market-friendly human rights (TRMFHR)"—that the UDHR paradigm is "being steadily, but surely, *supplanted*" by a paradigm that

> seeks to demote, even reverse, the notion that universal human rights are designed for the attainment of dignity and well-being of human beings and for enhancing the security and well-being of socially, economically and civilizationally vulnerable peoples and communities. The emergent paradigm insists upon the promotion and the protection of the collective human rights of global capital, in ways which "justify" corporate well-being and dignity even when it entails continuing gross and flagrant violation of human rights of actually existing human beings and communities.[23]

Baxi argues, in short, that human rights law and discourse have been "critically appropriated by global capital" and that a comparative sociology of human rights compels us to conclude that this "leaves us with no other credible option."[24]

It is important to contextualize this very serious claim (responding to the neoliberal transmutation of human rights law) against the characteristics and inherent design weaknesses of the UDHR paradigm itself. When we speak of the corporate subversion of the UDHR paradigm we are speaking of the exploitation of a regime already compromised in its ability to protect human beings from state and corporate violation. The international human rights regime is built around the UDHR, and its two related covenants, the International Covenant on Civil and Political Rights (ICCPR) and the International Covenant on Economic, Social and Cultural Rights (ICESCR). It comprises a system of standards and implementation procedures centered on the United Nations—in particular the Human Rights Council—supported by a small group of regional human rights regimes, key among which is the European Convention on Human Rights.[25] The international human rights regime, as is well known, has a central commitment to state sovereignty—and concomitantly weak enforcement mechanisms. The much vaunted postwar commitment to the high-minded ideals of the human rights standards promulgated by the UN still awaits the development of strong implementation and enforcement practices. Accordingly, the UDHR is, as Donnelly has noted, "a regime with extensive, coherent and widely accepted norms, but extremely limited international decision making powers—that is, a strong promotional regime."[26]

If the international human rights law regime is, in effect, predominantly a *promotional* regime, then it is being subverted by a corporation-friendly sensibility at its most potent point of purchase: its ethical and rhetorical appeal. Ethical and rhetorical appeal has in any case a poor track record of preventing human rights abuses,

22. Ronen Shamir, "Corporate Social Responsibility: A Case of Hegemony and Counter-Hegemony," in Boaventura de Sousa Santos and C. A. Rodríguez-Garavito, eds., *Law and Globalization from Below: Towards a Cosmopolitan Legality* (Cambridge: CUP, 2005), 92. It is not without persuasive reason that a 2014 42-page empirical research study from Princeton and Northwestern Universities concluded that the United States is either already or threatening to be an oligarchy, not a democracy. See J. C. Sevcik, "The US Is Not a Democracy But an Oligarchy, Study Concludes," UPI, 16 April 2014, http://www.upi.com/Top_News/US/2014/04/16/The-US-is-not-a-democracy-but-an-oligarchy-study-concludes/2761397680051 (accessed 21 June 2015).
23. Baxi, *The Future of Human Rights*, note 7, 234.

24. Ibid., 147.
25. For details, see Reading 27 (Weston) in Chapter 6, and Readings 30 (Marks) and 31 (Shelton) in Chapter 7.
26. Jack Donnelly, *Universal Human Rights in Theory and Practice* (Ithaca, N.Y.: Cornell University Press, 1989), 213.

as the spiraling global record of human rights violations in the so-called "age of human rights" reveals. When state interests (increasingly, the economic interests of a particular national elite enjoying international networks of solidarity) or the paramount imperative of national sovereignty seem to require the violation of human rights, then the apparent normative consensus around human rights tends to collapse. In such circumstances, the language of human rights is readily exploited by the state in the service of its "own" interests.

The state-centrism of the international human rights regime means it is inherently ill equipped to prevent human rights violations justified in the name of "national interest" or "national security" objectives, a tendency dramatically exacerbated post-9/11. And because the concepts of national interest and national security are determined increasingly by the market-friendly agenda of the current world order, it is highly likely that "enhanced competition for markets and for production niches in the current global restructuring of capital accumulation [will] fragment the conceptions of national self-interest even further, and augment the political aggressiveness that defends them against competing states."[27] State-centrism, in short, becomes a more problematic flaw in a context where the modern state "is not only (asymmetrically) subject to, but also agent of, the forces and logic of global capitalism."[28]

If traditional state justifications for the limitation or violation of human rights now operate in a setting where that interest is increasingly defined by the imperatives of neoliberalism, then this reality renders those human rights that collide with these imperatives even more vulnerable. The picture is especially discouraging for the prospects of human rights fulfillment. First, the prospect of TNC accountability is rendered less likely in light of the bottom-line reality of ongoing human rights abuses all over the world. Second, as Santos points out, there is the problem of the public/private divide: "Because of their private character, these economic actors can commit massive violations of human rights with total impunity in different parts of the world [and]

because such actors are at the core of the loss in economic national sovereignty, their actions, no matter how offensive to human rights, are *unlikely to collide with* consideration of national interest or security that might otherwise prompt the corrective or punitive intervention of the state."[29] Third, those agents that normally may be relied upon to raise resistance, such as NGOs and others, are increasingly forced, as Baxi has argued, to attempt to mitigate the harshness of neoliberal globalization from an essentially captive position "within the general imperatives of [the] ideology."[30] Indeed, Baxi contends, the very notion of the "global" in our age carries "connotations of the commercialization of humanity."[31] NGOs are themselves caught up in dynamics of a deepening dependency upon markets. There is a marked tendency, for example, for human rights movements to organize themselves in market-led terms, with NGOs operating as economic actors in competition for economic resources, producing in the process and in combination with other actors such as funding bodies something approaching a "human rights market rationality."[32] Overall, it is clear that market-led dynamics have more than superficial levels of purchase on human rights movements, creating in the process ethically fraught realities and practices, such as the "commodification" of human suffering,[33] whereby images of human suffering are deployed to raise money by increasingly market-led NGOs—a practice open to considerable ethical ambiguity.

The task for human rights proponents becomes even more daunting when we stop to consider the elusive nature of the domination with which we are concerned. Beck points out that one of the strategic advantages enjoyed by globalized capital is the power to refuse investment—a reality with the effect of transforming economic power into an elusive politics of "side-effect," a form of "domination by nobody." For Beck, this is a process in which the political meta-power of global capital is *increased* by the sense in which "Nobody is doing politics—yet they are doing so in a very effective and often

27. De Sousa Santos, *Toward a New Legal Common Sense*, note 5, 267.
28. Evans and Ayers, "In the Service of Power," note 21, 290.
29. De Sousa Santos, *Toward a New Legal Common Sense*, note 5, 268.
30. Baxi, *The Future of Human Rights*, note 7, 239.
31. Ibid., 240.
32. Ibid., 216–20.
33. Ibid., 223.

deliberate way."[34] The complexity of global power makes political and legal accountability all the more challenging to achieve, because, as Beck points out, "the political meta-power 'of capital' results from the collective impact of very heterogeneous actors, markets, capital flows, supranational organisations and so forth, each of which understands itself to be making decisions in its own interest on the basis of economic considerations."[35] Yet, at the same time, this very heterogeneous collection of actors reflects an ideological convergence with a deeply homogenizing effect on the policy choices of governments. This is a troubling state of affairs for human rights; it amounts to the "economic self-transformation of politics in the sense of self-colonisation."[36] It is the state that itself legitimates the power of capital, producing a *redefinition of the political on a global scale*. For Gill, this has resulted from the weakening of traditional political constraints and the production of frameworks specifically designed to secure a long-term commitment to the neoliberal path of development, ensuring that "disciplinary neoliberalism" will set the future (including the future of human rights) in capitalist terms by preventing future governments from undoing commitments to the neoliberal patterns of power.[37]

The global neoliberal constitutionalism identified by Gill, and the emptying out of politics by economic self-colonization identified by Beck, supports Baxi's argument concerning the emergence of a new paradigm of international human rights. The UDHR paradigm, as we have noted, assigned to *states* the principal responsibility for upholding human rights standards and of meeting the basic needs of human beings. The state, however, is shaped, as we have seen, by the imperatives of a neoliberal order. The new trade-related market-friendly paradigm calls upon the state to serve neoliberalism by pursuing *"de-regulation, de-nationalization and disinvestment"*— thus significantly reducing the state's traditional redistributive role. Indeed, the very meaning of the "redistributive state" may be changing. Despite the central importance of laissez-faire economics to the neoliberal order, states have

become far more interventionist in response to the 2008 financial crisis by redistributing debt to citizens and the costs of the crisis away from capitalist institutions. The relative demise of the traditional redistributive state—with its programs of social concern, however feeble—is not good news for human rights; it marks "in some important ways," as Baxi observes, "the end of the processes and regimes of *human rights-oriented, redistributionist governance practices* in ways that convert the mandate of 'progressive realization' of social, economic, and cultural rights of the people into an ongoing cruel hoax."[38]

It is not difficult to see how such realities particularly threaten the human rights futures of the poorer inhabitants of the most deeply cash-strapped nations. Where states are recalcitrant in embracing the new world order, they tend to be pressed into conformity. Beck notes that the few countries in the Global South that have attempted to reject neoliberal strictures have been effectively forced to submit under pressure from the World Bank and Western funding bodies.[39] Richardson has demonstrated that the World Bank and the IMF have most pressurized precisely those marginalized societies where poverty is most rife by insisting on structural adjustments such as deregulation, privatization, and the removal of human rights protective policies.[40] Such developments raise an important question concerning the degree to which organizations such as the IMF, the World Bank, and the WTO are simply "midwives" to the neoliberal order of power[41]—a question that becomes all the more important when we recall that WTO rules, in particular, were shaped, to an influential degree, by global corporations. Indeed, WTO rules have been described as providing the *formalization* of global corporate power.[42]

The situation is serious. The state and politics have mutated under the pressures of neoliberal-

34. Beck, *Power in the Global Age*, note 16, 117.
35. Ibid.
36. Ibid., 118.
37. Gill, "Constitutionalizing Inequality," 48.

38. Baxi, *The Future of Human Rights*, note 7, 248.
39. Beck, *Power in the Global Age*, note 16, 123.
40. James L. Richardson, "Contending Liberalisms: Past and Present," *European Journal of International Relations* 3 (1997): 5–33, 21.
41. Beck, *Power in the Global Age*, note 16, 120.
42. Ralph Nader, "Introduction," in Lori Wallach and Michelle Sforza, eds., *The WTO: Five Years of Reasons to Resist Corporate Globalization* (New York: Seven Stories Press, 1999), 7.

ism. Human rights are dependent for their real-ization upon a state that has been reconstituted as a market-driven, corporation-friendly actor. Indeed, Baxi argues that the realization of human rights may have become dependent on the prior realization of an order of rights for corporations.

Baxi's argument is substantiated by a range of examples concerning the *distortion* of human rights into an order of rights for corporate capi-tal. He notes, for example, that the war against hunger, in the 1998 Rome Declaration on the Right to Food, was implemented as an integrated system of food security dominated by a small group of multinational food corporations; that the struggle against homelessness, in the 1998 UN Social Summit, became a set of "mandates authorizing a whole range of human rights-violative practices of the construction industries and urban developers"; that "sustainable devel-opment" became the launch pad for massive projects primarily benefiting the imperatives of foreign investment and the "promotion and pro-tection of corporate governance 'greenwashing practices,'" while the Global Sustainable Devel-opment Facility inspired by the United Nations Development Programme is supported by money from "some of the most egregious multinational enterprise corporate human rights offenders."[43] Meanwhile, TNCs also undermine and infiltrate human rights discourse by seeking, increasingly, to have their rights promulgated in treaty re-gimes, such as the WTO Agreement, and the agreement on trade-related intellectual property rights (TRIPS); and, as Evans and Ayers note, "property and investment rights are protected in 'exquisite detail' under [the North American Free Trade Agreement (NAFTA), the General Agreement on Tariffs and Trade (GATT)] and more recently the WTO—with 20,000 pages of GATT/WTO regulations and 1,400 articles within NAFTA specifying exact rules to protect the rights of capitalist corporations."[44] The rights of corporations, in other words, are extensively protected, to the point where the "the promo-tion and protection of some of the most cher-ished contemporary human rights becomes

possible only when the order of rights for global capital stands fully recognized."[45]

Indeed, matters may be even worse for human rights futures. Ironically, the trade-related market-friendly paradigm means that human rights themselves now stand in danger of being recast as obstacles to be overcome in the name of guaranteeing their own future.[46] When the state unleashes forms of repression against its own population in the name of socioeco-nomic progress and of the "rule of law" in the interests of rights-violating corporate investors— and examples are legion—then human rights effectively turn against themselves, while being relatively dwarfed by a human rights-denying ideology constructed in the name of detailed, complicated, technically dense, and extensive corporate rights. The results produce multiple harms. These harms include the way corpora-tions have corrupted national regimes aimed at social and human development; engaged na-tional authorities in the co-option, corruption, or coercion of human rights communities whose activities subvert the imperatives of globaliza-tion; influenced law, medicine, media, science, and education; and created "human, bio, eco and genetic hazards . . . without obligation for reparation, restitution and rehabilitation."[47] Jochnick has argued that the impact of TNCs on human rights "ranges from a direct role in viola-tions, such as abuses of employees or the envi-ronment, to indirect support of governments guilty of widespread repression," and that the conduct of global corporations can also "have a

43. Baxi, *The Future of Human Rights*, note 7, 250.
44. Evans and Ayers, "In the Service of Power," note 21, 293.

45. Baxi, *The Future of Human Rights*, note 7, 256–57. For example, the right to health is thought best served by the overprotection of the research and development rights of the pharmaceutical and diagnostic industries and various forms of progress in female reproductive autonomy—that is, sustainable development and the management of environmental challenges are all thought best served by, among other things, the pro-tection of corporate property interests in various technologies.
46. Ibid., 258. There is a notable parallel here between market-friendly rights interpretations and national se-curity discourse post-9/11, in which human rights are frequently recast as obstacles to be overcome in the name of their own protection.
47. Ibid., 258–61, citing Upendra Baxi, "Justice as Emancipation: The Legacy of Babasaheb Ambedkar," in Upendra Baxi and Bikkhu Parekh, eds., *Crisis and Change in Contemporary India* (New Delhi: Sage, 1995), 122–49.

dramatic impact on poverty, either by directly undermining human welfare (for example, limiting a community's access to land or food) or influencing relevant government policies and laws (e.g., relating to agriculture, technology, employment and subsidies)."[48] Kinley and Joseph note that, while there is scope for corporations to have a positive impact, corporate activity has had a genuinely detrimental impact on human rights protection worldwide. The most egregious abuses have occurred in the developing world, abuses including complicity in the brutality of the police and military in host states, the use of forced and child labor, the suppression of human rights to free association and expression, violations of rights to cultural and religious practice, infringements of property rights (including the infringement of intellectual property rights), and environmental violations. Turning their attention to the developed world, Kinley and Joseph point out that abuses also occur in this context, most typically concerning the violation of environmental rights, privacy rights, consumer rights to health and information, and violation of rights to freedom of association.[49]

In light of all this behavior, does it not seem that there are genuine dangers in legitimating corporate interests by using the language of human rights *for* corporations? Is it possible, or even likely, that such legitimation can make it even more difficult than it already is to hold corporations to account? Consider, for example the impact of the "corporate human rights" of commercial free speech, privacy, and honor defended in lawsuits by corporations to silence objections to their activities—so-called Strategic Law Suits Against Public Participation (SLAPPS), a way of suing people for speaking out and thereby "effectively denying the equality of citizenship so

fundamental to informed decision making," a strategy that amounts to making "economic interests . . . the superior voice in determining public policy."[50]

This example brings us full circle to our earlier considerations of the emergence of a new constitutionalism. There is widespread evidence of the increasing use of legal, constitutional, and constitution-like limitations to prevent governments or citizens from intervening in the prioritization of the market. The aim seems to be to insulate "key aspects of the economy from the influence of politicians or the mass of citizens by imposing, internally and externally, 'binding constraints' on the conduct of fiscal, monetary, trade, and investment policies."[51] Corporations, one may conclude, have a plenitude of rights, including human rights. What then, of their responsibilities? Where does the situation just described leave corporate accountability to the human rights standards that TNCs and other corporate bodies are so systematically exploiting in their own favor?

A BRIEF ASSESSMENT OF CORPORATE ACCOUNTABILITY TO HUMAN RIGHTS STANDARDS

In general terms, TNCs have been remarkably successful at evading UN attempts to make them accountable to human rights standards.[52] For example, the UN attempt to produce a universal Code of Conduct for Transnationals was a failure. Corporations are exempt from the jurisdiction of the International Criminal Court. The draft UN Norms on the Responsibilities of Transnational Corporations and Other Business Enterprises with Regard to Human Rights were an attempt to mark a distinctive break with the ideology of voluntarism that generally has dogged

48. Chris Jochnick, "Confronting the Impunity of Non-State Actors: New Fields for the Promotion of Human Rights," *HRQ* 21, 1 (1999): 56–79, 65. See also Sarah Joseph, "Taming the Leviathans: Multinational Enterprises and Human Rights," *Netherlands International Law Review* 46, 2 (1999): 171–203, 173–74; also the reports of the Special Rapporteur to the Commission on Human Rights on the dumping of toxic waste, e.g., Commission on Human Rights, UN Doc. E/CN.4/1998/10 (20 January 1998).
49. David Kinley and Sarah Joseph, "Multinational Corporations and Human Rights: Questions About Their Relationship," *Alternative Law Journal* 27 (2002): 7–10, 7.

50. George W. Pring and Penelope Canan, *SLAPPs: Getting Sued for Speaking Out* (Philadelphia: Temple University Press, 1996), 221.
51. David Schneiderman, "Constitutional Approaches to Privatization: An Inquiry into the Magnitude of Neo-Liberal Constitutionalism," *Law and Contemporary Problems* 63 (2000): 83–109, 86, citing Stephen Gill, "Globalisation, Market Civilisation, and Disciplinary Neoliberalism," *Millennium Journal of International Studies* 24, 3 (1995): 399–423, 412.
52. This is well discussed in Chapter 8, Reading 35 (Simons) in this volume, so is treated here only briefly.

attempts to apply human rights standards to global corporations—but failed. More recently, Professor John Ruggie's appointment as UN Special Representative to the Secretary-General on the Issue of Human Rights and Transnational Corporations and Other Business Enterprises (SRSG), tasked with reviewing the whole question of corporations and human rights, resulted in yet another essentially voluntarist scheme. Ruggie's framework, presented in 2008, known as the "Protect, Respect, and Remedy" Framework, was unanimously endorsed by the Human Rights Council. Likewise, in 2011, his Guiding Principles were also unanimously adopted by the HRC.

Ruggie's approach and the initiatives that have followed his examination of the issues have certainly contributed significantly to the global conversation on corporate human rights accountability. However, his Protect, Respect, and Remedy policy framework and Guiding Principles fail to address a foundational problem. Simons has argued that Ruggie's underlying operative assumption was the conviction that the fundamental problem of ensuring corporate human rights accountability lies in "governance gaps."[53] Yet, Ruggie's approach fails to address the underlying structural orientation of international law and the pivotal fact that "corporate impunity" is "deeply embedded in the international legal system."[54] Anghie argues that international law (which developed in the context of the colonial and postcolonial eras) has at its heart the "promotion and protection of the economic interests of the [global] North."[55] Contemporary globalization is a continuation of earlier trajectories in the international legal order.

This fundamental question of radical tilt in the juridical order is completely unaddressed by Ruggie's work. Ruggie emphasizes the state's responsibility to protect human rights (with the "Protect" pillar of his framework). But how can his reassertion of state duty to ensure the protection of human rights—a duty that has, after all, long existed—bring any genuine hope of a shift in the ideological hegemony currently driving national and international policy choices? And

if, as Panitch suggests, states should now be understood as "the *authors* of a regime that defines and guarantees, through international treaties and constitutional effect, the global and domestic rights of capital,"[56] how does the reassertion of state duty, without engaging with the structural realities of contemporary globalization and the fundamental ideological structure of the international legal order, remotely address the *corporation- and state-compromised contemporary realities* of human rights?

CONCLUSION

The overall picture of the relationship between corporations and human rights in the context of contemporary globalization gives much cause for anxiety concerning the future of human rights. The UDHR paradigm is compromised, to an increasingly profound degree, by corporate global dominance. The market-friendly mutation of international human rights law accompanies a situation, moreover, in which TNCs have shown scant concern for human rights, particularly in the Global South. These developments cannot adequately be understood in all their seriousness without reference to certain global tendencies that have become particularly marked in the twenty-first century. In particular, the contemporary role of the state in the prioritization of corporate interests is decisive, especially in the context of a statecentric framework of international human rights law constructed with a public-private divide that makes it ill-equipped to hold powerful private entities to account.

Perhaps most problematical, the distorting effects of the imperatives of economic globalization are increasingly coupled with the rights-threatening and progressively more coercive state in the post-9/11 world order in the name of national interests and national security—a trend that surely will only deepen as the climate crisis presents ever more extreme exigencies, shortages, disasters, and mass destabilizing movements of climate refugees. The most recent example of the

---

53. Chapter 8, Reading 35 (Simons), 791–92.
54. Ibid., 805.
55. Ibid., 795 citing Antony Anghie, *Imperialism, Sovereignty and the Making of International Law* (Cambridge: CUP, 2005), 269.

56. Leo Panitch, "Rethinking the Role of the State," in James H. Mittelman, ed., *Globalization: Critical Reflections* (Boulder, Colo.: Lynne Reinner, 1995), 95, cited by Evans and Ayers, "In the Service of Power," 294 (emphasis added).

post-9/11 securitizing trend emerged in June 2013, with revelations of extensive electronic surveillance exercised by the United States and the United Kingdom over their own citizens and over political allies. What happens if the state drifts, in partnership with powerful corporate entities and lobbies, toward consolidating (as some commenters now suggest) a highly developed technical infrastructure for selective, totalitarian, securitizing impulses? In the light of such threats to human rights in the name of national security—particularly a national security shaped by economic and corporate imperatives—the question of whether or not human rights can survive as constructs genuinely capable of protecting vulnerable human beings and communities is, as we look forward to the rest of the twenty-first century, by no means clear.

QUESTIONS FOR REFLECTION AND DISCUSSION

1. Is globalization the necessary context against which to consider corporate human rights claims? Why? Why not? What does Grear say?

2. Grear poses this question: "Could it be that human rights discourse is somehow *implicated* in the complex inequalities and rights violations visible in the globalized economic order?" How do you answer this question, and why? Are there other readings in this book that assist you in making your argument? Which ones, and why?

3. "Is it possible that TNCs are in the process of accumulating rights and deploying *human rights* arguments and thereby gaining a complex form of legal humanity that endangers human beings and communities? Does such a possibility effect a mutation in the very meaning and potential of human rights?" How do you answer this question, and why? What sources and evidence can you draw upon? What evidence is there that giving the corporation human rights beneficiary status supports the promotion and protection of human beings and communities? What evidence to the contrary?

4. Does it make sense to grant human rights to corporations? Why and which ones? Why not?

5. Grear argues that "Contemporary globalization is increasingly characterized by a widening, savage gap between rich and poor; the looming threat of anthropogenic climate change; the emergence of pervasive state anxieties about global security post-9/11; the privatization of organized violence; apocalyptic misgivings about the future survival of the human race in the face of likely future global pandemics, water shortages, and other exigencies; the threat presented by the unprecedented mass movement of populations fleeing environmental disaster, and so forth. Globalization has also been convincingly linked to escalating global violence." What likely state reflexes accompany this situation? What, for example, does the example of the "war against terror" and its associated legal developments (see Reading 10) intimate concerning the likely state response to deepening social and environmental insecurity and pressure? What implications are there, in your view, for human rights?

6. Should economic rights be considered human rights? Do you think there needs to be more or less regulation relating to economic concerns? Does the state have any businesses participating in redistribution or should the market decide? Why? Why not? Do you see the increasing wealth gap as a problem? If so, is there anything states can do to control it?

7. Grear's analysis is directed at human rights for corporations, specifically TNCs. Should other entities such as small businesses be granted human rights? What about businesses not organized as an entity such as a family farm? Should economic protections such as anti-dumping be considered human rights? Why? Why not?

8. What do you understand to be the relationship between "state-centrism" in the international human rights regime and the ability of that regime to respond to (a) human rights violations justified in the name of national security and (b) human rights violations caused by non-state private actors?

9. How would you address the challenges of state-centrism and the question of corporate legal accountability for human rights abuses? Would you adopt the approach taken by SRSG Ruggie (see Reading 35)? Or would you opt for mandatory forms of accountability? Why? Why not?

10. Grear argues that "the state and politics have mutated under the pressures of neo-liberalism [and that] Human rights are dependent for their realization on a state that has been reconstituted as a market-driven, corporation-friendly actor." Can you point to any examples of this in the country in which you live? Do you think that markets are, on final analysis, the most effective way to deliver human rights outcomes? Why? And to what extent? Where is the balance to lie between commercializing human needs and simply meeting them because they matter, independent of market relations? If you do not think that markets are the most effective way to deliver human rights outcomes, why not and what is? In each case, defend your position with carefully constructed argument, drawing upon materials in this volume and elsewhere.

11. On balance, have corporations had a positive or negative effect on human rights worldwide? Upon what evidence do you draw in making your response?

12. Can human rights survive as constructs genuinely capable of protecting vulnerable human beings and communities in the future? Support your response as carefully as you can.

39. TONY EVANS *Citizenship and Human Rights in the Age of Globalization*

At the heart of the historic struggle over legitimate universal human rights are two questions. What kind of rights? And whom do they benefit? The standard answer to the first question is that lists of legitimate human rights can be found within the pages of international law, and to the second that these rights offer protection to the disempowered, the vulnerable, and the weak from governments and other powerful actors. This essay attempts to examine this standard answer from the perspective of the international political economy. It argues that far from offering protection to those unable to protect themselves, the once subversive idea of human rights is now used to lend legitimacy to the practices of powerful global economic actors. In particular, the neoliberal emphasis on individualism and limited government, which civil and political freedoms support, has seen the rich accumulate an even greater share of wealth and resources and offered a justification for withdrawing welfare and social entitlements from the poor.

THE HEGEMONY OF CIVIL AND POLITICAL RIGHTS

With the end of the Cold War, resistance to the neoliberal approach to rights seems to have

all but evaporated. The now-unmatched dominance of civil and political rights derives from a set of principles that emphasize the freedom of individual action, noninterference in the private sphere of economics, the right to own and dispose of property, and the important principle of laissez faire. In the absence of any champion for economic and social rights, the neoliberal consensus upon which the practices of globalization are built has succeeded in establishing the language of civil and political rights as the acceptable voice—indeed the only legitimate voice—of human rights talk. For neoliberals, economic, social, and cultural rights may be legitimate aspirations, but they can never be rights. The move to reduce state support for economic and social programs in all Western countries during the last two decades may be seen as indicative of the predominance of the neoliberal approach to rights.

Two broad arguments are used by neoliberals in support of human rights defined as civil and political rights, which I call, respectively, the altruistic argument and the pragmatic argument. Taken together, these arguments support the contention that neoliberals are concerned with promoting a particular set of human rights that places property rights at the top of any list of rights.

The altruistic argument for promoting civil and political freedoms at the expense of economic and social rights is that encouraging free trade and ever greater levels of economic interconnectedness has a positive and beneficial ef-

Excerpted with changes by permission of Sage Publications from Tony Evans, "Citizenship and Human Rights in the Age of Globalization," *Alternatives: Global, Local, Political* 25 (2000): 415–38. Copyright © 2000 Sage Publications.

fect on the human rights record of countries that do not comply with internationally recognized human rights standards. According to this argument, the social contacts generated by the unregulated exchange of goods and services are paralleled by an inevitable and unregulated exchange of moral values. If tyrannical governments want to enjoy the benefits of globalization and free trade, they cannot avoid the transmission of ideas that make people more aware of their rights and increase the demand to be treated in accordance with internationally agreed standards of civil and political rights. In short, free trade has a "civilizing" influence on the "uncivilized" and should be actively promoted in the name of human rights.

According to the pragmatic argument, disrupting free trade over human rights issues, perhaps by applying trade sanctions, has no practical value. First, under conditions of globalization, target countries have little difficulty in making alternative arrangements for the supply of essential goods, either legally or illegally. Second, to be effective, sanctions must be carefully targeted on those groups associated with tyrannical governments, rather than the wider population. The difficulties of achieving this task are immense and should not be underestimated. Third, and following from the above, the potential to "demonize" sanctioners offers a valuable propaganda opportunity, stimulating nationalist fervor and a greater resolve to resist external coercion. Sanctions may therefore help to prolong the life of an existing tyranny rather than bring about its reform or demise. Fourth, the international political frictions generated by sanctions may have implications for security if the target state and its allies decide to resist by whatever means at their disposal. Last, at the level of domestic politics, implementing sanctions brings economic consequences for manufacturing and service industries in the sanctioners' own country, and may harm the sanctioners' own economic interests.

Both the altruistic and pragmatic strands of the argument have been used in recent times to justify trading with those who are guilty of persistent gross violations of human rights. Indeed, such is the success of the neoliberal consensus that "in virtually all regions of the world there is broad acceptance of the triad of human rights, free markets, and democracy as desirable [and]

attainable policy objectives."[1] Although in achieving these aims it is accepted that some groups may suffer "high transition costs," neoliberals assert that future benefits far outweigh current sacrifices. The relentless spread of free market principles on a global scale is clearly reflected in the policies of all the major international organizations, including the World Bank and the World Trade Organization (WTO), and even the International Labour Organization (ILO), which has special responsibility for workers' rights.

The neoliberal defense for trading with human rights violators is therefore straightforward: if there is free trade, then there are human rights, or at least the conditions necessary for the protection of human rights. Even when the demands of globalization and international trade lead to forms of production, exchange, and finance that are the cause of violations of the right to life, liberty, work, sustenance, culture, and an adequate standard of living, neoliberals are reluctant to make the connection between the inconvenient facts of human rights violations and free trade. If the relationship is acknowledged at all, the "high transition costs" are seen as an acceptable price, to be endured stoically in the name of future generations, when all countries have fully developed economies. Reports of well-documented trade-related human rights violations in many regions of the world do not therefore trouble neoliberal thinking.

Although the neoliberal consensus accepts the universality and unity of all internationally agreed human rights in formal and legal terms, the political practice of promoting civil and political rights to the exclusion of economic and social rights has a long history. We have only to recall that the decision to draft a nonbinding Universal Declaration of Human Rights (UDHR), rather than a single, legally binding covenant, was itself a consequence of disagreements between Western countries who sought to prioritize civil and political rights and socialist and less-developed countries who favored economic, social, and cultural rights. However, with the collapse of the Cold War and the increasing pace

1. Marshall Conley and Daniel Livermore, "Human Rights, Development, and Democracy: The Linkage Between Theory and Practice," *Canadian Journal of Development Studies* 17, 4 (1996): 19–36.

of globalization, the role of universal human rights seems to have taken a new turn in world politics. Instead of fulfilling its intention of offering protection to the weak and the vulnerable, neoliberal interests have co-opted the idea of human rights as a justification for grabbing "even more of the world's [and their own nations'] resources than they previously had" and to "steal back the concessions to social democracy that were forced out of them at the end of the Second World War."[2] This is not to suggest that the discourse on universal human rights is of no further interest to the neoliberal consensus. On the contrary, the defense of human rights as civil and political rights, including the right to own and dispose of property freely, promotes the accumulation of capital at the expense of distributive policies that could have empowered the poor.

Underpinning the move to a global economy is an ideology of modernity, which rests upon the twin goals of economic growth and development, defined as increasing global capital accumulation and consumption. The central means of achieving these goals in all countries, whether the wealthy North or the impoverished South, are strategic planning at the global level, global management, and the creation of global regimes and agreements. Ideological convergence has the effect of homogenizing and limiting the policy choices of governments. The global human rights regime provides the quintessential values on which this program of convergence and homogenization is built. Global management requires adherence to rules that ensure all countries conform to the development model so that the "hidden hand" of the market can operate efficiently. But one of the consequences of adopting such strategies is growing inequality, and in some countries an "absolute decline in real income of the bottom forty to sixty percent of families."[3] Thus for economic and social rights, the conclusion is that "development processes (trade agreements, national economic development strategies, and so forth), individuals, or-

ganisations (multilateral lenders, multinational and national corporations), and governments, all deny human rights."[4] Furthermore, the imperatives of "efficiency" and increased profits often lead to violations of civil and political rights when people attempt to resist the worst excesses of globalization. The struggles of the Ogoni people in Nigeria and attempts to form free trade unions in Mexico offer good examples.

INTERNATIONAL CITIZENSHIP

To gain an insight into the move from human rights as protecting the vulnerable to human rights as legitimating the practices of globalization, an examination of the literature on citizenship and the idea of international citizenship is particularly instructive. In proposing the project of the good international citizen, the clear intention is to develop the "means of weakening the exclusionary character of the modern state and . . . overcoming an ancient tension between the rights of citizens and duties to the rest of the world,"[5] a project that has clear parallels with the post-World War II project for universal human rights. Making this connection allows the often-seen claim that the global human rights regime represents an "emerging constitution of the world."[6] Although at first reading such notions appear to offer a beguiling solution to the state-citizen versus humanity problem, upon further reflection the project can be seen to offer legitimacy to current practices that continue to deny human rights to the majority of the world's people. Before expanding on this argument, some brief outline of the notion of the international citizen is necessary.

2. Conor Gearty, "No Human Rights Please, We're Capitalists," *Independent on Sunday* (London), 13 December 1998, culture supp., 34.
3. Charles Beitz, "Economic Rights and Distributive Justice in Developing Societies," *World Politics* 33, 3 (1981): 321–46.
4. Barbara Rose Johnston and Gregory Button, "Human Environmental Rights Issues and the Multinational Corporation: Industrial Development in the Free Trade Zone," in Barbara Rose Johnston, ed., *Who Pays the Price?* (Washington, D.C.: Island Press, 1994), 213. See also UNDP, *Human Development Report 1996* (Oxford: OUP, 1996).
5. Andrew Linklater, "What Is a Good International Citizen?" in Paul Keal, ed., *Ethics and Foreign Policy* (Canberra: Allen and Unwin, 1992), 27.
6. Peter Weiss, "The Human Rights of the Underclass," in John Cavanagh, Daphne Wysham, and Marcos Arrunda, eds., *Beyond Bretton Woods* (London: Pluto, 1994), 30.

A well-known representation of this project is Andrew Linklater's essay on the "good international citizen." It begins by identifying three generally accepted characteristics that define citizenship: first, "primary legal rights," which guarantee the freedom of the individual in civil society; second, the "right to participation in political life," which guarantees the right to take part in government and the exercise of power; and third, "fundamental duties," which instill an obligation to ameliorate the real inequalities that underlie the formal equalities of civil and political rights.[7] The substance of these characteristics in any time or place is conditioned by the historic struggles for recognition in which "both the extent of the citizen body and the nature and extent of citizen rights are constantly contested and changed."[8] Citizenship should therefore be recognized for its dialectical qualities, which offer an opportunity for excluded groups to challenge the existing order in an effort to "generate additional claims for change and far-reaching, though not inevitable, patterns of political development."[9] Noting the dialectic of citizenship raises questions concerning the clamor for human rights under conditions of globalization, where the newly emerging structures of the political economy have seen the spread of both great wealth and great poverty, where the decisions and practices of governments, transnational corporations, and international organizations are often decoupled from the reality of many peoples' lives and experiences, and where new forms of exclusion continue to emerge. However, the task of providing answers to questions of globalization through a rearticulation of citizenship is severely constrained by the widely held assumption that the rights of the citizen cannot be divorced from the particularity of the state. Although the literature accepts that all individuals may possess rights as human beings, emphasis is more usually placed on the "tragic conflict between citizenship and humanity."[10]

Given these observations, Linklater attempts to reconsider the state-citizen versus humanity question and to offer a solution that navigates a pathway somewhere between the pessimism offered by realists and the optimism of cosmopolitans.[11] In this endeavor, Linklater develops the idea of international citizenship—a citizenship that seeks to undermine the arguments for continuing to legitimate the distinction between "insiders" and "outsiders" and thus weakens the exclusionary character of the modern state. What is important is Linklater's assertion that citizenship is not only invoked in defense of old rights, it also plays a prominent role in the continuing effort to affirm and realize new ones. Invoked in this context, citizenship is held to require support for collective action to assist the victims of unjustifiable forms of exclusion anchored in class, ethnicity, gender, and race.[12]

Under conditions of globalization, the cause, and therefore the resolution, of these exclusionary practices cannot be found solely within the state. Instead, Linklater proposes a system of overlapping citizenship, where the state-citizen, the international citizen, and the cosmopolitan citizen exist in harmony and mutual tolerance.

In 1998, Linklater attempted to develop his notion of a "post-Westphalian citizenship" in *The Transformation of Political Community*.[13] Noting the democratic deficit that is characteristic of the current era of global politics, where systems of national democracy no longer provide a sense of control over individual and collective lives and where the decisions of nonaccountable international organizations often have greater significance than domestic policy, Linklater calls for a form of citizenship that extends citizen rights "higher" than those of international institutions and "lower" than those of local institutions. This can be achieved, according to Linklater, by developing the rationalist or international society approach to international politics that takes ac-

7. Linklater, "What Is a Good International Citizen?" note 5, 23.
8. Kimberly Hutchings, "The Idea of International Citizenship," in Barry Holden, ed., *The Ethical Dimensions of Global Change* (Basingstoke: Macmillan, 1996), 117.
9. Linklater, "What Is a Good International Citizen?" note 5, 25.
10. Ibid.
11. *Eds.*—A cosmopolitan is a person whose relational identity is based not on local, provincial, or national bias or attachment, but instead, on an inclusive morality, a shared economic relationship, or a political structure that encompasses different nations—for example, a "world citizen." See, e.g., "Cosmopolitanism," in *Stanford Encyclopedia of Philosophy*, http://plato.stanford.edu/entries/cosmopolitanism (accessed 21 June 2015).
12. Linklater, "What Is a Good International Citizen?" 22.
13. Andrew Linklater, *The Transformation of Political Community* (Oxford: Polity, 1998).

count of the newly emerging conditions of globalization. Most important, Linklater argues that we must "break with the supposition that national populations have the sovereign right to withhold their consent from any developments within international organizations which clash with their conception of national interest."[14] Although the EU is held up as an early and, as yet, undeveloped model that includes many of the features of citizenship Linklater has in mind, it is also presented as a model that could eventually encompass the world. Like the Westphalian system of states, which also originated in Europe before embracing the whole of the globe, so, too, will the new institutions develop in the EU.

In proposing this project, Linklater attempts to take full account of both the legacy of the previous period, where the state remained the central actor on the international stage, and the new era of globalization, where the individual's identity and loyalty is no longer necessarily tied to the state. Linklater acknowledges that the tensions between the particular and universal claim for rights will not be resolved unless we redefine state citizenship to include tolerance of multiple loyalties, including those that develop as people engage in greater levels of interaction through nonstate institutions and organizations.

UNIVERSAL HUMAN RIGHTS AND INTERNATIONAL CITIZENSHIP

Although the account of international citizenship proposed by Linklater is intended to offer a possible solution to the pressing problems found in a rapidly changing world, any solution that relies on some notion of citizenship may also offer support for existing practices that are the cause of many human rights violations and much human misery. Three broad criticisms are important.

First, although the central aim in proposing an international citizenship is to find a solution to the statecitizen versus humanity problem, Linklater's project remains largely state-centric. As long as state citizenship remains integral to developing international citizenship, "international citizenship appears to depend on the idea of the state-citizen, with other notions of political iden-

tity and rights effectively only developing via the *permission* of the state."[15] This suggests that the rights attached to international citizenship are bestowed from above, rather than demanded and developed from below, notwithstanding recent reports of movements organized to resist further globalization in many regions of the world. Given that the idea of international citizenship is in part a response to the demand for greater democracy under conditions of globalization, conditions that alienate people from existing social institutions, the state-centric focus seems ambiguous. On the one hand, proponents argue that new forms of transnational association are stimulated by a desire to reestablish control over political life, following the perceived failure of the state to act in the interests of citizens, while on the other, the state is presented as integral to developing new forms of international political association.

Moreover, the observation that global politics is now characterized by a multiplicity of transnational actors, including nongovernmental organizations, transnational corporations, international financial institutions, and international organizations, is seen by proponents of international citizenship as an exciting and revolutionary phenomenon that demands a new democratic project for global governance. Following this observation, much academic and political energy has been put into proposals that seek to promote democracy within a framework of some kind of global governance in which the state permits the "development of multiple forms of citizenship."[16] What this project fails to acknowledge, however, is that the development of transnational association generates new forms of loyalty that may not be conducive to new forms of democracy, including the protection of human rights. Indeed, some of the new transnational associations, particularly those concerned with transnational corporations and financial institutions, may actually encourage the very practices that democracy and citizenship are supposed to ameliorate. Furthermore, although the idea of citizenship assumes some kind of equality, civil society is not free of social, political, and economic inequalities. By failing to note the undemocratic nature of transnational associational life, and capital's need to

14. Ibid., 192.

15. Hutchings, "The Idea of International Citizenship," 123 (emphasis in original).
16. Linklater, "What Is a Good International Citizen?" note 5, 31.

maintain inequality, proponents of international citizenship fail to take full account of social and economic power.

What is more, the state-centric approach to citizenship places the responsibility for promoting human rights onto states through the medium of international law. While acknowledging that the international law approach to promoting human rights remains the central focus of much human rights talk, the emerging conditions of globalization, including the recognition that the authority of the state is undergoing a radical transformation, suggest that implementing substantive international human rights through international law may not produce results. Even when commentators do acknowledge the challenge of globalization, and tacitly recognize that international law has limited potential for guaranteeing human rights, the natural and normal means for protecting human rights remains the creation of international law. In this way, human rights become a technical issue concerned with agreements and disagreements over the internal logic and elegance of the law, its coherence, extent, and meaning. More complex questions to do with efficacy, application, and obligations under the particular social, political, and economic conditions of globalization are therefore excluded. To expect more of international law overlooks the point that it is itself the product of traditional, state-centric thinking on world politics and cannot therefore resolve the more damaging aspects of an alternative globalized world order.

Second, the project for an international citizenship does not avoid the problems that arise in the relationship between the citizen and civil society described by the neoliberal conception of citizenship. Central to these problems is the notion that the neoliberal citizen is "defended from the state by a series of rights which enable a plurality of ways in which individuals can live their lives within the private sphere of civil society,"[17] thus separating public from private life. In this standard neoliberal interpretation of the state-citizen relationship, the task of protecting the freedom of the individual from interference in the pursuit of economic interests is assigned to the public sphere of the state. Citizenship is therefore concerned with protecting civil and political rights, rights that the state guarantees in the name of the private sphere of civil society. Although, in formal terms, economic and social rights are often afforded formal parity with civil and political rights, according to the neoliberal conception of citizenship, civil and political rights must be prioritized to provide the conditions for wealth creation. Citizens can turn their attention to honoring a duty to support the least fortunate only when these conditions are achieved.

This approach to universal rights has a long history, one that is readily found in the postwar debate on human rights. For example, although the well-known "Four Freedoms" speech made by President Roosevelt in 1941 included the freedom from want, he defined this to mean "economic understanding which will secure for every nation a healthy peace-time life for its inhabitants everywhere in the world."[18] Thus the freedom from want did not suggest that the deprived and excluded had a right to claim assistance from those who benefited most from the global economy, but rather that states accepted a duty to remove structural, commercial, and cultural barriers between states that threatened the potential expansion of neoliberalism on a global scale.

This is reflected in the general definition of citizenship adopted by neoliberals, which provides for legal *rights* and *rights* of participation but only "the *duty* to *promote* the widest possible good."[19] While the citizen has the right to seek legal protection if personal and political freedoms are threatened, those suffering economic deprivation have no such rights but must, instead, rely upon the good faith of duty holders. The duty placed on the citizen is not even one to *protect* the poor and vulnerable from further violations, a duty that implies positive action, but rather the lesser requirement to *promote* their cause in some indeterminate fashion. Furthermore, fostering a duty to promote human rights in the interest of the widest possible good tends to reinforce the centrality of the individual in the human rights debate at the expense of structural causes of violations. Current practices that are

17. Hutchings, "The Idea of International Citizenship," 116.

18. President's Annual Message to Congress, 6 January 1941.
19. Linklater, "What Is a Good International Citizen?" note 5, 36.

the cause of many human rights violations—practices legitimated by neoliberal freedoms exercised in existing structures—are marginalized and are less likely to present a challenge to the dominant value system.

These criticisms suggest that the attempt to secure universal civil, political, and economic rights through the medium of citizenship may, in fact, reinforce a set of values that support current exclusionary practices found in globalization. Notwithstanding the addition of duties as well as rights in the modern interpretation of citizenship, the idea of the international citizen does not offer a convincing argument for securing human rights in the age of globalization. It fails because it confuses the *rights of the individual* with the *rights of the citizen* and does not take full account of the relationship between civil society, the state, and the citizen.[20]

The conclusions to be drawn from this analysis suggest that the protection of human rights, particularly economic and social rights, cannot be achieved through mechanisms associated with the state, international law, and the idea of the international citizen. Indeed, far from offering a satisfactory response to globalization, the idea of the international citizen lends further support to neoliberal assertions that economic and social claims are aspirations, not universal human rights. In short, the vacuum left by the decline of the state as the main, if not the only, political actor in world politics, is not filled by civil society. Rather, civil society reflects the narrow self-interests of those in a structural position to take full advantage of the conditions of globalization, to the exclusion of the many.

Third, proponents of civil society and citizenship acknowledge that the new "politics of recognition demands new expressions of sensitivity to difference and new possibilities for expanding the range of permissible disagreements."[21] This is the virtue of tolerance, which is a fundamental principle of social pluralism. However, proponents of civil society do not intend that tolerance should be extended to all groups, ideas, and values. Instead, tolerance is extended to those who accept the general purposes of civil society by adopting its values and following the "correct" procedures

for realizing their particular vision of the "good life." Those who attempt to challenge the general principles of the dominant economic, social, and political order are tolerated only insofar as they "do not seek to make the transition from word to deed, from speech to action."[22] Those perceived as a threat to the principles manifest in civil society are marginalized, either by labeling them "mad" and therefore not worthy of "rational" consideration or by mobilizing official violence if that fails.

Tolerance and civility are therefore concerned with the preservation and management of a particular form of civil society, a narrowing of the political agenda, and the exclusion of actors whose voices appear as a threat. In neoliberal societies, tolerance is practiced by legitimating a set of civil liberties and freedoms that are granted to all citizens, regardless of "race, colour, sex, language, religion, political or other opinion, national or social origin, property, birth or other status."[23] Against this expression of formal equality and tolerance, however, is the actual practice of tolerance, which cannot be divorced from power relations that determine what will or will not be tolerated. An example of repressive tolerance operating at the global level can be seen in the treatment of new states following decolonization. Although the imperial powers withdrew from these countries, thereby removing the immediate threat of coercion if colonial peoples resisted the spread of globalization or failed to embrace the principles of a market economy, self-determination did not mean autonomy. Rather, self-determination meant freedom to embrace the rules, norms, and principles of the emerging neoliberal global order. That these rules and norms often lead to human rights violations—for example, by threatening economic, social, and cultural life, or denying the right to join a trade union or to sustenance—is rarely acknowledged and often tolerated in the name of "progress." To repeat, for the neoliberal consensus, the "high transition costs" of economic growth and development are a price worth paying for future benefits. Tolerance may therefore perform the task of "closure" by excluding alternatives that threaten the existing

---

20. *Eds.*—Emphases added.
21. Linklater, *The Transformation of Political Community*, note 13, 187.

22. Bhupinder S. Chimni, "Marxism and International Law," *Economic and Political Weekly* 34, 6 (1999): 337–49.
23. UDHR, art. 2.

order—for example, by defining peace in terms of the preparation for war, or human rights as a legal problem rather than one best understood within the context of the political economy.

Linklater's attempt to develop the idea of the good international citizen is already gaining wide acceptance. Although further attempts to develop and operationalize the concept exhibit detailed differences, they are all concerned with understanding democracy and human rights within the context of a changing world order. However, as this essay has attempted to demonstrate, the idea of the international citizen is not unproblematic and, in its current conceptualization, may not deliver the outcomes that proponents seek. The argument here is not that some form of citizenship cannot lend support to the protection of human rights, but, rather, that it cannot be done unless the critical points raised here are accommodated. In short, the success of the project to develop the idea of the international citizen depends upon our ability to understand the current configuration of social forces, forms of state and world order—understanding that seems to be lacking in much of the literature.

This essay set out to investigate how the idea of universal human rights was co-opted by the prevailing neoliberal consensus in support of processes associated with globalization. Civil and political rights form the core of neoliberal values upon which free market, laissez faire economics are based. Through an examination of the idea of the international citizen, it was argued that the attempt to introduce a duty to promote the widest possible social good falls far short of an obligation to respond to claims for economic and social rights. Indeed, while proponents of the idea of the international citizen might claim to be responding to the global political economy, it serves only to obfuscate important facets of the human-rights debate. Those who stand in the way of the "imperatives" of globalization risk violations of their rights—civil and political, economic and social.

As the state moves from being an active policy-maker to a passive unit of administration, the capacity of people to participate in defining a political agenda that expresses a genuine concern for human rights and human dignity declines. With the realization that the global rather than the national economy exercises greater influence on economic well-being and the prospects for rights, the state loses its significance as a center of authority through which people can express their preferences. Instead, the focus turns to international institutions and transnational organizations that have few democratic credentials, although they assume the task of providing the rules for action. In response to the new social formations that are characteristic of globalization, international citizenship seeks a pathway to promoting human rights. However, the discussion offered here suggests that the current project ends by giving greater legitimacy to practices that are the cause of human rights violations.

QUESTIONS FOR REFLECTION AND DISCUSSION

1. What justification, if any, consistent with human rights values, if any, is there for the "withdrawal of welfare and social entitlements from the poor"? (Specify what human rights values are, and what your conception of them relies upon.) Argue as fully and consistently as you can, drawing upon readings in this volume and elsewhere to support your position.

2. Evans argues that neoliberalism has "succeeded in establishing the language of civil and political rights as the acceptable voice—indeed the only legitimate voice—of human-rights talk." This statement contains two claims. The first claim is that neoliberalism has established the language of civil and political rights as "the acceptable" voice of human rights talk. What do you understand this to mean? The second claim is a stronger one: that neoliberalism has established the language of civil and political rights as "the only legitimate" voice of human rights talk. What do you understand this to mean? Do you agree with either/both of these two claims? Why and which one? Or, if not, why not?

3. Evans highlights two broad arguments neoliberals use to define human rights as civil and political rights. What are they? How do these arguments work together?

4. What is at stake in seeing socioeconomic needs as "legitimate aspirations" rather than "rights"?

5. Given the status of socioeconomic rights in the current international legal order, do you think that refusing to treat socioeconomic needs and entitlements as "rights" makes any real difference to outcomes? Why? Why not? Specify as fully as you can the status of socioeconomic rights today, why you characterize that status as you do, and what evidence you draw upon—including other readings in this volume.

6. Neoliberals justify trade with human rights violators by asserting that "If there is free trade, then there are human rights, or at least the conditions necessary for the protection of human rights." Do you find this argument convincing? Why or why not?

7. Does disrupting free trade over human rights issues have any practical value? Why not? Why? What definition of "free trade" are you using and why?

8. Evans argues that "Reports of well-documented trade-related human rights violations in many regions of the world do not . . . trouble neoliberal thinking." Should they? Is it acceptable, for example, to inflict abuse, environmental damage, and related violations of the human rights to life, health, and a decent standard of living on people in developing nations (and elsewhere) when they (or their communities or traditional ways of life) get in the way of free trade? Does some higher social goal justify ignoring such human and environmental costs? What is it? Or is it always unacceptable to ignore such harms in the pursuit of a goal? Upon what values do your answers rely, and what is assumed by those values? Defend your position as fully and consistently as you can.

9. Evans suggests that "To gain an insight into the move from human rights as protecting the vulnerable to human rights as legitimating the practices of globalization, an examination of the literature on citizenship and the idea of international citizenship is particularly instructive." Why? What does Evans argue?

10. What, in your view, are the strengths and limitations of the concept of "international citizenship"? What does Linklater say (discussed by Evans)?

11. What is Evans's view of Linklater's account and approach?

12. Evans identifies three criticisms of international citizenship. What are they? Can these criticisms be redressed? How? Or, if not, why not?

13. Returning to the argument made in Reading 15 (Benhabib) in Chapter 3, what would Benhabib argue? How do you think Evans would be likely to respond to Benhabib? And why? Upon what reasons and reasoning of Evans does your answer draw?

Postscript: Human Rights, Humane Governance, and the Future

IN its present-day collective form, the human journey is marked by the profound socio-cosmic challenges of globalization, in the face of mass poverty, persistent nuclear threat, and a looming planetary climate crisis. The human present is unparalleled in human history, and the human future is deeply uncertain. Given present negative trends, the human species—indeed, most current species—may not even survive.

But humans have the power to influence the present and future in decisive ways. Notwithstanding the complexity of the challenges, each person now has choices she or he can make—and, indeed, must make. Ours is an age that demands nothing less. At every daily opportunity, each person must choose to ensure a just, peaceful, and otherwise humane future for every man, woman, and child, and to do so wisely, fully cognizant of the fact that globalization and climate change bring humanity into a direct and intimate proximity and thus into levels of interdependence never before experienced. It matters little whether individuals are at the "highest" or "lowest" levels of societal influence; the most micro-situated of daily choices and actions are now inexorably linked to macro-issues and trends.

Of course, the process of globalization is not new. It has been with us in forms economic and political for centuries, since at least the fourth century B.C.E., when, eleven centuries before the European "Age of Exploration," Alexander the Great's empire extended to what we now call India and, a few hundred years later, to the Han Dynasty of China and the Roman Empire, which regularly traded with one another and even exchanged diplomats. Nevertheless, in its current form, globalization presents the most daunting challenge to transnational cooperation ever known to humankind. Since the Treaty of Westphalia in 1648, the effective end of the Holy Roman Empire and birth of the state system, international affairs have been guided by an essentially two-dimensional map according to which interstate relations travel by the compass of an international law system that, in defense of competing sovereignties and territories, looks upon interstate warfare and economic disparity as being inevitable ingredients of any political order that lacks a governmental center, the law of geopolitics. This Westphalian map is increasingly inadequate to the complexity of the challenges facing the present international legal system. Today, minimally, there is a need for a multidimensional map to reflect the multilayered relations and interdependencies among diverse forms of authority (qua governments, markets, individual citizens) and diverse doctrines, principles, and rules (qua treaties, laws, social norms) in a global order marked by intensifying interdependencies. Humans are being propelled ever more rapidly toward a world order that compels us to work together, however haltingly, but at our peril if we do not, toward new common objectives and new, humane modes of governance. Indeed, in an age of eco-crisis, humanity needs nothing short of a new sense of what "humanity" itself means—and a correspondingly rich, diversified, complexity-responsive notion of law itself.

Governance, let us be clear, is not the same as government. When we think of government, typically we think of public institutions (administrative, legislative, and judicial) that perform these functions backed by the coercive police powers of the state. Governance is a broader, more inclusive term. Political scientists define governance as a network of cooperative and integrative norms, institutions, and procedures that may or may not issue from formally constituted state power. Relying on consensus and consent more than coercion— indeed, commonly to the exclusion of coercion—governance is more about process than bureaucracy and includes within its embrace nongovernmental entities such as corporations, foundations, academic institutions, professional associations, NGOs, and social movements and grassroots community groups serving informally (though, for some, increasingly formally) as actors, claimants, and decision-makers alongside state and state-dominated intergovernmental institutions. Accordingly, while "The State necessarily remains focal for many purposes, non-State actors, territorial socioeconomic forces, globally organized media and communications networks, and new forms of global grassroots human solidarities are exerting a defining influence on large-scale social behavior."[1]

In his presidential address to the American Political Science Association in 2000, Robert O. Keohane observed that globalization can be good or bad depending on the cultivation of appropriate and effective governance and that if we earnestly want a benign globalized world we need to think in ethical, humane terms about our future.[2] Good governance depends on ethically humane visions of the decision-making norms, institutions, and procedures—local to global, formal and informal—that shape our lives.

In recent times, however, globalization has fallen into profound disrepute as the result of overbearing market forces, fundamentalist agendas, and hegemonic impulses through which the strong subdue the weak. The global age is marked by deepening levels of radical poverty (including hunger for 1.3 billion human beings, 70 percent of whom are ironically farmers), by spiraling levels of material inequality, and by the rise of totalitarian forces, whether politically or religiously inspired. The sheer complexity of climate change as a phenomenon, and of the dense global interdependencies characterizing the global order, makes it essential to challenge traditional logics with renewing possibilities. Meanwhile, the interstate system has remained stuck in the logic and time warp of an outdated geopolitics, the central focus of which is "a global security system in which the leadership and management role is played by a few dominant States and in which recurrent conflict tends to be resolved through wars and their outcomes."[3] This can no longer be thought of as a rational way forward.

1. Saul H. Mendlovitz and Burns H. Weston, "The United Nations at Fifty: Toward Humane Global Governance," in Saul H. Mendlovitz and Burns H. Weston, eds., *Preferred Futures for the United Nations* (Irvington-on-Hudson, N.Y.: Transnational, 1995), 3–20, 17.
2. Robert O. Keohane, "Governance in a Partially Globalized World," Presidential Address, American Political Science Association, 2000, *APSR* 95 (March 2001): 1–13, 1.
3. Mendlovitz and Weston, "The United Nations at Fifty," note 1, 17.

Happily, there are signs of hope: new modes of national, regional, and global governance are emerging, albeit hesitatingly and with some distressing backsliding,[4] to alleviate worldwide harm, because people everywhere are capable of envisioning the more compassionate and respectful quest for national and transnational justice—the global rule of just law and policy—or what some call "the law of humanity." Beyond governmental agreements to adhere to human rights norms, we see now a striving for justice in other layers of authoritative decision-making. On one hand, the energetic work of NGOs, the adoption of corporate codes and compacts, newly defined developmental and environmental rights, and the incorporation of human rights into codes of professional ethics—each of these and more can be seen to testify to the acceptance of interrelated humane principles of governance and the emergence of a holistic vision for human and world survival.

On the other hand, as we have seen throughout this volume, the reality is far more fractured. Forces of appropriation, control, and injustice are still powerfully at work, and—in any case—merely formal acceptance of a new ethos of species identity and solidarity will never be enough. There is an urgent need to detail the principles informing humane governance, and for the ethos that gives them direction to be given concrete outworking if an alternative vision for the future is truly to influence attitudes and behavior for the better.

That is the vision and program of *humane governance*, "a type of governance that is people- and human rights-oriented rather than statist and market-oriented."[5] Using the concept of "humane governance," international law and world order scholar Richard Falk has called for a global order that can secure essential human rights by transforming the world order as it now exists. His preliminary objective, shared by the editors of this volume, is to stimulate debate for the purpose of extending the boundaries of human rights beyond those set by the dictates of the still prevailing state system (and its operative codes linked to exclusive sovereignty and territoriality).[6]

The template for humane governance is implied by Article 28 of the 1948 Universal Declaration of Human Rights, which proclaims that "everyone is entitled to a social and international order in which the rights and freedoms set forth in this Declaration can be fully realized." In these terms, Falk's concept of humane governance refers to the right of every individual and group to live in societies that realize or conscientiously attempt to realize the overarching values that inform the International Bill of Rights: the 1948 UDHR, the 1966 International Covenant on Economic, Social and Cultural Rights (ICESCR), and the 1966 International Covenant on Civil and Political Rights (ICCPR). The notion of humane governance draws attention to the universal duty—the duty of everyone—to assist the realization of these values both alone and cooperatively, pursuing politics in the human interest and participating in the struggle for global justice.

However, given the seriousness of the context in which we write, it is clear that the struggle for global justice cannot be divorced from the three most profound challenges now facing humanity: the climate crisis; the continuing—and deepening—danger posed by the existence and spread of nuclear weapons (and the risk of terrorist appropriation of nuclear

---

4. See, e.g., Richard A. Falk, *The Declining World Order: America's Imperial Geopolitics* (New York: Routledge, 2004).

5. Mendlovitz and Weston, "The United Nations at Fifty," note 1, 18.

6. See, e.g., Richard Falk, *On Humane Governance: Toward a New Global Politics—The World Order Models Project Report of the Global Civilization Initiative* (University Park: Pennsylvania State University Press, 1995). See also Falk, *Human Rights and State Sovereignty* (New York: Holmes and Meier, 1981), esp. 180–83; *Human Rights Horizons, The Pursuit of Justice in a Globalizing World* (New York: Routledge, 2000), esp. 19–20, 34–35; *Achieving Human Rights* (New York: Routledge, 2008). Additionally, see Saul H. Mendlovitz, *On the Creation of a Just World Order* (New York: Free Press, 1975).

materials); and the existence of radical poverty. When we speak of global justice, therefore, we invoke a specifically *ecosensitive, peace-oriented, and economically humane* form of governance, thoroughly responsive to environmental, violence-driven, and poverty-inflicted injustice (including the entrenched injustices of globalization in its current hegemonic form). We want to think beyond the limits of the present into new possible futures—and to provoke thoughtful discussion on what the new multilayered maps of a humane future might be. Indeed, one of the fundamental problems facing the prospects for global justice is that global justice initiatives and conceptions have so far been considered, as Falk points out, "under the unideal conditions of the established world order."[7] Veiled by the failings of persistent geopolitics, he asserts, they therefore may or may not lead humanity toward a beneficial form of global governance.[8] Prospects for global justice are veiled, too, by the failings of human foresight and imagination. Who among us foresaw the end of the Cold War or the dismantling of the racist apartheid regime of South Africa? Implicitly, such changes insist that there are grounds for optimism.[9] As human beings we each have the capacity to envision and act upon a better future, a future premised on a culture of human solidarity, respect, and compassion—human rights as a way of life.

Indeed, for the sake of future generations, we all share a duty to build such a world—and human rights, for all their flaws, paradoxes, and betrayals, still contain radical seeds of hope for "worlds other." A renewing human rights vision—in which humans are understood as embodied, vulnerable beings intimately interdependent in and with a precarious living order and not simply as separative rational agents—can turn individuals and communities into forces of transformation. As stated by the People's Movement for Human Rights Education in its "Global Appeal for Human Rights Education" in December 2004 (on the close of the 1995–2004 United Nations Decade for Human Rights Education):

> All people must know their human rights in order to live together in justice and dignity; to become agents of transformation and establish human rights as a way of life. Humanity—standing on the brink of devastation, with millions of people mired in poverty, environmental destruction, violence and oppression—aspires to live in a world of human dignity, freedom, and social and economic justice. . . . To secure this vision, all people must learn and act according to our universal human rights, which define a shared moral and legal framework for living in dignity within our varied communities . . . , a shared global culture of human rights.[10]

And at a 1997 high-level communications conference, UN Secretary-General Kofi Annan put it this way: "What we must offer is a vision of human rights that is foreign to none and native to all."[11]

And this, in essence, is what humane global governance is all about. Humane governance and a social order accountable to human rights (in their most enriching and solidarity-enhancing formulations) amount to, on final analysis, the same thing. All that is needed is a belief in the possible and a willingness, despite the odds, to hazard the initiatives that

---

7. Falk, *Human Rights Horizons*, note 6, 34.
8. Ibid.
9. Falk demurs: "We do not understand political reality well enough to be pessimistic, or for that matter optimistic," ibid. (34).
10. For the complete Appeal, its history, and an opportunity to endorse it, see the website of the People's Movement at http://www.pdhre.org/global-appeal.html (accessed 3 June 2015).
11. Kofi Annan, "Ignorance, Not Knowledge, Makes Enemies of Man," Statement by Secretary-General Kofi Annan, delivered 18 October 1997 to the Communications Conference of the Aspen Institute, Colorado, UN Doc. SG/SM/6366, 20 October 1997. See also the frontispiece in this present volume.

can make it happen. In a very real sense, it is compassionate vision and firm resolve that we need. No small task, concededly. But what other conceivable way is there to ensure that humanity—both present and future generations—can flourish as inhabitants of a more peace-loving, humane, and ecologically wise future?

Robert F. Kennedy, in his 6 June 1966 "Day of Affirmation" speech at the University of Cape Town when South Africa was fully in the grip of an evil and seemingly invincible racist regime, put the challenge of forging history this way:

> Let no one be discouraged by the belief there is nothing one [person] can do against the enormous array of the world's ills—against misery and ignorance, injustice and violence. . . . Few will have the greatness to bend history itself; but each of us can work to change a small portion of events, and in the total of all those acts will be written the history of this generation. . . .
>
> It is from numberless diverse acts of courage and belief that human history is shaped. Each time a [human being] stands up for an ideal, or acts to improve the lot of others, or strikes out against injustice, [that human being] sends forth a tiny ripple of hope, and crossing each other from a million different centers of energy and daring those ripples build a current which can sweep down the mightiest walls of oppression and resistance.[12]

It is this message of everyday choice, of heroism even, on behalf of humane governance— "Not occasional heroism, a remarkable instance of it here and there, but constant heroism, systematic heroism, heroism as governing principle"[13]—that we hope this volume passes on to our companion travelers of the twenty-first century, every man, woman, and child who yearns for a compassionate, human rights respecting world.

12. As quoted in Arthur M. Schlesinger, Jr., *Robert Kennedy and His Times* (Boston: Houghton Mifflin, 1978), 745–46.
13. Russell Banks, *Continental Drift* (New York: Harper and Row, 1985), 40.

Index